PRAISE FOR MARK SOBELL'S BOOKS

"I keep searching for books that collect everything you want to know about a subject in one place, and keep getting disappointed. Usually the books leave out some important topic, while others go too deep in some areas and must skim lightly over the others. *A Practical Guide to Red Hat® Linux®* is one of those rare books that actually pulls it off. Mark G. Sobell has created a single reference for Red Hat Linux that cannot be beat! This marvelous text (with a 4-CD set of Linux Fedora Core 2 included) is well worth the price. This is as close to an "everything you ever needed to know" book that I've seen. It's just that good and rates 5 out of 5."

—*Ray Lodato*
Slashdot contributor

"Mark Sobell has written a book as approachable as it is authoritative."

—*Jeffrey Bianchine*
Advocate, Author, Journalist

"Excellent reference book, well suited for the sysadmin of a linux cluster, or the owner of a PC contemplating installing a recent stable linux. Don't be put off by the daunting heft of the book. Sobell has striven to be as inclusive as possible, in trying to anticipate your system administration needs."

—*Wes Boudville*
Inventor

"*A Practical Guide to Red Hat® Linux®* is a brilliant book. Thank you Mark Sobell."

—*C. Pozrikidis*
University of California
at San Diego

"This book presents the best overview of the Linux operating system that I have found. . . . [It] should be very helpful and understandable no matter what the reader's background is: traditional UNIX user, new

Linux devotee, or even Windows user. Each topic is presented in a clear, complete fashion and very few assumptions are made about what the reader knows. . . . The book is extremely useful as a reference, as it contains a 70-page glossary of terms and is very well indexed. It is organized in such a way that the reader can focus on simple tasks without having to wade through more advanced topics until they are ready."

—Cam Marshall
Marshall Information Service LLC
Member of Front Range UNIX
Users Group [FRUUG]
Boulder, Colorado

"Conclusively, this is THE book to get if you are a new Linux user and you just got into RH/Fedora world. There's no other book that discusses so many different topics and in such depth."

—Eugenia Loli-Queru
Editor in Chief
OSNews.com

A Practical Guide to Linux® Commands, Editors, and Shell Programming

A Practical Guide to Linux® Commands, Editors, and Shell Programming

Mark G. Sobell

Prentice Hall Professional Technical Reference

Upper Saddle River, NJ • Boston • Indianapolis • San Francisco
New York • Toronto • Montreal • London • Munich • Paris • Madrid
Capetown • Sydney • Tokyo • Singapore • Mexico City

Many of the designations used by manufacturers and sellers to distinguish their products are claimed as trademarks. Where those designations appear in this book, and the publisher was aware of a trademark claim, the designations have been printed with initial capital letters or in all capitals.

The author and publisher have taken care in the preparation of this book, but make no expressed or implied warranty of any kind and assume no responsibility for errors or omissions. No liability is assumed for incidental or consequential damages in connection with or arising out of the use of the information or programs contained herein.

The publisher offers excellent discounts on this book when ordered in quantity for bulk purchases or special sales, which may include electronic versions and/or custom covers and content particular to your business, training goals, marketing focus, and branding interests. For more information, please contact:

U.S. Corporate and Government Sales
(800) 382-3419
corpsales@pearsontechgroup.com

For sales outside the U.S., please contact:

International Sales
international@pearsoned.com

Visit us on the Web: www.phptr.com

Library of Congress Cataloging-in-Publication Data

Sobell, Mark G.
    A Practical Guide to Linux Commands, Editors, and Shell Programming / Mark G. Sobell
       p. cm.
    Includes bibliographical references and index.
    ISBN 0-13-147823-0 (alk. paper)
     1. Linux. 2. Operating systems (Computers) I. Title.
QA76.76.O63.S59483 2005
005.4'46—dc22

                                                       2005050051

Pearson Education, Inc.
Rights and Contracts Department
One Lake Street
Upper Saddle River, NJ 07458

ISBN 0-13-147823-0

Text printed in the United States on recycled paper at Courier in Stoughton, Massachusetts.

First printing, June 2005

With love for my guys,
Sam, Zach, and Max

BRIEF CONTENTS

CONTENTS

PART I   THE LINUX OPERATING SYSTEM   19

CHAPTER 4: THE LINUX FILESYSTEM 75

CHAPTER 5: THE SHELL   107

PART II   THE EDITORS   137

CHAPTER 6: THE vim EDITOR   139

CHAPTER 7: THE **emacs** EDITOR   195

PART III   THE SHELLS   253

CHAPTER 8: THE BOURNE AGAIN SHELL   255

CHAPTER 9: THE TC SHELL   339

PART IV   PROGRAMMING TOOLS   385

CHAPTER 10: PROGRAMMING TOOLS   387

PART V COMMAND REFERENCE 581

PREFACE

A Practical Guide to Linux® Commands, Editors, and Shell Programming explains how to work with the Linux operating system from the command line. The first few chapters quickly bring readers with little computer experience up to speed. The rest of the book is appropriate for more experienced computer users. This book does not describe a particular release or distribution of Linux but rather pertains to all recent versions of Linux.

Command line interface (CLI) In the beginning there was the command line (textual) interface (CLI), which enabled you to give Linux commands from the command line. There was no mouse or icons to drag and drop. Some programs, such as emacs, implemented rudimentary windows using the very minimal graphics available in the ASCII character set. Reverse video helped separate areas of the screen. Linux was born and raised in this environment.

Naturally all of the original Linux tools were invoked from the command line. The real power of Linux still lies in this environment, which explains why many Linux professionals work *exclusively* from the command line. Using clear descriptions and lots of examples, this book shows you how to get the most out of your Linux system using the command line interface.

Linux distributions A Linux distribution comprises the Linux kernel, utilities, and application programs. Many distributions are available, including Debian, Red Hat, Fedora Core, SUSE, Mandriva (formerly Mandrake), KNOPPIX, and Slackware. Although the distributions differ from one another in various ways, all of them rely on the Linux kernel, utilities, and applications. This book is based on the code that is common to most distributions. As a consequence you can use it regardless of which distribution you are running.

Overlap   If you read *A Practical Guide to Red Hat® Linux®: Fedora Core™ and Red Hat Enterprise Linux, Second Edition,* or a subsequent edition, you will notice some overlap between that book and the one you are reading now. The introduction, the appendix on regular expressions, and the chapters on the utilities (Chapter 3 of this book—*not* Part V), the filesystem, and programming tools are very similar in the two books. The three chapters that cover the Bourne Again Shell (bash) have been expanded and rewritten for this text. Chapters that appear in this book and but not in *A Practical Guide to Red Hat® Linux®, Second Edition,* include those covering the vim and emacs editors, the TC Shell (tcsh), the gawk and sed languages, and Part V, which describes 80 of the most useful Linux utility programs in detail.

Audience   This book is designed for a wide range of readers. It does not require programming experience, although some experience using a general-purpose computer is helpful. It is appropriate for the following readers:

- **Students** taking a class in which they use Linux

- **Power users** who want to explore the power of Linux from the command line

- **Professionals** who use Linux at work

- **System administrators** who need a deeper understanding of Linux and the tools that are available to them

- **Computer science students** who are studying the Linux operating system

- **Programmers** who need to understand the Linux programming environment

- **Technical executives** who want to get a grounding in Linux

Benefits   *A Practical Guide to Linux® Commands, Editors, and Shell Programming* gives you an in-depth understanding of how to use Linux from the command line. Regardless of your background, it offers the knowledge you need to get on with your work: You will come away from this book understanding how to use Linux, and this text will remain a valuable reference for years to come.

FEATURES OF THIS BOOK

This book is organized for ease of use in different situations. For example, you can read it from cover to cover to learn command line Linux from the ground up. Alternatively, once you are comfortable using Linux, you can use this book as a reference: Look up a topic of interest in the table of contents or index and read about it. Or, refer to one of the utilities covered in Part V, "Command Reference." You can also think of this book as a catalog of Linux topics: Flip through the pages until a topic catches your eye. The book also includes many pointers to Web sites where you can get additional information: Consider the Web an extension of this book.

A Practical Guide to Linux® Commands, Editors, and Shell Programming offers the following features:

- **Optional sections** allow you to read the book at different levels, returning to more difficult material when you are ready to tackle it.

- **Caution boxes** highlight procedures that can easily go wrong, giving you guidance *before* you run into trouble.

- **Tip boxes** highlight places in the text where you can save time by doing something differently or when it may be useful or just interesting to have additional information.

- **Security boxes** point out ways that you can make a system more secure.

- The **Supporting Web site** at www.sobell.com includes corrections to the book, downloadable examples from the book, pointers to useful Web sites, and answers to even-numbered exercises.

- Concepts are illustrated by **practical examples** found throughout the book.

- The many useful **URLs** (Internet addresses) identify sites where you can obtain software and information.

- **Chapter summaries** review the important points covered in each chapter.

- **Review exercises** are included at the end of each chapter for readers who want to hone their skills. Answers to even-numbered exercises are available at www.sobell.com.

- Important **GNU tools**, including gcc, gdb, GNU Configure and Build System, make, gzip, and many others, are described in detail.

- Pointers throughout the book provide help in obtaining **online documentation** from many sources, including the local system and the Internet.

CONTENTS

This section describes the information that each chapter covers and explains how that information can help you take advantage of the power of Linux. You may want to review the table of contents for more detail.

- **Chapter 1   Welcome to Linux**
  Presents background information on Linux. This chapter covers the **history of Linux,** explains how the GNU Project helped Linux get started, and discusses some of **Linux's important features** that distinguish it from other operating systems.

PART I: THE LINUX OPERATING SYSTEM

Experienced users may want to skim Part I

tip   If you have used a UNIX/Linux system before, you may want to skim or skip some or all of the chapters in Part I. All readers should take a look at "Conventions Used in This Book" (page 22), which explains the typographic conventions that this book uses, and "Getting the Facts: Where to Find Documentation" (page 29), which points you toward both local and remote sources of Linux documentation.

Part I introduces Linux and gets you started using it.

- **Chapter 2   Getting Started**
  Explains the **typographic conventions** that this book uses to make explanations clearer and easier to read. This chapter provides basic information and explains how to log in, **change your password**, give Linux commands using the shell, and **find system documentation**.

- **Chapter 3   Command Line Utilities**
  Explains the **command line interface** (CLI) and briefly introduces **more than 30 command line utilities**. Working through this chapter gives you a feel for Linux and introduces some of the tools you will use day in and day out. The utilities covered in this chapter include

  - grep, which **searches through files** for strings of characters;

  - unix2dos, which **converts Linux text files** to Windows format;

  - tar, which **creates archive files** that can hold many other files;

  - bzip2 and gzip, which **compress files** so that they take up less space on disk and allow you to transfer them over a network more quickly; and

  - diff, which **displays the differences** between two text files.

- **Chapter 4   The Linux Filesystem**
  Discusses the Linux hierarchical filesystem, covering files, filenames, **pathnames**, working with directories, **access permissions**, and hard and **symbolic links**. Understanding the filesystem allows you to **organize your data** so that you can find information quickly. It also enables you to **share some of your files** with other users while **keeping other files private**.

- **Chapter 5   The Shell**
  Explains how to use shell features to make your work faster and easier. All of the features covered in this chapter work with both bash and tcsh. This chapter discusses

- Using **command line options** to modify the way a command works;

- How a minor change in a command line can **redirect input** to a command to come from a file instead of the keyboard;

- How to **redirect output** from a command to go to a file instead of the screen;

- Using **pipes** to send the output of one utility directly to another utility so that you can solve problems right on the command line;

- Running programs in the **background** so that you can work on one task while Linux is working on a different one; and

- Using the shell to **generate filenames** to save you time spent on typing and help you when you do not remember the exact name of a file.

PART II: THE EDITORS

Part II covers two classic, powerful Linux command line text editors. Most Linux distributions include the vim text editor, an "improved" version of the widely used vi editor, as well as the popular GNU emacs editor. Text editors enable you to create and modify text files that can hold programs, shell scripts, memos, and input to text formatting programs. Because Linux system administration involves editing text-based configuration files, skilled Linux administrators are adept at using text editors.

- Chapter 6   The vim Editor
  Starts with a **tutorial** on vim and then explains how to use many of the **advanced features** of vim, including special characters in search strings, the General-Purpose and Named buffers, parameters, markers, and execution of commands from vim. The chapter concludes with a **summary of** vim **commands**.

- Chapter 7   The emacs Editor
  Opens with a **tutorial** and then explains many of the features of the emacs editor as well as how to use the META, ALT, and ESCAPE keys. The chapter also covers key bindings, buffers, and **incremental and complete searching** for both character strings and regular expressions. In addition, it details the relationship between Point, the cursor, Mark, and Region. It also explains how to take advantage of the extensive **online help** facilities available from emacs. Other topics covered include cutting and pasting, using multiple windows and frames, and working with emacs modes—specifically C **mode**, which aids programmers in writing and debugging C code. Chapter 7 concludes with a **summary of** emacs **commands**.

PART III: THE SHELLS

Part III goes into more detail about bash and introduces the TC Shell (tcsh).

- **Chapter 8   The Bourne Again Shell**
  Picks up where Chapter 5 leaves off, covering more advanced aspects of working with a shell. For examples it uses the Bourne Again Shell—bash, the shell used almost exclusively for system shell scripts. Chapter 8 describes how to

  - Use shell **startup files**, shell options, and shell features to **customize your shell**;
  - Use **job control** to stop jobs and move jobs from the foreground to the background and vice versa;
  - Modify and reexecute commands using the **shell history** list;
  - Create **aliases** to customize commands;
  - Work with **user-created and keyword variables** in shell scripts;
  - Set up **functions**, which are similar to shell scripts but can execute more quickly;
  - Write and execute simple **shell scripts**; and
  - **Redirect error messages** so that they go to a file instead of the screen.

- **Chapter 9   The TC Shell**
  Describes tcsh and covers features that are common to and different between bash and tcsh. This chapter explains how to

  - Run tcsh and **change your default shell** to tcsh;
  - **Redirect error messages** so that they go to files instead of the screen;
  - Use **control structures** to alter the flow of control within shell scripts;
  - Work with tcsh **array and numeric variables**; and
  - Use shell **builtin commands**.

PART IV: PROGRAMMING TOOLS

Part IV covers programming under Linux. It discusses the C programming environment, the use of bash as a programming language, and ways to write programs using gawk and sed.

- **Chapter 10   Programming Tools**
  Introduces Linux's exceptional programming environment. This chapter

- ◆ Explains how to invoke the GNU gcc compiler;

- ◆ Describes how to use make to keep a set of **programs up-to-date**;

- ◆ Explains how to **debug a C program** using gdb;

- ◆ Describes how to work with **shared libraries**;

- ◆ Explains how to set up and use CVS to **manage and track program modules** in a software development project; and

- ◆ Discusses **system calls** and explains how you can use them to initiate kernel operations.

Once you have mastered the basics of Linux, you can use your knowledge to build more complex and specialized programs, using the shell as a programming language.

- **Chapter 11   Programming the Bourne Again Shell**
Shows how to use bash to write advanced shell scripts. This chapter discusses

    - ◆ **Control structures** such as **if...then...else** and **case**;

    - ◆ **Variables**, including locality of variables;

    - ◆ **Arithmetic and logical (Boolean) expressions**; and

    - ◆ Some of the most useful **shell builtin commands**, including exec, trap, and getopts.

Chapter 11 poses two complete **shell programming problems** and then shows you how to solve them step by step. The first problem uses **recursion** to create a hierarchy of directories. The second problem develops a quiz program and shows you how to set up a shell script that **interacts with a user** and how the script processes data. (The examples in Part V also demonstrate many features of the utilities you can use in shell scripts.)

- **Chapter 12   The gawk Pattern Processing Language**
Explains how to write programs using the powerful gawk language that filter data, **write reports**, and **retrieve data from the Internet**. The advanced programming section describes how to set up **two-way communication** with another program using a **coprocess** and how to obtain input over a network instead of from a local file.

- **Chapter 13   The sed Editor**
Describes sed, the **noninteractive stream editor** that finds many applications as a filter within shell scripts. This chapter discusses how to use sed's buffers to write **simple yet powerful programs** and includes many examples.

PART V: COMMAND REFERENCE

Linux includes hundreds of utilities. Chapters 11 and 12 as well as Part V provide extensive examples of the use of more than 80 of the **most important utilities** with which you can solve problems without resorting to programming in C. If you are already familiar with UNIX/Linux, this part of the book will be a valuable, **easy-to-use reference**. If you are not an experienced user, it will serve as a useful supplement while you are mastering the earlier sections of the book.

Although the descriptions of the utilities in Chapters 11 and 12 and Part V are presented in a format similar to that used by the Linux manual (man) pages, they are much easier to read and understand. These utilities were chosen because you will work with them **day in and day out** (for example, ls and cp), because they are **powerful tools** that are especially useful in shell scripts (sort, paste, and test), because they help you **work with your Linux system** (ps, kill, and fsck), or because they enable you to **communicate with other systems** (ssh, scp, and ftp). Each utility description includes complete explanations of its most useful options. The "Discussion" and "Notes" sections present **tips and tricks** for using the utility to full advantage. The "**Examples**" **sections** demonstrate how to use these utilities in real life, alone and together with other utilities to generate reports, summarize data, and extract information. Take a look at the "Examples" sections for gawk (more than 20 pages, starting on page 537), ftp (page 674), and sort (page 764) to see how extensive these sections are.

PART VI: APPENDIXES

Part VI includes the appendixes, the glossary, and the index.

- **Appendix A   Regular Expressions**
  Explains how to use **regular expressions** to take advantage of the **hidden power of Linux**. Many utilities, including grep, sed, vim, and gawk, accept regular expressions in place of simple strings of characters. A single regular expression can match many simple strings.

- **Appendix B   Help**
  Details the steps typically used to **solve the problems** you may encounter with a Linux system. This appendix also includes many **links to Web sites** that offer **documentation**, useful Linux information, mailing lists, and **software**.

- **Appendix C   Keeping the System Up-to-date**
  Describes how to use tools to download software and **keep your system current**. This appendix includes information on

- yum   Downloads software from the Internet, keeping a system up-to-date and **resolving dependencies** as it goes.

- **Apt**   An alternative to yum for keeping a system current.

- **BitTorrent**   Good for distributing large amounts of data such as Linux installation CDs.

- Glossary
  Defines more than 500 terms that pertain to the use of Linux.

- Index
  Helps you find the information you want quickly.

SUPPLEMENTS

The author's home page (www.sobell.com) contains downloadable listings of the longer programs from this book as well as pointers to many interesting and useful Linux-related sites on the World Wide Web, a list of corrections to the book, answers to even-numbered exercises, and a solicitation for corrections, comments, and suggestions.

THANKS

First and foremost I want to thank my editor at Prentice Hall PTR, Mark L. Taub, who encouraged me and kept me on track. Mark is unique in my experience: He is an editor who works with the tools I am writing about. Because Mark runs Linux on his home computer, we could share experiences as I wrote. His comments and direction were invaluable. Thank you, Mark T.

A big "Thank You" to the folks who read through the drafts of the book and made comments that caused me to refocus parts of the book where things were not clear or were left out altogether: Lars Kellogg-Stedman, Harvard University; Jim A. Lola, Principal Systems Consultant, Privateer Systems, LLC; Eric S. Raymond, cofounder, Open Source Initiative; Scott Mann; Randall Lechlitner, Independent Computer Consultant; Jason Wertz, Computer Science Instructor, Montgomery County Community College; Justin Howell, Solano Community College; Ed Sawicki, The Accelerated Learning Center; David Mercer, Contechst; Jeffrey Bianchine, Advocate, Author, Journalist; John Kennedy; Chris Karr; and Jim Dennis, Starshine Technical Services.

Thanks to Molly Sharp of ContentWorks, the production manager who made sure the book came together as it was supposed to, and to Jill Hobbs, the copy editor who kept the various parts of the English language in their proper relative places. Thanks also to the folks at Prentice Hall PTR who helped bring this book to life: Heather Fox, Publicist; Suzette Ciancio, Marketing Manager; Robin O'Brien, Executive Marketing Manager; Julie Nahil, Full-Service Production Manager; Noreen Regina, Editorial Assistant; and everyone else who worked behind the scenes to make this book happen.

I am also indebted to Denis Howe, the editor of *The Free On-Line Dictionary of Computing* (FOLDOC). Dennis has graciously permitted me to use entries from his compilation. Be sure to visit the dictionary (www.foldoc.org).

Dr. Brian Kernighan and Rob Pike graciously allowed me to reprint the **bundle** script from their book, *The UNIX Programming Environment* (Prentice Hall, 1984).

Parts of *A Practical Guide to Linux® Commands, Editors, and Shell Programming* have grown from my previous Linux books and I want to thank the people who helped with those books.

Thank you to David Chisnall, computer scientist extraordinaire; Carsten Pfeiffer, Software Engineer and KDE Developer; Aaron Weber, Ximian; Matthew Miller, Boston University; Cristof Falk, Software Developer at CritterDesign; Scott Mann, IBM, Systems Managment and Integration Professional; Steve Elgersma, Computer Science Department, Princeton University; Scott Dier, University of Minnesota; and Robert Haskins, Computer Net Works.

Thanks also to Dustin Puryear, Puryear Information Technology; Gabor Liptak, Independent Consultant; Bart Schaefer, Chief Technical Officer, iPost; Michael J. Jordan, Web Developer, Linux Online Inc.; Steven Gibson, owner of SuperAnt.com; John Viega, founder and Chief Scientist, Secure Software, Inc.; K. Rachael Treu, Internet Security Analyst, Global Crossing; Kara Pritchard, K & S Pritchard Enterprises, Inc.; Glen Wiley, Capitol One Finances; Karel Baloun, Senior Software Engineer, Looksmart, Ltd.; Matthew Whitworth; Dameon D. Welch-Abernathy, Nokia Systems; Josh Simon, Consultant; Stan Isaacs; and Dr. Eric H. Herrin II, Vice President, Herrin Software Development, Inc. And thanks to Doug Hughes, long-time system designer and administrator, who gave me a big hand with the sections on system administration, networks, the Internet, and programming.

More thanks go to consultants Lorraine Callahan and Steve Wampler; Ronald Hiller, Graburn Technology, Inc.; Charles A. Plater, Wayne State University; Bob Palowoda; Tom Bialaski, Sun Microsystems; Roger Hartmuller, TIS Labs at Network Associates; Kaowen Liu; Andy Spitzer; Rik Schneider; Jesse St. Laurent; Steve Bellenot; Ray W. Hiltbrand; Jennifer Witham; Gert-Jan Hagenaars; and Casper Dik.

A Practical Guide to Linux® Commands, Editors, and Shell Programming is based in part on two of my previous UNIX books: *UNIX System V: A Practical Guide* and *A Practical Guide to the UNIX System*. Many people helped me with those books, and thanks here go to Pat Parseghian, Dr. Kathleen Hemenway, and Brian LaRose; Byron A. Jeff, Clark Atlanta University; Charles Stross; Jeff Gitlin, Lucent Technologies; Kurt Hockenbury; Maury Bach, Intel Israel Ltd.; Peter H. Salus; Rahul Dave, University of Pennsylvania; Sean Walton, Intelligent Algorithmic Solutions; Tim Segall, Computer Sciences Corporation; Behrouz Forouzan, DeAnza College; Mike Keenan, Virginia Polytechnic Institute and State University; Mike Johnson, Oregon State University; Jandelyn Plane, University of Maryland; Arnold Robbins and Sathis Menon, Georgia Institute of Technology; Cliff Shaffer, Virginia Polytechnic Institute and State University; and Steven Stepanek, California State University, Northridge, for reviewing the book.

I continue to be grateful to the many people who helped with the early editions of my UNIX books. Special thanks are due to Roger Sippl, Laura King, and Roy Harrington for introducing me to the UNIX system. My mother, Dr. Helen Sobell, provided invaluable comments on the original manuscript at several junctures. Also, thanks go to Isaac Rabinovitch, Professor Raphael Finkel, Professor Randolph Bentson, Bob Greenberg, Professor Udo Pooch, Judy Ross, Dr. Robert Veroff, Dr. Mike Denny, Joe DiMartino, Dr. John Mashey, Diane Schulz, Robert Jung, Charles Whitaker, Don Cragun, Brian Dougherty, Dr. Robert Fish, Guy Harris, Ping Liao, Gary Lindgren, Dr. Jarrett Rosenberg, Dr. Peter Smith, Bill Weber, Mike Bianchi, Scooter Morris, Clarke Echols, Oliver Grillmeyer, Dr. David Korn, Dr. Scott Weikart, and Dr. Richard Curtis.

I take responsibility for any errors and omissions in this book. If you find one or just have a comment, let me know (mgs@sobell.com) and I will fix it in the next printing. My home page (www.sobell.com) contains a list of errors and credits those who found them. It also offers copies of the longer scripts from the book and pointers to many interesting Linux pages.

Mark G. Sobell
San Francisco, California

WELCOME TO LINUX

The Linux *kernel* was developed by Finnish undergraduate student Linus Torvalds, who used the Internet to make the source code immediately available to others for free. Torvalds released Linux version 0.01 in September 1991.

The new operating system came together through a lot of hard work. Programmers around the world were quick to extend the kernel and develop other tools, adding functionality to match that already found in both BSD UNIX and System V UNIX (SVR4) as well as new functionality.

The Linux operating system, developed through the cooperation of many, many people around the world, is a *product of the Internet* and is a *free* operating system. In other words, all the source code is free. You are free to study it, redistribute it, and modify it. As a result, the code is available free of cost—no charge for the software, source, documentation, or support (via newsgroups, mailing lists, and other Internet resources). As the

GNU Free Software Definition (www.gnu.org/philosophy/free-sw.html) puts it:

Free beer

> "Free software" is a matter of liberty, not price. To understand the
> concept, you should think of "free" as in "free speech," not as in
> "free beer."

THE GNU–LINUX CONNECTION

An operating system is the low-level software that schedules tasks, allocates storage,
and handles the interfaces to peripheral hardware, such as printers, disk drives, the
screen, keyboard, and mouse. An operating system has two main parts: the *kernel*
and the *system programs*. The kernel allocates machine resources, including memory, disk space, and *CPU* (page 869) cycles, to all other programs that run on the
computer. The system programs perform higher-level housekeeping tasks, often acting as servers in a client/server relationship. *Linux* is the name of the kernel that
Linus Torvalds presented to the world in 1991 and that many others have worked
on since then to enhance, stabilize, expand, and make more secure.

THE HISTORY OF GNU–LINUX

This section presents some background on the relationship between GNU and
Linux.

FADE TO 1983

Richard Stallman (www.stallman.org) announces[1] the GNU Project for creating an
operating system, both kernel and system programs, and presents the GNU Manifesto,[2] which begins as follows:

> GNU, which stands for Gnu's Not UNIX, is the name for the com-
> plete UNIX-compatible software system which I am writing so that
> I can give it away free to everyone who can use it.

Some years later Stallman added a footnote to the preceding sentence when he real-
ized that it was creating confusion:

> The wording here was careless. The intention was that nobody
> would have to pay for *permission* to use the GNU system. But
> the words don't make this clear, and people often interpret them as
> saying that copies of GNU should always be distributed at little or

---

1. www.gnu.org/gnu/initial-announcement.html

2. www.gnu.org/gnu/manifesto.html

no charge. That was never the intent; later on, the manifesto mentions the possibility of companies providing the service of distribution for a profit. Subsequently I have learned to distinguish carefully between "free" in the sense of freedom and "free" in the sense of price. Free software is software that users have the freedom to distribute and change. Some users may obtain copies at no charge, while others pay to obtain copies—and if the funds help support improving the software, so much the better. The important thing is that everyone who has a copy has the freedom to cooperate with others in using it.

In the manifesto, after explaining a little about the project and what has been accomplished so far, Stallman continues:

Why I Must Write GNU

I consider that the golden rule requires that if I like a program I must share it with other people who like it. Software sellers want to divide the users and conquer them, making each user agree not to share with others. I refuse to break solidarity with other users in this way. I cannot in good conscience sign a nondisclosure agreement or a software license agreement. For years I worked within the Artificial Intelligence Lab to resist such tendencies and other inhospitalities, but eventually they had gone too far: I could not remain in an institution where such things are done for me against my will.

So that I can continue to use computers without dishonor, I have decided to put together a sufficient body of free software so that I will be able to get along without any software that is not free. I have resigned from the AI Lab to deny MIT any legal excuse to prevent me from giving GNU away.

NEXT SCENE, 1991

The GNU Project has moved well along toward its goal. Much of the GNU operating system, except for the kernel, is complete. Richard Stallman later writes:

By the early '90s we had put together the whole system aside from the kernel (and we were also working on a kernel, the GNU Hurd,[3] which runs on top of Mach[4]). Developing this kernel has been a lot harder than we expected, and we are still working on finishing it.[5]

---

3. www.gnu.org/software/hurd/hurd.html

4. www.gnu.org/software/hurd/gnumach.html

5. www.gnu.org/software/hurd/hurd-and-linux.html

> . . . [M]any believe that once Linus Torvalds finished writing
> the kernel, his friends looked around for other free software, and
> for no particular reason most everything necessary to make a
> UNIX-like system was already available.
>
> What they found was no accident—it was the GNU system.
> The available free software[6] added up to a complete system be-
> cause the GNU Project had been working since 1984 to make one.
> The GNU Manifesto had set forth the goal of developing a free
> UNIX-like system, called GNU. The Initial Announcement of the
> GNU Project also outlines some of the original plans for the GNU
> system. By the time Linux was written, the [GNU] system was al-
> most finished.[7]

Today the GNU "operating system" runs on top of the FreeBSD (www.freebsd.org)
and NetBSD (www.netbsd.org) kernels with complete Linux binary compatibility
and on top of Hurd pre-releases and Darwin (developer.apple.com/darwin) without
this compatibility.

THE CODE IS FREE

The tradition of free software dates back to the days when UNIX was released to
universities at nominal cost, which contributed to its portability and success. This
tradition died as UNIX was commercialized and manufacturers regarded the source
code as proprietary, making it effectively unavailable. Another problem with the
commercial versions of UNIX related to their complexity. As each manufacturer
tuned UNIX for a specific architecture, it became less portable and too unwieldy for
teaching and experimentation.

MINIX   Two professors created their own stripped-down UNIX look-alikes for educational
purposes: Doug Comer created XINU (www.cs.purdue.edu/research/xinu.html)
and Andrew Tanenbaum created MINIX (www.cs.vu.nl/~ast/minix.html). Linus
Torvalds created Linux to counteract the shortcomings in MINIX. Every time there
was a choice between code simplicity and efficiency/features Tanenbaum chose
simplicity (to make it easy to teach with MINIX), which meant that this system
lacked many of features people wanted. Linux goes in the opposite direction.

You can obtain Linux at no cost over the Internet. You can also obtain the GNU
code via the U.S. mail at a modest cost for materials and shipping. You can support
the Free Software Foundation by buying the same (GNU) code in higher-priced
packages, and you can buy commercial packaged releases of Linux (called *distributions*) that include installation instructions, software, and support.

---

6. www.gnu.org/philosophy/free-sw.html

7. www.gnu.org/gnu/linux-and-gnu.html

GPL Linux and GNU software are distributed under the terms of the GNU General Public License (GPL, www.gnu.org/licenses/licenses.html). The GPL says you have the right to copy, modify, and redistribute the code covered by the agreement. If you redistribute the code, you must also distribute the same license with the code, making the code and the license inseparable. If you get the source code off the Internet for an accounting program that is under the GPL, modify the code, and then redistribute an executable version of the program, you must also distribute the modified source code and the GPL agreement with it. Because this is the reverse of the way a normal copyright works (it gives rights instead of limiting them), it has been termed a *copyleft*. (This paragraph is not a legal interpretation of the GPL; it simply gives you an idea of how it works. Refer to the GPL itself when you want to make use of it.)

HAVE FUN!

Two key words for Linux are "Have Fun!" These words pop up in prompts and documentation. The UNIX—now Linux   culture is steeped in humor that can be seen throughout the system. For example, less is more—GNU has replaced the UNIX paging utility named more with an improved utility named less. The utility to view PostScript documents is named ghostscript, and one of several replacements for the vi editor is named elvis. While machines with Intel processors have "Intel Inside" logos on their outside, some Linux machines sport "Linux Inside" logos. And Torvalds himself has been seen wearing a T-shirt bearing a "Linus Inside" logo.

THE HERITAGE OF LINUX: UNIX

The UNIX system was developed by researchers who needed a set of modern computing tools to help them with their projects. The system allowed a group of people working together on a project to share selected data and programs while keeping other information private.

Universities and colleges played a major role in furthering the popularity of the UNIX operating system through the "four-year effect." When the UNIX operating system became widely available in 1975, Bell Labs offered it to educational institutions at nominal cost. The schools, in turn, used it in their computer science programs, ensuring that computer science students became familiar with it. Because UNIX was such an advanced development system, the students became acclimated to a sophisticated programming environment. As these students graduated and went into industry, they expected to work in a similarly advanced environment. As more of them worked their way up the ladder in the commercial world, the UNIX operating system found its way into industry.

In addition to introducing students to the UNIX operating system, the Computer Systems Research Group (CSRG) at the University of California at Berkeley made significant additions and changes to it. In fact, it made so many popular changes that one version of the system is called the Berkeley Software Distribution (BSD) of the UNIX system (or just Berkeley UNIX). The other major version is UNIX System V (SVR4), which descended from versions developed and maintained by AT&T and UNIX System Laboratories.

WHAT IS SO GOOD ABOUT LINUX?

In recent years Linux has emerged as a powerful and innovative UNIX work-alike. Its popularity is surpassing that of its UNIX predecessors. Although it mimics UNIX in many ways, the Linux operating system departs from UNIX in several significant ways: The Linux kernel is implemented independently of both BSD and System V, the continuing development of Linux is taking place through the combined efforts of many capable individuals throughout the world, and Linux puts the power of UNIX within easy reach of business and personal computer users. Using the Internet, today's skilled programmers submit additions and improvements to the operating system to Linus Torvalds, GNU, or one of the other authors of Linux.

Applications   A rich selection of applications is available for Linux—both free and commercial—as well as a wide variety of tools: graphical, word processing, networking, security, administration, Web server, and many others. Large software companies have recently seen the benefit in supporting Linux and have now on-staff programmers whose job it is to design and code the Linux kernel, GNU, KDE, or other software that runs on Linux For example, IBM (www.ibm.com/linux) is a major Linux supporter. Linux conforms increasingly more closely to POSIX standards, and some distributions and parts of others meet this standard. (See "Standards" on page 8 for more information.) These facts mean that Linux is becoming more mainstream and is respected as an attractive alternative to other popular operating systems.

Peripherals   Another aspect of Linux that appeals to users is the amazing range of peripherals that is supported and the speed with which support for new peripherals emerges. Linux often supports a peripheral or interface card before any company does. Unfortunately some types of peripherals—particularly proprietary graphics cards—lag in their support because the manufacturers do not release specifications or source code for drivers in a timely manner, if at all.

Software   Also important to users is the amount of software that is available—not just source code (which needs to be compiled) but also prebuilt binaries that are easy to install and ready to run. These include more than free software. Netscape, for example, has been available for Linux from the start and included Java support before it was available from many commercial vendors. Now its sibling Mozilla is also a viable browser, mail client, and newsreader, performing many other functions as well.

Platforms Linux is not just for Intel-based platforms but has been ported to and runs on the Power PC—including Apple computers (ppclinux), the Compaq's (née Digital Equipment Corporation) Alpha-based machines, MIPS-based machines, Motorola's 68K-based machines, and IBM's S/390. Nor is Linux just for single-processor machines: As of version 2.0, it runs on multiple processor machines (SMPs). As of version 2.5.2, Linux includes an O(1) scheduler, which dramatically increases scalability on SMP systems.

Emulators Linux supports programs, called *emulators*, that run code intended for other operating systems. By using emulators you can run some DOS, Windows, and Macintosh programs under Linux. Wine (www.winehq.com) is an open-source implementation of the Windows API on top of X and UNIX/Linux; QEMU (fabrice.bellard.free.fr/qemu) is a CPU-only emulator that executes x86 Linux binaries on non-x86 Linux systems.

WHY LINUX IS POPULAR WITH HARDWARE COMPANIES AND DEVELOPERS

Two trends in the computer industry set the stage for the popularity of UNIX and Linux. First, advances in hardware technology created the need for an operating system that could take advantage of available hardware power. In the mid-1970s, minicomputers began challenging the large mainframe computers because, in many applications, minicomputers could perform the same functions less expensively. More recently, powerful 64-bit processor chips, plentiful and inexpensive memory, and lower-priced hard disk storage have allowed hardware companies to install multiuser operating systems on desktop computers.

Proprietary operating systems Second, with the cost of hardware continually dropping, hardware manufacturers can no longer afford to develop and support proprietary operating systems. A *proprietary* operating system used to be written and owned by the manufacturer of the hardware (for example, DEC/Compaq owns VMS). Today's manufacturers need a generic operating system that they can easily adapt to their machines.

Generic operating systems A *generic* operating system is written outside of the company manufacturing the hardware and is sold (UNIX, Windows) or given (Linux) to the manufacturer. Linux is a generic operating system because it runs on different types of hardware produced by different manufacturers. Of course, if manufacturers can pay only for development and avoid per-unit costs (as they have to pay to Microsoft for each copy of Windows they sell), developers are much better off. In turn, software developers need to keep the prices of their products down; they cannot afford to convert their products to run under many different proprietary operating systems. Like hardware manufacturers, software developers need a generic operating system.

Although the UNIX system once met the needs of hardware companies and researchers for a generic operating system, over time it has become more proprietary as each manufacturer has added support for specialized features and introduced new software libraries and utilities.

Linux emerged to serve both needs. It is a generic operating system that takes advantage of available hardware power.

LINUX IS PORTABLE

A *portable* operating system is one that can run on many different machines. More than 95 percent of the Linux operating system is written in the C programming language, and C is portable because it is written in a higher-level, machine-independent language. (The C compiler is written in C.)

Because Linux is portable, it can be adapted (ported) to different machines and can meet special requirements. For example, Linux is used in embedded computers, such as the ones found in cellphones, PDAs, and the cable boxes on top of many TVs. The file structure takes full advantage of large, fast hard disks. Equally important, Linux was originally designed as a multiuser operating system—it was not modified to serve several users as an afterthought. Sharing the computer's power among many users and giving them the ability to share data and programs are central features of the system.

Because it is adaptable and takes advantage of available hardware, Linux now runs on many different microprocessor-based systems as well as mainframes. The popularity of the microprocessor-based hardware drives Linux; these microcomputers are getting faster all the time, at about the same price point. Linux on a fast microcomputer has become good enough to displace workstations on many desktops. Linux benefits both users, who do not like having to learn a new operating system for each vendor's hardware, and the system administrators, who like having a consistent software environment.

The advent of a standard operating system has aided the development of the software industry. Now software manufacturers can afford to make one version of a product available on machines from different manufacturers.

STANDARDS

Individuals from companies throughout the computer industry have joined together to develop the POSIX (Portable Operating System Interface for computer Environments) standard, which is based largely on the UNIX System V Interface Definition (SVID) and other earlier standardization efforts. These efforts have been spurred by the U.S. government, which needs a standard computing environment to minimize its training and procurement costs. Now that these standards are gaining acceptance, software developers are able to develop applications that run on all conforming versions of UNIX, Linux, and other operating systems.

THE C PROGRAMMING LANGUAGE

Ken Thompson wrote the UNIX operating system in 1969 in PDP-7 assembly language. Assembly language is machine dependent: Programs written in assembly language work on only one machine or, at best, one family of machines. The original UNIX operating system therefore could not easily be transported to run on other machines (it was not portable).

To make UNIX portable, Thompson developed the B programming language, a machine-independent language, from the BCPL language. Dennis Ritchie developed the C programming language by modifying B and, with Thompson, rewrote UNIX in C in 1973. The revised operating system could be transported more easily to run on other machines.

That development marked the start of C. Its roots reveal some of the reasons why it is such a powerful tool. C can be used to write machine-independent programs. A programmer who designs a program to be portable can easily move it to any computer that has a C compiler. C is also designed to compile into very efficient code. With the advent of C, a programmer no longer had to resort to assembly language to get code that would run well (that is, quickly, although an assembler will always generate more efficient code than a high-level language).

C is a good systems language. You can write a compiler or an operating system in C. It is highly structured but is not necessarily a high-level language. C allows a programmer to manipulate bits and bytes, as is necessary when writing an operating system. But it also has high-level constructs that allow efficient, modular programming.

In the late 1980s the American National Standards Institute (ANSI) defined a standard version of the C language, commonly referred to as *ANSI C* or *C89* (for the year the standard was published). Ten years later the C99 standard was published; it is mostly supported by the GNU Project's C compiler (named gcc). The original version of the language is often referred to as *Kernighan & Ritchie* (or *K&R*) C, named for the authors of the book that first described the C language.

Another researcher at Bell Labs, Bjarne Stroustrup, created an object-oriented programming language named C++, which is built on the foundation of C. Because object-oriented programming is desired by many employers today, C++ is preferred over C in many environments. The GNU Project's C compiler and its C++ compiler (g++) are integral parts of the Linux operating system.

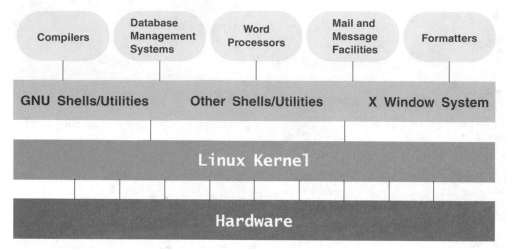

Figure 1-1   A layered view of the Linux operating system

OVERVIEW OF LINUX

The Linux operating system has many unique and powerful features. Like other operating systems, Linux is a control program for computers. But like UNIX, it is also a well-thought-out family of utility programs (Figure 1-1) and a set of tools allowing users to connect and use these utilities to build systems and applications.

LINUX HAS A KERNEL PROGRAMMING INTERFACE

The heart of the Linux operating system is the Linux kernel, which is responsible for allocating the computer's resources and scheduling user jobs so that each one gets its fair share of system resources, including access to the CPU; peripheral devices, such as disk, DVD, and CD-ROM storage; printers; and tape drives. Programs interact with the kernel through *system calls,* special functions with well-known names. A programmer can use a single system call to interact with many kinds of devices. For example, there is one **write** system call, not many device-specific ones. When a program issues a **write** request, the kernel interprets the context and passes the request to the appropriate device. This flexibility allows old utilities to work with devices that did not exist when the utilities were originally written. It also makes it possible to move programs to new versions of the operating system without rewriting them (provided that the new version recognizes the same system calls).

LINUX CAN SUPPORT MANY USERS

Depending on the hardware and what types of tasks the computer performs, a Linux system can support from 1 to more than 1,000 users, each concurrently running a different set of programs. The per-user cost of a computer that can be used by many people at the same time is less than that of a computer that can be used by only a single person at a time. It is less because one person cannot generally use all the resources a computer has to offer. No one can keep the printers going constantly, keep all the system memory in use, keep the disks busy reading and writing, keep the Internet connection in use, and keep all the terminals busy at the same time. A multiuser operating system allows many people to use these system resources almost simultaneously. The use of costly resources can be maximized, and the cost per user can be minimized. These are the primary objectives of a multiuser operating system.

LINUX CAN RUN MANY TASKS

Linux is a fully protected multitasking operating system, allowing each user to run more than one job at a time. Processes can communicate with one another but remain fully protected from one another, just as the kernel is protected from all processes. You can run several jobs in the background while giving all your attention to the job being displayed on your screen, and you can switch back and forth between jobs. If you are running the X Window System (page 15), you can run different programs in different windows on the same screen and watch all of them. This capability ensures that users can be more productive.

LINUX PROVIDES A SECURE HIERARCHICAL FILESYSTEM

A *file* is a collection of information, such as text for a memo or report, an accumulation of sales figures, an image, a song, or an executable program. Each file is stored under a unique identifier on a storage device, such as a hard disk. The Linux filesystem provides a structure whereby files are arranged under *directories,* which are like folders or boxes. Each directory has a name and can hold other files and directories. Directories, in turn, are arranged under other directories, and so forth, in a treelike organization. This structure helps users keep track of large numbers of files by grouping related files into directories. Each user has one primary directory and as many subdirectories as required (Figure 1-2).

Standards   With the idea of making life easier for system administrators and software developers, a group got together over the Internet and developed the Linux Filesystem Standard (FSSTND), which has since evolved into the Linux Filesystem Hierarchy Standard (FHS). Before this standard was adopted, key programs were located in different places in different Linux distributions. Today you can sit down at a Linux system and know where to expect to find any given standard program.

Links   A *link* allows a given file to be accessed by means of two or more different names. (Windows uses the term *shortcut* instead of *link*.) The alternative names can be located in the same directory as the original file or in another directory. Links can

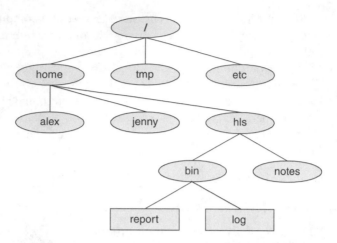

Figure 1-2 The Linux filesystem structure

be used to make the same file appear in several users' directories, enabling them to share the file easily.

Security Like most multiuser operating systems, Linux allows users to protect their data from access by other users. It also allows users to share selected data and programs with certain other users by means of a simple but effective protection scheme. This level of security is provided by file access permissions, which limit which users can read from, write to, or execute a file. Access Control Lists (ACLs) have recently been added to the Linux kernel. ACLs give users and administrators finer-grained control over file access permissions.

The Shell: Command Interpreter and Programming Language

In a textual environment, the shell—the command interpreter—acts as an interface between you and the operating system. When you enter a command on the screen, the shell interprets the command and calls the program you want. A number of shells are available for Linux including these two common ones:

- The Bourne Again Shell (bash), an enhanced version of the Bourne Shell, one of the original UNIX shells

- The TC Shell (tcsh), an enhanced version of the C Shell, developed as part of BSD UNIX

Because users often prefer different shells, multiuser systems can have a number of different shells in use at any given time. The choice of shells demonstrates one of the powers of the Linux operating system: the ability to provide a customized user interface.

Besides performing its function of interpreting commands from a keyboard and sending them to the operating system, the shell is a high-level programming language. Shell commands can be arranged in a file for later execution. Linux calls these files *shell scripts;* DOS and Windows call them *batch files.* Their flexibility allows users to perform complex operations with relative ease, often by using rather short commands, and to build with surprisingly little effort elaborate programs that perform highly complex operations.

FILENAME GENERATION

When you are typing commands to be processed by the shell, you can construct patterns using characters that have special meanings to the shell. The characters are called *wildcard* characters. These patterns represent a kind of shorthand: Rather than typing in complete filenames users can type in patterns, and the shell will expand them into matching filenames. These patterns are called *ambiguous file references.* An ambiguous file reference can save you the effort of typing a long filename or a long series of similar filenames. It can also be useful when you know only part of a filename or cannot remember its exact spelling.

DEVICE-INDEPENDENT INPUT AND OUTPUT

Redirection Devices (such as a printer or terminal) and disk files all appear as files to Linux programs. When you give a command to the Linux operating system, you can instruct it to send the output to any one of several devices or files. This diversion is called output *redirection.*

In a similar manner a program's input that normally comes from a keyboard can be redirected so that it comes from a disk file instead. Input and output are *device independent;* they can be redirected to or from any appropriate device.

As an example, the cat utility normally displays the contents of a file on the screen. When you run a cat command, you can easily redirect its output to go to a disk file instead of the screen.

SHELL FUNCTIONS

One of the most important features of the shell is that users can use it as a programming language. Because the shell is an interpreter, it does not compile programs written for it but rather interprets them each time they are loaded from the disk. Loading and interpreting programs can be time-consuming.

Many shells, including the Bourne Again Shell, include shell functions that the shell holds in memory so that it does not have to read them from the disk each time you want to execute them. The shell also keeps functions in an internal format so that it does not have to spend as much time interpreting them.

JOB CONTROL

Job control is a shell feature that allows users to work on several jobs at once, switching back and forth between them as desired. When you start a job it is frequently in the foreground, so it is connected to your terminal. Using job control, you can move the job you are working with into the background and continue running it there while working on or observing another job in the foreground. If a background job then needs your attention, you can move it into the foreground so that it is once again attached to the terminal. The concept of job control originated with BSD UNIX, where it appeared in the C Shell.

A LARGE COLLECTION OF USEFUL UTILITIES

Linux includes a family of several hundred utility programs, often referred to as *commands*. These utilities perform functions that are universally required by users. An example is sort. The sort utility puts lists (or groups of lists) in alphabetical or numerical order and can be used to sort by part number, last name, city, ZIP code, telephone number, age, size, cost, and so forth. The sort utility is an important programming tool and is part of the standard Linux system. Other utilities allow users to create, display, print, copy, search, and delete files, as well as to edit, format, and typeset text. The man (for manual) and info utilities provide online documentation of Linux itself.

INTERPROCESS COMMUNICATION

Pipes and filters — Linux allows users to establish both pipes and filters on the command line. A *pipe* sends the output of one program to another program as input. A *filter* is a special form of a pipe that processes a stream of input data to yield a stream of output data. A filter processes another program's output, altering it as a result. The filter's output then becomes input to another program.

Pipes and filters frequently join utilities to perform a specific task. For example, you can use a pipe to send the output of the cat utility to sort, a filter. You can then use another pipe to send the output of sort to a third utility, lpr, that sends the data to a printer. Thus, in one command line, you can use three utilities together to sort and print a file.

SYSTEM ADMINISTRATION

On a Linux system the system administrator is frequently the owner and only user of the system. This person has many responsibilities. The first responsibility may be to set up the system and install the software.

Once the system is up and running, the system administrator is responsible for downloading and installing software (including upgrading the operating system), backing up and restoring files, and managing such system facilities as printers, terminals, servers, and a local network. The system administrator is also responsible for setting up accounts for new users on a multiuser system, bringing the system up and down as needed, and taking care of any problems that arise.

ADDITIONAL FEATURES OF LINUX

The developers of Linux included features from BSD, System V, and Sun Microsystems' Solaris, as well as new features in their operating system. Although most of the tools found on UNIX exist for Linux, in many cases these tools have been replaced by more modern counterparts. The following sections describe many of the popular tools and features available under Linux.

GUIs: GRAPHICAL USER INTERFACES

The X Window System (also called X) was developed in part by researchers at the Massachusetts Institute of Technology and provides the foundation for the GUIs available with Linux. Given a terminal or workstation screen that supports X, a user can interact with the computer through multiple windows on the screen, display graphical information, or use special-purpose applications to draw pictures, monitor processes, or preview formatted output. X is an across-the-network protocol that allows a user to open a window on a workstation or computer system that is remote from the CPU generating the window.

Desktop manager
Usually two layers run under X: a desktop manager and a window manager. A *desktop manager* is a picture-oriented user interface that enables you to interact with system programs by manipulating icons instead of typing the corresponding commands to a shell. GNOME (www.gnome.org) and KDE (www.kde.org) are the most popular desktop managers.

Window manager
A *window manager* is a program that runs under the desktop manager and allows you to open and close windows, start programs running, and set up a mouse so it does different things depending on how and where you click. The window manager also gives the screen its personality. Microsoft Windows allows you to change the color of key elements in a window, but a window manager under X allows you to change the overall look and feel of your screen: change the way a window looks and works (by giving it different borders, buttons, and scrollbars), set up virtual desktops, create menus, and more.

Several popular window managers run under X and Linux, including Metacity (default under GNOME) and kwin (default under KDE). Other window managers, such as Sawfish and WindowMaker, are also available.

(INTER)NETWORKING UTILITIES

Linux network support includes many valuable utilities that enable you to access remote systems over a variety of networks. In addition to sending email to users on other systems, you can access files on disks mounted on other computers as if they were located on the local system, make your files available to other systems in a similar manner, copy files back and forth, run programs on remote systems while displaying the results on the local system, and perform many other operations across local area networks (LANs) and wide area networks (WANs), including the Internet.

Layered on top of this network access are a wide range of application programs that extend the computer's resources around the globe. You can carry on conversations with people throughout the world, gather information on a wide variety of subjects, and download new software over the Internet quickly and reliably.

SOFTWARE DEVELOPMENT

One of Linux's major strengths is its rich software development environment. You can find compilers and interpreters for many computer languages. Besides C and C++, languages available for Linux include Ada, Fortran, Java, Lisp, Pascal, Perl, and Python among many others. The bison utility generates parsing code that makes it easier to write programs to build compilers (tools that parse files containing structured information). The flex utility generates scanners, or code that recognizes lexical patterns in text. The make utility and GNU's automatic configuration utility (configure) make it easy to manage complex development projects. Source code management systems, such as CVS, simplify version control. Several debuggers, including ups and gdb, help in tracking down and repairing software defects. The GNU C compiler (gcc) works with the gprof profiling utility to help programmers identify potential bottlenecks in a program's performance. The C compiler includes options to perform extensive checking of C code that can make the code more portable and reduce debugging time.

CHAPTER SUMMARY

The Linux operating system grew out of the UNIX heritage to become a popular alternative to traditional systems (that is, Windows) available for microcomputer (PC) hardware. UNIX users will find a familiar environment in Linux. Distributions of Linux contain the expected complement of UNIX utilities, contributed by programmers around the world, including the set of tools developed as part of the GNU Project. The Linux community is committed to the continued development of this system. Support for new microcomputer devices and features is added soon after the hardware becomes available, and the tools available on Linux continue to be refined. With many commercial software packages available to run on Linux platforms and many hardware manufacturers offering Linux on their systems, it is clear that the system has evolved well beyond its origin as an undergraduate project to become an operating system of choice for academic, commercial, professional, and personal use.

EXERCISES

1. What is *free software?* List three characteristics of free software.

2. Why is Linux popular? Why is it popular in academia?

3. What are multiuser systems? Why are they successful?

4. What is the Free Software Foundation/GNU? What is Linux? Which parts of the Linux operating system did each provide? Who else has helped build and refine this operating system?

5. In what language is Linux written? What does the language have to do with the success of Linux?

6. What is a utility program?

7. What is a shell? How does it work with the kernel? With the user?

8. How can you use utility programs and a shell to create your own applications?

9. Why is the Linux filesystem referred to as *hierarchical?*

10. What is the difference between a multiprocessor and a multiprocessing system?

11. Give an example of when you would want to use a multiprocessing system.

12. Approximately how many people wrote Linux? Why is this unique?

13. What are the key terms of the GNU General Public License (GPL)?

PART I
THE LINUX OPERATING SYSTEM

2

GETTING STARTED

One way or another you are sitting in front of a screen that is connected to a computer that is running Linux. You may be working with a graphical user interface (GUI) or a textual interface. This book is about the textual, or command line, interface to Linux. If you are working with a GUI, you will need to use a terminal emulator such as xterm, Konsole, or GNOME Terminal, to follow along with the examples in this book.

This chapter starts with a discussion of the typographical conventions used in this book, followed by a section on logging in on the system. Next there is a brief reminder about the powers of Superuser (**root**) and how to avoid making mistakes that will make your system inoperable or hard to work with. The chapter continues with a discussion about where to find more information about Linux. It concludes with additional information on logging in, including how to change your password.

While heeding the warning about the dangers of misusing the powers of Superuser on page 28, feel free to experiment with your system: Give commands, create files, follow the examples in this book, and have fun.

CONVENTIONS USED IN THIS BOOK

This book uses conventions to make its explanations shorter and clearer. The following paragraphs describe these conventions.

Text and examples   The text is set in this type, whereas examples are shown in a monospace font (also called a fixed-width font):

```
$ cat practice
This is a small file I created
with a text editor.
```

The next paragraph explains why part of the first line is in a bold typeface.

Items you enter   Everything you enter at the keyboard is shown in a bold typeface: Within the text, **this bold typeface** is used; within examples and screens, **this one** is used. In the previous example, the dollar sign ($) on the first line is a prompt that Linux displays, so it is not bold; the remainder of the first line is entered by a user, so it is bold.

Utility names   Names of utilities are printed in this **bold sans serif typeface**. This book references the **emacs** editor and the **ls** utility or **ls** command (or just **ls**), but instructs you to enter **ls –a** on the command line. The text distinguishes between utilities, which are programs, and the instructions you give on the command line to invoke the utilities.

Filenames   Filenames appear in a **bold** typeface. Examples are **memo5, letter.1283**, and **reports**. Filenames may include uppercase and lowercase letters; however, Linux is *case sensitive* (page 866), so **memo5, MEMO5**, and **Memo5** name three different files.

Character strings   Within the text, characters and character strings are marked by putting them in a **bold** typeface. This convention avoids the need for quotation marks or other delimiters before and after a string. An example is the following string, which is displayed by the **passwd** utility: **Sorry, passwords do not match**.

Keys and characters   This book uses SMALL CAPS for three kinds of items:

- Important keyboard keys, such as the SPACE bar and the RETURN,[1] ESCAPE, and TAB keys.

- The characters that keys generate, such as the SPACEs generated by the SPACE bar.

- Keyboard keys that you press with the CONTROL key, such as CONTROL-D. (Even though D is shown as an uppercase letter, you do not have to press the SHIFT key. Enter CONTROL-D by holding down the CONTROL key and pressing **d**.)

---

1. Different keyboards use different keys to move the *cursor* (page 870) to the beginning of the next line. This book always refers to the key that ends a line as the RETURN key. Your keyboard may have a RET, NEWLINE, Enter, RETURN, or other key. Some keyboards have a key with a bent arrow on it. (The key with the bent arrow is not an arrow key. Arrow keys have straight shafts.) Use the corresponding key on your keyboard each time this book asks you to press RETURN.

Prompts and
RETURNS

Most examples include the *shell prompt*—the signal that Linux is waiting for a command—as a dollar sign ($). The prompt is not in boldface, because you do not enter it. Do not type the prompt on the keyboard when you are experimenting with examples from this book. If you do, the examples will not work.

Examples *omit* the RETURN keystroke that you must use to execute them. An example of a command line is

```
$ vim memo.1204
```

To use this example as a model for running the vim editor, give the command **vim memo.1204** and press the RETURN key. (Press ESCAPE **ZZ** to exit from vim; see page 141 for a vim tutorial.) This method of entering commands makes the examples in the book correspond to what appears on your screen.

Definitions

All entries marked with FOLDOC are courtesy of Denis Howe, editor of the Free Online Dictionary of Computing (www.foldoc.org), and are used with permission. This site is an ongoing work containing not just definitions but also anecdotes and trivia.

optional   Passages marked as optional are not central to the ideas presented in the chapter but often involve more challenging concepts. A good strategy when reading a chapter is to skip the optional sections and then return to them when you are comfortable with the main ideas presented in the chapter. This is an optional paragraph.

URLs (Web addresses)

Web addresses, or URLs, have an implicit **http://** prefix, unless **ftp://** or **https://** is shown. You do not normally need to specify a prefix when the prefix is **http://**, but you must use a prefix from a browser when you specify an FTP or secure HTTP site. Thus you can specify a URL in a browser exactly as shown in this book.

Tip, Caution, and Security boxes

The following boxes highlight information that may be helpful while you are using or administering a Linux system.

This is a tip box

tip   A tip box may help you avoid repeating a common mistake or may point toward additional information.

This box warns you about something

caution   A caution box warns you about a potential pitfall.

This box marks a security note

security   A security box highlights a potential security issue. These notes are usually for system administrators but some apply to all users.

LOGGING IN

To log in on a terminal, terminal emulator, or other text-based device, enter your username and password in response to the system prompts. If you are using a *terminal* (page 905) and your screen does not display **login:**, check whether the terminal is plugged in and turned on, and then press the RETURN key a few times. If **login:** still does not appear, try pressing CONTROL-Q. If you are using a *workstation* (page 910), make sure it is running. Run ssh, telnet, or whatever communications/emulation software you have to log in on the system. Try logging in, making sure that you enter your username and password as they were specified when your account was set up; the routine that verifies the username and password is case sensitive. Like most systems, Linux does not echo your password when you enter it.

Make sure **TERM** is set correctly

tip   The **TERM** shell variable establishes the pseudographical characteristics of a character-based terminal or terminal emulator. Typically **TERM** is set for you—you do not have to set it manually. If things on the screen do not look right, refer to "Specifying a Terminal" on page 844.

LOGGING IN FROM A TERMINAL

The following example shows what it looks like when you log in from a terminal. Max is logging in on the **bravo** system.

```
bravo login: max
Password:
Last login: Tue Mar  1 19:50:38 from kudos
[max@bravo max]$
```

After you log in, the *shell prompt* (or just *prompt*) appears, indicating that you have successfully logged in. It shows that the system is ready for you to give it a command. The shell prompt line may be preceded by one or two short messages called the *message of the day* (or **motd**) and *issue*. These messages generally identify the version of Linux that is running, along with local messages placed in either the **/etc/motd** or the **/etc/issue** file.

Did you log in last?

security   Immediately after you log in, the system may display information about the last login on this account, showing when it took place and where it originated. You can use this information to see whether anyone else may have accessed this account since you last used it. Perhaps an unauthorized user has learned your password and has logged in as you. In the interest of security, advise the system administrator of the circumstances that made you suspicious and change your password (page 37).

The usual prompt is a dollar sign ($). Do not be concerned if you have a different prompt; the examples in this book will work regardless of what your prompt looks like. In the previous example the $ prompt (last line) is preceded by the username (**max**), an at sign (@), the system name (**bravo**), and the name of the directory Max is working in (**max**). For information on how to change your prompt, refer to page 286 (bash) or page 363 (tcsh).

LOGGING IN REMOTELY: TERMINAL EMULATION, ssh, AND telnet

When you are not using the console, a terminal, or another device connected directly to the Linux system you are logging in on, you are probably connected to Linux using terminal emulation software on another system. This software runs on your computer, connects to the Linux system via a network (e.g., Ethernet, asynchronous phone line, PPP), and allows you to log in on the Linux system.

When you log in via a dial-up line, the connection is straightforward: You instruct the emulator program to contact the computer, it dials the phone, and you get a login prompt from the remote system. When you log in via a directly connected network, you use telnet (not secure, page 792) or ssh (secure, page 773) to connect to the remote system. One of the reasons that telnet is not secure is that it sends your username and password over the network in *cleartext* (page 867) when you log in, allowing someone to capture your login information and log in on your account. The ssh utility encrypts all information it sends over the network and, if available, is a better choice than telnet.

From an Apple, PC, UNIX, or other machine, give the command **ssh** or **telnet**, followed by the name or *IP address* (page 882) of the machine you want to log in on. Following is an example of logging in using ssh:

```
$ ssh bravo
max@bravo's password:
Permission denied, please try again.
max@bravo's password:
Last login: Wed Mar  2 21:21:49 2005 from bravo.example.com
[max@bravo max]$
```

In the preceding example the user mistyped his password, received an error message and another prompt, and retyped the password correctly.

WORKING WITH THE SHELL

When you log in and are working in a textual (nongraphical) environment, and when you are using a terminal emulator window in a graphical environment, you are using the shell as a command interpreter. That is, the shell displays a prompt, you type a command, and the shell executes the command and displays another prompt.

This section tells you how to identify the shell you are using and explains the keystrokes you can use to correct mistakes on the command line. It covers how to abort a running command and briefly discusses how to edit a command line. Several chapters of this book are dedicated to shells: Chapter 5 introduces shells, Chapter 8 goes into more detail about the Bourne Again Shell with some coverage of the TC Shell, Chapter 9 covers the TC Shell exclusively, and Chapter 11 discusses writing programs (shell scripts) using the Bourne Again Shell.

Which Shell Are You Running?

This book discusses both the Bourne Again Shell (bash) and the TC Shell (tcsh). You are probably running bash, but you may be running tcsh or another shell such as the Z Shell (zsh). You can identify the shell you are running by using the ps utility. Type **ps** in response to the shell prompt and press RETURN.

```
$ ps
  PID TTY          TIME CMD
 2402 pts/5     00:00:00 bash
 7174 pts/5     00:00:00 ps
```

This command shows that you are running two utilities or commands: bash and ps. If you are running tcsh, ps will display **tcsh** instead of **bash**. If you are running a different shell, ps will display its name.

Correcting Mistakes

This section explains how to correct typographical and other errors you may make while you are logged in on a character-based display. Because the shell does not begin to interpret the command line or other text until you press RETURN, you can correct typing mistakes before you press that key.

You can correct typing mistakes in several ways: You can erase one character at a time, back up a word at a time, or back up to the beginning of the command line in one step. After you press RETURN, it is too late to correct a mistake. You must either wait for the command to run to completion or abort execution of the program (page 27).

Erasing a Character

While entering characters from the keyboard, you can back up and erase a mistake by pressing the *erase key* once for each character you want to delete. The erase key backs over as many characters as you wish. Usually it will not back up past the beginning of the line.

The default erase key is BACKSPACE. If this key does not work, try DELETE or CONTROL-H. If these keys do not work, give the following command to set the erase and line kill keys (see "Deleting a Line" on page 27) to their defaults:

```
$ stty ek
```

For information on changing which key erases characters, refer to page 781.

CONTROL-Z **suspends a program**

tip Although not a way of correcting a mistake, you may press the suspend key (typically CONTROL-Z) by mistake and wonder what happened (you will see a message containing the word **Stopped**). You have just stopped the job you were running, using job control (page 271). Give the command fg to continue your job in the foreground, and you should return to where you were before you pressed the suspend key. For more information refer to "bg: Sends a Job to the Background" on page 273.

DELETING A WORD

You can delete a word you entered by pressing CONTROL-W. A *word* is any sequence of characters that does not contain a SPACE or TAB. When you press CONTROL-W, the cursor moves left to the beginning of the current word (as you are entering a word) or the previous word (when you have just entered a SPACE or TAB), removing the word it passes over.

DELETING A LINE

Any time before you press RETURN, you can delete a line you are entering by pressing the *line kill key,* also called the *kill key.* When you press this key, the cursor moves to the left, erasing characters as it goes, back to the beginning of the line. The default line kill key is CONTROL-U. If this key does not work, try CONTROL-X. If neither key works, give the following command to set the erase and line kill keys to their defaults:

```
$ stty ek
```

For information on changing which key deletes a line, refer to page 781.

ABORTING EXECUTION

Sometimes you may want to terminate a running program. For example, a Linux program may be performing a lengthy task such as displaying the contents of a file that is several hundred pages long or copying a file that is not the one you meant to copy.

To terminate a program from a character-based display, press the *interrupt key* (CONTROL-C or sometimes DELETE or DEL). When you press this key, the Linux operating system sends a terminal interrupt signal both to the program you are running and to the shell. Exactly what effect this signal has depends on the program. Some programs stop execution immediately; others ignore the signal. Some programs take other actions. When it receives a terminal interrupt signal, the shell displays a prompt and waits for another command. For information on changing which key aborts execution, refer to page 781.

If these methods do not terminate the program, try stopping the program with the suspend key (typically CONTROL-Z), giving the **jobs** command to verify the job number of the program, and using kill to abort the program. The job number is the number within the brackets at the left end of the line that **jobs** displays ([**1**]). The kill command sends a signal to the job specified as its argument. You must precede the job number with a percent sign (**%1**):

```
$ bigjob
^Z
[1]+  Stopped                 bigjob
$ jobs
[1]+  Stopped                 bigjob
$ kill %1

[1]+  Stopped                 bigjob
$ RETURN
[1]+  Killed                  bigjob
```

By default kill sends a software termination signal (**–TERM**). When this signal does not work, try using a kill (**–KILL**) signal:

```
$ kill -KILL %1
```

A running program cannot ignore a kill signal—it is sure to abort the program. The kill command returns a prompt; press RETURN again to see the confirmation message. For more information on job control, refer to "Running a Program in the Background" on page 125. For a list of signals, see Table 11-5 on page 494.

REPEATING/EDITING COMMAND LINES

To repeat a previous command on the command line, press the UP ARROW key. Each time you press UP ARROW, you see an earlier command line. To reexecute the displayed command line, press RETURN. Press DOWN ARROW to browse through the command lines in the other direction.

The RIGHT and LEFT ARROW keys move the cursor back and forth along the displayed command line. At any point along the command line, you can add characters by typing. Use the erase key to remove characters from the command line.

For more complex command line editing, see page 297 (bash) and page 353 (tcsh).

CURBING YOUR POWER: SUPERUSER ACCESS

While you are logged in as the user named **root**, you are referred to as *Superuser* or *administrator* and have extraordinary privileges. You can read from or write to any file on the system, execute programs that ordinary users cannot, and more. On a multiuser system you may not be permitted to know the **root** password, but someone—usually the *system administrator*—knows the **root** password and maintains the system. When you are running Linux on your own computer, you will assign a password to **root** when you install Linux.

Do not experiment as Superuser

caution Feel free to experiment when you are logged in as yourself. When you log in as Superuser, also called **root** or administrator, or whenever you give the Superuser password, do only what you have to do and make sure you know exactly what you are doing. After you have completed the task at hand, revert to working as yourself. When working as Superuser you can damage the Linux system to such an extent that you will need to reinstall Linux to get it working again.

GETTING THE FACTS: WHERE TO FIND DOCUMENTATION

Distributions of Linux typically do not come with hardcopy reference manuals. However, its online documentation has always been one of Linux's strengths. The manual (or man) and info pages have been available via the man and info utilities since early releases of the operating system. With the growth of Linux and the Internet, the sources of documentation have expanded. The following sections discuss some of the places you can look for information on various aspects of Linux.

THE --help OPTION

Most GNU utilities have a **--help** option that displays information about the utility.

```
$ cat --help
Usage: cat [OPTION] [FILE]...
Concatenate FILE(s), or standard input, to standard output.

  -A, --show-all          equivalent to -vET
  -b, --number-nonblank   number nonblank output lines
  -e                      equivalent to -vE
  -E, --show-ends         display $ at end of each line
...
```

If the information that **--help** displays runs off the screen, send the output through the less pager (page 30) using a pipe:

```
$ ls --help | less
```

More information about pipes appears on page 52. Non-GNU utilities may use a **-h** or **-help** option to display help information.

```
WHO(1)                        User Commands                        WHO(1)

NAME
    who - show who is logged on

SYNOPSIS
    who [OPTION]... [ FILE | ARG1 ARG2 ]

DESCRIPTION
    -a, --all
            same as -b -d --login -p -r -t -T -u

    -b, --boot
            time of last system boot

    -d, --dead
            print dead processes

    -H, --heading
            print line of column headings

    -i, --idle
            add idle time as HOURS:MINUTES, . or old (deprecated, use -u)
```

Figure 2-1   The man utility displaying information about who

man: DISPLAYS THE SYSTEM MANUAL

The man (manual) utility displays pages (man pages) from the system documentation. This documentation is helpful when you know which utility you want to use
but have forgotten exactly how to use it. You can also refer to the man pages to get
more information about specific topics or to determine which features are available
with Linux. Because the descriptions in the system documentation are often terse,
they are most helpful if you already understand basically what a utility does.

To find out more about a utility, including the man utility itself, give the command **man**,
followed by the name of the utility. Figure 2-1 shows the output of a **man who** command.

less (pager)   The command **man man** displays information about the man utility. The man utility
automatically sends the output through a *pager*, usually less (page 45), which
allows you to view a file one screen at a time. When you display a manual page in
this manner, less displays a prompt (:) at the bottom of the screen after each screen
of text and waits for you to request another screen by pressing the SPACE bar. Pressing
h (help) displays a list of less commands. Pressing **q** (quit) stops man and causes the
shell to display a prompt. You can search for topics covered by man pages by using
the apropos utility (page 62).

Manual sections   Based on the FHS (Filesystem Hierarchy Standard, page 86), the Linux system manual
and the man pages are divided into ten sections. Each section describes related tools:

1. User Commands
2. System Calls
3. Subroutines
4. Devices
5. File Formats
6. Games
7. Miscellaneous
8. System Administration
9. Local
10. New

This layout closely mimics the way the set of UNIX manuals has always been divided. Unless you specify a manual section, man displays the earliest occurrence in the manual of the word you provide on the command line. Most users find the information they need in sections 1, 6, and 7; programmers and system administrators frequently need to consult the other sections.

In some cases the manual contains entries for different tools with the same name. For example, the following command displays the manual page for the write utility (page 67) from section 1 of the system manual:

```
$ man write
```

To see the manual page for the **write** system call from section 2, enter

```
$ man 2 write
```

The preceding command instructs man to look only in section 2 for the manual page. Use the –a option (see the adjacent tip) to view all the man pages for a given subject (press **q** to move to the next section). Use **man –a write** to view all the man pages for write.

Options

tip An option modifies the way a utility or command works. Options are specified as one or more letters that are preceded by one or two hyphens (with some exceptions). The option appears following the name of the utility you are calling and a SPACE. Any other *arguments* (page 861) to the command follow the option and a SPACE. For more information refer to "Options" on page 109.

man **and** info **display different information**

tip The info utility displays more complete and up-to-date information on GNU utilities than does man. When a man page displays abbreviated information on a utility that is covered by info, the man page refers you to info. The man utility frequently displays the only information available on non-GNU utilities. When info displays information on non-GNU utilities, it is frequently a copy of the man page.

info: DISPLAYS INFORMATION ABOUT UTILITIES

The character-based info utility is a menu-based hypertext system developed by the GNU project and distributed with Linux. The info utility includes a tutorial on itself (give the command **info info** or go to www.gnu.org/software/texinfo/manual/info) and documentation on many Linux shells, utilities, and programs developed by the GNU project (page 2). Figure 2-2 shows the screen that info displays when you give the command **info**.

Because the information on this screen is drawn from an editable file, your display may differ. When you see the initial info screen, you can press

- **h** to go through an interactive tutorial on info
- **?** to list info commands
- SPACE to scroll through the menu of items for which information is available
- **m** followed by the name of the menu item you want to display
- **q** to quit

The notation info uses to describe keyboard keys may not be familiar to you. The notation **C-h** is the same as CONTROL-H. Similarly **M-x** means hold down the META or ALT key and press **x**. (On some systems you need to press ESCAPE and then **x** to duplicate the function of META-x.)

After giving the command **info**, press the SPACE bar a few times to scroll the display. Figure 2-3 shows the entry for sleep. The asterisk at the left end of the line means that this entry is the beginning of a menu item. Following the asterisk is the name of the menu item, followed by a colon, the name of the package (in parentheses) that the menu item belongs to, other information, and a description of the item on the right.

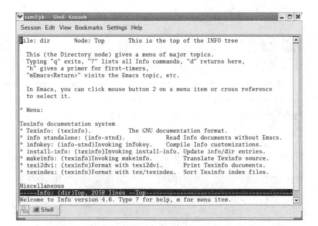

Figure 2-2   The first screen that info displays

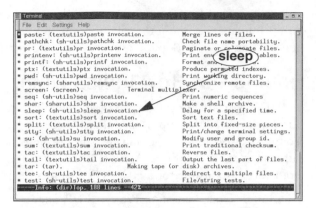

Figure 2-3   The screen that info displays after you press SPACE a few times

Each menu item is an active link to the info page that describes the item. To jump to that page, move the cursor to the line containing the menu item and press RETURN. Alternatively you can type the name of the menu item in a menu command to view the information. To get information on sleep, for example, you give the command **m sleep**, followed by a RETURN. When you type **m** (for *menu*), the cursor moves to the bottom line of the screen and displays **Menu item:**. Typing **sleep** displays **sleep** on that line, and pressing RETURN takes you to the menu item you have chosen.

Figure 2-4 shows the *top node* of information on sleep. A node is one group of information that you can scroll through with the SPACE bar. To get to the next node, press **n**. Press **p** to get to the previous node. You can always press **d** to display the initial menu (Figure 2-2).

As you read this book and learn about new utilities, you can use man or info to find out more about the utilities. If you can print PostScript documents, you can print a

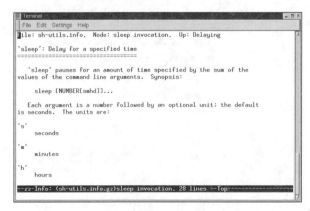

Figure 2-4   The info page on the sleep utility

manual page with the man utility using the **–t** option (for example, **man –t cat | lpr** prints information about the cat utility). Better yet, use a browser to look at the documentation at www.tldp.org and print the information from the browser.

HOWTOs: FINDING OUT HOW THINGS WORK

A HOWTO document explains in detail how to do something related to Linux—from setting up a specialized piece of hardware to performing a system administration task to setting up specific networking software. Mini-HOWTOs offer shorter explanations. As with Linux software, one person or a few people generally are responsible for a HOWTO document, yet many people contribute to it.

The Linux Documentation Project (LDP, page 35) site houses most HOWTO and mini-HOWTO documents. Use a browser to go to www.tldp.org, click **HOWTOs**, and pick the index you want to use to find a HOWTO or mini-HOWTO. Or use the LDP search feature on its home page to find HOWTOs and more.

USING THE INTERNET TO GET HELP

The Internet provides many helpful sites related to Linux. Aside from sites that carry various forms of documentation, you can enter an error message that you are having a problem with in a search engine such as Google (www.google.com). Enclose the error message within double quotation marks to improve the quality of your results. You will likely find a post concerning your problem and how to solve it. See Figure 2-5.

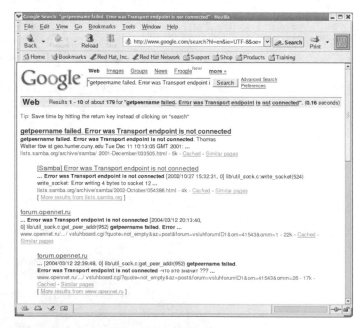

Figure 2-5   Google reporting on an error message

GNU   GNU makes many of its manuals available at www.gnu.org/manual. In addition, go to the GNU home page (www.gnu.org) for more documentation and other GNU resources. Many of the GNU pages and resources are available in a wide variety of languages.

The Linux Documentation Project   The Linux Documentation Project (www.tldp.org), which has been around for almost as long as Linux, houses a complete collection of guides, HOWTOs, FAQs, man pages, and Linux magazines. The home page is available in English, Portuguese, Spanish, Italian, Korean, and French and is easy to use, supporting local text searches. It also has a complete set of links (Figure 2-6) that can help you find almost anything you want that is related to Linux (click **Links** in the Search box or go to www.tldp.org/links). The links page includes sections on general information, events, getting started, user groups, mailing lists, and newsgroups, each containing many subsections.

MORE ABOUT LOGGING IN

This section covers what to do if you have a problem logging in, how to use virtual consoles, how to log in remotely, and how to change your password.

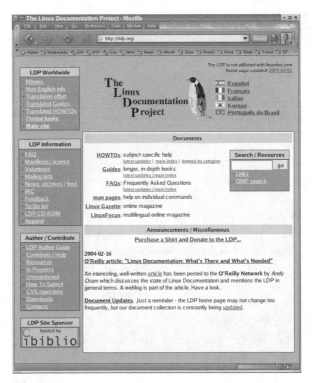

Figure 2-6 The Linux Documentation Project home page

WHAT TO DO IF YOU CANNOT LOG IN

When you enter your username or password incorrectly, the system displays an error message after you enter both your username *and* your password. This message indicates that you have entered either the login name *or* the password incorrectly or that they are not valid. It does not differentiate between an unacceptable login name and an unacceptable password to discourage unauthorized people from guessing names and passwords to gain access to the system. Some common reasons that logins fail are listed here:

- **Log In on the Right Machine**
  The login/password combination may not be valid if you are trying to log in on the wrong machine. On a larger, networked system, you may have to specify the machine that you want to connect to before you can log in.

- **Login Name and Password Are Case Sensitive**
  Make sure the CAPS LOCK key is off and that you enter your name and password exactly as specified or as you set them up.

- **Make Sure Your Login Name Is Valid**
  The login/password combination may not be valid if you have not been set up as a user.

Refer to "Changing Your Password" on page 37 when you want to change your password.

LOGGING OUT

To log out from a character-based interface, press CONTROL-D or give the command **exit** in response to the shell prompt.

USING VIRTUAL CONSOLES

When running Linux on a personal computer, you frequently work with the display and keyboard attached to the computer. Using this physical console, you can access as many as 63 *virtual consoles* (also called *virtual terminals*). Some are set up to allow logins, whereas others act as graphical displays. To switch between virtual consoles, hold down the CONTROL and ALT keys and press the function key that corresponds to the console you want to view. For example, CONTROL-ALT-F5 displays the fifth virtual console. This book refers to the console that you see when you first boot a system (or press CONTROL-ALT-F1) as the *system console* (or just *console*).

Typically, six virtual consoles are active and have text login sessions running. When you want to use both a character-based interface and a GUI, you can set up a character-based session on one virtual console and a graphical session on another. Whichever virtual console you start a graphical session from, the graphical session finds the first unused virtual console (typically number seven).

Changing Your Password

If someone else assigned you a password, it is a good idea to give yourself a new one. A good password is seven or eight characters long and contains a combination of numbers, uppercase and lowercase letters, and punctuation characters. Avoid using control characters (such as CONTROL-H) because they may have a special meaning to the system, making it impossible for you to log in. Do not use names, words from English or other languages, or other familiar words that someone can easily guess.

For security reasons none of the passwords you enter is ever displayed by any utility.

Protect your password

security   Do not allow someone to find out your password: *Do not* put your password in a file that is not encrypted, allow someone to watch you type your password, give it to someone you do not know (a system administrator never needs to know your password), or write it down.

Choose a password that is difficult to guess

security   Do not use phone numbers, names of pets or kids, birthdays, words from a dictionary (not even a foreign language), and so forth. Do not use permutations of these items.

Differentiate between important and less important passwords

security   It is important to differentiate between important and less important passwords. For example, Web site passwords for blogs or download access are not very important; it is not bad if you choose the same password for these types of sites. However, your login, mail server, and bank account Web site passwords are critical: Never use these passwords for an unimportant Web site.

To change your password, give the command **passwd** from a command line:

```
$ passwd
Changing password for user zach.
Changing password for zach
(current) UNIX password:
New UNIX password:
Retype new UNIX password:
passwd: all authentication tokens updated successfully.
```

The first item the system asks you for is your current (old) password. This password is verified to ensure that an unauthorized user is not trying to alter your password. Next the system requests the new password.

A password should meet the following criteria to be relatively secure. Only the first item is mandatory.

- It must be at least six characters long (or longer if the system administrator sets it up that way).

- It should not be a word in a dictionary of any language, no matter how seemingly obscure.

- It should not be the name of a person, place, pet, or other thing that might be discovered easily.
- It should contain at least two letters and one digit.
- It should not be your login name, the reverse of your login name, or your login name shifted by one or more characters.
- If you are changing your password, the new password should differ from the old one by at least three characters. Changing the case of a character does not make it count as a different character.

After you enter your new password, the system asks you to retype it to make sure you did not make a mistake when you entered it the first time. If the new password is the same both times you enter it, your password is changed. If the passwords differ, it means that you made an error in one of them, and the system displays an error message:

```
Sorry, passwords do not match
```

If your password is not long enough, the system displays the following message:

```
BAD PASSWORD: it is too short
```

When it is too simple, the system displays this message:

```
BAD PASSWORD: it is too simplistic/systematic
```

When it is formed from words, the system displays this message:

```
BAD PASSWORD: it is based on a dictionary word
```

If you get one of these messages you need to start over. Press RETURN a few times until the shell displays a prompt and run **passwd** again.

When you successfully change your password, you change the way you log in. If you forget your password, Superuser can change it and tell you your new password.

CHAPTER SUMMARY

As with many operating systems, your access to a Linux system is authorized when you log in. You enter your username in response to the **login:** prompt, followed by a password. You can change your password any time while you are logged in. Choose a password that is difficult to guess and that conforms to the criteria imposed by the utility that changes your password.

The system administrator is responsible for maintaining the system. On a single-user system, you are the system administrator. On a small, multiuser system, you or another user act as the system administrator, or this job may be shared. On a large, multiuser system or network of systems, there is frequently a full-time system administrator. When extra privileges are required to perform certain system tasks, the system administrator logs in as the **root** user by entering the username **root** and the **root** password; this user is called Superuser or administrator. On a multiuser system, several trusted users may be given the **root** password.

Do not work as Superuser as a matter of course. When you have to do something that requires Superuser privileges, work as Superuser for only as long as you need to; then revert to working as yourself as soon as possible.

The man utility provides online documentation on system utilities. This utility is helpful both to new Linux users and to experienced users who must often delve into the system documentation for information on the fine points of a utility's behavior. The info utility helps the beginner and the expert alike. It includes a tutorial on its use and documentation on many Linux utilities.

EXERCISES

1. The following message is displayed when you attempt to log in with an incorrect username *or* an incorrect password:

   ```
   Login incorrect
   ```

   This message does not indicate whether your username, your password, or both are invalid. Why does it not tell you this information?

2. Give three examples of poor password choices. What is wrong with each? Include one that is too short. Give the error message the system displays.

3. Is **fido** an acceptable password? Give several reasons why or why not.

4. What would you do if you could not log in?

5. Try to change your password to **dog**. What happens? Change it to a more secure password. What makes that password relatively secure?

ADVANCED EXERCISES

6. Change your login shell to tcsh without becoming **root** (Superuser).

7. How many man pages are in the **Devices** subsection of the system manual? (*Hint:* **Devices** is a subsection of **Special Files.**)

8. The example on page 31 shows that man pages for write appear in sections 1 and 2 of the system manual. Explain how you can use man to determine which sections of the system manual contain a manual page with a given name.

9. How would you find out which Linux utilities create and work with archive files?

3

COMMAND LINE UTILITIES

When Linus Torvalds introduced Linux and for a long time thereafter, Linux did not have a graphical user interface: It ran on character-based terminals only. All the tools ran from a command line. Today the Linux GUI is important, but many people—especially system administrators—run many command line programs. Command line utilities are often faster, more powerful, or more complete than their GUI counterparts. Sometimes there is no GUI counterpart to a text-based utility; some people just prefer the hands-on feeling of the command line.

When you work with a command line interface, you are working with a shell. Before you start working with a shell, it is important to understand something about the characters that are special to the shell, so this chapter starts with a discussion of shell special characters. The chapter then describes four basic utilities you can use to create and manipulate files (ls, cat, rm, and less) and one utility that tells you the name of the system you are using (hostname). It continues with a section on additional file manipulation utilities (including lpr, which prints files), followed by a brief discussion of how you can use a pipe on the command line. This chapter then describes utilities that compress and decompress files, locate other utilities, obtain user and system information, and allow you to communicate with other users. It concludes with a section on email.

Run these utilities from a command line

tip This chapter describes command line (i.e., text-based) utilities. You can experiment with these utilities from a terminal, a terminal emulator within a GUI, or a virtual console (page 36).

SPECIAL CHARACTERS

Special characters, which have a special meaning to the shell, are discussed in "Filename Generation/Pathname Expansion" on page 127. These characters are mentioned here so that you can avoid accidentally using them as regular characters until you understand how the shell interprets them. For example, it is best to avoid using any of the following characters in a filename (even though emacs and some other programs do) because they make the file harder to reference on the command line:

     & ; | * ? ' " ` [ ] ( ) $ < > { } ^ # / \ % ! ~ +

Whitespace Although not considered special characters, RETURN, SPACE, and TAB also have special meanings to the shell. RETURN usually ends a command line and initiates execution of a command. The SPACE and TAB characters separate elements on the command line and are collectively known as *whitespace* or *blanks*.

If you need to use one of the characters that has a special meaning to the shell as a regular character, you can *quote* (or *escape*) it. When you quote a special character, you keep the shell from giving it special meaning. The shell treats a quoted special character as a regular character.

Backslash To quote a character, precede it with a backslash (\). When you have two or more special characters together, you must precede each with a backslash (for example, enter ** as **). You can quote a backslash just as you would quote any other special character—by preceding it with a backslash (\\).

Single quotation marks Another way of quoting special characters is to enclose them between single quotation marks: ' ** '. You can quote many special and regular characters between a pair of single quotation marks: 'This is a special character: >'. The regular characters remain regular, and the shell also interprets the special characters as regular characters.

The only way to quote the erase character (CONTROL-H), the line kill character (CONTROL-U), and other control characters (try CONTROL-M) is by preceding it with a CONTROL-V. Single quotation marks and backslashes do not work. Try the following:

```
$ echo 'xxxxxxCONTROL-U'
$ echo xxxxxxCONTROL-V CONTROL-U
```

optional Although you cannot see the CONTROL-U displayed by the second of the preceding pair of commands, it is there. The following command sends the output of echo (page 647) through a pipe (page 52) to od (page 737) to display the CONTROL-U as an octal 25 (025):

```
$ echo xxxxxxCONTROL-V CONTROL-U | od -c
0000000   x   x   x   x   x   x 025  \n
0000010
```

The **\n** is the NEWLINE character that echo sends at the end of its output.

Basic Utilities

One of the important advantages of Linux is that it comes with thousands of utilities that perform myriad functions. You will use utilities whenever you use Linux, whether you use them directly by name from the command line or indirectly from a menu or icon. The following sections discuss some of the most basic and important utilities; these utilities are available from a character-based interface. Some of the more important utilities are also available from a GUI, and some are available only from a GUI.

The term *directory* is used extensively in the next sections. A directory is a resource that can hold files. On other operating systems, including Windows, Macintosh, and frequently Linux GUIs, a directory is referred to as a folder. That is a good analogy: A directory is a folder that can hold files.

In this chapter you work in your home directory

tip When you log in on the system, you are working in your *home directory*. In this chapter that is the only directory you use: All the files you create in this chapter are in your home directory. Chapter 4 goes into more detail about directories.

ls: Lists the Names of Files

Using the editor of your choice, create a small file named **practice**. (A tutorial on vim appears on page 141 and a tutorial on emacs appears on page 198.) After exiting from the editor, you can use the ls (list) utility to display a list of the names of the files in your home directory. In the first command in Figure 3-1 ls lists the name of the **practice** file. (You may also see files the system or a program created automatically.) Subsequent commands in Figure 3-1 display the contents of the file and remove the file. These commands are described next.

```
$ ls
practice
$ cat practice
This is a small file that I created
with a text editor.
$ rm practice
$ ls
$ cat practice
cat: practice: No such file or directory
$
```

Figure 3-1   Using ls, cat, and rm on the file named **practice**

cat: DISPLAYS A TEXT FILE

The cat utility displays the contents of a text file. The name of the command is derived from *catenate,* which means to join together, one after the other. (Figure 5-8 on page 118 shows how to use cat to string together the contents of three files.)

A convenient way to display the contents of a file to the screen is by giving the command **cat,** followed by a SPACE and the name of a file. Figure 3-1 shows cat displaying the contents of **practice.** This figure shows the difference between the ls and cat utilities: The ls utility displays the *name* of a file, whereas cat displays the *contents* of a file.

rm: DELETES A FILE

The rm (remove) utility deletes a file. Figure 3-1 shows rm deleting the file named **practice.** After rm deletes the file, ls and cat show that **practice** is no longer in the directory. The ls utility does not list its filename, and cat says that there is no such file. Use rm carefully.

A safer way of removing files

tip   You can use the interactive form of rm to make sure that you delete only the file(s) you intend to delete. When you follow rm with the **–i** option (see page 31 for a tip on options) and the name of the file you want to delete, rm displays the name of the file and then waits for you to respond with **y** (yes) before it deletes the file. It does not delete the file if you respond with a string that does not begin with **y.**

```
$ rm -i toollist
rm: remove regular file 'toollist'? y
```

Optional: You can create an alias (page 312) and put it in your startup file (page 83) so that rm always runs in interactive mode.

less **Is** more: DISPLAYING A TEXT FILE ONE SCREEN AT A TIME

Pagers   When you want to view a file that is longer than one screen, you can use either the less utility or the more utility. Each of these utilities pauses after displaying a screen of text. Because these utilities show one page at a time, they are called *pagers*. Although they are very similar, they have subtle differences. At the end of the file, for example, less displays an **EOF** (end of file) message and waits for you to press **q** before returning you to the shell. In contrast, more returns you directly to the shell. In both utilities you can press **h** to display a help screen that lists commands you can use while paging through a file. Replace the **cat** command in Figure 3-1 with **less practice** and **more practice** to see how these commands work. Use the command **less /etc/termcap** if you want to experiment with a long file. Refer to page 697 for more information on less.

Filename completion

tip   After you enter one or more letters of a filename (following a command) on a command line, press TAB and the shell will complete as much of the filename as it can. When only one filename starts with the characters you entered, the shell completes the filename and places a SPACE after it. You can keep typing or you can press RETURN to execute the command at this point. When the characters you entered do not uniquely identify a filename, the shell completes what it can and waits for more input. When pressing TAB does not change the display, press TAB again to display a list of possible completions. (Refer to "Pathname Completion" on page 308.)

The preceding description assumes you are running bash. Filename completion works a little differently if you are running tcsh; see "Word Completion" on page 350.

hostname: DISPLAYS THE SYSTEM NAME

The hostname command displays the name of the system you are working on. Use this command if you are not sure that you are logged in on the right system.

```
$ hostname
bravo.example.com
```

WORKING WITH FILES

The following sections describe utilities that copy, move, and print files.

cp: COPIES A FILE

The cp (copy) utility (Figure 3-2) makes a copy of a file. This utility can copy any file, including text and executable program (binary) files. You can use cp to make a backup copy of a file or a copy to experiment with.

The cp command line uses the following syntax to specify source and destination files:

cp source-file destination-file

The *source-file* is the name of the file that cp will copy. The *destination-file* is the name that cp assigns to the resulting (new) copy of the file.

cp can destroy a file

caution   If the *destination-file* exists *before* you give a cp command, cp overwrites it. Because cp over-writes (and destroys the contents of) an existing *destination-file* without warning, take care not to cause cp to overwrite a file that you need. The cp –i (interactive) option (see page 31 for a tip on options) prompts you before it overwrites a file.

The following example assumes that the file named **orange.2** exists before you give the cp command. The user answers **y** to overwrite the file:

```
$ cp –i orange orange.2
cp: overwrite 'orange.2'? y
```

The cp command line in Figure 3-2 copies the file named **memo** to **memo.copy**. The period is part of the filename—just another character. The initial ls command shows that **memo** is the only file in the directory. After the cp command, a second ls shows two files in the directory, **memo** and **memo.copy**.

Sometimes it is useful to incorporate the date in the name of a copy of a file. The following example includes the date January 30 (**0130**) in the copied file:

```
$ cp memo memo.0130
```

Although it has no significance to Linux, the date can help you find a version of a file that you created on a certain date. It can also help you avoid overwriting exist-ing files by providing a unique filename each day. Refer to "Filenames" on page 78.

Use scp (page 758) or ftp (page 671) when you need to copy a file from one system to another on a common network.

mv: CHANGES THE NAME OF A FILE

The mv (move) utility can rename a file without making a copy of it. The mv com-mand line specifies an existing file and a new filename using the same syntax as cp:

mv existing-filename new-filename

```
$ ls
memo
$ cp memo memo.copy
$ ls
memo memo.copy
```

Figure 3-2   cp copies a file

```
$ ls
memo
$ mv memo memo.0130
$ ls
memo.0130
```

Figure 3-3 mv renames a file

The command line in Figure 3-3 changes the name of the file **memo** to **memo.0130**. The initial ls command shows that **memo** is the only file in the directory. After you give the mv command, **memo.0130** is the only file in the directory. Compare this result to that of the earlier cp example.

The mv utility can be used for more than changing the name of a file. Refer to "mv, cp: Moves or Copies a File" on page 90.

mv **can destroy a file**

caution   Just as cp can destroy a file, so can mv. Also like cp, mv has a **–i** (interactive) option. See the caution box labeled "cp can destroy a file" on page 46.

lpr: PRINTS A FILE

The lpr (line printer) utility places one or more files in a print queue for printing. Linux provides print queues so that only one job is printed on a given printer at a time. A queue allows several people or jobs to send output simultaneously to a single printer with the expected results. On machines with access to more than one printer, you can use the **–P** option to instruct lpr to place the file in the queue for a specific printer, including one that is connected to another machine on the network. The following command prints the file named **report**:

```
$ lpr report
```

Because this command does not specify a printer, the output goes to the default printer, which is *the* printer when you have only one printer.

The next command line prints the same file on the printer named **mailroom**:

```
$ lpr -Pmailroom report
```

You can see what jobs are in the print queue by using the lpq utility:

```
$ lpq
lp is ready and printing
Rank   Owner   Job Files              Total Size
active alex     86 (standard input)     954061 bytes
```

In this example, Alex has one job that is being printed; no other jobs are in the queue. You can use the job number (86 in this case) with the lprm utility to remove the job from the print queue and stop it from printing:

```
$ lprm 86
```

You can send more than one file to the printer with a single command. The following command line prints three files on the printer named **laser1**:

```
$ lpr -Plaser1 05.txt 108.txt 12.txt
```

grep: FINDS A STRING

The grep (global regular expression print[1]) utility searches through one or more files to see whether any contain a specified string of characters. It does not change the file it searches but simply displays each line that contains the string.

The grep command in Figure 3-4 searches through the file **memo** for lines that contain the string **credit** and displays a single line that meets this criterion. If **memo** contained such words as **discredit, creditor,** or **accreditation,** grep would have displayed those lines as well because they contain the string it was searching for. The **–w** option causes grep to match only whole words. You do not need to enclose the string you are searching for in single quotation marks, but doing so allows you to put SPACEs and special characters in the search string.

The grep utility can do much more than search for a simple string in a single file. Refer to page 683 for more information on grep.

```
$ cat memo

Helen:

In our meeting on June 6 we
discussed the issue of credit.
Have you had any further thoughts
about it?

                    Alex
$ grep 'credit' memo
discussed the issue of credit.
```

Figure 3-4   grep searches for a string

---

1. Originally this utility's name was a play on an ed—an original UNIX editor, available on Linux—command: **g/re/p**. In this command the **g** stands for global, **re** is a regular expression delimited by slashes, and **p** means print.

head: DISPLAYS THE BEGINNING OF A FILE

By default the head utility displays the first ten lines of a file. You can use head to help you remember what a particular file contains. For example, if you have a file named **months** that lists the 12 months of the year in order, one to a line, head displays **Jan** through **Oct** (Figure 3-5).

This utility can display any number of lines, so you can use it to look at only the first line of a file, at a full screen, or even more. To specify the number of lines head displays, include a hyphen followed by the number of lines in the head command. For example, the following command displays only the first line of **months**:

```
$ head -1 months
Jan
```

The head utility can also display parts of a file based on a count of blocks or characters rather than lines. Refer to page 691 for more information on head.

tail: DISPLAYS THE END OF A FILE

The tail utility is similar to head but by default displays the *last* ten lines of a file. Depending on how you invoke it, this utility can display fewer or more than ten

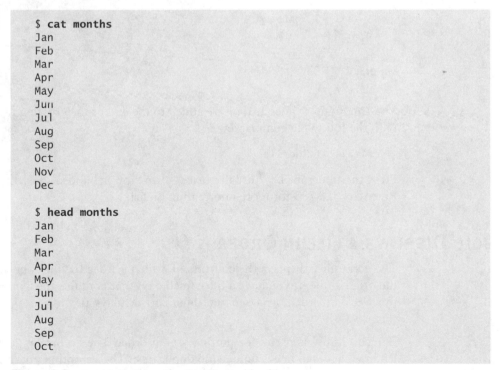

```
$ cat months
Jan
Feb
Mar
Apr
May
Jun
Jul
Aug
Sep
Oct
Nov
Dec

$ head months
Jan
Feb
Mar
Apr
May
Jun
Jul
Aug
Sep
Oct
```

Figure 3-5   head displays the first lines of a file

```
$ cat days
Monday
Tuesday
Wednesday
Thursday
Friday
Saturday
Sunday
$ sort days
Friday
Monday
Saturday
Sunday
Thursday
Tuesday
Wednesday
```

Figure 3-6   sort displays a file in order

lines, use a count of blocks or characters rather than lines to display parts of a file, and display lines being added to a file that is changing. The following command causes tail to display the last five lines, **Aug** through **Dec**, of the **months** file shown in Figure 3-5:

```
$ tail -5 months
Aug
Sep
Oct
Nov
Dec
```

You can monitor lines as they are added to the end of the growing file named **logfile** with the following command:

```
$ tail -f logfile
```

Press the interrupt key (usually CONTROL-C) to stop tail and display the shell prompt. Refer to page 783 for more information on tail.

sort: DISPLAYS A FILE IN ORDER

The sort utility displays the contents of a file in order by lines but does not change the original file. If you have a file named **days** that contains the name of each day of the week in order on a separate line, sort displays the file in alphabetical order (Figure 3-6).

The sort utility is useful for putting lists in order. The **–u** option generates a sorted list in which each line is unique (no duplicates). The **–n** option puts a list of numbers in order. Refer to page 762 for more information on sort.

```
$ cat dups
Cathy
Fred
Joe
John
Mary
Mary
Paula
$ uniq dups
Cathy
Fred
Joe
John
Mary
Paula
```

Figure 3-7   uniq removes duplicate lines

uniq: REMOVES DUPLICATE LINES FROM A FILE

The uniq (unique) utility displays a file, skipping adjacent duplicate lines, but does not change the original file. If a file contains a list of names and has two successive entries for the same person, uniq skips the extra line (Figure 3-7).

If a file is sorted before it is processed by uniq, this utility ensures that no two lines in the file are the same. (Of course, sort can do that all by itself with the –u option.) Refer to page 812 for more information on uniq.

diff: COMPARES TWO FILES

The diff (difference) utility compares two files and displays a list of the differences between them. This utility does not change either file, so it is useful when you want to compare two versions of a letter or a report or two versions of the source code for a program.

The diff utility with the –u (unified output format) option first displays two lines indicating which of the files you are comparing will be denoted by a plus sign (+) and which by a minus sign (–). In Figure 3-8, a minus sign indicates the **colors.1** file; a plus sign indicates the **colors.2** file.

The **diff –u** command breaks long, multiline text into *hunks*. Each hunk is preceded by a line starting and ending with two at signs (@@). This hunk identifier indicates the starting line number and the number of lines from each file for this hunk. In Figure 3-8, the **–1,6** indicates that the hunk covers the section of the **colors.1** file (indicated by a minus sign) from the first line and continuing for six lines (for a total of seven lines). Similarly the **+1,5** indicates that the hunk covers **colors.2** from the first line through five subsequent lines.

```
$ diff -u colors.1 colors.2
--- colors.1    Fri Nov 25 15:45:32 2005
+++ colors.2    Fri Nov 25 15:24:46 2005
@@ -1,6 +1,5 @@
 red
+blue
 green
 yellow
-pink
-purple
 orange
```

Figure 3-8   diff displaying the unified output format

Following these header lines, **diff –u** displays each line of text with a leading minus sign, plus sign, or nothing. The leading minus sign indicates that the line occurs only in the file denoted by the minus sign. The leading plus sign indicates that the line comes from the file denoted by the plus sign. A line that begins with neither a plus sign nor a minus sign occurs in both files in the same location. Refer to page 638 for more information on diff.

file: TESTS THE CONTENTS OF A FILE

You can use the file utility to learn about the contents of any file on a Linux system without having to open and examine the file yourself. In the following example, file reports that **letter_e.bz2** contains data that was compressed by the bzip2 utility (page 56):

```
$ file letter_e.bz2
letter_e.bz2: bzip2 compressed data, block size = 900k
```

Next file reports on two more files:

```
$ file memo zach.jpg
memo:     ASCII text
zach.jpg: JPEG image data, ... resolution (DPI), 72 x 72
```

Refer to page 653 for more information on file.

| (PIPE): COMMUNICATES BETWEEN PROCESSES

Because pipes are integral to the functioning of a Linux system, they are introduced here for use in examples. Pipes are covered in detail on page 122.

A *process* is the execution of a command by Linux (page 292). Communication between processes is one of the hallmarks of UNIX/Linux. A *pipe* (written as a vertical bar, |, on the command line and appearing as a solid or broken vertical line on keyboards) provides the simplest form of this kind of communication. Simply put, a pipe takes the output of one utility and sends that output as input to another utility. Using UNIX/Linux terminology, a pipe takes standard output of one process and redirects it to become standard input of another process. (See page 113 for more information on standard input and output.) Most of what a process displays on the screen is sent to standard output. If you do not redirect it, this output appears on the screen. Using a pipe, you can redirect the output so that it becomes instead standard input of another utility. A utility such as head can take its input from a file whose name you specify on the command line following the word **head,** or it can take its input from standard input. For example, you can give the command shown in Figure 3-5 on page 49 as follows:

```
$ cat months | head
Jan
Feb
Mar
Apr
May
Jun
Jul
Aug
Sep
Oct
```

The next command displays the first line of the **months** file:

```
$ cat months | head -1
Jan
```

You can use a pipe to send output of a program to the printer:

```
$ tail months | lpr
```

FOUR MORE UTILITIES

The echo and date utilities are two of the most frequently used from the large collection of Linux utilities. The script utility helps you record part of a session in a file, and unix2dos makes a copy of a text file that can be read on a Windows machine.

echo: DISPLAYS TEXT

The echo utility copies anything you put on the command line, after **echo,** to the screen. Some examples are shown in Figure 3-9. The last example shows what the shell does with an unquoted asterisk (*) on the command line: It expands the asterisk into a list of filenames in the directory.

```
$ ls
memo  memo.0714  practice
$ echo Hi
Hi
$ echo This is a sentence.
This is a sentence.
$ echo star: *
star: memo memo.0714 practice
$
```

Figure 3-9   echo copies the command line (but not the word **echo**) to the screen

The echo utility is a good tool for learning about the shell and other Linux programs. Some examples on page 129 use echo to illustrate how special characters, such as the asterisk, work. Throughout the chapters explaining the shells, echo helps explain how shell variables work and how you can send messages from shell scripts to the screen. Refer to page 647 for more information on echo.

date: DISPLAYS THE TIME AND DATE

The date utility displays the current date and time:

```
$ date
Thu Jan 20 10:24:00 PST 2005
```

The following example shows how you can choose the format and select the contents of the output of date. Refer to page 630 for more information on date.

```
$ date +"%A %B %d"
Thursday January 20
```

script: RECORDS A LINUX SESSION

The script utility records all or part of a login session, including your input and the system's responses. This utility is useful only from character-based devices, such as a terminal or a terminal emulator. It does capture a session with vim; however, because vim uses control characters to position the cursor and display different type-faces, such as bold, the output will be difficult to read and may not be useful. When you cat a file that has captured a vim session, the session quickly passes before your eyes.

By default script captures the session in a file named **typescript**. To use a different filename, follow the **script** command with a SPACE and the new filename. To append to a file, use the **–a** option after **script** but before the filename; otherwise, script overwrites an existing file. Following is a session being recorded by script:

```
$ script
Script started, file is typescript
$ date
Thu Jan 20 10:28:56 PST 2005
```

```
$ who am i
alex       pts/4     Jan  8 22:15
$
$ apropos mtools
mtools                 (1)  - utilities to access DOS disks in Unix
mtools.conf [mtools] (5)  - mtools configuration files
mtoolstest             (1)  - tests and displays the configuration
$ exit
Script done, file is typescript
$
```

Use the exit command to terminate a script session. You can view the file you created with cat, less, more, or an editor. Following is the file that was created by the preceding script command:

```
$ cat typescript
Script started on Thu Jan 20 10:28:56 2005
$ date
Thu Jan 20 10:28:56 PST 2005
$ who am i
alex       pts/4     Jan  8 22:15
$
$ apropos mtools
mtools                 (1)  - utilities to access DOS disks in Unix
mtools.conf [mtools] (5)  - mtools configuration files
mtoolstest             (1)  - tests and displays the configuration
$ exit
Script done on Thu Jan 20 10:29:58 2005
$
```

If you will be editing the file with vim, emacs, or another editor, you can use dos2unix to eliminate from the **typescript** file the ^M characters that appear at the ends of the lines.

unix2dos: CONVERTS LINUX FILES TO WINDOWS FORMAT

If you want to share a text file that you created on a Linux system with someone on a Windows system, you need to convert the file before the person on the Windows system can read it easily. The unix2dos utility converts a Linux text file so that it can be read on a Windows system. Give the following command to convert a file named **memo.txt** (created with a text editor) to a DOS-format file:

```
$ unix2dos memo.txt
```

Without any options unix2dos overwrites the original file. You can now email the file as an attachment to someone on a Windows system.

dos2unix   You can use the dos2unix utility to convert DOS files so they can be read on a Linux system:

```
$ dos2unix memo.txt
```

See the unix2dos and dos2unix man pages for more information.

You can also use tr (page 804) to change a DOS text file into a Linux text file. In the following example, the **–d** option causes tr to remove RETURNs (represented by \r) as it makes a copy of the file:

```
$ cat memo | tr -d '\r' > memo.txt
```

Converting a file the other way without unix2dos is not as easy.

COMPRESSING AND ARCHIVING FILES

Large files use a lot of disk space and take longer than smaller files to transfer from one system to another over a network. If you do not need to look at the contents of a large file very often, you may want to save it on a CD, DVD, or other medium and remove it from the hard disk. If you have a continuing need for the file, retrieving a copy from a CD may be inconvenient. To reduce the amount of disk space you use without removing the file entirely, you can compress the file without losing any of the information it holds. Also you may frequently download compressed files from the Internet. The utilities described in this section compress and decompress files.

bzip2: COMPRESSES A FILE

The bzip2 utility (sources.redhat.com/bzip2) compresses a file by analyzing it and recoding it more efficiently. The new version of the file looks completely different. In fact, because the new file contains many nonprinting characters, you cannot view it directly. The bzip2 utility works particularly well on files that contain a lot of repeated information, such as text and image data, although most image data is already in a compressed format.

The following example shows a boring file. Each of the 8,000 lines of this file, named **letter_e**, contains 72 e's and a NEWLINE character that marks the end of the line. The file occupies more than half a megabyte of disk storage.

```
$ ls -l
-rw-rw-r--  1 sam sam 584000 Mar  1 22:31 letter_e
```

The **–l** (long) option causes ls to display more information about a file. Here it shows that **letter_e** is 584,000 bytes long. The **––verbose** (or **–v**) option causes bzip2 to report how much it was able to reduce the size of the file. In this case, it shrank the file by 99.99 percent:

```
$ bzip2 -v letter_e
letter_e: 11680.00:1, 0.001 bits/byte, 99.99% saved, 584000 in, 50 out.
$ ls -l
-rw-rw-r--  1 sam sam 50 Mar  1 22:31 letter_e.bz2
```

.**bz2** filename
extension
Now the file is only 50 bytes long. The bzip2 utility also renamed the file, appending **.bz2** to its name. This naming convention reminds you that the file is compressed; you would not want to display or print it, for example, without first decompressing it. The bzip2 utility does not change the modification date associated with the file, even though it completely changes the file's contents.

In the following, more realistic example, the file **zach.jpg** contains a computer graphics image:

```
$ ls -l
-rw-r--r--  1 sam sam 33287 Mar  1 22:40 zach.jpg
```

The gzip utility can reduce the size of the file by only 28 percent because the image is already in a compressed format:

```
$ bzip2 -v zach.jpg
zach.jpg:  1.391:1,  5.749 bits/byte, 28.13% saved, 33287 in, 23922 out.

$ ls -l
-rw-r--r--  1 sam sam 23922 Mar  1 22:40 zach.jpg.bz2
```

Refer to page 596 and the *Bzip2 mini-HOWTO* (see page 34 for help finding it) for more information.

bunzip2 AND bzcat: DECOMPRESS A FILE

You can use the bunzip2 utility to restore a file that has been compressed with bzip2:

```
$ bunzip2 letter_e.bz2
$ ls -l
-rw-rw-r--  1 sam sam 584000 Mar  1 22:31 letter_e
$ bunzip2 zach.jpg.bz2
$ ls -l
-rw-r--r--  1 sam sam  33287 Mar  1 22:40 zach.jpg
```

The bzcat utility displays a file that has been compressed with bzip2. The equivalent of cat for **.bz2** files, bzcat decompresses the compressed data and displays the contents of the decompressed file. Like cat, bzcat does not change the source file. The pipe in the following example redirects the output of zcat so that instead of being displayed on the screen it becomes the input to head, which displays the first two lines of the file:

```
$ bzcat letter_e.bz2 | head -2
eeeeeeeeeeeeeeeeeeeeeeeeeeeeeeeeeeeeeeeeeeeeeeeeeeeeeeeeeeeeeeeeeeeeeeeee
eeeeeeeeeeeeeeeeeeeeeeeeeeeeeeeeeeeeeeeeeeeeeeeeeeeeeeeeeeeeeeeeeeeeeeeee
```

After bzcat is run, the contents of **letter_e.bz** is unchanged; the file is still stored on the disk in compressed form.

bzip2recover
The bzip2recover utility supports limited data recovery from media errors. Give the command **bzip2recover** followed by the name of the file from which you want to try to recover data.

gzip: COMPRESSES A FILE

gunzip and zcat The gzip (GNU zip) utility is older and less efficient than bzip2. Its flags and operation are very similar to those of bzip2. A file compressed by gzip is marked by a **.gz** filename extension. Linux stores manual pages in gzip format to save disk space; likewise, files you download from the Internet are frequently in gzip format. Use gzip, gunzip, and zcat just as you would use bzip2, bunzip2, and bzcat. Refer to page 688 for more information on gzip.

compress The compress utility can also compress files, albeit not as well as gzip. This utility marks a file it has compressed by adding .Z to its name.

gzip **versus** zip

tip Do not confuse gzip and gunzip with the zip and unzip utilities. These last two are used to pack and unpack zip archives containing several files compressed into a single file that has been imported from or is being exported to Windows. The zip utility constructs a zip archive, whereas unzip unpacks zip archives. The zip and unzip utilities are compatible with PKZIP, a Windows compress and archive program.

tar: PACKS AND UNPACKS FILES

The tar utility performs many functions. Its name is short for *tape archive,* as its original function was to create and read archive and backup tapes. Today it is used to create a single file (called a *tar file*) from multiple files or directory hierarchies and to extract files from a tar file.

In the following example, the first ls shows the existence and sizes of the files **g**, **b**, and **d**. Next tar uses −c (create), −v (verbose), and −f (write to or read from a file) options[2] to create an archive named **all.tar** from these files. Each line of the output from tar starts with the letter **a** to indicate that it is appending to the archive. This letter is followed by the name of the file tar is appending.

The tar utility does add overhead when it creates an archive. The next command shows that the archive file **all.tar** is about 9,700 bytes, whereas the sum of the sizes of the three files is about 6,000 bytes. This overhead is more appreciable on smaller files, such as the ones in this example.

```
$ ls -l g b d
-rw-r--r--   1 jenny jenny 1302 Aug 20 14:16 g
-rw-r--r--   1 jenny other 1178 Aug 20 14:16 b
-rw-r--r--   1 jenny jenny 3783 Aug 20 14:17 d
```

---

2. Although the original UNIX tar did not use a leading hyphen to indicate an option on the command line, it now accepts hyphens. The GNU tar described here will accept tar commands with or without a leading hyphen. This book uses the hyphen for consistency with most other utilities.

```
$ tar -cvf all.tar g b d
a g
a b
a d
$ ls -l all.tar
-rw-r--r--   1 jenny     jenny         9728 Aug 20 14:17 all.tar
$ tar -tvf all.tar
-rw-r--r-- jenny/jenny   1302 2003-08-20 14:16 2005 g
-rw-r--r-- jenny/other   1178 2003-08-20 14:16 2005 b
-rw-r--r-- jenny/jenny   3783 2003-08-20 14:17 2005 d
```

The final command in the preceding example uses the **–t** option to display a table of contents for the archive. Use **–x** instead of **–t** to extract files from a tar archive. Omit the **–v** option if you want tar to do its work silently.

You can use bzip2, compress, or gzip to compress tar files and make them easier to store and handle. Many files you download from the Internet are in one of these formats. Files that have been processed by tar and compressed by bzip2 frequently have a filename extension of **.tar.bz2**. Those processed by tar and gzip have an extension of **.tz** or **.tar.gz**, while files processed by tar and compress use **.tar.Z** as the extension.

You can unpack a tarred and gzipped file in two steps. (Follow the same procedure if the file was compressed by bzip2, but use bunzip2 instead of gunzip.) The next example shows how to unpack the GNU make utility after it has been downloaded (ftp.gnu.org/pub/gnu/make/make-3.80.tar.gz):

```
$ ls -l mak*
-rw-rw-r--  1 sam sam 1211924 Jan 20 11:49 make-3.80.tar.gz

$ gunzip mak*
$ ls -l mak*
-rw-rw-r--  1 sam sam 4823040 Jan 20 11:49 make-3.80.tar

$ tar -xvf mak*
make-3.80/
make-3.80/po/
make-3.80/po/Makefile.in.in
...
make-3.80/tests/run_make_tests.pl
make-3.80/tests/test_driver.pl
```

The first command lists the downloaded tarred and gzipped file: **make-3.80.tar.gz** (about 1.2 megabytes). The asterisk (*) in the filename matches any characters in any filenames (page 129), so you end up with a list of files whose names begin with **mak**; in this case there is only one. Using an asterisk saves typing and can improve accuracy with long filenames. The gunzip command decompresses the file and yields **make-3.80.tar** (no **.gz** extension), which is about 4.8 megabytes. The tar command creates the **make-3.80** directory in the working directory and unpacks the files into it.

```
$ ls -ld mak*
drwxrwxr-x  8 sam sam    4096 Oct  3  2002 make-3.80
-rw-rw-r--  1 sam sam 4823040 Jan 20 11:49 make-3.80.tar
$ ls -l make-3.80
total 1816
-rw-r--r--  1 sam sam   24687 Oct  3  2002 ABOUT-NLS
-rw-r--r--  1 sam sam    1554 Jul  8  2002 AUTHORS
-rw-r--r--  1 sam sam   18043 Dec 10  1996 COPYING
...
-rw-r--r--  1 sam sam   16520 Jan 21  2000 vmsify.c
-rw-r--r--  1 sam sam   16409 Aug  9  2002 vpath.c
drwxrwxr-x  5 sam sam    4096 Oct  3  2002 w32
```

After tar extracts the files from the archive, the working directory contains two files whose names start with **mak**: **make-3.80.tar** and **make-3.80**. The **−d** (directory) option causes ls to display only file and directory names, not the contents of directories as it normally does. The final ls command shows the files and directories in the **make-3.80** directory. Refer to page 786 for more information on tar.

tar: the −x option may extract a lot of files

caution Some tar archives contain many files. Run tar with the **−t** option and the name of the tar file to list the files in the archive without unpacking them. In some cases you may want to create a new directory (mkdir [page 80]), move the tar file into that directory, and expand it there. That way the unpacked files do not mingle with your existing files, and there is no confusion. This strategy also makes it easier to delete the extracted files. Some tar files automatically create a new directory and put the files into it. Refer to the preceding example.

tar: the −x option can overwrite files

caution The **−x** option to tar overwrites a file that has the same filename as a file you are extracting. Follow the suggestion in the preceding caution box to avoid overwriting files.

optional You can combine the gunzip and tar commands on one command line with a pipe (|), which redirects the output of gunzip so that it becomes the input to tar:

```
$ gunzip -c make-3.80.tar.gz | tar -xvf -
```

The **−c** option causes gunzip to send its output through the pipe instead of creating a file. Refer to "Pipes" (page 122), gzip (page 688), and tar (page 786) for more information about how this command line works.

A simpler solution is to use the **−z** option to tar. This option causes tar to call gunzip (or gzip when you are creating an archive) directly and simplifies the preceding command line to

```
$ tar -xvzf make-3.80.tar.gz
```

In a similar manner, the **−j** option calls bzip2 or bunzip2.

LOCATING COMMANDS

The whereis and apropos utilities help you find a command whose name you have forgotten or whose location you do not know. When there are multiple copies of a utility or program, which can tell you which copy you will run. The slocate utility searches for files on the local system.

which AND whereis: LOCATE A UTILITY

When you give Linux a command, the shell searches a list of directories for a program with that name and runs the first one it finds. This list of directories is called a *search path*. For information on how to change the search path, refer to "PATH: Where the Shell Looks for Programs" on page 284. If you do not change the search path, the shell searches only a standard set of directories and then stops searching. Other directories on the system may also contain useful utilities, however.

which   The which utility locates utilities (commands) by displaying the full pathname to the file for the utility. (Chapter 4 contains more information on pathnames and the structure of the Linux filesystem.) The local system may include several commands that have the same name. When you type the name of a command, the shell searches for the command in your search path and runs the first one it finds. You can find out which copy of the program the shell will run by using which. In the following example, which reports the location of the tar command:

```
$ which tar
/bin/tar
```

The which utility can be helpful when a command seems to be working in unexpected ways. By running which, you may discover that you are running a nonstandard version of a tool or a different one than you expected. (Refer to "Important Standard Directories and Files" on page 86 for a list of standard locations for executable files.) For example, if tar is not working properly and you find that you are running **/usr/local/bin/tar** instead of **/bin/tar**, you might suspect that the local version is broken.

whereis   The whereis utility searches for files related to a utility by looking in standard locations instead of using your search path. For example, you can find the locations for files related to tar:

```
$ whereis tar
tar: /bin/tar /usr/include/tar.h /usr/share/man/man1/tar.1.gz
```

In this example whereis finds three references to tar: the tar utility file, a tar header file, and the tar man page.

which, whereis, **and builtin commands**

caution   Both the which and whereis utilities report only the names for commands as they are found on disk and do not report shell builtins (utilities that are built into a shell; see page 132). When you use whereis to try to find out where the echo command (which exists as both a utility program and a shell builtin) is kept, you get the following result:

```
$ whereis echo
echo: /bin/echo /usr/share/man/man1/echo.1.gz /usr/share/man/man1p/echo.1p.
gz /usr/share/man/man3/echo.3x.gz
```

The whereis utility does not display the echo builtin. Even the which utility reports the wrong information:

```
$ which echo
/bin/echo
```

Under bash you can use the type builtin (page 487) to determine whether a command is a builtin.

```
$ type echo
echo is a shell builtin
```

which **versus** whereis

tip   Given the name of a program, which looks through the directories in your *search path,* in order, and locates the program. If more than one program with the specified name is in the search path, which displays the name of only the first one (the one you would run).

The whereis utility looks through a list of *standard directories* and works independently of your search path. Use whereis to locate a binary (executable) file, any manual pages, and source code for a program you specify; whereis displays all the files it finds.

apropos: SEARCHES FOR A KEYWORD

When you do not know the name of the command you need to carry out a particular task, you can use a keyword and the apropos utility to search for it. (The **whatis** database has to be set up and regularly maintained with makewhatis for apropos to work; this task is typically handled by cron. Refer to crontab on page 624 for more information.) This utility searches for the keyword in the short description line (the top line) of all of the man pages and displays those that contain a match. The man utility, when called with the **–k** (keyword) option, displays the same output as apropos (it is actually the same command).

The following example shows the output of apropos when you call it with the **who** keyword. The output includes the name of each command, the section of the manual that contains it, and the brief description from the top of the man page. This list includes the utility that you need (who) and identifies other, related tools that you might find useful:

```
$ apropos who
at.allow [at]        (5)  - determine who can submit jobs via at or batch
at.deny [at]         (5)  - determine who can submit jobs via at or batch
jwhois               (1)  - client for the whois service
ldapwhoami           (1)  - LDAP who am i? tool
w                    (1)  - Show who is logged on and what they are doing
who                  (1)  - show who is logged on
whoami               (1)  - print effective userid
```

whatis   The whatis utility is similar to apropos but finds only complete word matches for the name of the utility.

```
$ whatis who
who                      (1)  - show who is logged on
```

slocate: SEARCHES FOR A FILE

The slocate utility, a secure version of locate, searches for files on the local system:

```
$ slocate motd
/lib/security/pam_motd.so
/usr/share/man/man5/motd.5.gz
/etc/motd
```

Before you can use slocate the updatedb utility must build/update the slocate database. Typically the database is updated once a day by a cron script. Refer to crontab on page 624 for more information.

OBTAINING USER AND SYSTEM INFORMATION

If you are not on a network, skip the rest of this chapter

tip   If you are the only user on a system that is not connected to a network, you may want to skip the rest of this chapter. If you are not on a network but are set up to send and receive email, read "Email" on page 69.

This section covers utilities that display who is using the system, what those users are doing, and how the system is running. To find out who is using the local system, you can employ several utilities that vary in the details they provide and the options they support. The oldest utility, who, produces a list of users who are logged in on the local system, the device each person is using, and the time the person logged in.

The w and finger utilities show more detail, such as each user's full name and the command line each user is running. You can use the finger utility to retrieve information about users on remote systems if your computer is attached to a network. Table 3-1 on page 67 summarizes the output of these utilities.

```
$ who
root         console      Mar 27 05:00
alex         pts/4        Mar 27 12:23
alex         pts/5        Mar 27 12:33
jenny        pts/7        Mar 26 08:45
```

Figure 3-10   who lists who is logged in

who: LISTS USERS ON THE SYSTEM

The who utility displays a list of users who are logged in. In Figure 3-10, the first column shows Alex and Jenny logged in. (Alex is logged in from two locations.) The second column shows the device that each person's terminal, workstation, or terminal emulator is connected to. The third column shows the date and time the person logged in.

The information that who displays is useful when you want to communicate with a user at your installation. When the user is logged in, you can use write (page 67) to establish communication immediately. If who does not list the user or if you do not need to communicate immediately, you can send email to that person (page 69).

If the output of who scrolls off the screen, you can redirect the output through a pipe so that it becomes the input to less, which displays the output one page at a time. You can also use a pipe to redirect the output through grep to look for a specific name.

If you need to find out which terminal you are using or what time you logged in, you can use the command **who am i**:

```
$ who am i
alex         pts/5        Mar 27 12:33
```

finger: LISTS USERS ON THE SYSTEM

finger **can be a security risk**

security   On systems where security is a concern, the system administrator may disable finger. This utility can give information that can help a malicious user break into the system.

You can use finger to display a list of the users who are logged in on the system. In addition to login names, finger supplies each user's full name along with information about which device the person's terminal is connected to, how recently the user typed something on the keyboard, when the user logged in, and where the user is located (if the device appears in a system database). If the user has logged in over the network, the name of the remote system is shown as the user's location. For example, in Figure 3-11 **jenny** and **hls** are logged in from the remote system named

```
$ finger
Login      Name              Tty   Idle  Login Time   Office      Office
Phone
root       root              1     1:35  May 24 08:38
alex       Alex Watson       /0          Jun  7 12:46 (:0)
alex       Alex Watson       /1    19    Jun  7 12:47 (:0)
jenny      Jenny Chen        /2    2:24  Jun  2 05:33 (bravo.example.com)
hls        Helen Simpson     */2   2     Jun  2 05:33 (bravo.example.com)
```

Figure 3-11   finger I: lists who is logged in

bravo. The asterisk (*) in front of the name of Helen's device (TTY) indicates that she has blocked others from sending messages directly to her terminal (refer to "mesg: Denies or Accepts Messages" on page 68).

You can use finger to learn more about a particular individual by specifying that user on the command line. In Figure 3-12, finger displays detailed information about Alex. Alex is logged in and actively using one of his terminals (**pts/1**); he has not used his other terminal (**pts/0**) for 5 minutes and 52 seconds. You also learn from finger that if you want to set up a meeting with Alex, you should contact Jenny at extension 1693.

.plan and .project   Most of the information in Figure 3-12 was collected by finger from system files. The information shown after the heading **Plan:**, however, was supplied by Alex. The finger utility searched for a file named **.plan** in Alex's home directory and displayed its contents. (Filenames that begin with a period, such as **.plan**, are not normally listed by ls and are called invisible filenames [page 80].) You may find it helpful to create a **.plan** file for yourself; it can contain any information you choose, such as your typical schedule, interests, phone number, or address. In a similar manner finger displays the contents of the **.project** file in your home directory. If Alex had not been logged in, finger would have reported only his user information, the last time he logged in, the last time he read his email, and his plan.

```
$ finger alex
Login: alex                          Name: Alex Watson
Directory: /home/alex                Shell: /bin/tcsh
On since Wed Jun  7 12:46 (PDT) on pts/0 from :0
    5 minutes 52 seconds idle
On since Wed Jun  7 12:47 (PDT) on pts/1 from bravo
Last login Wed Jun  7 12:47 (PDT) on 1 from bravo
New mail received Wed Jun  7 13:16 2006 (PDT)
     Unread since Fri May 26 15:32 2006 (PDT)
Plan:
I will be at a conference in Hawaii all next week.  If you need
to see me, contact Jenny Chen, x1693.
```

Figure 3-12   finger II: lists details about one user

You can use finger to display a user's login name. For example, you might know that Helen's last name is Simpson but might not guess that her login name is **hls**. The finger utility, which is not case sensitive, can search for information on Helen using her first or last name. The following commands find the information you seek as well as information on other users whose names are Helen or Simpson.

```
$ finger HELEN
Login: hls                              Name: Helen Simpson.
...

$ finger simpson
Login: hls                              Name: Helen Simpson.
...
```

w: Lists Users on the System

The w utility displays a list of the users who are logged in. As discussed in the section on who, the information that w displays is useful when you want to communicate with someone at your installation.

The first column in Figure 3-13 shows that Alex, Jenny, and Scott are logged in. The second column shows the device number that each person's terminal is connected to. The third column shows the system that a remote user is logged in from. The fourth column shows the time each person logged in. The fifth column indicates how long each person has been idle (how much time has elapsed since the user pressed a key on the keyboard). The next two columns give measures of how much computer processor time each person has used during this login session and on the task that is running. The last column shows the command each person is running.

The first line that the w utility displays includes the time of day, the period of time the computer has been running (in days, hours, and minutes), the number of users logged in, and the load average (how busy the system is). The three load average numbers represent the number of jobs waiting to run, averaged over the past 1, 5, and 15 minutes. Use the uptime utility to display just this line. Table 3-1 compares the w, who, and finger utilities.

```
$ w
  8:20am  up 4 days,  2:28, 3 users,  load average: 0.04, 0.04, 0.00
USER      TTY      FROM          LOGIN@   IDLE   JCPU    PCPU   WHAT
alex      pts/4    :0            5:55am  13:45   0.15s   0.07s  w
alex      pts/5    :0            5:55am     27   2:55    1:01   bash
jenny     pts/7    bravo         5:56am  13:44   0.51s    30s   vim 3.txt
scott     pts/12   bravo         7:17pm          1.00s   0:14s  run_bdgt
```

Figure 3-13   The w utility

Table 3-1   Comparison of w, who, and finger

Information Displayed	w	who	finger
User login name	X	X	X
Terminal-line identification (tty)	X	X	X
Login day and time	X		X
Login date and time		X	
Idle time	X		X
What program the user is executing	X		
Where the user logged in from			X
CPU time used	X		
Full name (or other information from **/etc/passwd**)			X
User-supplied vanity information			X
System uptime and load average	X		

COMMUNICATING WITH OTHER USERS

The utilities discussed in this section exchange messages and files with other users either interactively or through email.

write: SENDS A MESSAGE

The write utility sends a message to another user who is logged in. When you and another user use write to send messages to each other, you establish two-way communication. Initially a write command (Figure 3-14) displays a banner on the other user's terminal, saying that you are about to send a message.

The syntax of a write command line is

*write **username** [terminal]*

```
$ write alex
Hi Alex, are you there? o
```

Figure 3-14   The write utility I

```
$ write alex
Hi Alex, are you there? o

Message from alex@bravo.example.com on pts/0 at 16:23 ...
Yes Jenny, I'm here. o
```

Figure 3-15   The write utility II

The *username* is the login name of the user you want to communicate with. The *terminal* is an optional terminal name that is useful if the user is logged in more than once. You can display the login and terminal names of the users who are logged in on your system by using who, w, or finger.

To establish two-way communication with another user, you and the other user must each execute write, specifying the other's login name as the *username*. The write utility then copies text, line by line, from one keyboard/display to the other (Figure 3-15). Sometimes it helps to establish a convention, such as typing o (for over) when you are ready for the other person to type and typing oo (for over and out) when you are ready to end the conversation. When you want to stop communicating with the other user, press CONTROL-D at the beginning of a line. Pressing CONTROL-D tells write to quit, displays **EOF** (end of file) on the other user's terminal, and returns you to the shell. The other user must do the same.

If the **Message from...** banner appears on your screen and obscures something you are working on, press CONTROL-L or CONTROL-R to refresh the screen and remove the banner. Then you can clean up, exit from your work, and respond to the person who is writing to you. You just have to remember who is writing to you, because the banner will no longer appear on the screen.

mesg: **DENIES OR ACCEPTS MESSAGES**

Give the following command when you do not wish to receive messages from another user:

```
$ mesg n
```

If Alex had given this command before Jenny tried to send him a message, she would have seen the following:

```
$ write alex
Permission denied
```

You can allow messages again by entering **mesg y**. Give the command **mesg** by itself to display **is y** (for yes, messages are allowed) or **is n** (for no, messages are *not* allowed).

EMAIL

You can use *email,* or *electronic mail,* to send and receive letters, memos, reminders, invitations, and even junk mail (unfortunately). Email can also transmit binary data, such as pictures or compiled code, as attachments. An *attachment* is a file that is attached to, but is not part of, a piece of email. Attachments are frequently opened by programs that are called by your mail program, so you may not be aware that they are not an integral part of an email message.

You can use email to communicate with users on your system and, if your installation is part of a network, with other users on the network. If you are connected to the Internet, you can communicate electronically with users around the world.

Email utilities differ from write in that email utilities can send a message when the recipient is not logged in. These utilities can also send the same message to more than one user at a time.

Many mail programs are available for Linux, including the original character-based mail program, Netscape/Mozilla mail, pine, mail through emacs, Kmail, evolution, and exmh, which are supplied with many Linux distributions. Another popular graphical mail program is sylpheed (sylpheed.good-day.net).

You can use two programs to make any mail program easier to use and more secure. The procmail program (www.procmail.org) creates and maintains mail servers and mailing lists; preprocesses mail by sorting it into appropriate files and directories; starts various programs depending on the characteristics of incoming mail; forwards mail; and so on. The GNU Privacy Guard (gpg or GNUpg) encrypts and decrypts email and makes it almost impossible for an unauthorized person to read.

Network addresses   If your system is part of a LAN, you can generally send mail to and receive mail from users on other systems on the LAN by using their login names. Someone sending Alex email on the Internet would need to specify his *domain name* (page 873) along with his login name. Use the following address to send email to the author of this book: **mgs@sobell.com**.

CHAPTER SUMMARY

The utilities introduced in this chapter and Chapter 2 constitute a small but powerful subset of the many utilities available on a typical Linux system. Because you will use them frequently and because they are integral to the following chapters, it is important that you become comfortable using them.

The utilities listed in Table 3-2 manipulate, display, compare, and print files.

Table 3-2   File utilities

Utility	Function
cp	Copies one or more files (page 45)
diff	Displays the differences between two files (page 51)
file	Displays information about the contents of a file (page 52)
grep	Searches file(s) for a string (page 48)
head	Displays the lines at the beginning of a file (page 49)
lpq	Displays a list of jobs in the print queue (page 47)
lpr	Places file(s) in the print queue (page 47)
lprm	Removes a job from the print queue (page 48)
mv	Renames a file or moves file(s) to another directory (page 46)
sort	Puts a file in order by lines (page 50)
tail	Displays the lines at the end of a file (page 49)
uniq	Displays the contents of a file, skipping successive duplicate lines (page 51)

To reduce the amount of disk space a file occupies, you can compress it with the bzip2 utility. The compression works especially well on files that contain patterns, such as most text files, but reduces the size of almost all files. The inverse of bzip2—bunzip2—restores a file to its original, decompressed form. Table 3-3 lists utilities that compress and decompress files. The bzip2 utility is the most efficient of these.

Table 3-3   (De)compression utilities

Utility	Function
bunzip2	Returns a file compressed with bzip2 to its original size and format (page 57)
bzcat	Displays a file compressed with bzip2 (page 57)
bzip2	Compresses a file (page 56)
compress	Compresses a file (not as well as gzip) (page 58)
gunzip	Returns a file compressed with gzip or compress to its original size and format (page 58)
gzip	Compresses a file (page 58)
zcat	Displays a file compressed with gzip (page 58)

An archive is a file, usually compressed, that contains a group of files. The tar utility (Table 3-4) packs and unpacks archives. The filename extensions **.tar.bz2, .tar.gz,** and **.tgz** identify compressed tar archive files and are often seen on software packages obtained over the Internet.

Table 3-4   Archive utility

Utility	Function
tar	Creates or extracts files from an archive file (page 58)

The utilities listed in Table 3-5 determine the location of a utility on the local system. For example, they can display the pathname of a utility or a list of C++ compilers available on the system.

Table 3-5   Location utilities

Utility	Function
apropos	Searches the man page one-line descriptions for a keyword (page 62)
slocate	Searches for files on the local system (page 63)
whereis	Displays the full pathnames of a utility, source code, or man page (page 61)
which	Displays the full pathname of a command you can run (page 61)

Table 3-6 lists utilities that display information about other users. You can easily learn a user's full name, the user's login status, the login shell of the user, and other information maintained by the system.

Table 3-6   User and system information utilities

Utility	Function
finger	Displays detailed information about users, including their full names (page 64)
w	Displays detailed information about users who are logged in (page 66)
who	Displays information about users who are logged in (page 64)

The utilities shown in Table 3-7 can help you stay in touch with other users on the local network.

Table 3-7   User communication utilities

mesg	Permits or denies messages sent by write (page 68)
write	Sends a message to another user who is logged in (page 67)

Table 3-8 lists miscellaneous utilities.

Table 3-8   Miscellaneous utilities

date	Displays the current date and time (page 54)
echo	Copies its *arguments* (page 861) to the screen (page 53)

EXERCISES

1. What commands can you use to determine who is logged in on a specific terminal?

2. How can you keep other users from using write to communicate with you? Why would you want to?

3. What happens when you give the following commands if the file named **done** already exists?

   ```
   $ cp to_do done
   $ mv to_do done
   ```

4. How can you find out which utilities are available on your system for editing files? Which utilities are available for editing on your system?

5. How can you find the phone number for Ace Electronics in a file named **phone** that contains a list of names and phone numbers? Which command can you use to display the entire file in alphabetical order? How can you remove adjacent duplicate lines from the file? How can you remove all duplicates?

6. What happens when you use diff to compare two binary files that are not identical? (You can use gzip to create the binary files.) Explain why the diff output for binary files is not the same as the diff output for ASCII files.

7. Create a **.plan** file in your home directory. Does finger on your system display the contents of your **.plan** file?

8. What is the result of giving the which utility the name of a command that resides in a directory that is *not* in your search path?

9. Are any of the utilities discussed in this chapter found in more than one directory on your system? If so, which ones?

10. Experiment by calling the file utility with names of files in **/usr/bin**. How many different types of files are there?

11. Which command can you use to look at the first few lines of a file named **status.report**? Which command can you use to look at the end of the file?

ADVANCED EXERCISES

12. Re-create the **colors.1** and **colors.2** files used in Figure 3-8 on page 52. Test your files by running **diff –u** on them, and see whether you get the same results as in the figure.

13. Try giving these two commands.

    ```
    $ echo cat
    $ cat echo
    ```

    Explain the differences between them.

14 Repeat exercise 5 using the file **phone.gz**, a compressed version of the list of names and phone numbers. Try to consider more than one approach to answer each question, and explain how you made your choices.

15. Find existing files or create files that

    a. gzip compresses by more than 80 percent

    b. gzip compresses by less than 10 percent

    c. get larger when compressed with gzip

    Use **ls –l** to determine the sizes of the files in question. Can you characterize the files in a, b, and c?

16. Some mailers—particularly older ones—are not able to handle binary files. Suppose that you are mailing a file that has been compressed with gzip, which produces a binary file, and you do not know what mailer the recipient is using. Refer to the man page for uuencode, which converts a binary file to an ASCII file. Learn about the utility and how to use it.

    a. Convert a compressed file to ASCII, using uuencode. Is the encoded file larger or smaller than the compressed file? Explain. (If uuencode is not on your system, you can download it from **rpmfind.net**; it is part of the GNU **sharutils** package.)

    b. Would it ever make sense to use uuencode on a file before compressing it? Explain.

4

THE LINUX FILESYSTEM

A *Filesystem* is a *data structure* (page 870) that usually resides on part of a disk and that holds directories of files. Filesystems store user and system data that are the basis of users' work on the system and the system's existence. This chapter discusses the organization and terminology of the Linux filesystem, defines ordinary and directory files, and explains the rules for naming them. It also shows how to create and delete directories, move through the filesystem, and use pathnames to access files in various directories. It includes a discussion of important files and directories as well as various types of files and ways to work with them. In addition, this chapter covers file access permissions, which allow you to share selected files with other users, and links, which can make a single file appear in more than one directory.

In addition to reading this chapter, you may want to refer to the df, fsck, mkfs, and tune2fs utilities in Part V for more information on filesystems.

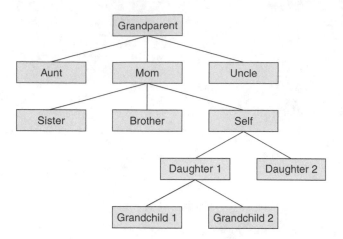

Figure 4-1   A family tree

THE HIERARCHICAL FILESYSTEM

Family tree   A *hierarchical* (page 878) structure frequently takes the shape of a pyramid. One example of this type of structure is found by tracing a family's lineage: A couple has a child, who may in turn have several children, each of whom may have more children. This hierarchical structure (shown in Figure 4-1) is called a *family tree*.

Directory tree   Like the family tree it resembles, the Linux filesystem is called a *tree*. It consists of a set of connected files. This structure allows you to organize files so you can easily find any particular one. On a standard Linux system, each user starts with one directory, to which the user can add subdirectories to any desired level. By creating multiple levels of subdirectories, a user can expand the structure as needed.

Subdirectories   Typically each subdirectory is dedicated to a single subject, such as a person, project, or event. The subject dictates whether a subdirectory should be subdivided further. For example, Figure 4-2 shows a secretary's subdirectory named **correspond**. This directory contains three subdirectories: **business**, **memos**, and **personal**. The **business** directory contains files that store each letter the secretary types. If you expect many letters to go to one client, as is the case with **milk_co**, you can dedicate a subdirectory to that client.

One major strength of the Linux filesystem is its ability to adapt to users' needs. You can take advantage of this strength by strategically organizing your files so they are most convenient and useful for you.

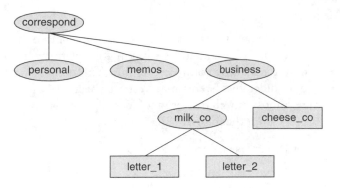

Figure 4-2   A secretary's directories

DIRECTORY AND ORDINARY FILES

Like a family tree, the tree representing the filesystem is usually pictured upside down, with its *root* at the top. Figures 4-2 and 4-3 show that the tree "grows" downward from the root, with paths connecting the root to each of the other files. At the end of each path is either an ordinary file or a directory file. *Ordinary files,* or simply *files,* appear at the ends of paths that cannot support other paths. *Directory files,* usually referred to as *directories* or *folders,* are points that other paths *can* branch off from. (Figures 4-2 and 4-3 show some empty directories.) When you refer to the tree, *up* is toward the root and *down* is away from the root. Directories directly connected by a path are called *parents* (closer to the root) or *children* (farther from the root). A *pathname* is a series of names that traces a path along branches from one file to another.

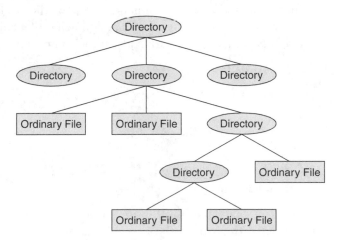

Figure 4-3   Directories and ordinary files

FILENAMES

Every file has a *filename*. The maximum length of a filename varies with the type of filesystem; Linux includes support for several types of filesystems. Most of today's filesystems allow you to create files with names up to 255 characters in length, but some older filesystems may restrict you to 14-character names. Although you can use almost any character in a filename, you will avoid confusion if you choose characters from the following list:

- Uppercase letters (A–Z)
- Lowercase letters (a–z)
- Numbers (0–9)
- Underscore (_)
- Period (.)
- Comma (,)

/ or root The *root* directory is always named **/** (slash) and referred to by this single character. No other file can use this name or have a **/** in its name. However, in a pathname, which is a string of filenames including directory names, the slash *separates* filenames (page 83).

Like the children of one parent, no two files in the same directory can have the same name. (Parents give their children different names because it makes good sense, but Linux requires it.) Files in different directories, like children of different parents, can have the same name.

The filenames you choose should mean something. Too often a directory is filled with important files with such unhelpful names as **hold1**, **wombat**, and **junk**, not to mention **foo** and **foobar**. Such names are poor choices because they do not help you recall what you stored in a file. The following filenames conform to the suggested syntax *and* convey information about the contents of the file:

- **correspond**
- **january**
- **davis**
- **reports**
- **2001**
- **acct_payable**

Filename length When you share files with users on other systems, you may need to make long filenames differ within the first 14 characters. If you keep the filenames short, they are easy to type; later you can add extensions to them without exceeding the

14-character limit imposed by some filesystems. The disadvantage of short filenames is that they are typically less descriptive than long filenames. When you share files with systems running DOS or older versions of Windows, you must respect the 8-character filename body length and 3-character filename extension length imposed by those systems.

Long filenames enable you to assign descriptive names to files. To help you select among files without typing entire filenames, shells support filename completion. For more information about this feature, see the "Filename completion" tip on page 45.

You can use uppercase and/or lowercase letters within filenames. Linux is case sensitive, so files named **JANUARY**, **January**, and **january** represent three distinct files.

Do not use SPACEs within filenames

caution   Although you can use SPACEs within filenames, it is a poor idea. Because a SPACE is a special character, you must quote it on a command line. Quoting a character on a command line can be difficult for a novice user and cumbersome for an experienced user. Use periods or underscores instead of SPACEs: **joe.05.04.26**, **new_stuff**.

FILENAME EXTENSIONS

In the filenames listed in Table 4-1, *filename extensions* help describe the contents of the file. A filename extension is the part of the filename following an embedded period. Some programs, such as the C programming language compiler, depend on specific filename extensions. In most cases, however, filename extensions are optional. Use extensions freely to make filenames easy to understand. You can use several periods within the same filename—for example, **notes.4.10.01** or **files.tar.gz**.

Table 4-1   Filename extensions

compute.c	A C programming language source file
compute.o	The object code for the program
compute	The same program as an executable file
memo.0410.txt	A text file
memo.pdf	A PDF file; view with xpdf under a GUI
memo.ps	A PostScript file; view with gs under a GUI
memo.Z	A file compressed with compress (page 58); use uncompress or gunzip (page 58) to decompress
memo.tgz or **memo.tar.gz**	A tar (page 58) archive of files compressed with gzip (page 58)
memo.gz	A file compressed with gzip (page 58); view with zcat or decompress with gunzip (both on page 58)

Table 4-1   Filename extensions (continued)

memo.bz2	A file compressed with bzip2 (page 56); view with bzcat or decompress with bunzip2 (both on page 57)
memo.html	A file meant to be viewed using a Web browser, such as Mozilla
photo.jpg or **photo.gif**	A file containing graphical information, such as a picture (also **.jpeg**)

INVISIBLE FILENAMES

A filename that begins with a period is called an *invisible filename* (or an *invisible file* or sometimes a *hidden file*) because ls does not normally display it. The command **ls –a** displays *all* filenames, even invisible ones. Names of startup files (page 83) usually begin with a period so that they are invisible and do not clutter a directory listing. The **.plan** file (page 65) is also invisible. Two special invisible entries—a single and double period (**.** and **..**)—appear in every directory (page 85).

mkdir: CREATES A DIRECTORY

The mkdir utility creates a directory. The *argument* (page 861) to mkdir becomes the pathname of the new directory. The following examples develop the directory structure shown in Figure 4-4. In the figure the directories that are added are a lighter shade than the others and are connected by dashes.

In Figure 4-5, ls shows the names of the files Alex has been working with in his home directory: **demo, names,** and **temp.** Using mkdir, Alex then creates a directory named **literature** as a child of the **/home/alex** directory. When you use mkdir, enter

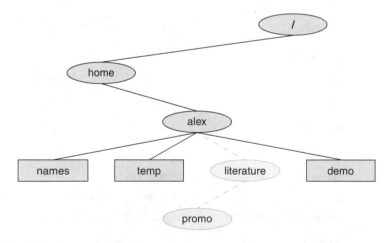

Figure 4-4   The file structure developed in the examples

```
$ ls
demo   names   temp
$ mkdir /home/alex/literature
$ ls
demo   literature   names   temp
$ ls -F
demo   literature/   names   temp
$ ls literature
$
```

Figure 4-5   The mkdir utility

the pathname of *your* home directory (page 82) in place of **/home/alex**. The second ls verifies the presence of the new directory.

You can use the –F option with ls to display a slash after the name of each directory and an asterisk after each executable file (shell script, utility, or program). When you call it with an argument that is the name of a directory, ls lists the contents of the directory. If the directory is empty, ls does not display anything.

THE WORKING DIRECTORY

pwd   While you are logged in on a character-based interface to a Linux system, you are always associated with a directory. The directory you are associated with, or are working in, is called the *working directory* or *current directory*. Sometimes this association is referred to in a physical sense: "You are *in* (or *working in*) the **jenny** directory." The pwd command displays the pathname of the working directory.

To access any file in the working directory, you need only a simple filename. To access a file in another directory, you *must* use a pathname.

SIGNIFICANCE OF THE WORKING DIRECTORY

Typing a long pathname is tedious and increases the chance of making a mistake. This possibility is less likely under a GUI, where you click filenames or icons. You can choose a working directory for any particular task to reduce the need for long pathnames. Your choice of a working directory does not allow you to do anything you could not do otherwise. Instead, it simply makes some operations easier.

Refer to Figure 4-6 as you read this paragraph. Files that are children of the working directory can be referenced by simple filenames. Grandchildren of the working directory can be referenced by short relative pathnames: two filenames separated by a slash. When you manipulate files in a large directory structure, short relative pathnames can save time and aggravation. If you choose a working directory that contains the files used most often for a particular task, you need to use fewer long, cumbersome pathnames.

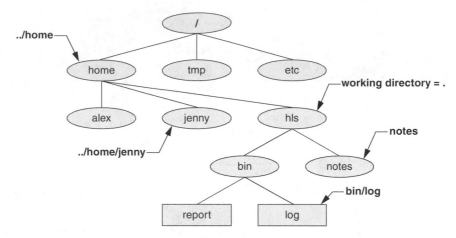

Figure 4-6   Relative pathnames

HOME DIRECTORY

When you first log in on a Linux system, your working directory is your *home directory*. To display the pathname of your home directory, use pwd just after you log in (see Figure 4-7).

When used without any arguments, the ls utility displays a list of the files in the working directory. Because your home directory has been the only working directory you have used so far, ls has always displayed a list of files in your home directory. (All the files you have created up to this point were created in your home directory.)

cd: CHANGES TO ANOTHER WORKING DIRECTORY

The cd (change directory) utility makes another directory the working directory but does *not* change the contents of the working directory. The first **cd** command in Figure 4-8 makes the **/home/alex/literature** directory the working directory, as verified by pwd.

When used without an argument, cd makes your home directory the working directory, as it was when you first logged in. The second **cd** command in Figure 4-8 does not have an argument and makes Alex's home directory the working directory.

```
login: alex
Password:
Last login: Wed Oct 20 11:14:21 from bravo
$ pwd
/home/alex
```

Figure 4-7   Logging in and displaying the pathname of your home directory

```
$ cd /home/alex/literature
$ pwd
/home/alex/literature
$ cd
$ pwd
/home/alex
```

Figure 4-8   cd changes your working directory

The working directory versus your home directory

tip The working directory is not the same as your home directory. Your home directory remains the same for the duration of your session and usually from session to session. Each time immediately after you log in, you are working in the same directory: your home directory.

Unlike your home directory, the working directory can change as often as you like. You have no set working directory, which is why some people refer to it as the *current directory.* When you log in and until you change directories by using cd, your home directory is your working directory. If you were to change directories to Scott's home directory, then Scott's home directory would be your working directory.

STARTUP FILES

Startup files, which appear in your home directory, give the shell and other programs information about you and your preferences. Frequently, one of these files tells the shell what kind of terminal you are using and executes the stty (set terminal) utility to establish your line kill and erase keys.

Either you or the system administrator can put a shell startup file containing shell commands in your home directory. The shell executes the commands in this file each time you log in. Because the startup files have invisible filenames, you must use the ls –a command to see whether one is in your home directory. See pages 257 and 342 for more information about startup files.

ABSOLUTE PATHNAMES

Every file has a pathname. Figure 4-9 shows the pathnames of directories and ordinary files in part of a filesystem hierarchy. An absolute pathname always starts with a slash (/), the name of the root directory. You can build the absolute pathname of a file by tracing a path from the root directory through all the intermediate directories to the file. String all the filenames in the path together, separating each from the next with a slash (/) and preceding the entire group of filenames with a slash (/). This path of filenames is called an *absolute pathname* because it locates a file absolutely by tracing a path from the root directory to the file. The part of a pathname following the final slash is called a *simple filename* or just *filename.*

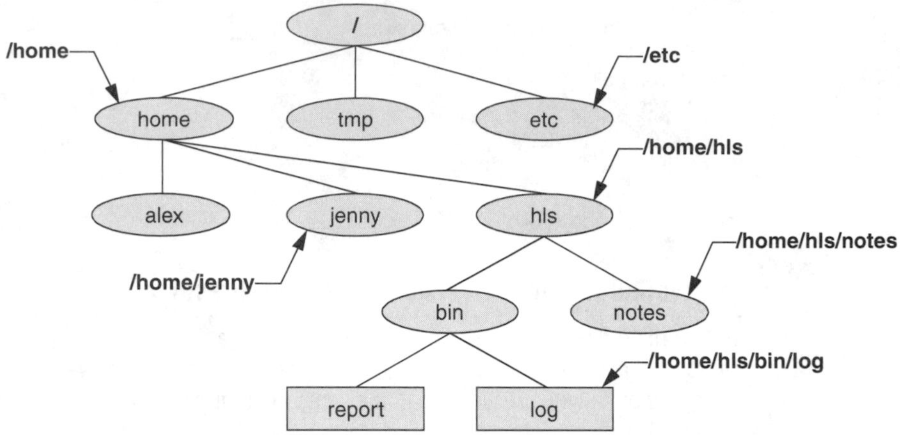

Figure 4-9   Absolute pathnames

Another form of absolute pathname begins with a tilde (~), which represents a home directory. For more information refer to "~ (Tilde) in Pathnames" on page 89.

RELATIVE PATHNAMES

A *relative pathname* traces a path from the working directory to a file. The pathname is *relative* to the working directory. Any pathname that does not begin with the root directory (/) or a tilde (~) is a relative pathname. Like absolute pathnames, relative pathnames can describe a path through many directories.

Alex could have created the **literature** directory in Figure 4-5 more easily by using a relative pathname:

```
$ pwd
/home/alex
$ mkdir literature
```

The pwd command shows that Alex's home directory (**/home/alex**) is the working directory. The mkdir utility displays an error message if a directory or file named **literature** exists: You cannot have two files or directories with the same name in the same directory. The pathname used in this example is a simple filename—a kind of relative pathname that specifies a file in the working directory.

The following commands show two ways to create the **promo** directory as a child of the newly created **literature** directory. The first way works when **/home/alex** is the working directory and uses a relative pathname.

```
$ pwd
/home/alex
$ mkdir literature/promo
```

When using a relative pathname, know which directory is the working directory

caution   The location of the file that you are accessing with a relative pathname depends on (is relative to) the working directory. Always make sure you know which directory is the working directory before you use a relative pathname. Use pwd to verify the directory. If you are using mkdir and you are not where you think you are in the file hierarchy, the new directory will end up in an unexpected location.

It does not matter which directory is the working directory when you use an absolute pathname.

The second way uses an absolute pathname:

```
$ mkdir /home/alex/literature/promo
```

Use the **–p** (parents) option to mkdir to create both the **literature** and **promo** directories with a single command.

```
$ pwd
/home/alex
$ ls
demo   names   temp
$ mkdir -p literature/promo
```

or

```
$ mkdir -p /home/alex/literature/promo
```

THE . AND .. DIRECTORY ENTRIES

The mkdir utility automatically puts two entries in each directory it creates: a single period (.) and a double period (..), representing the directory itself and the parent directory, respectively. These entries are invisible because each of their filenames begins with a period.

Because mkdir automatically places these entries in every directory, you can rely on their presence. The . is synonymous with the pathname of the working directory and can be used in its place; .. is synonymous with the pathname of the parent of the working directory.

With the **literature** directory as the working directory, the following example uses .. three times: first to list the contents of the parent directory (**/home/alex**), second to copy the **memoA** file to the parent directory, and third to list the contents of the parent directory again.

```
$ pwd
/home/alex/literature
$ ls ..
demo   literature   names   temp
$ cp memoA ..
$ ls ..
demo   literature   memoA   names   temp
```

While working in the **promo** directory, Alex can use a relative pathname to edit a file in his home directory. Before calling the editor, Alex checks which directory he is in:

```
$ pwd
/home/alex/literature/promo
$ vim ../../names
```

Virtually anywhere that a utility or program requires a filename or pathname, you can use an absolute or relative pathname or a simple filename. This usage holds true for ls, vim, mkdir, rm, and other Linux utilities.

IMPORTANT STANDARD DIRECTORIES AND FILES

Originally files on a Linux system were not located in standard places. The scattered files made it difficult to document and maintain a Linux system and just about impossible for someone to release a software package that would compile and run on all Linux systems. The first standard for the Linux filesystem, the FSSTND (Linux Filesystem Standard), was released on February 14, 1994. In early 1995 work was started on a broader standard covering many UNIX-like systems: FHS (Linux Filesystem Hierarchy Standard—www.pathname.com/fhs). More recently, FHS has been incorporated in LSB (Linux Standard Base—www.linuxbase.org), a workgroup of FSG (Free Standards Group—www.freestandards.org). Figure 4-10 shows the locations of some important directories and files as specified by FHS. The significance of many of these directories will become clear as you continue reading.

The following list describes the directories shown in Figure 4-10, some of the directories specified by FHS, and some other directories. Most Linux distributions do not use all the directories specified by FHS. You cannot always determine the function of a directory by its name. For example, although **/opt** stores add-on software, **/etc/opt** stores configuration files for the software in **/opt**.

/ **Root**   The root directory, present in all Linux system file structures, is the ancestor of all files in the filesystem.

/bin **Essential command binaries**   Holds the files needed to bring the system up and run it when it first comes up in single-user mode.

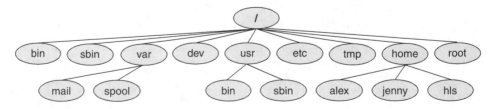

Figure 4-10   A typical FHS-based Linux system file structure

/boot   **Static files of the boot loader**   Contains most of the files needed to boot the system.

/dev   **Device files**   Contains all files that represent peripheral devices, such as disk drives, terminals, and printers.

/etc   **Machine–local system configuration**   Holds administrative, configuration, and other system files. One of the most important is **/etc/passwd,** which contains a list of all users who have permission to use the system.

/etc/X11   **Machine–local configuration for the X Window System**

/etc/opt   **Configuration files for add-on software packages kept in /opt**

/home   **User home directories**   Each user's home directory is typically one of many subdirectories of the **/home** directory. As an example, assuming that users' directories are under **/home,** the absolute pathname of Jenny's home directory is **/home/jenny.** On some systems the users' directories may not be under **/home** but instead might be spread among **/inhouse** and **/clients.**

/lib   **Shared libraries and kernel modules**

/lib/modules   **Loadable kernel modules**

/mnt   **Mount point for temporary mounting of filesystems**

/opt   **Add-on software packages (optional packages)**

/proc   **Kernel and process information virtual filesystem**

/root   **Home directory for root**

/sbin   **Essential system binaries**   Utilities used for system administration are stored in **/sbin** and **/usr/sbin.** The **/sbin** directory includes utilities needed during the booting process, and **/usr/sbin** holds utilities used after the system is up and running. In older versions of Linux, many system administration utilities were scattered through several directories that often included other system files (**/etc, /usr/bin, /usr/adm, /usr/include**).

/tmp   **Temporary files**   Used to hold temporary files.

/usr   **Second major hierarchy**   Traditionally includes subdirectories that contain information used by the system. Files in **/usr** subdirectories do not change often and may be shared by multiple systems.

/usr/bin   **Most user commands**   Contains the standard Linux utility programs—that is, binaries that are not needed in single-user mode.

/usr/bin/X11   **Symbolic link to /usr/X11R6/bin**

/usr/games   **Games and educational programs**

/usr/include   **Header files included by C programs**

/usr/include/X11   **Symbolic link to /usr/X11R6/include/X11**

/usr/lib	Libraries
/usr/lib/X11	Symbolic link to /usr/X11R6/lib/X11
/usr/local	**Local hierarchy** Holds locally important files and directories that are added to the system. Subdirectories can include **bin, games, include, lib, sbin, share,** and **src.**
/usr/man	Online manuals
/usr/sbin	Nonvital system administration binaries See **/sbin.**
/usr/share	**Architecture-independent data** Subdirectories can include **dict, doc, games, info, locale, man, misc, terminfo,** and **zoneinfo.**
/usr/share/doc	Miscellaneous documentation
/usr/share/info	GNU info system's primary directory
/usr/src	Source code
/usr/X11R6	X Window System, version 11 release 6
/var	**Variable data** Files with contents that vary as the system runs are found in subdirectories under **/var.** The most common examples are temporary files, system log files, spooled files, and user mailbox files. Subdirectories can include **cache, lib, lock, log, opt, run, spool, tmp,** and **yp.** Older versions of Linux scattered such files through several subdirectories of **/usr** (**/usr/adm, /usr/mail, /usr/spool, /usr/tmp**).
/var/log	**Log files** Contains **lastlog** (a record of the last login by each user), **messages** (system messages from **syslogd**), and **wtmp** (a record of all logins/logouts).
/var/spool	**Spooled application data** Contains **anacron, at, cron, lpd, mail, mqueue, news, samba,** and **uucp.** The file **/var/spool/mail** typically has a symbolic link in **/var.**

WORKING WITH DIRECTORIES

This section covers deleting directories, copying and moving files between directories, and moving directories. It also describes how to use pathnames to make your work with Linux easier.

rmdir: DELETES A DIRECTORY

The rmdir (remove directory) utility deletes a directory. You cannot delete the working directory or a directory that contains files other than . and .. entries. If you need to delete a directory with files in it, first use rm to delete the files and then delete the directory. You do not have to (nor can you) delete the . and .. entries; rmdir removes them automatically. The following command deletes the directory that was created in Figure 4-5 on page 81:

```
$ rmdir /home/alex/literature
```

The rm utility has a –r option (**rm –r** *filename*) that recursively deletes files, including directories, within a directory as well as the directory itself.

Use rm –r carefully, if at all

caution   Although **rm –r** is a handy command, you must use it carefully. Do not use it with an ambiguous file reference such as *. It is quite easy to wipe out your entire home directory with a single short command.

PATHNAMES

touch   Use a text editor to create a file named **letter** if you want to experiment with the examples that follow. Or you can use touch to create an empty file:

```
$ touch letter
```

With **/home/alex** as the working directory, the following example uses cp with a relative pathname to copy the file **letter** to the **/home/alex/literature/promo** directory. The copy of the file has the simple filename **letter.0610**:

```
$ pwd
/home/alex
$ cp letter literature/promo/letter.0610
```

If Alex does not change to another directory, he can use vim to edit the copy of the file he just made:

```
$ vim literature/promo/letter.0610
```

If Alex does not want to use a long pathname to specify the file, he can use cd to make **promo** the working directory before calling vim:

```
$ cd literature/promo
$ pwd
/home/alex/literature/promo
$ vim letter.0610
```

To make the parent of the working directory (named **/home/alex/literature**) become the new working directory, Alex can give the following command, which takes advantage of the **..** directory entry:

```
$ cd ..
$ pwd
/home/alex/literature
```

~ (TILDE) IN PATHNAMES

The shell expands the characters **~/** (a tilde followed by a slash) at the start of a pathname into the pathname of your home directory. Using this shortcut, you can display your **.bashrc** startup file (page 258) with the following command, no matter which directory is your working directory:

```
$ less ~/.bashrc
```

A tilde quickly references paths that start with your or someone else's home directory. The shell expands a tilde followed by a login name at the beginning of a pathname into the pathname of that user's home directory. Assuming he has permission to do so, Alex can examine Scott's **~/.bashrc** file with the following command:

```
$ less ~scott/.bashrc
```

Refer to "Tilde expansion" on page 326 for more information.

mv, cp: MOVES OR COPIES A FILE

Chapter 3 discussed the use of mv to rename files. However, mv is more general than that: You can use this utility to move files from one directory to another (change the pathname of a file) as well as to change a simple filename. When used to move one or more files to a new directory, the mv command has this syntax:

mv **existing-file-list directory**

If the working directory is **/home/alex**, Alex can use the following command to move the files **names** and **temp** from the working directory to the **literature** directory:

```
$ mv names temp literature
```

This command changes the absolute pathnames of the **names** and **temp** files from **/home/alex/names** and **/home/alex/temp** to **/home/alex/literature/names** and **/home/alex/literature/temp**, respectively (Figure 4-11). Like most Linux commands, mv accepts either absolute or relative pathnames.

As you work with Linux and create more and more files, you will need to create directories using mkdir to keep the files organized. The mv utility is a useful tool for moving files from one directory to another as you develop your file tree. The cp utility works in the same way that mv does, but it makes copies of the *existing-file-list* in the specified *directory*.

mv: MOVES A DIRECTORY

Just as it moves ordinary files from one directory to another, so mv can move directories. The syntax is similar except that you specify one or more directories, not ordinary files, to move:

mv **existing-directory-list new-directory**

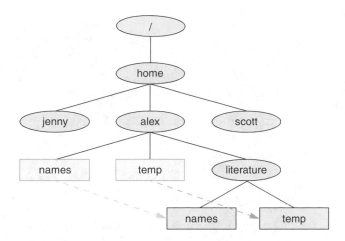

Figure 4-11   Using mv to move **names** and **temp**

If *new-directory* does not exist, the *existing-directory-list* must contain just one directory name, which mv changes to *new directory* (mv renames the directory). Although directories can be renamed using mv, their contents cannot be copied with cp unless you use the **–r** option. Refer to the explanations of tar (page 786) and cpio (page 619) for other ways to copy and/or move directories.

ACCESS PERMISSIONS

Three types of users can access a file: the owner of the file (*owner*), a member of a group to which the owner belongs (*group*), and everyone else (*other*). A user can attempt to access an ordinary file in three ways: by trying to *read from, write to,* or *execute* it. Three types of users, each of whom is able to access a file in three ways, equals a total of nine possible ways to access an ordinary file.

ls –l: Displays Permissions

When you call ls with the **–l** option and the name of an ordinary file, ls displays a line of information about the file. The following example displays information for two files. The file **letter.0610** contains the text of a letter, and **check_spell** contains a shell script, a program written in a high-level shell programming language:

```
$ ls -l letter.0610 check_spell
-rw-r--r-- 1 alex  pubs  3355  May  2 10:52 letter.0610
-rwxr-xr-x 2 alex  pubs   852  May  5 14:03 check_spell
```

From left to right, the lines that an ls –l command displays contain the following information (refer to Figure 4-12):

Figure 4-12 The columns displayed by the **ls –l** command

- The type of file (first character)
- The file's access permissions (the next nine characters)
- The number of links to the file (page 96)
- The name of the file's owner (usually the person who created the file)
- The name of the group that has group access to the file
- The size of the file in characters (bytes)
- The date and time the file was created or last modified
- The name of the file

The type of file (first column) for **letter.0610** is a hyphen (–) because it is an ordinary file (directory files have a **d** in this column).

The next three characters represent the access permissions for the *owner* of the file: **r** indicates read permission and **w** indicates write permission. The – in the next column indicates that the owner does *not* have execute permission; otherwise, an **x** would appear here.

In a similar manner the next three characters represent permissions for the *group,* and the final three characters represent permissions for *other* (everyone else). In the preceding example, the owner of **letter.0610** can read from and write to the file, whereas the group and others can only read from the file and no one is allowed to execute it. Although execute permission can be allowed for any file, it does not make sense to assign execute permission to a file that contains a document, such as a letter. The **check_spell** file is an executable shell script, and execute permission is appropriate. (The owner, the group, and others all have execute access permission.)

chmod: **CHANGES ACCESS PERMISSIONS**

The owner of a file controls which users have permission to access the file and how they can access it. When you own a file, you can use the **chmod** (change mode) utility to change access permissions for that file. In the following example, **chmod** adds (**+**) read and write permission (**rw**) for all (**a**) users:

```
$ chmod a+rw letter.0610
$ ls -l letter.0610
-rw-rw-rw- 1 alex pubs 3355  May  2 10:52 letter.0610
```

You must have read permission to execute a shell script

tip Because a shell needs to read a shell script (an ASCII file containing shell commands) before it can execute the commands within the script, you must have read permission to the file containing the script to execute it. You also need execute permission to execute a shell script directly on the command line. Binary (program) files do not need to be read; they are executed directly. You need only execute permission to run a binary (nonshell) program.

In the next example, chmod removes (–) read and execute (**rx**) permissions for users other (**o**) than the owner of the file (Alex) and members of the group associated with the file (**pubs**):

```
$ chmod o-rx check_spell
$ ls -l check_spell
-rwxr-x--- 2 alex pubs 852  May  5 14:03 check_spell
```

In addition to **a** (for *all*) and **o** (for *other*), you can use **g** (for *group*) and **u** (for *user*, although user refers to the owner of the file, who may or may not be the user of the file at any given time) in the argument to chmod. Refer to page 263 for more information on using chmod to make a file executable.

In addition to the symbolic arguments described in this section, you can use absolute, or numeric, arguments with chmod. See page 604 for information on absolute arguments and chmod in general.

The Linux file access permission scheme lets you give other users access to the files you want to share yet keep your private files confidential. You can allow other users to read from *and* write to a file (you may be one of several people working on a joint project). You can allow others only to read from a file (perhaps a project specification you are proposing). Or you can allow others only to write to a file (similar to an inbox or mailbox, where you want others to be able to send you mail but do not want them to read your mail). Similarly, you can protect entire directories from being scanned (covered shortly).

There is an exception to the access permissions just described. Anyone who knows the **root** password can log in as Superuser and have full access to *all* files, regardless of owner or access permissions.

chmod: **o** for other, **u** for owner

tip When using chmod, many people assume that the **o** stands for *owner;* it does not. The **o** stands for *other*, whereas **u** stands for *owner* (*user*).

SETUID AND SETGID PERMISSIONS

When you execute a file that has setuid (set user ID) permission, the process executing the file takes on the privileges of the file's owner. For example, if you run a setuid program that removes all files in a directory, you can remove files in any of the file owner's directories, even if you do not normally have permission to do so.

In a similar manner, setgid (set group ID) permission means that the process executing the file takes on the privileges of the group the file is associated with. The ls utility shows setuid permission by placing an **s** in the owner's executable position and setgid by placing an **s** in the group's executable position:

```
$ ls -l program1
-rwxr-xr-x   1 alex pubs 15828 Nov  5 06:28 program1
$ chmod u+s program1
$ ls -l program1
-rwsr-xr-x   1 alex pubs 15828 Nov  5 06:28 program1
$ chmod g+s program1
$ ls -l program1
-rwsr-sr-x   1 alex pubs 15828 Nov  5 06:28 program1
```

Minimize use of setuid and setgid programs owned by root

security   Executable files that are setuid and owned by **root** have Superuser privileges when they are run, even if they are not run by **root**. This type of program is very powerful because it can do anything that Superuser can do (that the program is designed to do). Similarly, executable files that are setgid and belong to the group **root** have extensive privileges.

Because of the power they hold and their potential for destruction, you should avoid creating and using setuid and setgid programs owned by **root** or belonging to the group **root** indiscriminately. Because of their inherent dangers, many sites do not allow these programs on their systems.

Do not write setuid shell scripts

security   Never give shell scripts setuid permission. Several techniques for subverting them are well known.

DIRECTORY ACCESS PERMISSIONS

Access permissions have slightly different meanings when they are used with directories. Although the three types of users can read from or write to a directory, the directory cannot be executed. Execute access permission is redefined for a directory: It means that you can cd into the directory and/or examine files that you have permission to read in the directory. It has nothing to do with executing a file.

When you have only execute permission for a directory, you can use ls to list a file in the directory if you know its name. You cannot use ls without an argument to list the entire contents of the directory. In the following exchange, Jenny first verifies that she is logged on as herself. Then she checks the permissions on Alex's **info** directory and cds into it. You can view the access permissions associated with a directory by running ls with the **–d** (directory) and **–l** (long) options:

```
$ who am i
jenny      pts/7   Aug 21 10:02
$ ls -ld /home/alex/info
drwx-----x   2 alex pubs 512 Aug 21 09:31 /home/alex/info
$ ls -l /home/alex/info
ls: /home/alex/info: Permission denied
```

The **d** at the left end of the line displayed by ls indicates that **/home/alex/info** is a directory. Alex has read, write, and execute permissions; members of the pubs group have no access permissions; and other users have execute permission only as indicated by the **x** at the right end of the permissions. Because Jenny does not have read permission for the directory, the ls –l command returns an error.

When Jenny specifies the names of the files she wants information about, she is not reading new directory information but searching for specific information, which she is allowed to do with execute access to the directory. She has read access to **notes,** so she has no problem using cat to display the file. She cannot display **financial** because she does not have read access to it:

```
$ ls -l /home/alex/info/financial /home/alex/info/notes
-rw-------   1 alex pubs 34 Aug 21 09:31 /home/alex/info/financial
-rw-r--r--   1 alex pubs 30 Aug 21 09:32 /home/alex/info/notes

$ cat /home/alex/info/notes
This is the file named notes.
$ cat /home/alex/info/financial
cat: /home/alex/info/financial: Permission denied
```

Next Alex gives others read access to his **info** directory:

```
$ chmod o+r /home/alex/info
```

When Jenny checks her access permissions on **info,** she finds that she has both read and execute access to the directory. Now ls –l works just fine without arguments, but she still cannot read **financial.** (This is an issue of file permissions, not directory permissions.)

Finally, Jenny tries to create a file named **newfile** by using touch. If Alex were to give her write permission to the **info** directory, she would be able to create new files in it:

```
$ ls -ld /home/alex/info
drwx---r-x   2 alex pubs 512 Aug 21 09:31 /home/alex/info
$ ls -l /home/alex/info
total 8
-rw-------   1 alex pubs 34 Aug 21 09:31 financial
-rw-r--r--   1 alex pubs 30 Aug 21 09:32 notes
$ cat financial
cat: financial: Permission denied
$ touch /home/alex/info/newfile
touch: cannot touch '/home/alex/info/newfile': Permission denied
```

LINKS

A *link* is a pointer to a file. Each time you create a file using vim, touch, cp, or any other means, you are putting a pointer in a directory. This pointer associates a filename with a place on the disk. When you specify a filename in a command, you are indirectly pointing to the place on the disk that holds the information you want.

Sharing files can be useful when two or more people are working on the same project and need to share information. You can make it easy for other users to access one of your files by creating additional links to the file.

To share a file with another user, first give the user permission to read from and write to the file. (You may also have to change the access permission of the parent directory of the file to give the user read, write, and/or execute permission.) Once the permissions are set appropriately, the user can create a link to the file so that each of you can access the file from your separate file trees.

A link can also be useful to a single user with a large file tree. You can create links to cross-classify files in your file tree, using different classifications for different tasks. For example, if your file tree is the one depicted in Figure 4-2, you might have a file named **to_do** in each subdirectory of the **correspond** directory—that is, in **personal**, **memos**, and **business**. If you later find it difficult to keep track of everything you need to do, you can create a separate directory named **to_do** in the **correspond** directory and link each subdirectory's to-do list into that directory. For example, you could link the file named **to_do** in the **memos** directory to a file named **memos** in the **to_do** directory. This set of links is shown in Figure 4-13.

Although it may sound complicated, this technique keeps all your to-do lists conveniently in one place. The appropriate list is easily accessible in the task-related directory when you are busy composing letters, writing memos, or handling personal business.

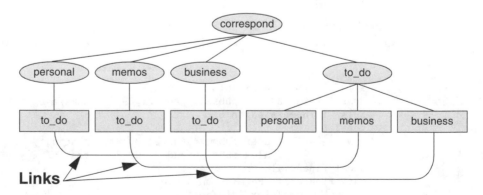

Figure 4-13   Using links to cross-classify files

About the discussion of hard links

tip Two kinds of links exist: hard links and symbolic (soft) links. Hard links are older and becoming dated. The section on hard links is marked as optional; you can skip it, although it discusses inodes and gives you insight into how the filesystem is structured.

optional

HARD LINKS

A hard link to a file appears as another file in the file structure. If the link appears in the same directory as the linked-to file, the links must have different filenames because two files in the same directory cannot have the same name.

ln: CREATES A HARD LINK

The ln (link) utility (without the –s or ––**symbolic** option) creates an additional hard link to an existing file using the following syntax:

ln existing-file new-link

The next command makes the link shown in Figure 4-14 by creating a new link named **/home/alex/letter** to an existing file named **draft** in Jenny's home directory:

```
$ pwd
/home/jenny
$ ln draft /home/alex/letter
```

The new link appears in the **/home/alex** directory with the filename **letter.** In practice Alex may need to change directory and file permissions as shown in the previous section for Jenny to be able to access the file.

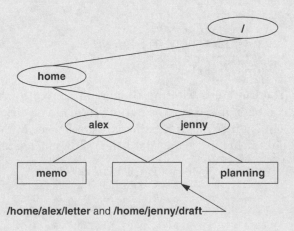

Figure 4-14   Two links to the same file: **/home/alex/letter** and **/home/jenny/draft**

The ln utility creates an additional pointer to an existing file but does *not* make another copy of the file. Because there is only one file, the file status information—such as access permissions, owner, and the time the file was last modified—is the same for all links. Only the filenames differ. When Jenny modifies **/home/jenny/draft**, Alex sees the changes in **/home/alex/letter**.

cp VERSUS ln

The following commands verify that ln does not make an additional copy of a file. Create a file, use ln to make an additional link to the file, change the contents of the file through one link, and verify the change through the other link:

```
$ cat file_a
This is file A.
$ ln file_a file_b
$ cat file_b
This is file A.
$ vim file_b
...
$ cat file_b
This is file B after the change.
$ cat file_a
This is file B after the change.
```

If you try the same experiment using cp instead of ln and change a *copy* of the file, the difference between the two utilities will become clearer. Once you change a *copy* of a file, the two files are different:

```
$ cat file_c
This is file C.
$ cp file_c file_d
$ cat file_d
This is file C.
$ vim file_d
...
$ cat file_d
This is file D after the change.
$ cat file_c
This is file C.
```

ls and link counts   You can use ls with the **–l** option, followed by the names of the files you want to compare, to see that the status information is the same for two links to the same file and is different for files that are not linked. In the following example, the **2** in the links field (just to the left of **alex**) shows there are two links to **file_a** and **file_b**:

```
$ ls -l file_a file_b file_c file_d
-rw-r--r-- 2 alex pubs 33  May 24 10:52 file_a
-rw-r--r-- 2 alex pubs 33  May 24 10:52 file_b
-rw-r--r-- 1 alex pubs 16  May 24 10:55 file_c
-rw-r--r-- 1 alex pubs 33  May 24 10:57 file_d
```

Although it is easy to guess which files are linked to one another in this example, ls does not explicitly tell you.

ls and inodes   Use ls with the –i option to determine definitively which files are linked. The –i option lists the *inode* (page 880) number for each file. An *inode* is the control structure for a file. If two filenames have the same inode number, they share the same control structure and are links to the same file. Conversely, when two filenames have different inode numbers, they are different files. The following example shows that **file_a** and **file_b** have the same inode number and that **file_c** and **file_d** have different inode numbers:

```
$ ls -i file_a file_b file_c file_d
3534 file_a    3534 file_b    5800 file_c    7328 file_d
```

All links to a file are of equal value: The operating system cannot distinguish the order in which multiple links were created. When a file has two links, you can remove either one and still access the file through the remaining link. You can remove the link used to create the file and, as long as one link remains, still access the file through that link.

SYMBOLIC LINKS

In addition to hard links, Linux supports links called *symbolic links, soft links,* or *symlinks*. A hard link is a pointer to a file (the directory entry points to the inode), whereas a symbolic link is an *indirect* pointer to a file (the directory entry contains the pathname of the pointed-to file—a pointer to the hard link to the file).

Limitations of hard links   Symbolic links were developed because of the limitations inherent in hard links. You cannot create a hard link to a directory, but you can create a symbolic link to a directory. A symbolic link can point to any file, regardless of where it is located in the file structure, but a hard link to a file must be in the same filesystem as the other hard link(s) to the file.

Often the Linux file hierarchy is composed of several filesystems. Because each filesystem keeps separate control information (that is, separate inode tables) for the files it contains, it is not possible to create hard links between files in different filesystems. When you create links only among files in your own directories, you will not notice these limitations.

One of the big advantages of a symbolic link is that it can point to a nonexistent file. This ability is useful if you need a link to a file that is periodically removed and re-created. A hard link keeps pointing to a "removed" file, which the hard link keeps alive even after a new file is created. A symbolic link always points to the newly created file and does not interfere with deleting the old file. For example, a symbolic link could point to a file that gets checked in and out under a source code control system, a .o file that is re-created by the C compiler each time you run make, or a log file that is periodically archived.

Although they are more general than hard links, symbolic links have some disadvantages. Whereas all hard links to a file have equal status, symbolic links do not have the same status as hard links. When a file has multiple hard links, it is analogous to a person having multiple full legal names, as many married women do. In contrast, symbolic links are analogous to nicknames. Anyone can have one or more nicknames but these nicknames have a lesser status than legal names. The following sections describe some of the peculiarities of symbolic links.

ln: CREATES A SYMBOLIC LINK

Use ln with the **--symbolic** (or **–s**) option to create a symbolic link. The following example creates the symbolic link **/tmp/s3** to the file **sum** in Alex's home directory. When you use the **ls –l** command to look at the symbolic link, ls displays the name of the link and the name of the file it points to. The first character of the listing is l (for link):

```
$ ln --symbolic /home/alex/sum /tmp/s3
$ ls -l /home/alex/sum /tmp/s3
-rw-rw-r--  1 alex alex 38 Jun 12 09:51 /home/alex/sum
lrwxrwxrwx  1 alex alex 14 Jun 12 09:52 /tmp/s3 -> /home/alex/sum
$ cat /tmp/s3
This is sum.
```

The sizes and times of the last modification of the two files are different. Unlike a hard link, a symbolic link to a file does not have the same status information as the file itself.

Similarly you can use ln to create a symbolic link to a directory. When you use the **--symbolic** option, ln does not care whether the file you are creating a link to is a regular file or a directory.

Use absolute pathnames with symbolic links

tip Symbolic links are literal and are not aware of directories. A link that points to a relative pathname, which includes simple filenames, assumes that the relative pathname is relative to the directory that the link was created *in* (not the directory the link was created *from*). In the following example, the link points to the file named **sum** in the **/tmp** directory. Because no such file exists, cat gives an error message:

```
$ pwd
/home/alex
$ ln --symbolic sum /tmp/s4
$ ls -l sum /tmp/s4
lrwxrwxrwx  1 alex     alex           3 Jun 12 10:13 /tmp/s4 -> sum
-rw-rw-r--  1 alex     alex          38 Jun 12 09:51 sum
$ cat /tmp/s4
cat: /tmp/s4: No such file or directory
```

optional cd AND SYMBOLIC LINKS

When you use a symbolic link as an argument to cd to change directories, the results can be confusing, particularly if you did not realize that you were using a symbolic link.

If you use cd to change to a directory that is represented by a symbolic link, the pwd builtin lists the name of the symbolic link. The pwd utility (**/bin/pwd**) lists the name of the linked-to directory, not the link, regardless of how you got there:

```
$ ln -s /home/alex/grades /tmp/grades.old
$ pwd
/home/alex
$ cd /tmp/grades.old
$ pwd
/tmp/grades.old
$ /bin/pwd
$/home/alex/grades
```

When you change directories back to the parent, you end up in the directory holding the symbolic link:

```
$ cd ..
$ pwd
/tmp
$ /bin/pwd
/tmp
```

rm: REMOVES A LINK

When you create a file, there is one hard link to it. You can delete the file or, using Linux terminology, remove the link with the rm utility. When you remove the last hard link to a file, you can no longer access the information stored there and the operating system releases for use by other files the space the file occupied on the disk. The space is released even if symbolic links to the file remain. When there is more than one hard link to a file, you can remove a hard link and still access the file from any remaining link. Unlike in DOS and Windows, there is no easy way in Linux to undelete a file once you have removed it. A skilled hacker can sometimes piece the file together with time and effort.

When you remove all the hard links to a file, you will not be able to access the file through a symbolic link. In the following example, cat reports that the file **total** does not exist because it is a symbolic link to a file that has been removed:

```
$ ls -l sum
-rw-r--r-- 1 alex pubs 981  May 24 11:05 sum
$ ln -s sum total
$ rm sum
$ cat total
cat: total: No such file or directory
$ ls -l total
lrwxrwxrwx 1 alex pubs 6  May 24 11:09 total -> sum
```

When you remove a file, be sure to remove all symbolic links to it. Remove a symbolic link the same way you remove other files:

```
$ rm total
```

CHAPTER SUMMARY

Linux has a hierarchical, or treelike, file structure that makes it possible to organize files so that you can find them quickly and easily. This file structure contains directory files and ordinary files. Directories contain other files, including other directories; ordinary files generally contain text, programs, or images. The ancestor of all files is the root directory named /.

This chapter introduced many important system files and directories, explaining what each does. The section on file types explained the difference between ordinary and directory files and the inodes that hold each. It also covered the use of hard and symbolic links.

Most Linux filesystems support 255-character filenames. Nonetheless, it is a good idea to keep filenames simple and intuitive. Filename extensions can help make filenames more meaningful.

An absolute pathname starts with the root directory and contains all the filenames that trace a path to a given file. Such a pathname starts with a slash representing the root directory and contains additional slashes between the other filenames in the path.

A relative pathname is similar to an absolute pathname but starts the path tracing from the working directory. A simple filename is the last element of a pathname and is a form of a relative pathname.

When you are logged in, you are always associated with a working directory. Your home directory is your working directory from the time you first log in until you use cd to change directories.

A Linux filesystem contains many important directories, including **/usr/bin**, which stores most of the Linux utility commands, and **/dev**, which stores device files, many of which represent physical pieces of hardware. An important standard file is **/etc/passwd**; it contains information about users, such as the user ID and full name.

Among the attributes associated with each file are access permissions. They determine who can access the file and the manner in which the file may be accessed. Three groups of user(s) can access the file: the owner, members of a group, and all other users. A regular file can be accessed in three ways: read, write, and execute. The ls utility with the –l option displays these permissions. For directories, execute access is redefined to mean that the directory can be searched.

The owner of a file or Superuser can use the chmod utility to change the access permissions of a file. This utility defines read, write, and execute permissions for the file's owner, the group, and all other users on the system.

A link is a pointer to a file. You can create several links to a single file so that you can share the file with other users or have the file appear in more than one directory. Because only one copy of a file with multiple links exists, changing the file through any one link causes the changes to appear in all the links. Hard links cannot link directories or span filesystems, whereas symbolic links can.

Table 4-2 lists the utilities introduced in this chapter.

Table 4-2 Utilities introduced in Chapter 4

cd	Associates you with another working directory (page 82)
chmod	Changes the access permissions on a file (page 92)
ln	Makes a link to an existing file (page 97)
mkdir	Creates a directory (page 80)
pwd	Displays the pathname of the working directory (page 81)
rmdir	Deletes a directory (page 88)

EXERCISES

1. Is each of the following an absolute pathname, a relative pathname, or a simple filename?

   a. **milk_co**

   b. **correspond/business/milk_co**

   c. **/home/alex**

   d. **/home/alex/literature/promo**

   e. **..**

   f. **letter.0610**

2. List the commands you can use to

   a. Make your home directory the working directory

   b. Identify the working directory

3. If your working directory is **/home/alex** with a subdirectory named **literature,** give three sets of commands that you can use to create a subdirectory named **classics** under **literature.** Also give several sets of commands you can use to remove the **classics** directory and its contents.

4. The df utility displays all mounted filesystems along with information about each. Use the df utility with the **–h** (humanly readable) option to answer the following questions.

   a. How many filesystems are on your Linux system?

   b. Which filesystem stores your home directory?

   c. Assuming that your answer to exercise 4a is two or greater, attempt to create a hard link to a file on another filesystem. What error message do you get? What happens when you attempt to create a symbolic link to the file instead?

5. Suppose that you have a file that is linked to a file owned by another user. What can you do so that changes to the file are no longer shared?

6. You should have read permission for the **/etc/passwd** file. To answer the following questions, use cat or less to display **/etc/passwd**. Look at the fields of information in **/etc/passwd** for the users on your system.

   a. Which character is used to separate fields in **/etc/passwd**?

   b. How many fields are used to describe each user?

   c. How many users are on your system?

   d. How many different login shells are in use on your system? (*Hint:* Look at the last field.)

   e. The second field of **/etc/passwd** stores user passwords in encoded form. If the password field contains an **x**, your system uses shadow passwords and stores the encoded passwords elsewhere. Does your system use shadow passwords?

7. If **/home/jenny/draft** and **/home/alex/letter** are links to the same file and the following sequence of events occurs, what will be the date in the opening of the letter?

   a. Alex gives the command **vim letter**.

   b. Jenny gives the command **vim draft**.

   c. Jenny changes the date in the opening of the letter to January 31, 2006, writes the file, and exits from vim.

   d. Alex changes the date to February 1, 2006, writes the file, and exits from vim.

8. Suppose that a user belongs to a group that has all permissions on a file named **jobs_list**, but the user, as the owner of the file, has no permissions. Describe what operations, if any, the user/owner can perform on **jobs_list**.

Which command can the user/owner give that will grant the user/owner all permissions on the file?

9. Does the root directory have any subdirectories that you cannot search? Does the root directory have any subdirectories that you cannot read? Explain.

10. Assume that you are given the directory structure shown in Figure 4-2 on page 77 and the following directory permissions:

```
d--x--x---    3 jenny pubs 512 Mar 10 15:16 business
drwxr-xr-x    2 jenny pubs 512 Mar 10 15:16 business/milk_co
```

For each category of permissions—owner, group, and other—what happens when you run each of the following commands? Assume that the working directory is the parent of **correspond** and that the file **cheese_co** is readable by everyone.

a. **cd correspond/business/milk_co**

b. **ls –l correspond/business**

c. **cat correspond/business/cheese_co**

ADVANCED EXERCISES

11. What is an inode? What happens to the inode when you move a file within a filesystem?

12. What does the .. entry in a directory point to? What does this entry point to in the root (/) directory?

13. How can you create a file named –i? Which techniques do not work, and why do they not work? How can you remove the file named –i?

14. Suppose that the working directory contains a single file named **andor**. What error message do you get when you run the following command line?

```
$ mv andor and\/or
```

Under what circumstances is it possible to run the command without producing an error?

15. The **ls –i** command displays a filename preceded by the inode number of the file (page 99). Write a command to output inode/filename pairs for the files in the working directory, sorted by inode number. (*Hint:* Use a pipe.)

16. Do you think that the system administrator has access to a program that can decode user passwords? Why or why not (see exercise 6)?

17. Is it possible to distinguish a file from a hard link to a file? That is, given a filename, can you tell whether it was created using an **ln** command? Explain.

18. Explain the error messages displayed in the following sequence of commands:

```
$ ls -l
total 1
drwxrwxr-x   2 alex pubs 1024 Mar  2 17:57 dirtmp
$ ls dirtmp
$ rmdir dirtmp
rmdir: dirtmp: Directory not empty
$ rm dirtmp/*
rm: No match.
```

5

THE SHELL

This chapter takes a close look at the shell and explains how to use some of its features. For example, it discusses command line syntax and also describes how the shell processes a command line and initiates execution of a program. The chapter also explains how to redirect input to and output from a command, construct pipes and filters on the command line, and run a command in the background. The final section covers filename expansion and explains how you can use this feature in your everyday work.

Except as noted everything in this chapter applies to the Bourne Again (bash) and TC (tcsh) Shells. The exact wording of the shell output differs from shell to shell: What your shell displays may differ slightly from what appears in this book. For shell-specific information, refer to Chapters 8 (bash) and 9 (tcsh). Chapter 11 covers writing and executing bash shell scripts.

THE COMMAND LINE

The shell executes a program when you give it a command in response to its prompt. For example, when you give the ls command, the shell executes the utility program named ls. You can cause the shell to execute other types of programs—such as shell scripts, application programs, and programs you have written—in the same way. The line that contains the command, including any arguments, is called the *command line*. In this book the term *command* refers to the characters you type on the command line as well as to the program that action invokes.

SYNTAX

Command line syntax dictates the ordering and separation of the elements on a command line. When you press the RETURN key after entering a command, the shell scans the command line for proper syntax. The syntax for a basic command line is

> *command* [*arg1*] [*arg2*] ... [*argn*] RETURN

One or more SPACEs must separate elements on the command line. The **command** is the name of the command, **arg1** through **argn** are arguments, and RETURN is the keystroke that terminates all command lines. The brackets in the command line syntax indicate that the arguments they enclose are optional. Not all commands require arguments: Some commands do not allow arguments; other commands allow a variable number of arguments; and others require a specific number of arguments. Options, a special kind of argument, are usually preceded by one or two hyphens (also called a dash or minus sign: –).

COMMAND NAME

Usage message   Some useful Linux command lines consist of only the name of the command without any arguments. For example, ls by itself lists the contents of the working directory. Most commands accept one or more arguments. Commands that require arguments typically give a short error message, called a *usage message,* when you use them without arguments, with incorrect arguments, or with the wrong number of arguments.

ARGUMENTS

On the command line each sequence of nonblank characters is called a *token* or *word*. An *argument* is a token, such as a filename, string of text, number, or other object that a command acts on. For example, the argument to a vim or emacs command is the name of the file you want to edit.

The following command line shows cp copying the file named **temp** to **tempcopy**:

```
$ cp temp tempcopy
```

Arguments are numbered starting with the command itself as argument zero. In this example **cp** is argument zero, **temp** is argument one, and **tempcopy** is argument two. The cp utility requires two arguments on the command line. (The utility can take more arguments but not fewer; see page 616.) Argument one is the name of an existing file. Argument two is the name of the file that cp is creating or overwriting. Here the arguments are not optional; both arguments must be present for the command to work. When you do not supply the right number or kind of arguments, cp displays a usage message. Try typing **cp** and then pressing RETURN.

OPTIONS

An *option* is an argument that modifies the effects of a command. You can frequently specify more than one option, modifying the command in several different ways. Options are specific to and interpreted by the program that the command line calls, not the shell.

By convention options are separate arguments that follow the name of the command and usually precede other arguments, such as filenames. Most utilities require you to prefix options with a single hyphen. However, this requirement is specific to the utility and not the shell. GNU program options are frequently preceded by two hyphens in a row. For example, **--help** generates a (sometimes extensive) usage message.

Figure 5-1 first shows what happens when you give an ls command without any options. By default ls lists the contents of the working directory in alphabetical order, vertically sorted in columns. Next the **–r** (reverse order; because this is a GNU utility, you can also use **--reverse**) option causes the ls utility to display the list of files in reverse alphabetical order, still sorted in columns. The **–x** option causes ls to display the list of files in horizontally sorted rows.

Combining options   When you need to use several options, you can usually group multiple single-letter options into one argument that starts with a single hyphen; do not put SPACEs between the options. You cannot combine options that are preceded by two

```
$ ls
alex  house  mark   office    personal  test
hold  jenny  names  oldstuff  temp
$ ls -r
test  personal  office  mark   house  alex
temp  oldstuff  names   jenny  hold
$ ls -x
alex    hold      house     jenny  mark   names
office  oldstuff  personal  temp   test
$ ls -rx
test  temp   personal  oldstuff  office  names
mark  jenny  house     hold      alex
```

Figure 5-1   Using options

hyphens in this way, however. Specific rules for combining options depend on the program you are running. Figure 5-1 shows both the **−r** and **−x** options with the **ls** utility. Together these options generate a list of filenames in horizontally sorted columns, in reverse alphabetical order. Most utilities allow you to list options in any order; thus **ls −xr** produces the same results as **ls −rx**. The command **ls −x −r** also generates the same list.

Displaying readable file sizes: the −h option

tip Most utilities that report on file sizes specify the size of a file in bytes. Bytes work well when you are dealing with smaller files, but the numbers can be difficult to read when you are working with file sizes that are measured in megabytes or gigabytes. Use the **−h** (or **−−human-readable**) option to display file sizes in kilo-, mega-, and gigabytes. Experiment with **df −h** (disk free) and **ls −lh** commands.

Option arguments   Some utilities have options that themselves require arguments. For example, the gcc utility has a **−o** option that must be followed by the name you want to give the executable file that gcc generates. Typically an argument to an option is separated from its option letter by a SPACE:

```
$ gcc -o prog prog.c
```

Arguments that start
with a hyphen
Another convention allows utilities to work with arguments, such as filenames, that start with a hyphen. If a file's name is **−l**, the following command is ambiguous:

```
$ ls -l
```

This command could mean a long listing of all files in the working directory or a listing of the file named **−l**. It is interpreted as the former. You should avoid creating files whose names begin with hyphens. If you do create them, many utilities follow the convention that a **−−** argument (two consecutive hyphens) indicates the end of the options (and the beginning of the arguments). To disambiguate the command, you can type

```
$ ls -- -l
```

You can use an alternative format in which the period refers to the working directory and the slash indicates that the name refers to a file in the working directory:

```
$ ls ./-l
```

Assuming that you are working in the **/home/alex** directory, the preceding command is functionally equivalent to

```
$ ls /home/alex/-l
```

You can give the following command to get a long listing of this file:

```
$ ls -l -- -l
```

These are conventions, not hard-and-fast rules, and a number of utilities do not follow them (e.g., find). Following such conventions is a good idea; it makes it much easier for users to work with your program. When you write shell programs that require options, follow the Linux option conventions.

The --help option

tip Many utilities display a (sometimes extensive) help message when you call them with an argument of **--help**. All GNU utilities accept this option. An example follows.

```
$ bzip2 --help
bzip2, a block-sorting file compressor.  Version 1.0.2, 30-Dec-2001.

   usage: bzip2 [flags and input files in any order]

   -h --help           print this message
   -d --decompress     force decompression
   -z --compress       force compression
   -k --keep           keep (don't delete) input files
   -f --force          overwrite existing output files
   -t --test           test compressed file integrity
   -c --stdout         output to standard out
   -q --quiet          suppress noncritical error messages
   -v --verbose        be verbose (a 2nd -v gives more)
   ...
```

PROCESSING THE COMMAND LINE

As you enter a command line, the Linux tty device driver (part of the Linux operating system kernel) examines each character to see whether it must take immediate action. When you press CONTROL-H (to erase a character) or CONTROL-U (to kill a line), the device driver immediately adjusts the command line as required; the shell never sees the character(s) you erased or the line you killed. Often a similar adjustment occurs when you press CONTROL-W (to erase a word). When the character you entered does not require immediate action, the device driver stores the character in a buffer and waits for additional characters. When you press RETURN, the device driver passes the command line to the shell for processing.

Parsing the command line   When the shell processes a command line, it looks at the line as a whole and *parses* (breaks) it into its component parts (Figure 5-2). Next the shell looks for the name of the command. Usually the name of the command is the first item on the command line after the prompt (argument zero). The shell takes the first characters on the command line up to the first blank (TAB or SPACE) and then looks for a command with that name. The command name (the first token) can be specified on the command line either as a simple filename or as a pathname. For example, you can call the ls command in either of the following ways:

```
$ ls
```

```
$ /bin/ls
```

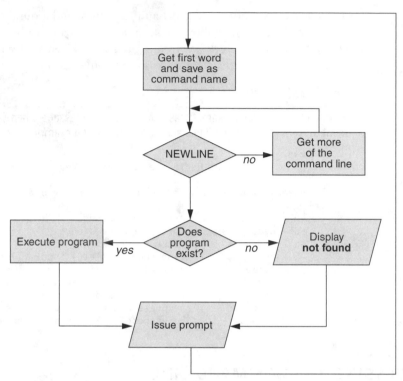

Figure 5-2   Processing the command line

optional   The shell does not require that the name of the program appear first on the command line. Thus you can structure a command line as follows:

optional   The shell does not require that the name of the program appear first on the command line. Thus you can structure a command line as follows:

```
$ >bb <aa cat
```

This command runs **cat** with standard input coming from the file named **aa** and standard output going to the file named **bb**. When the shell recognizes the redirect symbols (page 116), it recognizes and processes them and their arguments before finding the name of the program that the command line is calling. This is a properly structured—albeit rarely encountered and possibly confusing—command line.

Absolute versus   When you give an absolute pathname on the command line or a relative pathname
relative pathnames   that is not a simple filename (i.e., any pathname that includes at least one slash), the shell looks in the specified directory (**/bin** in the case of the **/bin/ls** command) for a file that has the name **ls** and that you have permission to execute. When you give a simple filename, the shell searches through a list of directories for a filename that matches the specified name and that you have execute permission for. The shell does not look through all directories but only the ones specified by the variable named **PATH**. Refer to page 284 (bash) or page 363 (tcsh) for more information on **PATH**. Also refer to the discussion of the which and whereis utilities on page 61.

When it cannot find the executable file, the Bourne Again Shell (bash) displays a message such as the following:

```
$ abc
bash: abc: command not found
```

One reason the shell may not be able to find the executable file is that it is not in a directory in your **PATH**. Under bash the following command temporarily adds the working directory (.) to your **PATH**:

```
$ PATH=$PATH:.
```

For security reasons, you may not want to add the working directory to **PATH** permanently; see the tip on page 285.

When the shell finds the program but cannot execute it (you do not have execute permission for the file that contains the program), it displays a message similar to

```
$ def
bash: ./def: Permission denied
```

See "ls –l: Displays Permissions" on page 91 for information on displaying access permissions for a file and "chmod: Changes Access Permissions" on page 92 for instructions on how to change file access permissions.

EXECUTING THE COMMAND LINE

Process   If it finds an executable file with the same name as the command, the shell starts a new process. A *process* is the execution of a command by Linux (page 292). The shell makes each command line argument, including options and the name of the command, available to the called program. While the command is executing, the shell waits for the process to finish. At this point the shell is in an inactive state called *sleep*. When the program finishes execution, it passes its exit status (page 479) to the shell. The shell then returns to an active state (wakes up), issues a prompt, and waits for another command.

The shell does not   Because the shell does not process command line arguments but only hands them to
process arguments   the called program, the shell has no way of knowing whether a particular option or other argument is valid for a given program. Any error or usage messages about options or arguments come from the program itself. Some utilities ignore bad options.

STANDARD INPUT AND STANDARD OUTPUT

Standard output is a place that a program can send information, such as text. The program never "knows" where the information it sends to standard output is going (Figure 5-3). The information can go to a printer, an ordinary file, or the screen.

Figure 5-3   The command does not know where standard input comes from or where standard output and standard error go

The following sections show that by default the shell directs standard output from a command to the screen[1] and describe how you can cause the shell to redirect this output to another file.

Standard input is a place that a program gets information from. As with standard output the program never "knows" where the information came from. The following sections also explain how to redirect standard input to a command so that it comes from an ordinary file instead of from the keyboard (the default).

In addition to standard input and standard output, a running program normally has a place to send error messages: *standard error*. Refer to page 260 (bash) and page 349 (tcsh) for more information on handling standard error.

chsh: **changes your login shell**

tip   The person who sets up your account determines which shell you will use when you first log in on the system or when you open a terminal emulator window in a GUI environment. You can run any shell you like once you are logged in. Enter the name of the shell you want to use (bash or tcsh) and press RETURN; the next prompt will be that of the new shell. Give an **exit** command to return to the previous shell. Because shells you call in this manner are nested (one runs on top of the other), you will be able to log out only from your original shell. When you have nested several shells, keep giving **exit** commands until you reach your original shell. You will then be able to log out.

Use the chsh utility when you want to change your login shell permanently. First give the command **chsh**. Then in response to the prompts enter your password and the absolute pathname of the shell you want to use (**/bin/bash** or **/bin/tcsh**). When you change your login shell in this manner using a terminal emulator PAGE under a GUI, subsequent terminal emulator windows will not reflect the change until you log out the system and log back in.

THE SCREEN AS A FILE

Chapter 4 introduced ordinary files, directory files, and hard and soft links. Linux has an additional type of file: a *device file*. A device file resides in the Linux file structure, usually in the **/dev** directory, and represents a peripheral device, such as a terminal emulator window, screen, printer, or disk drive.

---

1. The term *screen* is used throughout this book to mean screen, terminal emulator window, or workstation. *Screen* refers to the device that you see the prompt and messages displayed on.

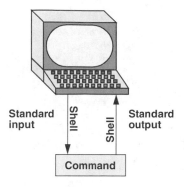

Figure 5-4   By default, standard input comes from the keyboard and
standard output goes to the screen

The device name that the who utility displays after your login name is the filename
of your screen. For example, when who displays the device name **pts/4**, the pathname of your screen is **/dev/pts/4**. When you work with multiple windows, each
window has its own device name. You can also use the tty utility to display the name
of the device that you give the command from. Although you would not normally
have occasion to do so, you can read from and write to this file as though it were a
text file. Writing to it displays what you wrote on the screen; reading from it reads
what you entered on the keyboard.

THE KEYBOARD AND SCREEN AS STANDARD INPUT AND STANDARD OUTPUT

When you first log in, the shell directs standard output of your commands to the
device file that represents your screen (Figure 5-4). Directing output in this manner
causes it to appear on your screen. The shell also directs standard input to come
from the same file, so that your commands receive as input anything you type on
your keyboard.

cat The cat utility provides a good example of the way the keyboard and the screen
function as standard input and standard output, respectively. When you use cat, it
copies a file to standard output. Because the shell directs standard output to the
screen, cat displays the file on the screen.

Up to this point cat has taken its input from the filename (argument) you specified
on the command line. When you do not give cat an argument (that is, when you
give the command cat followed immediately by RETURN), cat takes its input from standard input. Thus, when called without an argument, cat copies standard input to
standard output, one line at a time.

To see how cat works, type **cat** and press RETURN in response to the shell prompt.
Nothing happens. Enter a line of text and press RETURN. The same line appears just

```
$ cat
This is a line of text.
This is a line of text.
Cat keeps copying lines of text
Cat keeps copying lines of text
until you press CONTROL-D at the beginning
until you press CONTROL-D at the beginning
of a line.
of a line.
CONTROL-D
$
```

Figure 5-5   The cat utility copies standard input to standard output

under the one you entered. The cat utility is working. Because the shell associates cat's standard input with the keyboard and cat's standard output with the screen, when you type a line of text cat copies the text from standard input (the keyboard) to standard output (the screen). This exchange is shown in Figure 5-5.

CONTROL-D signals EOF   The cat utility keeps copying text until you enter CONTROL-D on a line by itself. Pressing CONTROL-D sends an EOF (end of file) signal to cat to indicate that it has reached the end of standard input and there is no more text for it to copy. The cat utility then finishes execution and returns control to the shell, which displays a prompt.

REDIRECTION

The term *redirection* encompasses the various ways you can cause the shell to alter where standard input of a command comes from and where standard output goes to. By default the shell associates standard input and standard output of a command with the keyboard and the screen as mentioned earlier. You can cause the shell to redirect standard input or standard output of any command by associating the input or output with a command or file other than the device file representing the keyboard or the screen. This section demonstrates how to redirect input from and output to ordinary text files and utilities.

REDIRECTING STANDARD OUTPUT

The *redirect output symbol* (>) instructs the shell to redirect the output of a command to the specified file instead of to the screen (Figure 5-6). The format of a command line that redirects output is

command [arguments] > filename

where **command** is any executable program (such as an application program or a utility), **arguments** are optional arguments, and **filename** is the name of the ordinary file the shell redirects the output to.

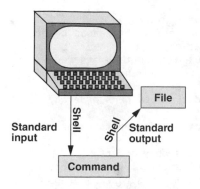

Figure 5-6 Redirecting standard output

Figure 5-7 uses cat to demonstrate output redirection. This figure contrasts with Figure 5-3 on page 114, where both standard input *and* standard output are associated with the keyboard and the screen. The input in Figure 5-7 comes from the keyboard. The redirect output symbol on the command line causes the shell to associate cat's standard output with the **sample.txt** file specified on the command line.

After giving the command and typing the text shown in Figure 5-7, the **sample.txt** file contains the text you entered. You can use cat with an argument of **sample.txt** to display this file. The next section shows another way to use cat to display the file.

Redirecting output can destroy a file I

caution Use caution when you redirect output to a file. If the file exists, the shell will overwrite it and destroy its contents. For more information, see the "Redirecting output can destroy a file II" caution on page 120.

Figure 5-7 shows that redirecting the output from cat is a handy way to create a file without using an editor. The drawback is that once you enter a line and press RETURN, you cannot edit the text. While you are entering a line, the erase and kill keys work to delete text. This procedure is useful for making short, simple files.

```
$ cat > sample.txt
This text is being entered at the keyboard and
cat is copying it to a file.
Press CONTROL-D to indicate the
end of file.
CONTROL-D
$
```

Figure 5-7 cat with its output redirected

```
$ cat stationery
2,000 sheets letterhead ordered:    10/7/05
$ cat tape
1 box masking tape ordered:         10/14/05
5 boxes filament tape ordered:      10/28/05
$ cat pens
12 doz. black pens ordered:         10/4/05

$ cat stationery tape pens > supply_orders

$ cat supply_orders
2,000 sheets letterhead ordered:    10/7/05
1 box masking tape ordered:         10/14/05
5 boxes filament tape ordered:      10/28/05
12 doz. black pens ordered:         10/4/05
$
```

Figure 5-8   Using cat to catenate files

Figure 5-8 shows how to use cat and the redirect output symbol to *catenate* (join one after the other—the derivation of the name of the cat utility) several files into one larger file. The first three commands display the contents of three files: **stationery**, **tape**, and **pens**. The next command shows cat with three filenames as arguments. When you call it with more than one filename, cat copies the files, one at a time, to standard output. In this case standard output is redirected to the file **supply_orders**. The final cat command shows that **supply_orders** contains the contents of all three files.

REDIRECTING STANDARD INPUT

Just as you can redirect standard output, so you can redirect standard input. The *redirect input symbol* (<) instructs the shell to redirect a command's input to come from the specified file instead of from the keyboard (Figure 5-9). The format of a command line that redirects input is

> *command [arguments] < filename*

where **command** is any executable program (such as an application program or a utility), **arguments** are optional arguments, and **filename** is the name of the ordinary file the shell redirects the input from.

Figure 5-10 shows cat with its input redirected from the **supply_orders** file that was created in Figure 5-8 and standard output going to the screen. This setup causes cat to display the sample file on the screen. The system automatically supplies an EOF (end of file) signal at the end of an ordinary file.

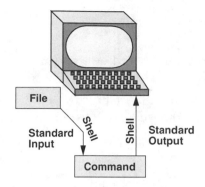

Figure 5-9   Redirecting standard input

```
$ cat < supply_orders
2,000 sheets letterhead ordered:    10/7/05
1 box masking tape ordered:         10/14/05
5 boxes filament tape ordered:      10/28/05
12 doz. black pens ordered:         10/4/05
```

Figure 5-10   cat with its input redirected

Utilities that take input from a file or standard input   Giving a cat command with input redirected from a file yields the same result as giving a cat command with the filename as an argument. The cat utility is a member of a class of Linux utilities that function in this manner. Other members of this class of utilities include lpr, sort, and grep. These utilities first examine the command line that you use to call them. If you include a filename on the command line, the utility takes its input from the file you specify. If you do not specify a filename, the utility takes its input from standard input. It is the utility or program—not the shell or operating system—that functions in this manner.

noclobber: AVOIDS OVERWRITING FILES

The shell provides a feature called **noclobber** that stops you from inadvertently overwriting an existing file using redirection. When you enable this feature by setting the **noclobber** variable and then attempt to redirect output to an existing file, the shell displays an error message and does not execute the command. If the preceding examples result in one of the following messages, the **noclobber** feature has been set. The following examples set **noclobber**, attempt to redirect the output from echo into an existing file, and then unset **noclobber** under bash and tcsh:

bash
```
$ set -o noclobber
$ echo "hi there" > tmp
bash: tmp: Cannot overwrite existing file
$ set +o noclobber
$ echo "hi there" > tmp
$
```

tcsh
```
tcsh $ set noclobber
tcsh $ echo "hi there" > tmp
tmp: File exists.
tcsh $ unset noclobber
tcsh $ echo "hi there" > tmp
$
```

You can override **noclobber** by putting a pipe symbol (tcsh uses an exclamation point) after the symbol you use for redirecting output (>|).

In the following example, the user first creates a file named **a** by redirecting the output of date to the file. Next the user sets the **noclobber** variable and tries redirecting output to **a** again. The shell returns an error message. Then the user tries the same thing but using a pipe symbol after the redirect symbol. This time the shell allows the user to overwrite the file. Finally, the user unsets **noclobber** (using a plus sign in place of the hyphen) and verifies that it is no longer set.

```
$ date > a
$ set -o noclobber
$ date > a
bash: a: Cannot overwrite existing file
$ date >| a
$ set +o noclobber
$ date > a
```

For more information on using **noclobber** under tcsh, refer to page 367.

Redirecting output can destroy a file II

caution   Depending on which shell you are using and how your environment has been set up, a command such as the following may give you undesired results:

```
$ cat orange pear > orange
cat: orange: input file is output file
```

Although cat displays an error message, the shell goes ahead and destroys the contents of the existing **orange** file. The new **orange** file will have the same contents as **pear** because the first action the shell takes when it sees the redirection symbol (>) is to remove the contents of the original **orange** file. If you want to catenate two files into one, use cat to put the two files into a temporary file and then use mv to rename this third file:

```
$ cat orange pear > temp
$ mv temp orange
```

What happens in the next example can be even worse. The user giving the command wants to search through files **a**, **b**, and **c** for the word **apple** and redirect the output from grep (page 48) to the file **a.output**. Unfortunately the user enters the filename as **a output**, omitting the period and inserting a SPACE in its place:

```
$ grep apple a b c > a output
grep: output: No such file or directory
```

The shell obediently removes the contents of **a** and then calls grep. The error message may take a moment to appear, giving you a sense that the command is running correctly. Even after you see the error message, it may take a while to realize that you destroyed the contents of **a**.

APPENDING STANDARD OUTPUT TO A FILE

The *append output symbol* (>>) causes the shell to add new information to the end of a file, leaving any existing information intact. This symbol provides a convenient way of catenating two files into one. The following commands demonstrate the action of the append output symbol. The second command accomplishes the catenation described in the preceding caution box:

```
$ cat orange
this is orange
$ cat pear >> orange
$ cat orange
this is orange
this is pear
```

You first see the contents of the **orange** file. Next the contents of the **pear** file is added to the end of (catenated with) the **orange** file. The final cat shows the result.

Do not trust **noclobber**

caution   Appending output is simpler than the two-step procedure described in the preceding caution box but you must be careful to include both greater than signs. If you accidentally use only one and the **noclobber** feature is not on, you will overwrite the **orange** file. Even if you have the **noclobber** feature turned on, it is a good idea to keep backup copies of files you are manipulating in these ways in case you make a mistake.

Although it protects you from making an erroneous redirection, **noclobber** does not stop you from overwriting an existing file using cp or mv. These utilities include the **–i** (interactive) option that helps protect you from this type of mistake by verifying your intentions when you try to overwrite a file. For more information, see the "cp can destroy a file" tip on page 46.

The next example shows how to create a file that contains the date and time (the output from date), followed by a list of who is logged in (the output from who). The first line in Figure 5-11 redirects the output from date to the file named **whoson**. Then cat displays the file. Next the example appends the output from who to the **whoson** file. Finally cat displays the file containing the output of both utilities.

```
$ date > whoson
$ cat whoson
Thu Mar 24 14:31:18 PST 2005
$ who >> whoson
$ cat whoson
Thu Mar 24 14:31:18 PST 2005
root       console      Mar 24 05:00(:0)
alex       pts/4        Mar 24 12:23(:0.0)
alex       pts/5        Mar 24 12:33(:0.0)
jenny      pts/7        Mar 23 08:45 (bravo.example.com)
```

Figure 5-11   Redirecting and appending output

/dev/null: MAKING DATA DISAPPEAR

The **/dev/null** device is a *data sink*, commonly referred to as a *bit bucket*. You can redirect output that you do not want to keep or see to **/dev/null**. The output disappears without a trace:

```
$ echo "hi there" > /dev/null
$
```

When you read from **/dev/null**, you get a null string. Give the following cat command to truncate a file named **messages** to zero length while preserving the ownership and permissions of the file:

```
$ ls -l messages
-rw-r--r--   1 alex pubs 25315 Oct 24 10:55 messages
$ cat /dev/null > messages
$ ls -l messages
-rw-r--r--   1 alex pubs 0 Oct 24 11:02 messages
```

PIPES

The shell uses a *pipe* to connect standard output of one command directly to standard input of another command. A pipe (sometimes referred to as a *pipeline*) has the same effect as redirecting standard output of one command to a file and then using that file as standard input to another command. A pipe does away with separate commands and the intermediate file. The symbol for a pipe is a vertical bar (|). The syntax of a command line using a pipe is

command_a [arguments] | *command_b [arguments]*

The preceding command line uses a pipe to generate the same result as the following group of command lines:

command_a [arguments] > *temp*
command_b [arguments] < *temp*
rm temp

In the preceding sequence of commands, the first line redirects standard output from *command_a* to an intermediate file named *temp*. The second line redirects standard input for *command_b* to come from *temp*. The final line deletes *temp*. The command using a pipe is not only easier to type, but is generally more efficient because it does not create a temporary file.

tr   You can use a pipe with any of the Linux utilities that accept input either from a file specified on the command line or from standard input. You can also use pipes with commands that accept input only from standard input. For example, the tr (translate) utility (page 804) takes its input from standard input only. In its simplest usage tr has the following format:

tr string1 string2

The tr utility accepts input from standard input and looks for characters that match one of the characters in *string1*. Upon finding a match, tr translates the matched character in *string1* to the corresponding character in *string2*. (The first character in *string1* translates into the first character in *string2*, and so forth.) The tr utility sends its output to standard output. In both of the following examples, tr displays the contents of the **abstract** file with the letters **a**, **b**, and **c** translated into **A**, **B**, and **C**, respectively:

```
$ cat abstract | tr abc ABC
```

```
$ tr abc ABC < abstract
```

The tr utility does not change the contents of the original file; it cannot change the original file because it does not "know" the source of its input.

lpr   The lpr (line printer) utility also accepts input from either a file or standard input. When you type the name of a file following lpr on the command line, it places that file in the print queue. When you do not specify a filename on the command line, lpr takes input from standard input. This feature enables you to use a pipe to redirect input to lpr. The first set of commands in Figure 5-12 shows how you can use ls and lpr with an intermediate file (**temp**) to send a list of the files in the working directory to the printer. If the **temp** file exists, the first command overwrites its contents. The second set of commands sends the same list (with the exception of **temp**) to the printer using a pipe.

The commands in Figure 5-13 redirect the output from the who utility to **temp** and then display this file in sorted order. The sort utility (page 50) takes its input from the file specified on the command line or, when a file is not specified, from standard input and sends its output to standard output. The sort command line in Figure 5-13 takes its input from standard input, which is redirected (<) to come from **temp**. The output that sort sends to the screen lists the users in sorted (alphabetical) order.

Because sort can take its input from standard input or from a filename on the command line, omitting the < symbol from Figure 5-13 yields the same result.

```
$ ls > temp
$ lpr temp
$ rm temp
```

or

```
$ ls | lpr
```

Figure 5-12   A pipe

```
$ who > temp
$ sort < temp
alex        pts/4       Mar 24 12:23
alex        pts/5       Mar 24 12:33
jenny       pts/7       Mar 23 08:45
root        console     Mar 24 05:00
$ rm temp
```

Figure 5-13   Using a temporary file to store intermediate results

Figure 5-14 achieves the same result without creating the **temp** file. Using a pipe the shell redirects the output from who to the input of sort. The sort utility takes input from standard input because no filename follows it on the command line.

When many people are using the system and you want information about only one of them, you can send the output from who to grep (page 48) using a pipe. The grep utility displays the line containing the string you specify—**root** in the following example:

```
$ who | grep 'root'
root        console     Mar 24 05:00
```

Another way of handling output that is too long to fit on the screen, such as a list of files in a crowded directory, is to use a pipe to send the output through less or more (both on page 45).

```
$ ls | less
```

The less utility displays text one screen at a time. To view another screen, press the SPACE bar. To view one more line, press RETURN. Press **h** for help and **q** to quit.

FILTERS

A *filter* is a command that processes an input stream of data to produce an output stream of data. A command line that includes a filter uses a pipe to connect standard output of one command to the filter's standard input. Another pipe connects the filter's standard output to standard input of another command. Not all utilities can be used as filters.

In the following example, sort is a filter, taking standard input from standard output of who and using a pipe to redirect standard output to standard input of lpr. This command line sends the sorted output of who to the printer:

```
$ who | sort | lpr
```

The preceding example demonstrates the power of the shell combined with the versatility of Linux utilities. The three utilities who, sort, and lpr were not specifically designed to work with each other, but they all use standard input and standard output in the conventional way. By using the shell to handle input and output, you can piece standard utilities together on the command line to achieve the results you want.

```
$ who | sort
alex        pts/4       Mar 24 12:23
alex        pts/5       Mar 24 12:33
jenny       pts/7       Mar 23 08:45
root        console     Mar 24 05:00
```

Figure 5-14   A pipe doing the work of a temporary file

tee: SENDS OUTPUT IN TWO DIRECTIONS

The tee utility copies its standard input both to a file and to standard output. The utility is aptly named: It takes a single input and sends the output in two directions. In Figure 5-15 the output of who is sent via a pipe to standard input of tee. The tee utility saves a copy of standard input in a file named **who.out** and also sends a copy to standard output. Standard output of tee goes via a pipe to standard input of grep, which displays lines containing the string **root**.

RUNNING A PROGRAM IN THE BACKGROUND

Foreground   In all the examples so far in this book, commands were run in the foreground. When you run a command in the *foreground,* the shell waits for it to finish before giving you another prompt and allowing you to continue. When you run a command in the *background,* you do not have to wait for the command to finish before you start running another command.

Jobs   A *job* is a series of one or more commands that can be connected by pipes. You can have only one foreground job in a window or on a screen, but you can have many background jobs. By running more than one job at a time, you are using one of Linux's important features: multitasking. Running a command in the background can be useful when the command will run for a long time and does not need supervision. It leaves the screen free so that you can use it for other work. Of course, when you are using a GUI, you can open another window to run another job.

Job number, PID number   To run a command in the background, type an ampersand (&) just before the RETURN that ends the command line. The shell assigns a small number to the job and displays

```
$ who | tee who.out | grep root
root        console     Mar 24 05:00
$ cat who.out
root        console     Mar 24 05:00
alex        pts/4       Mar 24 12:23
alex        pts/5       Mar 24 12:33
jenny       pts/7       Mar 23 08:45
```

Figure 5-15   Using tee

this *job number* between brackets. Following the job number, the shell displays the *process identification (PID) number*—a larger number assigned by the operating system. Each of these numbers identifies the command running in the background. Then the shell displays another prompt and you can enter another command. When the background job finishes running, the shell displays a message giving both the job number and the command line used to run the command.

The following examples use the Bourne Again Shell. The TC Shell produces almost identical results. The next example runs in the background and sends its output through a pipe to lpr, which sends it to the printer.

```
$ ls -l | lpr &
[1] 22092
$
```

The [**1**] following the command line indicates that the shell has assigned job number 1 to this job. The **22092** is the PID number of the first command in the job. (The TC Shell shows PID numbers for all commands in the job.) When this background job completes execution, you see the message

```
[1]+ Done            ls -l | lpr
```

(In place of **ls –l**, the shell may display something similar to **ls ––color=tty –l**. This difference is due to the fact that **ls** is aliased [page 312] to **ls ––color=tty**.)

Moving a Job from the Foreground to the Background

CONTROL-Z   You can suspend a foreground job (stop it from running) by pressing the suspend key, usually CONTROL-Z. The shell then stops the process and disconnects standard input from the keyboard. You can put a suspended job in the background and restart it by using the **bg** command followed by the job number. You do not need to use the job number when there is only one stopped job.

Only the foreground job can take input from the keyboard. To connect the keyboard to a program running in the background, you must bring it into the foreground. Type **fg** without any arguments when only one job is in the background. When more than one job is in the background, type **fg**, or a percent sign (%), followed by the number of the job you want to bring into the foreground. The shell displays the command you used to start the job (**promptme** in the following example), and you can enter any input the program requires to continue:

```
bash $ fg 1
promptme
```

Redirect the output of a job you run in the background to keep it from interfering with whatever you are doing on the screen. Refer to "Separating and Grouping Commands" on page 267 for more detail about background tasks.

kill: ABORTING A BACKGROUND JOB

The interrupt key (usually CONTROL-C) cannot abort a process you are running in the background; you must use kill (page 693) for this purpose. Follow **kill** on the command line with either the PID number of the process you want to abort or a percent sign (%) followed by the job number.

Determining a PID number with ps If you forget the PID number, you can use the ps (process status) utility (page 293) to display it. Using the TC Shell, the following example runs a **tail –f outfile** command (the **–f** option causes tail to watch **outfile** and display new lines as they are written to the file) as a background job, uses ps to display the PID number of the process, and aborts the job with kill. The same commands work under bash. So that it does not interfere with anything on the screen, the message saying that the job is terminated does not appear until you press RETURN after the RETURN that ends the kill command:

```
tcsh $ tail -f outfile &
[1] 22170
tcsh $ ps | grep tail
22170 pts/7    00:00:00 tail
tcsh $ kill 22170
tcsh $ RETURN
[1]    Terminated          tail -f outfile
tcsh $
```

If you forget the job number, you can use the jobs command to display a list of job numbers. The next example is similar to the previous one but uses the job number instead of the PID number to kill the job:

```
tcsh $ tail -f outfile &
[1] 3339
tcsh $ bigjob &
[2] 3340
tcsh $ jobs
[1]  + Running          tail -f outfile
[2]  - Running          bigjob
tcsh $ kill %1[1]    Terminated          tail -f outfile
tcsh $
```

FILENAME GENERATION/PATHNAME EXPANSION

Wildcards, globbing When you give the shell abbreviated filenames that contain special characters, also called *metacharacters*, the shell can generate filenames that match the names of existing files. These special characters are also referred to as *wildcards* because they act as the jokers do in a deck of cards. When one of these characters appears in an argument on the command line, the shell expands that argument in sorted order into a list of filenames and passes the list to the program that the command line calls. Filenames that contain these special characters are called *ambiguous file references* because they do not refer to any one specific file. The process that the shell performs on these filenames is called *pathname expansion* or *globbing*.

Ambiguous file references refer to a group of files with similar names quickly, saving you the effort of typing the names individually. They can also help you find a file whose name you do not remember in its entirety. If no filename matches the ambiguous file reference, the shell generally passes the unexpanded reference—special characters and all—to the command.

The ? Special Character

The question mark (?) is a special character that causes the shell to generate filenames. It matches any single character in the name of an existing file. The following command uses this special character in an argument to the lpr utility:

```
$ lpr memo?
```

The shell expands the **memo?** argument and generates a list of files in the working directory that have names composed of **memo** followed by any single character. The shell then passes this list to lpr. The lpr utility never "knows" that the shell generated the filenames it was called with. If no filename matches the ambiguous file reference, the shell passes the string itself (**memo?**) to lpr or, if it is set up to do so, passes a null string (see **nullglob**, page 322).

The following example uses ls first to display the names of all files in the working directory and then to display the filenames that **memo?** matches:

```
$ ls
mem     memo12  memo9   memoalex   newmemo5
memo    memo5   memoa   memos
$ ls memo?
memo5   memo9   memoa   memos
```

The **memo?** ambiguous file reference does not match **mem, memo, memo12, memoalex,** or **newmemo5.** You can also use a question mark in the middle of an ambiguous file reference:

```
$ ls
7may4report  may4report     mayqreport  may_report
may14report  may4report.79  mayreport   may.report
$ ls may?report
may.report  may4report  may_report  mayqreport
```

To practice generating filenames, you can use echo and ls. The echo utility displays the arguments that the shell passes to it:

```
$ echo may?report
may.report may4report may_report mayqreport
```

The shell first expands the ambiguous file reference into a list of all files in the working directory that match the string **may?report** and then passes this list to echo, as though you had entered the list of filenames as arguments to echo. Next echo displays the list of filenames.

A question mark does not match a leading period (one that indicates an invisible filename; see page 80). When you want to match filenames that begin with a period, you must explicitly include the period in the ambiguous file reference.

THE * SPECIAL CHARACTER

The asterisk (*) performs a function similar to that of the question mark but matches any number of characters, *including zero characters,* in a filename. The following example shows all of the files in the working directory and then shows three commands that display all the filenames that begin with the string **memo**, end with the string **mo**, and contain the string **alx**:

```
$ ls
amemo    memo        memoalx.0620  memosally   user.momo
mem      memo.0612   memoalx.keep  sallymemo
memalx   memoa       memorandum    typescript
$ echo memo*
memo memo.0612 memoa memoalx.0620 memoalx.keep memorandum memosally
$ echo *mo
amemo memo sallymemo user.memo
$ echo *alx*
memalx memoalx.0620 memoalx.keep
```

The ambiguous file reference **memo*** does not match **amemo, mem, sallymemo,** or **user.memo**. Like the question mark, an asterisk does *not* match a leading period in a filename.

The **−a** option causes ls to display invisible filenames. The command echo * does not display . (the working directory), .. (the parent of the working directory), **.aaa,** or **.profile**. In contrast, the command echo .* displays only those four names:

```
$ ls
aaa        memo.sally  sally.0612  thurs
memo.0612  report      saturday
$ ls -a
.    .aaa      aaa        memo.sally  sally.0612  thurs
..   .profile  memo.0612  report      saturday
$ echo *
aaa memo.0612 memo.sally report sally.0612 saturday thurs
$ echo .*
. .. .aaa .profile
```

In the following example **.p*** does not match **memo.0612, private, reminder,** or **report**. Next the ls .* command causes ls to list **.private** and **.profile** in addition to the contents of the . directory (the working directory) and the .. directory (the parent of the working directory). When called with the same argument, echo displays the names of files (including directories) in the working directory that begin with a dot (.), but not the contents of directories.

```
$ ls -a
.          .private   memo.0612   reminder
..         .profile   private     report
$ echo .p*
.private .profile
$ ls .*
.private .profile

.:
memo.0612   private    reminder    report

..:
.
.
$ echo .*
. .. .private .profile
```

You can take advantage of ambiguous file references when you establish conventions for naming files. For example, when you end all text filenames with **.txt**, you can reference that group of files with ***.txt**. The next command uses this convention to send all the text files in the working directory to the printer. The ampersand causes lpr to run in the background.

```
$ lpr *.txt &
```

THE [ ] SPECIAL CHARACTERS

A pair of brackets surrounding a list of characters causes the shell to match filenames containing the individual characters. Whereas **memo?** matches **memo** followed by any character, **memo[17a]** is more restrictive, and matches only **memo1**, **memo7**, and **memoa**. The brackets define a *character class* that includes all the characters within the brackets. (GNU calls this a *character list;* a GNU *character class* is something different.) The shell expands an argument that includes a character-class definition, by substituting each member of the character class, *one at a time*, in place of the brackets and their contents. The shell then passes the list of matching filenames to the program it is calling.

Each character-class definition can replace only a single character within a filename. The brackets and their contents are like a question mark that substitutes only the members of the character class.

The first of the following commands lists the names of all the files in the working directory that begin with a, e, i, o, or u. The second command displays the contents of the files named **page2.txt**, **page4.txt**, **page6.txt**, and **page8.txt**.

```
$ echo [aeiou]*
...
$ less page[2468].txt
...
```

A hyphen within brackets defines a range of characters within a character-class definition. For example, [6–9] represents [6789], [a–z] represents all lowercase letters in English, and [a–zA–Z] represents all letters, both uppercase and lowercase, in English.

The following command lines show three ways to print the files named **part0**, **part1**, **part2**, **part3**, and **part5**. Each of these command lines causes the shell to call lpr with five filenames:

```
$ lpr part0 part1 part2 part3 part5

$ lpr part[01235]

$ lpr part[0-35]
```

The first command line explicitly specifies the five filenames. The second and third command lines use ambiguous file references, incorporating character-class definitions. The shell expands the argument on the second command line to include all files that have names beginning with **part** and ending with any of the characters in the character class. The character class is explicitly defined as 0, 1, 2, 3, and 5. The third command line also uses a character-class definition but defines the character class to be all characters in the range 0–3 plus 5.

The following command line prints 39 files, **part0** through **part38**:

```
$ lpr part[0-9] part[12][0-9] part3[0-8]
```

The next two examples list the names of some of the files in the working directory. The first lists the files whose names start with **a** through **m**. The second lists files whose names end with **x**, **y**, or **z**.

```
$ echo [a-m]*
...
$ echo *[x-z]
...
```

optional When an exclamation point (!) or a caret (^) immediately follows the opening bracket ([) that defines a character class, the string enclosed by the brackets matches any character *not* between the brackets. Thus [^ab]* matches any filename that does not begin with **a** or **b**.

The following examples show that *[^ab] matches filenames that do not end with the letters **a** or **b** and that [b-d]* matches filenames that begin with **b**, **c**, or **d**.

```
$ ls
aa  ab  ac  ad  ba  bb  bc  bd  cc  dd
$ ls *[^ab]
ac  ad  bc  bd  cc  ddcc  dd
$ ls [b-d]*
ba  bb  bc  bd  cc  dd
```

You can match a hyphen (–) or a closing bracket (]) by placing it immediately before the final closing bracket.

The next example demonstrates that the ls utility cannot interpret ambiguous file references. First ls is called with an argument of ?old. The shell expands ?old into a matching filename, **hold,** and passes that name to ls. The second command is the same as the first, except the ? is quoted (refer to "Special Characters" on page 42). The shell does not recognize this question mark as a special character and passes it on to ls. The ls utility generates an error message saying that it cannot find a file named ?old (because there is no file named ?old).

```
$ ls ?old
hold
$ ls \?old
ls: ?old: No such file or directory
```

Like most utilities and programs, ls cannot interpret ambiguous file references; that work is left to the shell.

The shell expands ambiguous file references

tip *The shell does the expansion* when it processes an ambiguous file reference, not the program that the shell runs. In the examples in this section, *the utilities* (ls, cat, echo, lpr) *never see the ambiguous file references.* The shell expands the ambiguous file references and passes a list of ordinary filenames to the utility. In the previous examples, echo shows this to be true because it simply displays its arguments; it never displays the ambiguous file reference.

BUILTINS

A *builtin* is a utility (also called a *command*) that is built into a shell. Each of the shells has its own set of builtins. When it runs a builtin, the shell does not fork a new process. Consequently builtins run more quickly and can affect the environment of the current shell. Because builtins are used in the same way as utilities, you will not typically be aware of whether a utility is built into the shell or is a stand-alone utility.

The echo utility is a shell builtin. The shell always executes a shell builtin before trying to find a command or utility with the same name. See page 487 for an in-depth discussion of builtin commands, page 500 for a list of bash builtins, and page 377 for a list of tcsh builtins.

Listing bash
builtins

To get a complete list of bash builtins, give the command **info bash builtin**. To display a page with more information on each builtin, move the cursor to one of the lines listing a builtin command and press RETURN. Alternatively, after typing **info bash**, give the command **/builtin** to search the bash documentation for the string **builtin**. The cursor will rest on the word **Builtin** in a menu; press RETURN to display the builtins menu.

Because bash was written by GNU, the info page has better information than does the man page. If you want to read about builtins in the man page, give the command **man bash** and then search for the section on builtins with the command **/^SHELL BUILTIN COMMANDS** (search for a line that begins with **SHELL . . .**).

Listing tcsh builtins

For tcsh, give the command **man tcsh** to display the tcsh man page and then search for the second occurrence of **Builtin commands** with the following two commands: **/Builtin commands** (search for the string) and **n** (search for the next occurrence of the string).

CHAPTER SUMMARY

The shell is the Linux command interpreter. It scans the command line for proper syntax, picking out the command name and any arguments. The first argument is argument one, the second is argument two, and so on. The name of the command itself is argument zero. Many programs use options to modify the effects of a command. Most Linux utilities identify an option by its leading one or two hyphens.

When you give it a command, the shell tries to find an executable program with the same name as the command. When it does, the shell executes the program. When it does not, the shell tells you that it cannot find or execute the program. If the command is a simple filename, the shell searches the directories given in the variable **PATH** in an attempt to locate the command.

When it executes a command, the shell assigns one file to the command's standard input and another file to its standard output. By default the shell causes a command's standard input to come from the keyboard and its standard output to go to the screen. You can instruct the shell to redirect a command's standard input from or standard output to any file or device. You can also connect standard output of one command to standard input of another command using a pipe. A filter is a command that reads its standard input from standard output of one command and writes its standard output to standard input of another command.

When a command runs in the foreground, the shell waits for it to finish before it displays a prompt and allows you to continue. When you put an ampersand (&) at the end of a command line, the shell executes the command in the background and displays another prompt immediately. Run slow commands in the background when you want to enter other commands at the shell prompt. The jobs builtin displays a list of jobs and includes the job number of each.

The shell interprets special characters on a command line to generate filenames. A question mark represents any single character, and an asterisk represents zero or more characters. A single character may also be represented by a character class: a list of characters within brackets. A reference that uses special characters (wildcards) to abbreviate a list of one or more filenames is called an ambiguous file reference.

A builtin is a utility that is built into a shell. Each shell has its own set of builtins. When it runs a builtin, the shell does not fork a new process. Consequently builtins run more quickly and can affect the environment of the current shell.

UTILITIES AND BUILTINS INTRODUCED IN THIS CHAPTER

Table 5-1 lists the utilities introduced in this chapter.

Table 5-1   New utilities

Utility	Function
tr	Maps one string of characters into another (page 122)
tee	Sends standard input to both a file and standard output (page 125)
bg	Moves a process into the background (page 126)
fg	Moves a process into the foreground (page 126)
jobs	Displays a list of currently running jobs (page 127)

EXERCISES

1. What does the shell ordinarily do while a command is executing? What should you do if you do not want to wait for a command to finish before running another command?

2. Using sort as a filter, rewrite the following sequence of commands:

```
$ sort list > temp
$ lpr temp
$ rm temp
```

3. What is a PID number? Why are these numbers useful when you run processes in the background? Which utility displays the PID numbers of the commands you are running?

4. Assume that the following files are in the working directory:

```
$ ls
intro      notesb    ref2      section1    section3    section4b
notesa     ref1      ref3      section2    section4a   sentrev
```

Give commands for each of the following, using wildcards to express filenames with as few characters as possible.

a. List all files that begin with **section**.

b. List the **section1**, **section2**, and **section3** files only.

c. List the **intro** file only.

d. List the **section1**, **section3**, **ref1**, and **ref3** files.

5. Refer to the documentation of utilities in Part V or the man pages to determine which commands will

a. Output the number of lines in the standard input that contain the *word* **a** or **A**.

b. Output only the names of the files in the working directory that contain the pattern $(.

c. List the files in the working directory in their reverse alphabetical order.

d. Send a list of files in the working directory to the printer, sorted by size.

6. Give a command to

a. Redirect the standard output from a sort command into a file named **phone_list**. Assume that the input file is named **numbers**.

b. Translate all occurrences of the characters [and { to the character (, and all occurrences of the characters] and } to the character) in the file **permdemos.c**. (*Hint:* Refer to tr on page 804.)

c. Create a file named **book** that contains the contents of two other files: **part1** and **part2**.

7. The lpr and sort utilities accept input either from a file named on the command line or from standard input.

a. Name two other utilities that function in a similar manner.

b. Name a utility that accepts its input only from standard input.

8. Give an example of a command that uses grep

a. With both input and output redirected.

b. With only input redirected.

c. With only output redirected.

d. Within a pipe.

In which of the preceding is grep used as a filter?

9. Explain the following error message. What filenames would a subsequent
ls display?

```
$ ls
abc  abd  abe  abf  abg  abh
$ rm abc ab*
rm: cannot remove 'abc': No such file or directory
```

Advanced Exercises

10. When you use the redirect output symbol (>) with a command, the shell
creates the output file immediately, before the command is executed.
Demonstrate that this is true.

11. In experimenting with shell variables, Alex accidentally deletes his **PATH**
variable. He decides that he does not need the **PATH** variable. Discuss
some of the problems he may soon encounter and explain the reasons for
these problems. How could he *easily* return **PATH** to its original value?

12. Assume that your permissions allow you to write to a file but not to
delete it.

a. Give a command to empty the file without invoking an editor.

b. Explain how you might have permission to modify a file that you
cannot delete.

13. If you accidentally create a filename that contains a nonprinting character,
such as a CONTROL character, how can you rename the file?

14. Why does the **noclobber** variable *not* protect you from overwriting an
existing file with cp or mv?

15. Why do command names and filenames usually not have embedded SPACEs?
How would you create a filename containing a SPACE? How would you
remove it? (This is a thought exercise, not recommended practice. If you
want to experiment, create and work in a directory that contains only
your experimental file.)

16. Create a file named **answer** and give the following command:

```
$ > answers.0102 < answers cat
```

Explain what the command does and why. What is a more conventional
way of expressing this command?

PART II
THE EDITORS

6

THE vim EDITOR

This chapter begins with a history and description of vi, the original, powerful, sometimes cryptic, interactive, visually oriented text editor. The chapter continues with a tutorial that explains how to use vim (vi improved—a vi clone supplied with or available for most Linux distributions) to create and edit a file. Much of the tutorial and the balance of the chapter apply to vi and other vi clones. Following the tutorial, the chapter delves into the details of many vim commands and explains how to use parameters to customize vim to meet your needs. It concludes with a quick reference/summary of vim commands. The vim home page is www.vim.org.

HISTORY

Before vi was developed, the standard UNIX system editor was ed (still available on most Linux systems), a line-oriented editor that made it difficult to see the context of your editing. Next came ex,[1] a superset of ed. The most notable advantage that ex has over ed is a display-editing facility that allows you to work with a full screen of text instead of just a line. While using ex, you can bring up the display-editing facility by giving a **vi** (Visual mode) command. People used this display-editing facility so extensively that the developers of ex made it possible to start the editor with the display-editing facility already running, without having to start ex and then give a **vi** command. Appropriately they named the program vi. You can call the Visual mode from ex, and you can go back to ex while you are using vi. Start by running ex; give a **vi** command to switch to Visual mode, and give a **Q** command while in Visual mode to use ex. Give a **quit** command to exit from ex.

vi clones   Linux offers a number of versions, or *clones,* of vi. The most popular vi clones found on Linux are elvis (elvis.the-little-red-haired-girl.org), nvi (an implementation of the original vi editor, www.bostic.com/vi), vile (dickey.his.com/vile/vile.html), and vim (www.vim.org). Each clone offers additional features beyond those provided with the original vi.

The examples in this book are based on vim. Several Linux distributions support multiple versions of vim. For example, Red Hat provides **/bin/vi**, a minimal build of vim that is compact and faster to load but offers fewer features, and **/usr/bin/vim**, a full-featured version of vim.

If you use one of the clones other than vim, or vi itself, you may notice slight differences from the examples presented in this chapter. The vim editor is compatible with almost all vi commands and runs on many platforms, including Windows, Macintosh, OS/2, UNIX, and Linux. Refer to the vim home page (www.vim.org) for more information and a very useful Tips section.

What vim is not   The vim editor is not a text formatting program. It does not justify margins or provide the output formatting features of a sophisticated word processing system such as OpenOffice.org Writer. Rather, vim is a sophisticated text editor meant to be used to write code (C, HTML, Java, and so on), short notes, and input to a text formatting system, such as groff or troff. You can use fmt (page 664) to do minimal formatting on a text file that you create with vim.

Reading this chapter   Because vim is so large and powerful, this chapter describes only some of its features. Nonetheless, if vim is completely new to you, you may find even this limited set of commands overwhelming. The vim editor provides a variety of ways to accomplish any specified editing task. A useful strategy for learning vim is to begin by learning a subset of commands to accomplish basic editing tasks. Then, as you become more comfortable with the editor, you can learn other commands that enable you to do things more quickly and efficiently. The following tutorial section introduces a basic but useful set of vim commands and features that create and edit a file.

---

1. The ex program is usually a link to vi, which is a version of vim on some systems.

TUTORIAL: CREATING AND EDITING A FILE WITH vim

This section explains how to start vim, enter text, move the cursor, correct text, save the file to the disk, and exit from vim. The tutorial discusses two of the modes of operation of vim and explains how to switch from one mode to the other.

vimtutor In addition to working with this tutorial, you may want to try vim's tutor, named vimtutor: Give its name as a command to run it.

Specifying a terminal Because vim takes advantage of features that are specific to various kinds of terminals, you must tell it what type of terminal or terminal emulator you are using. On many systems, and usually when you work on a terminal emulator, your terminal type is set automatically. If you need to specify your terminal type, refer to "Specifying a Terminal" on page 844.

The vi command runs vim

tip On some systems the command **vi** runs a minimal build of vim that is compact and faster to load than vim but includes fewer features. See "The compatible Parameter" on page 148 for information on running vim in vi compatible mode.

STARTING vim

Start vim with the following command line to create and edit a file named **practice**:

```
$ vim practice
```

When you press RETURN, the command line disappears, and the screen looks similar to the one shown in Figure 6-1.

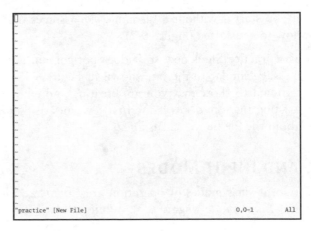

```
"practice" [New File]                      0,0-1      All
```

Figure 6-1   Starting vim

The tildes (~) at the left of the screen indicate that the file is empty. They disappear as you add lines of text to the file. If your screen looks like a distorted version of the one shown, your terminal type is probably not set correctly.

If you start vim with a terminal type that is not in the **terminfo** database, vim displays an error message and the terminal type defaults to **ansi**, which works on many terminals. In the following example, the user mistyped **vt100** and set the terminal type to **vg100**:

```
Terminal entry not found in terminfo
'vg100' not known. Available builtin terminals are:
    builtin_riscos
    builtin_amiga
    builtin_beos-ansi
    builtin_ansi
    builtin_pcansi
    builtin_win32
    builtin_vt320
    builtin_vt52
    builtin_xterm
    builtin_iris-ansi
    builtin_debug
    builtin_dumb
defaulting to 'ansi'
```

If you want to reset the terminal type, press ESCAPE and then give the following command to exit from vim and get the shell prompt back:

:q!

When you enter the colon (:), vim moves the cursor to the bottom line of the screen. The characters **q!** tell vim to quit without saving your work. (You will not ordinarily exit from vim this way because you typically want to save your work.) You must press RETURN after you give this command. Once you get the shell prompt back, refer to "Specifying a Terminal" on page 844, and then start vim again.

If you start it without a filename, vim assumes that you are a novice and tells you how to get started (Figure 6-2).

The **practice** file is new so it does not contain any text. The vim editor displays a message similar to the one shown in Figure 6-1 on the status (bottom) line of the terminal to show that you are creating and editing a new file. When you edit an existing file, vim displays the first few lines of the file and gives status information about the file on the status line.

COMMAND AND INPUT MODES

Two of vim's modes of operation are *Command mode* (also called *Normal mode*) and *Input mode* (Figure 6-3). While vim is in Command mode, you can give vim

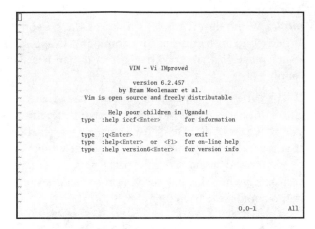

```
                            VIM - Vi IMproved

                               version 6.2.457
                            by Bram Moolenaar et al.
                      Vim is open source and freely distributable

                            Help poor children in Uganda!
                 type  :help iccf<Enter>          for information

                 type  :q<Enter>                  to exit
                 type  :help<Enter>  or  <F1>     for on-line help
                 type  :help version6<Enter>      for version info




                                                         0,0-1        All
```

Figure 6-2   Starting vim without a filename

commands. For example, you can delete text or exit from vim. You can also command vim to enter Input mode. In Input mode, vim accepts anything you enter as text and displays it on the screen. Press ESCAPE to return vim to Command mode.

By default the vim editor keeps you informed about which mode it is in. You will see **-- INSERT --** at the lower-left corner of the screen while vim is in Insert mode.

The following command causes vim to display line numbers next to the text you are editing:

`:set number` RETURN

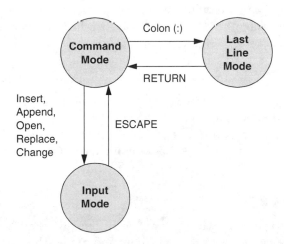

Figure 6-3   Modes in vim

Last Line mode | The colon (:) in the preceding command puts vim into another mode, *Last Line mode*. While in this mode, vim keeps the cursor on the bottom line of the screen. When you finish entering the command by pressing RETURN, vim restores the cursor to its place in the text. Give the command **:set nonumber** RETURN to turn off line numbers.

vim is case sensitive | When you give vim a command, remember that the editor is case sensitive. Thus vim editor interprets the same letter as two different commands, depending on whether you enter an uppercase or lowercase character. Beware of the CAPS LOCK (SHIFTLOCK) key. If you set this key to enter uppercase text while you are in Input mode and then exit to Command mode, vim interprets your commands as uppercase letters. It can be confusing when this happens because vim does not appear to be executing the commands you are entering.

ENTERING TEXT

Input mode (i/a) | When you start vim, you must put it in Input mode before you can enter text. To put vim in Input mode, press the **i** key (insert before the cursor) or the **a** key (append after the cursor).

If you are not sure whether vim is currently in Input mode, press the ESCAPE key; vim returns to Command mode if it was in Input mode or beeps, flashes, or does nothing if it is already in Command mode. You can put vim back in Input mode by pressing the **i** or **a** key again.

While vim is in Input mode, you can enter text by typing on the keyboard. If the text does not appear on the screen as you type, you are not in Input mode.

To continue with this tutorial, enter the sample paragraph shown in Figure 6-4, pressing the RETURN key to end each line. If you do not press RETURN before the cursor reaches the right side of the screen or window, vim will wrap the text so that it appears to start a new line. Physical lines will not correspond to programmatic (logical) lines in this situation, and editing will be more difficult.

While you are using vim, you can always correct any typing mistakes you make. If you notice a mistake on the line you are entering, you can correct it before you continue (page 146). You can correct other mistakes later. When you finish entering the paragraph, press ESCAPE to return vim to Command mode.

GETTING HELP

To get help while you are using vim, give the command **:help** [*feature*] followed by RETURN (you must be in Command mode when you give this command). The colon puts the cursor on the last line of the screen. If you type **:help**, vim displays an

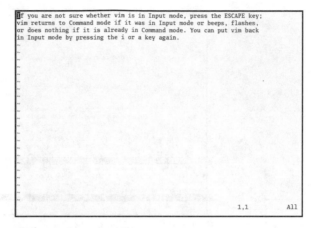

Figure 6-4   Entering text with vim

introduction to vim Help (Figure 6-5). Each dark band near the bottom of the screen names the file that is displayed above it. (Each area of the screen that displays a file, such as the two areas shown in Figure 6-5, is a vim "window.") The **help.txt** file occupies most of the screen (the upper window) in Figure 6-5. The file that is being edited (**practice**) occupies a few lines in the lower portion of the screen (the lower window).

Read through the introduction to Help by scrolling the text as you read. Pressing **j** or the DOWN ARROW key moves the cursor down one line at a time; pressing CONTROL-D or CONTROL-U scrolls the cursor down or up half a window at a time. Give the command **:q!** to close the Help window.

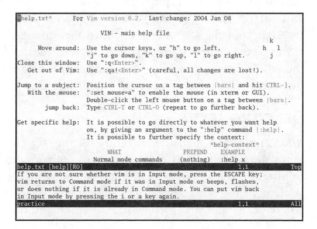

Figure 6-5   The main vim Help screen

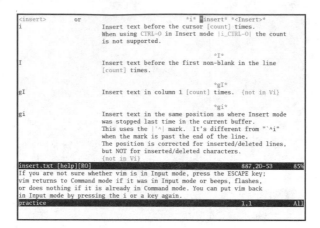

Figure 6-6   Help with insert

You can get help with the insert commands by giving the command **:help insert** while vim is in Command mode (Figure 6-6).

CORRECTING TEXT AS YOU INSERT IT

The keys that back up and correct a shell command line serve the same functions when vim is in Input mode. These keys include the erase, line kill, and word kill keys (usually CONTROL-H, CONTROL-U, and CONTROL-W, respectively). Although vim may not remove deleted text from the screen as you back up over it, the editor does remove it when you type over it or press RETURN.

MOVING THE CURSOR

You need to be able to move the cursor on the screen so that you can delete, insert, and correct text. While vim is in Command mode, you can use the RETURN key, the SPACE bar, and the ARROW keys to move the cursor. If you prefer to keep your hand closer to the center of the keyboard, if your terminal does not have ARROW keys, or if the emulator you are using does not support them, you can use the **h**, **j**, **k**, and **l** (lowercase "l") keys to move the cursor left, down, up, and right, respectively.

DELETING TEXT

Delete character (**x**)
Delete word (**dw**)
Delete line (**dd**)

You can delete a single character by moving the cursor until it is over the character you want to delete and then giving the command **x**. You can delete a word by positioning the cursor on the first letter of the word and then giving the command **dw** (Delete word). You can delete a line of text by moving the cursor until it is anywhere on the line and then giving the command **dd**.

UNDOING MISTAKES

Undo (**u**)
If you delete a character, line, or word by mistake or give any command you want to undo, give the command **u** (Undo) immediately after the command you want to

undo. The vim editor will restore the text to the way it was before you gave the last command. If you give the **u** command again, vim will undo the command you gave before the one it just undid. You can use this technique to back up over many of your actions. With the **compatible** parameter (page 148) set, vim can undo only the most recent change.

Redo (**:redo**)   If you undo a command you did not mean to undo, give a Redo command: CONTROL-R or **:redo** (followed by a RETURN). The vim editor will redo the undone command. As with the Undo command, you can give the Redo command many times in a row.

ENTERING ADDITIONAL TEXT

Insert (**i**)
Append (**a**)   When you want to insert new text within existing text, move the cursor so it is on the character that follows the new text you plan to enter. Then give the **i** (Insert) command to put vim in Input mode, enter the new text, and press ESCAPE to return vim to Command mode. Alternatively, you can position the cursor on the character that precedes the new text, and use the **a** (Append) command.

Open (**o** and **O**)   To enter one or more lines, position the cursor on the line above where you want the new text to go. Give the command **o** (Open). The vim editor opens a blank line, puts the cursor on it, and goes into Input mode. Enter the new text, ending each line with a RETURN. When you are finished entering text, press ESCAPE to return vim to Command mode. The **O** command works in the same way **o** works, except that it opens a line *above* the line the cursor is on.

CORRECTING TEXT

To correct text, use **dd**, **dw**, or **x** to remove the incorrect text. Then use **i**, **a**, **o**, or **O** to insert the correct text.

For example, to change the word **pressing** to **hitting** in Figure 6-4 on page 145 you might use the ARROW keys to move the cursor until it is on top of the **p** in **pressing**. Then give the command **dw** to delete the word **pressing**. Put vim in Input mode by giving an **i** command, enter the word **hitting** followed by a SPACE, and press ESCAPE. The word is changed and vim is in Command mode, waiting for another command. A shorthand for the two commands **dw** followed by the **i** command is **cw** (Change word). The command **cw** puts vim into Input mode.

Page breaks for the printer

tip   CONTROL-L is a signal to a printer to skip to the top of the next page. You can enter this character anywhere in a document by pressing CONTROL-L while you are in Input mode. If **^L** does not appear, press CONTROL-V before CONTROL-L.

ENDING THE EDITING SESSION

While you are editing, vim keeps the edited text in an area named the *Work buffer*. When you finish editing, you must write out the contents of the Work buffer to a disk file so that the edited text is saved and available when you next want it.

Make sure that vim is in Command mode, and then use the **ZZ** command (you must use uppercase **Z**'s) to write your newly entered text to the disk and end the editing session. After you give the **ZZ** command, vim returns control to the shell. You can exit with **:q!** if you do not want to save your work. Refer to page 188 for a summary of vim commands.

Do not confuse ZZ with CONTROL-Z

caution
When you exit from vim with **ZZ**, make sure that you type **ZZ** and not CONTROL-Z (typically the suspend key). When you press CONTROL-Z, vim disappears from your screen, almost as though you had exited from it. In fact, vim will continue running in the background with your work unsaved. Refer to "Job Control" on page 271. If you try to start editing the same file with a new **vim** command, vim displays a message about a swap file; refer to "File Locks" on page 152.

THE compatible PARAMETER

The **compatible** parameter makes vim more compatible with vi. By default this parameter is set so that vim works like vi. If you set up a **~/.vimrc** startup file (page 176), the **compatible** parameter is unset and vim works like vim. To get started with vim you can ignore this parameter.

Setting the **compatible** parameter changes many aspects of how vim works. For example, when the **compatible** parameter is set, the Undo command (page 146) can undo only your most recent change; with the **compatible** parameter unset, you can call undo repeatedly to undo many changes. This chapter notes when the **compatible** parameter affects a command. To obtain more details on the **compatible** parameter, give the command **:help compatible** RETURN. For a complete list of how vim differs from the original vi, use **:help vi-diff** RETURN. See page 144 for a discussion of the help command.

From the command line use the **–C** option to set the **compatible** parameter and the **–N** option to unset it. Refer to "Setting Parameters from Within vim" on page 175 for information on how to change the **compatible** parameter while you are running vim.

INTRODUCTION TO vim FEATURES

This section covers modes of operation, online help, the Work buffer, emergency procedures, and other vim features. To see which features are incorporated in a particular build, give a **vim** command followed by the **--version** option.

ONLINE HELP

As covered briefly earlier, vim provides help while you are using it. Give the command **:help** *feature* to display information about *feature*. As you scroll through the various help texts you will see words with a bar on either side, such as |tutor|. These words are *active links:* Move the cursor on top of an active link and press CONTROL-] to jump to the linked text. Use CONTROL-O (lowercase "o") to jump back to where you were in the help text. You can also use the active link words in place of *feature*. For example, you might see the reference |credits|; you could enter **:help credits** RETURN to read more about credits. Enter **:q!** to close a help window.

Some common *features* that you may want to look up using the help system are **insert**, **delete**, and **opening-window**. Although *opening-window* is not intuitive, you will get to know the names of *features* as you spend more time with vim. You can also give the command **:help doc-file-list** to view a complete list of the help files. Although vim is a free program, the author requests that you donate the money you would have spent on similar software to help the kids in Uganda (**:help uganda** for more information).

MODES OF OPERATION

The vim editor is part of the ex editor, which has five modes of operation:

- ex Command mode
- ex Input mode
- vim Command mode
- vim Input mode
- vim Last Line mode

While in Command mode, vim accepts keystrokes as commands, responding to each command as you enter it. It does not display the characters you type in this mode. While in Input mode, vim accepts and displays keystrokes as text that it eventually puts into the file you are editing. All commands that start with a colon (:) put vim in Last Line mode. The colon moves the cursor to the bottom line of the screen, where you enter the rest of the command.

In addition to the position of the cursor, there is another important difference between Last Line mode and Command mode. When you give a command in Command mode, you do not terminate the command with a RETURN. However, you must terminate all Last Line mode commands with a RETURN.

You do not normally use the ex modes. When this chapter refers to Input and Command modes, it means the vim modes, not the ex modes.

At the start of an editing session, vim is in Command mode. Several commands, including Insert and Append, put vim in Input mode. When you press the ESCAPE key, vim always reverts to Command mode.

The Change and Replace commands combine the Command and Input modes. The Change command deletes the text you want to change and puts vim in Input mode so you can insert new text. The Replace command deletes the character(s) you overwrite and inserts the new one(s) you enter. Figure 6-3 on page 143 shows the modes and the methods for changing between them.

Watch the mode and the CAPS LOCK **key**

tip Almost anything you type in Command mode means something to vim. If you think that vim is in Input mode when it is actually in Command mode, typing in text can produce confusing results. When learning vim, make sure that the **showmode** parameter (page 180) is set (it is by default) to remind you which mode you are using. You may also find it useful to turn on the status line by giving a **:set laststatus=2** command (page 178).

Also keep your eye on the CAPS LOCK key. In Command mode typing uppercase letters produces different results than typing lowercase ones. It can be disorienting to give commands and have vim give the "wrong" responses.

THE DISPLAY

The vim editor uses the status line and several special symbols to give information about what is happening during an editing session.

STATUS LINE

The vim editor displays status information on the bottom line of the display area. This information includes error messages, information about the deletion or addition of blocks of text, and file status information. In addition, vim displays Last Line mode commands on the status line.

REDRAWING THE SCREEN

Sometimes the screen becomes garbled or overwritten. When vim puts characters on the screen, it sometimes leaves @ on a line instead of deleting the line. When output from a program becomes intermixed with the display of the Work buffer things can get confusing. The output *does not* become part of the Work buffer but affects only the display. If the screen gets overwritten, press ESCAPE to make sure vim is in Command mode, and press CONTROL-L to redraw (refresh) the screen.

TILDE (~) SYMBOL

If the end of the file is displayed on the screen, vim marks lines that would appear past the end of the file with a tilde (~) at the left of the screen. When you start editing a new file, the vim editor marks each line on the screen (except for the first line) with this symbol.

CORRECTING TEXT AS YOU INSERT IT

While vim is in Input mode, you can use the erase and line kill keys to back up over text so you can correct it. You can also use CONTROL-W to back up over words.

WORK BUFFER

The vim editor does all of its work in the Work buffer. At the start of an editing session, vim reads the file you are editing from the disk into the Work buffer. During the editing session, it makes all changes to this copy of the file but does not change the file on the disk until you write the contents of the Work buffer back to the disk. Normally when you end an editing session, you command vim to write out the contents of the Work buffer, which makes the changes to the text final. When you edit a new file, vim creates the file when it writes the contents of the Work buffer to the disk, usually at the end of the editing session.

Storing the text you are editing in the Work buffer has both advantages and disadvantages. If you accidentally end an editing session without writing out the contents of the Work buffer, your work is lost. However, if you unintentionally make some major changes (such as deleting the entire contents of the Work buffer), you can end the editing session without implementing the changes.

If you want to use vim to look at a file but not to change it, you can use the view utility:

```
$ view filename
```

Calling the view utility is the same as calling the vim editor with the –R (readonly) option. Once you have invoked the editor in this way, you cannot write the contents of the Work buffer back to the file whose name appeared on the command line. You can always write the Work buffer out to a file with a different name.

LINE LENGTH AND FILE SIZE

The vim editor operates on any format file, provided the length of a single "line" (that is, the characters between two NEWLINE characters) can fit into available memory. The total length of the file is limited only by available disk space and memory.

WINDOWS

The vim editor allows you to open, close, and hide multiple windows, each of which allows you to edit a different file. Most of the window commands consist of CONTROL-W followed by another letter. For example, CONTROL-W s opens another window (splits the screen) that is editing the same file. CONTROL-W n opens a second window that is editing an empty file. CONTROL-W w moves the cursor between windows, and CONTROL-W q (or :q) quits (closes) a window. Give the command :help windows to display a complete list of windows commands.

```
E325: ATTENTION
Found a swap file by the name ".practice.swp"
          owned by: mark   dated: Mon Oct 18 16:16:15 2004
         file name: ~mark/practice
          modified: no
         user name: mark   host name: tuna.bogus.com
        process ID: 14171 (still running)
While opening file "practice"
             dated: Mon Oct 18 11:33:46 2004

(1) Another program may be editing the same file.
    If this is the case, be careful not to end up with two
    different instances of the same file when making changes.
    Quit, or continue with caution.

(2) An edit session for this file crashed.
    If this is the case, use ":recover" or "vim -r practice"
    to recover the changes (see ":help recovery").
    If you did this already, delete the swap file ".practice.swp"
    to avoid this message.

Swap file ".practice.swp" already exists!
[O]pen Read-Only, (E)dit anyway, (R)ecover, (Q)uit:█
```

Figure 6-7   Attempting to open a locked file

FILE LOCKS

When you edit an existing file, vim displays the first few lines of the file, gives status information about the file on the status line, and locks the file. When you try to open a locked file with vim, you will see a message similar to the one shown in Figure 6-7. You will see this type of message in two cases: when you try to edit a file that someone is already editing (perhaps you are editing it in another window or on another terminal) or when you try to edit a file that you were editing when vim or the system crashed.

Although it is advisable to follow the instructions that vim displays, a second user can edit a file and write it out with a different filename. Refer to the next sections for more information.

ABNORMAL TERMINATION OF AN EDITING SESSION

You can end an editing session in one of two ways: When you exit from vim, you can save the changes you made during the editing session or you can abandon those changes. You can use the **ZZ** or **:wq** command from Command mode to save your changes and exit from vim (see "Ending the Editing Session" on page 147).

To end an editing session without writing out the contents of the Work buffer, give the following command:

:q!

When you use this command to end an editing session, vim does not preserve the contents of the Work buffer, so you will lose all the work you did since the last time you wrote the Work buffer to disk. The next time you edit or use the file, it will appear as it did the last time you wrote the Work buffer to disk. Use the **:q!** command cautiously.

Sometimes you may find that you created or edited a file but vim will not let you exit. For example, if you forgot to specify a filename when you first called vim, you will get a message saying **No file name** when you give a **ZZ** command. If vim does not let you exit normally, you can use the Write command (**:w**) to name the file and write it to disk before you quit vim. Give the following command, substituting the name of the file for *filename* (remember to follow the command with a RETURN):

:w filename

After you give the Write command, you can use **:q** to quit using vim. You do not need to use the exclamation point (as in **q!**); it is necessary only when you have made changes since the last time you wrote the Work buffer to disk. Refer to page 174 for more information about the Write command.

When you cannot write to a file

tip   It may be necessary to write a file using *:w filename* if you do not have write permission for the file you are editing. If you give a **ZZ** command and see the message **"filename" is read only**, you do not have write permission for the file. Use the Write command with a temporary filename to write the file to disk under a different filename. If you do not have write permission for the working directory, vim may still not be able to write the file to the disk. Give the command again, using an absolute pathname of a dummy (nonexistent) file in your home directory in place of the filename. (For example, Alex might give the command **:w /home/alex/temp** or **:w ~/temp**.)

If vim reports **File exists**, you will need to use **:w!** *filename* to overwrite the existing file (make sure that you want to do this). Refer to page 175.

RECOVERING TEXT AFTER A CRASH

The vim editor temporarily stores the file you are working on in a *swap file*. If the system crashes while you are editing a file with vim, you can often recover its text from the swap file. When you attempt to edit a file that has a swap file, you will see a message similar to the one shown in Figure 6-7 on page 152. If someone else is editing the file, quit or open the file as a readonly file.

Alex checks whether the swap file exists for a file named **memo**, which he was editing when the system went down:

```
$ vim -r
Swap files found:
   In current directory:
1.    .memo.swp
            dated: Mon Oct 18 13:16:06 2004
         owned by: alex
        file name: ~alex/memo
        host name: bravo.example.com
        user name: alex
       process ID: 19786
   In directory ~/tmp:
      -- none --
   In directory /var/tmp:
      -- none --
   In directory /tmp:
      -- none --
```

With the **–r** option vim displays a list of any swap files that it has saved (some may be old). If your work was saved, give the same command followed by a SPACE and the name of the file. You will then be editing a recent copy of your Work buffer. Use **:w** *filename* immediately to save the salvaged copy of the Work buffer to disk under a name different from the original file. Then check the recovered file to make sure it is OK. Following is Alex's exchange with vim as he recovers **memo**. Subsequently he deletes the swap file:

```
$ vim -r memo
Using swap file ".memo.swp"
Original file "~/memo"
Recovery completed. You should check if everything is OK.
(You might want to write out this file under another name
and run diff with the original file to check for changes)
Delete the .swp file afterwards.

Hit ENTER or type command to continue
:w memo2
:q
$ rm .memo.swp
```

You must recover files on the system you were using

tip   The recovery feature of vim is specific to the system you were using when the crash occurred. If you are running on a cluster, you must log in on the system you were using before the crash to use the **–r** option.

COMMAND MODE: MOVING THE CURSOR

While vim is in Command mode, you can position the cursor over any character on the screen. You can also display a different portion of the Work buffer on the screen. By manipulating the screen and cursor position, you can place the cursor on any character in the Work buffer.

You can move the cursor forward or backward through the text. As illustrated in Figure 6-8, *forward* means toward the right and bottom of the screen and the end of the file. *Backward* means toward the left and top of the screen and the beginning of the file. When you use a command that moves the cursor forward past the end (right) of a line, the cursor generally moves to the beginning (left) of the next line. When you move it backward past the beginning of a line, the cursor moves to the end of the previous line.

Long lines   Sometimes a line in the Work buffer may be too long to appear as a single line on the screen. In such a case vim wraps the current line onto the next line (unless you set the **nowrap** option [page 178]).

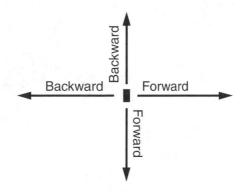

Figure 6-8   Forward and backward

You can move the cursor through the text by any *Unit of Measure* (that is, character, word, line, sentence, paragraph, or screen). If you precede a cursor-movement command with a number, called a *Repeat Factor,* the cursor moves that number of units through the text. Refer to pages 184 and 187 for more precise definitions of these terms.

MOVING THE CURSOR BY CHARACTERS

l/h   The SPACE bar moves the cursor forward, one character at a time, toward the right side of the screen. The l (lowercase "l") key and the RIGHT ARROW key (Figure 6-9) do the same thing. The command 7 SPACE or 7l moves the cursor seven characters to the right. These keys cannot move the cursor past the end of the current line to the beginning of the next line. The h and LEFT ARROW keys are similar to the l key but work in the opposite direction.

MOVING THE CURSOR TO A SPECIFIC CHARACTER

f/F   You can move the cursor to the next occurrence of a specified character on the current line by using the Find command. For example, the following command moves the cursor from its current position to the next occurrence of the character **a**, if one appears on the same line:

```
fa
```

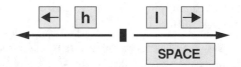

Figure 6-9   Moving the cursor by characters

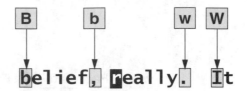

Figure 6-10   Moving the cursor by words

You can also find the previous occurrence by using a capital **F**. The following command moves the cursor to the position of the closest previous **a** in the current line:

    Fa

A semicolon (;) repeats the last Find command.

Moving the Cursor by Words

w/W The **w** (word) key moves the cursor forward to the first letter of the next word (Figure 6-10). Groups of punctuation count as words. This command goes to the next line if the next word is located there. The command **15w** moves the cursor to the first character of the fifteenth subsequent word.

The **W** key is similar to the **w** key but moves the cursor by blank-delimited words, including punctuation, as it skips forward. (Refer to "Blank-Delimited Word" on page 185.)

b/B The **b** (back) key moves the cursor backward to the first letter of the previous word. The **B** key moves the cursor backward by blank-delimited words. Similarly the **e** key moves the cursor to the end of the next word; **E** moves it to the end of the next blank-delimited word.

Moving the Cursor by Lines

j/k The RETURN key moves the cursor to the beginning of the next line; the **j** and DOWN ARROW keys move it down one line to the character just below the current character (Figure 6-11). If no character is immediately below the current character, the cursor moves to the end of the next line. The cursor will not move past the last line of text in the work buffer.

The **k** and UP ARROW keys are similar to the **j** key but work in the opposite direction. The minus (–) key is similar to the RETURN key but works in the opposite direction.

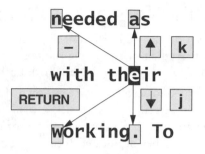

Figure 6-11   Moving the cursor by lines

MOVING THE CURSOR BY SENTENCES AND PARAGRAPHS

)/(The) and } keys move the cursor forward to the beginning of the next sentence or
}/{ the next paragraph, respectively (Figure 6-12). The (and { keys move the cursor
backward to the beginning of the current sentence or paragraph. You can find more
information on sentences and paragraphs starting on page 186.

MOVING THE CURSOR WITHIN THE SCREEN

H/M/L The **H** (home) key positions the cursor at the left end of the top line of the screen.
The **M** (middle) key moves the cursor to the middle line, and the **L** (lower) key
moves it to the bottom line (Figure 6-12).

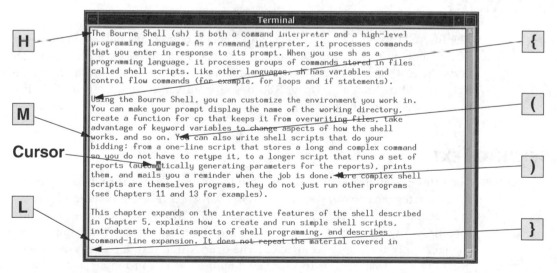

Figure 6-12   Moving the cursor by sentences, paragraphs, **H, M,** and L

VIEWING DIFFERENT PARTS OF THE WORK BUFFER

The screen displays a portion of the text that is in the Work buffer. You can display the text preceding or following the text on the screen by *scrolling* the display. You can also display a portion of the Work buffer based on a line number.

CONTROL-D
CONTROL-U

Press CONTROL-D to scroll the screen down (forward) through the file so that vim displays half a screen of new text. Use CONTROL-U to scroll the screen up (backward) by the same amount. If you precede either of these commands with a number, vim will scroll that number of lines each time you use CONTROL-D or CONTROL-U for the rest of the session (unless you again change the number of lines to scroll). See page 179 for a discussion of the **scroll** parameter.

CONTROL-F
CONTROL-B

The CONTROL-F (forward) and CONTROL-B (backward) keys display almost a *whole* screen of new text, leaving a couple of lines from the previous screen for continuity. On many keyboards you can use the PAGE DOWN and PAGE UP keys in place of CONTROL-F and CONTROL-B.

Line numbers (**G**)

When you enter a line number followed by **G** (goto), vim positions the cursor on that line in the Work buffer. If you press **G** without a number, vim positions the cursor on the last line in the Work buffer. Line numbers are implicit; your file does not need to have actual line numbers for this command to work. Refer to "Line numbers" on page 178 if you want vim to display line numbers.

INPUT MODE

The Insert, Append, Open, Change, and Replace commands put vim in Input mode. While vim is in this mode, you can put new text into the Work buffer. You need to press the ESCAPE key to return vim to Command mode when you finish entering text. Refer to "Show mode" on page 180 if you want vim to remind you when it is in Input mode (it does by default).

INSERTING TEXT

Insert (**i/I**)

The **i** (Insert) command puts vim in Input mode and places the text you enter before the character the cursor is on (the *current character*). The **I** command places text at the beginning of the current line (Figure 6-13). Although the **i** and **I** commands sometimes overwrite text on the screen, the characters in the Work buffer are not changed; only the display is affected. The overwritten text is redisplayed when you press ESCAPE and vim returns to Command mode. Use **i** or **I** to insert a few characters or words into existing text or to insert text in a new file.

Figure 6-13 The I, i, a, and A commands

APPENDING TEXT

Append (**a/A**) The **a** (Append) command is similar to the **i** command, except that it places the text you enter after the current character (Figure 6-13). The **A** command places the text after the last character on the current line.

OPENING A LINE FOR TEXT

Open (**o/O**) The **o** (Open) and **O** commands open a blank line within existing text, place the cursor at the beginning of the new (blank) line, and put vim in Input mode. The **O** command opens a line above the current line; **o** opens one below the current line. Use the Open commands when you are entering several new lines within existing text.

REPLACING TEXT

Replace (**r/R**) The **r** and **R** (Replace) commands cause the new text you enter to overwrite (replace) existing text. The single character you enter following an **r** command overwrites the current character. After you enter that character, vim automatically returns to Command mode—you do not need to press the ESCAPE key.

The **R** command causes *all* subsequent characters to overwrite existing text until you press ESCAPE to return vim to Command mode.

Replacing TABs

tip The Replace commands may appear to behave strangely when you replace TAB characters. TAB characters can appear as several SPACES—until you try to replace them. They are actually only one character and are replaced by a single character. Refer to "Invisible characters" on page 178 for information on how to display TABs as visible characters.

QUOTING SPECIAL CHARACTERS IN INPUT MODE

CONTROL-V While you are in Input mode, you can use the Quote command, CONTROL-V, to enter any character into the text, including characters that normally have special meaning to vim. Among these characters are CONTROL-L (or CONTROL-R), which redraws the screen; CONTROL-W, which backs the cursor up a word to the left; and ESCAPE, which ends Input mode.

To insert one of these characters into the text, type CONTROL-V followed by the character. CONTROL-V quotes the single character that follows it. For example, to insert the sequence ESCAPE[2J into a file you are creating in vim, you type the character sequence CONTROL-V ESCAPE[2J. This character sequence clears the screen of a DEC VT-100 and other similar terminals. Although you would not ordinarily want to type this sequence into a document, you might want to use it or another ESCAPE sequence in a shell script you are creating in vim. Refer to Chapter 11 for information about writing shell scripts.

Command Mode: Deleting and Changing Text

This section describes the commands to delete and replace, or change, text in the document you are editing. The Undo command is covered here because it allows you to restore deleted or changed text.

Undoing Changes

Undo (**u/U**)   The **u** command (Undo) restores text that you just deleted or changed by mistake. A single Undo command restores only the most recently deleted text. If you delete a line and then change a word, the first Undo restores only the changed word; you have to give a second Undo command to restore the deleted line. The **U** command restores the last line you changed to the way it was before you started changing it, even after several changes.

Deleting Characters

Delete character (**x/X**)   The **x** command deletes the current character. You can precede the **x** command by a Repeat Factor (page 187) to delete several characters on the current line, starting with the current character. The **X** command deletes characters to the left of the cursor.

Deleting Text

Delete (**d/D**)   The **d** (Delete) command removes text from the Work buffer. The amount of text that **d** removes depends on the Repeat Factor and the Unit of Measure (page 184) you enter after the **d**. After the text is deleted, vim is still in Command mode.

Use **dd** to delete a single line

tip   The command **d** RETURN deletes two lines: the current line and the following one. Use **dd** to delete just the current line, or precede **dd** by a Repeat Factor (page 187) to delete several lines.

You can delete from the current cursor position up to a specific character on the same line. To delete up to the next semicolon (;), give the command **dt;** (see page 164 for more information on the **t** command). To delete the remainder of the current line, use **D** or **d$**. Table 6-1 lists some Delete commands. Each command, except the last group that starts with **dd**, deletes *from/to* the current character.

Table 6-1   Delete command examples

Command	Result
dl	Deletes current character (same as the **x** command)
d0	Deletes from beginning of line
d^	Deletes from first character of the line (not including leading SPACES or TABS)
dw	Deletes to end of word
d3w	Deletes to end of third word
db	Deletes from beginning of word
dW	Deletes to end of blank-delimited word
dB	Deletes from beginning of blank-delimited word
d7B	Deletes from seventh previous beginning of blank-delimited word
d)	Deletes to end of sentence
d4)	Deletes to end of fourth sentence
d(	Deletes from beginning of sentence
d}	Deletes to end of paragraph
d{	Deletes from beginning of paragraph
d7{	Deletes from seventh paragraph preceding beginning of paragraph
d/*text*	Deletes up to the next occurrence of word ***text***
df*c*	Deletes on current line up to and including next occurrence of character ***c***
dt*c*	Deletes on current line up to next occurrence of ***c***
D	Deletes to end of line
d$	Deletes to end of line
dd	Deletes the current line
5dd	Deletes five lines starting with the current line
dL	Deletes through last line on screen
dH	Deletes from first line on screen
dG	Deletes through end of Work buffer
d1G	Deletes from beginning of Work buffer

Exchange characters and lines

tip   If two characters are out of order, position the cursor on the first character and give the commands **xp**.
If two lines are out of order, position the cursor on the first line and give the commands **ddp**.
See page 172 for more information on the Put commands.

Changing Text

Change (**c/C**)   The **c** (Change) command replaces existing text with new text. The new text does not have to occupy the same space as the existing text. You can change a word to several words, a line to several lines, or a paragraph to a single character. The C command replaces the text from the cursor position to the end of the line.

The **c** command deletes the amount of text specified by the Repeat Factor and the Unit of Measure (page 184) and puts vim in Input mode. When you finish entering the new text and press ESCAPE, the old word, line, sentence, or paragraph is changed to the new one. Pressing ESCAPE without entering new text deletes the specified text (replaces the specified text with nothing).

Table 6-2 lists some Change commands. Except for the last two, each command changes text *from/to* the current character.

Table 6-2   Change command examples

Command	Result
cl	Changes current character
cw	Changes to end of word
c3w	Changes to end of third word
cb	Changes from beginning of word
cW	Changes to end of blank-delimited word
cB	Changes from beginning of blank-delimited word
c7B	Changes from beginning of seventh previous blank-delimited word
c$	Changes to end of line
c0	Changes from beginning of line
c)	Changes to end of sentence
c4)	Changes to end of fourth sentence
c(	Changes from beginning of sentence
c}	Changes to end of paragraph

Table 6-2   Change command examples (continued)

c{	Changes from beginning of paragraph
c7{	Changes from beginning of seventh preceding paragraph
ct*c*	Changes on current line up to next occurrence of *c*
C	Changes to end of line
cc	Changes the current line
5cc	Changes five lines starting with the current line

dw works differently from cw

tip   The **dw** command deletes all the characters through (including) the SPACE at the end of a word. The **cw** command changes only the characters in the word, leaving the trailing SPACE intact.

REPLACING TEXT

Substitute (**s/S**)   The **s** and **S** (Substitute) commands also replace existing text with new text (Table 6-3). The **s** command deletes the character the cursor is on and puts vim into Input mode. It has the effect of replacing the single character that the cursor is on with whatever you type until you press ESCAPE. The **S** command does the same thing as the **cc** command: It changes the current line. The **s** command replaces characters only on the current line. If you specify a Repeat Factor before an **s** command and this action would replace more characters than exist on the current line, **s** changes characters only to the end of the line (same as **C**).

Table 6-3   Substitute command examples

Command	Result
s	Substitutes one or more characters for current character
S	Substitutes one or more characters for current line
5s	Substitutes one or more characters for five characters, starting with current character

CHANGING CASE

The tilde (~) character changes the case of the character under the cursor from uppercase to lowercase, or vice versa. You can precede the tilde with a number to specify the number of characters you want the command to affect. For example, 5~ will transpose the next five characters starting with the character under the cursor, but it will not transpose characters past the end of the line the cursor is on.

SEARCHING AND SUBSTITUTING

Searching for and replacing a character, a string of text, or a string that is matched by a regular expression is a key feature of any editor. The vim editor provides simple commands for searching for a character on the current line. It also provides more complex commands for searching for and optionally substituting for single and multiple occurrences of strings or regular expressions anywhere in the Work buffer.

SEARCHING FOR A CHARACTER

Find (f/F) You can search for and move the cursor to the next occurrence of a specified character on the current line using the f (Find) command. Refer to "Moving the Cursor to a Specific Character" on page 155.

t/T The next two commands are used in the same manner as the Find command. The t command places the cursor on the character before the next occurrence of the specified character. The T command places the cursor on the character after the previous occurrence of the specified character.

A semicolon (;) repeats the last f, F, t, or T command.

You can combine these search commands with other commands. For example, the command d2fq deletes the text from the location of the cursor to the second occurrence of the letter q on the current line.

SEARCHING FOR A STRING

The vim editor can search backward or forward through the Work buffer to find a string of text or a string that matches a regular expression (see Appendix A). To find the next occurrence of a string (forward), press the forward slash (/) key, enter the text you want to find (called the *search string*), and press RETURN. When you press the slash key, vim displays a slash on the status line. As you enter the string of text, it is also displayed on the status line. When you press RETURN, vim searches for the string. If this search is successful, vim positions the cursor on the first character of the string. If you use a question mark (?) in place of the forward slash, vim searches for the previous occurrence of the string. If you need to include a forward slash in a forward search or a question mark in a backward search, you must quote it by preceding it with a backslash (\).

Two distinct ways of quoting characters

tip You use CONTROL-V to quote special characters in text that you are entering into a file (page 159). This section discusses the use of a backslash (\) to quote special characters in a search string. The two techniques of quoting characters are not interchangeable.

The **N** and **n** keys repeat the last search without any need for you to reenter the search string. The **n** key repeats the original search exactly, and the **N** key repeats the search in the opposite direction of the original search.

If you are searching forward and vim does not find the search string before it gets to the end of the Work buffer, the editor typically *wraps around* and continues the search at the beginning of the Work buffer. During a backward search, vim wraps around from the beginning of the Work buffer to the end. Also, vim normally performs case-sensitive searches. Refer to "Wrap scan" (page 180) and "Ignore case in searches" (page 178) for information about how to change these search parameters.

NORMAL VERSUS INCREMENTAL SEARCHES

When vim performs a normal search (its default behavior), you enter a slash or question mark followed by the search string and press RETURN. The vim editor moves the cursor to the next or previous occurrence of the string you are searching for.

When vim performs an incremental search, you enter a slash or question mark. As you enter each character of the search string, vim moves the highlight to the next or previous occurrence of the string you have entered so far. When the highlight is on the string you are searching for, you must press RETURN to move the cursor to the highlighted string. If the string you enter does not match any text, vim does not highlight anything.

The type of search that vim performs depends on the **incsearch** parameter (page 178). Give the command **:set incsearch** to turn on incremental searching. Use **noincsearch** to turn it off. When you set the **compatible** parameter (page 148), vim turns off incremental searching.

SPECIAL CHARACTERS IN SEARCH STRINGS

Because the search string is a regular expression, some characters take on a special meaning within the search string. The following paragraphs list some of these characters. See also "Extended Regular Expressions" on page 834.

The first two items in the following list (^ and $) always have their special meanings within a search string unless you quote them by preceding them with a backslash (\). You can turn off the special meanings within a search string for the rest of the items in the list by setting the **nomagic** parameter. See "Allow special characters in searches" (page 177) for more information.

^ BEGINNING-OF-LINE INDICATOR

When the first character in a search string is a caret (also called a circumflex) it matches the beginning of a line. For example, the command **/^the** finds the next line that begins with the string **the**.

$ END-OF-LINE INDICATOR

A dollar sign matches the end of a line. For example, the command /!$ finds the next line that ends with an exclamation point and / $ matches the next line that ends with a SPACE.

.   ANY-CHARACTER INDICATOR

A period matches *any* character, anywhere in the search string. For example, the command /l..e finds **line, followed, like, included, all memory,** or any other word or character string that contains an l followed by any two characters and an e. To search for a period, use a backslash to quote the period (\.).

\>   END-OF-WORD INDICATOR

This pair of characters matches the end of a word. For example, the command /s\> finds the next word that ends with an s. Whereas a backslash (\) is typically used to *turn off* the special meaning of a character, the character sequence \> has a special meaning, while > alone does not.

\<   BEGINNING-OF-WORD INDICATOR

This pair of characters matches the beginning of a word. For example, the command /\<The finds the next word that begins with the string **The.** The beginning-of-word indicator uses the backslash in the same, atypical way as the end-of-word indicator.

*   ZERO OR MORE OCCURRENCES

This character is a modifier that will match zero or more occurrences of the character immediately preceding it. For example, the command /dis*m will match the string **di** followed by zero or more s characters followed by an **m.** Examples of successful matches are **dim** or **dism** or **dissm.**

[]   CHARACTER-CLASS DEFINITION

Brackets surrounding two or more characters match any *single* character located between the brackets. For example, the command /dis[ck] finds the next occurrence of *either* **disk** or **disc.**

There are two special characters you can use within a character-class definition. A caret (^) as the first character following the left bracket defines the character class to be *any except the following characters.* A hyphen between two characters indicates a range of characters. Refer to the examples in Table 6-4.

SUBSTITUTING ONE STRING FOR ANOTHER

A Substitute command combines the effects of a Search command and a Change command. That is, it searches for a string (regular expression) just as the / command does, allowing the same special characters discussed in the previous section. When it finds the string or matches the regular expression, the Substitute command

Table 6-4   Search examples

Search string	What it finds
/and	Finds the next occurrence of the string **and**
	Examples: sand and standard slander andiron
/\<and\>	Finds the next occurrence of the word **and**
	Example: and
/^The	Finds the next line that starts with **The**
	Examples:
	The . . .
	There . . .
/^[0-9][0-9])	Finds the next line that starts with a two-digit number followed by a right parenthesis
	Examples:
	77)...
	01)...
	15)...
/\<[adr]	Finds the next word that starts with an **a**, **d**, or **r**
	Examples: apple drive road argument right
/^[A-Za-z]	Finds the next line that starts with an uppercase or lowercase letter
	Examples:
	will not find a line starting with the number 7 . . .
	Dear Mr. Jones . . .
	In the middle of a sentence like this . . .

changes the string or regular expression it matches. The syntax of the Substitute command is

> *:[g][address]s/search-string/replacement-string[/option]*

As with all commands that begin with a colon, vim executes a Substitute command from the status line.

THE SUBSTITUTE ADDRESS

If you do not specify an *address*, Substitute searches only the current line. If you use a single line number as the *address*, Substitute searches that line. If the *address* is two line numbers separated by a comma, Substitute searches those lines and the lines between them. Refer to "Line numbers" on page 178 if you want vim to display line numbers. Wherever a line number is allowed in the address, you may also use an *address*-string enclosed between slashes. The vim editor operates on the next line that the *address*-string matches. When you precede the first slash of the *address*-string with the letter **g** (for global), vim operates on all lines in the file that the *address*-string matches. (This **g** is not the same as the one that goes at the end of the Substitute command to cause multiple replacements on a single line; see "Searching for and Replacing Strings" below).

Within the *address*, a period represents the current line, a dollar sign represents the last line in the Work buffer, and a percent sign represents the entire Work buffer. You can perform *address* arithmetic using plus and minus signs. Table 6-5 shows some examples of *address*es.

Table 6-5   Addresses

Address	Portion of Work buffer addressed
5	Line 5
77,100	Lines 77 through 100 inclusive
1,.	Beginning of Work buffer through current line
.,$	Current line through end of Work buffer
1,$	Entire Work buffer
%	Entire Work buffer
/pine/	The next line containing the word **pine**
g/pine/	All lines containing the word **pine**
.,.+10	Current line through tenth following line (11 lines in all)

SEARCHING FOR AND REPLACING STRINGS

An **s** comes after the *address* in the command syntax, indicating that this is a Substitute command. A delimiter follows the **s**, marking the beginning of the *search-string*. Although the examples in this book use a forward slash, you can use as a delimiter any character that is not a letter, number, blank, or backslash. You must use the same delimiter at the end of the *search-string*.

Next comes the *search-string*. It has the same format as the search string in the **/** command and can include the same special characters (page 165). (The *search-string* is a regular expression; refer to Appendix A for more information.) Another delimiter marks the end of the *search-string* and the beginning of the *replace-string*.

The *replace-string* replaces the text matched by the *search-string*. It should be followed by the delimiter character. You can omit the final delimiter when no option follows the *replace-string*; a final delimiter is required if an option is present.

Several characters have special meanings in the *search-string*, and other characters have special meanings in the *replace-string*. For example, an ampersand (**&**) in the *replace-string* represents the text that was matched by the *search-string*. A backslash in the *replace-string* quotes the character that follows it. Refer to Table 6-6 and Appendix A.

Table 6-6   Search and replace examples

Command	Result
:s/bigger/biggest/	Replaces the first occurrence of the string **bigger** on the current line with **biggest** **Example:** **bigger** $\longrightarrow$ **biggest**
:1,.s/Ch 1/Ch 2/g	Replaces every occurrence of the string **Ch 1**, before or on the current line, with the string **Ch 2** **Examples:** **Ch 1** $\longrightarrow$ **Ch 2** **Ch 12** $\longrightarrow$ **Ch 22**
:1,$s/ten/10/g	Replaces every occurrence of the string **ten** with the string **10** **Examples:** **ten** $\longrightarrow$ **10** **often** $\longrightarrow$ **of10** **tenant** $\longrightarrow$ **10ant**
:g/chapter/s/ten/10/	Replaces the first occurrence of the string **ten** with the string **10** on all lines containing the word **chapter** **Examples:** **chapter ten** $\longrightarrow$ **chapter 10** **chapters will often** $\longrightarrow$ **chapters will of10**
:%s/\<ten\>/10/g	Replaces every occurrence of the word **ten** with the string **10** **Example:** **ten** $\longrightarrow$ **10**
:.,.+10s/every/each/g	Replaces every occurrence of the string **every** with the string **each** on the current line through the tenth following line **Examples:** **every** $\longrightarrow$ **each** **everything** $\longrightarrow$ **eachthing**
:s/\<short\>/"&"/	Replaces the word **short** on the current line with **"short"** (enclosed within quotation marks) **Example:** **the shortest of the short** $\longrightarrow$ **the shortest of the "short"**

Normally, the Substitute command replaces only the first occurrence of any text that matches the *search-string* on a line. If you want a global substitution—that is, if you want to replace all matching occurrences of text on a line—append the **g** (global) option after the delimiter that ends the *replace-string*. Another useful option, **c** (check), causes vim to ask whether you would like to make the change each time it finds text that matches the *search-string*. Pressing y replaces the *search-string*, **q** terminates the command, **l** (last) makes the replacement and quits, **a** (all) makes all remaining replacements, and **n** continues the search without making that replacement.

The *address*-string need not be the same as the *search-string*. For example,

```
:/candle/s/wick/flame/
```

substitutes **flame** for the first occurrence of **wick** on the next line that contains the string **candle**. Similarly,

```
:g/candle/s/wick/flame/
```

performs the same substitution for the first occurrence of **wick** on each line of the file containing the string **candle** and

```
:g/candle/s/wick/flame/g
```

performs the same substitution for all occurrences of **wick** on each line that contains the string **candle**.

If the *search-string* is the same as the *address*, you can leave the *search-string* blank. For example, the command **:/candle/s//lamp/** is equivalent to the command **:/candle/s/candle/lamp/**.

MISCELLANEOUS COMMANDS

This section describes three commands that do not fit naturally into any other groups.

JOIN

Join (J)   The **J** (Join) command joins the line below the current line to the end of the current line, inserting a SPACE between what was previously two lines and leaving the cursor on this SPACE. If the current line ends with a period, vim inserts two SPACEs.

You can always "unjoin" (break) a line into two lines by replacing the SPACE or SPACEs where you want to break the line with a RETURN.

STATUS

Status (CONTROL-G) The Status command, CONTROL-G, displays the name of the file you are editing, information about whether the file has been modified, the total number of lines in the Work buffer, the percentage of the Work buffer preceding the current line, and the number of the line and character the cursor is on. You can also use :f to display status information. Following is a sample status line:

```
"termcap" 17103 lines --3%--                          569,1            3%
```

. (PERIOD)

. The . (period) command repeats the most recent command that made a change. If you had just given a **d2w** command (delete the next two words), for example, the . command would delete the next two words. If you had just inserted text, the . command would repeat the insertion of the same text. This command is useful if you want to change some occurrences of a word or phrase in the Work buffer. Search for the first occurrence of the word (use **/**) and then make the change you want (use **cw**). You can then use **n** to search for the next occurrence of the word and . to make the same change to it. If you do not want to make the change, use **n** again to find the next occurrence.

YANK, PUT, AND DELETE COMMANDS

The vim editor has a General-Purpose buffer and 26 Named buffers that can hold text during an editing session. These buffers are useful if you want to move or copy a portion of text to another location in the Work buffer. A combination of the Delete and Put commands removes text from one location in the Work buffer and places it in another location in the Work buffer. The Yank and Put commands copy text to another location in the Work buffer, without changing the original text.

THE GENERAL-PURPOSE BUFFER

The vim editor stores the text that you most recently changed, deleted, or yanked in the General-Purpose buffer. The Undo command retrieves text from the General-Purpose buffer when it restores text.

COPYING TEXT TO THE BUFFER

Yank (**y/Y**) The Yank command (**y**) is identical to the Delete (**d**) command except that it does not delete text from the Work buffer. The vim editor places a *copy* of the yanked text in the General-Purpose buffer. You can then use a Put command to place another copy of it elsewhere in the Work buffer. Use the Yank command just as you use the Delete command. The uppercase **Y** command yanks an entire line into the General-Purpose buffer.

Use yy to yank one line

tip Just as **d** RETURN deletes two lines, so **y** RETURN yanks two lines. Use the **yy** command to yank and **dd** to delete the current line.

D works differently from Y

tip The **D** command (page 160) does not work in the same manner as the **Y** command. Whereas **D** deletes to the end of the line, **Y** yanks the entire line regardless of the cursor position.

COPYING TEXT FROM THE BUFFER

Put (**p/P**) The Put commands, **p** and **P**, copy text from the General-Purpose buffer to the Work buffer. If you delete or yank characters or words into the General-Purpose buffer, **p** inserts them after the current *character,* and **P** inserts them before this character. If you delete or yank lines, sentences, or paragraphs, **P** inserts the contents of the General-Purpose buffer before the *line* the cursor is on, and **p** inserts them after this line.

Put commands do not destroy the contents of the General-Purpose buffer. Thus you can place the same text at several points within the file by using one Delete or Yank command and several Put commands.

DELETING TEXT COPIES IT INTO THE BUFFER

Any of the Delete commands described earlier in this chapter (page 160) place the deleted text in the General-Purpose buffer. Just as you can use the Undo command to put the deleted text back where it came from, so you can use a Put command to put the deleted text at another location in the Work buffer.

For example, if you delete a word from the middle of a sentence by using the **dw** command and then move the cursor to a SPACE between two words and give a **p** command, vim places the word you just deleted at the new location. If you delete a line using the **dd** command and then move the cursor to the line *below* the line where you want the deleted line to appear and give a **P** command, vim places the line at the new location.

optional

NAMED BUFFERS

You can use a Named buffer with any of the Delete, Yank, or Put commands. Each of the 26 Named buffers is named by a letter of the alphabet. Each Named buffer can store a different block of text so that you can recall each block as needed. Unlike the General-Purpose buffer, vim does not change the contents of a Named buffer unless you use a command that specifically overwrites that buffer. The vim editor maintains the contents of the Named buffers throughout an editing session.

The vim editor stores text in a Named buffer if you precede a Delete or Yank command with a double quotation mark (") and a buffer name (for example, "kyy yanks a copy of the current line into buffer k). You can use a Named buffer in two ways. First, if you give the name of the buffer as a lowercase letter, vim overwrites the contents of the buffer when it deletes or yanks text into the buffer. Second, if you use an uppercase letter for the buffer name, vim appends the newly deleted or yanked text to the end of the buffer. This feature enables you to collect blocks of text from various sections of a file and deposit them at one place in the file with a single command. Named buffers are also useful when you are moving a section of a file and do not want to use a Put command immediately after the corresponding Delete command, and when you want to insert a paragraph, sentence, or phrase repeatedly in a document.

If you have one sentence that you use throughout a document, you can yank that sentence into a Named buffer and put it wherever you need it by using the following procedure: After entering the first occurrence of the sentence and pressing ESCAPE to return to Command mode, leave the cursor on the line containing the sentence. (The sentence must appear on a line or lines by itself for this procedure to work.) Then yank the sentence into Named buffer **a** by giving the "ayy command (or "a2yy if the sentence takes up two lines). Now anytime you need the sentence, you can return to Command mode and give the command "ap to put a copy of the sentence below the line the cursor is on.

This technique provides a quick and easy way to insert text that you use frequently in a document. For example, if you were editing a legal document, you might store the phrase **The Plaintiff alleges that the Defendant** in a Named buffer to save yourself the trouble of typing it every time you want to use it. Similarly, if you were creating a letter that frequently used a long company name, such as **National Standards Institute**, you might put it into a Named buffer.

NUMBERED BUFFERS

In addition to the 26 Named buffers and 1 General-Purpose buffer, 9 Numbered buffers are available. They are, in one sense, readonly buffers. The vim editor fills them with the nine most recently deleted chunks of text that are at least one line long. The most recently deleted pattern is held in "1, the next most recent in "2, and so on. If you delete a block of text and then give other vim commands so that you cannot reclaim the deleted text with Undo, use "1p to paste the most recently deleted chunk of text below the location of the cursor. If you have deleted several blocks of text and want to reclaim a specific one, proceed as follows: Paste the contents of the first buffer with "1p. If the first buffer does not have the text you are looking for, undo the paste with **u** and then give the period (.) command to repeat the previous command. The Numbered buffers work in a unique way with the period command: Instead of pasting the contents of buffer "1, the period command pastes the contents of the next buffer ("2). Another **u** and period replace the contents of buffer "2 with that of buffer "3, and so on through the nine buffers.

READING AND WRITING FILES

Exit (**ZZ**)   The vim editor reads a disk file into the Work buffer when you specify a filename on the command line you use to call vim. The **ZZ** command that terminates the editing session writes the contents of the Work buffer back to the disk file. This section discusses other ways of reading text into the Work buffer and writing it to a file.

READING FILES

Read (**:r**)   The Read command reads a file into the Work buffer. The new file does not overwrite any text in the Work buffer but rather is positioned following the single address you specify (or the current line if you do not specify an address). You can use an address of 0 to read the file into the beginning of the Work buffer. The Read command has the following syntax:

> :*[address]r [filename]*

As with other commands that begin with a colon, when you enter the colon it appears on the status line. The *filename* is the pathname of the file that you want to read and must be terminated by RETURN. If you omit the *filename*, vim reads the file you are editing from the disk.

WRITING FILES

Write (**:w**)   The Write command writes part or all of the Work buffer to a file. You can use an address to write out part of the Work buffer and a filename to specify a file to receive the text. If you do not use an address or filename, vim writes the entire contents of the Work buffer to the file you are editing, updating the file on the disk.

During a long editing session, it is a good idea to use the Write command occasionally. If a problem later develops, a recent copy of the Work buffer is then safe on the disk. If you use a **:q!** command to exit from vim, the disk file reflects the version of the Work buffer at the time you last used the Write command. The Write command has two possible formats:

> :*[address]w[!] [filename]*
> :*[address]w>> filename*

The second format appends text to an existing file. The *address* specifies the portion of the Work buffer vim will write to the file. The *address* follows the form of the *address* that the Substitute command uses (page 167). If you do not specify an *address*, vim writes the entire contents of the Work buffer. The optional *filename* is the pathname of the file you are writing to. If you do not specify a *filename*, vim writes to the file you are editing.

w! Because the Write command can quickly destroy a large amount of work, vim demands that you enter an exclamation point (!) following the **w** as a safeguard against accidentally overwriting a file. The only times you do not need an exclamation point are when you are writing out the entire contents of the Work buffer to the file being edited (using no *address* and no filename) and when you are writing part or all of the Work buffer to a new file. When you are writing part of the file to the file being edited or when you are overwriting another file, you must use an exclamation point.

IDENTIFYING THE CURRENT FILE

The File command (:f) provides the same information as the Status command (CON-TROL-G, page 171). The filename the File command displays is the one the Write command uses if you give a :w command without a filename.

SETTING PARAMETERS

You can tailor the vim editor to your unique needs and habits by setting vim parameters. Parameters perform such functions as displaying line numbers, automatically inserting RETURNs for you, and establishing incremental and nonstandard searches.

You can set parameters in several ways. For example, you can set them to establish the environment for the current editing session while you are using vim. Alternatively, you can set the parameters in your **~/.bash_profile** (bash) or **~/.login** (tcsh) shell startup file or in the vim startup file, **~/.vimrc**. When you set the parameters in any of these files, each time you use vim, the environment has been established and you can begin editing immediately.

SETTING PARAMETERS FROM WITHIN vim

To set a parameter while you are using vim, enter a colon (:), the word **set**, a SPACE, and the parameter (refer to "Parameters" on page 177). The command appears on the status line as you type it and takes effect when you press RETURN. The following command establishes incremental searches for the current editing session:

```
:set incsearch
```

SETTING PARAMETERS IN A STARTUP FILE

VIMINIT   If you are using bash, you can put a line with the following format in your ~/.bash_profile startup file (page 257):

> *export VIMINIT='set param1 param2 ...'*

Replace *param1* and *param2* with parameters selected from Table 6-7. **VIMINIT** is a shell variable that vim reads. The following statement ignores the case of characters in searches, displays line numbers, uses the TC Shell to execute Linux commands, and wraps text 15 characters from the right edge of the screen:

```
export VIMINIT='set autoindent number shell=/bin/tcsh wrapmargin=15'
```

If you use the parameter abbreviations, it looks like this:

```
export VIMINIT='set ai nu sh=/bin/tcsh wm=15'
```

If you are using tcsh, put the following line in your ~/.tcshrc startup file (page 342).

> *setenv VIMINIT 'set param1 param2 ...'*

Again, replace *param1* and *param2* with parameters from Table 6-7. The values between the single quotation marks are the same as shown in the preceding examples.

THE .vimrc STARTUP FILE

Instead of setting vim parameters in your shell startup file, you can create a ~/.vimrc file in your home directory and set them there. Creating a .vimrc file causes vim to start with the **compatible** parameter unset (page 148). Lines in a .vimrc file use the following format:

> *set param1 param2 ...*

Following are examples of .vimrc files that perform the same function as **VIMINIT** described previously:

```
$ cat ~/.vimrc
set ignorecase
set number
set shell=/bin/tcsh
set wrapmargin=15

$ cat ~/.vimrc
set ic nu sh=/bin/tcsh wm=15
```

Parameters set by the **VIMINIT** variable take precedence over those set in the .vimrc file.

PARAMETERS

Table 6-7 lists some of the most useful vim parameters. The vim editor displays a complete list of parameters and indicates how they are currently set when you give the command **:set all** followed by a RETURN. The command **:set** RETURN displays a list of options that are set to values other than their default values. Two classes of parameters exist: those that contain an equal sign (and can take on a value) and those that are optionally prefixed with **no** (switches that are on or off). You can change the sense of a switch parameter by giving the command **:set [no]***param*. For example, give the command **:set number** (or **:set nonumber**) to turn on (or off) line numbering. To change the value of a parameter that takes on a value (and uses an equal sign), give a command such as **:set shiftwidth=15**.

Most parameters have abbreviations such as **nu** for **number, nonu** for no **number,** and **sw** for **shiftwidth**. The abbreviations are listed in the left column of Table 6-7, following the name of the parameter.

Table 6-7 Parameters

Parameter	Effect
Allow special characters in searches **magic**	Refer to "Special Characters in Search Strings" on page 165. By default the following characters have special meanings when used in a search string: . [ ] * When you set the **nomagic** parameter, these characters no longer have special meanings. The **magic** parameter restores their special meanings. The ^ and $ characters always have special meanings within search strings, regardless of how you set this parameter.
Automatic indention **autoindent, ai**	The automatic indention feature works with the **shiftwidth** parameter to provide a regular set of indentions for programs or tabular material. This feature is off by default. You can turn it on by setting **autoindent** and turn it off by setting **noautoindent**. When automatic indention is on and vim is in Input mode, CONTROL-T moves the cursor from the left margin (or an indention) to the next indention position, RETURN moves the cursor to the left side of the next line under the first character of the previous line, and CONTROL-D backs up over indention positions. The CONTROL-T and CONTROL-D keys work only before text is placed on a line.

Table 6-7   Parameters (continued)

Automatic write **autowrite**, **aw**	By default vim asks you before writing out the Work buffer when you have not explicitly told it to do so (as when you give a **:n** command to edit the next file). The **autowrite** option causes vim to write the Work buffer automatically when you use commands, such as **:n**, to edit to another file. You can disable this parameter by setting the **noautowrite** or **noaw** option.
Flash **flash**, **fl**	The vim editor normally causes the terminal to beep when you give an invalid command or press ESCAPE when it is in Command mode. Setting the parameter **flash** causes the terminal to flash instead of beep. Set **noflash** to cause it to beep. Not all terminals and emulators support this parameter.
Ignore case in searches **ignorecase**, **ic**	The vim editor normally performs case-sensitive searches, differentiating between uppercase and lowercase letters. It performs case-insensitive searches when you set the **ignorecase** parameter. Set **noignorecase** to restore case-sensitive searches.
Incremental search **incsearch**, **is**	Refer to "Normal Versus Incremental Searches" on page 165. By default vim does not perform incremental searches. To cause vim to perform incremental searches, set the parameter **incsearch**. To cause vim not to perform incremental searches, set the parameter **noincsearch**.
Invisible characters **list**	To cause vim to display each TAB as **^I** and to mark the end of each line with a **$**, set the **list** parameter. To display TABS as whitespace and not mark ends of lines, set **nolist**.
Status line **laststatus=**n, **ls=**n	Displays a status line that shows the name of the file you are editing, a **[+]** if the file has been changed since it was last written out, and the position of the cursor. Set the parameter **laststatus=**n, where n is **0** (zero) to turn off the status line, **1** to display the status line when at least two windows are displayed, or **2** to always display the status line.
Line numbers **number**, **nu**	The vim editor does not normally display the line number associated with each line. To display line numbers, set the parameter **number**. To cause line numbers not to be displayed, set the parameter **nonumber**. Line numbers are not part of the file, are not stored with the file, and are not displayed when the file is printed. They appear on the screen only while you are using vim.
Line wrap **wrap**	The line wrap controls how vim displays lines that are too long to fit on the screen. To cause vim to wrap long lines and continue them on the next line, set **wrap** (set by default). If you set **nowrap**, vim truncates long lines at the right edge of the screen.

Table 6-7   Parameters (continued)

Line wrap margin **wrapmargin=*nn*, wm=*nn***	The line wrap margin causes vim to break the text that you are inserting at approximately the specified number of characters from the right margin. The vim editor breaks the text by inserting a NEW-LINE character at the closest blank-delimited word boundary. Setting the line wrap margin is handy if you want all your text lines to be about the same length. It relieves you of having to remember to press RETURN to end each line of input. Set the parameter **wrapmargin=*nn***, where *nn* is the number of characters *from the right side of the screen* where you want vim to break the text. This number is not the column width of the text but the distance from the end of the text to the right edge of the screen. Setting the wrap margin to **0** (zero) turns this feature off. By default the line wrap margin is off (set to **0**).
Report **report=*nn***	Causes vim to display a report on the status line whenever you make a change that affects at least *nn* lines. For example, if **report** is set to **7** and you delete seven lines, vim displays the message **7 lines deleted**. When you delete six or fewer lines, vim does not display a message. The default for **report** is **5**.
Scroll **scroll=*nn*, scr=*nn***	Controls the number of lines that CONTROL-D and CONTROL-U (page 158) scroll text on the screen. By default **scroll** is set to half the window height. There are two ways to change the value of **scroll**. First you can enter a number before giving a CONTROL-D or CONTROL-U command; vim sets **scroll** to that number. Alternatively, you can set **scroll** explicitly with **scroll=*nn***, where *nn* is the number of lines you want to scroll with each CONTROL-D or CONTROL-U command.
Shell **shell=*path*, sh=*path***	While you are using vim, you can cause it to spawn a new shell. You can either create an interactive shell (if you want to run several commands) or run a single command. The **shell** parameter determines which shell vim invokes. By default vim sets the **shell** parameter to your login shell. To change it, set the parameter **shell=*path***, where ***path*** is the absolute pathname of the shell you want to use.
Shift width **shiftwidth=*nn*, sw=*nn***	Controls the functioning of CONTROL-T and CONTROL-D in Input mode when automatic indention is on (see "Automatic indention" in this table). Set the parameter **shiftwidth=*nn***, where *nn* is the spacing of the indention positions (**8** by default). Setting the shift width is similar to setting the TAB stops on a typewriter; with **shiftwidth**, however, the distance between TAB stops remains constant.

Table 6-7   Parameters (continued)

Show match **showmatch**, **sm**	Useful for programmers working in languages that use braces ({ }) or parentheses as expression delimiters (Lisp, C, Tcl, and so on). When **showmatch** is set and you are entering code (in Input mode) and type a closing brace or parenthesis, the cursor jumps briefly to the matching opening brace or parenthesis (that is, the preceding corresponding element at the same nesting level). After it highlights the matching element, the cursor resumes its previous position. When you type a right brace or parenthesis that does not have a match, vim beeps. Use **noshowmatch** to turn off automatic matching.
Show mode **showmode**, **smd**	Set the parameter **showmode** to display the mode in the lower-right corner of the screen when vim is in Input mode (default). Set **noshowmode** to cause vim not to display the mode.
vi compatibility **compatible**, **cp**	Refer to "The compatible Parameter" on page 148. By default, except when you have a **.vimrc** startup file (page 176), vim attempts to be compatible with vi. To cause vim to be compatible with vi, set the parameter **compatible**. To cause vim not to be compatible with vi, set the parameter **nocompatible**.
Wrap scan **wrapscan**, **ws**	By default, when a search for the next occurrence of a search string reaches the end of the Work buffer, vim continues the search at the beginning of the Work buffer. The reverse is true of a search for the previous occurrence of a search string. The **nowrapscan** parameter stops the search at either end of the Work buffer. Set the **wrapscan** parameter if you want searches to wrap around the ends of the Work buffer.

ADVANCED EDITING TECHNIQUES

This section presents several commands that you may find useful once you have become comfortable using vim.

optional

USING MARKERS

While you are using vim, you can set and use markers to make addressing more convenient. Set a marker by giving the command **m**c, where *c* is any character. (Letters are preferred because some characters, such as a single quotation mark, have special meanings when used as markers.) The vim editor does not preserve markers when you exit from vim.

Once you have set a marker, you can use it in a manner similar to a line number. You can move the cursor to the beginning of a line that contains a marker by preceding the marker name with a single quotation mark. For example, to set marker **t**, position the cursor on the line you want to mark and give the command **mt**. During this editing session, unless you reset marker **t** or delete the line it marks, you can return to the beginning of the line you marked with the command **'t**.

You can delete all text from the current line through the line containing marker **r** with the following command:

    d'r

You can use a back tick (**'**, also called a grave accent or reverse single quotation mark) to go to the exact position of the mark on the line. After setting marker **t**, you can move the cursor to the location of this marker (not the beginning of the line that holds the marker) with the command **'t**. The following command deletes all the text from the current line up to the character where the mark **r** was placed; the rest of the line containing the marker remains intact:

    d'r

You can use markers in addresses of commands instead of line numbers. The following command replaces all occurrences of **The** with **THE** on all lines from marker **m** to the current line (marker **m** must precede the current line):

    :'m,.s/The/THE/g

EDITING OTHER FILES

The following command causes vim to edit the file you specify with *filename*:

    :e[!] [filename]

If you want to save the contents of the Work buffer, you must write it out (using **:w**) before you give this command. If you do not want to save the contents of the Work buffer, vim insists that you use an exclamation point to acknowledge that you will lose the work you did since the last time you wrote out the Work buffer. If you do not supply a *filename*, vim edits the same file you are currently working on.

:e! The command **:e!** starts an editing session over again. This command returns the Work buffer to the state it was in the last time you wrote it out or, if you have not written it out, the state it was in when you started editing the file. It is useful when you make mistakes while editing a file and decide that it would be easier to start over than to fix the mistakes.

Because this command does not destroy the contents of the General-Purpose or Named buffers, you can store text from one file in a buffer, use a **:e** command to edit a second file, and put text from the buffer in the second file.

:e#   The command **:e#** closes the current file and opens the last file you were editing, placing the cursor on the line that it was on when you last closed the file. If you do not save the file you are working on before you give this command, vim prompts you to do so. Setting the **autowrite** parameter (page 178) will not stop vim from prompting you.

:n
:rew   The **:e#** command can help you copy blocks of text from one file to another. Call vim with the names of several files as arguments. You can use **:n** to edit the next file, **:e#** to edit the file you just edited, and **:rew** to rewind the sequence of files so that you are editing the first file again. As you move between files, you can copy text from one file into a buffer and paste that text into another file. You can use **:n!** to force vim to close a file without writing out changes before it opens the next file.

MACROS AND SHORTCUTS

:map   The vim editor allows you to create macros and shortcuts. The **:map** command defines a key or sequence of keys that perform some action in Command mode. The following command maps CONTROL-X to the commands that will find the next left bracket on the line the cursor is on (**f[**), delete all characters from that bracket to the next right bracket (**df]**) on the same line, delete the next character (**x**), move the cursor down two lines (**2j**), and finally move the cursor to the beginning of the line (**0**):

```
:map ^X f[df]x2j0
```

You can use ESCAPE and CONTROL sequences but try to avoid remapping characters or sequences that are vim commands. Type **:map** by itself to see a list of the current mappings. You may need to use CONTROL-V (page 159) to quote some of the characters you want to enter into the **:map** string.

:abbrev   The **:abbrev** command is similar to **:map** but creates abbreviations you can use while in Input mode. When you are in Input mode and type a string you have defined with **:abbrev**, followed by a SPACE, vim replaces the string and the SPACE with the characters you specified when you defined the string. For ease of use, do not use common sequences of characters when creating abbreviations. The following command defines **ZZ** as an abbreviation for **Mark G. Sobell**:

```
:abbrev ZZ Mark G. Sobell
```

Even though **ZZ** is a vim command, it is used only in Command mode. It has no special meaning in Input mode, where you use abbreviations.

EXECUTING SHELL COMMANDS FROM WITHIN vim

You can execute shell commands in several ways while you are using vim. You can spawn a new interactive shell by giving the following command and pressing RETURN:

```
:sh
```

The vim **shell** parameter (page 179) determines which shell is spawned (usually bash or tcsh). By default **shell** is the same as your login shell.

After you have finished your work in the shell, you can return to vim by exiting from the shell (press CONTROL-D or give an **exit** command).

If :sh does not work correctly

tip   The **:sh** command may behave strangely depending on how your shell has been configured. You may get warnings with the **:sh** command or it may even hang. Experiment with the **:sh** command to be sure it works with your configuration. If it does not, then you might want to set the vim **shell** parameter to another shell before using **:sh**. For example, the following command causes vim to use tcsh with the **:sh** command:

```
:set shell=/bin/tcsh
```

You may need to change the **SHELL** environment variable after starting **:sh** to show the correct shell.

Edit only one copy of a file

caution   When you create a new shell by using **:sh**, remember that you are still using vim. A common mistake is to try to edit the same file from the new shell, forgetting that vim is already editing the file from a different shell. Because you can lose information by editing the same file from two instances of an editor, vim warns you when you make this mistake. Refer to "File Locks" on page 152 to see an example of the message that vim displays.

You can execute a shell command line from vim by giving the following command, replacing *command* with the command line you want to execute and terminating the command with a RETURN:

> :!*command*

The vim editor spawns a new shell that executes the *command*. When the *command* runs to completion, the newly spawned shell returns control to the editor.

You can execute a command from vim and have it replace the current line with the output from the command. If you do not want to replace any text, put the cursor on a blank line before giving the following command:

> !!*command*

Nothing happens when you enter the first exclamation point. When you enter the second one, vim moves the cursor to the status line and allows you to enter the command you want to execute. Because this command puts vim in Last Line mode, you must end the command with a RETURN (as you would end most shell commands).

Finally you can execute a command from vim with standard input to the command coming from all or part of the file you are editing and standard output from the command replacing the input in the file you are editing. You can use this type of command to sort a list in place within a file.

To specify the block of text that will become standard input for the command, move the cursor to one end of the block of text. Then enter an exclamation point followed by a command that would normally move the cursor to the other end of the block of text. For example, if the cursor is at the beginning of the file and you want to specify the whole file, give the command **!G**. If you want to specify the part of the file between the cursor and marker **b**, give the command **! ' b**. After you give the cursor-movement command, vim displays an exclamation point on the status line and waits for you to enter a shell command.

To sort a list of names in a file, move the cursor to the beginning of the list and set marker **q** with an **mq** command. Then move the cursor to the end of the list and give the following command:

```
! ' sort
```

Press RETURN and wait. After a few seconds, the sorted list should replace the original list on the screen. If the command did not do what you expected, you can usually undo the change with a **u** command. Refer to page 762 for more information on sort.

! can destroy a file

caution   If you enter the wrong command or mistype a command, you can destroy a file (for example, if the command hangs or stops vim from working). For this reason it is a good idea to save your file before using this command. The Undo command (page 160) can be a lifesaver. A **:e!** command (page 181) will get rid of your changes, returning the buffer to the state it was in last time you saved it.

As with the **:sh** command, the default shell may not work properly with the **!** command. You may want to test the shell with a simple file before executing this command with your real work. If the usual shell does not work properly, change the **shell** parameter.

UNITS OF MEASURE

Many vim commands operate on a block of text—ranging from one character to many paragraphs. You specify the size of a block of text with a *Unit of Measure*. You can specify multiple Units of Measure by preceding a Unit of Measure with a Repeat Factor (page 187). This section defines the various Units of Measure.

CHARACTER

A character is one character—visible or not, printable or not—including SPACEs and TABs. Some examples of characters are

```
a  q  A  .  5  R  -  >  TAB SPACE
```

WORD

A word, similar to an ordinary word in the English language, is a string of one or more characters bounded on both sides by any combination of one or more of the following elements: a punctuation mark, SPACE, TAB, numeral, or NEWLINE. In addition, vim considers each group of punctuation marks to be a word (Table 6-8).

Table 6-8   Words

Word count	Text
1	pear
2	pear!
2	pear!)
3	pear!) The
4	pear!) "The
11	This is a short, concise line (no frills).

BLANK-DELIMITED WORD

A blank-delimited word is the same as a word but includes adjacent punctuation. Blank-delimited words are separated by one or more of the following elements: a SPACE, TAB, or NEWLINE (Table 6-9).

Table 6-9   Blank-delimited words

Word count	Text
1	pear
1	pear!
1	pear!)
2	pear!) The
2	pear!) "The
8	This is a short, concise line (no frills).

LINE

A line is a string of characters bounded by NEWLINEs that is not necessarily displayed as a single physical line on the screen. You can enter a very long single (logical) line that wraps around (continues on the next physical line) several times or disappears off the right edge of the display. It is a good idea to avoid long logical lines by terminating lines with a RETURN before they reach the right side of the screen. Terminating lines in this manner ensures that each physical line contains one logical line and avoids confusion when you edit and format text. Some commands do not *appear* to work properly on physical lines that are longer than the width of the screen. For example, with the cursor on a long logical line that wraps around several physical lines, pressing RETURN once appears to move the cursor down more than one line. You can use fmt (page 664) to break long logical lines into shorter ones.

SENTENCE

A sentence is an English sentence or the equivalent. A sentence starts at the end of the previous sentence and ends with a period, exclamation point, or question mark, followed by two SPACEs or a NEWLINE (Table 6-10).

Table 6-10 Sentences

Sentence count	Text
One: only one SPACE after the first period and a NEWLINE after the second period	That's it. This is one sentence.
Two: two SPACEs after the first period and a NEWLINE after the second period	That's it. This is two sentences.
Three: two SPACEs after the first two question marks and a NEWLINE after the exclamation point	What? Three sentences? One line!
One: NEWLINE after the period	This sentence takes up a total of three lines.

PARAGRAPH

A paragraph is preceded and followed by one or more blank lines. A blank line is composed of two NEWLINE characters in a row (Table 6-11).

Table 6-11 Paragraphs

Paragraph count	Text
| *One:* blank line before and after text | ```
One paragraph
``` |
| *One:* blank line before and after text | ```
          This may appear to be
more than one paragraph.
          Just because there are
two indentions does not mean
it qualifies as two paragraphs.
``` |
| *Three:* three blocks of text separated by blank lines | ```
Even though in

English this is only
one sentence,

vim considers it to be
three paragraphs.
``` |

WINDOW

Under vim, a screen or terminal emulator window can display one or more logical windows of information. A window displays all or part of a Work buffer. Figure 6-5 on page 145 shows a screen with two windows.

REPEAT FACTOR

A number that precedes a Unit of Measure (page 184) is a Repeat Factor. Just as the *5* in *5 inches* causes you to consider *5 inches* as a single Unit of Measure, so a Repeat Factor causes vim to group more than one Unit of Measure and consider it as a single Unit of Measure. For example, the command **w** moves the cursor forward 1 word, the command **5w** moves it forward 5 words, and the command **250w** moves it forward 250 words. If you do not specify a Repeat Factor, vim assumes a Repeat Factor of 1. If the Repeat Factor would move the cursor past the end of the file, the cursor is left at the end of the file.
```

CHAPTER SUMMARY

This summary of vim includes all the commands covered in this chapter, plus a few more. Table 6-12 lists some of the ways you can call vim from the command line.

Table 6-12   Calling vim

Command	Result
vim *filename*	Edits *filename* starting at line 1
vim +*n filename*	Edits *filename* starting at line *n*
vim + *filename*	Edits *filename* starting at the last line
vim +/*pattern filename*	Edits *filename* starting at the first line containing *pattern*
vim –r *filename*	Recovers *filename* after a system crash
vim –R *filename*	Edits *filename* readonly (same as opening the file with **view**)

You must be in Command mode to use commands that move the cursor by Units of Measure (Table 6-13). You can use these Units of Measure with Change, Delete, and Yank commands. Each of these commands can be preceded by a Repeat Factor.

Table 6-13   Moving the cursor by Units of Measure

Command	Moves the cursor
SPACE, **l** (ell), *or* RIGHT ARROW	Space to the right
h *or* LEFT ARROW	Space to the left
w	Word to the right
W	Blank-delimited word to the right
b	Word to the left
B	Blank-delimited word to the left
$	End of line
e	End of word to the right
E	End of blank-delimited word to the right
0 (zero)	Beginning of line (cannot be used with a Repeat Factor)
RETURN	Beginning of next line
j *or* DOWN ARROW	Down one line

Table 6-13 Moving the cursor by Units of Measure (continued)

−	Beginning of previous line
k *or* UP ARROW	Up one line
)	End of sentence
(	Beginning of sentence
}	End of paragraph
{	Beginning of paragraph
%	Move to matching brace of same type at same nesting level

Table 6-14 shows the commands that enable you to view different parts of the Work buffer.

Table 6-14 Viewing the Work buffer

Command	Moves the cursor
CONTROL-D	Forward one-half window
CONTROL-U	Backward one-half window
CONTROL-F *or* PAGE DOWN	Forward one window
CONTROL-B *or* PAGE UP	Backward one window
*n*G	To line *n* (without *n*, to the last line)
H	To top of window
M	To middle of window
L	To bottom of window

The commands in Table 6-15 enable you to add text to the buffer. All these commands, except **r**, leave vim in Input mode. You must press ESCAPE to return to Command mode.

Table 6-15 Adding text

Command	Adds text
i	Before cursor
I	Before first nonblank character on line
a	After cursor
A	At end of line

Table 6-15   Adding text (continued)

o	Open a line below current line
O	Open a line above current line
r	Replace current character (no ESCAPE needed)
R	Replace characters, starting with current character (overwrite until ESCAPE)

Table 6-16 lists commands that delete and change text. In this table *M* is a Unit of Measure that you can precede with a Repeat Factor, *n* is an optional Repeat Factor, and *c* is any character.

Table 6-16   Deleting and changing text

Command	Result
*n*x	Deletes the number of characters specified by *n*, starting with the current character
*n*X	Deletes *n* characters before the current character, starting with the character preceding the current character
d*M*	Deletes text specified by *M*
*n*dd	Deletes *n* lines
dt*c*	Deletes to the next character *c* on the current line
D	Deletes to end of the line
n~	Change case of the next *n* characters

The following commands leave vim in Input mode. You must press ESCAPE to return to Command mode.

*n*s	Substitutes *n* characters
S	Substitutes for the entire line
c*M*	Changes text specified by *M*
*n*cc	Changes *n* lines
ct*c*	Changes to the next character *c* on the current line
C	Changes to end of line

Table 6-17 lists search commands. Here **rexp** is a regular expression that can be a simple string of characters.

Table 6-17   Searching

Command	Result
/*rexp*RETURN	Searches forward for **rexp**
?*rexp* RETURN	Searches backward for **rexp**
n	Repeats original search exactly
N	Repeats original search, in the opposite direction
/RETURN	Repeats original search forward
?RETURN	Repeats original search backward
f*c*	Positions the cursor on the next character **c** on the current line
F*c*	Positions the cursor on the previous character **c** on the current line
t*c*	Positions the cursor on the character before (to the left of) the next character **c** on the current line
T*c*	Positions the cursor on the character after (to the right of) the previous character **c** on the current line
;	Repeats the last **f**, **F**, **t**, or **T** command

The format of a Substitute command is

:*[address]*s/*search-string*/*replacement-string*[/g]

where *address* is one line number or two line numbers separated by a comma. A
. (period) represents the current line, $ represents the last line, and % represents the
entire file. You can use a marker or a search string in place of a line number. The
search-string is a regular expression that can be a simple string of characters.
The *replacement-string* is the replacement string. A **g** indicates a global replacement
(more than one replacement per line).

Table 6-18 lists miscellaneous vim commands.

Table 6-18   Miscellaneous commands

Command	Result
J	Joins the current line and the following line
.	Repeats the most recent command that made a change
:w *filename*	Writes contents of Work buffer to **filename** (or to current file if there is no **filename**)
:q	Quits vim
ZZ	Writes contents of Work buffer to the current file and quits vim
:f *or* CONTROL-G	Displays the filename, status, current line number, number of lines in the Work buffer, and percentage of the Work buffer preceding the current line
CONTROL-V	Inserts the next character literally even if it is a vim command (use in Input mode)

Table 6-19 lists commands that yank and put text. In this table *M* is a Unit of Measure that you can precede with a Repeat Factor and *n* is a Repeat Factor. You can precede any of these commands with the name of a buffer using the form "*x*, where *x* is the name of the buffer (a–z).

Table 6-19   Yanking and putting text

Command	Result
y*M*	Yanks text specified by *M*
*n*yy	Yanks *n* lines
Y	Yanks to end of line
P	Puts text before or above
p	Puts text after or below

Table 6-20 lists advanced vim commands.

Table 6-20   Advanced commands

Command	Result
m*x*	Sets marker *x*, where *x* is a letter from **a** to **z**.
' ' (two single quotation marks)	Moves cursor back to its previous location.
' *x*	Moves cursor to line with marker *x*.
` *x*	Moves cursor to character with marker *x*.
:e *filename*	Edits *filename*, requiring you to write out changes to the current file (with **:w** or **autowrite**) before editing the new file. Use **:e!** *filename* to discard changes to the current file. Use **:e!** without a filename to discard changes to the current file and start editing the saved version of the current file.
:n	Edits the next file when **vim** is started with multiple filename arguments. Requires you to write out changes to the current file (with **:w** or **autowrite**) before editing the next file. Use **:n!** to discard changes to the current file and edit the next file.
:rew	Rewinds the filename list when **vim** is started with multiple filename arguments and starts editing with the first file. Requires you to write out changes to the current file (with **:w** or **autowrite**) before editing the first file. Use **:rew!** to discard changes to the current file and edit the first file.
:sh	Starts a shell. Exit from the shell to return to vim.
:!*command*	Starts a shell and executes *command*.
!!*command*	Starts a shell, executes *command*, and places output in the Work buffer, replacing the current line.

EXERCISES

1. How can you cause vim to enter Input mode? How can you make vim revert to Command mode?

2. What is the Work buffer? Name two ways of writing the contents of the Work buffer to the disk.

3. Suppose that you are editing a file that contains the following paragraph and the cursor is on the second tilde (~):

   ```
   The vim editor has a command, tilde (~),
   that changes lowercase letters to
   uppercase, and vice versa.
   The ~ command works with a Unit of Measure or
   a Repeat Factor, so you can change
   the case of more than one character at a time.
   ```

   How can you

   a. Move the cursor to the end of the paragraph?

   b. Move the cursor to the beginning of the word **Unit**?

   c. Change the word **character** to **letter**?

4. While working in vim, with the cursor positioned on the first letter of a word, you give the command **x** followed by **p**. Explain what happens.

5. What are the differences between the following commands?

   a. **i** and **I**

   b. **a** and **A**

   c. **o** and **O**

   d. **r** and **R**

   e. **u** and **U**

6. Which command would you use to search backward through the Work buffer for lines that start with the word **it**?

7. Which command substitutes all occurrences of the phrase **this week** with the phrase **next week**?

8. Consider the following scenario: You start vim to edit an existing file. You make many changes to the file and then realize that you deleted a critical section of the file early in your editing session. You want to get that section back but do not want to lose all the other changes you made. What would you do?

9. How can you move the line that the cursor is on to the beginning of the file?

10. Use vim to create the **letter_e** file of e's used on page 56. Use as few vim commands as possible. Which vim commands did you use?

ADVANCED EXERCISES

11. Which commands can you use to take a paragraph from one file and insert it in a second file?

12. Create a file that contains the following list, and then execute commands from within vim to sort the list and display it in two columns. (*Hint:* Refer to page 744 for more information on pr.)

```
Command mode
Input mode
Last Line mode
Work buffer
General-Purpose buffer
Named buffer
Regular Expression
Search String
Replacement String
Startup File
Repeat Factor
```

13. How do the Named buffers differ from the General-Purpose buffer?

14. Assume that your version of vim does not support multiple Undo commands. If you delete a line of text, then delete a second line, and then a third line, which commands would you use to recover the first two lines that you deleted?

15. Which command would you use to swap the words **hither** and **yon** on any line with any number of words between them? (You need not worry about special punctuation, just uppercase and lowercase letters and spaces.)

7

THE emacs EDITOR

In 1956 the Lisp (List processing) language was developed at MIT by John McCarthy. In its original conception, Lisp had only a few scalar (*atomic*) data types and only one *data structure* (page 870): a list. Lists could contain atomic data or perhaps other lists. Lisp supported recursion and nonnumeric data (exciting concepts in those FORTRAN and COBOL days) and, in the Cambridge culture at least, was once the favored implementation language. Richard Stallman and Guy Steele were part of this MIT Lisp culture. In 1975 they collaborated on emacs, which Stallman maintained by himself for a long time. This chapter discusses the emacs editor as implemented by the Free Software Foundation (GNU). The emacs home page is www.gnu.org/software/emacs.

HISTORY

The emacs editor was prototyped as a series of extension commands or macros for the late 1960s text editor TECO (Text Editor and COrrector). Its acronymic name, Editor MACroS, reflects this origin, although there have been many humorous reinterpretations, including ESCAPE META ALT CONTROL SHIFT, Emacs Makes All Computing Simple, and the unkind translation Eight Megabytes And Constantly Swapping.

EVOLUTION

Over time emacs has grown and evolved through more than 20 major revisions to the mainstream GNU version. The emacs editor, which is coded in C, contains a complete Lisp interpreter and fully supports the X Window System and mouse interaction. The original TECO macros are long gone, but emacs is still very much a work in progress. There are plans to support variable-width fonts, wide character sets, and the world's major languages as well as to move emacs in the direction of a WYSIWYG (what you see is what you get) word processor and make it easier for beginners to use.

The emacs editor has always been considerably more than a text editor. Not having been developed originally in a UNIX environment, it does not adhere to the UNIX/Linux philosophy. Whereas a UNIX/Linux utility is typically designed to do one thing and to be used in conjunction with other utilities, emacs is designed to "do it all." Taking advantage of the underlying programming language (Lisp), emacs users tend to customize and extend the editor rather than to use existing utilities or create new general-purpose tools. Instead they share their ~/.emacs (customization) files.

Well before the emergence of the X Window System, Stallman put a great deal of thought and effort into designing a window-oriented work environment, and he used emacs as his research vehicle. Over time he built facilities within emacs for reading and composing email messages, reading and posting netnews, giving shell commands, compiling programs and analyzing error messages, running and debugging these programs, and playing games. Eventually it became possible to enter the emacs environment and not come out all day, switching from window to window and from file to file. If you had only an ordinary serial, character-based terminal, emacs gave you tremendous leverage.

In an X Window System environment, emacs does not need to control the whole display. Instead, it usually operates only one or two windows. The original work environment is still available and is covered in this chapter.

As a *language-sensitive* editor, emacs has special features that you can turn on to help edit text, nroff, TeX, Lisp, C, Fortran, and so on. These feature sets are called *modes,* but they are not related in any way to the Command mode and Input mode found in vi, vim, and other editors. Because you never need to switch emacs between Input and Command modes, emacs is a *modeless* editor.

emacs VERSUS vim

Like vim, emacs is a display editor: It displays on the screen the text you are editing and changes the display as you type each command or insert new text. Unlike vim, emacs does not require you to keep track of whether you are in Command mode or Insert mode: Commands always use CONTROL or other special keys. The emacs editor inserts ordinary characters into the text you are editing (as opposed to using ordinary characters as commands), another trait of modeless editing. For many people this approach is convenient and natural.

Like vim, emacs has a rich, extensive command set for moving about in the buffer and altering text. This command set is not "cast in concrete"—you can change or customize commands at any time. Literally any key can be coupled (*bound*) to any command so as to match a particular keyboard better or just to fulfill a personal whim. Usually key bindings are set in the **.emacs** startup file, but they can also be changed interactively during a session. All the key bindings described in this chapter are standard on current GNU emacs versions, which also support many visual, mouse-oriented capabilities that are not covered here.

Too many key bindings

caution If you change too many key bindings, you may produce a command set that you will not remember or that will make it impossible for you to get back to the standard bindings again in the same session.

Finally, and *very* unlike vim, emacs allows you to use Lisp to write new commands or override old ones. Stallman calls this feature *online extensibility*, but it would take a gutsy Lisp guru to write and debug a new command while editing live text. It is much more common to add a few extra debugged commands to the **.emacs** file, where they are loaded when emacs starts up. Experienced emacs users often write modes, or environments, that are conditionally loaded by emacs for specific tasks.

The screen and emacs windows

tip In this chapter, the term *screen* denotes a character-based terminal screen or a terminal emulator window in a graphical environment. The term *window* refers to an emacs window within a screen.

emacs and the X Window System

tip With version 19, GNU emacs fully embraced the X Window System environment. If you start emacs from a terminal emulator window running in a graphical environment, you will bring up the X (GUI) interface to emacs. This book does not cover the graphical interface; use the **–nw** option when you start emacs to bring up the textual interface in any environment. See "Starting emacs" on page 198.

TUTORIAL: GETTING STARTED WITH emacs

The emacs editor has many, many features, and there are many ways to use it. Its complete manual includes more than 35 chapters. Nevertheless, you can do a considerable amount of meaningful work with a relatively small subset of the commands. This section describes a simple editing session, explaining how to start and exit from emacs and how to move the cursor and delete text. Some issues are postponed or simplified in the interest of clarity.

STARTING emacs

To edit a file named **sample** using emacs as a text-based editor, enter the following command. The **–nw** option, which must be the first option on the emacs command line, tells emacs not to use its X (GUI) interface.

```
$ emacs -nw -q sample
```

This command starts emacs, reads the file named **sample** into a buffer, and displays its contents on the screen or window. If no file has this name, emacs displays a blank screen with **New File** at the bottom (Figure 7-1). If the file exists, emacs displays another message (Figure 7-2, page 200). The **–q** option tells emacs *not* to read the **~/.emacs** startup file from your home directory. Not reading the startup file guarantees that you get standard, uncustomized behavior and is sometimes useful for beginners or for other users who want to bypass a **.emacs** file.

The screen starts with a single window. At the bottom of this window is a reverse-video titlebar called the *Mode Line*. At a minimum, the Mode Line shows which buffer the window is viewing, whether the buffer has been changed, what major and minor modes are in effect, and how far down the buffer the window is positioned. When you have more than one window, one Mode Line appears in each

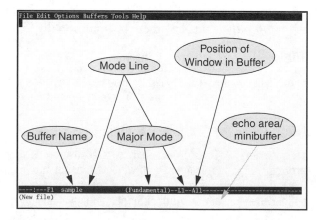

Figure 7-1   The emacs welcome screen

window. At the bottom of the screen, emacs leaves a single line open. This *Echo Area*, or *Minibuffer*, line is used for short messages and special one-line commands.

A cursor is in the window or Minibuffer. All input and nearly all editing takes place at the cursor. As you type ordinary characters, emacs inserts them at the cursor position. If characters are under the cursor or to its right, they get pushed to the right as you type, so no characters are lost.

STOPPING emacs

The command to exit from emacs is the two-key sequence CONTROL-X CONTROL-C. You can give this command at almost any time (in some modes you may have to press CONTROL-G first). It stops emacs gracefully, asking you to confirm changes if you made any during the editing session.

If you want to cancel a half-typed command or stop a running command before it is done, you can quit by pressing CONTROL-G. The emacs editor displays **Quit** in the Echo Area and waits for your next command.

INSERTING TEXT

Typing an ordinary (printing) character pushes the cursor and any characters to the right of the cursor one position to the right and inserts the new character in the position just opened. Backspacing pulls the cursor and any characters to the right of the cursor one position to the left, erasing the character that was there before.

DELETING CHARACTERS

Depending on the keyboard you are using and the emacs startup file, different keys may delete characters in different ways. CONTROL-D typically deletes the character under the cursor, as do DELETE and DEL. BACKSPACE typically deletes the character to the left of the cursor. Try each of these keys and see what it does.

More about deleting characters

tip   If the instructions described in this section do not work, read the emacs info section on **deletion**. Give this command from a shell prompt:

        $ **info emacs**

From info give the command **m deletion** to display a document that describes in detail how to delete small amounts of text. Use the SPACE bar to scroll through the document. Type **q** to exit from info.

Start emacs and type a few lines of text. If you make a mistake, use the deletion characters discussed previously. The RETURN key inserts an invisible end-of-line character in

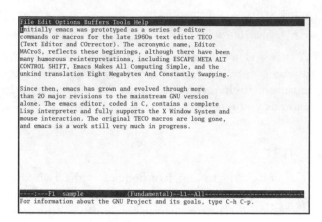

Figure 7-2   Sample buffer

the buffer and returns the cursor to the left margin, one line down. It is possible to back up past the start of a line and up to the end of the previous line. Figure 7-2 shows a sample buffer.

MOVING THE CURSOR

You can position the cursor over any character in the emacs window and move the window so it displays any portion of the buffer. You can move the cursor forward or backward through the text (Figure 6-8, page 155) by various textual units—for example, characters, words, sentences, lines, and paragraphs. Any of the cursor-movement commands can be preceded by a repetition count (CONTROL-U followed by a numeric argument), which causes the cursor to move that number of textual units through the text. Refer to page 205 for a discussion of numeric arguments.

Use the ARROW keys

tip   Sometimes the easiest way to move the cursor is by using the LEFT, RIGHT, UP, and DOWN ARROW keys.

MOVING THE CURSOR BY CHARACTERS

CONTROL-F   Pressing the RIGHT ARROW key or CONTROL-F moves the cursor forward one character. If the cursor is at the end of a line, these commands wrap it to the beginning of the next line. The command CONTROL-U 7 CONTROL-F moves the cursor seven characters forward (to the right).

CONTROL-B   Pressing the LEFT ARROW key or CONTROL-B moves the cursor backward one character. The command CONTROL-U 7 CONTROL-B moves the cursor seven characters backward (to the left). CONTROL-B works in a manner similar to CONTROL-F (Figure 7-3).

Figure 7-3   Moving the cursor by characters

MOVING THE CURSOR BY WORDS

META-f   Pressing META-f moves the cursor forward one word. To press META-f hold down the META or ALT key while you press f. If you do not have either of these keys, press ESCAPE, release it, and then press f. This command leaves the cursor on the first character that is not part of the word the cursor started on. The command CONTROL-U 4 META-f moves the cursor forward one space past the end of the fourth word. See page 204 for more about keys.

META-b   Pressing META-b moves the cursor backward one word so the cursor is on the first letter of the word it started on. If the cursor was on the first letter of a word, META-b moves the cursor to the first letter of the preceding word. It works in a manner similar to META-f (Figure 7-4).

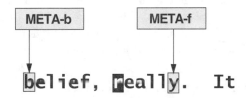

Figure 7-4   Moving the cursor by words

MOVING THE CURSOR BY LINES

CONTROL-A
CONTROL-E

CONTROL-P
CONTROL-N

Pressing CONTROL-A moves the cursor to the beginning of the line it is on; CONTROL-E moves it to the end. Pressing the UP ARROW key or CONTROL-P moves the cursor up one line to the position directly above where the cursor started; the DOWN ARROW key or CONTROL-N moves it down. As with the other cursor-movement keys, you can precede CONTROL-P and CONTROL-N with CONTROL-U and a numeric argument to move up or down multiple lines. You can use pairs of these commands to move the cursor up to the beginning of the previous line, down to the end of the following line, and so on (Figure 7-5).

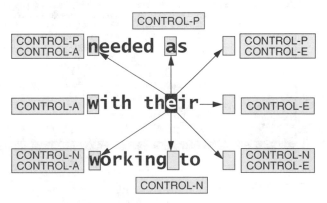

Figure 7-5   Moving the cursor by lines

MOVING THE CURSOR BY SENTENCES, PARAGRAPHS, AND WINDOW POSITION

META-a, META-e
META-{, META-}
Pressing META-a moves the cursor to the beginning of the sentence the cursor is on; META-e moves the cursor to the end. META-{ moves the cursor to the beginning of the paragraph the cursor is on; META-} moves it to the end. (Sentences and paragraphs are defined starting on page 227.) You can precede any of these commands with a repetition count (CONTROL-U and a numeric argument) to move the cursor that many sentences or paragraphs.

META-r
Pressing META-r moves the cursor to the beginning of the middle line of the window. You can precede this command with CONTROL-U and a line number (here CONTROL-U does not indicate a repetition count but a screen line number). The command CONTROL-U 0 META-r moves the cursor to the beginning of the top line (line zero) in the window. You can replace zero with the line number of the line you want to move the cursor to or with a minus sign (–), in which case the cursor moves to the beginning of the last line of the window (Figure 7-6).

EDITING AT THE CURSOR POSITION

With the cursor in the window you can type new text, pushing the existing text to the right. Entering new text requires no special commands once the cursor is positioned. If you type so many characters that the text in a line goes past the right edge

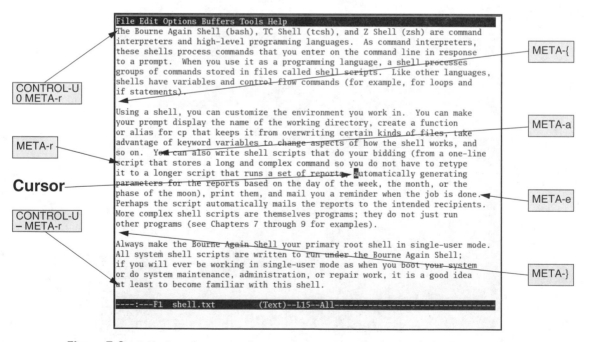

Figure 7-6   Moving the cursor by sentences, paragraphs, and window position

of the window, emacs puts a backslash (\) near the right edge of the window and wraps the text to the next line. The backslash appears on the screen but is not saved as part of the file and is never printed. Although you can create an arbitrarily long line, some UNIX tools have problems with text files containing such lines. You can split a line at any point by positioning the cursor and pressing RETURN.

Deleting text   Pressing DELETE removes characters to the left of the cursor. The cursor and the remainder of the text on this line both move to the left each time you press DELETE. To join a line with the line above it, position the cursor on the first character of the second line and press DELETE.

Press CONTROL-D to delete the character under the cursor. The cursor remains stationary, but the remainder of the text on the line moves left to replace the deleted character. See the tip "More about deleting characters" on page 199 if either of these keys does not work as described here.

Saving and Retrieving the Buffer

No matter what happens to a buffer during an emacs session, the associated file does not change until you save the buffer. If you leave emacs without saving the buffer (this *is* possible if you are insistent enough), the file is not changed and the session's work is discarded.

Backups   As mentioned previously, emacs prompts you about unsaved changes to the buffer contents. As it writes a buffer's edited contents back to the file, emacs may optionally first make a backup of the original file contents. You can choose to make no backups, one level (default), or an arbitrary number of levels. The one-level backup filenames are formed by appending a ~ character to the original filename. The multilevel backups append .~*n*~ to the filename, where *n* is the sequential backup number, starting with 1. The **version-control** variable dictates how emacs saves backups.

Saving the buffer   The command CONTROL-X CONTROL-S saves the current buffer in its associated file. The emacs editor confirms a successful save with a message in the Echo Area.

Visiting another file   If you are already editing a file with emacs and want to edit another file (also called *visiting* a file), you can copy the new file into a new emacs buffer by giving the command CONTROL-X CONTROL-F. The emacs editor prompts you for a filename, reads that file into a new buffer, and displays that buffer in the current window. Having two files open in one editing session is more convenient than exiting from emacs, returning to the shell, and then starting a new copy of emacs to edit a second file.

Visiting a file with CONTROL-X CONTROL-F

tip   When you use CONTROL-X CONTROL-F, emacs partially completes the path to the filename you are to enter. Normally it is the path to the working directory, but in some situations emacs may display a different path, such as the path to your home directory. You can edit this path if it is not pointing to the directory you want.

Basic Editing Commands

This section takes a more detailed look at the fundamental emacs editing commands. It covers straightforward editing of a single file in a single window.

Keys: Notation and Use

Mainstream emacs uses the 128-character ASCII character set. ASCII keyboards have a typewriter-style SHIFT key and a CONTROL key. Some keyboards also have a META (diamond or ALT) key that controls the eighth bit. It takes seven bits to describe an ASCII character; the eighth bit of an eight-bit byte can be used to communicate other information. Because so much of the emacs command set is in the nonprinting CONTROL or META case, Stallman was one of the first to confront the problem of developing a notation for writing about keystrokes.

His solution, although not popular outside the emacs community, is clear and unambiguous (Table 7-1). It uses the capital letters **C** and **M** to denote holding down the CONTROL and META (or ALT) keys, respectively, and a few simple acronyms for the most common special characters, such as RET (this book uses RETURN), LFD (LINEFEED), DEL (DELETE), ESC (ESCAPE), SPC (SPACE), and TAB. Most emacs documentation, including the online help, uses this notation.

Table 7-1　emacs key notation

Character	Classic emacs notation
(lowercase) a	a
(uppercase) SHIFT-a	A
CONTROL-a	C-a
CONTROL-A	C-a (do *not* use SHIFT), equivalent to CONTROL-a
META-a	M-a
META-A	M-A (*do* use SHIFT), different from M-a
CONTROL-META-a	C-M-a
META-CONTROL-a	M-C-a (not used frequently)

This use of keys had some problems. Many keyboards had no META key, and some operating systems discarded the META bit. In addition, the emacs character set clashes with XON-XOFF flow control, which also uses CONTROL-S and CONTROL-Q.

Although the flow-control problem still exists, the META key issue was resolved by making it an optional two-key sequence starting with ESCAPE. For instance, you can type ESCAPE-a instead of META-a or type ESCAPE CONTROL-A to get CONTROL-META-a. If the keyboard you are using does not have a META or ALT key, you can use the two-key ESCAPE sequence by pressing the ESCAPE key, releasing it, and then pressing the key following the META key in this book. For example, when this book says to press META-r, you can either press the META or ALT key while you press **r** or press and release ESCAPE and then press **r**.

The notation used in this book

tip This book uses an uppercase letter following the CONTROL key and a lowercase letter following the META key. In either case you *do not have to hold down the* SHIFT *key while entering a* CONTROL *or* META *character.* Although the META uppercase character (that is, META-A) is a different character, it is usually set up to cause no action or the same effect as its lowercase counterpart.

KEY SEQUENCES AND COMMANDS

In emacs the relationship between key sequences (one or more keys that are pressed together or in sequence to issue an emacs command) and commands is very flexible, and there is considerable opportunity for exercising your personal preference. You can translate and remap key sequences to other commands and replace or reprogram commands.

Although most emacs documentation glosses over the details and talks about keystrokes as though they were the commands, it is important to recognize that the underlying machinery remains separate from the key sequences and to understand that you can change the behavior of the key sequences and the commands. For more information refer to "Customizing emacs" on page 235.

META-x: RUNNING A COMMAND WITHOUT A KEY BINDING

The emacs keymaps (the tables, or vectors, that emacs uses to translate key sequences to commands [page 237]) are very crowded, and often it is not possible to bind every command to a key sequence. You can execute any command by name by preceding it with META-x. When you press META-x, the emacs editor prompts you for a command in the Echo Area. After you enter the command name and press RETURN, it executes the command.

Smart completion When a command has no common key sequence, it is sometimes described as META-x ***command-name***. The emacs editor has a *smart completion* for most prompted answers, using SPACE or TAB to complete, if possible, to the end of the current word or the whole command, respectively. Forcing a completion past the last unambiguous point or typing **?** displays a list of alternatives. You can find more details on smart completion in the online emacs manual.

NUMERIC ARGUMENTS

Some of the emacs editing commands accept a numeric argument as a repetition count. You place this argument immediately before the key sequence for the command. Absence of an argument almost always means a count of 1. Even an ordinary alphabetic character can have a numeric argument, which means "insert this many times." To give a command a numeric argument, you can do either of the following:

- Press META with each digit (0–9) or the minus sign (–). For example, to insert 10 z characters, type META-1 META-0 z.

- Use CONTROL-U to begin a string of digits, including the minus sign. For example, to move the cursor forward 20 words, type CONTROL-U 20 META-f.

CONTROL-U   For convenience, CONTROL-U defaults to *multiply by 4* when you do not follow it with a string of one or more digits. For example, entering CONTROL-U r means insert **rrrr** (4 * 1), whereas CONTROL-U CONTROL-U r means insert **rrrrrrrrrrrrrrrr** (4 * 4 * 1). For quick partial scrolling of a tall window, you may find it convenient to use repeated sequences of CONTROL-U CONTROL-V to scroll down four lines, CONTROL-U META-v to scroll up four lines, CONTROL-U CONTROL-U CONTROL-V to scroll down 16 lines, or CONTROL-U CONTROL-U META-v to scroll up 16 lines.

POINT AND THE CURSOR

Point is the place in a buffer where editing takes place and is where the cursor is positioned. Strictly speaking, Point is the left edge of the cursor—it is thought of as lying *between* two characters.

Each window has its own Point, but there is only one cursor. When the cursor is in a window, moving the cursor also moves Point. Switching the cursor out of a window does not change that window's Point; it is in the same place when you switch the cursor back to that window.

All of the cursor-movement commands described previously also move Point.

SCROLLING THROUGH A BUFFER

CONTROL-V   A buffer is likely to be much larger than the window through which it is viewed, so
META-v   you need a way of moving the display of the buffer contents up or down to position
CONTROL-L   the interesting part in the window. *Scrolling forward* refers to moving the text upward, with new lines entering at the bottom of the window. Use CONTROL-V or the PAGEDOWN key to scroll forward one window (minus two lines for context). *Scrolling backward* refers to moving the text downward, with new lines entering at the top of the window. Use META-v or the PAGEUP key to scroll backward one window (again leaving two lines for context). Pressing CONTROL-L clears the screen and repaints it, moving the current line to the center of the window. This command is useful if the screen becomes garbled.

A numeric argument to CONTROL-V or META-v means "scroll that many lines"; thus CONTROL-U 10 CONTROL-V means scroll forward ten lines. A numeric argument to CONTROL-L means "scroll the text so the cursor is on that line of the window," where 0 means the top line and −1 means the bottom, just above the Mode Line. Scrolling occurs automatically if you exceed the window limits with CONTROL-P or CONTROL-N.

META-<
META->
You can move the cursor to the beginning of the buffer with META-< or to the end of the buffer with META->.

ERASING TEXT

Delete versus kill When you erase text you can discard it or move it into a holding area and optionally bring it back later. The term *delete* means *permanently discard,* and the term *kill* means *move to a holding area.* The holding area, called the *Kill Ring,* can hold several pieces of killed text. You can use the text in the Kill Ring in many ways (refer to "Cut and Paste: Yanking Killed Text" on page 215).

The META-d command kills from the cursor forward to the end of the current word. CONTROL-K kills forward to the end of the current line. It does *not* delete the line-ending LINEFEED character unless Point and the cursor are just to the left of the LINEFEED. This setup allows you to reach the left end of a line with CONTROL-A, kill the whole line with CONTROL-K, and then immediately type a replacement line without having to reopen a hole for the new line. Another consequence is that, from the beginning of the line, it takes CONTROL-K CONTROL-K (or CONTROL-U 2 CONTROL-K) to kill the text and close the hole.

SEARCHING

The emacs editor has several types of search commands. You can search in the following ways:

- Incrementally for a character string
- Incrementally for a regular expression (possible but uncommon)
- For a complete character string
- For a complete regular expression (Appendix A)

You can run each of the four types of searches either forward or backward in the buffer.

The *complete* searches behave in the same manner as a search on other editors. Searching begins only when the search string is complete. In contrast, an *incremental* search begins when you type the first character of the search string and keeps going as you enter additional characters. Initially this approach may sound confusing, but it is surprisingly useful.

INCREMENTAL SEARCHES

CONTROL-S
CONTROL-R
A single command selects the direction of and starts an incremental search. CONTROL-S starts a forward incremental search, and CONTROL-R starts a reverse incremental search.

When you start an incremental search, emacs prompts you with **I-search:** in the Echo Area. When you enter a character, it immediately searches for that character in the buffer. If it finds that character, emacs moves Point and cursor to that position so you can see the search progress. If the search fails, emacs tells you so.

After you enter each character of the search string, you can take one of several actions depending on the result of the search to that point.

- The search finds the string you are looking for in the buffer, leaving the cursor positioned just to its right. Stop the search and leave the cursor in its new position by pressing RETURN. (Any emacs command not related to searching will also stop the search but remembering exactly which ones apply can be difficult. For a new user, RETURN is safer.)

- The search finds a string but it is not the one you are looking for. You can refine the search string by adding another letter, press CONTROL-R or CONTROL-S again to look for the next occurrence of this search string, or press RETURN to stop the search and leave the cursor where it is.

- The search hits the beginning or end of the buffer and reports **Failing I-Search.** You can proceed in several ways at this point.

  - If you mistyped the search string, press BACKSPACE as needed to remove characters from the search string. The text and cursor in the window jump backward in step with your removal of characters.

  - If you want to wrap past the beginning or end of the buffer and continue searching, you can force a wrap by pressing CONTROL-R or CONTROL-S again.

  - If the search has not found the string you are looking for but you want to leave the cursor at its current position, press RETURN to stop the search.

  - If the search has gone wrong and you just want to get back to where you started, press CONTROL-G (the quit character). From an unsuccessful search a single CONTROL-G backs out all the characters in the search string that could not be found. If this action returns you to a place you wish to continue searching from, you can add characters to the search string again. If you do not want to continue the search from that position, a second CONTROL-G stops the search and leaves the cursor where it was initially.

NONINCREMENTAL SEARCHES

CONTROL-S RETURN   If you prefer that your searches succeed or fail without showing all the intermediate
CONTROL-R RETURN   results, you can give the nonincremental command CONTROL-S RETURN to search forward

or CONTROL-R RETURN to search backward. Searching does not begin until you enter a search string in response to the emacs prompt and press RETURN again. Neither of these commands wraps past the end of the buffer.

REGULAR EXPRESSION SEARCHES

You can perform both incremental and nonincremental regular expression searching in emacs. Use the commands listed in Table 7-2 to begin a regular expression search.

Table 7-2   Searching for regular expressions

Command	Result
META-CONTROL-s	Incrementally searches forward for a regular expression; prompts for a regular expression one character at a time
META-x isearch-backward-regexp	Incrementally searches backward for a regular expression; prompts for a regular expression one character at a time
META-x isearch-complete RETURN	Prompts for and then searches forward for a complete regular expression
META-x isearch-backward-regexp RETURN	Prompts for and then searches backward for a complete regular expression

ONLINE HELP

The emacs help system is always available. With the default key bindings, you can start it with CONTROL-H. The help system then prompts you for a one-letter help command. If you do not know which help command you want, type ? or CONTROL-H to switch the current window to a list of help commands, each with a one-line description; emacs again requests a one-letter help command. If you decide you do not want help after all, type CONTROL-G to cancel your help request and return to the former buffer.

If the help output is only a single line, it appears in the Echo Area. If it consists of more text, the output appears in its own window. Use CONTROL-V and META-v to scroll forward and backward through the buffer (page 206). You can move the cursor between windows with CONTROL-X o (lowercase "o"). See page 222 for a discussion on working with multiple windows.

On many terminals the BACKSPACE or LEFT ARROW key generates CONTROL-H. If you forget that you are using emacs and try to back over a few characters, you may unintentionally enter the help system. This action does not pose a danger to the buffer you are editing, but it can be unsettling to lose the window contents and not have a clear picture

Closing the help window

tip   To delete the help window while the cursor is in the window that holds the text you are editing, type CONTROL-X **1** (one). Alternatively, you can move the cursor to the help window (CONTROL-X **o** [lowercase "o"]) and type CONTROL-X **0** (zero) to delete the current window.

If help displays a window that occupies the entire screen, as is the case with CONTROL-H **n** (emacs news) and CONTROL-H **t** (emacs tutorial), you can kill the help buffer with CONTROL-X **k** or use CONTROL-X **b** to switch buffers (both on page 220).

of how to restore it. While you are being prompted for the type of help you want you can type CONTROL-G to remove the prompt and return to editing the buffer. Some users elect to put help on a different key (page 237). Table 7-3 lists some of the help commands.

Table 7-3   Help commands

Command	Type of help offered
CONTROL-H a	Prompts for a string and displays a list of commands whose names contain that string.
CONTROL-H b	Displays a long table of the key bindings in effect.
CONTROL-H c **key-sequence**	Displays the name of the command bound to **key-sequence**. Multiple key sequences are allowed. For a long key sequence where only the first part is recognized, the command describes the first part and quietly inserts the unrecognized part into the buffer. This can happen with three-character function keys (F1, F2, and so on, on the keyboard) that generate character sequences such as ESCAPE [SHIFT.
CONTROL-H f	Prompts for the name of a Lisp function and displays the documentation for it. Because commands are Lisp functions, you can use a command name with this command.
CONTROL-H i	Displays the top info (page 32) menu where you can browse emacs or other documentation.
CONTROL-H k **key-sequence**	Displays the name and documentation of the command bound to **key-sequence**. (See the notes on CONTROL-H **c**.)
CONTROL-H l (lowercase "l")	Displays the last 100 characters typed. The record is kept *after* the first-stage keyboard translation. If you have customized the keyboard translation table, you must make a mental reverse translation.

Table 7-3   Help commands (continued)

CONTROL-H m	Displays the documentation and special key bindings for the current Major mode (Text, C, Fundamental, and so on, [page 226]).
CONTROL-H n	Displays the emacs news file which lists recent changes to emacs, ordered with the most recent changes first. See the tip "Closing the help window" on page 210.
CONTROL-H t	Runs an emacs tutorial session. See the tip "Closing the help window" on page 210.
CONTROL-H v	Prompts for a Lisp variable name and displays the documentation for that variable.
CONTROL-H w	Prompts for a command name and identifies any key sequence bound to that command. Multiple key sequences are allowed. (See the notes on CONTROL-H c.)

As this abridged presentation makes clear, you can use the help system to browse through the emacs internal Lisp system. For the curious, following is Stallman's list of strings that match many names in the Lisp system. To get a view of the internal functionality of emacs, you can use any of these strings with CONTROL-H **a** (help system list of commands) or META-x **apropos** (prompts for a string and lists variables whose names contain that string).

backward	dir	insert	previous	view
beginning	down	kill	region	what
buffer	end	line	register	window
case	file	list	screen	word
change	fill	mark	search	yank
char	find	mode	sentence	
defun	forward	next	set	
delete	goto	page	sexp	
describe	indent	paragraph	up	

ADVANCED EDITING

The basic emacs commands suffice for many editing tasks but the serious user will quickly discover the need for more power. This section presents some of the more advanced emacs capabilities.

UNDOING CHANGES

An editing session begins when you read a file into an emacs buffer. At that point the buffer content matches the file exactly. As you insert text and give editing commands, the buffer content becomes increasingly more different from the file. If you are satisfied with the changes, you can write the altered buffer back out to the file and end the session.

Near the left end of the Mode Line (Figure 7-1, page 198) is an indicator that shows the modification state of the buffer that is displayed in the window. The three possible states are –– (not modified), ✶✶ (modified), and %% (readonly).

The emacs editor keeps a record of all the keys you have pressed (text and commands) since the beginning of the editing session, up to a limit currently set at 20,000 characters. If you are within this limit, it is possible to undo the entire session for this buffer, one change at a time. If you have multiple buffers (page 220), each buffer has its own undo record.

Undoing is considered so important that it has a backup key sequence, just in case some keyboards cannot easily handle the primary sequence. The two sequences are CONTROL-_ (underscore, which on old ASR-33 TTY keyboards was LEFT ARROW) and CONTROL-X u. When you type CONTROL-_, emacs undoes the last command and moves the cursor to that position in the buffer so you can see what happened. If you type CONTROL-_ a second time, the next-to-last command is undone, and so on. If you keep typing CONTROL-_, eventually you will get the buffer back to its original unmodified state and the ✶✶ Mode Line indicator will change to ––.

When you break the string of Undo commands with *anything* (text or any command except Undo), all reverse changes you made during the string of undos become a part of the change record and can themselves be undone. This strategy offers a way to redo some or all the undo operations. If you decide you backed up too far, type a command (something innocuous, such as CONTROL-F, that does not change the buffer), and begin undoing in reverse. Table 7-4 lists some examples of Undo commands.

Table 7-4   Undo commands

Commands	Result
CONTROL-_	Undoes the last change
CONTROL-_ CONTROL-F CONTROL-_	Undoes the last change and changes it back again

Table 7-4   Undo commands (continued)

CONTROL-_ CONTROL-_	Undoes the last two changes
CONTROL-_ CONTROL-_ CONTROL-F CONTROL-_ CONTROL-_	Undoes two changes and changes them both back again
CONTROL-_ CONTROL-_ CONTROL-F CONTROL-_	Undoes two changes and changes one of them back again

If you do not remember the last change you made, you can type CONTROL-_ and undo it. If you wanted to make this change, type CONTROL-F CONTROL-_ and make it again. If you modified a buffer by accident, you can keep typing CONTROL-_ until the Mode Line indicator shows –– once more.

If the buffer is completely ruined and you want to start over, issue the command META-x **revert-buffer** to discard the current buffer contents and reread the associated file. The emacs editor asks you to confirm this command.

MARK AND REGION

Point is the current editing position in a buffer which you can move anywhere within the buffer by moving the cursor. It is also possible to set a marker called *Mark* in the buffer. The contiguous characters between Point and Mark (either one may come first) are called the *Region*. Many commands operate on a buffer's Region, not just on the characters near Point.

MOVING MARK AND ESTABLISHING A REGION

CONTROL-@
CONTROL-SPACE
CONTROL-X CONTROL-X

Mark is not as easy to move as Point. Once set, Mark can be moved only by setting it somewhere else. Each buffer has only one Mark. The CONTROL-@ (or CONTROL-SPACE) command explicitly sets Mark at the current cursor (and Point) position. Some keyboards generate CONTROL-@ when you type CONTROL-Q. Although this is not really a backup key binding, it is occasionally a convenient alternative. You can use CONTROL-X CONTROL-X to exchange Point and Mark (and move the cursor to the new Point).

To establish a Region, you usually position the cursor (and Point) at one end of the desired Region, set Mark with CONTROL-@, and then move the cursor (and Point) to the other end of the Region. If you forget where you left Mark, you can move the cursor back to it again with CONTROL-X CONTROL-X or hop back and forth with repeated CONTROL-X CONTROL-X to show the Region more clearly.

If a Region boundary is not to your liking, you can swap Point and Mark using CONTROL-X CONTROL-X to move the cursor from one end of the Region to the other and then move Point. Continue until you are satisfied with the Region.

OPERATING ON A REGION

Table 7-5 lists selected commands that operate on a Region. Give the command CONTROL-H **a region** to see a complete list of these commands.

Table 7-5   Operating on a region

Command	Result
META-w	Copies the Region nondestructively (without killing it) to the Kill Ring
CONTROL-W	Kills the Region
META-x print-region	Sends the Region to the printer
META-x append-to-buffer	Prompts for a buffer and appends the Region to that buffer
META-x append-to-file	Prompts for a filename and appends the Region to that file
META-x capitalize-region	Converts the Region to uppercase

THE MARK RING

Each time you set Mark in a buffer, you are also pushing Mark's former location onto the buffer's *Mark Ring*. The Mark Ring is organized as a FIFO (first-in-first-out) list and holds the 16 most recent locations where Mark was set. Each buffer has its own Mark Ring. This record of recent Mark history is useful because it often holds locations that you want to jump back to quickly. Jumping to a location pointed to by the Mark Ring can be faster and easier than scrolling or searching your way through the buffer to find the site of a previous change.

CONTROL-U CONTROL-@ To work your way backward along the trail of former Mark locations, give the command CONTROL-U CONTROL-@ one or more times. Each time you give the command, emacs

- Moves Point (and the cursor) to the current Mark location
- Saves the current Mark location at the *oldest* end of the Mark Ring
- Pops off the *youngest* (most recent) Mark Ring entry and sets Mark

Each additional CONTROL-U CONTROL-@ command causes emacs to move Point and the cursor to the previous entry on the Mark Ring.

Although this process may seem complex, it really just makes a safe jump to a previous Mark location. It is safe because each jump's starting point is recirculated through the Mark Ring, where it is easy to find again. You can jump to all previous locations on the Mark Ring (it may be fewer than 16) by giving the command CONTROL-U CONTROL-@ again and again. You can go around the ring as many times as you like and stop whenever you want.

SETTING MARK AUTOMATICALLY

Some commands set Mark automatically: The idea is to leave a bookmark before moving Point a long distance. For example, META-> sets Mark before jumping to the end of the buffer. You can then return to your starting position with CONTROL-U CONTROL-@. Searches behave similarly. To avoid surprises the message **Mark Set** appears in the Echo Area whenever Mark is set, either explicitly or implicitly.

CUT AND PASTE: YANKING KILLED TEXT

Recall that killed text is not discarded but rather is kept in the Kill Ring. The Kill Ring holds the last 30 pieces of killed text and is visible from all buffers.

Retrieving text from the Kill Ring is called *yanking*. This terminology is the opposite of that used in vim: In vim *yanking* pulls text from the buffer, and *putting* puts text into the buffer. Killing and yanking—which are roughly analogous to cutting and pasting—are emacs's primary mechanisms for moving and copying text. Table 7-6 lists the most common kill and yank commands.

Table 7-6   Common kill and yank commands

Command	Result
META-d	Kills to end of current word
META-D	Kills from beginning of previous word
CONTROL-K	Kills to end of line, not including LINEFEED
CONTROL-U 1 CONTROL-K	Kills to end of line, including LINEFEED
CONTROL-U 0 CONTROL-K	Kills from beginning of line
META-w	Copies the Region (between Point and Mark) to the Kill Ring but does *not* erase the Region from the buffer
CONTROL-W	Kills the Region (between Point and Mark)
META-z *char*	Kills up to next occurrence of *char*
CONTROL-Y	Yanks the most recently killed text into the current buffer at Point, sets Mark at the beginning of this text, and positions Point and the cursor at the end
META-y	Erases the just-yanked text, rotates the Kill Ring, and yanks the next item (only after CONTROL-Y or META-y)

To move two lines of text, move Point to the beginning of the first line and then enter CONTROL-U 2 CONTROL-K to kill two lines. Next move Point to the destination position, and enter CONTROL-Y.

To copy two lines of text, move Point to the beginning of the first line and give the commands CONTROL-U 2 CONTROL-K CONTROL-Y to kill and then yank back immediately. Then move Point to the destination position and type CONTROL-Y.

To copy a larger piece of the buffer, set the Region to cover this piece and then type CONTROL-W CONTROL-Y to kill and yank back at once. Next move Point to the destination, and type CONTROL-Y. You can also set the Region and use META-W to copy the Region to the Kill Ring.

The Kill Ring is organized as a fixed-length FIFO list, with each new entry causing the eldest to be discarded (once you build up to 30 entries). Simple cut-and-paste operations generally use only the newest entry. The older entries are retained to give you time to change your mind about a deletion. If you do change your mind you can "mine" the Kill Ring like an archaeological dig, working backward through time and down through the strata of killed material to copy a specific item back into the buffer.

To view every entry in the Kill Ring, begin a yanking session by pressing CONTROL-Y. This action copies the youngest entry to your buffer at the current cursor position. If this entry is not the item you want, continue the yanking session by pressing META-y. This action erases the previous yank and copies the next youngest entry to the buffer at the current cursor position. If this still is not the item you wanted, press META-y again to erase it and retrieve a copy of the next entry, and so on. You can continue giving META-y commands all the way back to the oldest entry. If you continue to press META-y, you wrap back to the youngest entry again. In this manner you can examine each entry as many times as you wish.

The sequence used in a yanking session consists of CONTROL-Y followed by any mixture of CONTROL-Y and META-y. If you type any other command after META-y, the sequence is broken and you must give the CONTROL-Y command again to start another yanking session.

As you work backward in the Kill Ring, it is useful to think of this process as advancing a Last Yank pointer back through history to increasingly older entries. This pointer is *not* reset to the youngest entry until you give a new kill command. Using this technique, you can work backward partway through the Kill Ring with CONTROL-Y and a few META-y commands, give some commands that do not kill, and then pick up where you left off with another CONTROL-Y and a succession of META-y commands.

It is also possible to position the Last Yank pointer with positive or negative numeric arguments to META-y. Refer to the online documentation for more information.

INSERTING SPECIAL CHARACTERS

As stated earlier, emacs inserts everything that is not a command into the buffer at the position of the cursor. To insert characters that would ordinarily be emacs commands, you can use the emacs escape character: CONTROL-Q. There are two ways of using this escape character:

- CONTROL-Q followed by any other character inserts that character in the buffer, no matter what command interpretation it was supposed to have.

- CONTROL-Q followed by three octal digits inserts a byte with that value in the buffer.

CONTROL-Q

tip Depending on the way your terminal is set up, CONTROL-Q may clash with software flow control. If CONTROL-Q seems to have no effect, it is most likely being used for flow control. In that case you must bind another key to the command **quoted-insert** (page 237).

GLOBAL BUFFER COMMANDS

The vim editor and its predecessors have global commands for bufferwide search and replace operations. Their default operating Region is the entire buffer. The emacs editor has a similar family of commands. Their operating Region begins at Point and extends to the end of the buffer. If you wish to operate on the entire buffer, use META-< to set Point at the beginning of the buffer before issuing the command.

LINE-ORIENTED OPERATIONS

The commands listed in Table 7-7 take a regular expression and apply it to the lines between Point and the end of the buffer.

Table 7-7   Line-oriented operations

Command	Result
META-x occur	Prompts for a regular expression and copies each line with a match for the expression in a buffer named *Occur*
META-x delete-matching-lines	Prompts for a regular expression and deletes each line with a match for the expression
META-x delete-non-matching-lines	Prompts for a regular expression and deletes each line that does *not* have a match for that expression

The META-x **occur** command puts its output in a special buffer named *Occur*, which you can peruse and discard or use as a jump menu to reach each line quickly. To use the *Occur* buffer as a jump menu, switch to it (CONTROL-X **o** [lowercase "o"]), move the cursor to the copy of the desired destination line, and type CONTROL-C CONTROL-C. This command moves the cursor to the buffer that was searched and positions it on the line that the regular expression matched.

As with any buffer change, you can undo the deletion commands.

UNCONDITIONAL AND INTERACTIVE REPLACEMENT

The commands listed in Table 7-8 operate on the characters between Point and the end of the buffer, changing every string match or regular expression match. An unconditional replacement makes all replacements automatically. An interactive replacement gives you the opportunity to see and approve each replacement before it is made.

Table 7-8   Replacement commands

Command	Result
META-x replace-string	Prompts for *string* and *newstring* and replaces every instance of *string* with *newstring*. Point is left at the site of the last replacement, but Mark is set when you give the command, so you can return to it with CONTROL-U CONTROL-@.
META-x replace-regexp	Prompts for *regexp* and *newstring* and replaces every match for *regexp* with *newstring*. Point is left at the site of the last replacement, but Mark is set when you give the command, so you can return to it with CONTROL-U CONTROL-@.
META-% *string* or META-x query-replace	The first form uses *string*, the second form prompts for *string*. Both forms prompt for *newstring*, query each instance of *string*, and, depending on your response, replace it with *newstring*. Point is left at the site of the last replacement, but Mark is set when you give the command, so you can return to it with CONTROL-U CONTROL-@.
META-x query-replace-regexp	Prompts for *regexp* and *newstring*, queries each match for *regexp*, and, depending on your response, replaces it with *newstring*. Point is left at the site of the last replacement, but Mark is set when you give the command, so you can return to it with CONTROL-U CONTROL-@.

If you perform an interactive replacement, emacs displays each instance of *string* or match for *regexp* and prompts you for an action to take. Table 7-9 lists some of the possible responses.

Table 7-9   Responses to interactive replacement prompts

Response	Meaning
RETURN	Do not do any more replacements; quit now.
SPACE	Make this replacement and go on.
DELETE	Do *not* make this replacement. Skip it and go on.

Table 7-9 Responses to interactive replacement prompts (continued)

, (comma)	Make this replacement, display the result, and ask for another command. Any command is legal except DELETE is treated like SPACE and does not undo the change.
. (period)	Make this replacement and quit searching.
! (exclamation point)	Replace this and all remaining instances without asking any more questions.

FILES

When you *visit* (emacs terminology for "call up") a file, emacs reads it into a buffer (page 220), allows you to edit the buffer, and eventually saves the buffer back to the file. The commands discussed here relate to visiting and saving files.

META-x **pwd**
META-x **cd**

Each emacs buffer keeps a record of its default directory (the directory the file was read from or the working directory, if it is a new file) that is prepended to any relative pathname you specify. This convenience is meant to save some typing. Enter META-x **pwd** to print the default directory for the current buffer or META-x **cd** to prompt for a new default directory and assign it to this buffer.

VISITING FILES

The emacs editor deals well with visiting a file that has already been called up and whose image is now in a buffer. After a check of the modification time to ensure that the file has not been changed since it was last called up, emacs simply switches to that buffer. Table 7-10 lists commands used to visit files.

Table 7-10 Visiting files

Command	Result
CONTROL-X CONTROL-F	Prompts for a filename and reads its contents into a freshly created buffer. Assigns the file's simple filename as the buffer name. Other buffers are unaffected. It is common and often useful to have several files open simultaneously for editing.
CONTROL-X CONTROL-V	Prompts for a filename and replaces the current buffer with a buffer containing the contents of the requested file. The current buffer is destroyed.
CONTROL-X 4 CONTROL-F	Prompts for a filename and reads its contents into a new buffer. Assigns the file's simple filename as the buffer name. Creates a new window for this buffer and selects that window. The window selected before the command still displays the buffer it was showing before this operation, although the new window may cover up part of the old window.

To create a new file, simply call it up. An empty buffer is created and properly named so you can eventually save it. The message (**New File**) appears in the Echo Area, reflecting emacs's understanding of the situation. Of course, if this "new file" grew out of a typographical error, you will probably want to issue CONTROL-X CONTROL-V with the correct name.

SAVING FILES

You save a buffer by copying its contents back to the original file you called up. The relevant commands are listed in Table 7-11.

Table 7-11   Saving files

Command	Result
CONTROL-X CONTROL-S	This workhorse file-saving command saves the current buffer into its original file. If the current buffer is not modified, you get the following message: **(No changes need to be saved)**.
CONTROL-X S	For each modified buffer, you are asked whether you wish to save it. Answer **y** or **n**. This command is given automatically as you exit from emacs and allows you to save any buffers that have been modified but not yet written out. If you want to save intermediate copies of your work, you can give this command at any time.
META-x set-visited-file-name	Prompts for a filename and sets this name as the current buffer's "original" name.
CONTROL-X CONTROL-W	Prompts for a filename, sets this name as the "original" name for the current buffer, and saves the current buffer into that file. It is equivalent to META-x **set-visited-file-name** followed by CONTROL-X CONTROL-S.
META-~ (tilde)	Clears modified flag from the current buffer. If you mistakenly typed META-~ against a buffer with changes you want to keep, you need to make sure that the modified condition and its ✶ ✶ indicator are turned back on before leaving emacs, or all the changes will be lost. One easy way to do this is to insert a SPACE into the buffer and then remove it again with DELETE.

BUFFERS

An emacs buffer is a storage object that you can edit. It often holds the contents of a file but can also exist without being associated with a file. You can select only one buffer at a time, designated as the *current buffer*. Most commands operate only on the current buffer, even when multiple windows show two or more buffers on the screen. For the most part each buffer is its own world: It has its own name, its own modes, its own file associations, its own modified state, and perhaps its own special key bindings. You can use the commands shown in Table 7-12 to create, select, list, and manipulate buffers.

Did you modify a buffer by mistake?

caution When you give a CONTROL-X **s** command, you may discover files whose buffers were modified by mistake as emacs tries to save the wrong changes back to the file. When emacs prompts you to confirm the save, *do not* answer **y** if you are not sure. First exit from the CONTROL-X **s** dialog by typing **n** to any saves you are not sure about. You then have several options:

- Save the suspicious buffer into a temporary file with CONTROL-X CONTROL-W and analyze it later.

- Undo the changes with a string of CONTROL-_ commands until the ✳✳ indicator disappears from the buffer's Mode Line.

- If you are sure that all the changes are wrong, use META-x **revert-buffer** to get a fresh copy of the file.

- Kill the buffer outright. Because it is modified, emacs asks whether you are sure before carrying out this command.

- Give the META-~ (tilde) command to clear the modified condition and ✳✳ indicator. A subsequent CONTROL-X **s** then believes that the buffer does not need to be written.

You can exit without first getting a warning

caution Clearing the modified flag (META-~) allows you to exit without saving a modified buffer with no warning. Make sure you know what you are doing when you use META-~.

Table 7-12   Work with buffers

Command	Result
CONTROL-X b	Prompts for a buffer name and selects it. If the buffer you name does not exist, this command creates it.
CONTROL-X 4 b	Prompts for a buffer name and selects it in another window. The existing window is not disturbed, although the new window may overlap it.
CONTROL-X CONTROL-B	Creates a buffer named ✳**Buffer List**✳ and displays it in another window. The existing window is not disturbed, although the new window may overlap it. The new buffer is not selected. In the ✳**Buffer List**✳ buffer, each buffer's data is shown along with the name, size, mode(s), and original filename. A % appears for a readonly buffer, a ✳ indicates a modified buffer, and **.** appears for the selected buffer.
META-x rename-buffer	Prompts for a new buffer name and gives this new name to the current buffer.
CONTROL-X CONTROL-Q	Toggles the current buffer's readonly status and the associated %% Mode Line indicator. This can be useful to prevent accidental buffer modification or to allow modification of a buffer when visiting a readonly file.

Table 7-12   Work with buffers (continued)

META-x append-to-buffer	Prompts for a buffer name and appends the Region (between Point and Mark) to the end of that buffer.
META-x prepend-to-buffer	Prompts for a buffer name and prepends the Region (between Point and Mark) to the beginning of that buffer.
META-x copy-to-buffer	Prompts for a buffer name and deletes the contents of the buffer before copying the Region (between Point and Mark) to that buffer.
META-x insert-buffer	Prompts for a buffer name and inserts the entire contents of that buffer into the current buffer at Point.
CONTROL-X k	Prompts for a buffer name and deletes that buffer. If the buffer is modified but unsaved, you are asked to confirm the operation.
META-x kill-some-buffers	Goes through the entire buffer list and offers the chance to delete each buffer. As with CONTROL-X **k**, you are asked to confirm the kill command if a modified buffer is not yet saved.

WINDOWS

An emacs *window* is a viewport that looks into a buffer. The emacs screen begins by displaying a single window, but this screen space can later be divided among two or more windows. On the screen the *current window* holds the cursor and views the *current buffer*. For a tip on terminology, see "The screen and emacs windows" on page 197.

A window views one buffer at a time. You can switch the buffer that a window views by giving the command CONTROL-X b *buffer-name* in the current window. Multiple windows can view one buffer; each window may view different parts of the same buffer; and each window has its own Point value. Any change to a buffer is reflected in all the windows viewing that buffer. Also, a buffer can exist without a window open on it.

SPLITTING A WINDOW

One way to divide the screen is to split the starting window explicitly into two or more pieces. The command CONTROL-X 2 splits the current window in two, with one new window appearing above the other. A numeric argument is taken as the size of the upper window in lines. The command CONTROL-X 3 splits the current window in two, with the new windows being arranged side by side (Figure 7-7). A numeric argument is taken as the number of columns to give the left window. For example, CONTROL-U CONTROL-X 2 splits the current window in two; because of the special "times 4" interpretation of CONTROL-U standing alone, the upper window is given four lines (barely enough to be useful).

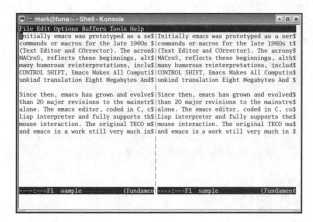

Figure 7-7 Splitting a window vertically

Although these commands split the current window, both windows continue to view the same buffer. You can select a new buffer in either or both new windows, or you can scroll each window to show different portions of the same buffer.

MANIPULATING WINDOWS

CONTROL-X o
META-CONTROL-V

You can use CONTROL-X o (lowercase "o") to select the other window. If more than two windows appear on the screen, a sequence of CONTROL-X o commands cycles through them in top-to-bottom, left-to-right order. The META-CONTROL-V command scrolls the other window. If more than two windows are visible, the command scrolls the window that CONTROL-X o would select next. You can use a positive or negative scrolling argument, just as with CONTROL-V scrolling in the current window.

OTHER-WINDOW DISPLAY

CONTROL-X 4b
CONTROL-X 4f

In normal emacs operation, explicit window splitting is not nearly as common as the implicit splitting done by the family of CONTROL-X 4 commands. The CONTROL-X 4b command, for example, prompts for a *buffer name* and selects it in the other window. If there is no other window, this command begins with a half-and-half split that arranges the windows one above the other. The CONTROL-X 4f command prompts for a *filename,* calls it up in the other window, and selects the other window. If there is no other window, this command begins with a half-and-half split that arranges the windows one above the other.

ADJUSTING AND DELETING WINDOWS

CONTROL-X 0
CONTROL-X 1

Windows may be destroyed when they get in the way. No data is lost in the window's associated buffer with this operation, and you can make another window whenever you like. The CONTROL-X 0 (zero) command deletes the current window and gives its space to its neighbors; CONTROL-X 1 deletes all windows except the current window.

META-x **shrink-window**
CONTROL-X ^
CONTROL-X }
CONTROL-X {

You can also adjust the dimensions of the current window, once again at the expense of its neighbors. To make a window shorter, use META-x **shrink-window**. Use CONTROL-X ^ to increase the height of a window, CONTROL-X } to make the window wider, and CONTROL-X { to make the window narrower. Each of these commands adds or subtracts one line or column to or from the window, unless you precede the command with a numeric argument.

The emacs editor has its own guidelines for a window's minimum useful size and may destroy a window before you force one of its dimensions to zero. Although the window may disappear, the buffer remains intact.

FOREGROUND SHELL COMMANDS

The emacs editor can run a subshell (a shell that is a child of the shell that is running emacs—refer to "Executing a Command" on page 294) to execute a single command line, optionally with standard input coming from the Region of the current buffer and optionally with standard output replacing the Region (Table 7-13). This process is analogous to executing a shell command from the vim editor and having the input come from the file you are editing and the output go back to the same file (page 183). As with vim, how well this process works depends in part on the capabilities of the shell.

Table 7-13   Foreground shell commands

Command	Result
META-! (exclamation point)	Prompts for a shell command, executes it, and displays the output
CONTROL-U META-! (exclamation point)	Prompts for a shell command, executes it, and inserts the output at Point
META-| (vertical bar)	Prompts for a shell command, gives the Region as input, filters it through the command, and displays the output
CONTROL-U META-| (vertical bar)	Prompts for a shell command, gives the Region as input, filters it through the command, deletes the old Region, and inserts the output in that position

The emacs editor can also start an interactive subshell that runs continuously in its own buffer. See "Shell Mode" on page 234 for more information.

BACKGROUND SHELL COMMANDS

The emacs editor can run processes in the background, with their output being fed into a growing emacs buffer that does not have to remain in view. You can continue editing while the background process runs and look at its output later. Any shell command can be run in this way.

The growing output buffer is always named *compilation*. You can read it, copy from it, or edit it in any way, without waiting for the background process to finish. Most commonly this buffer is used to review the output of program compilation and to correct any syntax errors found by the compiler.

META-x **compile** To run a process in the background, give the command META-x **compile** to prompt for a shell command and begin executing it as a background process. The screen splits in half to show the *compilation* buffer.

You can switch to the *compilation* buffer and watch the execution, if you wish. To make the display scroll as you watch, position the cursor at the very end of the text with a META-> command. If you are not interested in this display just remove the window with CONTROL-X 0 (zero) if you are in it or CONTROL-X 1 otherwise and keep working. You can switch back to the *compilation* buffer later with CONTROL-X **b**.

You can kill the background process with META-x **kill-compilation**. The emacs editor asks for confirmation and then kills the background process.

If standard format error messages appear in *compilation*, you can automatically visit the line in the file where each error occurred. Give the command CONTROL-X ` (back tick) to split the screen into two windows and visit the file and line of the next error message. Scroll the *compilation* buffer until this error message appears at the top of its window. Use CONTROL-U CONTROL-X ` to start over with the first error message and visit that file and line.

LANGUAGE-SENSITIVE EDITING

The emacs editor has a large collection of feature sets, each specific to a certain variety of text. The feature sets are called *Major modes*. A buffer can have only one Major mode at any time.

A buffer's Major mode is private to the buffer and does not affect editing in any other buffer. If you switch to a new buffer having a different mode, rules for the new mode immediately take effect. To avoid confusion, the name of a buffer's Major mode appears in the Mode Line of any window viewing that buffer (Figure 7-1 on page 198).

The three classes of Major modes are used for the following tasks:

- Editing human languages (for example, text, nroff, TeX)
- Editing programming languages (for example, C, Fortran, Lisp)
- Special purposes (for example, shell, mail, dired, ftp)

In addition, one Major mode—Fundamental—does nothing special. A Major mode usually sets up the following:

- Special commands unique to the mode, possibly with their own key bindings. Languages may have just a few special commands, but special-purpose modes may have dozens.

- Mode-specific character syntax and regular expressions defining word constituent characters, delimiters, comments, whitespace, and so on. This setup conditions the behavior of commands oriented to syntactic units, such as words, sentences, comments, or parenthesized expressions.

SELECTING A MAJOR MODE

META-x *modename*   The emacs editor chooses and sets a mode when a file is called up by matching the filename against a set of regular expression patterns describing the filename and filename extension. The explicit command to enter a Major mode is META-x *modename*. This command is rarely used except to correct wrong guesses.

A file can define its own mode by including the text – *– modename – *– somewhere in the first nonblank line, possibly inside a comment suitable for that programming language.

HUMAN-LANGUAGE MODES

A *human* language is meant eventually to be used by humans, possibly after being formatted by some text-formatting program. Human languages share many conventions about the structure of words, sentences, and paragraphs. With regard to these textual units, the major human language modes all behave in the same way.

Beyond this area of commonality, each mode offers additional functionality oriented to a specific text formatter, such as TeX, LaTeX, or nroff. Text-formatter extensions are beyond the scope of this presentation; the focus here is on the commands relating to human textual units (for example, words, sentences, and paragraphs).

WORDS

As a mnemonic aid, the bindings for words are defined parallel to the character-oriented bindings CONTROL-F, CONTROL-B, CONTROL-D, DELETE, and CONTROL-T.

Just as CONTROL-F and CONTROL-B move forward and backward over characters, META-f and META-b move forward and backward over words. They may start from a position inside or outside the word to be traversed, but in all cases Point finishes just beyond the word, adjacent to the last character skipped over. Both commands accept a numeric argument specifying the number of words to be traversed.

Just as CONTROL-D and DELETE delete characters forward and backward, the keys META-d and META-DELETE kill words forward and backward. They leave Point in exactly the same finishing position as META-f and META-b do, but they kill the words they pass over. They also accept a numeric argument.

META-t transposes the word before Point with the word after Point.

SENTENCES

As a mnemonic aid, three of the bindings for sentences are defined parallel to the line-oriented bindings: CONTROL-A, CONTROL-E, and CONTROL-K. The META-a command moves backward to the beginning of a sentence, and META-e moves forward to the end of a sentence. In addition, CONTROL-X DELETE kills backward to the beginning of a sentence; META-k kills forward to the end of a sentence.

The emacs editor recognizes the ends of sentences by referring to a regular expression that is kept in a variable named **sentence-end**. (If you are curious, give the command CONTROL-H **v sentence-end** RETURN to view this variable.) Briefly, it looks for the characters ., ?, or ! followed by two SPACEs or an end-of-line marker, possibly with close quotation marks or close braces.

The META-a and META-e commands leave Point adjacent to the first or last nonblank character in the sentence. They accept a numeric argument specifying the number of sentences to traverse; a negative argument runs them in reverse.

The META-k and CONTROL-X DELETE commands kill sentences forward and backward, in a manner analogous to CONTROL-K line kill. They leave Point in exactly the same finishing position as META-a and META-e do, but they kill the sentences they pass over. They also accept a numeric argument. CONTROL-X DELETE is useful for quickly backing out of a half-finished sentence.

PARAGRAPHS

The META-{ command moves backward to the most recent paragraph beginning, and META-} moves forward to the next paragraph ending. The META-h command marks the paragraph (that is, puts Point at the beginning and Mark at the end) that the cursor is currently on, or the next paragraph if it is between paragraphs.

The META-} and META-{ commands leave Point at the beginning of a line, adjacent to the first character or last character of the paragraph. They accept a numeric argument specifying the number of paragraphs to traverse and run in reverse if given a negative argument.

In human-language modes, paragraphs are separated by blank lines and text-formatter command lines, and an indented line starts a paragraph. Recognition is based on the regular expressions stored in the variables **paragraph-separate** and **paragraph-start**. A paragraph is composed of complete lines, including the final line terminator. If a paragraph starts following one or more blank lines, the last blank line before the paragraph belongs to the paragraph.

FILL

The emacs editor can *fill* a paragraph to fit a specified width, breaking lines and rearranging them as necessary. Breaking takes place only between words and no hyphenation occurs. Filling can be done automatically as you type or in response to an explicit command.

The META-x **auto-fill-mode** command toggles Auto Fill mode on and off. When Auto Fill mode is on, emacs automatically breaks lines when you press SPACE or RETURN and are currently beyond the specified line width. This feature is useful when you are entering new text.

Auto Fill mode does not automatically refill the entire paragraph you are currently working on. If you add new text in the middle of a paragraph, Auto Fill mode breaks your new text as you type but does not refill the complete paragraph. To refill a complete paragraph or Region of paragraphs, use either META-q to refill the current paragraph or META-x **fill-region** to refill each paragraph in the Region between Point and Mark.

You can change the filling width from its default value of 70 by setting the **fill-column** variable. Use CONTROL-X f to set **fill-column** to the current cursor position and CONTROL-U *nnn* CONTROL-X f to set **fill-column** to *nnn*, where 0 is the left margin.

CASE CONVERSION

The emacs editor can force words or Regions to all uppercase, all lowercase, or initial caps (the first letter of each word uppercase, the rest lowercase). Refer to Table 7-14.

Table 7-14   Case conversion

Command	Result
META-l (lowercase "l")	Converts word to the right of Point to lowercase
META-u	Converts word to the right of Point to uppercase
META-c	Converts word to the right of Point to initial caps
CONTROL-X CONTROL-L	Converts the Region (between Point and Mark) to lowercase
CONTROL-X CONTROL-U	Converts the Region (between Point and Mark) to uppercase

The word-oriented conversions move Point over the word just converted (just as META-f does), allowing you to walk through text and convert each word with META-l, META-u, or META-c, or skip over words to be left alone with META-f. A positive numeric argument converts that number of words to the right of Point, moving Point as it goes. A negative numeric argument converts that number of words to the left of Point but leaves Point stationary. This feature is useful for quickly changing the case of words you have just typed. Table 7-15 shows some examples.

Table 7-15 Examples of case conversion

Characters and commands	Result
HELLOMETA-–META-l (lowercase "l")	hello
helloMETA-–META-u	HELLO
helloMETA-–META-c	Hello

The word conversions are not picky about beginning in the middle of a word. In all cases, they consider the first word-constituent character to the right of Point as the beginning of the word to be converted.

TEXT MODE

With very few exceptions, the commands for human-language text units, such as words and sentences, are always turned on and available, even in the programming-language modes. Text mode adds very little to these basic commands but is still worth turning on just to get the TAB key. Use the command META-x **text-mode** to activate Text mode.

In Text mode TAB runs the function **tab-to-tab-stop**. By default TAB stops are set every eight columns. You can adjust them with META-x **edit-tab-stops**, which switches to a special *❋Tab Stops*❋ buffer. The current stops are laid out in this buffer on a scale for you to edit. The new stops are installed when or if you type CONTROL-C CONTROL-C. Of course, you are free to kill this buffer (CONTROL-X k) or switch away from it (CONTROL-X b) without ever changing the stops.

The tab stops you set with the META-x **edit-tab-stops** command affect only the interpretation of TAB characters arriving from the keyboard. The emacs editor automatically inserts enough spaces to reach the TAB stop. This command does not affect the interpretation of TAB characters already in the buffer or the underlying file. If you edit the TAB stops and then use them, you can still print the file and the hard copy will look the same as the text on the screen.

C MODE

Programming languages are read by humans but are interpreted by machines. Besides continuing to handle some of the human-language text units (for example, words and sentences), the major programming-language modes address several additional problems:

- *Balanced expressions* enclosed by parentheses, brackets, or braces as textual units
- Comments as textual units
- Indention

The emacs editor includes Major modes to support C, Fortran, and several variants of Lisp. In addition, many users have contributed modes for their favorite languages. In these modes the commands for human textual units are still available, with occasional redefinitions. For example, a paragraph is bounded only by blank lines and indention does not signal a paragraph start. In addition, each mode has custom coding to handle the language-specific conventions for balanced expressions, comments, and indention. This presentation discusses only C mode.

EXPRESSIONS

The emacs Major modes are limited to lexical analysis. They can recognize most tokens (for example, symbols, strings, and numbers) and all matched sets of parentheses, brackets, and braces. This is enough for Lisp but not for C. The C mode lacks a full-function syntax analyzer and is not prepared to recognize all of C's possible expressions.[1]

Table 7-16 lists the emacs commands applicable to parenthesized expressions and some tokens. By design the bindings run parallel to the CONTROL commands for characters and the META commands for words. All these commands accept a numeric argument and run in reverse if that argument is negative.

Table 7-16   Commands for expressions and tokens

Command	Result
CONTROL-META-f	Moves forward over an expression. The exact behavior depends on which character lies to the right of Point (or left of Point, depending on which direction you are moving Point).
	• If the first nonwhitespace is an opening delimiter (parenthesis, bracket, or brace), Point is moved just past the matching closing delimiter.
	• If the first nonwhitespace is a token, Point is moved just past the end of this token.
CONTROL-META-b	Moves backward over an expression.
CONTROL-META-k	Kills an expression forward. This command leaves Point at the same finishing position as CONTROL-META-f but kills the expression it traverses.
CONTROL-META-@	Sets Mark at the position CONTROL-META-f would move to but does not change Point. To see the marked Region clearly, give a pair of CONTROL-X CONTROL-X commands to interchange Point and Mark.

1. In the emacs documentation the recurring term *sexp* refers to the Lisp term *S-expression*. Unfortunately, it is sometimes used interchangeably with *expression,* even though the language might not be Lisp.

FUNCTION DEFINITIONS

In emacs a balanced expression at the outermost level is considered to be a function definition and is often called a *defun,* even though that term is specific to Lisp. More generally it is understood to be a function definition in the language at hand.

In C mode a function definition includes the return data type, the function name, and the argument declarations appearing before the { character. Table 7-17 shows the commands for operating on function definitions.

Table 7-17   Function definitions

Command	Result
CONTROL-META-a	Moves to the beginning of the most recent function definition. Use this command to scan backward through a buffer one function at a time.
CONTROL-META-e	Moves to the end of the next function definition. Use this command to scan forward through a buffer one function at a time.
CONTROL-META-h	Puts Point at the beginning and Mark at the end of the current function definition (or next function definition, if between two). This command sets up an entire function definition for a Region-oriented operation such as kill.

Function indention style

caution   The emacs editor assumes that an opening brace at the left margin is part of a function definition. This heuristic speeds up the reverse scan for a definition's leading edge. If your code has an indention style that puts that opening brace elsewhere, you may get unexpected results.

INDENTION

The emacs C mode has extensive logic to control the indention of C programs. Furthermore, you can adjust this logic for many different styles of C indention (Table 7-18).

Table 7-18   Indention commands

Command	Result
TAB	Adjusts the indention of the current line. TAB inserts or deletes whitespace at the beginning of the line until the indention conforms to the current context and rules in effect. Point is not moved unless it lies in the whitespace area; in that case it is moved to the end of the whitespace. TAB does not insert anything except leading whitespace, so you can hit it at any time and at any position in the line. If you really want to insert a tab in the text, use META-i or CONTROL-Q TAB.

Table 7-18   Indention commands (continued)

LINEFEED	Shorthand for RETURN followed by TAB. The LINEFEED key is a convenience for entering new code, giving you an autoindent as you begin each line.

The next two commands indent multiple lines with a single command.

CONTROL-META-q	Reindents all lines inside the next pair of matched braces. CONTROL-META-q assumes that the left brace is correctly indented and drives the indention from there. If you need to adjust the left brace type TAB just to the left of the brace before giving this command. All lines up to the matching brace are indented as if you had typed TAB on each one.
CONTROL-META-\	Reindents all lines in the Region (between Point and Mark). Put Point just to the left of a left brace and then give the command. All lines up to the matching brace are indented as if you had typed TAB on each one.

CUSTOMIZING INDENTION

Many styles of C programming have evolved, and emacs does its best to support automatic indention for all of them. The indention coding was completely rewritten for emacs version 19; it supports C, C++, Objective-C, and Java. The new emacs syntactic analysis is much more precise and can classify each syntactic element of each line of program text into a single syntactic category (out of about 50), such as *statement, string,* or *else-clause.* With the result of that analysis in hand, emacs goes to an offset table named **c-offsets-alist** and looks up how much each line should be indented from the preceding line.

To customize indention, you must change the offset table. It is possible to define a completely new offset table for each customized style but much more convenient to feed in a short list of exceptions to the standard rules. Each mainstream style (GNU, K&R [Kernighan and Ritchie], BSD, and so on) has such an exception list; all are collected in **c-style-alist.** Here is one entry from **c-style-alist:**

```
("gnu"
 (c-basic-offset . 2)
 (c-comment-only-line-offset . (0 . 0))
 (c-offsets-alist . ((statement-block-intro . +)
    (knr-argdecl-intro . 5)
    (substatement-open . +)
    (label . 0)
    (statement-case-open . +)
    (statement-cont . +)
    (arglist-intro . c-lineup-arglist-intro-after-paren)
    (arglist-close . c-lineup-arglist)
    ))
)
```

Constructing a custom style is beyond the scope of this book. If you are curious, the long story is available in emacs online info beginning at "Customizing C Indentation." The sample **.emacs** file given in this chapter (page 239) adds a very simple custom style and arranges to use it on every **.c** file that is edited.

COMMENTS

Each buffer has its own **comment-column** variable, which you can view with the CONTROL-H **v comment-column** RETURN help command. Table 7-19 lists commands that facilitate working with comments.

Table 7-19   Comments

Command	Result
META-;	Inserts a comment on the current line or aligns an existing comment. This command's behavior differs according to the situation. • If no comment is on this line, META-; creates an empty comment at the value of **comment-column**. • If text already on this line overlaps the position of **comment-column**, META-; creates an empty comment one SPACE after the end of the text. • If a comment is already on this line but not at the current value of **comment-column**, META-; realigns the comment at that column. If text is in the way, it places the comment one SPACE after the end of the text. Once an aligned (possibly empty) comment exists on the line, Point moves to the start of the comment text.
CONTROL-X ;	Sets **comment-column** to the column after Point. The left margin is column 0.
CONTROL-U – CONTROL-X ;	Kills the comment on the current line. This command sets **comment-column** from the first comment found above this line and then performs a META-; command to insert or align a comment at that position.
CONTROL-U CONTROL-X ;	Sets **comment-column** to the position of the first comment found above this line and then executes a META-; command to insert or align a comment on this line.

SPECIAL-PURPOSE MODES

The emacs editor includes a third family of Major modes that are not oriented toward a particular language or even toward ordinary editing. Instead, these modes perform some special function. The following modes may define their own key bindings and commands to accomplish that function:

- Rmail: reads, archives, and composes email
- Dired: moves around in an ls –l display and operates on files
- VIP: simulates a complete vi environment
- VC: allows you to drive version-control systems (including RCS, CVS, and Subversion) from within emacs
- GUD: Grand Unified Debugger; allows you to run and debug C (and other) programs from within emacs
- Tramp: allows you to edit files on any remote system you can reach with ftp or scp
- Shell: runs an interactive subshell from inside an emacs buffer

This book discusses only Shell mode.

SHELL MODE

One-time shell commands and Region filtering were discussed earlier; refer to "Foreground Shell Commands" on page 224. In Shell mode, however, each emacs buffer has an underlying interactive shell permanently associated with it. This shell takes its input from the last line of the buffer and sends its output back to the buffer, advancing Point as it goes. If you do not edit the buffer, it holds a record of the complete shell session.

The shell runs asynchronously, whether or not you have its buffer in view. The emacs editor uses idle time to read the shell's output and add it to the buffer.

Type META-x **shell** to create a buffer named ✳**shell**✳ and start a subshell. If a buffer named ✳**shell**✳ already exists, emacs just switches to that buffer. The shell that this command runs is taken from one of the following sources:

- The Lisp variable **explicit-shell-file-name**
- The environment variable **ESHELL**
- The environment variable **SHELL**

To start a second shell, first use META-x **rename-buffer** to change the name of the existing shell's buffer, and then use META-x **shell** to start another shell. You can create as many subshells and buffers as you like, all running in parallel.

A special set of commands is defined in Shell mode (Table 7-20). They are bound mostly to two-key sequences starting with CONTROL-C. Each sequence is similar to the ordinary control characters found in Linux but uses a leading CONTROL-C.

Table 7-20   Shell mode

Command	Result
RETURN	If Point is at the end of the buffer, emacs inserts the RETURN and sends this (the last) line to the shell. If Point is elsewhere, it copies this line to the end of the buffer, peeling off the old shell prompt (see the regular expression **shell-prompt-pattern**), if one existed. Then this copied line—now the last in the buffer—is sent to the shell.
CONTROL-C CONTROL-D	Sends CONTROL-D to the shell or its subshell.
CONTROL-C CONTROL-C	Sends CONTROL-C to the shell or its subshell.
CONTROL-C CONTROL-\	Sends a quit signal to the shell or its subshell.
CONTROL-C CONTROL-U	Kills the text on the current line not yet completed.
CONTROL-C CONTROL-R	Scrolls back to the beginning of the last shell output, putting the first line of output at the top of the window.
CONTROL-C CONTROL-O	Deletes the last batch of shell output.

optional

CUSTOMIZING emacs

At the heart of emacs is a Lisp interpreter written in C. This version of Lisp is significantly extended with many special commands specifically oriented to editing. The interpreter's main task is to execute the Lisp-coded system that implements the look-and-feel of emacs.

Reduced to its essentials, this system implements a continuous loop that watches keystrokes arrive, parses them into commands, executes those commands, and updates the screen. This behavior can be customized in a number of ways.

- As single keystrokes come in, they are mapped immediately through a keyboard translation table. By changing the entries in this table, it is possible to swap keys. If you are used to vi or vim, you can swap DELETE and CONTROL-H. Then CONTROL-H backspaces as it does in vim, and DELETE (which is not used by vim) is the help key. If you use DELETE as an interrupt key, you may want to choose another key to swap with CONTROL-H.

- The mapped keystrokes are gathered into small groups called *key sequences*. A key sequence may be only a single key, such as CONTROL-N, or may include two or more keys, such as CONTROL-X CONTROL-F. Once gathered the key sequences are used to select a particular procedure to be executed. The rules for gathering each key sequence and the specific procedure name to be executed when that sequence comes in are codified in a series of tables called *keymaps*. By altering the keymaps, you can change the gathering rules or change which procedure is associated with which sequence. If you are used to vi's or vim's use of CONTROL-W to back up over the word you are entering, you may want to change emacs's CONTROL-W binding from the standard **kill-region** to **delete-word-backward**.

- The command behavior is often conditioned by one or more global variables or options. It may be possible to get the behavior you want by setting some of these variables.

- The command itself is usually a Lisp program that can be reprogrammed to make it behave as desired. Although this task is not appropriate for beginners, the Lisp source to nearly all commands is available and the internal Lisp system is fully documented. As mentioned earlier, it is common practice to load customized Lisp code at startup time, even if you did not write it yourself.

Most emacs documentation glosses over all the translation, gathering, and procedure selection and talks about keystrokes as though they were commands. However, it is still important to know that the underlying machinery exists and to understand that its behavior can be changed.

THE .emacs STARTUP FILE

Each time you start emacs, it loads the file of Lisp code named ~/.emacs. Using this file is the most common way to customize emacs. Two command line options control the use of the .emacs file. The **–q** option ignores the .emacs file so that emacs starts up without it; this is one way to get past a bad .emacs file. The **–u** *user* option uses the ~*user*/.emacs file (the .emacs file from the home directory of *user*).

The .emacs startup file is generally concerned only with key bindings and option settings; it is possible to write the Lisp statements for this file in a straightforward style. Each parenthesized Lisp statement is a Lisp function call. Inside the parentheses the first symbol is the function name; the rest of the SPACE-separated tokens are arguments to that function. The most common function in the .emacs file, **setq**, is a simple assignment to a global variable. The first argument is the name of the variable to set and the second argument is its value. The following example sets the variable named **c-indent-level** to 8:

```
(setq c-indent-level 8)
```

You can set the default value for a variable that is buffer-private by using the function name **setq-default**. To set a specific element of a vector, use the function name

aset. The first argument is the name of the vector, the second is the target offset, and the third is the value of the target entry. In the startup file the new values are usually constants. Table 7-21 shows the formats of these constants.

Table 7-21   Formats of constants in **.emacs**

Command	Result
Numbers	Decimal integers, with an optional minus sign
Strings	Similar to C strings but with extensions for CONTROL and META characters: **\C-s** yields CONTROL-S, **\M-s** yields META-s, and **\M-\C-s** yields CONTROL-META-s
Characters	*Not* like C characters; start with **?** and continue with a printing character or with a backslash escape sequence (for example, **?a, ?\C-i, ?\033**)
Booleans	*Not* **1** and **0**; use **t** for *true* and **nil** for *false*
Other Lisp objects	Begin with a single quotation mark and continue with the object's name

Remapping Keys

The emacs command loop begins each cycle by translating incoming keystrokes into the name of the command to be executed. The basic translation operation uses the ASCII value of the incoming character to index a 128-element vector called a *keymap*.

Sometimes a character's eighth bit is interpreted as the META *case*, but this cannot always be relied on. At the point of translation all META characters appear with the ESCAPE prefix, whether or not they were actually typed that way.

Each position in this vector is one of the following:

- Not defined at all: No translation possible in this map.

- The name of another keymap: Switches to that keymap and waits for the next character to arrive.

- The name of a Lisp function to be called: Translation process is done; call this command.

Because keymaps can reference other keymaps, an arbitrarily complex recognition tree can be set up. The mainstream emacs bindings use at most three keys, with a very small group of well-known *prefix keys*, each with its well-known keymap name.

Each buffer can have a *local keymap* that is used first for any keystrokes arriving while a window into that buffer is selected. The local keymap allows the regular mapping to be extended or overridden on a per-buffer basis and is most often used to add bindings for a Major mode.

The basic translation flow runs as follows:

- Map the first character through the buffer's local keymap. If it is defined as a Lisp function name, translation is done and emacs executes that function. If it is not defined, use this same character to index the global top-level keymap.

- Map the first character through the top-level global keymap **global-map**. At this and each following stage, the following conditions hold:

  - If the entry for this character is not defined, it is an error. Send a bell to the terminal and discard all the characters entered in this key sequence.

  - If the entry for this character is defined as a Lisp function name, translation is done and the function is executed.

  - If the entry for this character is defined as the name of another keymap, switch to that keymap and wait for another character to select one of its elements.

Everything must be a command or an error. Ordinary characters that are to be inserted in the buffer are usually bound to the command **self-insert-command**. Each of the well-known prefix characters is each associated with a keymap (Table 7-22).

Table 7-22   Keymap prefixes

Keymap prefix	Applies to
ctl-x-map	For characters following CONTROL-X
ctl-x-4-map	For characters following CONTROL-X **4**
esc-map	For characters following ESCAPE (including META characters)
help-map	For characters following CONTROL-H
mode-specific-map	For characters following CONTROL-C

To see the current state of the keymaps, type CONTROL-H **b**. They appear in the following order: local, global, and shorter maps for each prefix key. Each line specifies the name of the Lisp function to be called; the documentation for that function can be retrieved with the commands CONTROL-H **f** *function-name* or CONTROL-H **k** *key-sequence*.

The most common type of keymap customization is making small changes to the global command assignments without creating any new keymaps or commands. This type of customization is most easily done in the **.emacs** file using the Lisp function **define-key**. The **define-key** function takes three arguments:

- The keymap name

- A single character defining a position in that map
- The command to be executed when this character appears

For instance, to bind the command **backward-kill-word** to CONTROL-W, use the statement

```
(define-key global-map "\C-w" 'backward-kill-word)
```

To bind the command **kill-region** to CONTROL-X CONTROL-K, use the statement

```
(define-key ctl-x-map "\C-k" 'kill-region)
```

The \ character causes **C-w** to be interpreted as CONTROL-W instead of three letters (equivalent to **\^w**). The unmatched single quotation mark in front of the command name is correct. This Lisp escape character keeps the name from being evaluated too soon.

A SAMPLE .emacs FILE

The following ~/.emacs file produces a plain editing environment that minimizes surprises for vi and vim users. Of course, if any section or any line is inapplicable or not to your liking, you can edit it out or comment it with one or more ; comment characters, beginning in column 1.

```
;;; Preference Variables

(setq make-backup-files nil)          ;Do not make backup files
(setq backup-by-copying t)            ;If you do, at least do not destroy links
(setq delete-auto-save-files t)       ;Delete autosave files when writing orig
(setq blink-matching-paren nil)       ;Do not blink opening delim
(setq-default case-fold-search nil)   ;Do not fold cases in search
(setq require-final-newline 'ask)     ;Ask about missing final newline

;; Reverse mappings for C-h and DEL.
(keyboard-translate ?\C-h ?\177)
(keyboard-translate ?\177 ?\C-h)

;; reassigning C-w to keep on deleting words backward

;; C-w is supposed to be kill-region, but it's a great burden for vi-trained fingers.
;; Bind it instead to backward-kill-word for more familiar, friendly behavior.
(define-key global-map "\^w" 'backward-kill-word)

;; for kill-region use a two-key sequence c-x c-k.
(define-key ctl-x-map "\^k" 'kill-region)

;; C mode customization: set vanilla (8-space bsd) indention style

(require 'cc-mode)                     ;kiss: be sure it's here

(c-add-style                          ;add indentation style
```

```
"bsd8"                                    ;old bsd (8 spaces)
 '((c-basic-offset . 8)
   (c-hanging-comment-ender-p . nil)      ;isolated "*/" ends blk comments
   (c-comment-only-line-offset . 0)
   (c-offsets-alist . ((statement-block-intro . +)
                       (knr-argdecl-intro . +)
                       (substatement-open . 0)
                       (label . 0)
                       (statement-cont . +)
                       ))
   ))
(add-hook                                 ;this is our default style,
 'c-mode-hook                             ;set it always in c-mode-hook
 (function
  (lambda ()
    (c-set-style "bsd8")))))

;; end of c mode style setup
```

MORE INFORMATION

A lot of emacs documentation is available in both paper and electronic form. The GNU emacs Web page is a good place to start: www.gnu.org/software/emacs.

The comp.emacs and gnu.emacs.help newsgroups offer support for and a general discussion about emacs.

ACCESS TO emacs

The emacs editor is included with most Linux distributions. You can download and install emacs with Apt (page 850) or yum (page 848). You can download the latest version of the source code from www.gnu.org.

The Free Software Foundation can be reached at these addresses:

Mail: Free Software Foundation, Inc.
        59 Temple Place, Suite 330
        Boston, MA 02111-1307, USA

E-mail: gnu@gnu.org

Phone: 1 617-542-5942

CHAPTER SUMMARY

You can precede many of the commands in the following tables with a numeric argument to make the command repeat the number of times specified by the argument. Precede a numeric argument with CONTROL-U to keep emacs from entering the argument as text.

Table 7-23 lists commands that move the cursor.

Table 7-23 Moving the cursor

Command	Result
CONTROL-F	Forward by characters
CONTROL-B	Backward by characters
META-f	Forward by words
META-b	Backward by words
META-e	To end of sentence
META-a	To beginning of sentence
META-}	To end of paragraph
META-{	To beginning of paragraph
META->	Forward to end of buffer
META-<	Backward to beginning of buffer
CONTROL-ESCAPE	To end of line
CONTROL-A	To beginning of line
CONTROL-N	Forward (down) one line
CONTROL-P	Backward (up) one line
CONTROL-V	Scroll forward (down) one window
META-v	Scroll backward (up) one window
CONTROL-L	Clear and repaint screen, and scroll current line to center of window
META-r	To beginning of middle line
CONTROL-U *num* META-r	To beginning of line number *num* (0 = top, − = bottom)

Table 7-24 lists commands that kill and delete text.

Table 7-24   Killing and deleting text

Command	Result
CONTROL-DELETE	Deletes character under cursor
DELETE	Deletes character to left of cursor
META-d	Kills forward to end of current word
META-DELETE	Kills backward to beginning of previous word
META-k	Kills forward to end of sentence
CONTROL-X DELETE	Kills backward to beginning of sentence
CONTROL-K	Kills forward to, but not including, line-ending LINEFEED; if there is no text between the cursor and the LINEFEED, kills the LINEFEED
CONTROL-U 1 CONTROL-K	Kills from cursor forward to and including LINEFEED
CONTROL-U 0 CONTROL-K	Kills from cursor backward to beginning of line
META-z *char*	Kills forward to, but not including, next occurrence of *char*
META-w	Copies Region to Kill Ring (does not delete Region from buffer)
CONTROL-W	Kills Region (deletes Region from buffer)
CONTROL-Y	Yanks most recently killed text into current buffer at Point; sets Mark at beginning of this text, with Point and cursor at the end
META-y	Erases just-yanked text, rotates Kill Ring, and yanks next item (only after CONTROL-Y or META-y)

Table 7-25 lists commands that search for strings and regular expressions.

Table 7-25   Search commands

Command	Result
CONTROL-S	Prompts incrementally for a string and searches forward
CONTROL-S RETURN	Prompts for a complete string and searches forward
CONTROL-R	Prompts incrementally for a string and searches backward
CONTROL-R RETURN	Prompts for a complete string and searches backward
META-CONTROL-S	Prompts incrementally for a regular expression and searches forward
META-−CONTROL-S RETURN	Prompts for a complete regular expression and searches forward
META-x isearch-backward-regexp	Prompts incrementally for a regular expression and searches forward
META-x isearch-backward-regexp RETURN	Prompts for a complete regular expression and searches backward

Table 7-26 lists commands that provide online help.

Table 7-26   Online help

Command	Result
CONTROL-H a	Prompts for *string* and displays a list of commands whose names contain *string*
CONTROL-H b	Displays a (long) table of all key bindings now in effect
CONTROL-H c *key-sequence*	Displays the name of the command bound to *key-sequence*
CONTROL-H k *key-sequence*	Displays the name of and documentation for the command bound to *key-sequence*
CONTROL-H f	Prompts for the name of a Lisp function and displays the documentation for that function
CONTROL-H i (lowercase "i")	Displays the top menu of info (page 32)
CONTROL-H l (lowercase "l")	Displays the last 100 characters typed
CONTROL-H m	Displays the documentation and special key bindings for the current Major mode
CONTROL-H n	Displays the emacs news file
CONTROL-H t	Starts an emacs tutorial session
CONTROL-H v	Prompts for a Lisp variable name and displays the documentation for that variable
CONTROL-H w	Prompts for a command name and displays the key sequence, if any, bound to that command

Table 7-27 lists commands that work with a Region.

Table 7-27   Working with a Region

Command	Result
META-W	Copies Region nondestructively to the Kill Ring
CONTROL-W	Kills (deletes) Region
META-x print-region	Copies Region to the print spooler
META-x append-to-buffer	Prompts for buffer name and appends Region to that buffer
META-x append-to-file	Prompts for filename and appends Region to that file
CONTROL-X CONTROL-U	Converts Region to uppercase
CONTROL-X CONTROL-L	Converts Region to lowercase

Table 7-28 lists commands that work with lines.

Table 7-28   Working with lines

Command	Result
META-x occur	Prompts for a regular expression and lists each line containing a match for the expression in a buffer named ✽**Occur**✽
META-x delete-matching-lines	Prompts for a regular expression and deletes lines from Point forward that have a match for the regular expression
META-x delete-non-matching-lines	Prompts for a regular expression and deletes lines from Point forward that do *not* have a match for the regular expression

Table 7-29 lists commands that replace strings and regular expressions unconditionally and interactively.

Table 7-29   Commands that replace text

Command	Result
META-x replace-string	Prompts for two strings and replaces each instance of the first string with the second string from Mark forward; sets Mark at the start of the command
META-% *or* META-x query-replace	As above but queries for each replacement (see Table 7-30 for a list of responses)
META-x replace-regexp	Prompts for a regular expression and a string, and replaces each match for the regular expression with the string; sets Mark at the start of the command
META-x query-replace-regexp	As above but queries for each replacement (see Table 7-30 for a list of responses)

Table 7-30 lists responses to replacement queries.

Table 7-30   Responses to replacement queries

Command	Result
RETURN	Quits searching (does not make or query for any more replacements)
SPACE	Makes this replacement and continues querying
DELETE	Does *not* make this replacement and continues querying
, (comma)	Makes this replacement, displays the result, and asks for another command

Table 7-30   Responses to replacement queries (continued)

. (period)	Makes this replacement and does not make or query for any more replacements
! (exclamation point)	Replaces this and all remaining instances without querying

Table 7-31 lists commands that work with windows.

Table 7-31   Working with windows

Command	Result
CONTROL-X b	Prompts for and displays a different buffer in current window
CONTROL-X 2	Splits current window vertically into two
CONTROL-X 3	Splits current window horizontally into two
CONTROL-X o (lowercase "o")	Selects other window
META-CONTROL-V	Scrolls other window
CONTROL-X 4b	Prompts for buffer name and selects it in other window
CONTROL-X 4f	Prompts for filename and selects it in other window
CONTROL-X 0 (zero)	Deletes current window
CONTROL-X 1 (one)	Deletes all windows except current window
META-x shrink-window	Makes current window one line shorter
CONTROL-X ^	Makes current window one line taller
CONTROL-X }	Makes current window one character wider
CONTROL-X {	Makes current window one character narrower

Table 7-32 lists commands that work with files.

Table 7-32   Working with files

Command	Result
CONTROL-X CONTROL-F	Prompts for a filename and reads its contents into a new buffer; assigns the file's simple filename as the buffer name.
CONTROL-X CONTROL-V	Prompts for a filename and reads its contents into the current buffer (overwriting the contents of the current buffer).
CONTROL-X 4 CONTROL-F	Prompts for a filename and reads its contents into a new buffer; assigns the file's simple filename as the buffer name. Creates a new window for the new buffer and selects that window. This command splits the screen in half if you begin with only one window.

Table 7-32   Working with files (continued)

CONTROL-X CONTROL-S	Saves the current buffer to the original file.
CONTROL-X S	Prompts for whether to save each modified buffer (**y/n**).
META-x set-visited-file-name	Prompts for a filename and sets the current buffer's "original" name to that filename.
CONTROL-X CONTROL-W	Prompts for a filename, sets the current buffer's "original" name to that filename, and saves the current buffer in that file.
META-~ (tilde)	Clears modified flag from the current buffer. Use with caution.

Table 7-33 lists commands that work with buffers.

Table 7-33   Working with buffers

Command	Result
CONTROL-X CONTROL-S	Saves current buffer in its associated file.
CONTROL-X CONTROL-F	Prompts for filename and visits (opens) that file.
CONTROL-X b	Prompts for buffer name and selects it. If that buffer does not exist, creates it.
CONTROL-X 4b	Prompts for buffer name and displays that buffer in another window. The existing window is not disturbed, although the new window may overlap it.
CONTROL-X CONTROL-B	Creates a buffer named ✷**Buffer List**✷ and displays it in another window. The existing window is not disturbed, although the new window may overlap it. The new buffer is not selected. In the ✷**Buffer List**✷ buffer, each buffer's data is displayed with its name, size, mode(s), and original filename.
META-x rename-buffer	Prompts for a new buffer name and assigns this new name to the current buffer.
CONTROL-X CONTROL-Q	Toggles the current buffer's readonly status and the associated %% Mode Line indicator.
META-x append-to-buffer	Prompts for buffer name and appends Region to the end of that buffer.
META-x prepend-to-buffer	Prompts for buffer name and prepends Region to beginning of that buffer.
META-x copy-to-buffer	Prompts for buffer name, deletes contents of that buffer, and copies the Region to that buffer.
META-x insert-buffer	Prompts for buffer name and inserts entire contents of that buffer in current buffer at Point.

Table 7-33 Working with buffers (continued)

CONTROL-X k	Prompts for buffer name and deletes that buffer.
META-x kill-some-buffers	Goes through the entire buffer list and offers the chance to delete each buffer.

Table 7-34 lists commands that run shell commands in the foreground. These commands may not work with all shells.

Table 7-34 Foreground shell commands

Command	Result
META-! (exclamation point)	Prompts for shell command, executes it, and displays the output
CONTROL-U META-! (exclamation point)	Prompts for shell command, executes it, and inserts the output at Point
META-| (vertical bar)	Prompts for shell command, supplies Region as input to that command, and displays output of command
CONTROL-U META-| (vertical bar)	Prompts for shell command, supplies Region as input to that command, deletes old Region, and inserts output of command in place of Region

Table 7-35 lists commands that run shell commands in the background.

Table 7-35 Background shell commands

Command	Result
META-x compile	Prompts for shell command and runs that command in the background, with output going to the buffer named *compilation*
META-x kill-compilation	Kills background process

Table 7-36 lists commands that convert text from uppercase to lowercase and vice versa.

Table 7-36 Case conversion commands

Command	Result
META-l (lowercase "l")	Converts word to right of Point to lowercase
META-u	Converts word to right of Point to uppercase
META-c	Converts word to right of Point to initial caps
CONTROL-X CONTROL-L	Converts Region to lowercase
CONTROL-X CONTROL-U	Converts Region to uppercase

Table 7-37 lists commands that work in C mode.

Table 7-37 C mode commands

Command	Result
CONTROL-META-f	Moves forward over expression
CONTROL-META-b	Moves backward over expression
CONTROL-META-k	Moves forward over expression and kills it
CONTROL-META-@	Sets Mark at the position CONTROL-META-f would move to, without changing Point
CONTROL-META-a	Moves to beginning of the most recent function definition
CONTROL-META-e	Moves to the end of the next function definition
CONTROL-META-h	Moves Point to beginning and Mark to end of current (or next, if between) function definition

Type META-x **shell** to create a buffer named ✳**shell**✳ and start a subshell. Table 7-38 lists commands that work on this buffer.

Table 7-38 Shell mode commands

Command	Result
RETURN	Sends current line to the shell
CONTROL-C CONTROL-D	Sends CONTROL-D to shell or its subshell
CONTROL-C CONTROL-C	Sends CONTROL-C to shell or its subshell
CONTROL-C CONTROL-\	Sends quit signal to shell or its subshell
CONTROL-C CONTROL-U	Kills text on the current line not yet completed
CONTROL-C CONTROL-R	Scrolls back to beginning of last shell output, putting first line of output at the top of the window
CONTROL-C CONTROL-O (uppercase "O")	Deletes last batch of shell output

EXERCISES

1. Given a buffer full of English text, answer the following questions:

    a. How would you change every instance of **his** to **hers**?

    b. How would you do this only in the final paragraph?

c. Is there a way to look at every usage in context before changing it?

d. How would you deal with the possibility that **His** might begin a sentence?

2. Which command moves the cursor to the end of the current paragraph? Can you use this command to skip through the buffer in one-paragraph steps?

3. Suppose that you get lost in the middle of typing a long sentence.

a. Is there an easy way to kill the botched sentence and start over?

b. What if only one word is incorrect? Is there an alternative to backspacing one letter at a time?

4. After you have been working on a paragraph for a while, most likely some lines will have become too short and others too long. Is there a command to "neaten up" the paragraph without rebreaking all the lines by hand?

5. Is there a way to change the entire contents of the buffer to capital letters? Can you think of a way to change just one paragraph?

6. How would you reverse the order of two paragraphs?

7. How would you reverse two words?

8. Imagine that you saw a Usenet posting with something particularly funny in it and saved the posting to a file. How would you incorporate this file into your own buffer? What if you wanted only a couple of paragraphs? How would you add > to the beginning of each included line?

9. On the keyboard alone emacs has always offered a full set of editing possibilities. Generally several techniques will accomplish the same goal for any editing task. In the X environment the choice is enlarged still further with a new group of mouse-oriented visual alternatives. From these options you must select the way that you like to solve a given editing puzzle best.

Consider this Shakespearean fragment:

```
1. Full fathom five thy father lies;
2.   Of his bones are coral made;
3. Those are pearls that were his eyes:
4.   Nothing of him that doth fade,
5. But doth suffer a sea-change
6. Into something rich and strange.
7. Sea-nymphs hourly ring his knell:
8.            Ding-dong.
9. Hark! now I hear them--
10.     Ding-dong, bell!
```

The following fragment has been typed with some errors:

```
 1. Full fathiom five tyy father lies;
 2. These are pearls that were his eyes:
 3.   Of his bones are coral made;
 4.   Nothin of him that doth fade,
 5. But doth susffer a sea-change
 6. Into something rich and strange.
 7. Sea-nymphs hourly ring his knell:
 8.          Ding=dong.
 9. Hard! now I hear them--
10.      Ding-dong, bell!
```

Use only the keyboard to answer the following:

a. How many ways can you think of to move the cursor to the spelling errors?

b. Once the cursor is on or near the errors, how many ways can you think of to fix them?

c. Are there ways to fix errors without explicitly navigating to/searching for them? How many can you think of?

d. Lines 2 and 3 are transposed. How many ways can you think of to correct this situation?

ADVANCED EXERCISES

10. Assume that your buffer contains the C code shown here, with the Major mode set for C and the cursor positioned at the end of the **while** line as shown by the black square:

```c
/*
 * Copy string s2 to s1.  s1 must be large enough
 * return s1
 */
char *
strcpy(s1, s2)
register char *s1, *s2;
{
     register char *os1;

     os1 = s1;
     while (*s1++ = *s2++)
     ;
return(os1);
}

/* Copy source into dest, stopping after '\0' is copied, and
```

```
    return a pointer to the '\0' at the end of dest.  Then our caller
    can concatenate to the dest string without another strlen call. */
char *
stpcpy (dest, source)
    char *dest;
    char *source;
{
  while ((*dest++ = *source++) != '\0') █
    ; /* void loop body */
  return (dest - 1);
}
```

a. Which command moves the cursor to the opening brace of **strcpy**? Which command moves the cursor past the closing brace? Can you use these commands to skip through the buffer in one-procedure steps?

b. Assume the cursor is just past the closing parenthesis of the **while** condition. How do you move to the matching opening parenthesis? How do you move back to the matching close parenthesis again? Does the same command set work for matched [] and {}? How does this differ from the vim % command?

c. One procedure is indented in the Berkeley indention style; the other is indented in the GNU style. Which command reindents a line in accordance with the current indention style you have set up? How would you reindent an entire procedure?

d. Suppose that you want to write five string procedures and intend to use **strcpy** as a starting point for further editing. How would you make five copies of the **strcpy** procedure?

e. How would you compile the code without leaving emacs?

PART III
The Shells

8

THE BOURNE AGAIN SHELL

This chapter picks up where Chapter 5 left off by focusing on the Bourne Again Shell (bash). It notes where tcsh implementation of a feature differs from that of bash; if appropriate, you are directed to the page where the alternative implementation is discussed. Chapter 11 expands on this chapter, exploring control flow commands and more advanced aspects of programming the Bourne Again Shell. The bash home page is www.gnu.org/software/bash. The bash info page is a complete Bourne Again Shell reference.

The Bourne Again Shell and TC Shell (tcsh) are command interpreters and high-level programming languages. As command interpreters, they process commands you enter on the command line in response to a prompt. When you use the shell as a programming language, it processes commands stored in files called *shell scripts*. Like other languages, shells have variables and control flow commands (for example, **for** loops and **if** statements).

When you use a shell as a command interpreter, you can customize the environment you work in. You can make your prompt display the name of the working directory, create a function or alias for cp that keeps it from overwriting certain kinds of files, take advantage of keyword variables to change aspects of how the shell works, and so on. You can also write shell scripts that do your bidding, from a one-line script that stores a long, complex command to a longer script that runs a set of reports, prints them, and mails you a reminder when the job is done. More complex shell scripts are themselves programs; they do not just run other programs. Chapter 11 has some examples of these types of scripts.

Most system shell scripts are written to run under the Bourne Again Shell. If you will ever work in single-user mode—as when you boot your system or do system maintenance, administration, or repair work, for example—it is a good idea to become familiar with this shell.

This chapter expands on the interactive features of the shell described in Chapter 5, explains how to create and run simple shell scripts, discusses job control, introduces the basic aspects of shell programming, talks about history and aliases, and describes command line expansion. Chapter 9 covers interactive use of the TC Shell and TC Shell programming, and Chapter 11 presents some more challenging shell programming problems.

BACKGROUND

The Bourne Again Shell is based on the Bourne Shell (the early UNIX shell; this book refers to it as the *original Bourne Shell* to avoid confusion), which was written by Steve Bourne of AT&T's Bell Laboratories. Over the years the original Bourne Shell has been expanded but it remains the basic shell provided with many commercial versions of UNIX.

sh Shell   Because of its long and successful history, the original Bourne Shell has been used to write many of the shell scripts that help manage UNIX systems. Some of these scripts appear in Linux as Bourne Again Shell scripts. Although the Bourne Again Shell includes many extensions and features not found in the original Bourne Shell, bash maintains compatibility with the original Bourne Shell so you can run Bourne Shell scripts under bash. On UNIX systems the original Bourne Shell is named sh. On Linux systems sh is a symbolic link to bash ensuring that scripts that require the presence of the Bourne Shell still run. When called as sh, bash does its best to emulate the original Bourne Shell.

Korn Shell   System V UNIX introduced the Korn Shell (ksh), written by David Korn. This shell extended many features of the original Bourne Shell and added many new features. Some features of the Bourne Again Shell, such as command aliases and command line editing, are based on similar features from the Korn Shell.

POSIX standards   The POSIX (the Portable Operating System Interface) family of related standards is being developed by PASC (IEEE's Portable Application Standards Committee, www.pasc.org). A comprehensive FAQ on POSIX, including many links, appears at www.opengroup.org/austin/papers/posix_faq.html.

POSIX standard 1003.2 describes shell functionality. The Bourne Again Shell provides the features that match the requirements of this POSIX standard. Efforts are under way to make the Bourne Again Shell fully comply with the POSIX standard. In the meantime, if you invoke bash with the --posix option, the behavior of the Bourne Again Shell will more closely match the POSIX requirements.

SHELL BASICS

This section covers writing and using startup files, redirecting standard error, writing and executing simple shell scripts, separating and grouping commands, implementing job control, and manipulating the directory stack.

STARTUP FILES

When a shell starts, it runs startup files to initialize itself. Which files the shell runs depends on whether it is a login shell, an interactive shell that is not a login shell (such as you get by giving the command **bash**), or a noninteractive shell (one used to execute a shell script). You must have read access to a startup file to execute the commands in it. Typically Linux distributions put appropriate commands in some of these files. This section covers bash startup files. See page 342 for information on tcsh startup files.

LOGIN SHELLS

The files covered in this section are executed by login shells and shells that you start with the --**login** option. Login shells are, by their nature, interactive.

/etc/profile   The shell first executes the commands in **/etc/profile**. Superuser can set up this file to establish systemwide default characteristics for bash users.

.bash_profile
.bash_login
.profile   Next the shell looks for ~/.bash_profile, ~/.bash_login, and ~/.profile (~/ is shorthand for your home directory), in that order, executing the commands in the first of these files it finds. You can put commands in one of these files to override the defaults set in **/etc/profile**.

.bash_logout   When you log out, bash executes commands in the ~/.bash_logout file. Frequently commands that clean up after a session, such as those that remove temporary files, go in this file.

INTERACTIVE NONLOGIN SHELLS

The commands in the preceding startup files are not executed by interactive, non-login shells. However, these shells inherit from the login shell variables that are set by these startup files.

/etc/bashrc   Although not called by bash directly, many **~/.bashrc** files call **/etc/bashrc**. This setup allows Superuser to establish systemwide default characteristics for nonlogin bash shells.

.bashrc   An interactive nonlogin shell executes commands in the **~/.bashrc** file. Typically a startup file for a login shell, such as **.bash_profile**, runs this file, so that both login and nonlogin shells benefit from the commands in **.bashrc**.

NONINTERACTIVE SHELLS

The commands in the previously described startup files are not executed by non-interactive shells, such as those that runs shell scripts. However, these shells inherit from the login shell variables that are set by these startup files.

BASH_ENV   Noninteractive shells look for the environment variable **BASH_ENV** (or **ENV**, if the shell is called as sh) and execute commands in the file named by this variable.

SETTING UP STARTUP FILES

Although many startup files and types of shells exist, usually all you need are the **.bash_profile** and **.bashrc** files in your home directory. Commands similar to the following in **.bash_profile** run commands from **.bashrc** for login shells (when **.bashrc** exists). With this setup, the commands in **.bashrc** are executed by login and non-login shells.

```
if [ -f ~/.bashrc ]; then source ~/.bashrc; fi
```

The [**–f ~/.bashrc**] tests whether the file named **.bashrc** in your home directory exists. See page 794 for more information on test and its synonym [ ].

Use .bash_profile to set PATH

tip   Because commands in **.bashrc** may be executed many times, and because subshells inherit exported variables, it is a good idea to put commands that add to existing variables in the **.bash_profile** file. For example, the following command adds the **bin** subdirectory of the **home** directory to **PATH** (page 284) and should go in **.bash_profile**:

```
PATH=$PATH:$HOME/bin
```

When you put this command in **.bash_profile** and not in **.bashrc**, the string is added to the **PATH** variable only once, when you log in.

Modifying a variable in **.bash_profile** allows changes you make in an interactive session to propagate to subshells. In contrast, modifying a variable in **.bashrc** overrides changes inherited from a parent shell.

Sample **.bash_profile** and **.bashrc** files follow. Some of the commands used in these files are not covered until later in this chapter. In any startup file, you must export variables and functions that you want to be available to child processes. For more information refer to "Locality of Variables" on page 475.

```
$ cat ~/.bash_profile
if [ -f ~/.bashrc ]; then
    source ~/.bashrc              # read local startup file if it exists
fi
PATH=$PATH:.                      # add the working directory to PATH
export PS1='[\h \W \!]\$ '        # set prompt
```

The first command in the preceding **.bash_profile** file executes the commands in the user's **.bashrc** file if it exists. The next command adds to the **PATH** variable (page 284). Typically **PATH** is set and exported in **/etc/profile** so it does not need to be exported in a user's startup file. The final command sets and exports **PS1** (page 286), which controls the user's prompt.

Next is a sample **.bashrc** file. The first command executes the commands in the **/etc/bashrc** file if it exists. Next the **LANG** (page 290) and **VIMINIT** (page 176) variables are set and exported and several aliases (page 312) are established. The final command defines a function (page 315) that swaps the names of two files.

```
$ cat ~/.bashrc
if [ -f /etc/bashrc ]; then
    source /etc/bashrc            # read global startup file if it exists
fi

set -o noclobber                 # prevent overwriting files
unset MAILCHECK                  # turn off "you have new mail" notice
export LANG=C                    # set LANG variable
export VIMINIT='set ai aw'       # set vim options
alias df='df -h'                 # set up aliases
alias rm='rm -i'                 # always do interactive rm's
alias lt='ls -ltrh | tail'
alias h='history | tail'
alias ch='chmod 755 '

function switch()                # a function to exchange the names
{                                # of two files
    local tmp=$$switch
    mv "$1" $tmp
    mv "$2" "$1"
    mv $tmp "$2"
}
```

. (DOT) OR source: RUNS A STARTUP FILE IN THE CURRENT SHELL

After you edit a startup file such as **.bashrc**, you do not have to log out and log in again to put the changes into effect. You can run the startup file using the . (dot) or source builtin (they are the same command under bash; only source is available under tcsh [page 380]). As with all other commands, the . must be followed by a SPACE on the command line. Using the . or source builtin is similar to running a shell script, except that these commands run the script as part of the current process. Consequently, when you use . or source to run a script, changes you make to variables from within the script affect the shell that you run the script from. You can use the . or source command to run any shell script—not just a startup file—but undesirable side effects (such as changes in the values of shell variables you rely on) may occur. If you ran a startup file as a regular shell script and did not use the . or source builtin, the variables created in the startup file would remain in effect only in the subshell running the script—not in the shell you ran the script from. For more information refer to "Locality of Variables" on page 475.

In the following example, **.bashrc** sets several variables and sets **PS1**, the prompt, to the name of the host. The . builtin puts the new values into effect.

```
$ cat ~/.bashrc
export TERM=vt100              # set the terminal type
export PS1="$(hostname -f): " # set the prompt string
export CDPATH=:$HOME          # add HOME to CDPATH string
stty kill '^u'                # set kill line to control-u
$ . ~/.bashrc
bravo.example.com:
```

COMMANDS THAT ARE SYMBOLS

The Bourne Again Shell uses the symbols (,), [,], and $ in a variety of ways. To minimize confusion, Table 8-1 lists the most common use of each of these symbols, even though some of them are not introduced until later.

REDIRECTING STANDARD ERROR

Chapter 5 covered the concept of standard output and explained how to redirect standard output of a command. In addition to standard output, commands can send output to *standard error*. A command can send error messages to standard error to keep them from getting mixed up with the information it sends to standard output.

Just as it does with standard output, by default the shell sends a command's standard error to the screen. Unless you redirect one or the other, you may not know the difference between the output a command sends to standard output and the output it sends to standard error. This section covers the syntax used by the Bourne Again Shell. See page 349 if you are using the TC Shell.

File descriptors   A *file descriptor* is the place a program sends its output to and gets its input from. When you execute a program, the process running the program opens three file descriptors: 0 (standard input), 1 (standard output), and 2 (standard error). The redirect output symbol (> [page 116]) is shorthand for **1>**, which tells the shell to

Table 8-1 Builtin commands that are symbols

Symbol	Command
( )	Subshell (page 270)
$( )	Command substitution (page 329)
(( ))	Arithmetic evaluation; a synonym for **let** (use when the enclosed value contains an equal sign) (page 501)
$(( ))	Arithmetic expansion (not for use with an enclosed equal sign) (page 327)
[ ]	The **test** command. (pages 437, 440, 453, and 794)
[[ ]]	Conditional expression; similar to [ ] but adds string comparisons (page 503)

redirect standard output. Similarly **<** (page 118) is short for **0<**, which redirects standard input. The symbols **2>** redirect standard error. For more information refer to "File Descriptors" on page 470.

The following examples demonstrate how to redirect standard output and standard error to different files and to the same file. When you run the **cat** utility with the name of a file that does not exist and the name of a file that does exist, **cat** sends an error message to standard error and copies the file that does exist to standard output. Unless you redirect them, both messages appear on the screen.

```
$ cat y
This is y.
$ cat x
cat: x: No such file or directory

$ cat x y
cat: x: No such file or directory
This is y.
```

When you redirect standard output of a command, output sent to standard error is not affected and still appears on the screen.

```
$ cat x y > hold
cat: x: No such file or directory
$ cat hold
This is y.
```

Similarly, when you send standard output through a pipe, standard error is not affected. The following example sends standard output of **cat** through a pipe to **tr** (page 804), which in this example converts lowercase characters to uppercase. The text that **cat** sends to standard error is not translated because it goes directly to the screen rather than through the pipe.

```
$ cat x y | tr "[a-z]" "[A-Z]"
cat: x: No such file or directory
THIS IS Y.
```

The following example redirects standard output and standard error to different files. The notation **2>** tells the shell where to redirect standard error (file descriptor 2). The **1>** tells the shell where to redirect standard output (file descriptor 1). You can use **>** in place of **1>**.

```
$ cat x y 1> hold1 2> hold2
$ cat hold1
This is y.
$ cat hold2
cat: x: No such file or directory
```

Duplicating a file descriptor   In the next example, **1>** redirects standard output to **hold**. Then **2>&1** declares file descriptor 2 to be a duplicate of file descriptor 1. As a result both standard output and standard error are redirected to **hold**.

```
$ cat x y 1> hold 2>&1
$ cat hold
cat: x: No such file or directory
This is y.
```

In the preceding example, **1> hold** precedes **2>&1**. If they had been listed in the opposite order, standard error would have been made a duplicate of standard output before standard output was redirected to **hold**. In that case only standard output would have been redirected to **hold**.

The next example declares file descriptor 2 to be a duplicate of file descriptor 1 and sends the output for file descriptor 1 through a pipe to the tr command.

```
$ cat x y 2>&1 | tr "[a-z]" "[A-Z]"
CAT: X: NO SUCH FILE OR DIRECTORY
THIS IS Y.
```

Sending errors to standard error   You can also use **1>&2** to redirect standard output of a command to standard error. This technique is often used in shell scripts to send the output of echo to standard error. In the following script, standard output of the first echo is redirected to standard error:

```
$ cat message_demo
echo This is an error message. 1>&2
echo This is not an error message.
```

If you redirect standard output of **message_demo**, error messages such as the one produced by the first echo will still go to the screen because you have not redirected standard error. Because standard output of a shell script is frequently redirected to another file, you can use this technique to display on the screen error messages generated by the script. The **lnks** script (page 445) uses this technique. You can also use the exec builtin to create additional file descriptors and to redirect standard input, standard output, and standard error of a shell script from within the script (page 491).

The Bourne Again Shell supports the redirection operators shown in Table 8-2.

Table 8-2   Redirection operators

Operator	Meaning
< *filename*	Redirects standard input from *filename*.
> *filename*	Redirects standard output to *filename* unless *filename* exists and **noclobber** (page 119) is set. If **noclobber** is not set, this redirection creates *filename* if it does not exist.
>| *filename*	Redirects standard output to *filename*, even if the file exists and **noclobber** (page 119) is set.
>> *filename*	Redirects and appends standard output to *filename* unless *filename* exists and **noclobber** (page 119) is set. If **noclobber** is not set, this redirection creates *filename* if it does not exist.
<&*m*	Duplicates standard input from file descriptor *m* (page 471).
[*n*]>&*m*	Duplicates standard output or file descriptor *n* if specified from file descriptor *m* (page 471).
[*n*]<&–	Closes standard input or file descriptor *n* if specified (page 471).
[*n*]>&–	Closes standard output or file descriptor *n* if specified.

WRITING A SIMPLE SHELL SCRIPT

A *shell script* is a file that contains commands that the shell can execute. The commands in a shell script can be any commands you can enter in response to a shell prompt. For example, a command in a shell script might run a Linux utility, a compiled program, or another shell script. Like the commands you give on the command line, a command in a shell script can use ambiguous file references and can have its input or output redirected from or to a file or sent through a pipe (page 122). You can also use pipes and redirection with the input and output of the script itself.

In addition to the commands you would ordinarily use on the command line, *control flow* commands (also called *control structures*) find most of their use in shell scripts. This group of commands enables you to alter the order of execution of commands in a script just as you would alter the order of execution of statements using a structured programming language. Refer to "Control Structures" on page 436 (bash) and page 368 (tcsh) for specifics.

The shell interprets and executes the commands in a shell script, one after another. Thus a shell script enables you to simply and quickly initiate a complex series of tasks or a repetitive procedure.

chmod: MAKES A FILE EXECUTABLE

To execute a shell script by giving its name as a command, you must have permission to read and execute the file that contains the script (refer to "Access Permissions" on page 91). Read permission enables you to read the file that holds the script. Execute permission tells the shell and the system that the owner, group, and/or public has permission to execute the file; it implies that the content of the file is executable.

When you create a shell script using an editor, the file does not typically have its execute permission set. The following example shows a file named **whoson** that contains a shell script:

```
$ cat whoson
date
echo "Users Currently Logged In"
who

$ whoson
bash: ./whoson: Permission denied
```

You cannot execute **whoson** by giving its name as a command because you do not have execute permission for the file. The shell does not recognize **whoson** as an executable file and issues an error message when you try to execute it. When you give the filename as an argument to bash (**bash whoson**), bash takes the argument to be a shell script and executes it. In this case **bash** is executable and **whoson** is an argument that bash executes so you do not need to have permission to execute **whoson**. You can do the same with tcsh script files.

Command not found?

tip If you get the message

```
$ whoson
bash: whoson: command not found
```

the shell is not set up to search for executable files in the working directory. Give this command instead:

```
$ ./whoson
```

The ./ tells the shell explicitly to look for an executable file in the working directory. To change the environment so that the shell searches the working directory automatically, see page 284.

The chmod utility changes the access privileges associated with a file. Figure 8-1 shows ls with the –l option displaying the access privileges of **whoson** before and after chmod gives execute permission to the file's owner.

The first ls displays a hyphen (–) as the fourth character, indicating that the owner does not have permission to execute the file. Next chmod gives the owner execute permission: The **u+x** causes chmod to add (+) execute permission (**x**) for the owner (**u**). (The **u** stands for *user*, although it means the owner of the file who may be the user of the file at any given time.) The second argument is the name of the file. The second ls shows an **x** in the fourth position, indicating that the owner now has execute permission.

If other users will execute the file, you must also change group and/or public access permissions for the file. Any user must have execute access to use the file's name as

```
$ ls -l whoson
-rw-rw-r--    1 alex group 40 May 24 11:30 whoson

$ chmod u+x whoson
$ ls -l whoson
-rwxrw-r--    1 alex group 40 May 24 11:30 whoson

$ whoson
Tue May 24 11:40:49 PDT 2005
Users Currently Logged In
jenny     pts/7     May 23 18:17
hls       pts/1     May 24 09:59
scott     pts/12    May 24 06:29 (bravo.example.com)
alex      pts/4     May 24 09:08
```

Figure 8-1   Using chmod to make a shell script executable

a command. If the file is a shell script, the user trying to execute the file must also have read access to the file. You do not need read access to execute a binary executable (compiled program).

The final command in Figure 8-1 shows the shell executing the file when its name is given as a command. For more information refer to "Access Permissions" on page 91 and to ls and chmod in Part V.

#! SPECIFIES A SHELL

You can put a special sequence of characters on the first line of a file to tell the operating system which shell should execute the file. Because the operating system checks the initial characters of a program before attempting to **exec** it, these characters save the system from making an unsuccessful attempt. If **#!** are the first two characters of a script, the system interprets the characters that follow as the absolute pathname of the utility that should execute the script. This can be the pathname of any program, not just a shell. The following example specifies that bash should run the script:

```
$ cat bash_script
#!/bin/bash
echo "This is a Bourne Again Shell script."
```

The **#!** characters are useful if you have a script that you want to run with a shell other than the shell you are running the script from. The following example shows a script that should be executed by tcsh:

```
$ cat tcsh_script
#!/bin/tcsh
echo "This is a tcsh script."
set person = jenny
echo "person is $person"
```

Because of the #! line, the operating system ensures that tcsh executes the script no matter which shell you run it from.

You can use **ps –f** within a shell script to display the name of the shell that is executing the script. The three lines that ps displays in the following example show the process running the parent bash shell, the process running the tcsh script, and the process running the ps command:

```
$ cat tcsh_script2
#!/bin/tcsh
ps -f

$ tcsh_script2
UID        PID  PPID  C STIME TTY          TIME CMD
alex       3031 3030  0 Nov16 pts/4    00:00:00 -bash
alex       9358 3031  0 21:13 pts/4    00:00:00 /bin/tcsh ./tcsh_script2
alex       9375 9358  0 21:13 pts/4    00:00:00 ps -f
```

If you do not follow #! with the name of an executable program, the shell reports that it cannot find the command that you asked it to run. You can optionally follow #! with SPACEs. If you omit the #! line and try to run, for example, a tcsh script from bash, the shell may generate error messages or the script may not run properly.

See page 576 for an example of a stand-alone sed script that uses #!.

BEGINS A COMMENT

Comments make shell scripts and all code easier to read and maintain by you and others. The comment syntax is common to both the Bourne Again and the TC Shells.

If a pound sign (#) in the first character position of the first line of a script is not immediately followed by an exclamation point (!) or if a pound sign occurs in any other location in a script, the shell interprets it as the beginning of a comment. The shell then ignores everything between the pound sign and the end of the line (the next NEWLINE character).

RUNNING A SHELL SCRIPT

fork and **exec** system calls A command on the command line causes the shell to **fork** a new process, creating a duplicate of the shell process (a subshell). The new process attempts to **exec** (execute) the command. Like **fork**, the **exec** routine is executed by the operating system (a system call). If the command is a binary executable program, such as a compiled C program, **exec** succeeds and the system overlays the newly created subshell with the executable program. If the command is a shell script, **exec** fails. When **exec** fails, the command is assumed to be a shell script, and the subshell runs the commands in the script. Unlike a login shell, which expects input from the command line, the subshell takes its input from a file: the shell script.

As discussed earlier, if you have a shell script in a file that you do not have execute permission for, you can run the commands in the script by using a bash command to **exec** a shell to run the script directly. In the following example, bash creates a new shell that takes its input from the file named **whoson**:

```
$ bash whoson
```

Because the bash command expects to read a file containing commands, you do not need execute permission for **whoson**. (You do need read permission.) Even though bash reads and executes the commands in **whoson**, standard input, standard output, and standard error remain connected to the terminal.

Although you can use bash to execute a shell script, this technique causes the script to run more slowly than giving yourself execute permission and directly invoking the script. Users typically prefer to make the file executable and run the script by typing its name on the command line. It is also easier to type the name, and this practice is consistent with the way other kinds of programs are invoked (so you do not need to know whether you are running a shell script or another kind of program). However, if bash is not your interactive shell or if you want to see how the script runs with different shells, you may want to run a script as an argument to **bash** or **tcsh**.

sh does not call the original Bourne Shell

caution   The original Bourne Shell was invoked with the command **sh**. Although you can call bash with an **sh** command, it is not the original Bourne Shell. The **sh** command (**/bin/sh**) is a symbolic link to **/bin/bash**, so it is simply another name for the **bash** command. When you call bash using the command **sh**, bash tries to mimic the behavior of the original Bourne Shell as closely as possible. It does not always succeed.

SEPARATING AND GROUPING COMMANDS

Whether you give the shell commands interactively or write a shell script, you must separate commands from one another. This section, which applies to the Bourne Again and the TC Shells, reviews the ways to separate commands that were covered in Chapter 5 and introduces a few new ones.

; AND NEWLINE SEPARATE COMMANDS

The NEWLINE character is a unique command separator because it initiates execution of the command preceding it. You have seen this throughout this book each time you press the RETURN key at the end of a command line.

The semicolon (;) is a command separator that *does not* initiate execution of a command and *does not* change any aspect of how the command functions. You can execute a series of commands sequentially by entering them on a single command line and separating each from the next with a semicolon (;). You initiate execution of the sequence of commands by pressing RETURN:

```
$ x ; y ; z
```

If x, y, and z are commands, the preceding command line yields the same results as the next three commands. The difference is that in the next example the shell issues a prompt after each of the commands (x, y, and z) finishes executing, whereas the preceding command line causes the shell to issue a prompt only after z is complete:

```
$ x
$ y
$ z
```

Whitespace   Although the whitespace around the semicolons in the earlier example makes the command line easier to read, it is not necessary. None of the command separators needs to be surrounded by SPACEs or TABs.

\ CONTINUES A COMMAND

When you enter a long command line and the cursor reaches the right side of the screen, you can use a backslash (\) character to continue the command on the next line. The backslash quotes, or escapes, the NEWLINE character that follows it so that the shell does not treat the NEWLINE as a command terminator. Enclosing a backslash within single quotation marks turns off the power of a backslash to quote special characters such as NEWLINE. Enclosing a backslash within double quotation marks has no effect on the power of the backslash.

Although you can break a line in the middle of a word (token), it is typically easier to break a line just before or after whitespace.

optional   You can enter a RETURN in the middle of a quoted string on a command line without using a backslash. The NEWLINE (RETURN) that you enter will then be part of the string:

```
$ echo "Please enter the three values
> required to complete the transaction."
Please enter the three values
required to complete the transaction.
```

In the three examples in this section, the shell does not interpret RETURN as a command terminator because it occurs within a quoted string. The > is a secondary prompt indicating that the shell is waiting for you to continue the unfinished command. In the next example, the first RETURN is quoted (escaped) so the shell treats it as a separator and does not interpret it literally.

```
$ echo "Please enter the three values \
> required to complete the transaction."
Please enter the three values required to complete the transaction.
```

Single quotation marks cause the shell to interpret a backslash literally:

```
$ echo 'Please enter the three values \
> required to complete the transaction.'
Please enter the three values \
required to complete the transaction.
```

| AND & SEPARATE COMMANDS AND DO SOMETHING ELSE

The pipe symbol (|) and the background task symbol (&) are also command separators. They *do not* start execution of a command but *do* change some aspect of how the command functions. The pipe symbol alters the source of standard input or the destination of standard output. The background task symbol causes the shell to execute the task in the background so you get a prompt immediately and can continue working on other tasks.

Each of the following command lines initiates a single job comprising three tasks:

```
$ x | y | z
$ ls -l | grep tmp | less
```

In the first job, the shell redirects standard output of task **x** to standard input of task **y** and redirects **y**'s standard output to **z**'s standard input. Because it runs the entire job in the foreground, the shell does not display a prompt until task **z** runs to completion: Task **z** does not finish until task **y** finishes, and task **y** does not finish until task **x** finishes. In the second job, task **x** is an **ls –l** command, task **y** is **grep tmp**, and task **z** is the pager **less**. The shell displays a long (wide) listing of the files in the working directory that contain the string **tmp**, piped through **less**.

The next command line executes tasks **d** and **e** in the background and task **f** in the foreground:

```
$ d & e & f
[1] 14271
[2] 14272
```

The shell displays the job number between brackets and the PID (process identification) number for each process running in the background. You get a prompt as soon as **f** finishes, which may be before **d** or **e** finishes.

Before displaying a prompt for a new command, the shell checks whether any background jobs have completed. For each job that has completed, the shell displays its job number, the word **Done**, and the command line that invoked the job; then the shell displays a prompt. When the job numbers are listed, the number of the last job started is followed by a + character and the job number of the previous job is followed by a – character. Any other jobs listed show a SPACE character. After running the last command, the shell displays the following before issuing a prompt:

```
[1]-  Done                    d
[2]+  Done                    e
```

The next command line executes all three tasks as background jobs. You get a shell prompt immediately:

```
$ d & e & f &
[1] 14290
[2] 14291
[3] 14292
```

You can use pipes to send the output from one task to the next task and an ampersand (&) to run the entire job as a background task. Again the prompt comes back immediately. The shell regards the commands joined by a pipe as being a single job. That is, it treats all pipes as single jobs, no matter how many tasks are connected with the pipe (|) symbol or how complex they are. The Bourne Again Shell shows only one process placed in the background:

```
$ d | e | f &
[1] 14295
```

The TC Shell shows three processes (all belonging to job 1) placed in the background:

```
tcsh $ d | e | f &
[1] 14302 14304 14306
```

optional () GROUPS COMMANDS

You can use parentheses to group commands. The shell creates a copy of itself, called a *subshell,* for each group. It treats each group of commands as a job and creates a new process to execute each command (refer to "Process Structure" on page 293 for more information on creating subshells). Each subshell (job) has its own environment, meaning that it has its own set of variables with values that can differ from those of other subshells.

The following command line executes commands **a** and **b** sequentially in the background while executing **c** in the background. The shell prompt returns immediately.

```
$ (a ; b) & c &
[1] 15520
[2] 15521
```

The preceding example differs from the earlier example **d & e & f &** in that tasks **a** and **b** are initiated sequentially, not concurrently.

Similarly the following command line executes **a** and **b** sequentially in the background and, at the same time, executes **c** and **d** sequentially in the background. The subshell running **a** and **b** and the subshell running **c** and **d** run concurrently. The prompt returns immediately.

```
$ (a ; b) & (c ; d) &
[1] 15528
[2] 15529
```

The next script copies one directory to another. The second pair of parentheses creates a subshell to run the commands following the pipe. Because of these parentheses, the output of the first tar command is available for the second tar command despite the intervening cd command. Without the parentheses, the output of the first tar command would be sent to cd and lost because cd does not process input from standard input. The shell variables **$1** and **$2** represent the first and second command line arguments (page 481), respectively. The first pair of parentheses, which creates a subshell to run the first two commands, allows users to call **cpdir** with relative pathnames. Without them the first cd command would change the working directory of the script (and consequently the working directory of the second cd command). With them only the working directory of the subshell is changed.

```
$ cat cpdir
(cd $1 ; tar -cf - . ) | (cd $2 ; tar -xvf - )
$ cpdir /home/alex/sources /home/alex/memo/biblio
```

The **cpdir** command line copies the files and directories in the **/home/alex/sources** directory to the directory named **/home/alex/memo/biblio**. This shell script is almost the same as using cp with the **–r** option. Refer to Part V for more information on cp (page 616) and tar (page 786).

JOB CONTROL

A job is a command pipeline. You run a simple job whenever you give Linux a command. For example, type **date** on the command line and press RETURN: You have run a job. You can also create several jobs with multiple commands on a single command line:

```
$ find . -print | sort | lpr & grep -l alex /tmp/* > alexfiles &
[1] 18839
[2] 18876
```

The portion of the command line up to the first & is one job consisting of three processes connected by pipes: find (page 655), sort (page 50), and lpr (page 47). The second job is a single process running grep. Both jobs have been put into the background by the trailing & characters, so bash does not wait for them to complete before displaying a prompt.

Using job control you can move commands from the foreground to the background (and vice versa), stop commands temporarily, and list all the commands that are running in the background or stopped.

jobs: LISTS JOBS

The jobs builtin lists all background jobs. The following sequence demonstrates what happens when you give a **jobs** command. Here the sleep command runs in the background and creates a background job that jobs reports on:

```
$ sleep 60 &
[1] 7809
$ jobs
[1] + Running                    sleep 60 &
```

fg: BRINGS A JOB TO THE FOREGROUND

The shell assigns job numbers to commands you run in the background (page 269). Several jobs are started in the background in the next example. For each job the shell lists the job number and PID number immediately, just before it issues a prompt.

```
$ xclock &
[1] 1246
$ date &
[2] 1247
$ Sun Dec 4 11:44:40 PST 2005
[2]+ Done            date
$ find /usr -name ace -print > findout &
[2] 1269
$ jobs
[1]- Running          xclock &
[2]+ Running          find /usr -name ace -print > findout &
```

Job numbers, which are discarded when a job is finished, can be reused. When you start or put a job in the background, the shell assigns a job number that is one more than the highest job number in use.

In the preceding example, the jobs command lists the first job, xclock, as job 1. The date command does not appear in the jobs list because it finished before jobs was run. Because the date command was completed before find was run, the find command became job 2.

To move a background job into the foreground, use the fg builtin followed by the job number. Alternatively, you can give a percent sign (%) followed immediately by the job number as a command. Either of the following commands moves job 2 into the foreground:

```
$ fg 2
```

or

```
$ %2
```

You can also refer to a job by following the percent sign with a string that uniquely identifies the beginning of the command line used to start the job. Instead of the preceding command, you could have used either **fg %find** or **fg %f** because both uniquely identify job 2. If you follow the percent sign with a question mark and a string, the string can match any part of the command line. In the preceding example, **fg %?ace** also brings job 2 into the foreground.

Often the job you wish to bring into the foreground is the only job running in the background or is the job that jobs lists with a plus (+). In these cases you can use fg without an argument.

bg: SENDS A JOB TO THE BACKGROUND

To move the foreground job to the background, you must first suspend (temporarily stop) the job by pressing the suspend key (usually CONTROL-Z). Pressing the suspend key immediately suspends the job in the foreground. You can then use the bg builtin to resume execution of the job in the background.

```
$ bg
```

If a background job attempts to read from the terminal, the shell stops it and notifies you that the job has been stopped and is waiting for input. You must then move the job into the foreground so that it can read from the terminal. The shell displays the command line when it moves the job into the foreground.

```
$ (sleep 5; cat > mytext) &
[1] 1343
$ date
Sun Dec  4 11:58:20 PST 2005
[1]+ Stopped                    ( sleep 5; cat >mytext )
$ fg
( sleep 5; cat >mytext )
Remember to let the cat out!
CONTROL-D
$
```

In the preceding example, the shell displays the job number and PID number of the background job as soon as it starts, followed by a prompt. Demonstrating that you can give a command at this point, the user gives the command date and its output appears on the screen. The shell waits until just before it issues a prompt (after date has finished) to notify you that job 1 is stopped. When you give an **fg** command, the shell puts the job in the foreground and you can enter the input that the command is waiting for. In this case the input needs to be terminated with a CONTROL-D to signify EOF (end of file). The shell then displays another prompt.

The shell keeps you informed about changes in the status of a job, notifying you when a background job starts, completes, or is stopped, perhaps waiting for input from the terminal. The shell also lets you know when a foreground job is suspended. Because notices about a job being run in the background can disrupt your work, the shell delays displaying these notices until just before it displays a prompt. You can set **notify** (page 321) to make the shell display these notices without delay.

If you try to exit from a shell while jobs are stopped, the shell issues a warning and does not allow you to exit. If you then use jobs to review the list of jobs or you immediately try to leave the shell again, the shell allows you to leave and terminates the stopped jobs. Jobs that are running (not stopped) in the background continue to run. In the following example, find (job 1) continues to run after the second exit terminates the shell, but cat (job 2) is terminated:

```
$ find / -size +100k > $HOME/bigfiles 2>&1 &
[1] 1426
$ cat > mytest &
[2] 1428
$ exit
exit
There are stopped jobs.
$ exit
exit

login:
```

MANIPULATING THE DIRECTORY STACK

Both the Bourne Again and the TC Shells allow you to store a list of directories you are working with, enabling you to move easily among them. This list is referred to as a *stack*. It is analogous to a stack of dinner plates: You typically add plates to and remove plates from the top of the stack, creating a first-in last-out, (*FILO*) stack.

dirs: DISPLAYS THE STACK

The dirs builtin displays the contents of the directory stack. If you call dirs when the directory stack is empty, it displays the name of the working directory:

```
$ dirs
~/literature
```

The dirs builtin uses a tilde (~) to represent the name of the home directory. The examples in the next several sections assume that you are referring to the directory structure shown in Figure 8-2.

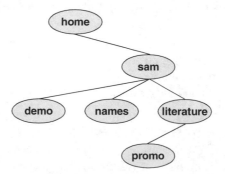

Figure 8-2   The directory structure in the examples

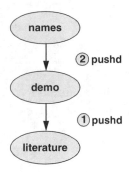

Figure 8-3 Creating a directory stack

pushd: PUSHES A DIRECTORY ON THE STACK

To change directories and at the same time add a new directory to the top of the stack, use the pushd (push directory) builtin. In addition to changing directories, the pushd builtin displays the contents of the stack. The following example is illustrated in Figure 8-3:

```
$ pushd ../demo
~/demo ~/literature
$ pwd
/home/sam/demo
$ pushd ../names
~/names ~/demo ~/literature
$ pwd
/home/sam/names
```

When you use pushd without an argument, it swaps the top two directories on the stack and makes the new top directory (which was the second directory) become the new working directory (Figure 8-4):

```
$ pushd
~/demo ~/names ~/literature
$ pwd
/home/sam/demo
```

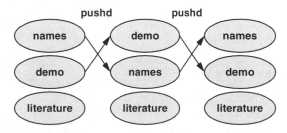

Figure 8-4 Using pushd to change working directories

Using pushd in this way, you can easily move back and forth between two directories. You can also use **cd –** to change to the previous directory, whether or not you have explicitly created a directory stack. To access another directory in the stack, call pushd with a numeric argument preceded by a plus sign. The directories in the stack are numbered starting with the top directory, which is number 0. The following pushd command continues with the previous example, changing the working directory to **literature** and moving **literature** to the top of the stack:

```
$ pushd +2
~/literature ~/demo ~/names
$ pwd
/home/sam/literature
```

popd: POPS A DIRECTORY OFF THE STACK

To remove a directory from the stack, use the popd (pop directory) builtin. As the following example and Figure 8-5 show, popd used without an argument removes the top directory from the stack and changes the working directory to the new top directory:

```
$ dirs
~/literature ~/demo ~/names
$ popd
~/demo ~/names
$ pwd
/home/sam/demo
```

To remove a directory other than the top one from the stack, use popd with a numeric argument preceded by a plus sign. The following example removes directory number 1, **demo**:

```
$ dirs
~/literature ~/demo ~/names
$ popd +1
~/literature ~/names
```

Removing a directory other than directory number 0 does not change the working directory.

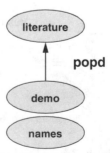

Figure 8-5   Using popd to remove a directory from the stack

PARAMETERS AND VARIABLES

Variables   Within a shell, a *shell parameter* is associated with a value that is accessible to the user. There are several kinds of shell parameters. Parameters whose names consist of letters, digits, and underscores are often referred to as *shell variables,* or simply *variables.* A variable name must start with a letter or underscore, not with a number. Thus A76, MY_CAT, and ___X___ are valid variable names, whereas 69TH_STREET (starts with a digit) and MY-NAME (contains a hyphen) are not.

User-created variables   Shell variables that you name and assign values to are *user-created variables.* You can change the values of user-created variables at any time, or you can make them *readonly* so that their values cannot be changed. You can also make user-created variables *global.* A global variable (also called an *environment variable*) is available to all shells and other programs you fork from the original shell. One naming convention is to use only uppercase letters for global variables and to use mixed-case or lowercase letters for other variables. Refer to "Locality of Variables" on page 475 for more information on global variables.

To assign a value to a variable in the Bourne Again Shell, use the following syntax:

VARIABLE=value

There can be no whitespace on either side of the equal sign (=). An example assignment follows:

```
$ myvar=abc
```

Under the TC Shell the assignment must be preceded by the word **set** and the SPACEs on either side of the equal sign are optional:

```
$ set myvar = abc
```

The Bourne Again Shell permits you to put variable assignments on a command line. These assignments are local to the command shell—that is, they apply to the command only. The **my_script** shell script displays the value of **TEMPDIR**. The following command runs **my_script** with **TEMPDIR** set to **/home/sam/temp**. The echo builtin shows that the interactive shell has no value for **TEMPDIR** after running **my_script**. If **TEMPDIR** had been set in the interactive shell, running **my_script** in this manner would have had no effect on its value.

```
$ cat my_script
echo $TEMPDIR
$ TEMPDIR=/home/sam/temp my_script
/home/sam/temp
$ echo $TEMPDIR

$
```

Keyword variables   *Keyword shell variables* (or simply *keyword variables*) have special meaning to the shell and usually have short, mnemonic names. When you start a shell (by logging in, for example), the shell inherits several keyword variables from the environment. Among these variables are **HOME**, which identifies your home directory, and **PATH**, which determines which directories the shell searches and in what order to locate commands that you give the shell. The shell creates and initializes (with default values) other keyword variables when you start it. Still other variables do not exist until you set them.

You can change the values of most of the keyword shell variables at any time but it is usually not necessary to change the values of keyword variables initialized in the **/etc/profile** or **/etc/csh.cshrc** systemwide startup files. If you need to change the value of a bash keyword variable, do so in one of your startup files (for bash see page 257; for tcsh see page 342). Just as you can make user-created variables global, so you can make keyword variables global; this is usually done automatically in the startup files. You can also make a keyword variable readonly.

Positional parameters   The names of one group of parameters do not resemble variable names. Most of these parameters have one-character names (for example, **1**, **?**, and **#**) and are refer-

Special parameters   enced (as are all variables) by preceding the name with a dollar sign (**$1**, **$?**, and **$#**). The values of these parameters reflect different aspects of your ongoing interaction with the shell.

Whenever you give a command, each argument on the command line becomes the value of a *positional parameter*. Positional parameters (page 480) enable you to access command line arguments, a capability that you will often require when you write shell scripts. The set builtin (page 484) enables you to assign values to positional parameters.

Other frequently needed shell script values, such as the name of the last command executed, the number of command line arguments, and the status of the most recently executed command, are available as *special parameters*. You cannot assign values to special parameters.

USER-CREATED VARIABLES

The first line in the following example declares the variable named **person** and initializes it with the value **alex** (use **set person = alex** in tcsh):

```
$ person=alex
$ echo person
person
$ echo $person
alex
```

Because the echo builtin copies its arguments to standard output, you can use it to display the values of variables. The second line of the preceding example shows that

person does not represent **alex**. Instead, the string **person** is echoed as **person**. The shell substitutes the value of a variable only when you precede the name of the variable with a dollar sign ($). The command **echo $person** displays the value of the variable **person**; it does not display **$person** because the shell does not pass **$person** to echo as an argument. Because of the leading $, the shell recognizes that **$person** is the name of a variable, *substitutes* the value of the variable, and passes that value to echo. The echo builtin displays the value of the variable—not its name—never knowing that you called it with a variable.

Quoting the $ You can prevent the shell from substituting the value of a variable by quoting the leading $. Double quotation marks do not prevent the substitution; single quotation marks or a backslash (\) do.

```
$ echo $person
alex
$ echo "$person"
alex
$ echo '$person'
$person
$ echo \$person
$person
```

SPACES   Because they do not prevent variable substitution but do turn off the special meanings of most other characters, double quotation marks are useful when you assign values to variables and when you use those values. To assign a value that contains SPACEs or TABs to a variable, use double quotation marks around the value. Although double quotation marks are not required in all cases, using them is a good habit.

```
$ person="alex and jenny"
$ echo $person
alex and jenny

$ person=alex and jenny
bash: and: command not found
```

When you reference a variable that contains TABs or multiple adjacent SPACEs, you need to use quotation marks to preserve the spacing. If you do not quote the variable, the shell collapses each string of blank characters into a single SPACE before passing the variable to the utility:

```
$ person="alex    and    jenny"
$ echo $person
alex and jenny
$ echo "$person"
alex    and    jenny
```

When you execute a command with a variable as an argument, the shell replaces the name of the variable with the value of the variable and passes that value to the program being executed. If the value of the variable contains a special character, such as * or ?, the shell *may* expand that variable.

Pathname expansion in assignments
The first line in the following sequence of commands assigns the string **alex*** to the variable **memo**. The Bourne Again Shell does *not expand the string* because bash does not perform pathname expansion (page 127) when assigning a value to a variable. All shells process a command line in a specific order. Within this order bash (but not tcsh) expands variables before it interprets commands. In the following echo command line, the double quotation marks quote the asterisk (*) in the expanded value of **$memo** and prevent bash from performing pathname expansion on the expanded **memo** variable before passing its value to the echo command:

```
$ memo=alex*
$ echo "$memo"
alex*
```

All shells interpret special characters as special when you reference a variable that contains an unquoted special character. In the following example, the shell expands the value of the **memo** variable because it is not quoted:

```
$ ls
alex.report
alex.summary
$ echo $memo
alex.report alex.summary
```

Here the shell expands **$memo** to **alex***, expands **alex*** to **alex.report** and **alex.summary**, and passes these two values to echo.

optional

Braces
The *$VARIABLE* syntax is a special case of the more general syntax *${VARIABLE}*, in which the variable name is enclosed by ${}. The braces insulate the variable name. Braces are necessary when catenating a variable value with a string:

```
$ PREF=counter
$ WAY=$PREFclockwise
$ FAKE=$PREFfeit
$ echo $WAY $FAKE

$
```

The preceding example does not work as planned. Only a blank line is output because, although the symbols **PREFclockwise** and **PREFfeit** are valid variable names, they are not set. By default the shell evaluates an unset variable as an empty (null) string and displays this value (bash) or generates an error message (tcsh). To achieve the intent of these statements, refer to the **PREF** variable using braces:

```
$ PREF=counter
$ WAY=${PREF}clockwise
$ FAKE=${PREF}feit
$ echo $WAY $FAKE
counterclockwise counterfeit
```

The Bourne Again Shell refers to the arguments on its command line by position, using the special variables **$1, $2, $3,** and so forth up to **$9.** If you wish to refer to arguments past the ninth argument, you must use braces: **${10}.** The name of the command is held in **$0** (page 481).

unset: REMOVES A VARIABLE

Unless you remove a variable, it exists as long as the shell in which it was created exists. To remove the *value* of a variable but not the variable itself, set the value to null (use **set person =** in tcsh):

```
$ person=
$ echo $person

$
```

You can remove a variable with the unset builtin. To remove the variable **person,** give the following command:

```
$ unset person
```

VARIABLE ATTRIBUTES

This section discusses attributes and explains how to assign them to variables.

readonly: MAKES THE VALUE OF A VARIABLE PERMANENT

You can use the readonly builtin (not in tcsh) to ensure that the value of a variable cannot be changed. The next example declares the variable **person** to be readonly. You must assign a value to a variable *before* you declare it to be readonly; you cannot change its value after the declaration. When you attempt to unset or change the value of a readonly variable, the shell displays an error message:

```
$ person=jenny
$ echo $person
jenny
$ readonly person
$ person=helen
bash: person: readonly variable
```

If you use the readonly builtin without an argument, it displays a list of all readonly shell variables. This list includes keyword variables that are automatically set as readonly as well as keyword or user-created variables that you have declared as readonly. See "Listing variable attributes" on page 282 for an example (**readonly** and **declare –r** produce the same output).

declare AND typeset: ASSIGN ATTRIBUTES TO VARIABLES

The declare and typeset builtins (two names for the same command, neither of which is available in tcsh) set attributes and values for shell variables. Table 8-3 lists five of these attributes.

Table 8-3   Variable attributes (typeset or declare)

Attribute	Meaning
–a	Declares a variable as an array (page 474)
–f	Declares a variable to be a function name (page 315)
–i	Declares a variable to be of type integer (page 283)
–r	Makes a variable readonly; also readonly (page 281)
–x	Exports a variable (makes it global); also export (page 475)

The following commands declare several variables and set some attributes. The first line declares **person1** and assigns it a value of **alex**. This command has the same effect with or without the word **declare**.

```
$ declare person1=alex
$ declare -r person2=jenny
$ declare -rx person3=helen
$ declare -x person4
```

The readonly and export builtins are synonyms for the commands **declare –r** and **declare –x**, respectively. It is legal to declare a variable without assigning a value to it, as the preceding declaration of the variable **person4** illustrates. This declaration makes **person4** available to all subshells (makes it global). Until an assignment is made to the variable, it has a null value.

You can list the options to declare separately in any order. The following is equivalent to the preceding declaration of **person3**:

```
$ declare -x -r person3=helen
```

Use the **+** character in place of **–** when you want to remove an attribute from a variable. You cannot remove a readonly attribute, however. After the following command is given, the variable **person3** is no longer exported but it is still readonly.

```
$ declare +x person3
```

You can also use typeset instead of declare.

Listing variable attributes   Without any arguments or options, the declare builtin lists all shell variables. The same list is output when you run set (page 484) without any arguments.

If you use a declare builtin with options but no variable names as arguments, the command lists all shell variables that have the indicated attributes set. For example, the option **–r** with declare gives a list of all readonly shell variables. This list is the same as that produced by a **readonly** command without any arguments. After the declarations in the preceding example have been given, the results are as follows:

```
$ declare -r
declare -ar BASH_VERSINFO='([0]="2" [1]="05b" [2]="0" [3]="1" ... )'
declare -ir EUID="500"
declare -ir PPID="936"
declare -r SHELLOPTS="braceexpand:emacs:hashall:histexpand:history:..."
declare -ir UID="500"
declare -r person2="jenny"
declare -rx person3="helen"
```

The first five entries are keyword variables that are automatically declared as read-only. Some of these variables are stored as integers (–i). The –a option indicates that **BASH_VERSINFO** is an array variable; the value of each element of the array is listed to the right of an equal sign.

Integer   By default the values of variables are stored as strings. When you perform arithmetic on a string variable, the shell converts the variable into a number, manipulates it, and then converts it back to a string. A variable with the integer attribute is stored as an integer. Assign the integer attribute as follows:

```
$ typeset -i COUNT
```

KEYWORD VARIABLES

Keyword variables either are inherited or are declared and initialized by the shell when it starts. You can assign values to these variables from the command line or from a startup file. Typically you want these variables to apply to all subshells you start as well as to your login shell. For those variables not automatically exported by the shell, you must use export (bash, page 475) or setenv (tcsh, page 356) to make them available to child shells.

HOME: YOUR HOME DIRECTORY

By default your home directory is your working directory when you log in. Your home directory is determined when you establish your account; its name is stored in the **/etc/passwd** file.

```
$ grep sam /etc/passwd
sam:x:501:501:Sam S. x301:/home/sam:/bin/bash
```

When you log in, the shell inherits the pathname of your home directory and assigns it to the variable **HOME**. When you give a **cd** command without an argument, cd makes the directory whose name is stored in **HOME** the working directory:

```
$ pwd
/home/alex/laptop
$ echo $HOME
/home/alex
$ cd
$ pwd
/home/alex
```

This example shows the value of the **HOME** variable and the effect of the cd builtin. After you execute cd without an argument, the pathname of the working directory is the same as the value of **HOME**: your home directory.

Tilde (~)   The shell uses the value of **HOME** to expand pathnames that use the shorthand tilde (~) notation (page 89) to denote a user's home directory. The following example uses echo to display the value of this shortcut and then uses ls to list the files in Alex's **laptop** directory, which is a subdirectory of his home directory:

```
$ echo ~
/home/alex
$ ls ~/laptop
tester      count      lineup
```

PATH: WHERE THE SHELL LOOKS FOR PROGRAMS

When you give the shell an absolute or relative pathname rather than a simple filename as a command, it looks in the specified directory for an executable file with the specified filename. If the file with the pathname you specified does not exist, the shell reports **command not found**. If the file exists as specified but you do not have execute permission for it, or in the case of a shell script you do not have read and execute permission for it, the shell reports **Permission denied.**

If you give a simple filename as a command, the shell searches through certain directories for the program you want to execute. It looks in several directories for a file that has the same name as the command and that you have execute permission for (a compiled program) or read and execute permission for (a shell script). The **PATH** shell variable controls this search.

The default value of **PATH** is determined when bash or tcsh is compiled. It is not set in a startup file, although it may be modified there. Normally the default specifies that the shell search several system directories used to hold common commands and then search the working directory. These system directories include **/bin** and **/usr/bin** and other directories appropriate to the local system. When you give a command, if the shell does not find the executable—and, in the case of a shell script, readable—file named by the command in any of the directories listed in **PATH**, the shell generates one of the aforementioned error messages.

Working directory   The **PATH** variable specifies the directories in the order the shell should search them. Each directory must be separated from the next by a colon. The following command sets **PATH** so that a search for an executable file starts with the **/usr/local/bin** directory. If it does not find the file in this directory, the shell first looks in **/bin,** and then in **/usr/bin**. If the search fails in those directories, the shell looks in the **bin** director, a subdirectory of the user's home directory. Finally the shell looks in the working directory. Exporting **PATH** makes its value accessible to subshells:

```
$ export PATH=/usr/local/bin:/bin:/usr/bin:~/bin:
```

A null value in the string indicates the working directory. In the preceding example, a null value (nothing between the colon and the end of the line) appears as the last element of the string. The working directory is represented by a leading colon (not recommended; see the following security tip), a trailing colon (as in the example), or two colons next to each other anywhere in the string. You can also represent the working directory explicitly with a period (.).

See "**PATH**" on page 363 for a tcsh example. Because Linux stores many executable files in directories named **bin** (*binary*), users typically put their own executable files in their own **~/bin** directories. If you put your own **bin** directory at the end of your **PATH**, as in the preceding example, the shell looks there for any commands that it cannot find in directories listed earlier in **PATH**.

PATH and security

security   Do not put the working directory first in **PATH** when security is a concern. If you are running as Superuser, you should *never* put the working directory first in **PATH**. It is common for Superuser **PATH** to omit the working directory entirely. You can always execute a file in the working directory by prepending **./** to the name: **./ls**.

Putting the working directory first in **PATH** can create a security hole. Most people type **ls** as the first command when entering a directory. If the owner of a directory places an executable file named **ls** in the directory, and the working directory appears first in a user's **PATH**, the user giving an **ls** command from the directory executes the **ls** program in the working directory instead of the system **ls** utility, possibly with undesirable results.

If you want to add directories to **PATH**, you can reference the old value of the **PATH** variable while you are setting **PATH** to a new value (but see the preceding security tip). The following command adds **/usr/X11R6/bin** to the beginning of the current **PATH** and **/usr/local/bin** and the working directory to the end:

```
$ PATH=/usr/X11R6/bin:$PATH:/usr/local/bin:
```

MAIL: WHERE YOUR MAIL IS KEPT

The **MAIL** variable (**mail** under tcsh) contains the pathname of the file that holds your mail (your *mailbox*, usually **/var/spool/mail/***name*, where *name* is your login name). If **MAIL** is set and **MAILPATH** (next) is not set, the shell informs you when mail arrives in the file specified by **MAIL**. In a graphical environment you can unset **MAIL** so that the shell does not display mail reminders in a terminal emulator window (assuming you are using a graphical mail program).

The **MAILPATH** variable (not available under tcsh) contains a list of filenames separated by colons. If this variable is set, the shell informs you when any one of the files is modified (for example, when mail arrives). You can follow any of the filenames in the list with a question mark (**?**), followed by a message. The message replaces the **you have mail** message when you get mail while you are logged in.

The **MAILCHECK** variable (not available under tcsh) specifies how often, in seconds, the shell checks for new mail. The default is 60 seconds. If you set this variable to zero, the shell checks before each prompt.

PS1: USER PROMPT (PRIMARY)

The default Bourne Again Shell prompt is a dollar sign ($). When you run bash as **root,** you may have a pound sign (#) prompt. The **PS1** variable (**prompt** under tcsh, page 363) holds the prompt string that the shell uses to let you know that it is waiting for a command. When you change the value of **PS1** or **prompt,** you change the appearance of your prompt.

You can customize the prompt displayed by **PS1.** For example, the assignment

```
$ PS1="[\u@\h \W \!]$ "
```

displays the following prompt:

[user@host directory event]$

where *user* is the username, *host* is the hostname up to the first period, *directory* is the basename of the working directory, and *event* is the event number of the current command.

If you are working on more than one system, it can be helpful to incorporate the system name into your prompt. For example, you might change the prompt to the name of the system you are using, followed by a colon and a SPACE (a SPACE at the end of the prompt makes the commands that you enter after the prompt easier to read):

```
$ PS1="$(hostname): "
bravo.example.com: echo test
test
bravo.example.com:
```

Use the following command under tcsh:

```
tcsh $ set prompt = "`hostname`: "
```

The first example that follows changes the prompt to the name of the local host, a SPACE, and a dollar sign (or, if the user is running as **root,** a pound sign). The second example changes the prompt to the time followed by the name of the user. The third example changes the prompt to the one used in this book (a pound sign for **root** and a dollar sign otherwise):

```
$ PS1='\h \$ '
bravo $

$ PS1='\@ \u $ '
09:44 PM alex $

$ PS1='\$ '
$
```

Table 8-4 describes some of the symbols you can use in **PS1**. For a complete list of special characters you can use in the prompt strings, open the bash man page and search for the second occurrence of **PROMPTING** (give the command **/PROMPTING** and then press **n**).

Table 8-4   PS1 symbols

Symbol	Display in prompt
\$	# if the user is running as **root**; otherwise, **$**
\w	Pathname of the working directory
\W	Basename of the working directory
\!	Current event (history) number (page 300)
\d	Date in Weekday Month Date format
\h	Machine hostname, without the domain
\H	Full machine hostname, including the domain
\u	Username of the current user
\@	Current time of day in 12-hour, AM/PM format
\T	Current time of day in 12-hour HH:MM:SS format
\A	Current time of day in 24-hour HH:MM format
\t	Current time of day in 24-hour HH:MM:SS format

PS2: User Prompt (Secondary)

Prompt String 2 is a secondary prompt that the shell stores in **PS2** (not under tcsh). On the first line of the next example, an unclosed quoted string follows echo. The shell assumes that the command is not finished and, on the second line, gives the default secondary prompt (>). This prompt indicates that the shell is waiting for the user to continue the command line. The shell waits until it receives the quotation mark that closes the string and then executes the command:

```
$ echo "demonstration of prompt string
> 2"
demonstration of prompt string
2
$ PS2="secondary prompt: "
$ echo "this demonstrates
secondary prompt: prompt string 2"
this demonstrates
prompt string 2
```

The second command changes the secondary prompt to **secondary prompt:** followed by a SPACE. A multiline echo demonstrates the new prompt.

PS3: Menu Prompt

PS3 holds the menu prompt for the **select** control structure (page 467).

PS4: Debugging Prompt

PS4 holds the bash debugging symbol (page 449).

Be careful when changing IFS

caution   Changing **IFS** has a variety of side effects so work cautiously. You may find it useful to first save the value of **IFS** before changing it; you can easily then restore the original value if you get unexpected results. Alternatively, you can fork a new shell with a **bash** command before experimenting with **IFS**; if you get into trouble, you can **exit** back to the old shell, where **IFS** is working properly. You can also set **IFS** to its default value with the following command:

```
$ IFS=' \t\n'
```

IFS: Separates Input Fields (Word Splitting)

The **IFS** (Internal Field Separator) shell variable (not under tcsh) specifies the characters that you can use to separate arguments on a command line and has the default value of SPACE TAB NEWLINE. Regardless of the value of **IFS**, you can always use one or more SPACE or TAB characters to separate arguments on the command line, provided that these characters are not quoted or escaped. When you assign **IFS** character values, these characters can also separate fields but only if they undergo expansion. This type of interpretation of the command line is called *word splitting*.

The following example demonstrates how setting **IFS** can affect the interpretation of a command line:

```
$ a=w:x:y:z
$ cat $a
cat: w:x:y:z: No such file or directory
$ IFS=":"
$ cat $a
cat: w: No such file or directory
cat: x: No such file or directory
cat: y: No such file or directory
cat: z: No such file or directory
```

The first time cat is called, the shell expands the variable **a**, interpreting the string **w:x:y:z** as a single word to be used as the argument to cat. The cat utility cannot find a file named **w:x:y:z** and reports an error for that filename. After **IFS** is set to a colon (:), the shell expands the variable **a** into four words, each of which is an argument to cat. Now cat reports an error for four separate files: **w**, **x**, **y**, and **z**. Word splitting based on the colon (:) takes place only *after* the variable **a** is expanded.

The shell splits all *expanded* words on a command line according to the separating characters found in **IFS**. When there is no expansion, there is no splitting. Consider the following commands:

```
$ IFS="p"
$ export VAR
```

Although **IFS** is set to **p**, the **p** on the **export** command line is not expanded so the word **export** is not split.

The next example uses variable expansion in an attempt to produce an **export** command:

```
$ IFS="p"
$ aa=export
$ echo $aa
ex ort
```

This time expansion occurs so that the character **p** in the token **export** is interpreted as a separator as the preceding echo command shows. Now when you try to use the value of the **aa** variable to export the **VAR** variable, the shell parses the **$aa VAR** command line as **ex ort VAR**. The effect is that the command line starts the **ex** editor with two filenames: **ort** and **VAR**.

```
$ $aa VAR
2 files to edit
"ort" [New File]
Entering Ex mode.  Type "visual" to go to Normal mode.
:q
E173: 1 more file to edit
:q
$
```

If you unset **IFS**, only SPACEs and TABs work as field separators.

CDPATH: BROADENS THE SCOPE OF cd

The **CDPATH** variable (**cdpath** under tcsh) allows you to use a simple filename as an argument to the **cd** builtin to change the working directory to a directory other than a child of the working directory. If you have several directories you like to work out of, this variable can speed things up and save you the tedium of using **cd** with longer pathnames to switch among them.

When **CDPATH** or **cdpath** is not set and you specify a simple filename as an argument to **cd**, **cd** searches the working directory for a subdirectory with the same name as the argument. If the subdirectory does not exist, **cd** displays an error message. When **CDPATH** or **cdpath** is set, **cd** searches for an appropriately named subdirectory in the directories in the **CDPATH** list. If **cd** finds one, that directory becomes the working directory. With **CDPATH** or **cdpath** set, you can use **cd** and a simple filename to change the working directory to a child of any of the directories listed in **CDPATH** or **cdpath**.

The **CDPATH** or **cdpath** variable takes on the value of a colon-separated list of directory pathnames (similar to the **PATH** variable). It is usually set in the

~/.**bash_profile** (bash) or ~/.**tcshrc** (tcsh) startup file with a command line such as the following:

```
export CDPATH=$HOME:$HOME/literature
```

Use the following format for tcsh:

```
setenv cdpath $HOME\:$HOME/literature
```

These commands cause cd to search your home directory, the **literature** directory, and then the working directory when you give a cd command. If you do not include the working directory in **CDPATH** or **cdpath**, cd searches the working directory if the search of all the other directories in **CDPATH** or **cdpath** fails. If you want cd to search the working directory first (which you should never do when you are logged in as **root**—refer to the security tip on page 285), include a null string, represented by two colons (::), as the first entry in **CDPATH**:

```
export CDPATH=::$HOME:$HOME/literature
```

If the argument to the cd builtin is an absolute filename—one starting with a slash (/)—the shell does not consult **CDPATH** or **cdpath**.

Keyword Variables: A Summary

Table 8-5 lists the bash keyword variables.

Table 8-5   bash keyword variables

Variable	Value
BASH_ENV	The pathname of the startup file for noninteractive shells (page 258)
CDPATH	The cd search path (page 289)
COLUMNS	The width of the display used by **select** (page 466)
FCEDIT	The name of the editor that fc uses by default (page 298)
HISTFILE	The pathname of the file that holds the history list (default: ~/.**bash_history**; page 295)
HISTFILESIZE	The maximum number of entries saved in **HISTFILE** (default: 500; page 295)
HISTSIZE	The maximum number of entries saved in the history list (default: 500; page 295)
HOME	The pathname of the user's home directory (page 283); used as the default argument for cd and in tilde expansion (page 89)
IFS	Internal Field Separator (page 288); used for word splitting (page 330)
INPUTRC	The pathname of the Readline startup file (default: ~/.**inputrc**; page 309)
LANG	The locale category when that category is not specifically set with an **LC_**✶ variable

Table 8-5   bash keyword variables (continued)

LC_*	A group of variables that specify locale categories including **LC_COLLATE**, **LC_CTYPE**, **LC_MESSAGES**, and **LC_NUMERIC**; use the locale builtin to display a complete list with values
LINES	The height of the display used by **select** (page 466)
MAIL	The pathname of the file that holds a user's mail (page 285)
MAILCHECK	How often, in seconds, bash checks for mail (page 285)
MAILPATH	A colon-separated list of file pathnames that bash checks for mail in (page 285)
PATH	A colon-separated list of directory pathnames that bash looks for commands in (page 284)
PROMPT_COMMAND	A command that bash executes just before it displays the primary prompt
PS1	Prompt String 1; the primary prompt (default: **'\s–\v\$ '**; page 286)
PS2	Prompt String 2; the secondary prompt (default: **'> '**; page 287)
PS3	The prompt issued by **select** (page 466)
PS4	The bash debugging symbol (page 449)
REPLY	Holds the line that read accepts (page 488); also used by **select** (page 466)

SPECIAL CHARACTERS

Table 8-6 lists most of the characters that are special to the bash and tcsh shells.

Table 8-6   Shell special characters

Character	Use
NEWLINE	Initiates execution of a command (page 267)
;	Separates commands (page 267)
( )	Groups commands (page 270) for execution by a subshell or identifies a function (page 315)
&	Executes a command in the background (pages 125 and 269)
|	Sends standard output of preceding command to standard input of following command (pipe; page 269)
>	Redirects standard output (page 116)
>>	Appends standard output (page 121)
<	Redirects standard input (page 118)

Table 8-6   Shell special characters *(continued)*

Character	Use
<<	Here document (page 468)
*	Any string of zero or more characters in an ambiguous file reference (page 129)
?	Any single character in an ambiguous file reference (page 128)
\	Quotes the following character (page 42)
'	Quotes a string, preventing all substitution (page 42)
"	Quotes a string, allowing only variable and command substitution (pages 42 and 279)
` ... `	Performs command substitution (page 329)
[ ]	Character class in an ambiguous file reference (page 130)
$	References a variable (page 277)
. (dot builtin)	Executes a command (only at the beginning of a line, page 259)
#	Begins a comment (page 266)
{ }	Used to surround the contents of a function (page 315)
: (null builtin)	Returns *true* (page 495)
&& (Boolean AND)	Executes command on right only if command on left succeeds (returns a zero exit status, page 507)
|| (Boolean OR)	Executes command on right only if command on left fails (returns a nonzero exit status; page 507)
! (Boolean NOT)	Reverses exit status of a command
$() (not in tcsh)	Performs command substitution (preferred form; page 329)
[ ]	Evaluates an arithmetic expression (page 327)

PROCESSES

A *process* is the execution of a command by Linux. The shell that starts when you log in is a command, or a process, like any other. When you give the name of a Linux utility on the command line, you initiate a process. When you run a shell script, another shell process is started and additional processes are created for each command in the script. Depending on how you invoke the shell script, the script is run either by the current shell or, more typically, by a subshell (child) of the current shell. A process is not started when you run a shell builtin, such as cd.

PROCESS STRUCTURE

fork system call   Like the file structure, the process structure is hierarchical, with parents, children, and even a *root*. A parent process *forks* a child process, which in turn can fork other processes. (The term *fork* indicates that, as with a fork in the road, one process turns into two. Initially the two forks are identical except that one is identified as the parent and one as the child. You can also use the term *spawn;* the words are interchangeable.) The operating system routine, or *system call,* that creates a new process is named **fork**.

When Linux begins execution when a system is started, it starts init, a single process called a *spontaneous process,* with PID number 1. This process holds the same position in the process structure as the root directory does in the file structure: It is the ancestor of all processes that the system and users work with. When the system is in multiuser mode, init runs getty or mingetty processes, which display **login:** prompts on terminals and virtual consoles. When someone responds to the prompt and presses RETURN, getty hands control over to a utility named login, which checks the username and password combination. After the user logs in, the login process becomes the user's shell process.

PROCESS IDENTIFICATION

PID number   Linux assigns a unique PID (process identification) number at the inception of each process. As long as a process exists, it keeps the same PID number. During one session the same process is always executing the login shell. When you fork a new process—for example, when you use an editor—the PID number of the new (child) process is different from that of its parent process. When you return to the login shell, it is still being executed by the same process and has the same PID number as when you logged in.

The following example shows that the process running the shell forked (is the parent of) the process running ps (page 127). When you call it with the –f option, ps displays a full listing of information about each process. The line of the ps display with **bash** in the **CMD** column refers to the process running the shell. The column headed by **PID** identifies the PID number. The column headed **PPID** identifies the PID number of the *parent* of the process. From the PID and PPID columns you can see that the process running the shell (PID 21341) is the parent of the process running sleep (PID 22789). The parent PID number of sleep is the same as the PID number of the shell (21341).

```
$ sleep 10 &
[1] 22789
$ ps -f
UID        PID  PPID  C STIME TTY          TIME CMD
alex      21341 21340  0 10:42 pts/16   00:00:00 bash
alex      22789 21341  0 17:30 pts/16   00:00:00 sleep 10
alex      22790 21341  0 17:30 pts/16   00:00:00 ps -f
```

Refer to page 746 for more information on ps and the columns it displays with the –f option. A second pair of **sleep** and **ps –f** commands shows that the shell is still being run by the same process but that it forked another process to run sleep:

```
$ sleep 10 &
[1] 22791
$ ps -f
UID        PID  PPID  C STIME TTY         TIME CMD
alex     21341 21340  0 10:42 pts/16  00:00:00 bash
alex     22791 21341  0 17:31 pts/16  00:00:00 sleep 10
alex     22792 21341  0 17:31 pts/16  00:00:00 ps -f
```

You can also use pstree (or **ps --forest**, with or without the –e option) to see the parent–child relationship of processes. The next example shows the –p option to pstree, which causes it to display PID numbers:

```
$ pstree -p
init(1)-+-acpid(1395)
        |-atd(1758)
        |-crond(1702)
   ...
        |-kdeinit(2223)-+-firefox(8914)---run-mozilla.sh(8920)---firefox-bin(8925)
        |               |-gaim(2306)
        |               |-gqview(14062)
        |               |-kdeinit(2228)
        |               |-kdeinit(2294)
        |               |-kdeinit(2314)-+-bash(2329)---ssh(2561)
        |               |               |-bash(2339)
        |               |               '-bash(15821)---bash(16778)
        |               |-kdeinit(16448)
        |               |-kdeinit(20888)
        |               |-oclock(2317)
        |               '-pam-panel-icon(2305)---pam_timestamp_c(2307)
   ...
        |-login(1823)---bash(20986)-+-pstree(21028)
        |                           '-sleep(21026)
   ...
```

The preceding output is abbreviated. The line that starts with **–kdeinit** shows a graphical user running many processes, including **firefox**, **gaim**, and **oclock**. The line that starts with **–login** shows a textual user running sleep in the background while running pstree in the foreground. Refer to "$$: PID Number" on page 478 for a description of how to instruct the shell to report on PID numbers.

EXECUTING A COMMAND

fork and sleep   When you give the shell a command, it usually forks (spawns) a child process to execute the command. While the child process is executing the command, the parent process *sleeps*. While a process is sleeping, it does not use any computer time but remains inactive, waiting to wake up. When the child process finishes executing the command, it tells its parent of its success or failure via its exit status and then dies. The parent process (which is running the shell) wakes up and prompts for another command.

Background process When you run a process in the background by ending a command with an ampersand (&), the shell forks a child process without going to sleep and without waiting for the child process to run to completion. The parent process, which is executing the shell, reports the job number and PID number of the child and prompts for another command. The child process runs in the background, independent of its parent.

Builtins Although the shell forks a process to run most of the commands you give it, some commands are built into the shell. The shell does not need to fork a process to run builtins. For more information refer to "Builtins" on page 132.

Variables Within a given process, such as your login shell or a subshell, you can declare, initialize, read, and change variables. By default, however, a variable is local to a process. When a process forks a child process, the parent does not pass the value of a variable to the child. You can make the value of a variable available to child processes (global) by using the export builtin under bash (page 475) or the setenv builtin under tcsh (page 356).

HISTORY

The history mechanism, a feature adapted from the C Shell, maintains a list of recently issued command lines, also called *events,* providing a quick way to reexecute any of the events in the list. This mechanism also enables you to execute variations of previous commands and to reuse arguments from them. You can replicate complicated commands and arguments that you used earlier in this login session or in a previous one and enter a series of commands that differ from one another in minor ways. The history list also serves as a record of what you have done. It can prove helpful when you have made a mistake and are not sure what you did or when you want to keep a record of a procedure that involved a series of commands.

The history builtin (both in bash and tcsh) displays the history list. If it does not, read on—you need to set some variables.

history **can help track down mistakes**

tip When you have made a command line mistake (not an error within a script or program) and are not sure what you did wrong, look at the history list to review your recent commands. Sometimes this list can help you figure out what went wrong and how to fix things.

VARIABLES THAT CONTROL HISTORY

The TC Shell's history mechanism is similar to bash's but uses different variables and has other differences. See page 344 for more information.

The value of the **HISTSIZE** variable determines the number of events preserved in the history list during a session. A value in the range of 100 to 1,000 is normal.

When you exit from the shell, the most recently executed commands are saved in the file given by the **HISTFILE** variable (the default is **~/.bash_history**). The next time you start the shell, this file initializes the history list. The value of the **HISTFILESIZE** variable determines the number of lines of history saved in **HISTFILE** (not necessarily the same as **HISTSIZE**). **HISTSIZE** holds the number of events remembered during a session, **HISTFILESIZE** holds the number remembered between sessions, and the file designated by **HISTFILE** holds the history list. See Table 8-7.

Table 8-7   History variables

Variable	Default	Function
HISTSIZE	500 events	Maximum number of events saved during a session
HISTFILE	~/.bash_history	Location of the history file
HISTFILESIZE	500 events	Maximum number of events saved between sessions

Event number   The Bourne Again Shell assigns a sequential *event number* to each command line. You can display this event number as part of the bash prompt by including \! in **PS1** (page 286). Examples in this section show numbered prompts when they help to illustrate the behavior of a command.

Give the following command manually or place it in **~/.bash_profile** (to affect future sessions) to establish a history list of the 100 most recent events:

```
$ HISTSIZE=100
```

The following command causes bash to save the 100 most recent events across login sessions:

```
$ HISTFILESIZE=100
```

After you set **HISTFILESIZE**, you can log out and log in again, and the 100 most recent events from the previous login session will appear in your history list.

Give the command **history** to display the events in the history list. The list of events is ordered with oldest events at the top of the list. A tcsh history list includes the time the command was executed. The following history list includes a command to modify the bash prompt so that it displays the history event number. The last event in the history list is the **history** command that displayed the list.

```
32 $ history | tail
   23  PS1="\! bash$ "
   24  ls -l
   25  cat temp
   26  rm temp
   27  vim memo
   28  lpr memo
   29  vim memo
   30  lpr memo
   31  rm memo
   32  history | tail
```

As you run commands and your history list becomes longer, it may run off the top of the screen when you use the history builtin. Pipe the output of history through less to browse through it, or give the command **history 10** to look at the ten most recent commands.

REEXECUTING AND EDITING COMMANDS

You can reexecute any event in the history list. This feature can save you time, effort, and aggravation. Not having to reenter long command lines allows you to reexecute events more easily, quickly, and accurately than you could if you had to retype the entire command line. You can recall, modify, and reexecute previously executed events in three ways: You can use the fc builtin (covered next); the exclamation point commands (page 300); or the Readline Library, which uses a one-line vi- or emacs-like editor to edit and execute events (page 305).

Which method to use?

tip If you are more familiar with vi or emacs and less familiar with the C or TC Shell, use fc or the Readline Library. If you are more familiar with the C or TC Shell and less familiar with vi and emacs, use the exclamation point commands. If it is a toss-up, try the Readline Library; it will benefit you in other areas of Linux more than learning the exclamation point commands will.

fc: DISPLAYS, EDITS, AND REEXECUTES COMMANDS

The fc (fix command) builtin (not in tcsh) enables you to display the history list and to edit and reexecute previous commands. It provides many of the same capabilities as the command line editors.

VIEWING THE HISTORY LIST

When you call fc with the –l option, it displays commands from the history list. Without any arguments, fc –l lists the 16 most recent commands in a numbered list, with the oldest appearing first:

```
$ fc -l
1024    cd
1025    view calendar
1026    vim letter.adams01
1027    aspell -c letter.adams01
1028    vim letter.adams01
1029    lpr letter.adams01
1030    cd ../memos
1031    ls
1032    rm *0405
1033    fc -l
1034    cd
1035    whereis aspell
1036    man aspell
1037    cd /usr/share/doc/*aspell*
1038    pwd
1039    ls
1040    ls man-html
```

The fc builtin can take zero, one, or two arguments with the –l option. The arguments specify the part of the history list to be displayed:

fc –l [first [last]]

The fc builtin lists commands beginning with the most recent event that matches *first*. The argument can be an event number, the first few characters of the command line, or a negative number, which is taken to be the *n*th previous command. If you provide *last*, fc displays commands from the most recent event that matches *first* through the most recent event that matches *last*. The next command displays the history list from event 1030 through event 1035:

```
$ fc -l 1030 1035
1030    cd ../memos
1031    ls
1032    rm *0405
1033    fc -l
1034    cd
1035    whereis aspell
```

The following command lists the most recent event that begins with **view** through the most recent command line that begins with **whereis**:

```
$ fc -l view whereis
1025    view calendar
1026    vim letter.adams01
1027    aspell -c letter.adams01
1028    vim letter.adams01
1029    lpr letter.adams01
1030    cd ../memos
1031    ls
1032    rm *0405
1033    fc -l
1034    cd
1035    whereis aspell
```

To list a single command from the history list, use the same identifier for the first and second arguments. The following command lists event 1027:

```
$ fc -l 1027 1027
1027    aspell -c letter.adams01
```

EDITING AND REEXECUTING PREVIOUS COMMANDS

You can use fc to edit and reexecute previous commands.

fc [–e editor] [first [last]]

When you call fc with the –e option followed by the name of an editor, fc calls the editor with event(s) in the Work buffer. Without *first* and *last*, fc defaults to the most recent command. The next example invokes the vi(m) editor to edit the most recent command:

```
$ fc -e vi
```

The fc builtin uses the stand-alone vi(m) editor. If you set the **FCEDIT** variable, you do not need to use the –e option to specify an editor on the command line. Because the value of **FCEDIT** has been changed to **/usr/bin/emacs** and fc has no arguments, the following command edits the most recent command with the emacs editor:

```
$ export FCEDIT=/usr/bin/emacs
$ fc
```

If you call it with a single argument, fc invokes the editor on the specified command. The following example starts the editor with event 21 in the Work buffer. When you exit from the editor, the shell executes the command:

```
$ fc 21
```

Again you can identify commands with numbers or by specifying the first few characters of the command name. The following example calls the editor to work on events from the most recent event that begins with the letters **vim** through event 206:

```
$ fc vim 206
```

Clean up the fc buffer

caution   When you execute an fc command, the shell executes whatever you leave in the editor buffer, possibly with unwanted results. If you decide you do not want to execute a command, delete everything from the buffer before you exit from the editor.

REEXECUTING COMMANDS WITHOUT CALLING THE EDITOR

You can reexecute previous commands without going into an editor. If you call fc with the –s option, it skips the editing phase and reexecutes the command. The following example reexecutes event 1029:

```
$ fc -s 1029
lpr letter.adams01
```

The next example reexecutes the previous command:

```
$ fc -s
```

When you reexecute a command you can tell fc to substitute one string for another. The next example substitutes the string **john** for the string **adams** in event 1029 and executes the modified event:

```
$ fc -s adams=john 1029
lpr letter.john01
```

USING AN EXCLAMATION POINT (!) TO REFERENCE EVENTS

The C Shell history mechanism uses an exclamation point to reference events and is available under bash and tcsh. It is frequently more cumbersome to use than fc but nevertheless has some useful features. For example, the !! command reexecutes the previous event, and the !$ token represents the last word on the previous command line.

You can reference an event by using its absolute event number, its relative event number, or the text it contains. All references to events, called event designators, begin with an exclamation point (!). One or more characters follow the exclamation point to specify an event.

You can put history events anywhere on a command line. To escape an exclamation point so that it is treated literally instead of as the start of a history event, precede it with a backslash (\) or enclose it within single quotation marks.

EVENT DESIGNATORS

An event designator specifies a command in the history list. See Table 8-8 on page 301 for a list of event designators.

!! reexecutes the previous event You can always reexecute the previous event by giving a !! command. In the following example, event 45 reexecutes event 44:

```
44 $ ls -l text
-rw-rw-r--   1 alex group 45 Apr 30 14:53 text
45 $ !!
ls -l text
-rw-rw-r--   1 alex group 45 Apr 30 14:53 text
```

The !! command works whether or not your prompt displays an event number. As this example shows, when you use the history mechanism to reexecute an event, the shell displays the command it is reexecuting.

!n event number A number following an exclamation point refers to an event. If that event is in the history list, the shell executes it. Otherwise, the shell displays an error message. A negative number following an exclamation point references an event relative to the current event. For example, the command !−3 refers to the third preceding event. After you issue a command, the relative event number of a given event changes (event −3 becomes event −4). Both of the following commands reexecute event 44:

```
51 $ !44
ls -l text
-rw-rw-r--   1 alex group 45 Nov 30 14:53 text
52 $ !-8
ls -l text
-rw-rw-r--   1 alex group 45 Nov 30 14:53 text
```

!string event text When a string of text follows an exclamation point, the shell searches for and executes the most recent event that *began* with that string. If you enclose the string between question marks, the shell executes the most recent event that *contained* that string. The final question mark is optional if a RETURN would immediately follow it.

```
68 $ history 10
   59  ls -l text*
   60  tail text5
   61  cat text1 text5 > letter
   62  vim letter
   63  cat letter
   64  cat memo
   65  lpr memo
   66  pine jenny
   67  ls -l
   68  history
69 $ !l
ls -l
...
70 $ !lpr
lpr memo
71 $ !?letter?
cat letter
...
```

Table 8-8 Event designators

Designator	Meaning
!	Starts a history event unless followed immediately by SPACE, NEWLINE, **=**, or **(**.
!!	The previous command.
!*n*	Command number *n* in the history list.
!–*n*	The *n*th preceding command.
!*string*	The most recent command line that started with *string*.
!?*string*[**?**]	The most recent command that contained *string*. The last **?** is optional.
!#	The current command (as you have it typed so far).
!{*event***}**	The *event* is an event designator. The braces isolate *event* from the surrounding text. For example, **!{–3}3** is the third most recently executed command followed by a **3**.

optional WORD DESIGNATORS

A *word designator* specifies a word or series of words from an event. Table 8-9 on page 303 lists word designators.

The words are numbered starting with 0 (the first word on the line—usually the command), continuing with 1 (the first word following the command), and going through *n* (the last word on the line).

To specify a particular word from a previous event, follow the event designator (such as **!14**) with a colon and the number of the word in the previous event. For example, !14:3 specifies the third word following the command from event 14. You can specify the first word following the command (word number 1) by using a caret (^) and the last word by using a dollar sign ($). You can specify a range of words by separating two word designators with a hyphen.

```
72 $ echo apple grape orange pear
apple grape orange pear
73 $ echo !72:2
echo grape
grape
74 $ echo !72:^
echo apple
apple
75 $ !72:0 !72:$
echo pear
pear
76 $ echo !72:2-4
echo grape orange pear
grape orange pear
77 $ !72:0-$
echo apple grape orange pear
apple grape orange pear
```

As the next example shows, !$ refers to the last word of the previous event. You can use this shorthand to edit, for example, a file you just displayed with cat:

```
$ cat report.718
...
$ vim !$
vim report.718
...
```

If an event contains a single command, the word numbers correspond to the argument numbers. If an event contains more than one command, this correspondence does not hold true for commands after the first. In the following example event 78 contains two commands separated by a semicolon so that the shell executes them sequentially; the semicolon is word number 5.

```
78 $ !72 ; echo helen jenny barbara
echo apple grape orange pear ; echo helen jenny barbara
apple grape orange pear
helen jenny barbara
79 $ echo !78:7
echo helen
helen
80 $ echo !78:4-7
echo pear ; echo helen
pear
helen
```

Table 8-9	Word designators
Designator	**Meaning**
n	The *nth* word. Word 0 is normally the command name.
^	The first word (after the command name).
$	The last word.
m–n	All words from word number *m* through word number *n; m* defaults to 0 if you omit it (0–*n*).
n∗	All words from word number *n* through the last word.
∗	All words except the command name. The same as **1**∗.
%	The word matched by the most recent **?** *string* **?** search.

MODIFIERS

On occasion you may want to change an aspect of an event you are reexecuting. Perhaps you entered a complex command line with a typo or incorrect pathname or you want to specify a different argument. You can modify an event or a word of an event by putting one or more modifiers after the word designator, or after the event designator if there is no word designator. Each modifier must be preceded by a colon (:).

Substitute modifier   The *substitute modifier* is more complex than the other modifiers. The following example shows the substitute modifier correcting a typo in the previous event:

```
$ car /home/jenny/memo.0507 /home/alex/letter.0507
bash: car: command not found
$ !!:s/car/cat
cat /home/jenny/memo.0507 /home/alex/letter.0507
...
```

The substitute modifier has the following syntax:

    [g]s/*old*/*new*/

where *old* is the original string (not a regular expression), and *new* is the string that replaces *old*. The substitute modifier substitutes the first occurrence of *old* with *new*. Placing a **g** before the **s** (as in g*s/old/new/*) causes a global substitution, replacing all occurrences of *old*. The **/** is the delimiter in the examples but you can use any character that is not in either *old* or *new*. The final delimiter is optional if a RETURN would immediately follow it. As with the vim Substitute command, the history mechanism replaces an ampersand (&) in *new* with *old*. The shell replaces a null old string (*s//new/*) with the previous old string or string within a command that you searched for with **?***string***?**.

Quick substitution An abbreviated form of the substitute modifier is *quick substitution*. Use it to reexecute the most recent event while changing some of the event text. The quick substitution character is the caret (^). For example, the command

```
$ ^old^new^
```

produces the same results as

```
$ !!:s/old/new/
```

Thus substituting **cat** for **car** in the previous event could have been entered as

```
$ ^car^cat
cat /home/jenny/memo.0507 /home/alex/letter.0507
...
```

You can omit the final caret if it would be followed immediately by a RETURN. As with other command line substitutions, the shell displays the command line as it appears after the substitution.

Other modifiers Modifiers (other than the substitute modifier) perform simple edits on the part of the event that has been selected by the event designator and the optional word designators. You can use multiple modifiers, each preceded by a colon (:).

The following series of commands uses ls to list the name of a file, repeats the command without executing it (**p** modifier), and repeats the last command, removing the last part of the pathname (**h** modifier) again without executing it:

```
$ ls /etc/sysconfig/harddisks
/etc/sysconfig/harddisks
$ !!:p
ls /etc/sysconfig/harddisks
$ !!:h:p
ls /etc/sysconfig
$
```

Table 8-10 lists event modifiers other than the substitute modifier.

Table 8-10   Modifiers

Modifier	Function
e (extension)	Removes all but the filename extension
h (head)	Removes the last part of a pathname
p (print-not)	Displays the command, but does not execute it
q (quote)	Quotes the substitution to prevent further substitutions on it
r (root)	Removes the filename extension
t (tail)	Removes all elements of a pathname except the last
x	Like **q** but quotes each word in the substitution individually

THE READLINE LIBRARY

Command line editing under the Bourne Again Shell is implemented through the *Readline Library,* which is available to any application written in C. Any application that uses the Readline Library supports line editing that is consistent with that provided by bash. Programs that use the Readline Library, including bash, read ~/.inputrc (page 309) for key binding information and configuration settings. The --noediting command line option turns off command line editing in bash.

vi mode   You can choose one of two editing modes when using the Readline Library in bash: emacs or vi(m). Both modes provide many of the commands available in the stand-alone versions of the vi(m) and emacs editors. You can also use the ARROW keys to move around. Up and down movements move you backward and forward through the history list. In addition, Readline provides several types of interactive word completion (page 307). The default mode is emacs; you can switch to vi mode with the following command:

```
$ set -o vi
```

emacs mode   The next command switches back to emacs mode:

```
$ set -o emacs
```

vi EDITING MODE

Before you start make sure you are in vi mode.

When you enter bash commands while in vi editing mode, you are in Input mode (page 142). As you enter a command, if you discover an error before you press RETURN, you can press ESCAPE to switch to vi Command mode. This setup is different from the stand-alone vi(m) editor's initial mode. While in Command mode you can use many vi(m) commands to edit the command line. It is as though you were using vi(m) to edit a copy of the history file with a screen that has room for only one command. When you use the k command or the UP ARROW to move up a line, you access the previous command. If you then use the j command or the DOWN ARROW to move down a line, you will return to the original command. To use the k and j keys to move between commands you must be in Command mode; you can use the ARROW keys in both Command and Input modes.

The stand-alone editor starts in Command mode

tip   The stand-alone vim editor starts in Command mode, whereas the command line vi(m) editor starts in Input mode. If commands display characters and do not work properly, you are in Input mode. Press ESCAPE and enter the command again.

In addition to cursor-positioning commands, you can use the search-backward (?) command followed by a search string to look *back* through your history list for the most recent command containing that string. If you have moved back in your history list, use a forward slash (/) to search *forward* toward your most recent command. Unlike the search strings in the stand-alone vi(m) editor, these search strings cannot contain regular expressions. You can, however, start the search string with a caret (^) to force the shell to locate commands that start with the search string. As in vi(m), pressing **n** after a successful search looks for the next occurrence of the same string.

You can also access events in the history list by using event numbers. While you are in Command mode (press ESCAPE), enter the event number followed by a **G** to go to the command with that event number.

When you use **/**, **?**, or **G** to move to a command line, you are in Command mode, not Input mode. Now you can edit the command as you like or press RETURN to execute it.

Once the command you want to edit is displayed, you can modify the command line using vi(m) Command mode editing commands such as **x** (delete character), **r** (replace character), **~** (change case), and **.** (repeat last change). To change to Input mode, use an Insert (**i**, **I**), Append (**a**, **A**), Replace (**R**), or Change (**c**, **C**) command. You do not have to return to Command mode to run a command; simply press RETURN, even if the cursor is in the middle of the command line.

Refer to page 188 for a summary of vim commands.

emacs EDITING MODE

Unlike the vi(m) editor, emacs is modeless. You need not switch between Command mode and Input mode because most emacs commands are control characters (page 204), allowing emacs to distinguish between input and commands. Like vi(m), the emacs command line editor provides commands for moving the cursor on the command line and through the command history list and for modifying part or all of a command. The emacs command line editor commands differ in a few cases from the commands in the stand-alone emacs editor.

In emacs you perform cursor movement by using both CONTROL and ESCAPE commands. To move the cursor one character backward on the command line, press CONTROL-B. Press CONTROL-F to move one character forward. As in vi, you may precede these movements with counts. To use a count you must first press ESCAPE; otherwise, the numbers you type will appear on the command line.

Like vi(m), emacs provides word and line movement commands. To move backward or forward one word on the command line, press ESCAPE b or ESCAPE f. To move several words by using a count, press ESCAPE followed by the number and the appropriate escape sequence. To get to the beginning of the line, press CONTROL-A; to the end of the line, press CONTROL-E; and to the next instance of the character *c*, press CONTROL-X CONTROL-F followed by *c*.

You can add text to the command line by moving the cursor to the correct place and typing the desired text. To delete text, move the cursor just to the right of the characters that you want to delete and press the erase key (page 26) once for each character you want to delete.

CONTROL-D can terminate your screen session

If you want to delete the character directly under the cursor, press CONTROL-D. If you enter CONTROL-D at the beginning of the line, it may terminate your shell session.

If you want to delete the entire command line, type the line kill character (page 27). You can type this character while the cursor is anywhere in the command line. If you want to delete from the cursor to the end of the line, use CONTROL-K.

Refer to page 241 for a summary of emacs commands.

READLINE COMPLETION COMMANDS

You can use the TAB key to complete words you are entering on the command line. This facility, called *completion*, works in both vi and emacs editing modes and is similar to the completion facility available in tcsh. Several types of completion are possible, and which one you use depends on which part of a command line you are typing when you press TAB.

COMMAND COMPLETION

If you are typing the name of a command (the first word on the command line), pressing TAB results in *command completion*. That is, bash looks for a command whose name starts with the part of the word you have typed. If no command starts with what you have entered, bash beeps. If there is one such command, bash completes the command name for you. If there is more than one choice, bash does nothing in vi mode and beeps in emacs mode. Pressing TAB a second time causes bash to display a list of commands whose names start with the prefix you typed and allows you to finish typing the command name.

In the following example, the user types **bz** and presses TAB. The shell beeps (the user is in emacs mode) to indicate that several commands start with the letters **bz**. The user enters another TAB to cause the shell to display a list of commands that start with **bz** followed by the command line as the user had entered it so far:

```
$ bz ⟶ TAB (beep) ⟶ TAB
bzcat          bzdiff       bzip2          bzless
bzcmp          bzgrep       bzip2recover bzmore
$ bz█
```

Next the user types **c** and presses TAB twice. The shell displays the two commands that start with **bzc**. The user types **a** followed by TAB and the shell then completes the command because only one command starts with **bzca**.

```
$ bzc ⟶ TAB (beep) ⟶ TAB
bzcat bzcmp
$ bzca ⟶ TAB ⟶t █
```

PATHNAME COMPLETION

Pathname completion, which also uses TABs, allows you to type a portion of a pathname and have bash supply the rest. If the portion of the pathname that you have typed is sufficient to determine a unique pathname, bash displays that pathname. If more than one pathname would match it, bash completes the pathname up to the point where there are choices so that you can type more.

When you are entering a pathname, including a simple filename, and press TAB, the shell beeps (if the shell is in emacs mode—in vi mode there is no beep). It then extends the command line as far as it can.

```
$ cat films/dar → TAB (beep) cat films/dark_█
```

In the **films** directory every file that starts with **dar** has **k_** as the next characters, so bash cannot extend the line further without making a choice among files. You are left with the cursor just past the _ character. At this point you can continue typing the pathname or press TAB twice. In the latter case bash beeps, displays your choices, redisplays the command line, and again leaves the cursor just after the _ character.

```
$ cat films/dark_ → TAB (beep) → TAB
dark_passage   dark_victory
$ cat films/dark_█
```

When you add enough information to distinguish between the two possible files and press TAB, bash displays the unique pathname. If you enter **p** followed by TAB after the _ character, the shell completes the command line:

```
$ cat films/dark_p → TAB → assage
```

Because there is no further ambiguity, the shell appends a SPACE so you can finish typing the command line or just press RETURN to execute the command. If the complete pathname is that of a directory, bash appends a slash (/) in place of a SPACE.

VARIABLE COMPLETION

When typing a variable name, pressing TAB results in *variable completion,* where bash tries to complete the name of the variable. In case of an ambiguity, pressing TAB twice displays a list of choices:

```
$ echo $HO → TAB → TAB
$HOME       $HOSTNAME $HOSTTYPE
$ echo $HOM → TAB → E
```

Pressing RETURN executes the command

caution   Pressing RETURN causes the shell to execute the command regardless of where the cursor is on the command line.

.inputrc: CONFIGURING READLINE

The Bourne Again Shell and other programs that use the Readline Library read the file specified by the **INPUTRC** environment variable to obtain initialization information. If **INPUTRC** is not set, these programs read the ~/.inputrc file. They ignore lines of .inputrc that are blank or that start with a pound sign (#).

VARIABLES

You can set variables in .inputrc to control the behavior of the Readline Library using the following syntax:

set variable value

Table 8-11 lists some variables and values you can use. See **Readline Variables** in the bash man or info page for a complete list.

Table 8-11   Readline variables

Variable	Effect
editing-mode	Set to **vi** to start Readline in vi mode. Set to **emacs** to start Readline in emacs mode (the default). Similar to the **set –o vi** and **set –o emacs** shell commands (page 305).
horizontal-scroll-mode	Set to **on** to cause long lines to extend off the right edge of the display area. Moving the cursor to the right when it is at the right edge of the display area shifts the line to the left so you can see more of the line. You can shift the line back by moving the cursor back past the left edge. The default value is **off**, which causes long lines to wrap onto multiple lines of the display.
mark-directories	Set to **off** to cause Readline not to place a slash (/) at the end of directory names it completes. Normally it is **on**.
mark-modified-lines	Set to **on** to cause Readline to precede modified history lines with an asterisk. The default value is **off**.

KEY BINDINGS

You can specify bindings that map keystroke sequences to Readline commands, allowing you to change or extend the default bindings. As in emacs, the Readline Library includes many commands that are not bound to a keystroke sequence. To use an unbound command, you must map it using one of the following forms:

keyname: command_name
"keystroke_sequence": command_name

In the first form, you spell out the name for a single key. For example, CONTROL-U would be written as **control-u**. This form is useful for binding commands to single keys.

In the second form, you specify a string that describes a sequence of keys that will be bound to the command. You can use the emacs-style backslash escape sequences to represent the special keys CONTROL (**\C**), META (**\M**), and ESCAPE (**\e**). Specify a backslash by escaping it with another backslash: ****. Similarly, a double or single quotation mark can be escaped with a backslash: **\"** or **\'** .

The **kill-whole-line** command, available in emacs mode only, deletes the current line. Put the following command in **.inputrc** to bind the **kill-whole-line** command (which is unbound by default) to the keystroke sequence CONTROL-R.

```
control-r: kill-whole-line
```

bind   Give the command **bind –P** to display a list of all Readline commands. If a command is bound to a key sequence, that sequence is shown. Commands you can use in vi mode start with **vi**. For example, **vi-next-word** and **vi-prev-word** move the cursor to the beginning of the next and previous words, respectively. Commands that do not begin with **vi** are generally available in emacs mode.

Use **bind –q** to determine which key sequence is bound to a command:

```
$ bind -q kill-whole-line
kill-whole-line can be invoked via "\C-r".
```

You can also bind text by enclosing it within double quotation marks (emacs mode only):

```
"QQ": "The Linux Operating System"
```

This command causes bash to insert the string **The Linux Operating System** when you type **QQ**.

CONDITIONAL CONSTRUCTS

You can conditionally select parts of the **.inputrc** file using the **$if** directive. The syntax of the conditional construct is

$if [test[=value]]

    commands

  [$else

    commands

  $endif

where *test* is **mode, term,** or **bash.** If *test* equals *value* or if *test* is *true,* this structure executes the first set of *commands.* If *test* does not equal *value* or if *test* is *false,* it executes the second set of *commands* if they are present or exits from the structure if they are not present.

The power of the **$if** directive lies in the three types of tests it can perform.

1. You can test to see which mode is currently set.

   ```
   $if mode=vi
   ```

   The preceding test is *true* if the current Readline mode is **vi** and *false* otherwise. You can test for **vi** or **emacs**.

2. You can test the type of terminal.

   ```
   $if term=xterm
   ```

   The preceding test is *true* if the **TERM** variable is set to **xterm**. You can test for any value of **TERM**.

3. You can test the application name.

   ```
   $if bash
   ```

   The preceding test is *true* when you are running bash and not another program that uses the Readline Library. You can test for any application name.

These tests can customize the Readline Library based on the current mode, the type of terminal, and the application you are using. They give you a great deal of power and flexibility when using the Readline Library with bash and other programs.

The following commands in **.inputrc** cause CONTROL-Y to move the cursor to the beginning of the next word regardless of whether bash is in vi or emacs mode:

```
$ cat ~/.inputrc
set editing-mode vi
$if mode=vi
     "\C-y": vi-next-word
   $else
     "\C-y": forward-word
$endif
```

Because bash reads the preceding conditional construct when it is started, you must set the editing mode in **.inputrc**. Changing modes interactively using set will not change the binding of CONTROL-Y.

For more information on the Readline Library, open the bash man page and give the command **/^READLINE**, which searches for the word **READLINE** at the beginning of a line.

If Readline commands do not work, log out and log in again

tip The Bourne Again Shell reads **~/.inputrc** when you log in. After you make changes to this file, you should log out and log in again before testing the changes.

ALIASES

An *alias* is a (usually short) name that the shell translates into another (usually longer) name or (complex) command. Aliases allow you to define new commands by substituting a string for the first token of a simple command. They are typically placed in the ~/.bashrc (bash) or ~/.tcshrc (tcsh) startup files so that they are available to interactive subshells.

Under bash the syntax of the alias builtin is

> *alias [name[=value]]*

Under tcsh the syntax is

> *alias [name[value]]*

In the bash syntax there are no SPACEs around the equal sign. If **value** contains SPACEs or TABs, you must enclose **value** between quotation marks. Unlike aliases under tcsh, a bash alias does not accept an argument from the command line in **value**. Use a bash function (page 315) when you need to use an argument.

An alias does not replace itself, which avoids the possibility of infinite recursion in handling an alias such as the following:

```
$ alias ls='ls -F'
```

You can nest aliases. Aliases are disabled for noninteractive shells (that is, shell scripts). To see a list of the current aliases, give the command **alias**. To view the alias for a particular name, use alias followed by the name and nothing else. You can use the unalias builtin to remove an alias.

When you give an alias builtin without any arguments, the shell displays a list of all defined aliases:

```
$ alias
alias ll='ls -l'
alias l='ls -ltr'
alias ls='ls -F'
alias zap='rm -i'
```

Most Linux distributions define at least some aliases. Give an **alias** command to see which aliases are in effect. You can delete the aliases you do not want from the appropriate startup file.

SINGLE VERSUS DOUBLE QUOTATION MARKS IN ALIASES

The choice of single or double quotation marks is significant in the alias syntax when the alias includes variables. If you enclose **value** within double quotation marks, any variables that appear in *value* are expanded when the alias is created. If you enclose *value* within single quotation marks, variables are not expanded until the alias is used. The following example illustrates the difference.

The **PWD** keyword variable holds the pathname of the working directory. Alex creates two aliases while he is working in his home directory. Because he uses double quotation marks when he creates the **dirA** alias, the shell substitutes the value of the working directory when he creates this alias. The **alias dirA** command displays the **dirA** alias and shows that the substitution has already taken place:

```
$ echo $PWD
/home/alex
$ alias dirA="echo Working directory is $PWD"
$ alias dirA
alias dirA='echo Working directory is /home/alex'
```

When Alex creates the **dirB** alias, he uses single quotation marks, which prevent the shell from expanding the **$PWD** variable. The **alias dirB** command shows that the **dirB** alias still holds the unexpanded **$PWD** variable:

```
$ alias dirB='echo Working directory is $PWD'
$ alias dirB
alias dirB='echo Working directory is $PWD'
```

After creating the **dirA** and **dirB** aliases, Alex uses cd to make **cars** his working directory and gives each of the aliases as commands. The alias that he created with double quotation marks displays the name of the directory that he created the alias in as the working directory (which is wrong) and the **dirB** alias displays the proper name of the working directory:

```
$ cd cars
$ dirA
Working directory is /home/alex
$ dirB
Working directory is /home/alex/cars
```

How to prevent the shell from invoking an alias

tip The shell checks only simple, unquoted commands to see if they are aliases. Commands given as relative or absolute pathnames and quoted commands are not checked. When you want to give a command that has an alias but do not want to use the alias, precede the command with a backslash, specify the command's absolute pathname, or give the command as *./command*.

EXAMPLES OF ALIASES

The following alias allows you to type **r** to repeat the previous command or **r abc** to repeat the last command line that began with **abc**:

```
$ alias r='fc -s'
```

If you use the command **ls −ltr** frequently, you can create an alias that substitutes **ls −ltr** when you give the command **l**:

```
$ alias l='ls -ltr'
$ l
total 41
-rw-r--r--  1 alex    group      30015 Mar  1 2004 flute.ps
-rw-r-----  1 alex    group       3089 Feb 11 2005 XTerm.ad
-rw-r--r--  1 alex    group        641 Apr  1 2005 fixtax.icn
-rw-r--r--  1 alex    group        484 Apr  9 2005 maptax.icn
drwxrwxr-x  2 alex    group       1024 Aug  9 17:41 Tiger
drwxrwxr-x  2 alex    group       1024 Sep 10 11:32 testdir
-rwxr-xr-x  1 alex    group        485 Oct 21 08:03 floor
drwxrwxr-x  2 alex    group       1024 Oct 27 20:19 Test_Emacs
```

Another common use of aliases is to protect yourself from mistakes. The following example substitutes the interactive version of the rm utility when you give the command **zap**:

```
$ alias zap='rm -i'
$ zap f*
rm: remove 'fixtax.icn'? n
rm: remove 'flute.ps'? n
rm: remove 'floor'? n
```

The −i option causes rm to ask you to verify each file that would be deleted, to help you avoid accidentally deleting the wrong file. You can also alias rm with the **rm −i** command: **alias rm='rm −i'**.

The aliases in the next example cause the shell to substitute **ls −l** each time you give an **ll** command and **ls −F** when you use **ls**:

```
$ alias ls='ls -F'
$ alias ll='ls -l'
$ ll
total 41
drwxrwxr-x  2 alex    group       1024 Oct 27 20:19 Test_Emacs/
drwxrwxr-x  2 alex    group       1024 Aug 9 17:41 Tiger/
-rw-r-----  1 alex    group       3089 Feb 11 2005 XTerm.ad
-rw-r--r--  1 alex    group        641 Apr 1 2005 fixtax.icn
-rw-r--r--  1 alex    group      30015 Mar 1 2004 flute.ps
-rwxr-xr-x  1 alex    group        485 Oct 21 08:03 floor*
-rw-r--r--  1 alex    group        484 Apr 9 2005 maptax.icn
drwxrwxr-x  2 alex    group       1024 Sep 10 11:32 testdir/
```

The −F option causes ls to print a slash (/) at the end of directory names and an asterisk (*) at the end of the names of executable files. In this example, the string that replaces the alias ll (ls −l) itself contains an alias (ls). When it replaces an alias with its value, the shell looks at the first word of the replacement string to see whether it is an alias. In the preceding example, the replacement string contains the alias ls, so a second substitution occurs to produce the final command ls −F −l. (To avoid a *recursive plunge*, the ls in the replacement text, although an alias, is not expanded a second time.)

When given a list of aliases without the *=value* or *value* field, the alias builtin responds by displaying the value of each defined alias. The alias builtin reports an error if an alias has not been defined:

```
$ alias ll l ls zap wx
alias ll='ls -l'
alias l='ls -ltr'
alias ls='ls -F'
alias zap='rm -i'
bash: alias: wx: not found
```

You can avoid alias substitution by preceding the aliased command with a back-slash (\):

```
$ \ls
Test_Emacs XTerm.ad  flute.ps  maptax.icn
Tiger      fixtax.icn floor     testdir
```

Because the replacement of an alias name with the alias value does not change the rest of the command line, any arguments are still received by the command that gets executed:

```
$ ll f*
-rw-r--r--  1 alex    group      641 Apr  1 2005 fixtax.icn
-rw-r--r--  1 alex    group    30015 Mar  1 2004 flute.ps
-rwxr-xr-x  1 alex    group      485 Oct 21 08:03 floor*
```

You can remove an alias with the unalias builtin. When the **zap** alias is removed, it is no longer displayed with the alias builtin and its subsequent use results in an error message:

```
$ unalias zap
$ alias
alias ll='ls -l'
alias l='ls -ltr'
alias ls='ls -F'
$ zap maptax.icn
bash: zap: command not found
```

FUNCTIONS

A shell function (tcsh does not have functions) is similar to a shell script in that it stores a series of commands for execution at a later time. However, because the shell stores a function in the computer's main memory (RAM) instead of in a file on the disk, the shell can access it more quickly than the shell can access a script. The shell also preprocesses (parses) a function so that it starts up more quickly than a script. Finally the shell executes a shell function in the same shell that called it. If you define too many functions, the overhead of starting a subshell (as when you run a script) can become unacceptable.

You can declare a shell function in the ~/.bash_profile startup file, in the script that uses it, or directly from the command line. You can remove functions with the unset builtin. The shell does not keep functions once you log out.

Removing variables and functions

tip   If you have a shell variable and a function with the same name, using unset removes the shell variable. If you then use unset again with the same name, it removes the function.

The syntax that declares a shell function is

[function] function-name ()
{
    commands
}

where the word *function* is optional, *function-name* is the name you use to call the function, and *commands* comprise the list of commands the function executes when you call it. The *commands* can be anything you would include in a shell script, including calls to other functions.

The first brace ({) can appear on the same line as the function name. Aliases and variables are expanded when a function is read, not when it is executed. You can use the **break** statement (page 459) within a function to terminate its execution.

Shell functions are useful as a shorthand as well as to define special commands. The following function starts a process named **process** in the background, with the output normally displayed by **process** being saved in **.process.out**:

```
start_process() {
process > .process.out 2>&1 &
}
```

The next example shows how to create a simple function that displays the date, a header, and a list of the people who are using the system. This function runs the same commands as the **whoson** script described on page 264. In this example the function is being entered from the keyboard. The greater-than (>) signs are secondary shell prompts (**PS2**); do not enter them.

```
$ function whoson ()
> {
>    date
>    echo "Users Currently Logged On"
>    who
> }
$ whoson
Sun Aug  7 15:44:58 PDT 2005
Users Currently Logged On
hls       console    Aug  6 08:59  (:0)
alex      pts/4      Aug  6 09:33  (0.0)
jenny     pts/7      Aug  6 09:23  (bravo.example.com)
```

Functions in
startup files

If you want to have the **whoson** function always be available without having to enter it each time you log in, put its definition in **~/.bash_profile**. Then run **.bash_profile**, using the . (dot) command to put the changes into effect immediately:

```
$ cat ~/.bash_profile
export TERM=vt100
stty kill '^u'
whoson ()
{
    date
    echo "Users Currently Logged On"
    who
}
$ . ~/.bash_profile
```

You can specify arguments when you call a function. Within the function these arguments are available as positional parameters (page 480). The following example shows the **arg1** function entered from the keyboard.

```
$ arg1 ( ) {
> echo "$1"
> }

$ arg1 first_arg
first_arg
```

See the function **switch** () on page 259 for another example of a function. "Functions" on page 477 discusses the use of local and global variables within a function.

optional   The following function allows you to export variables using tcsh syntax. The env builtin lists all environment variables and their values and verifies that **setenv** worked correctly:

```
$ cat .bash_profile
...
# setenv - keep tcsh users happy
function setenv()
{
    if [ $# -eq 2 ]
        then
            eval $1=$2
            export $1
        else
            echo "Usage: setenv NAME VALUE" 1>&2
    fi
}
$ . ~/.bash_profile
$ setenv TCL_LIBRARY /usr/local/lib/tcl
$ env | grep TCL_LIBRARY
TCL_LIBRARY=/usr/local/lib/tcl
```

eval   The $# special parameter (page 480) takes on the value of the number of command line arguments. This function uses the eval builtin to force bash to scan the command $1=$2 *twice*. Because $1=$2 begins with a dollar sign ($), the shell treats the entire string as a single token—a command. With variable substitution performed, the command name becomes TCL_LIBRARY=/usr/local/lib/tcl, which results in an error. Using eval, a second scanning splits the string into the three desired tokens, and the correct assignment occurs.

CONTROLLING bash FEATURES AND OPTIONS

This section explains how to control bash features and options using command line options and the set and shopt builtins.

COMMAND LINE OPTIONS

Two kinds of command line options are available: short and long. Short options consist of a hyphen followed by a letter; long options have two hyphens followed by multiple characters. Long options must appear before short options on a command line that calls bash. Table 8-12 lists some commonly used command line options.

Table 8-12   Command line options

Option	Explanation	Syntax
Help	Displays a usage message.	**--help**
No edit	Prevents users from using the Readline Library (page 305) to edit command lines in an interactive shell.	**--noediting**
No profile	Prevents reading these startup files (page 257): **/etc/profile**, **~/.bash_profile**, **~/.bash_login**, and **~/.profile**.	**--noprofile**
No rc	Prevents reading the **~/.bashrc** startup file (page 258). This option is on by default if the shell is called as **sh**.	**--norc**
POSIX	Runs bash in POSIX mode.	**--posix**
Version	Displays bash version information and exits.	**--version**
Login	Causes bash to run as though it were a login shell.	**-l** (lowercase "l")
shopt	Runs a shell with the **opt** shopt option (page 319). A **-O** (uppercase "O") sets the option; **+O** unsets it.	**[±]O [opt]**
End of options	On the command line, signals the end of options. Subsequent tokens are treated as arguments even if they begin with a hyphen (–).	**--**

SHELL FEATURES

You can control the behavior of the Bourne Again Shell by turning features on and off. Different features use different methods to turn features on and off. The set builtin controls one group of features, while the shopt builtin controls another group. You can also control many features from the command line you use to call bash.

Features, options, variables?

tip To avoid confusing terminology, this book refers to the various shell behaviors that you can control as *features*. The bash info page refers to them as "options" and "values of variables controlling optional shell behavior."

set ±o: TURNS SHELL FEATURES ON AND OFF

The set builtin (there is a set builtin in tcsh, but it works differently), when used with the **−o** or **+o** option, enables, disables, and lists certain bash features. For example, the following command turns on the **noclobber** feature (page 119):

```
$ set -o noclobber
```

You can turn this feature off (the default) by giving the command

```
$ set +o noclobber
```

The command **set −o** without an option lists each of the features controlled by set followed by its state (on or off). The command **set +o** without an option lists the same features in a form that you can use as input to the shell. Table 8 13 lists bash features.

shopt: TURNS SHELL FEATURES ON AND OFF

The shopt (shell option) builtin (not available in tcsh) enables, disables, and lists certain bash features that control the behavior of the shell. For example, the following command causes bash to include filenames that begin with a period (.) when it expands ambiguous file references (the **−s** stands for *set*):

```
$ shopt -s dotglob
```

You can turn this feature off (the default) by giving the command (the **−u** stands for *unset*)

```
$ shopt -u dotglob
```

The shell displays how a feature is set if you give the name of the feature as the only argument to shopt:

```
$ shopt dotglob
dotglob         off
```

The command **shopt** without any options or arguments lists the features controlled by shopt and their state. The command **shopt −s** without an argument lists the features controlled by shopt that are set or on. The command **shopt –u** lists the features that are unset or off. Table 8-13 lists bash features.

Setting set ±o features using shopt

tip You can use shopt to set/unset features that are otherwise controlled by **set ±o**. Use the regular shopt syntax with **–s** or **–u** and include the **–o** option. For example, the following command turns on the **noclobber** feature:

```
$ shopt -o -s noclobber
```

Table 8-13 bash features

Feature	Description	Syntax	Alternate syntax
allexport	Automatically exports all variables and functions that you create or modify after giving this command.	**set –o allexport**	**set –a**
braceexpand	Causes bash to perform brace expansion (the default; page 324).	**set –o braceexpand**	**set –B**
cdspell	Corrects minor spelling errors in directory names used as arguments to cd.	**shopt –s cdspell**	
cmdhist	Saves all lines of a multiline command in the same history entry, adding semicolons as needed.	**shopt –s cmdhist**	
dotglob	Causes shell special characters (wildcards; page 127) in an ambiguous file reference to match a leading period in a filename. By default special characters do not to match a leading period. You must always specify the filenames . and .. explicitly because no pattern ever matches them.	**shopt –s dotglob**	
emacs	Specifies emacs editing mode for command line editing (the default; page 306).	**set –o emacs**	
errexit	Causes bash to exit when a simple command (not a control structure) fails.	**set –o errexit**	**set –e**
execfail	Causes a shell script to continue running when it cannot find the file that is given as an argument to exec. By default a script terminates when exec cannot find the file that is given as its argument.	**shopt –s execfail**	

Table 8-13   bash features (continued)

expand_aliases	Causes aliases (page 312) to be expanded (by default it is on for interactive shells and off for noninteractive shells).	**shopt –s expand_alias**	
hashall	Causes bash to remember where commands it has found using **PATH** (page 284) are located (default).	**set –o hashall**	**set –h**
histappend	Causes bash to append the history list to the file named by **HISTFILE** (page 295) when the shell exits. By default bash overwrites this file.	**shopt –s histappend**	
histexpand	Causes the history mechanism (which uses exclamation points; page 300) to work (default). Turn this feature off to turn off history expansion.	**set –o histexpand**	**set –H**
history	Enable command history (on by default; page 295).	**set –o history**	
ignoreeof	Specifies that bash must receive ten EOF characters before it exits. Useful on noisy dial-up lines.	**set –o ignoreeof**	
monitor	Enables job control (on by default, page 271).	**set –o monitor**	**set –m**
nocaseglob	Causes ambiguous file references (page 127) to match filenames without regard to case (off by default).	**shopt –s nocaseglob**	
noclobber	Helps prevent overwriting files (off by default; page 119).	**set –o noclobber**	**set –C**
noglob	Disables pathname expansion (off by default; page 127).	**set –o noglob**	**set –f**
notify	With job control (page 271) enabled, reports the termination status of background jobs immediately. The default behavior is to display the status just before the next prompt.	**set –o notify**	**set –b**
nounset	Displays an error and exits from a shell script when you use an unset variable in an interactive shell. The default is to display a null value for an unset variable.	**set –o nounset**	**set –u**

Table 8-13   bash features (continued)

nullglob	Causes bash to expand ambiguous file references (page 127) that do not match a filename to a null string. By default bash passes these file references without expanding them.	**shopt –s nullglob**	
posix	Runs bash in POSIX mode.	**set –o posix**	
verbose	Displays command lines as bash reads them.	**set –o verbose**	**set –v**
vi	Specifies vi editing mode for command line editing (page 305).	**set –o vi**	
xpg_echo	Causes the echo builtin to expand back-slash escape sequences without the need for the **–e** option (page 463).	**shopt –s xpg_echo**	
xtrace	Turns on shell debugging (page 448).	**set –o xtrace**	**set –x**

Processing the Command Line

Whether you are working interactively or running a shell script, bash needs to read a command line before it can start processing it—bash always reads at least one line before processing a command. Some bash builtins, such as **if** and **case**, as well as functions and quoted strings, span multiple lines. When bash recognizes a command that covers more than one line, it reads the entire command before processing it. In interactive sessions bash prompts you with the secondary prompt (**PS2**, **>** by default; page 287) as you type each line of a multiline command until it recognizes the end of the command:

```
$ echo 'hi
> end'
hi
end
$ function hello () {
> echo hello there
> }
$
```

After reading a command line, bash applies history expansion and alias substitution to the line.

HISTORY EXPANSION

"Reexecuting and Editing Commands" on page 297 discusses the commands you can give to modify and reexecute command lines from the history list. History expansion is the process that bash uses to turn a history command into an executable command line. For example, when you give the command !!, history expansion changes that command line so it is the same as the previous one. History expansion is turned on by default for interactive shells; **set +o histexpand** turns it off. History expansion does not apply to noninteractive shells (shell scripts).

ALIAS SUBSTITUTION

Aliases (page 312) substitute a string for the first word of a simple command. By default aliases are turned on for interactive shells and off for noninteractive shells. Give the command **shopt –u expand_aliases** to turn aliases off.

PARSING AND SCANNING THE COMMAND LINE

After processing history commands and aliases, bash does not execute the command immediately. One of the first things the shell does is to *parse* (isolate strings of characters in) the command line into tokens or words. The shell then scans each token for special characters and patterns that instruct the shell to take certain actions. These actions can involve substituting one word or words for another. When the shell parses the following command line, it breaks it into three tokens (**cp**, **~/letter**, and **.**):

```
$ cp ~/letter .
```

After separating tokens and before executing the command, the shell scans the tokens and performs *command line expansion*.

COMMAND LINE EXPANSION

In both interactive and noninteractive use, the shell transforms the command line using *command line expansion* before passing the command line to the program being called. You can use a shell without knowing much about command line expansion, but you can use what a shell has to offer to a better advantage with an understanding of this topic. This section covers Bourne Again Shell command line expansion; TC Shell command line expansion is covered starting on page 344.

The Bourne Again Shell scans each token for the various types of expansion and substitution in the following order. Most of these processes expand a word into a single word. Only brace expansion, word splitting, and pathname expansion can change the number of words in a command (except for the expansion of the variable "$@"—page 482).

1. Brace expansion (page 324)

2. Tilde expansion (page 326)

3. Parameter and variable expansion (page 326)

4. Arithmetic expansion (page 327)

5. Command substitution (page 329)

6. Word splitting (page 330)

7. Pathname expansion (page 330)

8. Process substitution (page 332)

Quote removal   After bash finishes with the preceding list, it removes from the command line single quotation marks, double quotation marks, and backslashes that are not a result of an expansion. This process is called *quote removal*.

ORDER OF EXPANSION

The order in which bash carries out these steps affects the interpretation of commands. For example, if you set a variable to a value that looks like the instruction for output redirection and then enter a command that uses the variable's value to perform redirection, you might expect bash to redirect the output.

```
$ SENDIT="> /tmp/saveit"
$ echo xxx $SENDIT
xxx > /tmp/saveit
$ cat /tmp/saveit
cat: /tmp/saveit: No such file or directory
```

In fact, the shell does *not* redirect the output—it recognizes input and output redirection before it evaluates variables. When it executes the command line, the shell checks for redirection and, finding none, evaluates the **SENDIT** variable. After replacing the variable with **> /tmp/saveit**, bash passes the arguments to echo, which dutifully copies its arguments to standard output. No **/tmp/saveit** file is created.

The following sections provide more detailed descriptions of the steps involved in command processing. Keep in mind that double and single quotation marks cause the shell to behave differently when performing expansions. Double quotation marks permit parameter and variable expansion but suppress other types of expansion. Single quotation marks suppress all types of expansion.

BRACE EXPANSION

Brace expansion, which originated in the C Shell, provides a convenient way to specify filenames when pathname expansion does not apply. Although brace expansion is almost always used to specify filenames, the mechanism can be used to generate arbitrary strings; the shell does not attempt to match the brace notation with the names of existing files.

Brace expansion is turned on in interactive and noninteractive shells by default; you can turn it off with **set +o braceexpand**. The shell also uses braces to isolate variable names (page 280).

The following example illustrates how brace expansion works. The ls command does not display any output because there are no files in the working directory. The echo builtin displays the strings that the shell generates with brace expansion. In this case the strings do not match filenames (there are no files in the working directory.)

```
$ ls
$ echo chap_{one,two,three}.txt
chap_one.txt chap_two.txt chap_three.txt
```

The shell expands the comma-separated strings inside the braces in the echo command into a SPACE-separated list of strings. Each string from the list is prepended with the string **chap_**, called the *preamble,* and appended with the string **.txt,** called the *postscript.* Both the preamble and the postscript are optional. The left-to-right order of the strings within the braces is preserved in the expansion. For the shell to treat the left and right braces specially and for brace expansion to occur, at least one comma and no unquoted whitespace characters must be inside the braces. You can nest brace expansions.

Brace expansion is useful when there is a long preamble or postscript. The following example copies the four files **main.c, f1.c, f2.c,** and **tmp.c** located in the **/usr/local/src/C** directory to the working directory:

```
$ cp /usr/local/src/C/{main,f1,f2,tmp}.c .
```

You can also use brace expansion to create directories with related names:

```
$ ls -F
file1  file2  file3
$ mkdir vrs{A,B,C,D,E}
$ ls -F
file1  file2  file3  vrsA/  vrsB/  vrsC/  vrsD/  vrsE/
```

The **–F** option causes ls to display a slash (/) after a directory and an asterisk (*) after an executable file.

If you tried to use an ambiguous file reference instead of braces to specify the directories, the result would be different (and not what you wanted):

```
$ rmdir vrs*
$ mkdir vrs[A-E]
$ ls -F
file1  file2  file3  vrs[A-E]/
```

An ambiguous file reference matches the names of existing files. Because it found no filenames matching **vrs[A–E]**, bash passed the ambiguous file reference to mkdir, which created a directory with that name. Page 130 has a discussion of brackets in ambiguous file references.

TILDE EXPANSION

Chapter 4 (page 89) showed a shorthand notation to specify your home directory or the home directory of another user. This section provides a more detailed explanation of *tilde expansion*.

The tilde (~) is a special character when it appears at the start of a token on a command line. When it sees a tilde in this position, bash looks at the following string of characters—up to the first slash (/) or to the end of the word if there is no slash—as a possible login name. If this possible login name is null (that is, if the tilde appears as a word by itself or if it is immediately followed by a slash), the shell substitutes the value of the **HOME** variable for the tilde. The following example demonstrates this expansion, where the last command copies the file named **letter** from Alex's home directory to the working directory:

```
$ echo $HOME
/home/alex
$ echo ~
/home/alex
$ echo ~/letter
/home/alex/letter
$ cp ~/letter .
```

If the string of characters following the tilde forms a valid login name, the shell substitutes the path of the home directory associated with that login name for the tilde and name. If it is not null and not a valid login name, the shell does not make any substitution:

```
$ echo ~jenny
/home/jenny
$ echo ~root
/root
$ echo ~xx
~xx
```

Tildes are also used in directory stack manipulation (page 274). In addition, ~+ is a synonym for **PWD** (the name of the working directory), and ~– is a synonym for **OLDPWD** (the name of the previous working directory).

PARAMETER AND VARIABLE EXPANSION

On a command line a dollar sign ($) that is not followed by an open parenthesis introduces parameter or variable expansion. *Parameters* include command line, or positional, parameters (page 480) and special parameters (page 478). *Variables* include user-created variables (page 278) and keyword variables (page 283). The bash man and info pages do not make this distinction, however.

Parameters and variables are not expanded if they are enclosed within single quotation marks or if the leading dollar sign is escaped (preceded with a backslash). If they are enclosed within double quotation marks, the shell expands parameters and variables.

ARITHMETIC EXPANSION

The shell performs *arithmetic expansion* by evaluating an arithmetic expression and replacing it with the result. See page 358 for information on arithmetic expansion under tcsh. Under bash the syntax for arithmetic expansion is

$((expression))$

The shell evaluates *expression* and replaces *$((expression))* with the result of the evaluation. This syntax is similar to the syntax used for command substitution [*$(...)*] and performs a parallel function. You can use *$((expression))* as an argument to a command or in place of any numeric value on a command line.

The rules for forming *expression* are the same as those found in the C programming language; all standard C arithmetic operators are available (see Table 11-8 on page 505). Arithmetic in bash is done using integers. Unless you use variables of type integer (page 283) or actual integers, however, the shell must convert string-valued variables to integers for the purpose of the arithmetic evaluation.

You do not need to precede variable names within *expression* with a dollar sign ($). In the following example, an arithmetic expression determines how many years are left until age 60:

```
$ cat age_check
#!/bin/bash
echo -n "How old are you? "
read age
echo "Wow, in $((60-age)) years, you'll be 60!"

$ age_check
How old are you? 55
Wow, in 5 years, you'll be 60!
```

You do not need to enclose the *expression* within quotation marks because bash does not perform filename expansion on it. This feature makes it easier for you to use an asterisk (✶) for multiplication, as the following example shows:

```
$ echo There are $((60✶60✶24✶365)) seconds in a non-leap year.
There are 31536000 seconds in a non-leap year.
```

The next example uses wc, cut, arithmetic expansion, and command substitution to estimate the number of pages required to print the contents of the file **letter.txt**. The

Fewer dollar signs ($)

tip   When you use variables within $((and)), the dollar signs that precede individual variable references are optional:

```
$ x=23 y=37
$ echo $((2*$x + 3*$y))
157
$ echo $((2*x + 3*y))
157
```

output of the wc utility (page 816) used with the –l option is the number of lines in the file, in columns 1 through 4, followed by a SPACE and the name of the file (the first command following). The cut utility (page 627) with the –c1-4 option extracts the first four columns.

```
$ wc -l letter.txt
351 letter.txt
$ wc -l letter.txt | cut -c1-4
351
```

The dollar sign and single parenthesis instruct the shell to perform command substitution; the dollar sign and double parentheses indicate arithmetic expansion:

```
$ echo $(( $(wc -l letter.txt | cut -c1-4)/66 + 1))
6
```

The preceding example sends standard output from wc to standard input of cut via a pipe. Because of command substitution, the output of both commands replaces the commands between the $(and the matching) on the command line. Arithmetic expansion then divides this number by 66, the number of lines on a page. A 1 is added at the end because the integer division results in any remainder being discarded.

Another way to get the same result without using cut is to redirect the input to wc instead of having wc get its input from a file you name on the command line. When you redirect its input, wc does not display the name of the file:

```
$ wc -l < letter.txt
   351
```

It is common practice to assign the result of arithmetic expansion to a variable:

```
$ numpages=$(( $(wc -l < letter.txt)/66 + 1))
```

let builtin   The let builtin (not available in tcsh) evaluates arithmetic expressions just as the $(( )) syntax does. The following command is equivalent to the preceding one:

```
$ let "numpages=$(wc -l < letter.txt)/66 + 1"
```

The double quotation marks keep the SPACEs (both those you can see and those that result from the command substitution) from separating the expression into separate arguments to let. The value of the last expression determines the exit status of let. If the value of the last expression is 0, the exit status of let is 1; otherwise, the exit status is 0.

You can give multiple arguments to let on a single command line:

```
$ let a=5+3 b=7+2
$ echo $a $b
8 9
```

When you refer to variables when doing arithmetic expansion with let or $(( )), the shell does not require you to begin the variable name with a dollar sign ($). Nevertheless, it is a good practice to do so, as in most places you must include this symbol.

COMMAND SUBSTITUTION

Command substitution replaces a command with the output of that command. The preferred syntax for command substitution under bash follows:

$(command)

Under bash you can also use the following syntax, which is the only syntax allowed under tcsh:

` *command* `

The shell executes *command* within a subshell and replaces *command*, along with the surrounding punctuation, with standard output of *command*.

In the following example, the shell executes pwd and substitutes the output of the command for the command and surrounding punctuation. Then the shell passes the output of the command, which is now an argument, to echo, which displays it.

```
$ echo $(pwd)
/home/alex
```

The next script assigns the output of the pwd builtin to the variable **where** and displays a message containing the value of this variable:

```
$ cat where
where=$(pwd)
echo "You are using the $where directory."
$ where
You are using the /home/jenny directory.
```

Although it illustrates how to assign the output of a command to a variable, this example is not realistic. You can more directly display the output of pwd without using a variable:

```
$ cat where2
echo "You are using the $(pwd) directory."
$ where2
You are using the /home/jenny directory.
```

The following command uses find to locate files with the name **README** in the directory tree with its root at the working directory. This list of files is standard output of find and becomes the list of arguments to ls.

```
$ ls -l $(find . -name README -print)
```

The next command line shows the older `command` syntax:

```
$ ls -l `find . -name README -print`
```

One advantage of the newer syntax is that it avoids the rather arcane rules for token handling, quotation mark handling, and escaped back ticks within the old syntax. Another advantage of the new syntax is that it can be nested, unlike the old syntax. For example, you can produce a long listing of all **README** files whose size exceeds the size of **./README** with the following command:

```
$ ls -l $(find . -name README -size +$(echo $(cat ./README | wc -c)c ) -print )
```

Try giving this command after giving a **set −x** command (page 448) to see how bash expands it. If there is no **README** file, you just get the output of **ls −l**.

For additional scripts that use command substitution, see pages 444, 464, and 496.

$((Versus $(

tip   The symbols **$((** constitute a separate token. They introduce an arithmetic expression, not a command substitution. Thus, if you want to use a parenthesized subshell (page 270) within **$()**, you must insert a SPACE between the **$(** and the next **(**.

WORD SPLITTING

The results of parameter and variable expansion, command substitution, and arithmetic expansion are candidates for word splitting. Using each character of **IFS** (page 288) as a possible delimiter, bash splits these candidates into words or tokens. If **IFS** is unset, bash uses its default value (SPACE-TAB-NEWLINE). If **IFS** is null, bash does not split words.

PATHNAME EXPANSION

Pathname expansion (page 127), also called *filename generation* or *globbing,* is the process of interpreting ambiguous file references and substituting the appropriate list of filenames. Unless **noglob** (page 321) is set, the shell performs this function when it encounters an ambiguous file reference—a token containing any of the unquoted characters *, ?, [, or]. If bash cannot locate any files that match the specified pattern, the token with the ambiguous file reference is left alone. The shell does not delete the token or replace it with a null string but rather passes it to the program as is (except see **nullglob**, page 322). The TC Shell generates an error message.

In the first echo command in the following example, the shell expands the ambiguous file reference **tmp*** and passes three tokens (**tmp1**, **tmp2**, and **tmp3**) to echo. The echo builtin displays the three filenames it was passed by the shell. After rm removes the three **tmp*** files, the shell finds no filenames that match **tmp*** when it tries to expand it. Thus it passes the unexpanded string to the echo builtin, which displays the string it was passed.

```
$ ls
tmp1 tmp2 tmp3
$ echo tmp*
tmp1 tmp2 tmp3
$ rm tmp*
$ echo tmp*
tmp*
```

By default the same command causes the TC Shell to display an error message:

```
tcsh $ echo tmp*
echo: No match
```

A period that either starts a pathname or follows a slash (/) in a pathname must be matched explicitly unless you have set **dotglob** (page 320). The option **nocaseglob** (page 321) causes ambiguous file references to match filenames without regard to case.

Quotation marks   Putting double quotation marks around an argument causes the shell to suppress pathname and all other expansion except parameter and variable expansion. Putting single quotation marks around an argument suppresses all types of expansion. The second echo command in the following example shows the variable $alex between double quotation marks, which allow variable expansion. As a result the shell expands the variable to its value: **sonar**. This expansion does not occur in the third echo command, which uses single quotation marks. Because neither single nor double quotation marks allow pathname expansion, the last two commands display the unexpanded argument **tmp***.

```
$ echo tmp* $alex
tmp1 tmp2 tmp3 sonar
$ echo "tmp* $alex"
tmp* sonar
$ echo 'tmp* $alex'
tmp* $alex
```

The shell distinguishes between the value of a variable and a reference to the variable and does not expand ambiguous file references if they occur in the value of a variable. As a consequence you can assign to a variable a value that includes special characters, such as an asterisk (*).

Levels of expansion   In the next example, the working directory has three files whose names begin with **letter**. When you assign the value **letter*** to the variable **var**, the shell does not expand the ambiguous file reference because it occurs in the value of a variable (in the assignment statement for the variable). No quotation marks surround the string **letter***; context alone prevents the expansion. After the assignment the set builtin (with the help of grep) shows the value of **var** to be **letter***.

The three echo commands demonstrate three levels of expansion. When $var is quoted with single quotation marks, the shell performs no expansion and passes the character string $var to echo, which displays it. When you use double quotation marks, the shell performs variable expansion only and substitutes the value of the **var** variable for its name, preceded by a dollar sign. No pathname expansion is performed on this command because double quotation marks suppress it. In the final command, the shell, without the limitations of quotation marks, performs variable substitution and then pathname expansion before passing the arguments to echo.

```
$ ls letter*
letter1  letter2  letter3
$ var=letter*
$ set | grep var
var='letter*'
$ echo '$var'
$var
$ echo "$var"
letter*
$ echo $var
letter1 letter2 letter3
```

PROCESS SUBSTITUTION

A special feature of the Bourne Again Shell is the ability to replace filename arguments with processes. An argument with the syntax <*(command)* causes *command* to be executed and the output written to a named pipe (FIFO). The shell replaces that argument with the name of the pipe. If that argument is then used as the name of an input file during processing, the output of *command* is read. Similarly an argument with the syntax >*(command)* is replaced by the name of a pipe that *command* reads as standard input.

The following example uses sort (page 762) with the **–m** (merge, which works correctly only if the input files are already sorted) option to combine two word lists into a single list. Each word list is generated by a pipe that extracts words matching a pattern from a file and sorts the words in that list.

```
$ sort -m -f <(grep "[^A-Z]..$" memo1 | sort) <(grep ".*aba.*" memo2 |sort)
```

CHAPTER SUMMARY

The shell is both a command interpreter and a programming language. As a command interpreter, the shell executes commands you enter in response to its prompt. As a programming language, the shell executes commands from files called shell scripts. When you start a shell, it typically runs one or more startup files.

Running a shell script   Assuming that the file holding a shell script is in the working directory, there are three basic ways to execute the shell script from the command line.

1. Type the simple filename of the file that holds the script.

2. Type a relative pathname, including the simple filename preceded by ./.

3. Type **bash** or **tcsh** followed by the name of the file.

Technique 1 requires that the working directory be in the **PATH** variable. Techniques 1 and 2 require that you have execute and read permission for the file holding the script. Technique 3 requires that you have read permission for the file holding the script.

Job control   A job is one or more commands connected by pipes. You can bring a job running in the background into the foreground by using the fg builtin. You can put a foreground job into the background by using the bg builtin, provided that you first suspend the job by pressing the suspend key (typically CONTROL-Z). Use the jobs builtin to see which jobs are running or suspended.

Variables   The shell allows you to define variables. You can declare and initialize a variable by assigning a value to it; you can remove a variable declaration by using unset. Variables are local to a process unless they are exported using the export (bash) or setenv (tcsh) builtin to make them available to child processes. Variables you declare are called *user-created* variables. The shell also defines called *keyword* variables. Within a shell script you can work with the command line (*positional*) parameters the script was called with.

Process   Each process has a unique identification (PID) number and is the execution of a single Linux command. When you give it a command, the shell forks a new (child) process to execute the command, unless the command is built into the shell (page 132). While the child process is running, the shell is in a state called sleep. By ending a command line with an ampersand (&), you can run a child process in the background and bypass the sleep state so that the shell prompt returns immediately after you press RETURN. Each command in a shell script forks a separate process, each of which may in turn fork other processes. When a process terminates, it returns its exit status to its parent process. An exit status of zero signifies success and nonzero signifies failure.

History   The history mechanism, a feature adapted from the C Shell, maintains a list of recently issued command lines, also called *events*, that provides a way to reexecute previous commands quickly. There are several ways to work with the history list; one of the easiest is to use a command line editor.

Command line editors   When using an interactive Bourne Again Shell, you can edit your command line and commands from the history file, using either of the Bourne Again Shell's command line editors (vi[m] or emacs). When you use the vi(m) command line editor, you start in Input mode, unlike the way you normally enter vi(m). You can switch between Command and Input modes. The emacs editor is modeless and distinguishes commands from editor input by recognizing control characters as commands.

Aliases   An alias is a name that the shell translates into another name or (complex) command. Aliases allow you to define new commands by substituting a string for the first token of a simple command. The Bourne Again and TC Shells use different syntaxes to define an alias, but aliases in both shells work similarly.

Functions   A shell function is a series of commands that, unlike a shell script, are parsed prior to being stored in memory so that they run faster than shell scripts. Shell scripts are parsed at runtime and are stored on disk. A function can be defined on the command line or within a shell script. If you want the function definition to remain in effect across login sessions, you can define it in a startup file. Like the functions of a programming language, a shell function is called by giving its name followed by any arguments.

Shell features   There are several ways to customize the shell's behavior. You can use options on the command line when you call bash and you can use the bash set and shopt builtins to turn features on and off.

Command line expansion   When it processes a command line, the Bourne Again Shell may replace some words with expanded text. Most types of command line expansion are invoked by the appearance of a special character within a word (for example, a leading dollar sign denotes a variable). See Table 8-6 on page 291 for a list of special characters. The expansions take place in a specific order. Following the history and alias expansions, the common expansions are parameter and variable expansion, command substitution, and pathname expansion. Surrounding a word with double quotation marks suppresses all types of expansion except parameter and variable expansion. Single quotation marks suppress all types of expansion, as does quoting (escaping) a special character by preceding it with a backslash.

EXERCISES

1. Explain the following unexpected result:

   ```
   $ whereis date
   date: /bin/date
   $ echo $PATH
   .:/usr/local/bin:/usr/bin:/bin
   $ cat > date
   echo "This is my own version of date."
   $ date
   Tue May 24 11:45:49 PDT 2005
   ```

2. What are two ways you can execute a shell script when you do not have execute access permission for the file containing the script? Can you execute a shell script if you do not have read access permission for the file containing the script?

3. What is the purpose of the **PATH** variable?

   a. Set the **PATH** variable so that it causes the shell to search the following directories in order:

- /usr/local/bin

- /usr/bin/X11

- /usr/bin

- /bin

- /usr/kerberos/bin

- The **bin** directory in your home directory

- The working directory

b. If there is a file named **doit** in **/usr/bin** and another file with the same name in your **~/bin,** which one will be executed? (Assume that you have execute permission for both files.)

c. If your **PATH** variable is not set to search the working directory, how can you execute a program located there?

d. Which command can you use to add the directory **/usr/games** to the end of the list of directories in **PATH**?

4. Assume that you have made the following assignment:

```
$ person=jenny
```

Give the output of each of the following commands:

a. echo $person

b. echo ' $person '

c. echo "$person"

5. The following shell script adds entries to a file named **journal-file** in your home directory. This script helps you keep track of phone conversations and meetings.

```
$ cat journal
# journal: add journal entries to the file
# $HOME/journal-file

file=$HOME/journal-file
date >> $file
echo -n "Enter name of person or group: "
read name
echo "$name" >> $file
echo >> $file
cat >> $file
echo "------------------------------------------------------" >> $file
echo >> $file
```

a. What do you have to do to the script to be able to execute it?

b. Why does the script use the read builtin (page 487) the first time it accepts input from the terminal and the cat utility the second time?

6. Assume that the **/home/jenny/grants/biblios** and **/home/jenny/biblios** directories exist. Give Jenny's working directory after she executes each sequence of commands given. Explain what happens in each case.

   a.

   ```
   $ pwd
   /home/jenny/grants
   $ CDPATH=$(pwd)
   $ cd
   $ cd biblios
   ```

   b.

   ```
   $ pwd
   /home/jenny/grants
   $ CDPATH=$(pwd)
   $ cd $HOME/biblios
   ```

7. Name two ways you can identify the PID number of your login shell.

8. Give the following command:

   ```
   $ sleep 30 | cat /etc/inittab
   ```

   Is there any output from sleep? Where does cat get its input from? What has to happen before the shell displays another prompt?

ADVANCED EXERCISES

9. Write a sequence of commands or a script that demonstrates that variable expansion occurs before pathname expansion.

10. Write a shell script that outputs the name of the shell that is executing it.

11. Explain the behavior of the following shell script:

    ```
    $ cat quote_demo
    twoliner="This is line 1.
    This is line 2."
    echo "$twoliner"
    echo $twoliner
    ```

    a. How many arguments does each echo command see in this script? Explain.

    b. Redefine the **IFS** shell variable so that the output of the second echo is the same as the first.

12. Add the exit status of the previous command to your prompt so that it behaves similarly to the following:

```
$ [0] ls xxx
ls: xxx: No such file or directory
$ [1]
```

13. The dirname utility treats its argument as a pathname and writes to standard output the path prefix—that is, everything up to but not including the last component:

```
$ dirname a/b/c/d
a/b/c
```

If you give **dirname** a simple filename (no / characters) as an argument, **dirname** writes a . to standard output:

```
$ dirname simple
.
```

Implement dirname as a bash function. Make sure that it behaves sensibly when given such arguments as /.

14. Implement the basename utility, which writes the last component of its pathname argument to standard output, as a bash function. For example, given the pathname a/b/c/d, basename writes d to standard output:

```
$ basename a/b/c/d
d
```

15. The Linux basename utility has an optional second argument. If you give the command **basename** *path suffix*, basename removes the *suffix* and the prefix from *path*:

```
$ basename src/shellfiles/prog.bash .bash
prog
$ basename src/shellfiles/prog.bash .c
prog.bash
```

Add this feature to the function you wrote for exercise 14.

9

THE TC SHELL

The TC Shell (tcsh) performs the same function as the Bourne Again Shell and other shells: It provides an interface between you and the Linux operating system. The TC Shell is an interactive command interpreter as well as a high-level programming language. Although you use only one shell at any given time, you should be able to switch back and forth comfortably between shells as the need arises (you may want to run different shells in different windows). Chapters 8 and 11 apply to tcsh as well as to bash so they provide a good background for this chapter. This chapter explains tcsh features that are not found in bash and those that are implemented differently from their bash counterparts. The tcsh home page is www.tcsh.org.

The TC Shell is an expanded version of the C Shell (csh), which originated on Berkeley UNIX. The "T" in TC Shell comes from the TENEX and TOPS-20 operating systems, which inspired command completion and other features in the TC Shell. A number of features not found in csh are present in tcsh, including file and username completion, command line editing, and spelling correction. As with csh, you can customize tcsh to make it more tolerant of mistakes and easier to use. By setting the proper shell variables, you can have tcsh warn you when you appear to be accidentally logging out or overwriting a file. Many popular features of the original C Shell are now shared by bash and tcsh.

Assignment statement   Although some of the functionality of tcsh is present in bash, differences arise in the syntax of some commands. For example, the tcsh assignment statement has the following syntax:

> set *variable* = *value*

Having SPACEs on either side of the equal sign, although illegal in bash, is allowed in tcsh. By convention shell variables in tcsh are generally named with lowercase letters, not uppercase (you can use either). If you reference an undeclared variable (one that has had no value assigned to it), tcsh will give you an error message, whereas bash will not. Finally the default tcsh prompt is a greater than sign (>), but it is frequently set to a single $ character followed by a SPACE. The examples in this chapter use a prompt of **tcsh $** to avoid confusion with the bash prompt.

Do not use tcsh as a programming language

tip   If you have used UNIX and are comfortable with the C or TC Shell, you may want to use tcsh as your login shell. However, you may find that the TC Shell is not as good a programming language as bash. If you are going to learn only one shell programming language, learn bash. The Bourne Again Shell is used throughout Linux to program many system administration scripts.

SHELL SCRIPTS

With tcsh you can execute files containing TC Shell commands, just as bash can execute files containing Bourne Again Shell commands. The concepts of writing and executing scripts in the two shells are similar. However, the methods of declaring and assigning values to variables and the syntax of control structures are different.

You can run bash and tcsh scripts while using any one of the shells as a command interpreter. Various methods exist for selecting the shell that runs a script. Refer to "#! Specifies a Shell" on page 265 for more information.

If the first character of a shell script is a pound sign (#) and the following character is *not* an exclamation point (!), the TC Shell executes the script under tcsh. If the first character is anything other than #, tcsh calls the sh link to bash to execute the script.

echo: **getting rid of the** RETURN

tip   The tcsh echo builtin accepts either a **−n** option or a trailing **\c** to get rid of the RETURN that echo normally displays at the end of a line. The bash echo builtin accepts only the **−n** option (refer to "read: Accepts User Input" on page 487).

Shell game

tip   When you are working with an interactive TC Shell, if you run a script in which # is *not* the first character of the script and you call the script *directly* (without preceding its name with tcsh), tcsh calls the sh link to bash to run the script. The following script was written to be run under tcsh but, when called from a tcsh command line, is executed by bash. The set builtin (page 484) works differently under bash and tcsh. As a result the following example (from page 361) issues a prompt but does not wait for you to respond:

```
tcsh $ cat user_in
echo -n "Enter input: "
set input_line = "$<"
echo $input_line

tcsh $ user_in
Enter input:
```

Although in each case the examples are run from a tcsh command line, the following one calls tcsh explicitly so that tcsh executes the script and it runs correctly.

```
tcsh $ tcsh user_in
Enter input: here is some input
here is some input
```

ENTERING AND LEAVING THE TC SHELL

chsh   You can execute tcsh by giving the command **tcsh**. If you are not sure which shell you are using, use the ps utility to find out. It shows whether you are running tcsh, bash, sh (linked to bash), or possibly another shell. The finger command followed by your username displays the name of your login shell, which is stored in the /etc/passwd file. If you want to use tcsh as a matter of course, you can use the chsh (change shell) utility to change your login shell:

```
bash $ chsh
Changing shell for sam.
Password:
New shell [/bin/bash]: /bin/tcsh
Shell changed.
bash $
```

The shell you specify will be in effect for your next login and all subsequent logins until you specify a different login shell. The /etc/passwd file stores the name of your login shell.

You can leave tcsh in several ways. The approach you choose depends on two factors: whether the shell variable **ignoreeof** is set and whether you are using the shell that you logged in on (your login shell) or another shell that you created after you logged in. If you are not sure how to exit from tcsh, press CONTROL-D on a line by itself with no leading SPACEs, just as you would to terminate standard input to another program. You will either exit or receive instructions on how to exit. If you have not set **ignoreeof** (page 366) and it has not been set for you in a startup file, you can exit from any shell by using CONTROL-D (the same procedure you use to exit from the Bourne Again Shell).

When **ignoreeof** is set, CONTROL-D does not work. The **ignoreeof** variable causes the shell to display a message telling you how to exit. You can always exit from tcsh by giving an **exit** command. A **logout** command allows you to exit from your login shell only.

STARTUP FILES

When you log in on the TC Shell, it automatically executes various startup files. These files are normally executed in the order described in this section, but you can compile tcsh so that it uses a different order. You must have read access to a startup file to execute the commands in it.

/etc/csh.cshrc and /etc/csh.login   The shell first executes the commands in **/etc/csh.cshrc** and **/etc/csh.login**. Superuser can set up these files to establish systemwide default characteristics for tcsh users. They contain systemwide configuration information, such as the default **path**, the location to check for mail, and so on.

.tcshrc and .cshrc   Next the shell looks for **~/.tcshrc** or, if it does not exist, **~/.cshrc** (**~/** is shorthand for your home directory). You can use these files to establish variables and parameters that are local to your shell. Each time you create a new shell, tcsh reinitializes these variables for the new shell. The following **.tcshrc** file sets several shell variables, establishes two aliases (page 347), and adds two new directories to **path**—one at the start of the list and one at the end:

```
tcsh $ cat ~/.tcshrc
set noclobber
set dunique
set ignoreeof
set history=256
set path = (~/bin $path /usr/games)
alias h history
alias ll ls -l
```

.history   Login shells rebuild the history list from the contents of **~/.history**. If the **histfile** variable exists, tcsh uses the file that **histfile** points to in place of **.history**.

.login   Login shells read and execute the commands in **~/.login**. This file contains commands that you want to execute once, at the beginning of each session. You can use setenv (page 356) to declare environment (global) variables here. You can also declare the type of terminal you are using and set some terminal characteristics in your **.login** file.

```
tcsh $ cat ~/.login
setenv history 200
```

```
setenv mail /var/spool/mail/$user
if ( -z $DISPLAY ) then
        setenv TERM vt100
    else
        setenv TERM xterm
endif
stty erase '^h' kill '^u' -lcase tab3
date '+Login on %A %B %d at %I:%M %p'
```

The preceding **.login** file establishes the type of terminal you are using by setting the **TERM** variable (the **if** statement [page 368] determines whether you are using a graphical interface and therefore what value should be assigned to **TERM**). It then runs stty (page 778) to set terminal characteristics and date (page 630) to display the time you logged in.

/etc/csh.logout
and .logout
The TC Shell runs the **/etc/csh.logout** and **~/.logout** files, in that order, when you exit from a login shell. The following sample **.logout** file uses date to display the time you logged out. The sleep command ensures that echo has time to display the message before the system logs you out. The delay may be useful for dial-up lines that take some time to display the message.

```
tcsh $ cat ~/.logout
date '+Logout on %A %B %d at %I:%M %p'
sleep 5
```

FEATURES COMMON TO THE BOURNE AGAIN AND TC SHELLS

Most of the features common to both bash and tcsh are derived from the original C Shell:

- Command line expansion (also called substitution; page 344)
- History (page 344)
- Aliases (page 347)
- Job control (page 348)
- Filename substitution (page 348)
- Directory stack manipulation (page 349)
- Command substitution (page 349)

Because the chapters on bash discuss these features in detail, this section focuses on the differences between the bash and tcsh implementations.

COMMAND LINE EXPANSION (SUBSTITUTION)

Refer to "Processing the Command Line" on page 322 for an introduction to command line expansion in the Bourne Again Shell. The tcsh man page uses the term *substitution* instead of *expansion,* which is used by bash. The TC Shell scans each token for possible expansion in the following order:

1. History substitution (page 344)

2. Alias substitution (page 347)

3. Variable substitution (page 356)

4. Command substitution (page 349)

5. Filename substitution (page 348)

6. Directory stack substitution (page 349)

HISTORY

The TC Shell assigns a sequential *event number* to each command line. You can display this event number as part of the tcsh prompt (refer to "prompt" on page 363). Examples in this section show numbered prompts when they help illustrate the behavior of a command.

history BUILTIN

As in bash, the tcsh history builtin displays the events in your history list. The list of events is ordered with the oldest events at the top. The last event in the history list is the **history** command that displayed the list. In the following history list, which is limited to ten lines by the argument of **10** to the **history** command, command 23 modifies the tcsh prompt to display the history event number. The time each command was executed appears to the right of the event number.

```
32 $ history 10
   23  23:59   set prompt = "! $ "
   24  23:59   ls -l
   25  23:59   cat temp
   26  0:00    rm temp
   27  0:00    vim memo
   28  0:00    lpr memo
   29  0:00    vim memo
   30  0:00    lpr memo
   31  0:00    rm memo
   32  0:00    history
```

HISTORY EXPANSION

The same event and word designators work in both shells. For example, **!!** refers to the previous event in tcsh, just as it does in bash. The command **!328** executes event number **328** and **!?txt?** executes the most recent event containing the string **txt**. For more information refer to "Using an Exclamation Point (!) to Reference Events" on page 300. Table 9-1 lists the few tcsh word modifiers not found in bash.

Table 9-1   Word modifiers

Modifier	Function
u	Converts the first lowercase letter into uppercase
l	Converts the first uppercase letter into lowercase
a	Applies the next modifier globally within a single word

You can use more than one word modifier in a command. For instance, the **a** modifier, in combination with the **u** or **l** modifier, enables you to change the case of an entire word.

```
tcsh $ echo $VERSION
VERSION: Undefined variable.
tcsh $ echo !!:1:al
echo $version
tcsh 6.12.00 (Astron) 2002-07-23 (i386-intel-linux) options 8b,nls,...
```

In addition to using event designators to access the history list, you can use the command line editor to access, modify, and execute previous commands (page 353).

VARIABLES

The variables that you set to control history in tcsh are different from those used in bash. Whereas bash uses **HISTSIZE** and **HISTFILESIZE** to determine the number of events that are preserved during and between sessions, tcsh uses **history** and **savehist** (Table 9-2) for these purposes.

Table 9-2   History variables

Variable	Default	Function
history	100 events	Maximum number of events saved during a session
histfile	~/.history	Location of the history file
savehist	not set	Maximum number of events saved between sessions

history and savehist   When you exit from a tcsh shell, the most recently executed commands are saved in your **~/.history** file. The next time you start the shell this file initializes the history list. The value of the **savehist** variable determines the number of lines saved in the **.history** file (not necessarily the same as the **history** variable). If **savehist** is not set, tcsh does not save history between sessions. The **history** and **savehist** variables must be local (declared with set, not setenv). The **history** variable holds the number of events remembered during a session and the **savehist** variable holds the number remembered between sessions. See Table 9-2.

If you set the value of **history** too high, it can use too much memory. If it is unset or set to zero, the shell does not save any commands. To establish a history list of the 500 most recent events, give the following command manually or place it in your ~/.tcshrc startup file:

```
tcsh $ set history = 500
```

The following command causes tcsh to save the 200 most recent events across login sessions:

```
tcsh $ set savehist = 200
```

You can combine these two assignments into a single command:

```
tcsh $ set history=500 savehist=200
```

After you set **savehist** you can log out and log in again, and the 200 most recent events from the previous login sessions will appear in your history list. Set **savehist** in your ~/.tcshrc file if you want to maintain your event list from login to login.

histlit   If you set the variable **histlit** (history literal), history displays the commands in the history list exactly as they were typed in without any shell interpretation. The following example shows the effect of this variable (compare the lines numbered 32):

```
tcsh $ cat /etc/csh.cshrc
...
tcsh $ cp !!:1 ~
cp /etc/csh.cshrc ~
tcsh $ set histlit
tcsh $ history
...
    31  9:35    cat /etc/csh.cshrc
    32  9:35    cp !!:1 ~
    33  9:35    set histlit
    34  9:35    history
tcsh $ unset histlit
tcsh $ history
...
    31  9:35    cat /etc/csh.cshrc
    32  9:35    cp /etc/csh.cshrc ~
    33  9:35    set histlit
    34  9:35    history
    35  9:35    unset histlit
    36  9:36    history
```

optional   There is a difference in how bash and tcsh expand history event designators. If you give the command !250w, bash replaces it with command number 250 with a character **w** appended to it. In contrast, tcsh looks back through your history list for an event that begins with the string **250w** to execute. The reason for the difference: bash interprets the first three characters of **250w** as the number of a command, whereas tcsh interprets those characters as part of the search string **250w**. (If the 250 stands alone, tcsh treats it as a command number.)

If you want to append **w** to command number 250, you can insulate the event number from the **w** by surrounding it with braces:

```
!{250}w
```

Aliases

The alias/unalias feature in tcsh closely resembles its counterpart in bash (page 312). However, the alias builtin has a slightly different syntax:

> alias **name value**

The following command creates an alias for **ls**:

```
tcsh $ alias ls "ls -lF"
```

The tcsh alias allows you to substitute command line arguments, whereas bash does not:

```
$ alias nam "echo Hello, \!^ is my name"
$ nam Sam
Hello, Sam is my name
```

The string **\!*** within an alias expands to all command line arguments:

```
$ alias sortprint "sort \!* | lpr"
```

The next alias displays its second argument:

```
$ alias n2 "echo \!:2"
```

Special Aliases

Some alias names, called *special aliases*, have special meaning to tcsh. If you define an alias with one of these names, tcsh executes it automatically as explained in Table 9-3. Initially all special aliases are undefined.

To see a list of current aliases, give the command **alias**. To view the alias for a particular name, give the command **alias** followed by the name.

Table 9-3   Special aliases

Alias	When executed
beepcmd	Whenever the shell would normally ring the terminal bell. Gives you a way to have other visual or audio effects take place at those times.
cwdcmd	Whenever you change to another working directory.
periodic	Periodically, as determined by the number of minutes in the **tperiod** variable. If **tperiod** is unset or has the value 0, **periodic** has no meaning.
precmd	Just before the shell displays a prompt.
shell	Gives the absolute pathname of the shell that you want to use to run scripts that do not start with **#!** (page 265).

HISTORY SUBSTITUTION IN ALIASES

You can substitute command line arguments by using the history mechanism, where a single exclamation point represents the command line containing the alias. Modifiers are the same as those used by history (page 300). In the following example, the exclamation points are quoted so that the shell does not interpret them when building the aliases:

```
21 $ alias last echo \!:$
22 $ last this is just a test
test
23 $ alias fn2 echo \!:2:t
24 $ fn2 /home/jenny/test /home/alex/temp /home/barbara/new
temp
```

Event 21 defines for **last** an alias that displays the last argument. Event 23 defines for **fn2** an alias that displays the simple filename, or tail, of the second argument on the command line.

JOB CONTROL

Job control is similar in both bash (page 271) and tcsh. You can move commands between the foreground and background, suspend jobs temporarily, and get a list of the current jobs. The % character references a job when followed by a job number or a string prefix that uniquely identifies the job. You will see a minor difference when you run a multiple-process command line in the background from each shell. Whereas bash displays only the PID number of the last background process in each job, tcsh displays the numbers for all processes belonging to a job. The example from page 271 looks like this under tcsh:

```
tcsh $ find . -print | sort | lpr & grep -l alex /tmp/* > alexfiles &
[1] 18839   18840   18841
[2] 18876
```

FILENAME SUBSTITUTION

The TC Shell expands the characters *, ?, and [] in a pathname just as bash does (page 127). The * matches any string of zero or more characters, ? matches any single character, and [] defines a character class, which is used to match single characters appearing within a pair of brackets.

The TC Shell expands command line arguments that start with a tilde (~) into filenames in much the same way that bash does (page 351), with the ~ standing for the user's home directory or the home directory of the user whose name follows the tilde. The bash special expansions ~+ and ~– are not available in tcsh.

Brace expansion (page 324) is available in tcsh. Like tilde expansion, it is regarded as an aspect of filename substitution even though brace expansion can generate strings that are not the names of actual files.

In tcsh and its predecessor csh, the process of using patterns to match filenames is referred to as *globbing* and the pattern itself is called a *globbing pattern*. If tcsh is unable to identify one or more files that match a globbing pattern, it reports an error (unless the pattern contains a brace). Setting the shell variable **noglob** suppresses filename substitution, including both tilde and brace interpretation.

MANIPULATING THE DIRECTORY STACK

Directory stack manipulation in tcsh does not differ much from that in bash (page 274). The dirs builtin displays the contents of the stack, and the pushd and popd builtins push directories onto and pop directories off of the stack.

COMMAND SUBSTITUTION

The $(...) format for command substitution is *not* available in tcsh. In its place you must use the original ` ... ` format. Otherwise, the implementation in bash and tcsh is identical. Refer to page 329 for more information on command substitution.

REDIRECTING STANDARD ERROR

Both bash and tcsh use a greater than symbol (>) to redirect standard output, but tcsh does not use the bash notation 2> to redirect standard error. Under tcsh you use a greater than symbol followed by an ampersand (>&) to combine and redirect standard output and standard error. Although you can use this notation under bash, it is not common. The following examples, like the bash examples on page 261, reference file **x**, which does not exist, and file **y**, which contains a single line.

```
tcsh $ cat x
cat: x: No such file or directory
tcsh $ cat y
This is y.
tcsh $ cat x y >& hold
tcsh $ cat hold
cat: x: No such file or directory
This is y.
```

With an argument of **y** in the preceding example, cat sends a string to standard output. An argument of **x** causes cat to send an error message to standard error.

Unlike bash, tcsh does not provide a simple way to redirect standard error separately from standard output. A work-around frequently provides a reasonable solution. The following example runs cat with arguments of **x** and **y** in a subshell (the parentheses ensure that the command within them runs in a subshell—see page 270). Also within the subshell a > redirects standard output to the file **outfile**. Output sent to standard error is not touched by the subshell but rather is sent to the parent shell, where both it and standard output are sent to **errfile**. Because standard output has already been redirected, **errfile** contains only output sent to standard error.

```
tcsh $ (cat x y > outfile) >& errfile
tcsh $ cat outfile
This is y.
tcsh $ cat errfile
cat: x: No such file or directory
```

It can be useful to combine and redirect output when you want to run a slow command in the background and do not want its output cluttering up the terminal screen. For example, because the find utility (page 655) often takes some time to complete, it may be a good idea to run it in the background. The next command finds in the filesystem hierarchy all files that contain the string **biblio** in their name. The command runs in the background and sends its output to the **findout** file. Because the find utility sends to standard error a report of directories that you do not have permission to search, the **findout** file contains a record of any files that are found as well as a record of the directories that could not be searched.

```
tcsh $ find / -name "*biblio*" -print >& findout &
```

In this example, if you did not combine standard error with standard output and redirected only standard output, the error messages would appear on the screen and **findout** would list only files that were found.

While a command that has its output redirected to a file is running in the background, you can look at the output by using tail (page 783) with the –f option. The –f option causes tail to display new lines as they are written to the file:

```
tcsh $ tail -f findout
```

To terminate the tail command, press the interrupt key (usually CONTROL-C).

WORKING WITH THE COMMAND LINE

This section covers word completion, editing the command line, and correcting spelling.

WORD COMPLETION

The TC Shell completes filenames, commands, and variable names on the command line when you prompt it to do so. The generic term used to refer to all these features under tcsh is *word completion*.

FILENAME COMPLETION

The TC Shell can complete a filename after you specify a unique prefix. Filename completion is similar to filename generation, but the goal of filename completion is to select a single file. Together they make it practical to use long, descriptive filenames.

To use filename completion when you are entering a filename on the command line, type enough of the name to identify the file in the directory uniquely and press TAB; tcsh fills in the name and adds a SPACE, leaving the cursor so you can enter additional arguments or press RETURN. In the following example, the user types the command **cat trig1A** and presses TAB; the system fills in the rest of the filename that begins with **trig1A**:

```
tcsh $ cat trig1A ⟶ TAB ⟶ cat trig1A.302488 ∎
```

If two or more filenames match the prefix that you have typed, tcsh cannot complete the filename without obtaining more information from you. The shell attempts to maximize the length of the prefix by adding characters, if possible, and then beeps to signify that additional input is needed to resolve the ambiguity:

```
tcsh $ ls h*
help.hist  help.trig01  help.txt
tcsh $ cat h ⟶ TAB ⟶ cat help. (beep)
```

You can fill in enough characters to resolve the ambiguity and then press the TAB key again. Alternatively, you can press CONTROL-D to cause tcsh to display a list of matching filenames:

```
tcsh $ cat help. ⟶ CONTROL-D
help.hist     help.trig01  help.txt
tcsh $ cat help.∎
```

After displaying the filenames tcsh redraws the command line so you can disambiguate the filename (and press TAB again) or finish typing the filename manually.

TILDE COMPLETION

The TC Shell parses a tilde (~) appearing as the first character of a word and attempts to expand it to a username when you enter a TAB:

```
tcsh $ cd ~al ⟶ TAB ⟶ cd ~alex/∎ ⟶ RETURN
tcsh $ pwd
/home/alex
```

By appending a slash (/), tcsh indicates that the completed word is a directory. The slash also makes it easy to continue specifying the pathname.

COMMAND AND VARIABLE COMPLETION

You can use the same mechanism that you use to list and complete filenames with command and variable names. Unless you give a full pathname, the shell uses the variable **path** in an attempt to complete a command name. The choices listed are likely to be located in different directories.

```
tcsh $ up —→ TAB (beep) —→ CONTROL-D
up2date              updatedb                  uptime
up2date-config       update-mime-database
up2date-nox          updmap
tcsh $ up —→ t —→ TAB —→ uptime ■ —→ RETURN
9:59am up 31 days, 15:11, 7 users, load average: 0.03, 0.02, 0.00
```

If you set the **autolist** variable as in the following example, the shell lists choices automatically when you invoke completion by pressing TAB. You do not have to press CONTROL-D.

```
tcsh $ set autolist
tcsh $ up —→ TAB (beep)
up2date              updatedb                  uptime
up2date-config       update-mime-database
up2date-nox          updmap
tcsh $ up —→ t —→ TAB —→ uptime ■ —→ RETURN
10:01am up 31 days, 15:14, 7 users, load average: 0.20, 0.06, 0.02
```

If you set **autolist** to **ambiguous**, the shell lists the choices when you press TAB *only* if the word you enter is the longest prefix of a set of commands. Otherwise, pressing TAB causes the shell to add one or more characters to the word until it is the longest prefix; pressing TAB again then lists the choices:

```
tcsh $ set autolist=ambiguous
tcsh $ echo $h —→ TAB (beep)
histfile history home
tcsh $ echo $h■ —→ i —→ TAB —→ echo $hist■ —→ TAB
histfile history
tcsh $ echo $hist■ —→ o —→ TAB —→ echo $history ■ —→ RETURN
1000
```

The shell must rely on the context of the word within the input line to determine whether it is a filename, a username, a command, or a variable name. The first word on an input line is assumed to be a command name; if a word begins with the special character $, it is viewed as a variable name; and so on. In the following example, the second which command does not work properly: The context of the word **up** makes it look like the beginning of a filename rather than the beginning of a command. The TC Shell supplies which with an argument of **updates** (a nonexecutable file) and which displays an error message:

```
tcsh $ ls up*
updates
tcsh $ which updatedb ups uptime
/usr/bin/updatedb
/usr/local/bin/ups
/usr/bin/uptime
tcsh $ which up —→ TAB —→ which updates
updates: Command not found.
```

EDITING THE COMMAND LINE

bindkey The tcsh command line editing feature is similar to that available under bash. You can use either emacs mode commands (default) or vi(m) mode commands. Change to vi(m) mode commands by using **bindkey –v** and to emacs mode commands by using **bindkey –e**. The ARROW keys are bound to the obvious motion commands in both modes, so you can move back and forth (up and down) through your history list as well as left and right on the current command line.

Without an argument, the bindkey builtin displays the current mappings between editor commands and the key sequences you can enter at the keyboard:

```
tcsh $ bindkey
Standard key bindings
"^@"            ->   set-mark-command
"^A"            ->   beginning-of-line
"^B"            ->   backward-char
"^C"            ->   tty-sigintr
"^D"            ->   delete-char-or-list-or-eof
...
Multi character bindings
"^[[A"          -> up-history
"^[[B"          -> down-history
"^[[C"          -> forward-char
"^[[D"          -> backward-char
"^[[H"          -> beginning-of-line
"^[[F"          -> end-of-line
...
Arrow key bindings
down            -> down-history
up              -> up-history
left            -> backward-char
right           -> forward-char
home            -> beginning-of-line
end             -> end-of-line
```

The ^ indicates a CONTROL character (^B = CONTROL-B). The ^[indicates a META or ALT character; you press and hold the META or ALT key while you press the key for the next character. If this substitution does not work or if the keyboard you are using does not have a META or ALT key, press and release the ESCAPE key and then press the key for the next character. For ^[[F you would press META-[or ALT-[followed by the F key or else ESCAPE [F). The **down/up/left/right** indicate ARROW keys, and **home/end** indicate the HOME and END keys on the numeric keypad.

The preceding example shows the output from bindkey with the user in emacs mode. Change to vi(m) mode (**bindkey –v**) and give another bindkey command to display the vi(m) key bindings. You can pipe the output of bindkey through less to make it easier to read the list.

CORRECTING SPELLING

You can have tcsh attempt to correct the spelling of command names, filenames, and variables (but only using emacs-style key bindings). Spelling correction can take place only at two times: before and after you press RETURN.

BEFORE YOU PRESS RETURN

For tcsh to correct a word or line before you press RETURN, you must indicate that you want it to do so. The two functions for this purpose are **spell-line** and **spell-word**:

```
$ bindkey | grep spell
"^[$"           -> spell-line
"^[S"           -> spell-word
"^[s"           -> spell-word
```

The output from bindkey shows that **spell-line** is bound to META-$ (ALT-$ or ESCAPE $) and **spell-word** is bound to META-S and META-s (ALT-s or ESCAPE s and ALT-S or ESCAPE S). To correct the spelling of the word to the left of the cursor, enter META-s. Entering META-$ invokes the **spell-line** function, which attempts to correct all words on a command line:

```
tcsh $ ls
bigfile.gz
tcsh $ gunzipp  →  META-s  →  gunzip bigfele.gz  →  META-s  →  gunzip bigfile.gz
tcsh $ gunzip bigfele.gz  →  META-$  →  gunzip bigfile.gz
tcsh $ ecno $usfr  →  META-$  →  echo $user
```

AFTER YOU PRESS RETURN

The variable named **correct** controls what tcsh attempts to correct or complete *after* you press RETURN and before it passes the command line to the command being called. If you do not set **correct**, tcsh will not correct anything:

```
tcsh $ unset correct
tcsh $ ls morning
morning
tcsh $ ecno $usfr morbing
usfr: Undefined variable.
```

The shell reports the error in the variable name and not the command name because it expands variables before it executes the command (page 344). When you give a bad command name without any arguments, the shell reports on the bad command name.

Set **correct** to **cmd** to correct only commands; **all** to correct commands, variables, and filenames; or **complete** to complete commands:

```
tcsh $ set correct = cmd
tcsh $ ecno $usfr morbing

CORRECT>echo $usfr morbing (y|n|e|a)? y
usfr: Undefined variable.
```

```
tcsh $ set correct = all
tcsh $ echo $usfr morbing

CORRECT>echo $user morning (y|n|e|a)? y
alex morning
```

With **correct** set to **cmd**, tcsh corrects the command name from **ecno** to **echo**. With **correct** set to **all**, tcsh corrects both the command name and the variable. It would also correct a filename if one was present on the command line.

Automatic spell checking displays a special prompt that lets you enter **y** to accept the modified command line, **n** to reject it, **e** to edit it, or **a** to abort the command. Refer to "prompt3" on page 364 for a discussion of the special prompt used in spelling correction.

In the next example, after setting the **correct** variable the user mistypes the name of the ls command; tcsh then prompts for a correct command name. Because the command that tcsh has offered as a replacement is not ls, the user chooses to edit the command line. The shell leaves the cursor following the command so the user can correct the mistake:

```
tcsh $ set correct=cmd
tcsh $ lx -l ⟶ RETURN (beep)
CORRECT>lex -l (y|n|e|a)? e
tcsh $ lx -l▮
```

If you assign the value **complete** to the variable **correct**, tcsh attempts command name completion in the same manner as filename completion (page 350). In the following example, after setting **correct** to **complete** the user enters the command **up**. The shell responds with **Ambiguous command** because several commands start with these two letters but differ in the third letter. The shell then redisplays the command line. The user could press TAB at this point to get a list of commands that start with **up** but decides to enter **t** and press RETURN. The shell completes the command because these three letters uniquely identify the uptime utility:

```
tcsh $ set correct = complete
tcsh $ upRETURN
Ambiguous command
tcsh $ up ⟶ tRETURN ⟶ uptime
4:45pm  up 5 days,  9:54,  5 users,  load average: 1.62, 0.83, 0.33
```

VARIABLES

Although tcsh stores variable values as strings, you can work with these variables as numbers. Expressions in tcsh can use arithmetic, logical, and conditional operators. The @ builtin can evaluate integer arithmetic expressions.

This section uses the term *numeric variable* to describe a string variable that contains a number that tcsh uses in arithmetic or logical arithmetic computations. However, no true numeric variables exist in tcsh.

Variable name   A tcsh variable name consists of 1 to 20 characters, which can be letters, digits, and underscores (_). The first character cannot be a digit but can be an underscore.

VARIABLE SUBSTITUTION

Three builtins declare, display, and assign values to variables: set, @, and setenv. The set and setenv builtins both assume nonnumeric string variables. The @ builtin works only with numeric variables. Both set and @ declare local variables. The setenv builtin declares a variable *and* places it in the calling environment of all child processes (makes it global). Using setenv is similar to assigning a value to a variable and then using export in the Bourne Again Shell. See "Locality of Variables" on page 475 for a discussion of local and environment variables.

Once the value—or merely the existence—of a variable has been established, tcsh substitutes the value of that variable when the name of the variable, preceded by a dollar sign ($), appears on a command line. If you quote the dollar sign by preceding it with a backslash or enclosing it within single quotation marks, the shell does not perform the substitution. When a variable is within double quotation marks, the substitution occurs even if you quote the dollar sign by preceding it with a backslash.

STRING VARIABLES

The TC Shell treats string variables similarly to the way the Bourne Again Shell does. The major difference is in their declaration and assignment: tcsh uses an explicit command, set (or setenv), to declare and/or assign a value to a string variable.

```
tcsh $ set name = fred
tcsh $ echo $name
fred
tcsh $ set
argv    ()
cwd     /home/alex
home    /home/alex
name    fred
path    (/usr/local/bin /bin /usr/bin /usr/X11R6/bin)
prompt  $
shell   /bin/tcsh
status  0
term    vt100
user    alex
```

The first line in the example declares the variable **name** and assigns the string **fred** to it. Unlike bash, tcsh allows but does not demand SPACEs around the equal sign. The next line displays this value. When you give a set command without any arguments, it displays a list of all local shell variables and their values (your list will be longer than the one in the example). When you give a set command with the name of a variable and no value, the command sets the value of the variable to a null string.

You can use the unset builtin to remove a variable:

```
tcsh $ set name
tcsh $ echo $name

tcsh $ unset name
tcsh $ echo $name
name: Undefined variable.
```

With setenv you must separate the variable name from the string being assigned to it by one or more SPACEs and *no* equal sign. The **tcsh** command creates a subshell, echo shows that the variable and its value are known to the subshell, and **exit** returns to the original shell. Try this example, using set in place of setenv:

```
tcsh $ setenv SCRDIR /usr/local/src
tcsh $ tcsh
tcsh $ echo $SCRDIR
/usr/local/src
tcsh $ exit
```

If you use setenv with no arguments, it displays a list of the environment (global) variables—variables that are passed to the shell's child processes. By convention, environment variables are named using uppercase letters.

As with set, giving setenv a variable name without a value sets the value of the variable to a null string. Although you can use unset to remove environment and local variables, unsetenv can remove *only* environment variables.

ARRAYS OF STRING VARIABLES

An *array* is a collection of strings, each of which is identified by its index (1, 2, 3, and so on). Arrays in tcsh use one-based indexing (the first element of the array has the subscript 1). Before you can access individual elements of an array, you must declare the entire array by assigning a value to each element of the array. The list of values must be enclosed in parentheses and separated by SPACEs:

```
8 $ set colors = (red green blue orange yellow)
9 $ echo $colors
red green blue orange yellow
10 $ echo $colors[3]
blue
11 $ echo $colors[2-4]
green blue orange
12 $ set shapes = ('' '' '' '' '')
13 $ echo $shapes

14 $ set shapes[4] = square
15 $ echo $shapes[4]
square
```

Event 8 declares the array of string variables named **colors** to have five elements and assigns values to each of them. If you do not know the values of the elements at the time you declare an array, you can declare an array containing the necessary number of null elements (event 12).

You can reference an entire array by preceding its name with a dollar sign (event 9). A number in brackets following a reference to the array refers to an element of the array (events 10, 14, and 15). Two numbers in brackets, separated by a hyphen, refer to two or more adjacent elements of the array (event 11). Refer to "Special Variable Forms" on page 361 for more information on arrays.

NUMERIC VARIABLES

The **@** builtin assigns the result of a numeric calculation to a numeric variable (as described under "Variables" [page 355], tcsh has no true numeric variables). You can declare single numeric variables with **@**, just as you can use **set** to declare nonnumeric variables. However, if you give it a nonnumeric argument, **@** displays an error message. Just as **set** does, the **@** command used without any arguments lists all shell variables.

Many of the expressions that the **@** builtin can evaluate and the operators it recognizes are derived from the C programming language. The following format shows a declaration or assignment using **@** (the SPACE after the **@** is required):

> **@** *variable-name operator expression*

The *variable-name* is the name of the variable that you are assigning a value to. The *operator* is one of the C assignment operators: =, +=, −=, *=, /=, or %=. (See page 533 for an explanation of these operators.) The *expression* is an arithmetic expression that can include most C operators (see the next section). You can use parentheses within the expression for clarity or to change the order of evaluation. Parentheses must surround parts of the expression that contain any of the following characters: <, >, &, or |.

EXPRESSIONS

An expression is composed of constants, variables, and most any of the bash operators (page 505). Expressions that involve files rather than numeric variables or strings are described in Table 9-8 on page 368.

Expressions follow these rules:

1. The shell evaluates a missing or null argument as 0.

2. All results are decimal numbers.

3. Except for != and ==, the operators act on numeric arguments.

4. You must separate each element of an expression from adjacent elements by a SPACE, unless the adjacent element is &, |, <, >, (, or).

Do not use $ when assigning a value to a variable

tip As with bash, variables having a value assigned to them (those on the left of the operator) must not be preceded by a dollar sign ($). Thus

```
tcsh $ @ $answer = 5 + 5
```

will yield

```
answer: Undefined variable.
```

or, if **answer** is defined,

```
@: Variable name must begin with a letter.
```

whereas

```
tcsh $ @ answer = 5 + 5
```

assigns the value 10 to the variable **answer**.

Following are some examples that use @:

```
216 $ @ count = 0
217 $ echo $count
0
218 $ @ count = ( 10 + 4 ) / 2
219 $ echo $count
7
220 $ @ result = ( $count < 5 )
221 $ echo $result
0
222 $ @ count += 5
223 $ echo $count
12
224 $ @ count++
225 $ echo $count
13
```

Event 216 declares the variable **count** and assigns it a value of 0. Event 218 shows the result of an arithmetic operation being assigned to a variable. Event 220 uses @ to assign the result of a logical operation involving a constant and a variable to **result**. The value of the operation is *false* (= 0) because the variable **count** is not less than 5. Event 222 is a compressed form of the following assignment statement:

```
tcsh $ @ count = $count + 5
```

Event 224 uses a postfix operator to increment **count** by 1.

Postincrement and postdecrement operators You can use the postincrement (++) and postdecrement (−−) operators only in expressions containing a single variable name, as shown in the following example:

```
tcsh $ @ count = 0
tcsh $ @ count++
tcsh $ echo $count
1
tcsh $ @ next = $count++
@: Badly formed number.
```

Unlike in the C programming language and bash, expressions in tcsh cannot use preincrement and predecrement operators.

ARRAYS OF NUMERIC VARIABLES

You must use the set builtin to declare an array of numeric variables before you can use @ to assign values to the elements of that array. The set builtin can assign any values to the elements of a numeric array, including zeros, other numbers, and null strings.

Assigning a value to an element of a numeric array is similar to assigning a value to a simple numeric variable. The only difference is that you must specify the element, or index, of the array. The syntax is

@ *variable-name[index] operator expression*

The *index* specifies the element of the array that is being addressed. The first element has an index of 1. The *index* cannot be an expression but must be either a numeric constant or a variable. In the preceding syntax the brackets around *index* are part of the syntax and do not indicate that *index* is optional. If you specify an *index* that is too large for the array you declared with set, tcsh displays **@: Subscript out of range**.

```
226 $ set ages = (0 0 0 0 0)
227 $ @ ages[2] = 15
228 $ @ ages[3] = ($ages[2] + 4)
229 $ echo $ages[3]
19
230 $ echo $ages
0 15 19 0 0
231 $ set index = 3
232 $ echo $ages[$index]
19
233 $ echo $ages[6]
ages: Subscript out of range.
```

Elements of a numeric array behave as though they were simple numeric variables. Event 226 declares an array with five elements, each having a value of 0. Events 227 and 228 assign values to elements of the array, and event 229 displays the value of one of the elements. Event 230 displays all the elements of the array, 232 specifies an element by using a variable, and 233 demonstrates the out-of-range error message.

BRACES

Like with bash, tcsh allows you to use braces to distinguish a variable from surrounding text without the use of a separator:

```
$ set bb=abc
$ echo $bbdef
bbdef: Undefined variable.
$ echo ${bb}def
abcdef
```

SPECIAL VARIABLE FORMS

The special variable with the following syntax has the value of the number of elements in the *variable-name* array:

$#variable-name

You can determine whether *variable-name* has been set by looking at the value of the variable with the following syntax:

$?variable-name

This variable has a value of 1 if *variable-name* is set and 0 otherwise:

```
tcsh $ set days = (mon tues wed thurs fri)
tcsh $ echo $#days
5
tcsh $ echo $?days
1
tcsh $ unset days
tcsh $ echo $?days
0
```

READING USER INPUT

Within a tcsh shell script, you can use the set builtin to read a line from the terminal and assign it to a variable. The following portion of a shell script prompts the user and reads a line of input into the variable **input_line**:

```
echo -n "Enter input: "
set input_line = "$<"
```

The value of the shell variable $< is a line from standard input. The quotation marks around $< keep the shell from assigning only the first word of the line of input to the variable **input_line**.

SHELL VARIABLES

TC Shell variables may be set by the shell, inherited by the shell from the environment, or set by the user and used by the shell. Some variables take on significant values (for example, the PID number of a background process). Other variables act as switches: *on* if they are declared and *off* if they are not. Many of the shell variables are often set from one of tcsh's two startup files: **~/.login** and **~/.tcshrc** (page 342).

SHELL VARIABLES THAT TAKE ON VALUES

argv   Contains the command line arguments (positional parameters) from the command line that invoked the shell. Like all tcsh arrays, this array uses one-based indexing; **argv[1]** contains the first command line argument. You can abbreviate references to

$argv[n]$ as $n. The token **argv[*]** references all the arguments together; you can abbreviate it as **$***. Use **$0** to reference the name of the calling program. Refer to "Positional Parameters" on page 480. The Bourne Again Shell does not use the **argv** form, only the abbreviated form.

$#argv *or* **$#**   Holds the number of elements in the **argv** array. Refer to "Special Variable Forms" on page 361.

autolist   Controls command and variable completion (page 351).

autologout   Enables tcsh's automatic logout facility, which logs you out if you leave the shell idle for too long. The value of the variable is the number of minutes of inactivity that tcsh waits before logging you out. The default is 60 minutes if you are Superuser. This variable is initially unset for other users.

cdpath   Affects the operation of cd in the same way as the **CDPATH** variable does in bash (page 289). The **cdpath** variable is assigned an array of absolute pathnames (see **path**, later in this section) and is usually set in the **~/.login** file with a command line such as the following:

```
tcsh $ set cdpath = (/home/scott /home/scott/letters)
```

When you call cd with a simple filename, it searches the working directory for a subdirectory with that name. If one is not found, cd searches the directories listed in **cdpath** for the subdirectory.

correct   Set to **cmd** for automatic spelling correction of command names, to **all** to correct the entire command line, and to **complete** for automatic completion of command names. This variable works on corrections that are made after you press RETURN. Refer to "After You Press RETURN" on page 354.

cwd   The shell sets this variable to the name of the working directory. When you access a directory through a symbolic link (page 99), tcsh sets **cwd** to the name of the symbolic link.

dirstack   The shell keeps the stack of directories used with the pushd, popd, and dirs builtins in this variable. For more information refer to "Manipulating the Directory Stack" on page 274.

fignore   Holds an array of suffixes that tcsh ignores during filename completion.

gid   The shell sets this variable to your group ID.

histfile   Holds the full pathname of the file that saves the history list between login sessions (page 345). The defaults is **~/.history**.

history   Specifies the size of your history list. Refer to "History" on page 344.

home *or* **HOME**   Holds the pathname of the user's home directory. The cd builtin refers to this variable, as does the filename substitution of ~ (page 326).

mail   Specifies files and directories to check for mail. The TC Shell checks for new mail every 10 minutes unless the first word of **mail** is a number, in which case that number specifies how often the shell should check in seconds.

owd The shell keeps the name of your previous (old) working directory in this variable, which is equivalent to ~− in bash.

path *or* **PATH** Holds a list of directories that tcsh searches for executable commands (page 284). If this array is empty or unset, you can execute commands only by giving their full pathnames. You can set **path** with a command such as the following:

```
tcsh $ set path = ( /usr/bin /bin /usr/local/bin /usr/bin/X11 ~/bin . )
```

prompt Holds the primary prompt, similar to the bash **PS1** variable (page 286). If it is not set, the prompt is >, or # for **root** (Superuser). The shell expands an exclamation point in the prompt string to the current event number. The following is a typical line from a **.tcshrc** file that sets the value of **prompt**:

```
set prompt = '! $ '
```

Table 9-4 lists a number of special formatting sequences you can use in **prompt** to achieve special effects.

Table 9-4 **prompt** formatting sequences

Sequence	Displays in prompt
%/	Value of **cwd** (the working directory)
%~	Same as %/, but replaces the path of the user's home directory with a tilde
%! *or* %h *or* !	Current event number
%m	Hostname without the domain
%M	Full hostname, including the domain
%n	User's username
%t	Time of day through the current minute
%p	Time of day through the current second
%d	Day of the week
%D	Day of the month
%W	Month as **mm**
%y	Year as **yy**
%Y	Year as **yyyy**
%#	A pound sign (#) if the user is running as **root** (Superuser); otherwise a greater than sign (>)
%?	Exit status of the preceding command

prompt2   Holds the prompt used in **foreach** and **while** control structures (pages 373 and 375). The default value is '**%R?** ', where **R** is replaced by the word **while** if you are inside a **while** structure and **foreach** if you are inside a **foreach** structure.

prompt3   Holds the prompt used during automatic spelling correction. The default value is '**CORRECT>%R** (y|n|e|a)?', where **R** is replaced by the corrected string.

savehist   Specifies the number of commands saved from the history list when you log out. These events are saved in a file named **~/.history**. The shell uses these events as the initial history list when you log in again, causing your history list to continue across login sessions (page 345).

shell   Holds the pathname of the shell you are using.

shlvl   Is incremented each time you start a subshell and decremented each time you exit a subshell. The value is set to 1 for login a shell.

status   Contains the exit status returned by the last command. Similar to **$?** in bash (page 479).

tcsh   Holds the version number of tcsh that you are running.

time   Provides two functions: automatic timing of commands using the time builtin and the format used by time. You can set this variable to either a single numeric value or an array holding a numeric value and a string. The numeric value is used to control automatic timing; any command that takes more than that number of CPU seconds to run has time display the command statistics when it finishes execution. A value of 0 results in statistics being displayed after every command. The string controls the formatting of the statistics using special formatting sequences, including those listed in Table 9-5.

Table 9-5   time formatting sequences

Sequence	Displays
%U	Time the command spent running user code, in CPU seconds (user mode)
%S	Time the command spent running system code, in CPU seconds (kernel mode)
%E	Wall clock time (total elapsed) taken by the command
%P	Percentage of time the CPU spent on this task during this period, computed as (%U+%S)/%E
%W	Number of times the command's processes were swapped out to disk
%X	Average amount of shared code memory used by the command, in kilobytes
%D	Average amount of data memory used by the command, in kilobytes

Table 9-5   time formatting sequences (continued)

%K	Total memory used by the command (as %X+%D), in kilobytes
%M	Maximum amount of memory used by the command, in kilobytes
%F	Number of major page faults (pages of memory that had to be read from disk)
%I	Number of input operations
%O	Number of output operations

By default the time builtin uses the string

```
"%Uu %Ss %E %P%   %X+%Dk %I+%Oio %Fpf+%Ww"
```

which generates output in the following format:

```
tcsh $ time
0.200u 0.340s 17:32:33.27 0.0%        0+0k 0+0io 1165pf+0w
```

You can time commands when you are concerned about system performance. If your commands consistently show many page faults and swaps, your system is probably memory starved and you should consider adding more memory to the system. You can use the information that time reports to compare the performance of various system configurations and program algorithms.

tperiod Controls how often, in minutes, the shell executes the special **periodic** alias (page 347).

user The shell sets this variable to your username.

version The shell sets this variable to contain detailed information about the version of tcsh you are using.

watch Set to an array of user and terminal pairs to watch for logins and logouts. The word **any** means any user or any terminal, so (**any any**) monitors all logins and logouts on all terminals, and (**scott ttyS1 any console $user any**) watches for **scott** on **ttyS1**, any user who accesses the system console, and any logins and logouts that use your account (presumably to catch intruders). By default logins and logouts are checked once every 10 minutes, but you can change this value by beginning the array with a numeric value giving the number of minutes between checks. If you set **watch** to (**1 any console**), logins and logouts by any user on the console will be checked once a minute. Reports are displayed just before a new shell prompt is issued. Also, the log builtin forces an immediate check whenever it is executed. See **who** for information about how you can control the format of the **watch** messages.

who Controls the format of the information displayed in **watch** messages (Table 9-6).

Table 9-6 who formatting sequence

Sequence	Displays
%n	Username
%a	Action taken by user
%l	Terminal on which action took place
%M	Full hostname of remote host (or **local** if none) from which action took place
$m	Hostname without domain name

The default string used for watch messages when **who** is unset is "**%n has %a %l from %m**", which generates the following line:

```
jenny has logged on tty2 from local
```

$ As in bash, this variable contains the PID number of the current shell; use it as **$$**.

SHELL VARIABLES THAT ACT AS SWITCHES

The following shell variables act as switches; their values are not significant. If the variable has been declared, the shell takes the specified action. If not, the action is not taken or is negated. You can set these variables in your ~/.tcshrc startup file, in a shell script, or from the command line.

autocorrect Causes the shell to attempt spelling correction automatically, just before each attempt at completion.

dunique Normally pushd blindly pushes the new working directory onto the directory stack, meaning that you can end up with many duplicate entries on this stack. Set **dunique** to cause the shell to look for and delete any entries that duplicate the one it is about to push.

echo Causes the shell to display each command before it executes that command. Set **echo** by calling tcsh with the **–x** option or by using set.

filec Enables filename completion (page 350) when running tcsh as csh (and csh is linked to tcsh).

histlit Displays the commands in the history list exactly as entered, without interpretation by the shell (page 346).

ignoreeof Prevents you from using CONTROL-D to exit from a shell so you cannot accidentally log out. When this variable is declared, you must use **exit** or **logout** to leave a shell.

listjobs Causes the shell to list all jobs whenever a job is suspended.

listlinks Causes the ls–F builtin to show the type of file each symbolic link points to instead of marking the symbolic link with an @ symbol.

loginsh Set by the shell if the current shell is running as a login shell.

nobeep Disables all beeping by the shell.

noclobber Prevents you from accidentally overwriting a file when you redirect output and prevents you from creating a file when you attempt to append output to a nonexistent file (Table 9-7). To override **noclobber**, add an exclamation point to the symbol you use for redirecting or appending output (for example, **>!** and **>>!**). For more information see page 119.

Table 9-7 How **noclobber** works

Command line	noclobber not declared	noclobber declared
x > *fileout*	Redirects standard output from process **x** to *fileout*. Overwrites *fileout* if it exists.	Redirects standard output from process **x** to *fileout*. The shell displays an error message if *fileout* exists and does not overwrite the file.
x >> *fileout*	Redirects standard output from process **x** to *fileout*. Appends new output to the end of *fileout* if it exists. Creates *fileout* if it does not exist.	Redirects standard output from process **x** to *fileout*. Appends new output to the end of *fileout* if it exists. The shell displays an error message if *fileout* does not exist and does not create the file.

noglob Prevents the shell from expanding ambiguous filenames. Allows you to use *, ?, ~, and [] on the command line or in a shell script without quoting them.

nonomatch Causes the shell to pass an ambiguous file reference that does not match a filename to the command that is being called. The shell does not expand the file reference. When you do not set **nonomatch**, tcsh generates a **No match** error message and does not execute the command.

```
tcsh $ cat questions?
cat: No match
tcsh $ set nonomatch
tcsh $ cat questions?
cat: questions?: No such file or directory
```

notify When set, tcsh sends a message to the screen immediately whenever a background job completes. Ordinarily tcsh notifies you about job completion just before displaying the next prompt. Refer to "Job Control" on page 271.

pushdtohome Causes a call to pushd without any arguments to change directories to your home directory (equivalent to **pushd –**).

pushdsilent Causes pushd and popd not to display the directory stack.

rmstar Causes the shell to request confirmation when you give an **rm *** command.

verbose Causes the shell to display each command after a history expansion (page 344). Set **verbose** by calling tcsh with the **–v** option or by using set.

visiblebell Causes audible beeps to be replaced by flashing the screen.

CONTROL STRUCTURES

The TC Shell uses many of the same control structures as the Bourne Again Shell. In each case the syntax is different, but the effects are the same. This section summarizes the differences between the control structures in the two shells. For more information refer to "Control Structures" on page 436.

if

The syntax of the **if** control structure is

if (expression) simple-command

The **if** control structure works only with simple commands, not with pipes or lists of commands. You can use the **if...then** control structure (page 372) to execute more complex commands.

```
tcsh $ cat if_1
#!/bin/tcsh
# Routine to show the use of a simple if control structure.
#
if ( $#argv == 0 ) echo "if_1: there are no arguments"
```

The **if_1** script checks whether it was called without any arguments. If the expression enclosed in parentheses evaluates to *true*—that is, if zero arguments were on the command line—the **if** structure displays a message.

In addition to logical expressions such as the one the **if_1** script uses, you can use expressions that return a value based on the status of a file. The syntax for this type of expression is

–n filename

where *n* is from the list in Table 9-8.

Table 9-8   Value of *n*

n	Meaning
b	File is a block special file
c	File is a character special file
d	File is a directory file
e	File exists
f	File is an ordinary or directory file

Table 9-8 Value of *n* (continued)

g	File has the set-group-ID bit set
k	File has the sticky bit (page 903) set
l	File is a symbolic link
o	File is owned by user
p	File is a named pipe (FIFO)
r	The user has read access to the file
s	File is not empty (has nonzero size)
S	File is a socket special file
t	File descriptor (a single digit replacing *filename*) is open and connected to the screen
u	File has the set-user-ID bit set
w	User has write access to the file
x	User has execute access to the file
X	File is either a builtin or an executable found by searching the directories in **$path**
z	File is 0 bytes long

If the result of the test is *true,* the expression has a value of 1; if it is *false,* the expression has a value of 0. If the specified file does not exist or is not accessible, tcsh evaluates the expression as 0. The following example checks whether the file specified on the command line is an ordinary or directory file (and not a device or other special file):

```
tcsh $ cat if_2
#!/bin/tcsh
if -f $1 echo "Ordinary or Directory file"
```

You can combine operators where it makes sense. For example, **–ox filename** is *true* if you own and have execute permission for the file. This expression is equivalent to **–o filename && –x filename**.

Some operators return useful information about a file other than reporting *true* or *false.* They use the same **–n filename** format, where **n** is one of the values shown in Table 9-9.

You can use only one of these operators in a given test, and it must appear as the last operator in a multiple-operator sequence. Because 0 can be a valid response

Table 9-9   Value of *n*

n	Meaning
A	The last time the file was accessed.*
A:	The last time the file was accessed displayed in a human-readable format.
M	The last time the file was modified.*
M:	The last time the file was modified displayed in a human-readable format.
C	The last time the file's inode was modified.*
C:	The last time the file's inode was modified displayed in a human-readable format.
D	Device number for the file. This number uniquely identifies the device (disk partition, for example) on which the file resides.
I	Inode number for the file. The inode number uniquely identifies a file on a particular device.
F	A string of the form **device:inode**. This string uniquely identifies a file anywhere on the system.
N	Number of hard links to the file.
P	The file's permissions, shown in octal, without a leading 0.
U	Numeric user ID of the file's owner.
U:	Username of the file's owner.
G	Numeric group ID of the file's group.
G:	Name of the file's group.
Z	Number of bytes in the file.

*Time measured in seconds from the *epoch* (usually the start of January 1, 1970).

from some of these operators (for instance, the number of bytes in a file might be 0), most return −1 on failure instead of the 0 that the logical operators return on failure. The one exception is F, which returns a colon if it cannot determine the device and inode for the file.

When you want to use one of these operators outside of a control structure expression, you can use the filetest builtin to evaluate a file test and report the result:

```
tcsh $ filetest -z if_1
0
tcsh $ filetest -F if_1
2051:12694
tcsh $ filetest -Z if_1
131
```

goto

The **goto** statement has the following syntax:

goto label

A **goto** builtin transfers control to the statement beginning with *label:*. The following script fragment demonstrates the use of **goto**:

```
tcsh $ cat goto_1
#!/bin/tcsh
#
# test for 2 arguments
#
if ($#argv == 2) goto goodargs
echo "Usage: goto_1 arg1 arg2"
exit 1
goodargs:
...
```

The **goto_1** script displays a usage message (page 440) when it is called with more or fewer than two arguments.

INTERRUPT HANDLING

The **onintr** statement transfers control when you interrupt a shell script. The format of an **onintr** statement is

onintr label

When you press the interrupt key during execution of a shell script, the shell transfers control to the statement beginning with *label:*. This statement allows you to terminate a script gracefully when it is interrupted. You can use it to ensure that when you interrupt a shell script, the script removes temporary files before returning control to the parent shell.

The following script demonstrates **onintr**. It loops continuously until you press the interrupt key, at which time it displays a message and returns control to the shell:

```
tcsh $ cat onintr_1
#!/bin/tcsh
# demonstration of onintr
onintr close
while ( 1 )
    echo "Program is running."
    sleep 2
end
close:
echo "End of program."
```

If a script creates temporary files, you can use **onintr** to remove them.

```
close:
rm -f /tmp/$$*
```

The ambiguous file reference **/tmp/$$*** matches all files in **/tmp** that begin with the PID number of the current shell. Refer to page 478 for a description of this technique for naming temporary files.

if...then...else

The **if...then...else** control structure has three forms. The first form, an extension of the simple **if** structure, executes more complex *commands* or a series of *commands* if *expression* is *true*. This form is still a one-way branch.

if (expression) then
    commands
endif

The second form is a two-way branch. If *expression* is *true,* the first set of *commands* is executed. If it is *false,* the set of *commands* following **else** is executed.

if (expression) then
    commands
else
    commands
endif

The third form is similar to the **if...then...elif** structure (page 442). It performs tests until it finds an *expression* that is *true* and then executes the corresponding *commands*.

if (expression) then
    commands
else if (expression) then
    commands

    . . .
else
    commands
endif

The following program assigns a value of 0, 1, 2, or 3 to the variable **class** based on the value of the first command line argument. The program declares the variable **class** at the beginning for clarity; you do not need to declare it before its first use. Also for clarity, the script assigns the value of the first command line argument to **number**.

```
tcsh $ cat if_else_1
#!/bin/tcsh
# routine to categorize the first
# command line argument
```

```
set class
set number = $argv[1]
#
if ($number < 0) then
    @ class = 0
else if (0 <= $number && $number < 100) then
    @ class = 1
else if (100 <= $number && $number < 200) then
    @ class = 2
else
    @ class = 3
endif
#
echo "The number $number is in class ${class}."
```

The first **if** statement tests whether **number** is less than 0. If it is, the script assigns 0 to **class** and transfers control to the statement following **endif**. If it is not, the second **if** tests whether the number is between 0 and 100. The **&&** is the Boolean AND operator, yielding a value of *true* if the expression on each side is *true*. If the number is between 0 and 100, 1 is assigned to **class** and control is transferred to the statement following **endif**. A similar test determines whether the number is between 100 and 200. If it is not, the final **else** assigns 3 to **class**. The **endif** closes the **if** control structure. The final statement uses braces ({}) to isolate the variable **class** from the following period. The braces isolate the period for clarity; the shell does not consider a punctuation mark to be part of a variable name. The braces would be required if you wanted other characters to follow immediately after the variable.

foreach

The **foreach** structure parallels the bash **for...in** structure (page 449). The syntax is

> *foreach* **loop-index** *(argument-list)*
>   ***commands***
> *end*

This structure loops through *commands*. The first time through the loop, the structure assigns the value of the first argument in *argument-list* to *loop-index*. When control reaches the **end** statement, the shell assigns the value of the next argument from *argument-list* to *loop-index* and executes the commands again. The shell repeats this procedure until it exhausts *argument-list*.

The following tcsh script uses a **foreach** structure to loop through the files in the working directory containing a specified string of characters in their filename and to change the string. For example, you can use it to change the string **memo** in filenames to **letter**. The filenames **memo.1**, **dailymemo**, and **memories** would change to **letter.1**, **dailyletter**, and **letterries**.

This script requires two arguments: the string to be changed (the old string) and the new string. The *argument-list* of the **foreach** structure uses an ambiguous file reference to loop through all filenames that contain the first argument. For each filename that matches the ambiguous file reference, the mv utility changes the filename. The echo and sed commands appear within back ticks (`) that indicate command substitution: Executing the commands within the back ticks replaces the back ticks and everything between them. Refer to "Command Substitution" on page 329 for more information. The sed utility (page 563) substitutes the first argument for the second argument in the filename. The **$1** and **$2** are abbreviated forms of **$argv[1]** and **$argv[2]**.

```
tcsh $ cat ren
#!/bin/tcsh
# Usage:        ren arg1 arg2
#               changes the string arg1 in the names of files
#               in the working directory into the string arg2
if ($#argv != 2) goto usage
foreach i ( *$1* )
    mv $i `echo $i | sed -n s/$1/$2/p`
end
exit 0

usage:
echo "Usage: ren arg1 arg2"
exit 1
```

optional   The next script uses a **foreach** loop to assign the command line arguments to the elements of an array named **buffer**:

```
tcsh $ cat foreach_1
#!/bin/tcsh
# routine to zero-fill argv to 20 arguments
#
set buffer = (0 0 0 0 0 0 0 0 0 0 0 0 0 0 0 0 0 0 0 0)
set count = 1
#
if ($#argv > 20) goto toomany
#
foreach argument ($argv[*])
    set buffer[$count] = $argument
    @ count++
end
# REPLACE command ON THE NEXT LINE WITH
# THE PROGRAM YOU WANT TO CALL.
exec command $buffer[*]
#
toomany:
echo "Too many arguments given."
echo "Usage: foreach_1 [up to 20 arguments]"
exit 1
```

The **foreach_1** script calls another program named **command** with a command line guaranteed to contain 20 arguments. If **foreach_1** is called with fewer than 20 arguments, it fills the command line with zeros to complete the 20 arguments for **command**. Providing more than 20 arguments causes it to display a usage message and exit with an error status of 1.

The **foreach** structure loops through the commands one time for each command line argument. Each time through the loop, **foreach** assigns the value of the next argument from the command line to the variable **argument**. Then the script assigns each of these values to an element of the array **buffer**. The variable **count** maintains the index for the **buffer** array. A postfix operator increments the **count** variable using @ (**@ count++**). The exec builtin (bash and tcsh; page 491) calls **command** so that a new process is not initiated. (Once **command** is called, the process running this routine is no longer needed so a new process is not required.)

while

The syntax of the **while** structure is

> *while (**expression**)*
> > *commands*
> *end*

This structure continues to loop through *commands* while *expression* is *true*. If *expression* is *false* the first time it is evaluated, the structure never executes *commands*.

```
tcsh $ cat while_1
#!/bin/tcsh
# Demonstration of a while control structure.
# This routine sums the numbers between 1 and n,
# with n being the first argument on the command # line.
#
set limit = $argv[1]
set index = 1
set sum = 0
#
while ($index <= $limit)
    @ sum += $index
    @ index++
end
#
echo "The sum is $sum"
```

This program computes the sum of all integers up to and including *n*, where *n* is the first argument on the command line. The **+=** operator assigns the value of **sum + index** to **sum**.

break AND continue

You can interrupt a **foreach** or **while** structure with a **break** or **continue** statement. These statements execute the remaining commands on the line before they transfer control. The **break** statement transfers control to the statement after the **end** statement, terminating execution of the loop. The **continue** statement transfers control to the **end** statement, which continues execution of the loop.

switch

The **switch** structure is analogous to the bash **case** structure (page 459):

*switch (**test-string**)*

> *case **pattern:***
> > ***commands***
> *breaksw*
>
> *case **pattern:***
> > ***commands***
> *breaksw*
> *...*
> *default:*
> > ***commands***
> *breaksw*

endsw

The **breaksw** statement transfers control to the statement following the **endsw** statement. If you omit a **breaksw**, control falls through to the next command. You can use any of the special characters listed in Table 11-2 on page 462 within **pattern** except the pipe symbol (|).

```
tcsh $ cat switch_1
#!/bin/tcsh
# Demonstration of a switch control structure.
# This routine tests the first command line argument
# for yes or no in any combination of uppercase and
# lowercase letters.
#
#
# test that argv[1] exists
if ($#argv != 1) then
    echo "Usage: switch_1 [yes|no]"
    exit 1
else
# argv[1] exists, set up switch based on its value
```

```
        switch ($argv[1])
        # case of YES
            case [yY][eE][sS]:
            echo "Argument one is yes."
            breaksw
        #
        # case of NO
            case [nN][oO]:
            echo "Argument one is no."
        breaksw
        #
        # default case
            default:
            echo "Argument one is neither yes nor no."
            breaksw
        endsw
    endif
```

BUILTINS

Builtins are commands that are part of (built into) the shell. When you give a simple filename as a command, the shell first checks whether it is the name of a builtin. If it is, the shell executes it as part of the calling process; the shell does not fork a new process to execute the builtin. The shell does not need to search the directory structure for builtin programs because they are immediately available to the shell.

If the simple filename you give as a command is not a builtin, the shell searches the directory structure for the program you want, using the **PATH** variable as a guide. When it finds the program the shell forks a new process to execute the program.

Although they are not listed in Table 9-10, the control structure keywords (**if, foreach, endsw,** and so on) are builtins. The table describes many of the tcsh builtins, some of which are also built into other shells.

Table 9-10   tcsh builtins

Builtin	Function
% *job*	A synonym for the fg builtin. The *job* is the job number of the job you want to bring to the foreground (page 272).
% *job* &	A synonym for the bg builtin. The *job* is the number of the job you want to put in the background (page 273).
@	Similar to the set builtin but evaluates numeric expressions. Refer to "Numeric Variables" on page 358.
alias	Creates and displays aliases; bash uses a different syntax than tcsh. Refer to "Aliases" on page 347.

Table 9-10   tcsh builtins (continued)

alloc	Displays a report of the amount of free and used memory.
bg	Moves a suspended job into the background (page 273).
bindkey	Controls the mapping of keys to the tcsh command line editor commands.
bindkey	Without any arguments, bindkey lists all key bindings (page 353).
bindkey −l	Lists all available editor commands along with a short description of each.
bindkey −e	Puts the command line editor in emacs mode (page 353).
bindkey −v	Puts the command line editor in vi(m) mode (page 353).
bindkey *key* command	Attaches the editor command ***command*** to the key ***key***.
bindkey −b *key* command	Similar to the previous form but allows you to specify control keys by using the form C–x (where x is the character you type while you press the CONTROL key), specify meta key sequences as M–x (on most keyboards used with Linux, the ALT key is the meta key), and specify function keys as F-x.
bindkey −c *key* command	Binds the key ***key*** to the command ***command***. Here the ***command*** is not an editor command but either a shell builtin or an executable program.
bindkey −s *key* string	Whenever you type ***key***, ***string*** is substituted.
builtins	Displays a list of all builtins.
cd or chdir	Changes working directories (page 82).
dirs	Displays the directory stack (page 274).
echo	Displays its arguments. You can prevent echo from displaying a RETURN at the end of a line by using the **−n** option (see "Reading User Input" on page 361) or by using a trailing **\c** (see "read: Accepts User Input" on page 487). The echo builtin is similar to the echo utility (page 647).
eval	Scans and evaluates the command line. When you put eval in front of a command, the command is scanned twice by the shell before it is executed. This feature is useful with a command that is generated by command or variable substitution. Because of the order in which the shell processes a command line, it is sometimes necessary to repeat the scan to achieve the desired result (page 318).
exec	Overlays the program currently being executed with another program in the same shell. The original program is lost. Refer to "exec: Executes a Command" on page 491 for more information; also refer to source (page 380).
exit	Exits from a TC Shell. When you follow it with a numeric argument, tcsh returns that number as the exit status (page 479).

Table 9-10 tcsh builtins (continued)

fg	Moves a job into the foreground (page 271).
filetest	Takes one of the file inquiry operators followed by one or more filenames and applies the operator to each filename (page 370). Returns the results as a space-separated list.
glob	Like echo, but does not display SPACEs between its arguments and does not follow its display with a NEWLINE.
hashstat	Reports on the efficiency of tcsh's hash mechanism. The hash mechanism speeds the process of searching through the directories in your search path. See also rehash (page 380) and unhash (page 381).
history	Displays a list of recent commands (page 344).
jobs	Displays a list of jobs (suspended commands and those running in the background).
kill	Terminates a job or process (page 497).
limit	Limits the computer resources that the current process and any processes it creates can use. You can put limits on the number of seconds of CPU time the process can use, the size of files that the process can create, and so forth.
log	Immediately produces the report that the watch shell variable (page 365) would normally produce every 10 minutes.
login	Logs in a user. Can be followed by a username.
logout	Ends a session if you are using your original (login) shell.
ls–F	Similar to **ls –F** but faster. (This builtin is the characters **ls–F** without any SPACEs.)
nice	Lowers the processing priority of a command or a shell. It is useful if you want to run a command that makes large demands on the system and you do not need the output right away. If you are Superuser, you can use nice to raise the priority of a command. Refer to page 734 for more information on the nice builtin and the nice utility, which is available from bash.
nohup	Allows you to log out without terminating processes running in the background. Some systems are set up to do this automatically. Refer to page 736 for information on the nohup builtin and the nohup utility, which is available from bash.
notify	Causes the shell to notify you immediately when the status of one of your jobs changes (page 271).
onintr	Controls what action an interrupt causes within a script (page 371). See "trap: Catches a Signal" on page 493 for information on the equivalent command in bash.

Table 9-10   tcsh builtins (continued)

popd	Removes a directory from the directory stack (page 274).
printenv	Displays all environment variable names and values.
pushd	Changes the working directory and places the new directory at the top of the directory stack (page 274).
rehash	Re-creates the internal tables used by the hash mechanism. Whenever a new instance of tcsh is invoked, the hash mechanism creates a sorted list of all available commands based on the value of **path**. After you add a command to a directory in **path**, use rehash to re-create the sorted list of commands. If you do not, tcsh may not be able to find the new command. Also refer to hashstat (page 379) and unhash (page 381).
repeat	Takes two arguments—a count and simple command (no pipes or lists of commands)—and repeats the command the number of times specified by the count.
sched	Executes a command at a specified time. For example, the following command causes the shell to print the message **Dental appointment.** at 10 AM: tcsh $ `sched 10:00 echo "Dental appointment."` Without any arguments, sched prints the list of scheduled commands. When the time to execute a scheduled command arrives, tcsh executes the command just before it displays a prompt.
set	Declares, initializes, and displays local variables (page 355).
setenv	Declares, initializes, and displays environment variables (page 355).
shift	Analogous to the bash shift builtin (page 483). Without an argument, shift promotes the indexes of the **argv** array. You can use it with an argument of an array name to perform the same operation on that array.
source	Executes the shell script given as its argument: source does not fork another process. It is similar to the bash . (dot) builtin (page 259). The source builtin expects a TC Shell script so no leading **#!** is required in the script. The current shell executes source so that the script can contain commands, such as set, that affect the current shell. After you make changes to your **.tcshrc** or **.login** file, you can use source to execute it from the shell and thereby put the changes into effect without logging off and on. You can nest source builtins.
stop	Stops a job or process that is running in the background. The stop builtin accepts multiple arguments.
suspend	Stops the current shell and puts it in the background. It is similar to the suspend key, which stops jobs running in the foreground.

Table 9-10 tcsh builtins (continued)

time	Executes the command that you give it as an argument. It displays a summary of time-related information about the executed command, according to the **time** shell variable (page 364). Without an argument, time displays the times for the current shell and its children.
umask	Identifies or changes the access permissions that are assigned to files you create (page 810).
unalias	Removes an alias (page 347).
unhash	Turns off the hash mechanism. See also hashstat (page 379) and rehash (page 380).
unlimit	Removes limits (page 379) on the current process.
unset	Removes a variable declaration (page 355).
unsetenv	Removes an environment variable declaration (page 355).
wait	Causes the shell to wait for all child processes to terminate. When you give a wait command in response to a shell prompt, tcsh does not display a prompt until all background processes have finished execution. If you interrupt it with the interrupt key, wait displays a list of outstanding processes before tcsh displays a prompt.
where	When given the name of a command as an argument, locates all occurrences of the command and, for each, tells you whether it is an alias, a builtin, or an executable program in your path.
which	Similar to where but reports on only the command that would be executed, not all occurrences. This builtin is much faster than the Linux which utility and knows about aliases and builtins.

CHAPTER SUMMARY

Like the Bourne Again Shell, the TC Shell is both a command interpreter and a programming language. The TC Shell, which is based on the C Shell that was developed at the University of California at Berkeley, includes popular features such as history, alias, and job control.

You may prefer to use tcsh as a command interpreter, especially if you are familiar with the C Shell. You can use chsh to change your login shell to tcsh. However, running tcsh as your interactive shell does *not* cause tcsh to run shell scripts; they will continue to be run by bash unless you explicitly specify another shell on the first line of the script or specify the script name as an argument to tcsh. Specifying the shell on the first line of a shell script ensures the behavior you expect.

If you are familiar with bash, you will notice some differences between the two shells. For instance, the syntax you use to assign a value to a variable differs and tcsh allows SPACEs around the equal sign. Both numeric and nonnumeric variables are created and given values using the set builtin. The @ builtin can evaluate numeric expressions for assignment to numeric variables.

setenv   Because there is no export builtin in tcsh, you must use the setenv builtin to create an environment (global) variable. You can also assign a value to the variable with the setenv command. The command unset removes both local and environment variables, whereas the command unsetenv removes only environment variables.

Aliases   The syntax of the tcsh alias builtin is slightly different from that of alias in bash. Unlike bash, the tcsh aliases permit you to substitute command line arguments using the history mechanism syntax.

Most other tcsh features, such as history, word completion, and command line editing, closely resemble their bash counterparts. The syntax of the tcsh control structures is slightly different but provides functionality equivalent to that found in bash.

Globbing   The term *globbing*, a carryover from the original Bourne Shell, refers to the matching of strings containing special characters (such as * and ?) to filenames. If tcsh is unable to generate a list of filenames matching a globbing pattern, it displays an error message. This behavior contrasts with that of bash, which simply leaves the pattern alone.

Standard input and standard output can be redirected in tcsh, but there is no straightforward way to redirect them independently. Doing so requires the creation of a subshell that redirects standard output to a file while making standard error available to the parent process.

EXERCISES

1. Assume that you are working with the following history list:

```
37   mail alex
38   cd /home/jenny/correspondence/business/cheese_co
39   less letter.0321
40   vim letter.0321
41   cp letter.0321 letter.0325
42   grep hansen letter.0325
43   vim letter.0325
44   lpr letter*
45   cd ../milk_co
46   pwd
47   vim wilson.0321 wilson.0329
```

Using the history mechanism, give commands to

a. Send mail to Alex.

b. Use vim to edit a file named **wilson.0329**.

c. Send **wilson.0329** to the printer.

d. Send both **wilson.0321** and **wilson.0329** to the printer.

2. How can you display the aliases currently in effect? Write an alias named **homedots** that lists the names (only) of all invisible files in your home directory.

3. How can you prevent a command from sending output to the terminal when you start it in the background? What can you do if you start a command in the foreground and later decide that you want it to run in the background?

4. What statement can you put in your **~/.tcshrc** file to prevent accidentally overwriting a file when you redirect output? How can you override this feature?

5. Assume that the working directory contains the following files:

```
adams.ltr.03
adams.brief
adams.ltr.07
abelson.09
abelson.brief
anthony.073
anthony.brief
azevedo.99
```

What happens if you press TAB after typing the following commands?

a. **less adams.l**

b. **cat a**

c. **ls ant**

d. **file az**

What happens if you press CONTROL-D after typing the following commands?

e. **ls ab**

f. **less a**

6. Write an alias named **backup** that takes a filename as an argument and creates a copy of that file with the same name and a filename extension of **.bak**.

7. Write an alias named **qmake** (quiet make) that runs make with both standard output and standard error redirected to the file named **make.log**. The command **qmake** should accept the same options and arguments as make.

8. How can you make tcsh always display the pathname of the working directory as part of its prompt?

ADVANCED EXERCISES

9. What lines do you need to change in the Bourne Again Shell script **command_menu** (page 462) to turn it into a TC Shell script? Make the changes and verify that the new script works.

10. Users often find rm (and even **rm –i**) too unforgiving because it removes files irrevocably. Create an alias named **delete** that moves files specified by its argument(s) into the **~/.trash** directory. Create a second alias named **undelete** that moves a file from the **~/.trash** directory into the working directory. Put the following line in your **~/.logout** file to remove any files that you deleted during the login session:

    ```
    /bin/rm -f $HOME/.trash/* >& /dev/null
    ```

    Explain what could be different if the following line were put in your **~/.logout** file instead:

    ```
    rm $HOME/.trash/*
    ```

11. Modify the **foreach_1** script (page 374) so that it takes the command to exec as an argument.

12. Rewrite the program **while_1** (page 375) so that it runs faster. Use the time builtin to verify the improvement in execution time.

13. Write your own version of find named **myfind** that writes output to the file **findout** but without the clutter of error messages, such as those generated when you do not have permission to search a directory. The **myfind** command should accept the same options and arguments as find. Can you think of a situation in which **myfind** does not work as desired?

14. When the **foreach_1** script (page 374) is supplied with 20 or fewer arguments, why are the commands following **toomany:** not executed? (Why is there no exit command?)

PART IV
PROGRAMMING TOOLS

10

PROGRAMMING TOOLS

With its rich set of languages and development tools, the Linux operating system provides an outstanding environment for programming. C is one of the most popular system programming languages to use in conjunction with Linux, in part because the operating system itself is written mostly in C. Using C, programmers can easily access system services using function libraries and system calls. In addition, a variety of helpful tools can facilitate the development and maintenance of programs.

This chapter explains how to compile and link C programs. It introduces the GNU gdb debugger and tools that provide feedback about memory, disk, and CPU resources. It also covers some of the most useful software development tools: the make utility and CVS. The make utility helps you keep track of which program modules have been updated and helps to ensure that you use the latest versions of all program modules when you compile a program. CVS (Concurrent Versions System) is a source code management system that tracks the versions of files involved in a project.

PROGRAMMING IN C

A major reason that the Linux system provides an excellent C programming environment is that C programs can easily access the services of the operating system. The system calls—the routines that make operating system services available to programmers—can be called from C programs. These system calls provide such services as creating files, reading from and writing to files, collecting information about files, and sending signals to processes. When you write a C program, you can use system calls in the same way you use ordinary C program modules, or *functions,* that you have written. For more information refer to "System Calls" on page 417.

Several *libraries* of functions have been developed to support programming in C. The libraries are collections of related functions that you can use just as you use your own functions and the system calls. Many of the library functions access basic operating system services through the system calls, providing the services in ways that are more suited to typical programming tasks. Other library functions, such as the math library functions, serve special purposes.

This chapter describes the processes of writing and compiling C programs. However, it will *not* teach you to program in C.

CHECKING YOUR COMPILER

The C compiler in common use on Linux is GNU gcc (www.gnu.org/software/gcc/gcc.html), which comes as part of most distributions. Give the following command to see if you have access to the gcc compiler:

```
$ gcc --version
bash: gcc: command not found
```

If you get a response other than version information, either the compiler is not installed or your **PATH** variable does not contain the necessary pathname (usually gcc is installed in **/usr/bin**). If you get version information from the gcc command, the GNU C compiler is installed.

Next make sure that the compiler is functioning. As a simple test, create a file named **Makefile** with the following lines. The line that starts with **gcc** must be indented by using a TAB, not SPACEs.

```
$ cat Makefile
morning: morning.c
TAB gcc -o morning morning.c
```

Now create a source file named **morning.c** with the following lines:

```
$ cat morning.c
#include <stdio.h>
int main(int argc, char** argv) {
    printf("Good Morning\n");
    return 0;
}
```

Compile the file with the command **make morning**. When it compiles successfully, run the program by giving the command **morning** or **./morning**. When you get output from this program, you know that you have a working C compiler:

```
$ make morning
gcc -o morning morning.c
$ morning
Good Morning
```

A C Programming Example

You must use an editor, such as emacs or vim, to create or change a C program. The name of the C program file must end in .c. Entering the source code for a program is similar to typing a memo or shell script. Although emacs and vim "know" that you are editing a C program, many editors do not know whether your file is a C program, a shell script, or an ordinary text document. You are responsible for making the contents of the file syntactically suitable for the C compiler to process.

Figure 10-1 illustrates the structure of a simple C program named **tabs.c**. The first two lines of the program are comments that describe what the program does. The string /* identifies the beginning of the comment, and the string */ identifies the end of the comment; the C compiler ignores all the characters between them. Because a comment can span two or more lines, the */ at the end of the first line and the /* at the beginning of the second line are not necessary but are included for clarity. As the comment explains, the program reads standard input, converts TAB characters into the appropriate number of spaces, and writes the transformed input to standard output. Like many Linux utilities, this program is a filter.

Following the comments at the top of **tabs.c** are *preprocessor directives*, which are instructions for the C preprocessor. During the initial phase of compilation the C preprocessor expands these directives, making the program ready for the later stages of the compilation process. Preprocessor directives begin with the pound sign (#) and may optionally be preceded by SPACE and TAB characters.

Symbolic constants   You can use the **#define** preprocessor directive to define symbolic constants and macros. *Symbolic constants* are names that you can use in a program in place of constant values. For example, **tabs.c** uses a **#define** preprocessor directive to associate the symbolic constant **TABSIZE** with the constant 8. **TABSIZE** is used in the program in place of the constant 8 as the distance between TAB stops. By convention the names of symbolic constants consist of all uppercase letters.

```
 1  /* convert tabs in standard input to spaces in */
 2  /* standard output while maintaining columns */
 3
 4  #include        <stdio.h>
 5  #define         TABSIZE         8
 6
 7  /* prototype for function findstop */
 8  int findstop(int *);
 9
10  int main()
11  {
12  int c;          /* character read from stdin */
13  int posn = 0;   /* column position of character */
14  int inc;        /* column increment to tab stop */
15
16  while ((c = getchar()) != EOF)
17       switch(c)
18            {
19            case '\t':              /* c is a tab */
20                 inc = findstop(&posn);
21                 for( ; inc > 0; inc-- )
22                      putchar(' ');
23                 break;
24            case '\n':              /* c is a newline */
25                 putchar(c);
26                 posn = 0;
27                 break;
28            default:                /* c is anything else */
29                 putchar(c);
30                 posn++;
31                 break;
32            }
33  return 0;
34  }
35
36  /* compute size of increment to next tab stop */
37
38  int findstop(int *col)
39  {
40  int retval;
41  retval = (TABSIZE - (*col % TABSIZE));
42
43  /* increment argument (current column position) to next tabstop */
44  *col += retval;
45
46  return retval;           /* main gets how many blanks for filling */
47  }
```

Comments

Preprocessor Directives

Function Prototype

Main Function

Function

Figure 10-1   A simple C program: **tabs.c** (The line numbers are not part of the source code.)

By defining symbolic names for constant values you can make a program easier to read and easier to modify. If you later decide to change a constant, you need to change only the preprocessor directive rather than the value everywhere it occurs in the program. If you replace the **#define** directive for **TABSIZE** in Figure 10-1 with the following directive, the program will place TAB stops every four columns rather than every eight:

```
#define    TABSIZE    4
```

A symbolic constant, which is a type of *macro*, maps a symbolic name to *replacement text*. Macros are handy when the replacement text is needed at multiple points throughout the source code or when the definition of the macro is subject to change. The process of substituting the replacement text for the symbolic name is called *macro expansion*.

Macros | You can also use **#define** directives to define macros with arguments. Use of such a macro resembles a function call. Unlike C functions, however, macros are replaced with C code prior to compilation into object files.

The NEXTTAB macro computes the distance to the next TAB stop, given the current column position **curcol**:

```
#define NEXTTAB(curcol) (TABSIZE - ((curcol) % TABSIZE))
```

This definition uses the macro TABSIZE, whose definition must appear prior to NEXTTAB in the source code. The macro NEXTTAB could be used in **tabs.c** to assign a value to **retval** in the function **findstop**:

```
retval = NEXTTAB(*col);
```

Headers (include files) | When modules of a program use several macro definitions, the definitions are typically collected together in a single file called a *header file* or an *include file*. Although the C compiler does not place constraints on the names of header files, by convention they end in **.h**. The name of the header file is listed in an **#include** preprocessor directive in each program source file that uses any of the macros. The program in Figure 10-1 uses **getchar** and **putchar**, which are macros defined in **stdio.h**. The **stdio.h** header file defines a variety of general-purpose macros and is used by many C library functions.

The angle brackets (< and >) that surround **stdio.h** in **tabs.c** instruct the C preprocessor to look for the header file in a standard list of directories (such as **/usr/include**). To include a header file from another directory, enclose its pathname between double quotation marks. You can specify an absolute pathname within the double quotation marks or you can give a relative pathname. If you give a relative pathname, searching begins with the working directory and then moves to the same directories that are searched when the header file is surrounded by angle brackets. By convention header files that you supply are surrounded by double quotation marks.

You can also specify directories to be searched for header files by using the –I option to the C compiler. Assume that you want to compile the program **deriv.c**, which contains the following preprocessor directive:

```
#include "eqns.h"
```

If the header file **eqns.h** is located in the subdirectory **myincludes**, you can compile **deriv.c** with the –I option to tell the C preprocessor to look for the file **eqns.h** there:

```
$ gcc -I./myincludes deriv.c
```

When the C preprocessor encounters the #include directive in the **deriv.c** file, it will look for **eqns.h** in the **myincludes** subdirectory of the working directory.

Use relative pathnames for include files

tip Using absolute pathnames for include files does not work if the location of the header file within the filesystem changes. Using relative pathnames for header files works as long as the location of the header file relative to the working directory remains the same. Relative pathnames also work with the **–I** option on the **gcc** command line and allow header files to be moved.

Function prototype Preceding the definition of the function **main** is a *function prototype*. This declaration tells the compiler what type a function returns, how many arguments a function expects, and what the types of those arguments are. In **tabs.c** the prototype for the function **findstop** informs the compiler that **findstop** returns type *int* and that it expects a single argument of type *pointer to int*:

```
int findstop(int *);
```

Once the compiler has seen this declaration, it can detect and flag inconsistencies in the definition and the uses of the function. As an example, suppose that the reference to **findstop** in **tabs.c** was replaced with the following statement:

```
inc = findstop();
```

The prototype for **findstop** would cause the compiler to detect a missing argument and issue an error message. You could then easily fix the problem. When a function is present in a separate source file or is defined after it is referenced in a source file (as **findstop** is in the example), the function prototype helps the compiler check that the function is being called properly. Without the prototype, the compiler would not issue an error message and the problem might manifest itself as unexpected behavior during execution. At this late point, finding the bug might be difficult and time-consuming.

Functions Although you can call most C functions anything you want, each program must have exactly one function named **main**. The function **main** is the control module: A program begins execution with the function **main**, which typically calls other functions, which in turn may call still other functions, and so forth. By putting different operations into separate functions, you can make a program easier to read and maintain. For example, the program in Figure 10-1 uses the function **findstop** to compute the distance to the next TAB stop. Although the few statements of **findstop** could easily have been included in the **main** function, isolating them in a separate function draws attention to a key computation.

Functions can make both development and maintenance of the program more efficient. By putting a frequently used code segment into a function, you avoid entering the same code into the program over and over again. When you later want to make changes to the code, you need change it only once.

If a program is long and includes several functions, you may want to split it into two or more files. Regardless of its size, you may want to place logically distinct parts of a program in separate files. A C program can be split into any number of different files; however, each function must be wholly contained within a single file.

Use a header file for multiple source files

tip When you are creating a program that takes advantage of multiple source files, put **#define** preprocessor directives into a header file and use an include statement with the name of the header file in any source file that uses the directives.

COMPILING AND LINKING A C PROGRAM

To compile **tabs.c** and create an executable file named **a.out**, give the following command:

```
$ gcc tabs.c
```

The gcc utility calls the C preprocessor, the C compiler, the assembler, and the linker. Figure 10-2 shows these four components of the compilation process. The C preprocessor expands macro definitions and includes header files. The compilation phase creates assembly language code corresponding to the instructions in the source file. Then the assembler creates machine-readable object code. One object file is created for each source file. Each object file has the same name as the source file, except that the .c extension is replaced with a .o. The preceding example creates a single object file named **tabs.o**. After successfully completing all phases of the compilation process for a program, the C compiler creates the executable file and then removes any .o files.

During the final phase of the compilation process, the linker searches specified libraries for functions the program uses and combines object modules for those functions with the program's object modules. By default the C compiler links the standard C library **libc.so** (usually found in **/lib**), which contains functions that handle input and

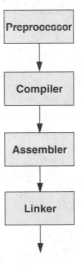

Figure 10-2   The compilation process

output and provides many other general-purpose capabilities. If you want the linker to search other libraries, you must use the –l (lowercase "l") option to specify the libraries on the command line. Unlike most options to Linux system utilities, the –l option does not come before all filenames on the command line but usually appears after the filenames of all modules that it applies to. In the next example, the C compiler searches the math library **libm.so** (usually found in **/lib**):

```
$ gcc calc.c -lm
```

The –l option uses abbreviations for library names, appending the letter following –l to **lib** and adding a **.so** or **.a** extension. The **m** in the example stands for **libm.so**.

Using the same naming mechanism, you can have a graphics library named **libgraphics.a**, which can be linked with the following command:

```
$ gcc pgm.c -lgraphics
```

When you use this convention to name libraries, gcc knows to search for them in **/usr/lib** and **/lib**. You can have gcc also search other directories by using the –L option:

```
$ gcc pgm.c -L. -L/usr/X11R6/lib -lgraphics
```

The preceding command causes gcc to search for the library file **libgraphics.a** in the working directory and in **/usr/X11R6/lib** before searching **/usr/lib** and **/lib**.

As the last step of the compilation process, the linker creates an executable file named **a.out** unless you specify a different filename with the –o option. Object files are deleted after the executable is created.

ELF format   You may occasionally encounter references to the **a.out** format, an old UNIX binary format. Linux uses the Executable and Linking Format (ELF) for binaries; recent versions of gcc produce this format—not the **a.out** format, in spite of the filename. Use the file utility (page 653) to determine the format of the executable that gcc generates:

```
$ file a.out
a.out: ELF 32-bit LSB executable, Intel 80386, version 1 (SYSV), for
GNU/Linux 2.2.5, dynamically linked (uses shared libs), not stripped
```

In the next example, the –O3 option causes gcc to use the C compiler *optimizer*. The optimizer makes object code more efficient so that the executable program runs more quickly. Optimization has many facets, including locating frequently used variables and taking advantage of processor-specific features. The number after the –O indicates the level of optimization, where a higher number specifies more optimization. See the gcc info page for specifics. The following example also shows that the **.o** files are not present after **a.out** is created:

```
$ ls
acctspay.c  acctsrec.c  ledger.c
$ gcc -O3 ledger.c acctspay.c acctsrec.c
$ ls
a.out  acctspay.c  acctsrec.c  ledger.c
```

You can use the executable **a.out** in the same way you use shell scripts and other programs: by typing its name on the command line. The program in Figure 10-1 on page 390 expects to read from standard input, so once you have created the executable **a.out** you can use a command such as the following to run it:

```
$ ./a.out < mymemo
```

If you want to save the **a.out** file, you should change the name to a more descriptive one. Otherwise, you might accidentally overwrite it during a later compilation:

```
$ mv a.out accounting
```

To save yourself the trouble of renaming an **a.out** file, you can specify the name of the executable file when you use gcc. The –o option causes the C compiler to give the executable the name you specify rather than **a.out**. In the next example, the executable is named **accounting**:

```
$ gcc -o accounting ledger.c acctspay.c acctsrec.c
```

If **accounting** does not require arguments, you can run it with the following command:

```
$ accounting
```

You can suppress the linking phase of compilation by using the –c option with the gcc command. The –c option does not treat unresolved external references as errors; this capability enables you to compile and debug the syntax of the modules of a program as you create them. Once you have compiled and debugged all the modules, you can run gcc again with the object files as arguments to produce an executable program. In the next example, gcc produces three object files but no executable:

```
$ gcc -c ledger.c acctspay.c acctsrec.c
$ ls
acctspay.c  acctspay.o  acctsrec.c  acctsrec.o  ledger.c  ledger.o
```

If you then run gcc again and name the object files on the command line, gcc will produce the executable. Because it recognizes the filename extension .o, the C compiler knows that the files need only to be linked. You can also include both .c and .o files on a single command line:

```
$ gcc -o accounting ledger.o acctspay.c acctsrec.o
```

The C compiler recognizes that the .c file needs to be preprocessed and compiled, whereas the .o files do not. The C compiler also accepts assembly language files ending in .s and assembles and links them. This feature makes it easy to modify and recompile a program.

You can use separate files to divide a project into functional groups. For instance, you might put graphics routines in one file, string functions in another, and database calls in a third. Multiple files can enable several engineers to work on the same project concurrently and can speed up compilation. If all functions are in one file and you make a change, the compiler must recompile all functions in the file. Thus the entire program will be recompiled, which may take considerable time even if you made only a small change. When you use separate files, only the file that you change must be recompiled. For large programs with many source files (for example, the C compiler or emacs), the time lost by recompiling one huge file for every small change would be enormous. For more information, refer to "make: Keeps a Set of Programs Current" on page 399.

What not to name a program

tip Do not name a program **test** or any other name of a builtin or other executable on the local system. If you do, you will likely execute the builtin or other program instead of the program you intend to run. Use which (page 61) to determine which program you will run when you give a command.

USING SHARED LIBRARIES

Most modern operating systems use *shared* libraries, also called *dynamic* libraries. These libraries are not linked into a program at compile time but rather are loaded when the program starts (or later in some cases). The names of files housing shared libraries have filename extensions of **.so** (shared object)—for example libc.so. Usually **libaaa.so** is a symbolic link to **libaaa.so.x**, where x is a small number representing the version of the library. Many of these libraries are kept in **/usr/lib**: A typical Linux installation has more than 300 shared libraries in **/usr/lib** and more than 30 in **/usr/X11R6/lib**. Applications can have their own shared libraries. For example, the gcc compiler might keep its libraries in **/usr/lib/gcc-lib/i386-redhat-linux/3.4.0**.

Archived libraries In contrast to shared libraries are the older, *statically linked* libraries (with a **.a** filename extension), also called *archived* libraries. Archived libraries are added to the executable file during the last (link) phase of compilation. This addition can make a program run slightly faster the first time it is run, albeit at the expense of program maintainability and size. Taken together, the combined size of several executables that use a shared library and the size of the shared library are smaller than the combined size of the same executables with static libraries. When a running program has already loaded a dynamic library, a second program that requires the same dynamic library starts slightly faster.

Reducing memory usage and increasing maintainability are the primary reasons for using shared object libraries; they have largely replaced statically linked libraries as the library type of choice. Consider what happens when you discover an error in a library. With a static library, you need to relink every program that uses the library once the library has been fixed and recompiled. With a dynamic library, you need to fix and recompile only the library itself.

Shared object libraries also make dynamic loading of program libraries on the fly possible (for example, perl, python, and tcl extensions and modules). The Apache (HTTP) Web server specifies modules in the **httpd.conf** file and loads them as needed.

ldd   The ldd (list dynamic dependencies) utility tells you which shared libraries a program needs. The following example shows that cp uses **libacl**, the Access Control Lists library; **libc**, the C library; **libattr**, the Extended Attributes library; and **ld-linux**, the runtime linker:

```
$ ldd /bin/cp
        libacl.so.1 => /lib/libacl.so.1 (0x40026000)
        libc.so.6 => /lib/i686/libc.so.6 (0x42000000)
        libattr.so.1 => /lib/libattr.so.1 (0x4002d000)
        /lib/ld-linux.so.2 => /lib/ld-linux.so.2 (0x40000000)
```

Running ldd on **/usr/bin/gnome-session** (a program that starts a graphical GNOME session) lists 59 libraries from **/usr/lib**, **/usr/X11R6/lib**, and **/lib**.

The program that does the dynamic runtime linking, ld-linux.so, always looks in **/usr/lib** for libraries. The other directories that ld searches vary depending on how ld is set up. You can add directories for ld to look in by specifying a search path at compile (actually link) time, using the **–r** option followed by a colon-separated list of directories (do not put a SPACE after **–r**). Use only absolute pathnames in the search path. Although you use this option on the gcc command line, it is passed to the linker (ld). The gnome-session desktop manager was likely linked with a command such as the following:

gcc flags –o gnome-session objects –r/lib:/usr/X11R6/lib libraries

This command line allows ld.so (and ldd) to search **/lib** and **/usr/X11R6/lib** in addition to the standard **/usr/lib** for the libraries needed by the executable.

The compiler needs to see the shared libraries at link time to make sure that the needed functions and procedures are present as promised by the header (**.h**) files. Use the **–L** option to tell the compile-time linker to look in the directory **mylib** for shared or static libraries: **–L mylib**. Unlike the search path, **–L** can use relative pathnames such as **–L ../lib**—handy when a program builds its own shared library. The library can be in one location at build time (**–L**) but in another location at runtime after it is installed (**–r***path*). The SPACE after **–L** is optional and is usually omitted; **–r** must not be followed by a SPACE. You can repeat the **–L** and the **–r** options multiple times on the link line.

FIXING BROKEN BINARIES

The command line search path is a fairly new idea. The search path was traditionally created by using the **LD_LIBRARY_PATH** and, more recently, the **LD_RUN_PATH** environment variables. These variables have the same format as **PATH** (page 284).

The directories in **LD_LIBRARY_PATH** are normally searched before the usual library locations. Newer Linux releases extend the function of **LD_LIBRARY_PATH** to specify directories to be searched either before or after the normal locations. See the ld man page for details. The **LD_RUN_PATH** variable behaves similarly to **LD_LIBRARY_PATH**. If you use –r, however, **LD_LIBRARY_PATH** supersedes anything in **LD_RUN_PATH**.

The use of **LD_LIBRARY_PATH** brings up several problems. Because only one environment variable exists, it must be shared among all programs. If two programs have the same name for a library or use different, incompatible versions of the same library, only the first will be found. As a result one of the programs will not run or—worse—will not run correctly.

LD_LIBRARY_PATH

security Under certain circumstances a malicious user can create a Trojan horse named **libc.so** and place it in a directory that is searched before **/usr/lib** (any directory in **LD_LIBRARY_PATH**, which appears before **/usr/lib**). The fake **libc** will then be used instead of the real **libc**.

Wrappers **LD_LIBRARY_PATH** still has its place in the scripts, called *wrappers,* that are used to fix broken binaries. Suppose that the broken binary **bb** uses the shared library **libbb.so**, which you want to put in **/opt/bb/lib** and not in **/usr/lib**, as the **bb** programmer requested. The command **ldd bb** will tell you which libraries are missing. Not a problem: Rename **bb** to **bb.broken**, and create a **/bin/sh** wrapper named **bb**.

```
#!/bin/sh
LD_LIBRARY_PATH=/opt/bb/lib
export LD_LIBRARY_PATH
exec bb.broken "$@"
```

(Using $@ rather than $* preserves SPACEs in the parameters; see page 482.) A wrapper can also allow you to install programs in arbitrary locations.

CREATING SHARED LIBRARIES

Building a dynamically loadable shared library is not a trivial matter: It involves using reentrant function calls, defining a library entrance routine, and performing other tasks. When you want to create a shared object library, you must at a minimum compile the source files with the **–fPIC** (position-independent code) option to gcc and link the resulting object files into the **lib*xx*.so** file using the **–shared –x** options to the linker (for example, **ld –shared –x –o libmylib.so *.o**). The best resource for investigating shared library construction and usage is existing code on the Internet. For example, you can look at the source files for zlib (www.gzip.org/zlib).

C++ C++ files have special needs, and libraries (shared or not) often have to be made by the compiler rather than ld or ar. Shared libraries can depend on other shared libraries and have their own search paths. If you set **LD_LIBRARY_PATH**, add the **–i** flag to the link phase when compiling to ignore the current **LD_LIBRARY_PATH** or you may have unexpected results. Ideally, you would not have **LD_LIBRARY_PATH** set on a global level but would use it only in wrappers as needed.

make: Keeps a Set of Programs Current

This section covers the GNU make program

tip This section describes the GNU make program. Other make tools (BSN make, GNUStep make, Borland make, and so on) are available as well as similar tools such as ant (the Apache build tool). Makefiles created for GNU make are often incompatible with other make tools, which can be problematic if you are trying to compile code targeted for another platform.

In a large program with many source and header files, the files typically depend on one another in complex ways. When you change a file that other files depend on, you *must* recompile all dependent files. For example, you might have several source files, all of which use a single header file. When you change the header file, you must recompile each of the source files. The header file might depend on other header files, and so forth. Figure 10-3 shows a simple example of dependency relationships. Each arrow in this figure points from a file to another file that depends on it.

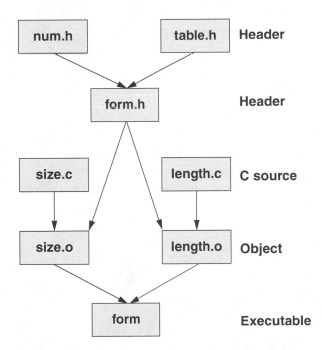

Figure 10-3   Dependency graph for the target **form**

When you are working on a large program, it can be difficult, time-consuming, and tedious to determine which modules need to be recompiled because of their dependency relationships. The make utility automates this process.

Dependency lines: target files and prerequisite files

At its simplest, make looks at *dependency lines* in a file named **Makefile** or **makefile** in the working directory. The dependency lines indicate relationships among files, specifying a *target file* that depends on one or more *prerequisite files*. If you have modified any of the prerequisite files more recently than their target file, make updates the target file based on construction commands that follow the dependency line. The make utility normally stops if it encounters an error during the construction process.

The file containing the updating information for the make utility is called a *makefile*. (See page 388 for a trivial example.) A simple makefile has the following syntax:

target: prerequisite-list
TAB *construction-commands*

The dependency line consists of the **target** and the **prerequisite-list**, separated by a colon. Each **construction-commands** line (you may have more than one) must start with a TAB and must follow the dependency line. Long lines can be continued with a BACKSLASH (\) as the last character on the line.

The **target** is the name of the file that depends on the files in the **prerequisite-list**. The **construction-commands** are regular shell commands that construct (usually compile and/or link) the target file. The make utility executes the **construction-commands** when the modification time of one or more files in the **prerequisite-list** is more recent than that of the target file.

The following example shows the dependency line and construction commands for the file named **form** in Figure 10-3. The **form** file depends on the prerequisites **size.o** and **length.o**. An appropriate gcc command constructs the **target**:

```
form: size.o length.o
TAB     gcc -o form size.o length.o
```

Each of the prerequisites on one dependency line can be a target on another dependency line. For example, both **size.o** and **length.o** are targets on other dependency lines. Although the example in Figure 10-3 is simple, the nesting of dependency specifications can create a complex hierarchy that dictates relationships among many files.

The following makefile (named **Makefile**) corresponds to the complete dependency structure shown in Figure 10-3. The executable file **form** depends on two object files, and the object files each depend on their respective source files and a header file, **form.h**. In turn, **form.h** depends on two other header files.

```
$ cat Makefile
form: size.o length.o
    gcc -o form size.o length.o
size.o: size.c form.h
    gcc -c size.c
```

```
length.o: length.c form.h
    gcc -c length.c
form.h: num.h table.h
    cat num.h table.h > form.h
```

Although the last line would not normally be seen in a makefile, it illustrates the fact that you can put any shell command on a construction line. Because the shell processes makefiles, the command line should be one that you could enter in response to a shell prompt.

The following command builds the default target **form** if any of its prerequisites are more recent than their corresponding targets or if any of the targets do not exist:

```
$ make
```

Thus, if the file **form** has been deleted, make will rebuild it, regardless of the modification dates of its prerequisite files. The first target in a makefile is the default and is built when you call make without any arguments.

If you want make to rebuild a target other than the first in the makefile, you must provide that target as an argument to make. The following command rebuilds only **form.h** if it does not exist or if its prerequisites are more recent than the target:

```
$ make form.h
```

IMPLIED DEPENDENCIES

You can rely on *implied* dependencies and construction commands to facilitate the job of writing a makefile. For instance, if you do not include a dependency line for an object file, make assumes that it depends on a compiler or assembler source code file. Thus, if a prerequisite for a target file is **xxx.o** and no dependency line identifies **xxx.o** as a target, make looks at the extension to determine how to build the .o file. If it finds an appropriate source file, make provides a default construction command line that calls the proper compiler or the assembler to create the object file. Table 10-1 lists some filename extensions that make recognizes and the type of file that corresponds to each suffix.

Table 10-1   Filename extensions

Filename with extension	Type of file
filename.c	C programming language source code
filename.C, filename.cc, filename.cxx, filename.c++, filename.cpp	C++ programming language source code
filename.f	Fortran programming language source code

Table 10-1   Filename extensions (continued)

filename.h	Header file
filename.l	flex, lex lexical analyzer generator source code
filename.o	Object module
filename.s	Assembler code
filename.sh	Shell script
filename.y	bison, yacc parser generator source code

C and C++ are traditional programming languages that are available with many Linux distributions. The bison and flex tools create command languages.

In the next example a makefile keeps the file named **compute** up-to-date. The make utility ignores any line that begins with a pound sign (#). Thus the first three lines of the following makefile are comment lines. The first dependency line shows that **compute** depends on two object files: **compute.o** and **calc.o**. The corresponding construction line gives the command make needs to produce **compute**. The second dependency line shows that **compute.o** depends not only on its C source file but also on the **compute.h** header file. The construction line for **compute.o** uses the C compiler optimizer (–O3 option). The third set of dependency and construction lines is not required. In their absence, make infers that **calc.o** depends on **calc.c** and produces the command line needed for the compilation:

```
$ cat Makefile
#
# Makefile for compute
#
compute: compute.o calc.o
        gcc -o compute compute.o calc.o

compute.o: compute.c compute.h
        gcc -c -O3 compute.c

calc.o: calc.c
        gcc -c calc.c

clean:
    rm *.o *core* *~
```

There are no prerequisites for **clean,** the last target. This target is commonly used to get rid of extraneous files that may be out-of-date or no longer needed, such as .o files.

Following are some sample executions of make based on the previous makefile. As the ls command shows, **compute.o, calc.o,** and **compute** are not up-to-date. Consequently the make command runs the construction commands that re-create them.

```
$ ls -ltr
total 22
-rw-rw----  1 alex   pubs   311 Jun 21 15:56 makefile
-rw-rw----  1 alex   pubs   354 Jun 21 16:02 calc.o
-rwxrwx---  1 alex   pubs  6337 Jun 21 16:04 compute
-rw-rw----  1 alex   pubs    49 Jun 21 16:04 compute.h
-rw-rw----  1 alex   pubs   880 Jun 21 16:04 compute.o
-rw-rw----  1 alex   pubs   780 Jun 21 18:20 compute.c
-rw-rw----  1 alex   pubs   179 Jun 21 18:20 calc.c

$ make
gcc -c -O3 compute.c
gcc -c calc.c
gcc -o compute compute.o calc.o
```

If you run make once and then run it again without making any changes to the prerequisite files, make indicates that the program is up-to-date and does not execute any commands:

```
$ make
make: 'compute' is up to date.
```

touch The next example uses the touch utility to change the modification time of a prerequisite file. This simulation shows what happens when you alter the file. The make utility executes only the commands necessary to bring the out-of-date targets up-to-date:

```
$ touch calc.c
$ make
gcc -c calc.c
gcc -o compute compute.o calc.o
```

In the next example, touch changes the modification time of **compute.h**. The make utility re-creates **compute.o** because it depends on **compute.h** and re-creates the executable because it depends on **compute.o**:

```
$ touch compute.h
$ make
gcc -c -O3 compute.c
gcc -o compute compute.o calc.o
```

-n If you want to see what make *would* do if you ran it, run make with the **–n** (no execute) option. The **–n** option shows the commands that make would execute but it does not execute them.

-t As these examples illustrate, touch is useful when you want to fool make either into recompiling programs or into *not* recompiling them. You can use touch to update the modification times of all source files so that make considers nothing to be up-to-date; make will then recompile everything. Alternatively, you can use touch or the **–t** option to make to touch all relevant files; make then considers everything to be up-to-date. Using touch in this manner is useful if the modification times of files have changed yet the files remain up-to-date (as can happen when you copy a set of files from one directory to another).

The following example uses **make –n** several times to see what make *would* do if you gave a **make** command. The first command shows that the target, **compute**, is up-to-date. Next touch makes the modification dates on all the ***.c** files more recent than their targets and **make –n** shows what make would do if you called it without the **–n** option. The **make –t** command then brings all the targets up-to-date. The final **make –n** confirms that **compute** is up-to-date.

```
$ make -n
make: 'compute' is up to date.
$ touch *.c
$ make -n
gcc -c -O3 compute.c
gcc -c calc.c
gcc -o compute compute.o calc.o
$ make -t
touch compute.o
touch calc.o
touch compute
$ make -n
make: 'compute' is up to date.
```

–j The **–j** (jobs) option performs a number of tasks in parallel; the numeric argument to **–j** specifies the number of jobs or processes. Most make tasks hit the disk first and then the CPU, resulting in CPU usage dropping between compiles. On a multi-processor system, you can reduce CPU usage by using **make –j** *n*, where *n* is the number of CPUs plus 1. Running tasks in parallel can significantly reduce the build time for a large project.

Once you are satisfied with the program you have created, you can use the makefile to remove extraneous files. It is helpful to keep intermediate files around while you are writing and debugging a program so that you need to rebuild only the ones that change. When you will not be working on the program for a while, you can release the disk space. Using a **clean** target in a makefile means that you do not have to remember all the little pieces that can safely be deleted. The next example simply removes all object (**.o**) files:

```
$ make clean
rm *.o
```

optional

MACROS

The make utility's macro facility enables you to create and use macros within a makefile. The syntax of a macro definition is

ID = list

Replace *ID* with an identifying name, and replace *list* with a list of filenames. After this macro definition, $(ID) represents *list* in the makefile.

With a macro you can compile a program with any of several C compilers, making only a minor change to the makefile. By using the CC macro and replacing all occurrences of **gcc** in the makefile on page 402 with $(CC), for example, you need to assign a value only to CC to use the compiler of your choice:

```
$ cat Makefile
#
# Makefile for compute
#
CC=gcc

compute: compute.o calc.o
        $(CC) -o compute compute.o calc.o

compute.o: compute.c compute.h
        $(CC) -c -O3 compute.c

calc.o: calc.c
        $(CC) -c calc.c

clean:
        rm *.o
```

This example assumes that the compiler/loader flags are the same across compilers/loaders. In a more complex situation, you need to create macros for these flags or use the default values. Several commercial, high-performance compilers are available for Linux. You could specify the compiler from the Portland Group, **pgcc**, by replacing the **CC=gcc** assignment with **CC=pgcc**. If you do not assign a value to the CC macro, it defaults to **gcc** under Linux. The CC macro invokes the C compiler with only the options that you specify.

Several other macro definitions are commonly used. The **CFLAGS** macro sends arguments to the C compiler, **LDFLAGS** sends arguments to the linker (**ld**, or **gcc –o**), and **CPPFLAGS** sends arguments to the C preprocessor and programs that use it, including **gcc**. The **COMPILE.c** macro expands to $(CC) –c $(CFLAGS) $(CPPFLAGS). The **LINK.c** macro expands to $(CC) $(CFLAGS) $(CPPFLAGS) $(LDFLAGS).

By default **make** invokes the C compiler without any options (except the –c option when it is appropriate to compile but not to link a file). You can use the **CFLAGS** macro definition to cause **make** to call the C compiler with specific options. Replace *options* with the options you want to use:

CFLAGS = options

The following makefile uses macros as well as implied dependencies and constructions:

```
# makefile: report, print, printf, printh
#
CC=gcc
CFLAGS = -O3
# comment out the two lines above and uncomment the
# two below when you are using the Portland Group's compiler
#CC=pgcc
#CFLAGS = -fast
FILES = in.c out.c ratio.c process.c tally.c
OBJECTS = in.o out.o ratio.o process.o tally.o
HEADERS = names.h companies.h conventions.h

report: $(OBJECTS)
        $(LINK.c) -o report $(OBJECTS)

ratio.o: $(HEADERS)

process.o: $(HEADERS)

tally.o: $(HEADERS)

print:
    pr $(FILES) $(HEADERS) | lpr

printf:
    pr $(FILES) | lpr

printh:
    pr $(HEADERS) | lpr
```

Following the comment lines in this example, the makefile uses the **CFLAGS** macro to cause make always to use the optimizer (**–O3** option) when it invokes the C compiler as the result of an implied construction. (The **CC** and **CFLAGS** definitions for the pgcc C compiler perform the same functions when they are uncommented and you are working with pgcc, except that you use **–fast** with pgcc where you use **–O3** with gcc.) A construction line in a makefile overrides the corresponding implied construction line, if one exists. If you want to apply a macro to a construction command, you must include the macro in that command; see **OBJECTS** in the construction command for the **report** target. Following **CFLAGS**, the makefile defines the **FILES**, **OBJECTS**, and **HEADERS** macros. Each of these macros defines a list of files.

The first dependency line in the preceding example shows that **report** depends on the list of files that **OBJECTS** defines. The corresponding construction line links the **OBJECTS** and creates an executable file named **report**.

The next three dependency lines show that three object files depend on the list of files that **HEADERS** defines. Because there are no construction lines, make looks for a source code file corresponding to each object file and compiles it. These three dependency lines ensure that the object files are recompiled if any header files change.

Finally the **LINK.c** macro is invoked to link the executable file. If you specify any **LDFLAGS**, they are used in this step.

You can combine several targets on one dependency line, so these three dependency lines could have been combined into one line as follows:

```
ratio.o process.o tally.o: $(HEADERS)
```

The three final dependency lines in the preceding example send source and header files to the printer. They have nothing to do with compiling the **report** file. None of these targets (**print, printf,** and **printh**) depends on anything. When you call one of these targets from the command line, make executes the construction line following it. The following command prints all the source files that **FILES** defines:

```
$ make printf
```

You can override macros in a makefile by specifying them on the command line. The following command adds debugging symbols to all object files:

```
$ make CFLAGS=-g ...
```

DEBUGGING C PROGRAMS

The C compiler is liberal about the kinds of constructs it allows in programs. In keeping with the UNIX philosophy that "no news is good news" and that the user knows what is best, gcc, like many other Linux utilities, accepts almost anything that is logically possible according to the definition of the language. Although this approach gives the programmer a great deal of flexibility and control, it can make debugging difficult.

Figure 10-4 on page 409 shows **badtabs.c,** a flawed version of the **tabs.c** program discussed earlier. It contains some errors and does not run properly. This section uses this program to illustrate some debugging techniques.

In the following example, **badtabs.c** is compiled and then run with input from the **testtabs** file. Inspection of the output shows that the TAB character has not been replaced with the proper number of SPACEs:

```
$ gcc -o badtabs badtabs.c
$ cat testtabs
abcTABxyz
$ badtabs < testtabs
abc   xyz
```

One way to debug a C program is to insert print statements at critical points throughout the source code. To learn more about the behavior of **badtabs.c** when it runs, you can replace the contents of the **switch** statement with

```
        case '\t':                /* c is a tab */
            fprintf(stderr, "before call to findstop, posn is %d\n", posn);
            inc = findstop(&posn);
            fprintf(stderr, "after call to findstop, posn is %d\n", posn);
            for( ; inc > 0; inc-- )
                putchar(' ');
            break;
        case '\n':                /* c is a newline */
            fprintf(stderr, "got a newline\n");
            putchar(c);
            posn = 0;
            break;
        default:                  /* c is anything else */
            fprintf(stderr, "got another character\n");
            putchar(c);
            posn++;
            break;
```

The **fprintf** statements in this code send their messages to standard error. Thus, if you redirect standard output of this program, it will not be interspersed with the output sent to standard error. The next example demonstrates the operation of this program on the input file **testtabs**:

```
$ gcc -o badtabs badtabs.c
$ badtabs < testtabs > testspaces
got another character
got another character
got another character
before call to findstop, posn is 3
after call to findstop, posn is 3
got another character
got another character
got another character
got a newline
$ cat testspaces
abcTABxyz
```

The **fprintf** statements provide additional information about the execution of **tabs.c**. The value of the variable **posn** is not incremented in **findstop**, as it should be. This clue might be enough to lead you to the bug in the program. If not, you might attempt to "corner" the offending code by inserting print statements in **findstop**.

For simple programs or when you have an idea of what is wrong with a program, adding **print** statements that trace the execution of the code can often help you solve the problem quickly. A better strategy may be to take advantage of the tools that Linux provides to help you debug programs.

gcc: Compiler Warning Options

The gcc compiler includes many of the features of lint, the classic C program verifier, and then some. (The lint utility is not available under Linux; use splint [secure

```
 1  /* convert tabs in standard input to spaces in */
 2  /* standard output while maintaining columns */
 3
 4  #include         <stdio.h>
 5  #define          TABSIZE          8
 6
 7  /* prototype for function findstop */
 8  int findstop(int *);
 9
10  main()
11  {
12  int c;           /* character read from stdin */
13  int posn = 0;    /* column position of character */
14  int inc;         /* column increment to tab stop */
15
16  while ((c = getchar()) != EOF)
17          switch(c)
18                  {
19                  case '\t':                  /* c is a tab */
20                          inc = findstop(&posn);
21                          for( ; inc > 0; inc-- )
22                                  putchar(' ');
23                          break;
24                  case '\n':                  /* c is a newline */
25                          putchar(c);
26                          posn = 0;
27                          break;
28                  default:                    /* c is anything else */
29                          putchar(c);
30                          posn++;
31                          break;
32                  }
33
34  }
35
36  /* compute size of increment to next tab stop */
37
38  int findstop(int *col)
39  {
40  int colindex, retval;
41  retval = (TABSIZE - (*col % TABSIZE));
42
43  /* increment argument (current column position) to next tabstop */
44  *col += retval;
45
46  return retval;           /* main gets how many blanks for filling */
47  }
```

Comments

Preprocessor
Directives

Function
Prototype

Main
Function

Function

Figure 10-4 The **badtabs.c** program (The line numbers are not part
of the source code; the arrows point to errors in the program.)

programming lint; www.splint.org] instead.) The gcc compiler can identify many C
program constructs that pose potential problems, even for programs that conform to
the syntax rules of the language. For instance, you can request that the compiler
report whether a variable is declared but not used, a comment is not properly terminated, or a function returns a type not permitted in older versions of C. Options that
enable this stricter compiler behavior all begin with the uppercase letter **W** (Warning).

Among the **–W** options is a class of warnings that typically result from programmer
carelessness or inexperience (see Table 10-2). The constructs that generate these
warnings are generally easy to fix and easy to avoid.

Table 10-2   **gcc –W** options

Option	Reports an error when
–Wimplicit	A function or parameter is not explicitly declared
–Wreturn-type	A function that is not void does not return a value or the type of a function defaults to **int**
–Wunused	A variable is declared but not used
–Wcomment	The characters /*, which normally begin a comment, occur within a comment
–Wformat	Certain input/output statements contain format specifications that do not match the arguments

The **–Wall** option displays warnings about all the errors listed in Table 10-2, along with other, similar errors.

The program **badtabs.c** is syntactically correct: It compiles without generating an error. However, if you compile it (**–c** causes gcc to compile but not to link) with the **–Wall** option, gcc displays several problems. (Warning messages do not stop the program from compiling, whereas error messages do.)

```
$ gcc -c -Wall badtabs.c
badtabs.c:47: warning: '/*' within comment
badtabs.c:11: warning: return-type defaults to 'int'
badtabs.c: In function 'main':
badtabs.c:34: warning: control reaches end of non-void function
badtabs.c: In function 'findstop':
badtabs.c:40: warning: unused variable 'colindex'
badtabs.c:49: warning: control reaches end of non-void function
```

The first warning message references line 47. Inspection of the code for **badtabs.c** around that line reveals a comment that is not properly terminated. The compiler sees the string /* in the following line as the beginning of a comment:

```
/* increment argument (current column position) to next tabstop * /
```

However, because the characters * and / at the end of the line are separated by a SPACE, they do not signify the end of the comment to the compiler. Instead the compiler interprets all the statements—including the statement that increments the argument—through the string */ at the very end of the **findstop** function as part of the comment.

Compiling with the **–Wall** option can be very helpful when you are debugging a program. After you remove the SPACE between the characters * and /, **badtabs** produces the correct output.

The next few paragraphs discuss the remaining warning messages. Although most do not cause problems in the execution of **badtabs**, you can generally improve a program by rewriting those parts of the code that produce such warnings.

Because the definition of the function **main** does not include an explicit type, the compiler assumes type **int**, the default. This results in the warning message referencing line 11 in **badtabs.c**, the top of the function **main**. An additional warning is given when the compiler encounters the end of the function **main** (line 34) without seeing a value returned.

If a program runs successfully, by convention it should return a zero value; if no value is returned, the exit code is undefined. Although many C programs do not return a value, this oversight can cause problems when the program is executed. When you add the following statement at the end of the function **main** in **badtabs.c**, the warning referencing line 34 disappears:

```
return 0;
```

Line 40 of **badtabs.c** contains the definition for the local variable **colindex** in the function **findstop**. The warning message referencing that line occurs because the **colindex** variable is never used. Removing its declaration eliminates the warning message.

The final warning message, referencing line 49, results from the improperly terminated comment discussed earlier. The compiler issues the warning message because it never sees a **return** statement in **findstop**. (The compiler ignores commented text.) Because the function **findstop** returns type **int**, the compiler expects a **return** statement before reaching the end of the function. The warning disappears when the comment is properly terminated.

Many other **–W** options are available with the gcc compiler. The ones not covered in the **Wall** class often deal with portability differences; modifying the code causing these warnings may not be appropriate. The warnings usually result from programs that are written in different C dialects as well as from constructs that may not work well with other (especially older) C compilers. The **–pedantic-errors** option turns warnings into errors, causing a build to fail if it contains items that would generate warnings. To learn more about these and other warning options, refer to the gcc info page.

SYMBOLIC DEBUGGER

Many debuggers are available to tackle problems that evade the simpler debugging methods such as print statements and compiler warning options. These debuggers include gdb, kdbg, xxgdb mxgdb, ddd, and ups, which are available from the Web (refer to Appendix B). All are high-level symbolic debuggers that enable you to analyze the execution of a program in terms of C language statements. The debuggers also provide a lower-level view for analyzing the execution of a program in terms of the machine instructions. Except for gdb, each of these debuggers provides a GUI.

A debugger enables you to monitor and control the execution of a program. You can step through a program line by line while you examine the state of the execution environment.

Core dumps   A debugger also allows you to examine *core* files. (Core files are named **core**.) When a serious error occurs during the execution of a program, the operating system can create a core file containing information about the state of the program and the system when the error occurred. This file comprises a dump of the computer's memory (it was previously called *core memory*—hence the term *core dump*) that was being used by the program. To conserve disk space, your system may not save core files automatically. You can use the ulimit builtin to enable core files to be saved. If you are running bash, the following command allows core files of unlimited size to be saved to disk:

```
$ ulimit -c unlimited
```

The operating system advises you when it dumps core. You can use a symbolic debugger to read information from the core file to identify the line in the program where the error occurred, to check the values of variables at that point, and so forth. Because core files tend to be large and take up disk space, be sure to remove these files when you no longer need them.

gdb: SYMBOLIC DEBUGGER

The following examples demonstrate the use of the GNU gdb debugger. Other symbolic debuggers offer a different interface but operate in a similar manner. To make full use of a symbolic debugger with a program, you must compile the program with the –g option, which causes gcc to generate additional information that the debugger uses. This information includes a *symbol table*—a list of variable names used in the program and their associated values. Without the symbol table information, the debugger cannot display the values and types of variables. If a program is compiled without the –g option, gdb cannot identify source code lines by number, as many gdb commands require.

Always use –g

tip   It can be helpful always to use the –g option even when you are releasing software. Including debugging symbols makes a binary a bit bigger. Debugging symbols do not make a program run more slowly, but they do make it much easier to find problems identified by users.

Avoid using optimization flags with the debugger

tip   Limit the optimization flags to –O or –O2 when you compile a program for debugging. Because debugging and optimizing inherently have different goals, it may be best to avoid combining the two operations.

The following example uses the –g option when creating the executable file **tabs** from the C program **tabs.c**, discussed at the beginning of this chapter:

```
$ gcc -g tabs.c -o tabs
```

Optimization should work

tip Turning optimization off completely can sometimes eliminate errors. Eliminating errors in this way should not be seen as a permanent solution, however. When optimization is not enabled, the compiler may automatically initialize variables and perform certain other checks for you, resulting in more stable code. Correct code should work correctly when compiled with at least **–O** and almost certainly **–O2**. The **–O3** setting often includes experimental optimizations so it may not generate correct code in all cases.

Input for **tabs** is contained in the file **testtabs**, which consists of a single line:

```
$ cat testtabs
xyzTABabc
```

You cannot specify the input file to **tabs** when you first call the debugger. Specify the input file once you have called the debugger and started execution with the **run** command.

To run the debugger on the sample executable, give the name of the executable file on the command line when you run gdb. You will see some introductory statements about gdb, followed by the gdb prompt [(**gdb**)]. At this point the debugger is ready to accept commands. The **list** command displays the first ten lines of source code. A subsequent **list** command displays the next ten lines of source code.

```
$ gdb tabs
GNU gdb 4.18
...
(gdb) list
4         #include        <stdio.h>
5         #define         TABSIZE         8
6
7         /* prototype for function findstop */
8         int findstop(int *);
9
10        int main()
11        {
12        int c;          /* character read from stdin */
13        int posn = 0;   /* column position of character */
(gdb) list
14        int inc;        /* column increment to tab stop */
15
16        while ((c = getchar()) != EOF)
17                switch(c)
18                        {
19                        case '\t':              /* c is a tab */
20                                inc = findstop(&posn);
21                                for( ; inc > 0; inc-- )
22                                        putchar(' ');
23                                break;
(gdb)
```

One of the most important features of a debugger is its ability to run a program in a controlled environment. You can stop the program from running whenever you want. While it is stopped, you can check the state of an argument or variable. For example, you can give the **break** command a source code line number, an actual memory address, or a function name as an argument. The following command tells gdb to stop the process whenever the function **findstop** is called:

```
(gdb) break findstop
Breakpoint 1 at 0x804849f: file tabs.c, line 41.
(gdb)
```

The debugger acknowledges the request by displaying the breakpoint number, the hexadecimal memory address of the breakpoint, and the corresponding source code line number (41). The debugger numbers breakpoints in ascending order as you create them, starting with 1.

After setting a breakpoint you can issue a **run** command to start execution of **tabs** under the control of the debugger. The **run** command syntax allows you to use angle brackets to redirect input and output (just as the shells do). In the following example, the **testtabs** file is specified as input. When the process stops (at the breakpoint), you can use the **print** command to check the value of ∗**col**. The **backtrace** (or **bt**) command displays the function stack. The example shows that the currently active function has been assigned the number 0. The function that called **findstop** (**main**) has been assigned the number 1:

```
(gdb) run < testtabs
Starting program: /home/mark/book/10/tabs < testtabs

Breakpoint 1, findstop (col=0xbffffc70) at tabs.c:41
41      retval = (TABSIZE - (*col % TABSIZE));
(gdb) print *col
$1 = 3
(gdb) backtrace
#0  findstop (col=0xbffffc70) at tabs.c:41
#1  0x804843a in main () at tabs.c:20
(gdb)
```

You can examine anything in the current scope—variables and arguments in the active function as well as globals. In the next example, the request to examine the value of the variable **posn** at breakpoint 1 results in an error. The error is generated because the variable **posn** is defined locally in the function **main**, not in the function **findstop**:

```
(gdb) print posn
No symbol "posn" in current context.
```

The **up** command changes the active function to the caller of the currently active function. Because **main** calls the function **findstop**, the function **main** becomes the active function when the **up** command is given. (The **down** command does the inverse.) The **up** command may be given an integer argument specifying the number of levels in the function stack to backtrack, with **up 1** having the same meaning as **up**. (You can use the **backtrace** command to determine the argument to use with **up**.)

```
(gdb) up
#1  0x804843a in main () at tabs.c:20
20                              inc = findstop(&posn);
(gdb) print posn
$2 = 3
(gdb) print *col
No symbol "col" in current context.
(gdb)
```

The **cont** (continue) command causes the process to continue running from where it left off. The **testtabs** file contains only one line; the process finishes executing and the results appear on the screen. The debugger reports the exit code of the program. A **cont** command given after a program has finished executing reminds you that execution of the program is complete. The debugging session is then ended with a **quit** command.

```
(gdb) cont
Continuing.
abc     xyz

Program exited normally.
(gdb) cont
The program is not being run.
(gdb) quit
$
```

The gdb debugger supports many commands that are designed to make debugging easier. Type **help** at the **(gdb)** prompt to get a list of the command classes available under gdb:

```
(gdb) help
List of classes of commands:

aliases -- Aliases of other commands
breakpoints -- Making program stop at certain points
data -- Examining data
files -- Specifying and examining files
internals -- Maintenance commands
obscure -- Obscure features
running -- Running the program
stack -- Examining the stack
status -- Status inquiries
support -- Support facilities
tracepoints -- Tracing of program execution without stopping the program
user-defined -- User-defined commands

Type "help" followed by a class name for a list of commands in that class.
Type "help" followed by command name for full documentation.
Command name abbreviations are allowed if unambiguous.
(gdb)
```

As explained in the instructions following the list, entering **help** followed by the name of a command class or command name will display more information. The following lists the commands in the class **data**:

```
(gdb) help data
Examining data.

List of commands:                      .

call -- Call a function in the program
delete display -- Cancel some expressions to be displayed when program stops
disable display -- Disable some expressions to be displayed when program stops
disassemble -- Disassemble a specified section of memory
display -- Print value of expression EXP each time the program stops
enable display -- Enable some expressions to be displayed when program stops
inspect -- Same as "print" command
output -- Like "print" but don't put in value history and don't print newline
print -- Print value of expression EXP
printf -- Printf "printf format string"
ptype -- Print definition of type TYPE
set -- Evaluate expression EXP and assign result to variable VAR
set variable -- Evaluate expression EXP and assign result to variable VAR
undisplay -- Cancel some expressions to be displayed when program stops
whatis -- Print data type of expression EXP
x -- Examine memory: x/FMT ADDRESS

Type "help" followed by command name for full documentation.
Command name abbreviations are allowed if unambiguous.
(gdb)
```

The following requests information on the command **whatis**, which takes a variable name or other expression as an argument:

```
(gdb) help whatis
Print data type of expression EXP.
```

GRAPHICAL SYMBOLIC DEBUGGERS

Several graphical interfaces to gdb exist. The xxgdb graphical version of gdb provides a number of windows, including a Source Listing window, a Command window that contains a set of commonly used commands, and a Display window for viewing the values of variables. The left mouse button selects commands from the Command window. You can click the desired line in the Source Listing window to set a breakpoint, and you can select variables by clicking them in the Source Listing window. Selecting a variable and clicking **print** in the Command window will display the value of the variable in the Display window. You can view lines of source code by scrolling (and resizing) the Source Listing window.

The GNU ddd debugger (www.gnu.org/software/ddd) also provides a GUI to gdb. Unlike xxgdb, ddd can graphically display complex C structures and the links between them. This display makes it easier to see errors in these structures. Otherwise, the ddd interface is very similar to that of xxgdb.

Unlike xxgdb, ups (ups.sourceforge.net) was designed from the ground up to work as a graphical debugger; the graphical interface was not added after the debugger was complete. The resulting interface is simple yet powerful. For example, ups automatically displays the value of a variable when you click it and provides a built-in C interpreter that allows you to attach C code to the program you are debugging. Because this attached code has access to the variables and values in the program, you can use it to perform sophisticated checks, such as following and displaying the links in a complex *data structure* (page 870).

THREADS

A *thread* is a single sequential flow of control within a process. Threads are the basis for multithreaded programs, which allow a single program to control concurrently running threads, each performing a different task. Multithreaded programs generally use *reentrant* code (code that multiple threads can use simultaneously) and are most valuable when run on multiple-CPU machines. Under Linux, multithreaded servers, such as NFS, can provide a cleaner interface and may be easier to write than multiple server processes. When applied judiciously, multithreading can also serve as a lower-overhead replacement for the traditional fork-exec idiom for spawning processes. See the FAQ at tldp.org/FAQ/Threads-FAQ.

Multiple threads are not always better

tip   If you write a multithreaded program with no clear goal or division of effort for a single-CPU system (for example, a parallel-server process), the resulting program will likely run more slowly than a nonthreaded program on the same system.

SYSTEM CALLS

Three fundamental responsibilities of the Linux kernel are to control processes, manage the filesystem, and operate peripheral devices. As a programmer you have access to these kernel operations through system calls and library functions. This section discusses system calls at a general level; a detailed treatment is beyond the scope of this book.

As the name implies, a system call instructs the system (kernel) to perform some work directly on your behalf. The request is a message that tells the kernel what work needs to be done and includes the necessary arguments. For example, a system call to open a file includes the name of the file. A library routine is indirect; it issues system calls for you. The advantages of a library routine are that it may insulate you from the low-level details of kernel operations and that it has been written carefully to make sure that it performs efficiently.

For example, it is straightforward to use the standard I/O library function **fprintf( )** to send text to standard output or standard error. Without this function, you would need to issue several system calls to achieve the same result. The calls to the library routines **putchar**( ) and **getchar**( ) in Figure 10-1 on page 390 ultimately use the **write**( ) and **read**( ) system calls to perform the I/O operations.

strace: TRACES SYSTEM CALLS

The strace utility is a debugging tool that displays a trace of all system calls made by a process or program. Because you do not need to recompile the program that you want to trace, you can use strace on binaries that you do not have source for.

System calls are events that take place at the interface (boundary) between user code and kernel code. Examining this boundary can help you isolate bugs, track down race conditions, and perform sanity checking. The Linux kernel does not fully cooperate with strace. See the strace home page (www.liacs.nl/~wichert/strace) for kernel patches that improve kernel cooperation with strace.

CONTROLLING PROCESSES

When you enter a command line at a shell prompt, the shell process calls the **fork** system call to create a copy of itself (spawn a child) and then uses an **exec** system call to overlay that copy in memory with a different program (the command you asked it to run). Table 10-3 lists system calls that affect processes.

Table 10-3   System calls: processes control

System call	Function
fork( )	Creates a copy of a process
exec( )	Overlays a program in memory with another
getpid( )	Returns the PID number of the calling process
wait( )	Causes the parent process to wait for the child to finish running before it resumes execution
exit( )	Causes a process to exit
nice( )	Changes the priority of a process
kill( )	Sends a signal to a process

ACCESSING THE FILESYSTEM

Many operations take place when a program reads from or writes to a file. The program needs to know where the file is located; the filename must be converted to an inode number on the correct filesystem. Your access permissions must be checked not only for the file itself but also for all intervening directories in the path to the file. The file is not stored in one continuous piece on the disk so all disk blocks that contain pieces of the file must be located. The appropriate kernel device driver must be called to control the operation of the disk. Once the file has been found, the program may need to find a particular location within the file rather than working with it sequentially from beginning to end. Table 10-4 lists some of the most common system calls for filesystem operations.

Table 10-4   System calls: filesystem

System call	Function
stat( )	Gets status information from an inode, such as the inode number, the device on which it is located, owner and group information, and the size of the file
lseek( )	Moves to a position in the file
creat( )	Creates a new file
open( )	Opens an existing file
read( )	Reads a file
write( )	Writes a file
close( )	Closes a file
unlink( )	Unlinks a file (deletes a name reference to the inode)
chmod( )	Changes file access permissions
chown( )	Changes file ownership

Access to peripheral devices on a Linux system is handled through the filesystem interface. Each peripheral device is represented by one or more special files, usually located under **/dev**. When you read or write to one of these special files, the kernel passes your requests to the appropriate kernel device driver. As a result you can use the standard system calls and library routines to interact with these devices; you do not need to learn a new set of specialized functions. This ability is one of the most powerful features of a Linux system because it allows users to use the same basic utilities on a wide range of devices.

The availability of standard system calls and library routines is the key to the portability of Linux tools. For example, as an applications programmer, you can rely on the read and write system calls working the same way on different versions of the

Linux system and on different types of computers. The systems programmer who writes a device driver or ports the kernel to run on a new computer, however, must understand the details at their lowest level.

Source Code Management

When you work on a project involving many files that evolve over long periods of time, it can be difficult to keep track of the different versions of the files, particularly if several people are updating the files. This problem frequently occurs in large software development projects. Source code and documentation files change frequently as you fix bugs, enhance programs, and release new versions of the software. The task becomes even more complex when more than one version of each file is active. Frequently customers are using one version of a file while a newer version is being modified. You can easily lose track of the versions and accidentally undo changes or duplicate earlier work.

To help avoid these kinds of problems, Linux includes CVS (Concurrent Versions System; www.cvshome.org) for managing and tracking changes to files. Although CVS can be used on any file, it is most often used to manage source code and software documentation. CVS is based on RCS (GNU's Revision Control System) and is designed to control the concurrent access and modification of source files by multiple users.

A graphical front end to CVS named TkCVS (page 429) simplifies the use of CVS, especially if you do not use it frequently enough to memorize its many commands and options.

CVS controls who is allowed to update files. For each update, CVS records who made the changes and why the changes were made. Because CVS stores the most recent version of a file and the information needed to re-create all previous versions, it is possible to regenerate any version of a file.

A set of versions for several files may be grouped together to form a *release*. An entire release can be re-created from the change information stored with each file. Saving the changes for a file rather than saving a complete copy of the file generally conserves a lot of disk space, well in excess of the space required to store each update in the CVS files themselves.

This section provides an overview of CVS and TkCVS. See the *CVS-RCS-HOW-TO Document for Linux* for more information.

CVS: Concurrent Versions System

CVS treats collections of files as single units, making it easy to work on large projects and permitting multiple users to work on the same file. CVS also provides valuable self-documenting features for its utilities.

Built-in CVS Help

CVS uses a single utility, cvs, for all its functions. To display the instructions for getting help, use the **--help** option:

```
$ cvs --help
Usage: cvs [cvs-options] command [command-options-and-arguments]
  where cvs-options are -q, -n, etc.
    (specify --help-options for a list of options)
  where command is add, admin, etc.
    (specify --help-commands for a list of commands
     or --help-synonyms for a list of command synonyms)
  where command-options-and-arguments depend on the specific command
    (specify -H followed by a command name for command-specific help)
  Specify --help to receive this message

The Concurrent Versions System (CVS) is a tool for version control.
For CVS updates and additional information, see
    the CVS home page at http://www.cvshome.org/ or Pascal Molli's CVS
    site at http://www.loria.fr/~molli/cvs-index.html
```

To get help with a cvs command, use the **--help** option followed by the name of the utility. The following example shows help for the log command:

```
$ cvs --help log
Usage: cvs log [-lRhtNb] [-r[revisions]] [-d dates] [-s states]
    [-w[logins]] [files...]
      -l        Local directory only, no recursion.
      -R        Only print name of RCS file.
      -h        Only print header.
      -t        Only print header and descriptive text.
      -N        Do not list tags.
      -b        Only list revisions on the default branch.
      -r[revisions]    Specify revision(s)s to list.
        rev1:rev2   Between rev1 and rev2, including rev1 and rev2.
        rev1::rev2  Between rev1 and rev2, excluding rev1 and rev2.
        rev:        rev and following revisions on the same branch.
        rev::       After rev on the same branch.
        :rev        rev and previous revisions on the same branch.
        ::rev       Before rev on the same branch.
        rev         Just rev.
        branch      All revisions on the branch.
        branch.     The last revision on the branch.
      -d dates      Specify dates (D1<D2 for range, D for latest before).
      -s states     Only list revisions with specified states.
      -w[logins]    Only list revisions checked in by specified logins.
(Specify the --help global option for a list of other help options)
```

Options for individual cvs commands (command options) go to the *right* of the individual command names. Options to the cvs utility itself, such as the **--help** option to the **log** command, go to the *left* of all individual command names (that is, they follow the word **cvs** on the command line). The two types of options sometimes use the same letter yet may have an entirely different meaning.

HOW CVS STORES REVISION FILES

With CVS, revision files are kept in a common area called a *source repository*. This area is identified by the value of the environment variable **CVSROOT**, which holds the absolute pathname of the repository. The system administrator can tell you what value of **CVSROOT** to use, or you can create your own private repository and have **CVSROOT** point to it.

The source repository is organized as a hierarchical collection of files and directories. CVS does not limit you to checking out one file at a time; you can check out an entire subdirectory containing many files—typically all the files for a particular project. A subdirectory of **CVSROOT** that can be checked out as a single unit is called a *module*. Several people can check out and simultaneously modify the files within a single module.

CVS users typically store all the modules they are currently working on in a special directory. If you want to follow this practice, you must use cd to make that special directory the working directory before you check out a module. When you check out a module, *CVS replicates the module's tree structure in the working directory*. Multiple developers can check out and edit CVS files simultaneously because the originals are retained in the source repository; the files in the repository undergo relatively infrequent modification in a controlled manner.

BASIC CVS COMMANDS

Although many cvs commands are available, a handful of commands allows a software developer to use CVS and to contribute changes to a module. A discussion of some useful commands follows. All examples assume that the appropriate modules have been installed in the CVS source repository. "Adding a Module to the Repository" (page 426) explains how to install a module.

Of the commands discussed in this section, **cvs commit** is the only one that changes the source repository. The other commands affect only the files in the working directory.

To simplify examples in the following sections, the pathname of the working directory is given by the variable **CVSWORK**; all modules can be assumed to be subdirectories of **CVSWORK**. Although this variable has no special meaning to CVS, you may find it helpful to define such a variable for your own work.

CHECKING OUT FILES FROM THE SOURCE REPOSITORY

To check out a module from the CVS source repository, use the **cvs checkout** command. The following example checks out the **Project2** module, which consists of four source files. First use cd to change working directories to the directory you want the module copied into (**CVSWORK** in this case). The cvs utility always copies into the working directory.

```
$ cd $CVSWORK
$ ls
Project1
$ cvs checkout Project2
cvs checkout: Updating Project2
U Project2/adata.h
U Project2/compute.c
U Project2/randomfile.h
U Project2/shuffle.c
$ ls
Project1 Project2
$ ls Project2
CVS adata.h compute.c randomfile.h shuffle.c
```

The name of the module, **Project2**, is given as an argument to **cvs checkout**. Because the **Project2** directory does not already exist, cvs creates it in the working directory and places copies of all source files for the **Project2** module into it: The name of the module and the name of the directory holding the module are the same. The **checkout** command preserves the tree structure of the cvs module, creating subdirectories as needed.

The second ls command after **checkout** reveals, in addition to the four source files for **Project2**, a directory named **CVS**. The CVS system uses this directory for administrative purposes; you do not normally access it.

Once you have your own copies of the source files, you can edit them as you see fit. You can change files within the module even if other developers are modifying the same files at the same time.

MAKING YOUR CHANGES AVAILABLE TO OTHERS

To check in your changes so that others have access to them, you need to run the **cvs commit** command. When you give this command, cvs prompts you to provide a brief log message describing the changes, unless you use the **–m** option. With this option, cvs uses the string following the option as the log message. The file or files that you want to commit follow the optional log message on the command line:

```
$ cvs commit -m "function shuffle inserted" compute.c
cvs commit: Up-to-date check failed for 'compute.c'
cvs [commit aborted]: correct above errors first!
```

Here the cvs utility reports an error because the version of **compute.c** that you modified is not up-to-date. A newer version of **compute.c** has been committed by someone else since you last checked it out of the source repository. After informing you of the problem, cvs exits without storing your changes in the source repository.

To make your version of **compute.c** current, you need to run the update command. A subsequent **commit** will then succeed, and your changes will apply to the latest revision in the source repository.

Updating Your Copies with Changes by Others

As the preceding example shows, CVS does not notify you when another developer checks in a new revision of a file after you have checked out your working copy. You learn this fact only when you attempt to commit your changes to the source repository. To incorporate up-to-date revisions of a CVS source file, use the **cvs update** command:

```
$ cvs update compute.c
RCS file: /usr/local/src/master/Project2/compute.c,v
retrieving revision 1.9
retrieving revision 1.10
Merging differences between 1.9 and 1.10 into compute.c
M compute.c
```

The changes made to the working copy of **compute.c** remain intact because the **update** command merges the latest revision in the source repository with the version specified on the **update** command line. The result of the merge is not always perfect, however. The **cvs update** command informs you if it detects overlapping changes.

Adding New Files to the Repository

You can use the **cvs add** command to schedule new files to be added to the source repository as part of the module you are working on. Once you have moved to the directory containing the files, give the **cvs add** command, listing the files you want to add as arguments:

```
$ cd $CVSWORK/Project2
$ ls
CVS compute.c shuffle.c tabout2.c
adata.h randomfile.h tabout1.c
$ cvs add tabout[1-2].c
cvs add: scheduling file 'tabout1.c' for addition
cvs add: scheduling file 'tabout2.c' for addition
cvs add: use 'cvs commit' to add these files permanently
```

The **add** command marks the files **tabout1.c** and **tabout2.c** for entry into the repository. These files will not be available for others until you give a **commit** command. This staging allows you to prepare several files before others incorporate the changes into their working copies with the **cvs update** command.

Removing Files from the Repository

The **cvs remove** command records the fact that you wish to remove a file from the source repository. Like the **add** command, it does not affect the source repository. To delete a file from the repository, you must first delete your working copy of the file, as the following example shows:

```
$ cvs remove shuffle.c
cvs remove: file 'shuffle.c' still in working directory
cvs remove: 1 file exists; use 'rm' to remove it first
$ rm shuffle.c
$ cvs remove shuffle.c
cvs remove: scheduling 'shuffle.c' for removal
cvs remove: use 'cvs commit' to remove this file permanently
```

After using rm to delete the working copy of **shuffle.c**, invoke a **cvs remove** command. Again, you must give the **commit** command before the file is actually removed from the source repository.

OTHER CVS COMMANDS

Although the commands given earlier are sufficient for most work on a module, you may find some other commands to be useful as well.

TAGGING A RELEASE

You can apply a common label, or *tag*, to the files in a module as they currently exist. Once you have tagged files of a module, you can re-create them in exactly the same form even if they have been modified, added, or deleted since that time. This ability enables you to *freeze* a release yet allows development to continue on the next release:

```
$ cvs rtag Release_1 Project1
cvs rtag: Tagging Project1
```

Here the **Project1** module has been tagged with the label **Release_1**. You can use this tag with the **cvs export** command to extract the files as they were frozen at this time.

EXTRACTING A RELEASE

The **cvs export** command lets you extract files as they were frozen and tagged:

```
$ cvs export -r Release_1 -d R1 Project1
cvs export: Updating R1
U R1/scm.txt
```

This command works like the **cvs checkout** command but does not create the CVS support files. You must give either the –r option to identify the release (as shown above) or a date with the –D option. The –d R1 option instructs cvs to place the files for the module into the directory **R1** instead of using the module name as the directory.

REMOVING WORKING FILES

When you are finished making changes to the files you have checked out of the repository, you may decide to remove your copy of the module from your working directory. One simple method is to move into the working directory and recursively remove the module. For example, if you want to remove your working copy of **Project2**, you could use the following commands:

```
$ cd $CVSWORK
$ rm -rf Project2
```

The repository will not be affected by removing these files. However, if you had made changes to the files but had not yet committed those changes, they would be lost if you used this approach. The **cvs release** command is helpful in this situation:

```
$ cd $CVSWORK
$ cvs release -d Project2
```

The **release** command also removes the working files but first checks each one to see whether it has been marked for addition into the repository but has not yet been committed. If that is the case, the **release** command warns you and asks you to verify your intention to delete the file. You can fix the problem at this point if you like and redo the **release** command. The **release** command also warns you if the repository holds a newer version of the file than the one in your working directory. Thus you have the opportunity to update and commit your file before deleting it. (Without the **–d** option, your working files will not be deleted, but the same sequence of warning messages will be given.)

ADDING A MODULE TO THE REPOSITORY

The discussion of CVS to this point assumes that a module is already present in the CVS source repository. If you want to install a directory hierarchy as a new module in the repository or update an existing module with a new release that was developed elsewhere, go to the directory that holds the files for the project and run the **cvs import** command. The following example installs the files for **Project1** in the source repository:

```
$ cvs import -m "My first project" Project1 ventag reltag
```

The **–m** option allows you to enter a brief description of the module on the command line. Following the description is the directory or the pathname of the directory under **CVSROOT** that you want to hold the module. The last two fields are symbolic names for the vendor branch and the release. Although they are not significant here, they can be useful when releases of software are supplied by outside sources.

You can now use the **cvs checkout** command to check out the **Project1** module:

```
$ cvs checkout Project1
```

CVS ADMINISTRATION

Before you install a CVS repository, think about how you would like to administer it. Many installations have a single repository where separate projects are kept as separate modules. You may choose to have more than one repository. The CVS system supports a single repository that is shared across several computer systems using NFS.

Inside a repository is a module, named CVSROOT that contains administrative files (here CVSROOT is the name of a module and is different from the **CVSROOT** directory). Although the files in this module are not required to use CVS, they can simplify access to the repository.

Do not change any files in the CVSROOT module by editing them directly. Instead, check out the file you want to change, edit the checked-out copy, and then check it back in, just as you would with files in any other module in the repository. For example, to check out the **modules** file from the CVSROOT module, use the command

```
$ cvs checkout CVSROOT/modules
```

This command creates the directory **CVSROOT** in your working directory and places a checked-out copy of **modules** in that directory. After checking it out, you can edit the **modules** file in the **CVSROOT** directory:

```
$ cd CVSROOT
$ vim modules
```

After you edit the **modules** file, check it back into the repository:

```
$ cd ..
$ cvs checkin CVSROOT/modules
```

Of all the administrative files in the CVSROOT module, the **modules** file is the most important. You can use this file to attach symbolic names to modules in the repository, allow access to subdirectories of a module as if they were themselves modules, and specify actions to take when checking specific files in or out.

Most repositories start with a **modules** file that allows you to check out the **modules** file with the following command, instead of the one shown earlier:

```
$ cvs checkout modules
```

With the preceding command CVS creates a subdirectory named **modules** within the working directory, instead of one named **CVSROOT**. The **modules** file is then checked out into this directory.

The following is an example of a **modules** file (the lines that start with # are comment lines and, along with blank lines, are ignored by CVS):

```
# The CVS modules file
#
# Three different line formats are valid:
#   key -a aliases...
#   key [options] directory
#   key [options] directory files...
#
# Where "options" are composed of:
#   -i prog   Run "prog" on "cvs commit" from top-level of module.
#   -o prog   Run "prog" on "cvs checkout" of module.
#   -t prog   Run "prog" on "cvs rtag" of module.
#   -u prog   Run "prog" on "cvs update" of module.
#   -d dir    Place module in directory "dir" instead of module name.
#   -l        Top-level directory only -- do not recurse.
#
# And "directory" is a path to a directory relative to $CVSROOT.
#
# The "-a" option specifies an alias.  An alias is interpreted as if
# everything on the right of the "-a" had been typed on the command line.
#
#
# You can encode a module within a module by using the special '&'
# character to interpose another module into the current module.  This
# can be useful for creating a module that consists of many directories
# spread out over the entire source repository.



# Convenient aliases
world      -a .

# CVSROOT support; run mkmodules whenever anything changes.
CVSROOT    -i mkmodules CVSROOT
modules    -i mkmodules CVSROOT modules
loginfo    -i mkmodules CVSROOT loginfo
commitinfo -i mkmodules CVSROOT commitinfo
rcsinfo    -i mkmodules CVSROOT rcsinfo
editinfo   -i mkmodules CVSROOT editinfo
# Add other modules here...
testgen    testgen
testdata1  testdata1
testdata2  testdata2
testdata3  testdata3
testdata4  testdata4
testcode   testgen/_code
cvs        cvs
```

The lines after the comment and blank lines define symbolic names for many modules. For example, the following line defines **world** to be an alias for the root of the CVS repository:

```
world      -a .
```

You can use such names in CVS commands as the names of modules. For example, the following command checks out the entire repository (probably not a good idea):

```
$ cvs checkout world
```

In the sample **modules** file, the administrative files have been given definitions that attach both a symbolic name to the file and an action (**–i mkmodules**) to take when each file is checked into the repository. The **–i mkmodules** action causes CVS to run the **mkmodules** program when the file is checked in. This program ensures that a copy of the checked-in file exists in a location where CVS can locate it.

Following the action is the name of the subdirectory in **CVSROOT** where any files associated with the symbolic name are located. Any remaining arguments on the line are the names of specific files within that directory.

The following line identifies CVSROOT as the name for the module in the directory **$CVSROOT/CVSROOT**—that is, for all the administrative files for CVS:

```
CVSROOT     -i mkmodules CVSROOT
```

Similarly the following line associates the **modules** module with the **modules** file within the **CVSROOT** directory:

```
modules     -i mkmodules CVSROOT modules
```

The preceding line allows the following command to find and check out the **modules** file:

```
$ cvs checkout modules
```

The last set of lines in the sample **modules** file associates symbolic module names with directories and files in the repository.

USING TkCVS

The cvs utility is useful enough that an X Window System interface, TkCVS (www.twobarleycorns.net/tkcvs.html), has been written for it using the Tk extension to the Tcl programming language (tcl.sourceforge.net). It provides a convenient point-and-click interface to CVS (Figure 10-5). After you have downloaded and installed TkCVS, start it by using cd to change to the directory you want to work in and entering the following command:

```
$ tkcvs &
```

All operations are available through the pull-down menus at the top of the window. Along the bottom are buttons for accessing the most common actions. A description of the action bound to a button appears when you position the mouse pointer on top of a button.

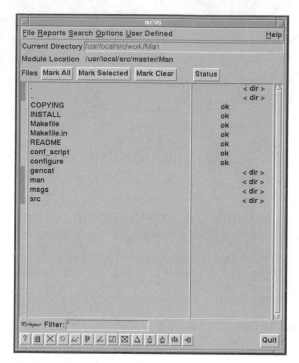

Figure 10-5   The TkCVS utility

In the middle of the window is a *browse list*. Move into a subdirectory by double-clicking the left mouse button while the mouse pointer is on the directory name in the list. Edit a file by double-clicking the filename. To select more than one file, hold down the left mouse button and drag the mouse pointer across several names. Clicking the right mouse button will *mark* all selected files. Some of the operations (such as viewing the revision log messages) will work on all marked files.

The Help pull-down menu in the upper-right corner is an excellent way to learn how TkCVS works. For example, when you select the Help menu item **CVS modules file...**, an explanation of the lines that you can add to the CVS **modules** file to support TkCVS better appears in a window. If you choose not to add these lines to the **modules** file, some TkCVS commands, such as browsing the repository, may not display all available modules.

CHAPTER SUMMARY

The operating system interface to C programs and a variety of software development tools make the Linux system well suited to programming in C. The C libraries provide general-purpose C functions that make operating system services and other functionality available to C programmers. The standard C library **libc** is always accessible to C programs, and you can specify other libraries by using the –l option to the gcc compiler.

You can write a C program using a text editor, such as vim or emacs. C programs always have a function named **main** and often include several other functions. Preprocessor directives define symbolic constants and macros and instruct the preprocessor to include header files.

gcc When you use gcc, it calls the C preprocessor followed by the C compiler and the assembler. The compiler creates assembly language code, which the assembler uses to create object modules. The linker combines these object modules into an executable file. You can use the **–Wall** option to gcc to detect *risky* constructs—ones that are legal but suggest the possibility of later problems. Other options to gcc can help locate areas of your code that might not be portable.

gdb Although using **printf** statements and the **–Wall** option can help in tracking program bugs, it is a good practice to compile C programs routinely with the **–g** option. This option causes information that can be interpreted by gdb, a symbolic debugger, to be generated as part of the executable file. When you run a program under the control of gdb, you can specify points where you want gdb to pause the program, inquire about the values of variables, display the program stack, and use a wide range of commands to learn about many other aspects of the program's behavior.

make The make utility uses a file named **Makefile** (or **makefile**) that documents the relationships among files. It determines which modules of a program are out-of-date and compiles files to keep all modules up-to-date. The dependency line, which specifies the exact dependency relationship between target and prerequisite files, is the key to the operation of a makefile. Following the dependency line are construction commands that can bring the target up-to-date. Implied dependencies, construction commands, and the make macro facility are available to simplify the writing of complex makefiles.

The Linux system includes utilities that assist in keeping track of groups of files that undergo multiple revisions, often at the hands of multiple developers. These source code management systems include CVS, the Concurrent Versions System. CVS is built on top of RCS but provides a much more extensive set of operations for managing directories of files that may be accessed and modified by many users. It is a good choice for large-scale projects and for maintaining software releases that are sent to and from other sites.

Exercises

1. What function does every C program have? Why should you split large programs into several functions?

2. What command could you use to compile **prog.c** and **func.c** into an executable named **cprog**?

3. Show two ways to instruct the C preprocessor to include the header file **/usr/include/math.h** in your C program. Assuming that the **declar.h** header file is located in the subdirectory named **headers** of your home directory, describe two ways to instruct the C preprocessor to include this header file in your C program.

4. How are the names of system libraries abbreviated on the gcc command line? Where does gcc search for libraries named in this manner? Describe how to specify your own library on the gcc command line.

5. Write a makefile that reflects the following relationships:

   a. The C source files **transactions.c** and **reports.c** are compiled to produce an executable **accts**.

   b. Both **transactions.c** and **reports.c** include a header file **accts.h**.

   c. The header file **accts.h** is composed of two other header files: **trans.h** and **reps.h**.

6. If you retrieve version 4.1 of the file **answer** for editing and then attempt to retrieve the same version again, what will CVS do? Why is CVS set up this way?

ADVANCED EXERCISES

7. Modify the **badtabs.c** program (page 409) so that it exits cleanly (with a specific return value). Compile the program and run it using gdb or another debugger. What values does the debugger report when the program finishes executing?

8. For the makefile

   ```
   $ cat Makefile
   leads: menu.o users.o resellers.o prospects.o
               gcc -o leads menu.o users.o resellers.o prospects.o

   menu.o: menu.h dialog.h inquiry.h

   users.o: menu.h dialog.h

   prospects.o: dialog.h
   ```

   identify:

   a. Targets.

b. Construction commands.

c. Prerequisites.

9. Refer to **Makefile** in exercise 8 to answer the following questions:

a. If the target **leads** is up-to-date and you then change **users.c**, what happens when you run make again? Be specific.

b. Rewrite the makefile to include the following macros:

```
OBJECTS = menu.o users.o resellers.o prospects.o
HFILES = menu.h dialog.h
```

10. Review the make info page to answer the following questions:

a. What does the –t option do?

b. If you have files named **makefile** and **Makefile** in the working directory, how can you instruct make to use **Makefile**?

c. Give two ways to define a variable so that you can use it inside a makefile.

11. Refer to the makefile for **compute** on page 402.

a. Suppose that a file in the working directory is named **clean**. What is the effect of giving the following command? Explain.

```
$ make clean
```

b. The discussion on page 401 states that the following command is not normally seen in makefiles:

```
cat num.h table.h > form.h
```

Discuss the effect of removing this construction command from the makefile while retaining the dependency line.

c. The preceding construction command works only because the file **form.h** is made up of **num.h** and **table.h**. More often **#include** directives in the target define the dependencies. Suggest a more general technique that updates **form.h** whenever **num.h** or **table.h** has a more recent modification date.

PROGRAMMING THE BOURNE AGAIN SHELL

Chapter 5 introduced the shells and Chapter 8 went into detail about the Bourne Again Shell. This chapter introduces additional Bourne Again Shell commands, builtins, and concepts that carry shell programming to a point where it can be useful. The first part of this chapter covers programming control structures, which are also known as control flow constructs. These structures allow you to write scripts that can loop over command line arguments, make decisions based on the value of a variable, set up menus, and more. The Bourne Again Shell uses the same constructs found in such high-level programming languages as C.

The next part of this chapter discusses parameters and variables, going into detail about array variables, local versus global variables, special parameters, and positional parameters. The exploration of builtin commands covers type, which displays information about a command, and read, which allows you to accept user input in a shell script. The section on the exec builtin demonstrates how exec provides an efficient way to execute a command by replacing a process and explains how you can use it to redirect input and output from within a script. The next section covers the trap builtin, which provides a way to detect and respond to operating system signals (such as that which is generated when you press CONTROL-C). The discussion of builtins concludes with a discussion of kill, which can abort a process, and getopts, which makes it easy to parse options for a shell script. (Table 11-6 on page 500 lists some of the more commonly used builtins.)

Next the chapter examines arithmetic and logical expressions and the operators that work with them. The final section walks through the design and implementation of two major shell scripts.

This chapter contains many examples of shell programs. Although they illustrate certain concepts, most use information from earlier examples as well. This overlap not only reinforces your overall knowledge of shell programming but also demonstrates how you can combine commands to solve complex tasks. Running, modifying, and experimenting with the examples in this book is a good way to become comfortable with the underlying concepts.

Do not name a shell script test

tip You can unwittingly create a problem if you give a shell script the name **test** because a Linux utility has the same name. Depending on how the **PATH** variable is set up and how you call the program, you may run your script or the utility, leading to confusing results.

This chapter illustrates concepts with simple examples, which are followed by more complex ones in sections marked "Optional." The more complex scripts illustrate traditional shell programming practices and introduce some Linux utilities often used in scripts. You can skip these sections without loss of continuity the first time you read the chapter. Return to them later when you feel comfortable with the basic concepts.

CONTROL STRUCTURES

The *control flow* commands alter the order of execution of commands within a shell script. The TC Shell uses a different syntax for these commands (page 368) than the Bourne Again Shell does. Control structures include the if...then, for...in, while, until, and case statements. In addition, the break and continue statements work in conjunction with the control structures to alter the order of execution of commands within a script.

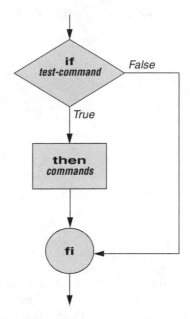

Figure 11-1   An **if...then** flowchart

if...then

The **if...then** control structure has the following syntax:

if **test-command**
    then
        commands
fi

The ***bold*** words in the syntax description are the items you supply to cause the structure to have the desired effect. The *nonbold* words are the keywords the shell uses to identify the control structure.

test builtin Figure 11-1 shows that the **if** statement tests the status returned by the ***test-command*** and transfers control based on this status. The end of the **if** structure is marked by a **fi** statement, (*if* spelled backward). The following script prompts for two words, reads them, and then uses an **if** structure to execute commands based on the result returned by the test builtin (tcsh uses the test utility) when it compares the two words. (See page 794 for information on the test utility, which is similar to the test builtin.) The test builtin returns a status of *true* if the two words are the same and *false* if they are not. Double quotation marks around **$word1** and **$word2** make sure that test works properly if you enter a string that contains a SPACE or other special character:

```
$ cat if1
echo -n "word 1: "
read word1
echo -n "word 2: "
read word2

if test "$word1" = "$word2"
    then
        echo "Match"
fi
echo "End of program."
$ if1
word 1: peach
word 2: peach
Match
End of program.
```

In the preceding example the *test-command* is **test "$word1" = "$word2"**. The test builtin returns a *true* status if its first and third arguments have the relationship specified by its second argument. If this command returns a *true* status (= 0), the shell executes the commands between the **then** and **fi** statements. If the command returns a *false* status (not = 0), the shell passes control to the statement following **fi** without executing the statements between **then** and **fi**. The effect of this **if** statement is to display **Match** if the two words are the same. The script always displays **End of program.**

Builtins   In the Bourne Again Shell, test is a builtin—part of the shell. It is also a stand-alone utility kept in **/usr/bin/test**. This chapter discusses and demonstrates many Bourne Again Shell builtins. Each bash builtin may or may not be a builtin in tcsh. You usually use the builtin version if it is available and the utility if it is not. Each version of a command may vary slightly from one shell to the next and from the utility to any of the shell builtins. See page 487 for more information on shell builtins.

Checking arguments   The next program uses an **if** structure at the beginning of a script to check that you have supplied at least one argument on the command line. The **–eq** test operator compares two integers, where the **$#** special parameter (page 480) takes on the value of the number of command line arguments. This structure displays a message and exits from the script with an exit status of 1 if you do not supply at least one argument:

```
$ cat chkargs
if test $# -eq 0
    then
        echo "You must supply at least one argument."
        exit 1
fi
echo "Program running."
```

```
$ chkargs
You must supply at least one argument.
$ chkargs abc
Program running.
```

A test like the one shown in **chkargs** is a key component of any script that requires arguments. To prevent the user from receiving meaningless or confusing information from the script, the script needs to check whether the user has supplied the appropriate arguments. Sometimes the script simply tests whether arguments exist (as in **chkargs**). Other scripts test for a specific number or specific kinds of arguments.

You can use test to ask a question about the status of a file argument or the relationship between two file arguments. After verifying that at least one argument has been given on the command line, the following script tests whether the argument is the name of a regular file (not a directory or other type of file) in the working directory. The test builtin with the –f option and the first command line argument (**$1**) check the file:

```
$ cat is_regfile
if test $# -eq 0
    then
        echo "You must supply at least one argument."
        exit 1
fi
if test -f "$1"
    then
        echo "$1 is a regular file in the working directory"
    else
        echo "$1 is NOT a regular file in the working directory"
fi
```

You can test many other characteristics of a file with test and various options. Table 11-1 lists some of these options.

Table 11-1 Options to the test builtin

Option	Tests file to see if it
–d	Exists and is a directory file
–e	Exists
–f	Exists and is a regular file (not a directory)
–r	Exists and is readable
–s	Exists and has a size greater than 0 bytes
–w	Exists and is writable
–x	Exists and is executable

Other test options provide ways to test relationships between two files, such as whether one file is newer than another. Refer to later examples in this chapter and to test on page 794 for more detailed information.

Always test the arguments

tip To keep the examples in this book short and focused on specific concepts, the code to verify arguments is often omitted or abbreviated. It is a good practice to test arguments in shell programs that other people will use. Doing so results in scripts that are easier to run and debug.

[] is a synonym for test   The following example—another version of **chkargs**—checks for arguments in a way that is more traditional for Linux shell scripts. The example uses the bracket ([]) synonym for test. Rather than using the word test in scripts, you can surround the arguments to test with brackets. The brackets must be surrounded by whitespace (SPACEs or TABs).

```
$ cat chkargs2
if [ $# -eq 0 ]
    then
        echo "Usage: chkargs2 argument..." 1>&2
        exit 1
fi
echo "Program running."
exit 0
$ chkargs2
Usage: chkargs2 arguments
$ chkargs2 abc
Program running.
```

Usage message   The error message that **chkargs2** displays is called a *usage message* and uses the **1>&2** notation to redirect its output to standard error (page 260). After issuing the usage message, **chkargs2** exits with an exit status of 1, indicating that an error has occurred. The **exit 0** command at the end of the script causes **chkargs2** to exit with a 0 status after the program runs without an error. The Bourne Again Shell returns a 0 status if you omit the status code.

The usage message is commonly employed to specify the type and number of arguments the script takes. Many Linux utilities provide usage messages similar to the one in **chkargs2**. If you call a utility or other program with the wrong number or kind of arguments, you will often see a usage message. Following is the usage message that cp displays when you call it without any arguments:

```
$ cp
cp: missing file argument
Try 'cp --help' for more information.
```

if...then...else

The introduction of an **else** statement turns the **if** structure into the two-way branch shown in Figure 11-2. The **if...then...else** control structure (available in tcsh with a slightly different syntax) has the following syntax:

if **test-command**
    then
        commands
    else
        commands
fi

Because a semicolon (;) ends a command just as a NEWLINE does, you can place **then** on the same line as **if** by preceding it with a semicolon. (Because **if** and **then** are separate builtins, they require a command separator between them; a semicolon and NEWLINE work equally well.) Some people prefer this notation for aesthetic reasons, while others like it because it saves space:

if **test-command**; *then*
        commands
    else
        commands
fi

If the **test-command** returns a *true* status, the **if** structure executes the commands between the **then** and **else** statements and then diverts control to the statement following **fi**. If the **test-command** returns a *false* status, the **if** structure executes the commands following the **else** statement.

When you run the next script, named **out**, with arguments that are filenames, it displays the files on the terminal. If the first argument is **–v** (called an option in this

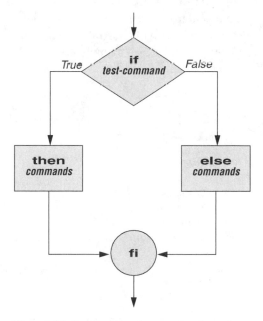

Figure 11-2   An **if**...**then**...**else** flowchart

case), **out** uses less (page 45) to display the files one page at a time. After determining that it was called with at least one argument, **out** tests its first argument to see whether it is **–v**. If the result of the test is *true* (if the first argument is **–v**), **out** uses the shift builtin to shift the arguments to get rid of the **–v** and displays the files using less. If the result of the test is *false* (if the first argument is *not* **–v**), the script uses cat to display the files:

```
$ cat out
if [ $# -eq 0 ]
    then
        echo "Usage: out [-v] filenames..." 1>&2
        exit 1
fi
if [ "$1" = "-v" ]
    then
        shift
        less -- "$@"
    else
        cat -- "$@"
fi
```

optional In **out** the –– argument to cat and less tells these utilities that no more options follow on the command line and not to consider leading hyphens (–) in the following list as indicating options. Thus –– allows you to view a file with a name that starts with a hyphen. Although not common, filenames beginning with a hyphen do occasionally occur. (You can create such a file by using the command **cat > –fname**.) The –– argument works with all Linux utilities that use the getopts builtin (page 497) to parse their options; it does not work with more and a few other utilities. This argument is particularly useful when used in conjunction with rm to remove a file whose name starts with a hyphen (**rm –– –fname**), including any that you create while experimenting with the –– argument.

if...then...elif

The **if...then...elif** control structure (Figure 11-3; not available in tcsh) has the following syntax:

if test-command
    then
        commands
    elif test-command
        then
            commands
  . . .
    else
        commands
fi

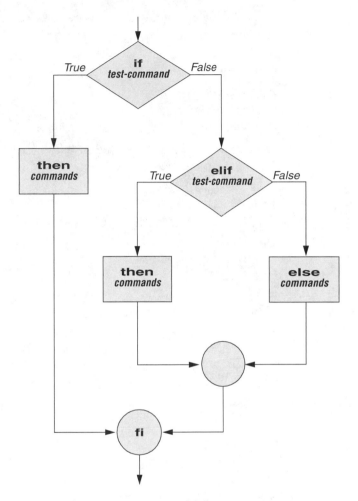

Figure 11-3   An if...then...elif flowchart

The **elif** statement combines the **else** statement and the **if** statement and allows you to construct a nested set of **if...then...else** structures (Figure 11-3). The difference between the **else** statement and the **elif** statement is that each **else** statement must be paired with a **fi** statement, whereas multiple nested **elif** statements require only a single closing **fi** statement.

The following example shows an **if...then...elif** control structure. This shell script compares three words that the user enters. The first **if** statement uses the Boolean operator AND (**–a**) as an argument to test. The test builtin returns a *true* status only if the first and second logical comparisons are *true* (that is, if **word1** matches **word2** and **word2** matches **word3**). If test returns a *true* status, the script executes the command following the next **then** statement, passes control to the statement following **fi**, and terminates:

```
$ cat if3
echo -n "word 1: "
read word1
echo -n "word 2: "
read word2
echo -n "word 3: "
read word3
if [ "$word1" = "$word2" -a "$word2" = "$word3" ]
    then
        echo "Match: words 1, 2, & 3"
    elif [ "$word1" = "$word2" ]
    then
        echo "Match: words 1 & 2"
    elif [ "$word1" = "$word3" ]
    then
        echo "Match: words 1 & 3"
    elif [ "$word2" = "$word3" ]
    then
        echo "Match: words 2 & 3"
    else
        echo "No match"
fi

$ if3
word 1: apple
word 2: orange
word 3: pear
No match
$ if3
word 1: apple
word 2: orange
word 3: apple
Match: words 1 & 3
$ if3
word 1: apple
word 2: apple
word 3: apple
Match: words 1, 2, & 3
```

If the three words are not the same, the structure passes control to the first **elif**, which begins a series of tests to see if any pair of words is the same. As the nesting continues, if any one of the **if** statements is satisfied, the structure passes control to the next **then** statement and subsequently to the statement following **fi**. Each time an **elif** statement is not satisfied, the structure passes control to the next **elif** statement. The double quotation marks around the arguments to echo that contain ampersands (&) prevent the shell from interpreting the ampersands as special characters.

optional THE lnks SCRIPT

The following script, named **lnks**, demonstrates the **if...then** and **if...then...elif** control structures. This script finds hard links to its first argument, a filename. If you provide the name of a directory as the second argument, **lnks** searches for links in that directory and all subdirectories. If you do not specify a directory, **lnks** searches the working directory and its subdirectories. This script does not locate symbolic links.

```bash
$ cat lnks
#!/bin/bash
# Identify links to a file
# Usage: lnks file [directory]

if [ $# -eq 0 -o $# -gt 2 ]; then
    echo "Usage: lnks file [directory]" 1>&2
    exit 1
fi
if [ -d "$1" ]; then
    echo "First argument cannot be a directory." 1>&2
    echo "Usage: lnks file [directory]" 1>&2
    exit 1
else
    file="$1"
fi
if [ $# -eq 1 ]; then
        directory="."
    elif [ -d "$2" ]; then
        directory="$2"
    else
        echo "Optional second argument must be a directory." 1>&2
        echo "Usage: lnks file [directory]" 1>&2
        exit 1
fi

# Check that file exists and is a regular file:
if [ ! -f "$file" ]; then
    echo "lnks: $file not found or special file" 1>&2
    exit 1
fi
# Check link count on file
set -- $(ls -l "$file")

linkcnt=$2
if [ "$linkcnt" -eq 1 ]; then
    echo "lnks: no other hard links to $file" 1>&2
    exit 0
fi

# Get the inode of the given file
set $(ls -i "$file")

inode=$1

# Find and print the files with that inode number
echo "lnks: using find to search for links..." 1>&2
find "$directory" -xdev -inum $inode -print
```

Alex has a file named **letter** in his home directory. He wants to find links to this file in his and other users' home directory file trees. In the following example, Alex calls **lnks** from his home directory to perform the search. The second argument to **lnks**, **/home**, is the pathname of the directory he wants to start the search in. The **lnks** script reports that **/home/alex/letter** and **/home/jenny/draft** are links to the same file:

```
$ lnks letter /home
lnks: using find to search for links...
/home/alex/letter
/home/jenny/draft
```

In addition to the **if...then...elif** control structure, **lnks** introduces other features that are commonly used in shell programs. The following discussion describes **lnks** section by section.

Specify the shell   The first line of the **lnks** script uses **#!** (page 265) to specify the shell that will execute the script:

```
#!/bin/bash
```

In this chapter the **#!** notation appears only in more complex examples. It ensures that the proper shell executes the script, even when the user is running a different shell or the script is called from another shell script.

Comments   The second and third lines of **lnks** are comments; the shell ignores the text that follows a pound sign up to the next NEWLINE character. These comments in **lnks** briefly identify what the file does and how to use it:

```
# Identify links to a file
# Usage: lnks file [directory]
```

Usage messages   The first **if** statement tests whether **lnks** was called with zero arguments or more than two arguments:

```
if [ $# -eq 0 -o $# -gt 2 ]; then
    echo "Usage: lnks file [directory]" 1>&2
    exit 1
fi
```

If either of these conditions is *true*, **lnks** sends a usage message to standard error and exits with a status of 1. The double quotation marks around the usage message prevent the shell from interpreting the brackets as special characters. The brackets in the usage message indicate that the **directory** argument is optional.

The second **if** statement tests whether the first command line argument (**$1**) is a directory (the **–d** argument to test returns a *true* value if the file exists and is a directory):

```
if [ -d "$1" ]; then
    echo "First argument cannot be a directory." 1>&2
    echo "Usage: lnks file [directory]" 1>&2
    exit 1
else
    file="$1"
fi
```

If the first argument is a directory, **lnks** displays a usage message and exits. If it is not a directory, **lnks** saves the value of **$1** in the **file** variable because later in the script **set** resets the command line arguments. If the value of **$1** is not saved before the **set** command is issued, its value will be lost.

Test the arguments | The next section of **lnks** is an **if...then...elif** statement:

```
if [ $# -eq 1 ]; then
        directory="."
    elif [ -d "$2" ]; then
        directory="$2"
    else
        echo "Optional second argument must be a directory." 1>&2
        echo "Usage: lnks file [directory]" 1>&2
        exit 1
fi
```

The first *test-command* determines whether the user specified a single argument on the command line. If the *test-command* returns 0 (*true*), the user-created variable named **directory** is assigned the value of the working directory (.). If the *test-command* returns *false,* the **elif** statement tests whether the second argument is a directory. If it is a directory, the **directory** variable is set equal to the second command line argument, **$2**. If **$2** is not a directory, **lnks** sends a usage message to standard error and exits with a status of 1.

The next **if** statement in **lnks** tests whether **$file** does not exist. This test keeps **lnks** from wasting time looking for links to a nonexistent file.

The **test** builtin with the three arguments **!**, **–f**, and **$file** evaluates to *true* if the file **$file** does *not* exist:

```
[ ! -f "$file" ]
```

The **!** operator preceding the **–f** argument to **test** negates its result, yielding *false* if the file **$file** *does* exist and is a regular file.

Next **lnks** uses **set** and **ls –l** to check the number of links **$file** has:

```
# Check link count on file
set -- $(ls -l "$file")

linkcnt=$2
if [ "$linkcnt" -eq 1 ]; then
    echo "lnks: no other hard links to $file" 1>&2
    exit 0
fi
```

The **set** builtin uses command substitution (page 329) to set the positional parameters to the output of **ls –l**. The second field in this output is the link count, so the user-created variable **linkcnt** is set equal to **$2**. The **––** used with **set** prevents **set** from interpreting as an option the first argument produced by **ls –l** (the first argument is the access permissions for the file and typically begins with –). The **if** statement checks whether **$linkcnt** is equal to 1; if it is, **lnks** displays a message and exits. Although this message is not truly an error message, it is redirected to standard error. The way **lnks** has been written, all informational messages are sent to standard error. Only the final product of **lnks**—the pathnames of links to the specified file—is sent to standard output, so you can redirect the output as you please.

If the link count is greater than one, **lnks** goes on to identify the *inode* (page 880) for **$file**. As explained on page 99, comparing the inodes associated with filenames is a good way to determine whether the filenames are links to the same file. The **lnks** script uses **set** to set the positional parameters to the output of **ls –i**. The first argument to **set** is the inode number for the file, so the user-created variable named **inode** is assigned the value of **$1**:

```
# Get the inode of the given file
set $(ls -i "$file")

inode=$1
```

Finally **lnks** uses the find utility (page 655) to search for files having inode numbers that match **$inode**:

```
# Find and print the files with that inode number
echo "lnks: using find to search for links..." 1>&2
find "$directory" -xdev -inum $inode -print
```

The find utility searches for files that meet the criteria specified by its arguments, beginning its search with the directory specified by its first argument (**$directory**) and searching all subdirectories. The remaining arguments specify that the filenames of files having inodes matching **$inode** should be sent to standard output. Because files in different filesystems can have the same inode number and not be linked, find must search only directories in the same filesystem as **$directory**. The **–xdev** argument prevents find from searching directories on other filesystems. Refer to page 96 for more information about filesystems and links.

The echo command preceding the find command in **lnks**, which tells the user that find is running, is included because find frequently takes a long time to run. Because **lnks** does not include a final exit statement, the exit status of **lnks** is that of the last command it runs, find.

DEBUGGING SHELL SCRIPTS

When you are writing a script such as **lnks**, it is easy to make mistakes. You can use the shell's **–x** option to help debug a script. This option causes the shell to display each command before it runs the command. Tracing a script's execution in this way can give you information about where a problem lies.

You can run **lnks** as in the previous example and cause the shell to display each command before it is executed. Either set the **–x** option for the current shell (**set –x**) so that all scripts display commands as they are run or use the **–x** option to affect only the shell that is running the script called by the command line.

```
$ bash -x lnks letter /home
+ '[' 2 -eq 0 -o 2 -gt 2 ']'
+ '[' -d letter ']'
+ file=letter
+ '[' 2 -eq 1 ']'
+ '[' -d /home ']'
+ directory=/home
+ '[' '!' -f letter ']'
...
```

PS4 Each command that the script executes is preceded by the value of the **PS4** variable—a plus sign (**+**) by default, so you can distinguish debugging output from script-produced output. You must export **PS4** if you set it in the shell that calls the script. The next command sets **PS4** to **>>>>** followed by a SPACE and exports it:

```
$ export PS4='>>>> '
```

You can also set the **–x** option of the shell running the script by putting the following **set** command at the top of the script:

```
set -x
```

Put **set –x** anywhere in the script you want to turn debugging on. Turn the debugging option off with a plus sign.

```
set +x
```

The **set –o xtrace** and **set +o xtrace** commands do the same things as **set –x** and **set +x**, respectively.

for...in

The **for...in** control structure (tcsh uses **foreach**) has the following syntax:

> *for loop-index in argument-list*
> *do*
> > *commands*
> *done*

The **for...in** structure (Figure 11-4) assigns the value of the first argument in the *argument-list* to the *loop-index* and executes the *commands* between the **do** and **done** statements. The **do** and **done** statements mark the beginning and end of the **for** loop.

After it passes control to the **done** statement, the structure assigns the value of the second argument in the *argument-list* to the *loop-index* and repeats the *commands*. The structure repeats the *commands* between the **do** and **done** statements one time

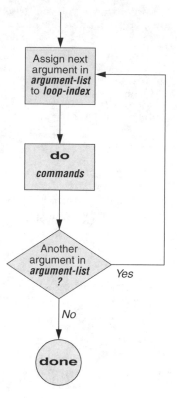

Figure 11-4 A **for...in** flowchart

for each argument in the **argument-list**. When the structure exhausts the **argument-list**, it passes control to the statement following **done**.

The following **for...in** structure assigns **apples** to the user-created variable **fruit** and then displays the value of **fruit**, which is **apples**. Next the structure assigns **oranges** to **fruit** and repeats the process. When it exhausts the argument list, the structure transfers control to the statement following **done**, which displays a message.

```
$ cat fruit
for fruit in apples oranges pears bananas
do
    echo "$fruit"
done
echo "Task complete."
$ fruit
apples
oranges
pears
bananas
Task complete.
```

The next script lists the names of the directory files in the working directory by looping over all the files, using **test** to determine which files are directories:

```
$ cat dirfiles
for i in *
do
    if [ -d "$i" ]
        then
            echo "$i"
    fi
done
```

The ambiguous file reference character * matches the names of all files (except invisible files) in the working directory. Prior to executing the **for** loop, the shell expands the * and uses the resulting list to assign successive values to the index variable **i**.

for

The **for** control structure (not available in tcsh) has the following syntax:

for loop-index
do
    commands
done

In the **for** structure the *loop-index* takes on the value of each of the command line arguments, one at a time. It is the same as the **for...in** structure (Figure 11-4) except for where it gets values for the *loop-index*. The **for** structure performs a sequence of commands, usually involving each argument in turn.

The following shell script shows a **for** structure displaying each command line argument. The first line of the script, **for arg**, implies **for arg in "$@"**, where the shell expands **"$@"** into a list of quoted command line arguments **"$1" "$2" "$3"** and so on. The balance of the script corresponds to the **for...in** structure.

```
$ cat for_test
for arg
do
    echo "$arg"
done
$ for_test candy gum chocolate
candy
gum
chocolate
```

optional

THE whos SCRIPT

The following script, named **whos**, demonstrates the usefulness of the implied **"$@"** in the **for** structure. You give **whos** one or more user or login names as arguments, and **whos** displays information about the users. The **whos** script gets the information it displays from the first and fifth fields in the **/etc/passwd** file. The first field always contains a username, and the fifth field typically contains the user's full name. You can provide a login name as an argument to **whos** to identify the user's name or provide a name as an argument to identify the username. The **whos** script is similar to the finger utility, although **whos** delivers less information.

```
$ cat whos
#!/bin/bash
# adapted from finger.sh by Lee Sailer
# UNIX/WORLD, III:11, p. 67, Fig. 2

if [ $# -eq 0 ]
    then
        echo "Usage: whos id..." 1>&2
        exit 1
fi
for id
do
    gawk -F: '{print $1, $5}' /etc/passwd |
    grep -i "$id"
done
```

Below **whos** identifies the user whose username is **chas** and the user whose name is **Marilou Smith**:

```
$ whos chas "Marilou Smith"
chas Charles Casey
msmith Marilou Smith
```

Use of "$@" The **whos** script uses a **for** statement to loop through the command line arguments. In this script the implied use of **"$@"** in the **for** loop is particularly beneficial because it causes the **for** loop to treat an argument that contains a SPACE as a single argument. This example quotes **Marilou Smith**, which causes the shell to pass it to the script as a single argument. Then the implied **"$@"** in the **for** statement causes the shell to regenerate the quoted argument **Marilou Smith** so that it is again treated as a single argument.

gawk For each command line argument, **whos** searches the **/etc/passwd** file. Inside the **for** loop the gawk utility (Chapter 12) extracts the first (**$1**) and fifth (**$5**) fields from the lines in **/etc/passwd**. The **–F:** option causes gawk to use a colon (:) as a field separator when it reads **/etc/passwd**, allowing it to break each line into fields. The gawk command sets and uses the **$1** and **$5** arguments; they are included within single quotation marks and are not interpreted by the shell. Do not confuse these arguments with positional parameters, which correspond to command line arguments. The first and fifth fields are sent to grep (page 683) via a pipe. The grep utility searches for **$id** (which has taken on the value of a command line argument) in its input. The **–i** option causes grep to ignore case as it searches; grep displays each line in its input that contains **$id**.

| at the end of a line An interesting syntactical exception that bash gives the pipe symbol (|) appears on the line with the gawk command: You do not have to quote a NEWLINE that immediately

follows a pipe symbol (that is, a pipe symbol that is the last thing on a line) to keep the NEWLINE from executing a command. Try giving the command **who |** and pressing RETURN. The shell (not tcsh) displays a secondary prompt. If you then enter **sort** followed by another RETURN, you see a sorted who list. The pipe works even though a NEWLINE follows the pipe symbol.

while

The **while** control structure (not available in tcsh) has the following syntax:

*while **test-command***
do
    commands
done

As long as the ***test-command*** (Figure 11-5) returns a *true* exit status, the **while** structure continues to execute the series of ***commands*** delimited by the **do** and **done** statements. Before each loop through the ***commands***, the structure executes the ***test-command***. When the exit status of the ***test-command*** is *false*, the structure passes control to the statement after the **done** statement.

test builtin   The following shell script first initializes the **number** variable to zero. The test builtin then determines whether **number** is less than 10. The script uses test with the **–lt** argument to perform a numerical test. For numerical comparisons, you must use **–ne** (not equal), **–eq** (equal), **–gt** (greater than), **–ge** (greater than or equal to), **–lt** (less than), or **–le** (less than or equal to). For string comparisons use = (equal) or != (not equal) when you are working with test. In this example, test has an exit status of 0 (*true*) as long as **number** is less than 10. As long as test returns *true*, the structure executes the commands between the **do** and **done** statements. See page 794 for information on the test utility, which is very similar to the test builtin.

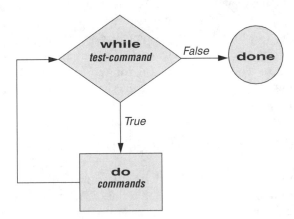

Figure 11-5   A **while** flowchart

```
$ cat count
#!/bin/bash
number=0
while [ "$number" -lt 10 ]
    do
        echo -n "$number"
        ((number +=1))
    done
echo
$ count
0123456789
$
```

The echo command following **do** displays **number**. The **–n** prevents echo from issu-ing a NEWLINE following its output. The next command uses arithmetic evaluation [((...)); page 501] to increment the value of **number** by 1. The **done** statement termi-nates the loop and returns control to the **while** statement to start the loop over again. The final echo causes **count** to send a NEWLINE character to standard output, so that the next prompt occurs in the leftmost column on the display (rather than immediately following 9).

optional   THE spell_check SCRIPT

The aspell utility checks the words in a file against a dictionary of correctly spelled words. With the **–l** option, aspell runs in list mode: Input comes from standard input and aspell sends each potentially misspelled word to standard output. The following command produces a list of possible misspellings in the file **letter.txt**:

```
$ aspell -l < letter.txt
quikly
portible
frendly
```

The next shell script, named **spell_check**, shows another use of a **while** structure. To find the incorrect spellings in a file, you can use **spell_check**, which calls aspell to check a file against a system dictionary but goes a step further: It enables you to specify a list of correctly spelled words and removes these words from the output of aspell. This script is useful for removing words that you use frequently, such as names and technical terms, that are not in a standard dictionary. Although you can duplicate the functionality of **spell_check** by using additional aspell dictionaries, the script is included here for its instructive value.

The **spell_check** script requires two filename arguments: a file containing the list of correctly spelled words and a file that you want to check. The first **if** statement ver-ifies that the user specified two arguments. The next two **if** statements verify that both arguments are readable files. (The exclamation point negates the sense of the following operator; the **–r** operator causes test to determine whether a file is read-able. The result is a test that determines whether a file is *not readable*.)

```
$ cat spell_check
#!/bin/bash
# remove correct spellings from aspell output

if [ $# -ne 2 ]
    then
        echo "Usage: spell_check file1 file2" 1>&2
        echo "file1: list of correct spellings" 1>&2
        echo "file2: file to be checked" 1>&2
        exit 1
fi

if [ ! -r "$1" ]
    then
        echo "spell_check: $1 is not readable" 1>&2
        exit 1
fi

if [ ! -r "$2" ]
    then
        echo "spell_check: $2 is not readable" 1>&2
        exit 1
fi

aspell -l < "$2" |
while read line
do
    if ! grep "^$line$" "$1" > /dev/null
        then
            echo $line
    fi
done
```

The **spell_check** script sends the output from aspell (with the −l option so that it produces a list of misspelled words on standard output) through a pipe to standard input of a **while** structure, which reads one line at a time (each line has one word on it) from standard input. The *test-command* (that is, **read line**) returns a *true* exit status as long as it receives a line from standard input.

Inside the **while** loop an **if** statement[1] monitors the return value of grep, which determines whether the line that was read is in the user's list of correctly spelled words. The pattern that grep searches for (the value of **$line**) is preceded and followed by special characters that specify the beginning and end of a line (^ and $, respectively). These special characters ensure that grep finds a match only if the

---

1. This **if** statement can also be written as

```
if ! grep -qw "$line" "$1"
```

The −q option suppresses the output from grep so that only an exit code is returned. The −w option causes grep to match only a whole word.

$line variable matches an entire line in the file of correctly spelled words. (Otherwise, grep would match a string, such as **paul**, in the output of aspell if the file of correctly spelled words contained the word **paulson**.) These special characters, together with the value of the **$line** variable, form a regular expression (Appendix A).

The output of grep is redirected to **/dev/null** (page 122) because the output is not needed; only the exit code is important. The **if** statement checks the negated exit status of grep (the leading exclamation point negates or changes the sense of the exit status—*true* becomes *false*, and vice versa), which is 0 or *true* (*false* when negated) when a matching line is found. If the exit status is *not* 0 or *false* (*true* when negated), the word was *not* in the file of correctly spelled words. The echo builtin sends a list of words that are not in the file of correctly spelled words to standard output.

Once it detects the EOF (end of file), the read builtin returns a *false* exit status. Control then passes out of the **while** structure, and the script terminates.

Before you use **spell_check**, create a file of correct spellings containing words that you use frequently but that are not in a standard dictionary. For example, if you work for a company named **Blinkenship and Klimowski, Attorneys,** you would put **Blinkenship** and **Klimowski** into the file. The following example shows how **spell_check** checks the spelling in a file named **memo** and removes **Blinkenship** and **Klimowski** from the output list of incorrectly spelled words:

```
$ aspell -l < memo
Blinkenship
Klimowski
targat
hte
$ cat word_list
Blinkenship
Klimowski
$ spell_check word_list memo
targat
hte
```

Refer to page 589 for more information on aspell.

until

The **until** (not available in tcsh) and **while** (available in tcsh with a slightly different syntax) structures are very similar, differing only in the sense of the test performed at the top of the loop. Figure 11-6 shows that **until** continues to loop *until* the *test-command* returns a *true* exit status. The **while** structure loops *while* the *test-command* continues to return a *true* or nonerror condition. The **until** control structure has the following syntax:

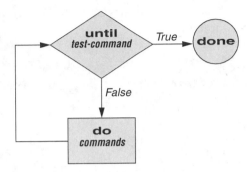

Figure 11-6 An until flowchart

*until **test-command***
do
    commands
done

The following script demonstrates an **until** structure that includes read. When the user enters the correct string of characters, the *test command* is satisfied and the structure passes control out of the loop.

```
$ cat until1
secretname=jenny
name=noname
echo "Try to guess the secret name!"
echo
until [ "$name" = "$secretname" ]
do
    echo -n "Your guess: "
    read name
done
echo "Very good."

$ until1
Try to guess the secret name!

Your guess: helen
Your guess: barbara
Your guess: rachael
Your guess: jenny
Very good
```

The following **locktty** script is similar to the lock command on Berkeley UNIX and the **Lock Screen** menu selection in GNOME. The script prompts you for a key (password) and uses an **until** control structure to lock the terminal. The **until** statement causes the system to ignore any characters typed at the keyboard until the user types in the key on a line by itself, which unlocks the terminal. The **locktty** script can keep people from using your terminal while you are away from it for short periods of time. It saves you from having to log out if you are concerned about other users using your login.

```
$ cat locktty
#! /bin/bash
# UNIX/WORLD, III:4

trap '' 1 2 3 18
stty -echo
echo -n "Key: "
read key_1
echo
echo -n "Again: "
read key_2
echo
key_3=
if [ "$key_1" = "$key_2" ]
    then
        tput clear
        until [ "$key_3" = "$key_2" ]
        do
            read key_3
        done
    else
        echo "locktty: keys do not match" 1>&2
fi
stty echo
```

Forget your password for locktty?

tip   If you forget your key (password), you will need to log in from another (virtual) terminal and kill the process running **locktty**.

trap builtin   The trap builtin (page 493; not available in tcsh) at the beginning of the **locktty** script stops a user from being able to terminate the script by sending it a signal (for example, by pressing the interrupt key). Trapping signal 18 means that no one can use CONTROL-Z (job control, a stop from a tty) to defeat the lock. (See Table 11-5 on page 494 for a list of signals.) The **stty –echo** command (page 778) causes the terminal not to display characters typed at the keyboard, thereby preventing the key that the user enters from appearing on the screen. After turning off keyboard echo, the script prompts the user for a key, reads it into the user-created variable **key_1**, prompts the user to enter the same key again, and saves it in **key_2**. The statement **key_3=** creates a variable with a NULL value. If **key_1** and **key_2** match, **locktty** clears the screen (with the **tput** command) and starts an **until** loop. The **until** loop keeps attempting to read from the terminal and assigning the input to the **key_3** variable. Once the user types in a string that matches one of the original keys (**key_2**), the **until** loop terminates and keyboard echo is turned on again.

break **AND** continue

You can interrupt a **for, while,** or **until** loop by using a **break** or **continue** statement. The **break** statement transfers control to the statement after the **done** statement, which terminates execution of the loop. The **continue** command transfers control to the **done** statement, which continues execution of the loop.

The following script demonstrates the use of these two statements. The **for...in** structure loops through the values 1–10. The first **if** statement executes its commands when the value of the index is less than or equal to 3 (**$index –le 3**). The second **if** statement executes its commands when the value of the index is greater than or equal to 8 (**$index –ge 8**). In between the two **ifs**, echo displays the value of the index. For all values up to and including 3, the first **if** statement displays **continue** and executes a **continue** statement that skips **echo $index** and the second **if** statement and continues with the next **for** statement. For the value of 8, the second **if** statement displays **break** and executes a **break** statement that exits from the **for** loop:

```
$ cat brk
for index in 1 2 3 4 5 6 7 8 9 10
    do
        if [ $index -le 3 ] ; then
            echo "continue"
            continue
        fi
#
    echo $index
#
    if [ $index -ge 8 ] ; then
        echo "break"
        break
    fi
done

$ brk
continue
continue
continue
4
5
6
7
8
break
```

case

The **case** structure (Figure 11-7, page 461) is a multiple-branch decision mechanism. The path taken through the structure depends on a match or lack of a match between the *test-string* and one of the *patterns*. The **case** control structure (tcsh uses **switch**) has the following syntax:

> *case test-string in*
>   *pattern-1)*
>   *commands-1*
>   *;;*
>   *pattern-2)*
>   *commands-2*
>   *;;*
>   *pattern-3)*
>   *commands-3*
>   *;;*
> *. . .*
> *esac*

The following **case** structure examines the character that the user enters as the *test-string*. This value is held in the variable **letter**. If the *test-string* has a value of **A**, the structure executes the command following the *pattern* **A**. The right parenthesis is part of the **case** control structure, not part of the *pattern*. If the *test-string* has a value of **B** or **C**, the structure executes the command following the matching *pattern*. The asterisk (*) indicates *any string of characters* and serves as a catchall in case there is no match. If no *pattern* matches the *test-string* and if there is no catchall (*) *pattern*, control passes to the command following the **esac** statement, without the **case** structure taking any action.

```
$ cat case1
echo -n "Enter A, B, or C: "
read letter
case "$letter" in
    A)
        echo "You entered A"
        ;;
    B)
        echo "You entered B"
        ;;
    C)
        echo "You entered C"
        ;;
    *)
        echo "You did not enter A, B, or C"
        ;;
esac

$ case1
Enter A, B, or C: B
You entered B
```

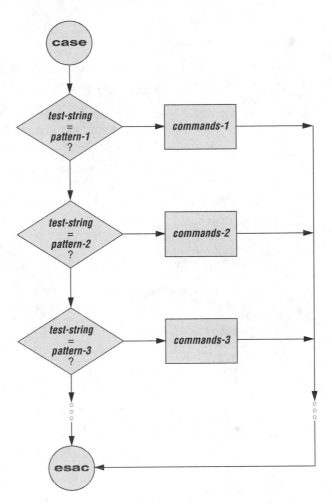

Figure 11-7 A case flowchart

The next execution of **case1** shows the user entering a lowercase **b**. Because the *test-string* **b** does not match the uppercase **B** *pattern* (or any other *pattern* in the **case** statement), the program executes the commands following the catchall *pattern* and displays a message:

```
$ case1
Enter A, B, or C: b
You did not enter A, B, or C
```

The *pattern* in the **case** structure is analogous to an ambiguous file reference. It can include any of the special characters and strings shown in Table 11-2.

Table 11-2   Patterns

Pattern	Function
*	Matches any string of characters. Use for the default case.
?	Matches any single character.
[...]	Defines a character class. Any characters enclosed within brackets are tried, one at a time, in an attempt to match a single character. A hyphen between two characters specifies a range of characters.
|	Separates alternative choices that satisfy a particular branch of the **case** structure.

The next script accepts both uppercase and lowercase letters:

```
$ cat case2
echo -n "Enter A, B, or C: "
read letter
case "$letter" in
    a|A)
        echo "You entered A"
        ;;
    b|B)
        echo "You entered B"
        ;;
    c|C)
        echo "You entered C"
        ;;
    *)
        echo "You did not enter A, B, or C"
        ;;
esac

$ case2
Enter A, B, or C: b
You entered B
```

optional   The following example shows how you can use the **case** structure to create a simple menu. The **command_menu** script uses echo to present menu items and prompt the user for a selection. (The **select** control structure [page 466] makes it much easier to code a menu.) The **case** structure then executes the appropriate utility depending on the user's selection.

```
$ cat command_menu
#!/bin/bash
# menu interface to simple commands

echo -e "\n        COMMAND MENU\n"
echo "  a.  Current date and time"
echo "  b.  Users currently logged in"
echo "  c.  Name of the working directory"
echo -e "  d.  Contents of the working directory\n"
echo -n "Enter a, b, c, or d: "
```

```
                    read answer
                    echo
                    case "$answer" in
                        a)
                            date
                            ;;
                        b)
                            who
                            ;;
                        c)
                            pwd
                            ;;
                        d)
                            ls
                            ;;
                        *)
                            echo "There is no selection: $answer"
                            ;;
                    esac

                $ command_menu

                            COMMAND MENU

                    a.  Current date and time
                    b.  Users currently logged in
                    c.  Name of the working directory
                    d.  Contents of the working directory

                Enter a, b, c, or d: a

                Wed Jan  5 12:31:12 PST 2005
```

echo –e   The –e option causes echo to interpret \n as a NEWLINE character. If you do not include this option, echo does not output the extra blank lines that make the menu easy to read but instead outputs the (literal) two-character sequence \n. The –e option causes echo to interpret several other backslash-quoted characters (Table 11-3). Remember to quote (i.e., place double quotation marks around the string) the backslash-quoted character so that the shell does not interpret it but passes the backslash and the character to echo. See **xpg_echo** (page 322) for a way to avoid using the –e option.

Table 11-3   Special characters in echo (must use **–e**)

Quoted character	echo **displays**
\a	Alert (bell)
\b	BACKSPACE
\c	Suppress trailing NEWLINE
\f	FORMFEED
\n	NEWLINE

Table 11-3   Special characters in echo (must use **–e**) (continued)

\r	RETURN
\t	Horizontal TAB
\v	Vertical TAB
\\	Backslash
\nnn	The character with the ASCII octal code *nnn;* if *nnn* is not valid, echo displays the string literally

You can also use the **case** control structure to take various actions in a script, depending on how many arguments the script is called with. The following script, named **safedit**, uses a **case** structure that branches based on the number of command line arguments (**$#**). It saves a backup copy of a file you are editing with vim.

```
$ cat safedit
#!/bin/bash
# UNIX/WORLD, IV:11
PATH=/bin:/usr/bin
script=$(basename $0)
case $# in

    0)
        vim
        exit 0
        ;;


    1)
        if [ ! -f "$1" ]
            then
                vim "$1"
                exit 0
        fi
        if [ ! -r "$1" -o ! -w "$1" ]
            then
                echo "$script: check permissions on $1" 1>&2
                exit 1
            else
                editfile=$1
        fi
        if [ ! -w "." ]
            then
                echo "$script: backup cannot be " \
                    "created in the working directory" 1>&2
                exit 1
        fi
        ;;
    *)
        echo "Usage: $script [file-to-edit]" 1>&2
        exit 1
        ;;
esac
```

```
            tempfile=/tmp/$$.$script
            cp $editfile $tempfile
            if vim $editfile
                then
                    mv $tempfile bak.$(basename $editfile)
                    echo "$script: backup file created"
                else
                    mv $tempfile editerr
                    echo "$script: edit error--copy of " \
                        "original file is in editerr" 1>&2
            fi
```

If you call **safedit** without any arguments, the **case** structure executes its first branch and calls vim without a filename argument. Because an existing file is not being edited, **safedit** does not create a backup file. (See the **:w** command on page 153 for an explanation of how to exit from vim when you have called it without a filename.) If you call **safedit** with one argument, it runs the commands in the second branch of the **case** structure and verifies that the file specified by **$1** does not yet exist or is the name of a file for which the user has read and write permission. The **safedit** script also verifies that the user has write permission for the working directory. If the user calls **safedit** with more than one argument, the third branch of the **case** structure presents a usage message and exits with a status of 1.

Set **PATH**   In addition to using a **case** structure for branching based on the number of command line arguments, the **safedit** script introduces several other features. First, at the beginning of the script, the **PATH** variable is set to search **/bin** and **/usr/bin**. Setting **PATH** in this way ensures that the commands executed by the script are standard utilities, which are kept in those directories. By setting **PATH** inside a script, you can avoid the problems that might occur if users have set **PATH** to search their own directories first and have scripts or programs with the same names as the utilities the script calls. You can also include absolute pathnames within a script to achieve this end, but this practice can make a script less portable.

Name of the   In a second **safedit** feature, the following line creates a variable named **script** and
program   assigns the simple filename of the script to it:

```
            script=$(basename $0)
```

The basename utility sends the simple filename component of its argument to standard output, which is assigned to the **script** variable, using command substitution. The **$0** holds the command the script was called with (page 481). No matter which of the following commands the user calls the script with, the output of basename is the simple filename **safedit**:

```
            $ /home/alex/bin/safedit memo
            $ ./safedit memo
            $ safedit memo
```

After the **script** variable is set, it replaces the filename of the script in usage and error messages. By using a variable that is derived from the command that invoked the script rather than a filename that is hardcoded into the script, you can create links to the script or rename it, and the usage and error messages will still provide accurate information.

Naming temporary files

A third significant feature of **safedit** relates to the use of the **$$** variable in the name of a temporary file. The statement following the **esac** statement creates and assigns a value to the **tempfile** variable. This variable contains the name of a temporary file that is stored in the **/tmp** directory, as are many temporary files. The temporary filename begins with the PID number of the shell and ends with the name of the script. Use of the PID number ensures that the filename is unique, and **safedit** will not attempt to overwrite an existing file, as might happen if two people were using **safedit** at the same time. The name of the script is appended so that, should the file be left in **/tmp** for some reason, you can figure out where it came from.

The PID number is used in front of—rather than after—**$script** in the filename because of the 14-character limit placed on filenames by some older versions of UNIX. Linux systems do not have this limitation. Because the PID number ensures the uniqueness of the filename, it is placed first so that it cannot be truncated. (If the **$script** component is truncated, the filename is still unique.) For the same reason, when a backup file is created inside the **if** control structure a few lines down in the script, the filename is composed of the string **bak.** followed by the name of the file being edited. On an older system, if **bak** were used as a suffix rather than a prefix and the original filename were 14 characters long, **.bak** might be lost and the original file would be overwritten. The **basename** utility extracts the simple filename of **$editfile** before it is prefixed with **bak.**

Fourth, **safedit** uses an unusual *test-command* in the **if** structure: **vim $editfile**. The *test-command* calls vim to edit **$editfile**. When you finish editing the file and exit from vim, vim returns an exit code. The **if** control structure uses that exit code to determine which branch to take. If the editing session completed successfully, vim returns 0 and the statements following the **then** statement are executed. If vim does not terminate normally (as would occur if the user killed [page 693] the vim process), vim returns a nonzero exit status and the script executes the statements following **else**.

select

The **select** control structure (not available in tcsh) is based on the one found in the Korn Shell. It displays a menu, assigns a value to a variable based on the user's choice of items, and executes a series of commands. The **select** control structure has the following syntax:

```
select varname [in arg . . . ]
do
    commands
done
```

The **select** structure displays a menu of the *arg* items. If you omit the keyword **in** and the list of arguments, **select** uses the positional parameters in place of the *arg* items. The menu is formatted with numbers before each item. For example, a **select** structure that begins with

```
select fruit in apple banana blueberry kiwi orange watermelon STOP
```

displays the following menu:

```
1) apple      3) blueberry   5) orange       7) STOP
2) banana     4) kiwi        6) watermelon
```

The **select** structure uses the values of the **LINES** and **COLUMNS** variables to determine the size of the display. (**LINES** has a default value of 24; **COLUMNS** has a default value of 80.) With **COLUMNS** set to 20, the menu looks like this:

```
1) apple
2) banana
3) blueberry
4) kiwi
5) orange
6) watermelon
7) STOP
```

PS3 After displaying the menu **select** displays the value of **PS3**, the special **select** prompt. The default value of **PS3** is ?# but you typically set **PS3** to a more meaningful value. When you enter a valid number (one in the menu range) in response to the **PS3** prompt, **select** sets *varname* to the argument corresponding to the number you entered. If you make an invalid entry, *varname* is set to null. Either way **select** stores your response in the keyword variable **REPLY** and then executes the *commands* between **do** and **done**. If you press RETURN without entering a choice, the shell redisplays the menu and the **PS3** prompt.

The **select** structure continues to issue the **PS3** prompt and execute the *commands* until something causes it to exit—typically a **break** or **exit** statement. A **break** statement exits from the loop and an **exit** statement exits from the script.

The following script illustrates the use of **select**:

```
$ cat fruit2
#!/bin/bash
PS3="Choose your favorite fruit from these possibilities: "
select FRUIT in apple banana blueberry kiwi orange watermelon STOP
do
    if [ "$FRUIT" == "" ]; then
        echo -e "Invalid entry.\n"
        continue
    elif [ $FRUIT = STOP ]; then
        echo "Thanks for playing!"
        break
    fi
echo "You chose $FRUIT as your favorite."
echo -e "That is choice number $REPLY.\n"
done
```

```
$ fruit2
1) apple       3) blueberry   5) orange       7) STOP
2) banana      4) kiwi        6) watermelon
Choose your favorite fruit from these possibilities: 3
You chose blueberry as your favorite.
That is choice number 3.

Choose your favorite fruit from these possibilities: 99
Invalid entry.

Choose your favorite fruit from these possibilities: 7
Thanks for playing!
```

After setting the **PS3** prompt and establishing the menu with the **select** statement, **fruit2** executes the *commands* between **do** and **done**. If the user makes an invalid entry, the shell sets *varname* (**$FRUIT**) to a null value, so **fruit2** first tests whether **$FRUIT** is null. If it is, echo displays an error and **continue** causes the shell to redisplay the **PS3** prompt. If the entry is valid, the script tests whether the user wants to stop. If so, echo displays a message and **break** exits from the **select** structure (and from the script). If the user entered a valid response and does not want to stop, the script displays the name and number of the user's response. (See page 463 for information about the –e option to echo.)

Here Document

A Here document allows you to redirect input to a shell script from within the shell script itself. A Here document is so called because it is *here*—immediately accessible in the shell script—instead of *there,* perhaps in another file.

The following script, named **birthday**, contains a Here document. The two less than (**<<**) symbols in the first line indicate that a Here document follows. One or more characters that delimit the Here document follow the less than symbols—this example uses a plus sign. Whereas the opening delimiter must appear adjacent to the less than symbols, the closing delimiter must be on a line by itself. The shell sends everything between the two delimiters to the process as standard input. In the example it is as though you had redirected standard input to grep from a file, except that the file is embedded in the shell script:

```
$ cat birthday
grep -i "$1" <<+
Alex    June 22
Barbara February 3
Darlene May 8
Helen   March 13
Jenny   January 23
Nancy   June 26
+
$ birthday Jenny
Jenny   January 23
```

```
$ birthday june
Alex    June 22
Nancy   June 26
```

When you run **birthday**, it lists all the Here document lines that contain the argument you called it with. In this case the first time **birthday** is run, it displays Jenny's birthday because it is called with an argument of **Jenny**. The second run displays all the birthdays in June. The –i argument causes grep's search not to be case sensitive.

optional   The next script, named **bundle**,[2] includes a clever use of a Here document. The **bundle** script is an elegant example of a script that creates a shell archive (**shar**) file. The script creates a file that is itself a shell script containing several other files as well as the code to re-create the original files:

```
$ cat bundle
#!/bin/bash
# bundle:  group files into distribution package

echo "# To unbundle, bash this file"
for i
do
    echo "echo $i 1>&2"
    echo "cat >$i <<'End of $i'"
    cat $i
    echo "End of $i"
done
```

Just as the shell does not treat special characters that occur in standard input of a shell script as special, so the shell does not treat the special characters that occur between the delimiters in a Here document as special.

As the following example shows, the output of **bundle** is a shell script, which is redirected to a file named **bothfiles**. It contains the contents of each file given as an argument to **bundle** (**file1** and **file2** in this case) inside a Here document. To extract the original files from **bothfiles**, you simply run it as an argument to a bash command. Before each Here document is a cat command that causes the Here document to be written to a new file when **bothfiles** is run:

```
$ cat file1
This is a file.
It contains two lines.
$ cat file2
This is another file.
It contains
three lines.
```

---

2. Thanks to Brian W. Kernighan and Rob Pike, *The Unix Programming Environment* (Englewood Cliffs, N.J.: Prentice-Hall, 1984), 98. Reprinted with permission.

```
$ bundle file1 file2 > bothfiles
$ cat bothfiles
# To unbundle, bash this file
echo file1 1>&2
cat >file1 <<'End of file1'
This is a file.
It contains two lines.
End of file1
echo file2 1>&2
cat >file2 <<'End of file2'
This is another file.
It contains
three lines.
End of file2
```

In the next example, **file1** and **file2** are removed before **bothfiles** is run. The **both-files** script echoes the names of the files it creates as it creates them. The ls command then shows that **bothfiles** has re-created **file1** and **file2**:

```
$ rm file1 file2
$ bash bothfiles
file1
file2
$ ls
bothfiles
file1
file2
```

FILE DESCRIPTORS

As discussed on page 260, before a process can read from or write to a file it must open that file. When a process opens a file, Linux associates a number (called a *file descriptor*) with the file. Each process has its own set of open files and its own file descriptors. After opening a file, a process reads from and writes to that file by referring to its file descriptor. When it no longer needs the file, the process closes the file, freeing the file descriptor.

A typical Linux process starts with three open files: standard input (file descriptor 0), standard output (file descriptor 1), and standard error (file descriptor 2). Often those are the only files the process needs. Recall that you redirect standard output with the symbol > or the symbol **1>** and that you redirect standard error with the symbol **2>**. Although you can redirect other file descriptors, because file descriptors other than 0, 1, and 2 do not have any special conventional meaning, it is rarely useful to do so.

The exception is in programs that you write yourself, in which case you control the meaning of the file descriptors and can take advantage of redirection.

Opening a file descriptor   The Bourne Again Shell opens files using the exec builtin as follows:

> *exec n> outfile*
> *exec m< infile*

The first line opens *outfile* for output and holds it open, associating it with file descriptor *n*. The second line opens *infile* for input and holds it open, associating it with file descriptor *m*.

Duplicating a file descriptor   The <& token duplicates an input file descriptor; use >& to duplicate an output file descriptor. You can duplicate a file descriptor by making it refer to the same file as another open file descriptor, such as standard input or output. Use the following format to open or redirect file descriptor *n* as a duplicate of file descriptor *m:*

> *exec n<&m*

Once you have opened a file, you can use it for input and output in two different ways. First, you can use I/O redirection on any command line, redirecting standard output to a file descriptor with >&*n* or redirecting standard input from a file descriptor with <&*n*. Second, you can use the read (page 487) and echo builtins. If you invoke other commands, including functions (page 315), they inherit these open files and file descriptors. When you have finished using a file, you can close it with

> *exec n<&–*

When you invoke the shell function in the next example, named **mycp**, with two arguments, it copies the file named by the first argument to the file named by the second argument. If you supply only one argument, the script copies the file named by the argument to standard output. If you invoke **mycp** with no arguments, it copies standard input to standard output.

A function is not a shell script

tip   The **mycp** example is a shell function; it will not work as you expect if you execute it as a shell script. (It will work: The function will be created in a very short-lived subshell, which is probably of little use.) You can enter this function from the keyboard. If you put the function in a file, you can run it as an argument to the . (dot) builtin (page 259). You can also put the function in a startup file if you want it to be always available (page 317).

```
function mycp ()
{
case $# in
    0)
        # zero arguments
        # file descriptor 3 duplicates standard input
        # file descriptor 4 duplicates standard output
        exec 3<&0 4<&1
        ;;
    1)
        # one argument
        # open the file named by the argument for input
        # and associate it with file descriptor 3
        # file descriptor 4 duplicates standard output
        exec 3< $1 4<&1
        ;;
    2)
        # two arguments
        # open the file named by the first argument for input
        # and associate it with file descriptor 3
        # open the file named by the second argument for output
        # and associate it with file descriptor 4
        exec 3< $1 4> $2
        ;;
    *)
        echo "Usage: mycp [source [dest]]"
        return 1
        ;;
esac

# call cat with input coming from file descriptor 3
# and output going to file descriptor 4
cat <&3 >&4

# close file descriptors 3 and 4
exec 3<&- 4<&-
}
```

The real work of this function is done in the line that begins with cat. The rest of the script arranges for file descriptors 3 and 4, which are the input and output of the cat command, to be associated with the appropriate files.

optional   The next program takes two filenames on the command line, sorts both, and sends the output to temporary files. The program then merges the sorted files to standard output, preceding each line by a number that indicates which file it came from.

```
$ cat sortmerg
#!/bin/bash
usage ()
{
if [ $# -ne 2 ]; then
    echo "Usage: $0 file1 file2" 2>&1
    exit 1
    fi
}
```

```
# Default temporary directory
: ${TEMPDIR:=/tmp}

# Check argument count
usage "$@"

# Set up temporary files for sorting
file1=$TEMPDIR/$$.file1
file2=$TEMPDIR/$$.file2

# Sort
sort $1 > $file1
sort $2 > $file2

# Open $file1 and $file2 for reading. Use file descriptors 3 and 4.
exec 3<$file1
exec 4<$file2

# Read the first line from each file to figure out how to start.
read Line1 <&3
status1=$?
read Line2 <&4
status2=$?

# Strategy: while there is still input left in both files:
#    Output the line that should come first.
#    Read a new line from the file that line came from.
while [ $status1 -eq 0 -a $status2 -eq 0 ]
    do
        if [[ "$Line2" > "$Line1" ]]; then
            echo -e "1.\t$Line1"
            read -u3 Line1
            status1=$?
        else
            echo -e "2.\t$Line2"
            read -u4 Line2
            status2=$?
        fi
    done

# Now one of the files is at end-of-file.
# Read from each file until the end.
# First file1:
while [ $status1 -eq 0 ]
    do
        echo -e "1.\t$Line1"
        read Line1 <&3
        status1=$?
    done
# Next file2:
while [[ $status2 -eq 0 ]]
    do
        echo -e "2.\t$Line2"
        read Line2 <&4
        status2=$?
    done
```

```
                     # Close and remove both input files
                     exec 3<&- 4<&-
                     rm -f $file1 $file2
                     exit 0
```

Parameters and Variables

Shell parameters and variables were introduced on page 277. This section adds to the previous coverage with a discussion of array variables, global versus local variables, special and positional parameters, and expanding null and unset variables.

Array Variables

The Bourne Again Shell supports one-dimensional array variables. The subscripts are integers with zero-based indexing (i.e., the first element of the array has the subscript 0). The following format declares and assigns values to an array:

> *name=(element1 element2 ...)*

The following example assigns four values to the array **NAMES**:

```
$ NAMES=(max helen sam zach)
```

You reference a single element of an array as follows:

```
$ echo ${NAMES[2]}
sam
```

The subscripts [*] and [@] both extract the entire array but work differently when used within double quotation marks. An @ produces an array that is a duplicate of the original array; an * produces a single element of an array (or a plain variable) that holds all the elements of the array separated by the first character in **IFS** (normally a SPACE). In the following example, the array **A** is filled with the elements of the **NAMES** variable using an *, and **B** is filled using an @. The declare builtin with the **–a** option displays the values of the arrays (and reminds you that bash uses zero-based indexing for arrays):

```
$ A=("${NAMES[*]}")
$ B=("${NAMES[@]}")

$ declare -a
declare -a A='([0]="max helen sam zach")'
declare -a B='([0]="max" [1]="helen" [2]="sam" [3]="zach")'
...
declare -a NAMES='([0]="max" [1]="helen" [2]="sam" [3]="zach")'
```

From the output of declare, you can see that **NAMES** and **B** have multiple elements. In contrast, **A**, which was assigned its value with an * within double quotation marks, has only one element: **A** has all its elements enclosed between double quotation marks.

In the next example, echo attempts to display element 1 of array **A**. Nothing is displayed because **A** has only one element and that element has an index of 0. Element 0 of array **A** holds all four names. Element 1 of **B** holds the second item in the array and element 0 holds the first item.

```
$ echo ${A[1]}

$ echo ${A[0]}
max helen sam zach
$ echo ${B[1]}
helen
$ echo ${B[0]}
max
```

You can apply the ${#*name*[*]} operator to array variables, returning the number of elements in the array:

```
$ echo ${#NAMES[*]}
4
```

The same operator, when given the index of an element of an array in place of *, returns the length of the element:

```
$ echo ${#NAMES[1]}
5
```

You can use subscripts on the left side of an assignment statement to replace selected elements of the array:

```
$ NAMES[1]=alex
$ echo ${NAMES[*]}
max alex sam zach
```

LOCALITY OF VARIABLES

By default variables are local to the process in which they are declared. Thus a shell script does not have access to variables declared in your login shell unless you explicitly make the variables available (global). Under bash, export makes a variable available to child processes. Under tcsh, setenv (page 356) assigns a value to a variable and makes it available to child processes. The examples in this section use the bash syntax but the theory applies to both shells.

Once you use the export builtin with a variable name as an argument, the shell places the value of the variable in the calling environment of child processes. This *call by value* gives each child process a copy of the variable for its own use.

The following **extest1** shell script assigns a value of **american** to the variable named **cheese** and then displays its filename (**extest1**) and the value of **cheese**. The **extest1** script then calls **subtest**, which attempts to display the same information. Next **subtest** declares a **cheese** variable and displays its value. When **subtest** finishes, it returns control to the parent process, which is executing **extest1**. At this point **extest1** again displays the value of the original **cheese** variable.

```
$ cat extest1
cheese=american
echo "extest1 1: $cheese"
subtest
echo "extest1 2: $cheese"
$ cat subtest
echo "subtest 1: $cheese"
cheese=swiss
echo "subtest 2: $cheese"
$ extest1
extest1 1: american
subtest 1:
subtest 2: swiss
extest1 2: american
```

The **subtest** script never receives the value of **cheese** from **extest1**, and **extest1** never loses the value. Unlike in the real world, a child can never affect its parent's attributes. When a process attempts to display the value of a variable that has not been declared, as is the case with **subtest**, the process displays nothing; the value of an undeclared variable is that of a null string.

The following **extest2** script is the same as **extest1** except that it uses export to make **cheese** available to the **subtest** script:

```
$ cat extest2
export cheese=american
echo "extest2 1: $cheese"
subtest
echo "extest2 2: $cheese"
$ extest2
extest2 1: american
subtest 1: american
subtest 2: swiss
extest2 2: american
```

Here the child process inherits the value of **cheese** as **american** and, after displaying this value, changes *its copy* to **swiss**. When control is returned to the parent, the parent's copy of **cheese** retains its original value: **american**.

An export builtin can optionally include an assignment:

```
export cheese=american
```

The preceding statement is equivalent to the following two statements:

```
cheese=american
export cheese
```

Although it is rarely done, you can export a variable before you assign a value to it. You do not need to export an already-exported variable a second time after you change its value. For example, you do not usually need to export **PATH** when you assign a value to it in **~/.bash_profile** because it is typically exported in the **/etc/profile** global startup file.

FUNCTIONS

Because functions run in the same environment as the shell that calls them, variables are implicitly shared by a shell and a function it calls.

```
$ function nam () {
> echo $myname
> myname=zach
> }

$ myname=sam
$ nam
sam
$ echo $myname
zach
```

In the preceding example, the **myname** variable is set to **sam** in the interactive shell. Then the **nam** function is called. It displays the value of **myname** it has (**sam**) and sets **myname** to **zach**. The final echo shows that, in the interactive shell, the value of **myname** has been changed to **zach**.

Function local variables

Local variables are helpful in a function written for general use. Because the function is called by many scripts that may be written by different programmers, you need to make sure that the names of the variables used within the function do not interact with variables of the same name in the programs that call the function. Local variables eliminate this problem. When used within a function, the typeset builtin declares a variable to be local to the function it is defined in.

The next example shows the use of a local variable in a function. It uses two variables named **count**. The first is declared and assigned a value of 10 in the interactive shell. Its value never changes, as echo verifies after **count_down** is run. The other **count** is declared, using typeset, to be local to the function. Its value, which is unknown outside the function, ranges from 4 to 1, as the echo command within the function confirms.

The example shows the function being entered from the keyboard; it is not a shell script. (See the tip "A function is not a shell script" on page 471).

```
$ function count_down () {
> typeset count
> count=$1
> while [ $count -gt 0 ]
> do
> echo "$count..."
> ((count=count-1))
> sleep 1
> done
> echo "Blast Off."
> }
$ count=10
$ count_down 4
4...
3...
2...
1...
Blast Off\!
$ echo $count
10
```

The ((**count=count–1**)) assignment is enclosed between double parentheses, which cause the shell to perform an arithmetic evaluation (page 501). Within the double parentheses you can reference shell variables without the leading dollar sign (**$**).

SPECIAL PARAMETERS

Special parameters enable you to access useful values pertaining to command line arguments and the execution of shell commands. You reference a shell special parameter by preceding a special character with a dollar sign (**$**). As with positional parameters, it is not possible to modify the value of a special parameter by assignment.

$$: PID NUMBER

The shell stores in the **$$** parameter the PID number of the process that is executing it. In the following interaction, echo displays the value of this variable and the ps utility confirms its value. Both commands show that the shell has a PID number of 5209:

```
$ echo $$
5209
$ ps
  PID TTY          TIME CMD
 5209 pts/1    00:00:00 bash
 6015 pts/1    00:00:00 ps
```

Because echo is built into the shell, the shell does not have to create another process when you give an echo command. However, the results are the same whether echo is a builtin or not, because the shell substitutes the value of **$$** *before* it forks a new process to run a command. Try using the echo utility (**/bin/echo**), which is run by another process, and see what happens. In the following example, the shell substitutes the value of $$ and passes that value to cp as a prefix for a filename:

```
$ echo $$
8232
$ cp memo $$.memo
$ ls
8232.memo memo
```

Incorporating a PID number in a filename is useful for creating unique filenames when the meanings of the names do not matter; it is often used in shell scripts for creating names of temporary files. When two people are running the same shell script, these unique filenames keep them from inadvertently sharing the same temporary file.

The following example demonstrates that the shell creates a new shell process when it runs a shell script. The **id2** script displays the PID number of the process running it (not the process that called it—the substitution for $$ is performed by the shell that is forked to run **id2**):

```
$ cat id2
echo "$0 PID= $$"
$ echo $$
8232
$ id2
./id2 PID= 8362
$ echo $$
8232
```

The first echo displays the PID number of the interactive shell. Then **id2** displays its name (**$0**) and the PID of the subshell that it is running in. The last echo shows that the PID number of the interactive shell has not changed.

$!** The value of the PID number of the last process that you ran in the background is stored in **$! (not available in tcsh). The following example executes sleep as a background task and uses echo to display the value of **$!**:

```
$ sleep 60 &
8376
$ echo $!
8376
```

$?: EXIT STATUS

When a process stops executing for any reason, it returns an *exit status* to the parent process. The exit status is also referred to as a *condition code* or a *return code*. The **$?** (**$status** under tcsh) variable stores the exit status of the last command.

By convention a nonzero exit status represents a *false* value and means that the command failed. A zero is *true* and indicates that the command was successful. In the following example, the first ls command succeeds and the second fails:

```
$ ls es
es
$ echo $?
0
$ ls xxx
ls: xxx: No such file or directory
$ echo $?
1
```

You can specify the exit status that a shell script returns by using the exit builtin, followed by a number, to terminate the script. If you do not use exit with a number to terminate a script, the exit status of the script is that of the last command the script ran.

```
$ cat es
echo This program returns an exit status of 7.
exit 7
$ es
This program returns an exit status of 7.
$ echo $?
7
$ echo $?
0
```

The es shell script displays a message and terminates execution with an exit command that returns an exit status of 7, the user-defined exit status in this script. The first echo then displays the value of the exit status of es. The second echo displays the value of the exit status of the first echo. The value is 0 because the first echo was successful.

Positional Parameters

The *positional* parameters comprise the command name and command line arguments. They are called *positional* because within a shell script, you refer to them by their position on the command line. Only the set builtin (page 484) allows you to change the values of positional parameters with one exception: You cannot change the value of the command name from within a script. The tcsh set builtin does not change the values of positional parameters.

$#: Number of Command Line Arguments

The $# parameter holds the number of arguments on the command line (positional parameters), not counting the command itself:

```
$ cat num_args
echo "This script was called with $# arguments."
$ num_args sam max zach
This script was called with 3 arguments.
```

$0: NAME OF THE CALLING PROGRAM

The shell stores the name of the command you used to call a program in parameter $0. This parameter is numbered zero because it appears before the first argument on the command line:

```
$ cat abc
echo "The command used to run this script is $0"
$ abc
The command used to run this script is ./abc
$ /home/sam/abc
The command used to run this script is /home/sam/abc
```

The preceding shell script uses echo to verify the name of the script you are executing. You can use the basename utility and command substitution to extract and display the simple filename of the command:

```
$ cat abc2
echo "The command used to run this script is $(basename $0)"
$ /home/sam/abc2
The command used to run this script is abc2
```

$1 – $n: COMMAND LINE ARGUMENTS

The first argument on the command line is represented by parameter $1, the second argument by $2, and so on up to $n. For values of n over 9, the number must be enclosed within braces. For example, the twelfth command line argument is represented by ${12}. The following script displays positional parameters that hold command line arguments:

```
$ cat display_5args
echo First 5 arguments are $1 $2 $3 $4 $5

$ display_5args jenny alex helen
First 5 arguments are jenny alex helen
```

The **display_5args** script displays the first five command line arguments. The shell assigns a null value to each parameter that represents an argument that is not present on the command line. Thus the $4 and $5 variables have null values in this example.

$*   The $* variable represents all the command line arguments, as the **display_all** program demonstrates:

```
$ cat display_all
echo All arguments are $*

$ display_all a b c d e f g h i j k l m n o p
All arguments are a b c d e f g h i j k l m n o p
```

Enclose references to positional parameters between double quotation marks. The quotation marks are particularly important when you are using positional parameters as arguments to commands. Without double quotation marks, a positional parameter that is not set or that has a null value disappears:

```
$ cat showargs
echo "$0 was called with $# arguments, the first is :$1:."

$ showargs a b c
./showargs was called with 3 arguments, the first is :a:.
$ echo $xx

$ showargs $xx a b c
./showargs was called with 3 arguments, the first is :a:.
$ showargs "$xx" a b c
./showargs was called with 4 arguments, the first is ::.
```

The **showargs** script displays the number of arguments (**$#**) followed by the value of the first argument enclosed between colons. The preceding example first calls **showargs** with three simple arguments. Next the echo command demonstrates that the **$xx** variable, which is not set, has a null value. In the final two calls to **showargs**, the first argument is **$xx**. In the first case the command line becomes **showargs a b c**; the shell passes **showargs** three arguments. In the second case the command line becomes **showargs "" a b c**, which results in calling **showargs** with four arguments. The difference in the two calls to **showargs** illustrates a subtle potential problem that you should keep in mind when using positional parameters that may not be set or that may have a null value.

"$*" versus "$@"   The **$*** and **$@** parameters work the same way except when they are enclosed within double quotation marks. Using **"$***" yields a single argument (with SPACEs or the value of **IFS** [page 288] between the positional parameters), whereas **"$@"** produces a list wherein each positional parameter is a separate argument. This difference typically makes **"$@"** more useful than **"$***" in shell scripts.

The following scripts help to explain the difference between these two special parameters. In the second line of both scripts, the single quotation marks keep the shell from interpreting the enclosed special characters so they can be displayed as themselves. The **bb1** script shows that **set "$***" assigns multiple arguments to the first command line parameter:

```
$ cat bb1
set "$*"
echo $# parameters with '"$*"'
echo 1: $1
echo 2: $2
echo 3: $3
```

```
$ bb1 a b c
1 parameters with "$*"
1: a b c
2:
3:
```

The **bb2** script shows that **set "$@"** assigns each argument to a different command line parameter:

```
$ cat bb2
set "$@"
echo $# parameters with '"$@"'
echo 1: $1
echo 2: $2
echo 3: $3
$
$ bb2 a b c
3 parameters with "$@"
1: a
2: b
3: c
```

shift: PROMOTES COMMAND LINE ARGUMENTS

The shift builtin promotes each command line argument. The first argument (which was **$1**) is discarded. The second argument (which was **$2**) becomes the first argument (now **$1**), the third becomes the second, and so on. Because no "unshift" command exists, you cannot bring back arguments that have been discarded. An optional argument to shift specifies the number of positions to shift (and the number of arguments to discard); the default is 1.

The following **demo_shift** script is called with three arguments. Double quotation marks around the arguments to echo preserve the spacing of the output. The program displays the arguments and shifts them repeatedly until there are no more arguments left to shift:

```
$ cat demo_shift
echo "arg1= $1     arg2= $2     arg3= $3"
shift
echo "arg1= $1     arg2= $2     arg3= $3"
shift
echo "arg1= $1     arg2= $2     arg3= $3"
shift
echo "arg1= $1     arg2= $2     arg3= $3"
shift
$ demo_shift alice helen jenny
arg1= alice    arg2= helen    arg3= jenny
arg1= helen    arg2= jenny    arg3=
arg1= jenny    arg2=     arg3=
arg1=     arg2=     arg3=
```

Repeatedly using shift is a convenient way to loop over all the command line arguments in shell scripts that expect an arbitrary number of arguments. See page 442 for a shell script that uses shift.

set: INITIALIZES COMMAND LINE ARGUMENTS

When you call the set builtin with one or more arguments, it assigns the values of the arguments to the positional parameters, starting with $1 (not available in tcsh). The following script uses set to assign values to the positional parameters $1, $2, and $3:

```
$ cat set_it
set this is it
echo $3 $2 $1
$ set_it
it is this
```

Combining command substitution (page 329) with the set builtin is a convenient way to get standard output of a command in a form that can be easily manipulated in a shell script. The following script shows how to use date and set to provide the date in a useful format. The first command shows the output of date. Then cat displays the contents of the **dateset** script. The first command in this script uses command substitution to set the positional parameters to the output of the date utility. The next command, **echo $***, displays all positional parameters resulting from the previous set. Subsequent commands display the values of parameters $1, $2, $3, and $4. The final command displays the date in a format you can use in a letter or report:

```
$ date
Wed Jan  5 23:39:18 PST 2005
$ cat dateset
set $(date)
echo $*
echo
echo "Argument 1: $1"
echo "Argument 2: $2"
echo "Argument 3: $3"
echo "Argument 6: $6"
echo
echo "$2 $3, $6"

$ dateset
Wed Jan 5 23:39:25 PST 2005

Argument 1: Wed
Argument 2: Jan
Argument 3: 5
Argument 6: 2005

Jan 5, 2005
```

You can also use the +*format* argument to date (page 630) to modify the format of its output.

When used without any arguments, set displays a list of the shell variables that are set, including user-created variables and keyword variables. Under bash, this list is the same as that displayed by declare and typeset when they are called without any arguments.

The set builtin also accepts options that let you customize the behavior of the shell (not available in tcsh). For more information refer to "set ±o: Turns Shell Features On and Off" on page 319.

EXPANDING NULL AND UNSET VARIABLES

The expression ${name} (or just $name if it is not ambiguous) expands to the value of the **name** variable. If **name** is null or not set, bash expands ${name} to a null string. The Bourne Again Shell provides the following alternatives to accepting the expanded null string as the value of the variable:

- Use a default value for the variable.
- Use a default value and assign that value to the variable.
- Display an error.

You can choose one of these alternatives by using a modifier with the variable name. In addition, you can use set –o nounset (page 321) to cause bash to display an error and exit from a script whenever an unset variable is referenced.

:– USES A DEFAULT VALUE

The :– modifier uses a default value in place of a null or unset variable while allowing a nonnull variable to represent itself:

> ${name:–default}

The shell interprets :– as "If *name* is null or unset, expand *default* and use the expanded value in place of *name*; else use *name*." The following command lists the contents of the directory named by the **LIT** variable. If **LIT** is null or unset, it lists the contents of **/home/alex/literature**:

```
$ ls ${LIT:-/home/alex/literature}
```

The default can itself have variable references that are expanded:

```
$ ls ${LIT:-$HOME/literature}
```

:= ASSIGNS A DEFAULT VALUE

The :– modifier does not change the value of a variable. You may want to change the value of a null or unset variable to its default in a script, however. You can do so with the := modifier:

> ${name:=default}

The shell expands the expression ${name:=default} in the same manner as it expands ${name:–default} but also sets the value of *name* to the expanded value of *default*. If a script contains a line such as the following and **LIT** is unset or null at the time this line is executed, **LIT** is assigned the value **/home/alex/literature**:

> `$ ls ${LIT:=/home/alex/literature}`

: builtin   Shell scripts frequently start with the : (colon) builtin followed on the same line by the := expansion modifier to set any variables that may be null or unset. The : builtin evaluates each token in the remainder of the command line but does not execute any commands. Without the leading colon (:), the shell evaluates and attempts to execute the "command" that results from the evaluation.

Use the following syntax to set a default for a null or unset variable in a shell script (there is a SPACE following the first colon):

> : ${name:=default}

When a script needs a directory for temporary files and uses the value of **TEMPDIR** for the name of this directory, the following line makes **TEMPDIR** default to **/tmp**:

> `: ${TEMPDIR:=/tmp}`

:? DISPLAYS AN ERROR MESSAGE

Sometimes a script needs the value of a variable but you cannot supply a reasonable default at the time you write the script. If the variable is null or unset, the :? modifier causes the script to display an error message and terminate with an exit status of 1:

> ${name:?message}

You must quote *message* if it contains SPACEs. If you omit *message,* the shell displays the default error message (**parameter null or not set**). Interactive shells do not exit when you use :?. In the following command, **TESTDIR** is not set so the shell displays on standard error the expanded value of the string following :?. In this case the string includes command substitution for date, with the **%T** format being followed by the string **error, variable not set.**

```
cd ${TESTDIR:?$(date +%T) error, variable not set.}
bash: TESTDIR: 16:16:14 error, variable not set.
```

BUILTIN COMMANDS

Builtin commands were introduced in Chapter 5. Commands that are built into a shell do not fork a new process when you execute them. This section discusses the type, read, exec, trap, kill, and getopts builtins and concludes with Table 11-6 on page 500, which lists many bash builtins. See Table 9-10 on page 377 for a list of tcsh builtins.

type: DISPLAYS INFORMATION ABOUT A COMMAND

The type builtin (use which under tcsh) provides information about a command:

```
$ type cat echo who if lt
cat is hashed (/bin/cat)
echo is a shell builtin
who is /usr/bin/who
if is a shell keyword
lt is aliased to 'ls -ltrh | tail'
```

The preceding output shows the files that would be executed if you gave **cat** or **who** as a command. Because cat has already been called from the current shell, it is in the *hash table* (page 878) and type reports that **cat is hashed**. The output also shows that a call to **echo** runs the echo builtin, **if** is a keyword, and **lt** is an alias.

read: ACCEPTS USER INPUT

When you begin writing shell scripts, you soon realize that one of the most common tasks for user-created variables is storing information a user enters in response to a prompt. Using read, scripts can accept input from the user and store that input in variables. See page 361 for information about reading user input under tcsh. The read builtin reads one line from standard input and assigns the words on the line to one or more variables:

```
$ cat read1
echo -n "Go ahead: "
read firstline
echo "You entered: $firstline"
$ read1
Go ahead: This is a line.
You entered: This is a line.
```

The first line of the **read1** script uses echo to prompt you to enter a line of text. The **–n** option suppresses the following NEWLINE, allowing you to enter a line of text on the same line as the prompt. The second line reads the text into the variable **firstline**. The third line verifies the action of read by displaying the value of **firstline**. The variable is quoted (along with the text string) in this example because you, as the script writer, cannot anticipate which characters the user might enter in response to the prompt. Consider what would happen if the variable were not quoted and the user entered * in response to the prompt:

```
$ cat read1_no_quote
echo -n "Go ahead: "
read firstline
echo You entered: $firstline
$ read1_no_quote
Go ahead: *
You entered: read1 read1_no_quote script.1
$ ls
read1    read1_no_quote    script.1
```

The ls command lists the same words as the script, demonstrating that the shell expands the asterisk into a list of files in the working directory. When the variable $firstline is surrounded by double quotation marks, the shell does not expand the asterisk. Thus the read1 script behaves correctly:

```
$ read1
Go ahead: *
You entered: *
```

If you want the shell to interpret the special meanings of special characters, do not use quotation marks.

REPLY The read builtin has features that can make it easier to use. When you do not specify a variable to receive read's input, bash puts the input into the variable named **REPLY**. You can use the **–p** option to prompt the user instead of using a separate echo command. The following **read1a** script performs exactly the same task as **read1**:

```
$ cat read1a
read -p "Go ahead: "
echo "You entered: $REPLY"
```

The **read2** script prompts for a command line and reads the user's response into the variable **cmd**. The script then attempts to execute the command line that results from the expansion of the **cmd** variable:

```
$ cat read2
read -p "Enter a command: " cmd
$cmd
echo "Thanks"
```

In the following example, **read2** reads a command line that calls the echo builtin. The shell executes the command and then displays **Thanks**. Next **read2** reads a command line that executes the who utility:

```
$ read2
Enter a command: echo Please display this message.
Please display this message.
Thanks
```

```
$ read2
Enter a command: who
alex       pts/4        Jun 17 07:50 (:0.0)
scott      pts/12       Jun 17 11:54 (bravo.example.com)
Thanks
```

If **cmd** does not expand into a valid command line, the shell issues an error message:

```
$ read2
Enter a command: xxx
./read2: line 2: xxx: command not found
Thanks
```

The **read3** script reads values into three variables. The read builtin assigns one word (a sequence of nonblank characters) to each variable:

```
$ cat read3
read -p "Enter something: " word1 word2 word3
echo "Word 1 is: $word1"
echo "Word 2 is: $word2"
echo "Word 3 is: $word3"

$ read3
Enter something: this is something
Word 1 is: this
Word 2 is: is
Word 3 is: something
```

When you enter more words than read has variables, read assigns one word to each variable, with all leftover words going to the last variable. Both **read1** and **read2** assigned the first word and all leftover words to the one variable they each had to work with. In the following example, read accepts five words into three variables, assigning the first word to the first variable, the second word to the second variable, and the third through fifth words to the third variable:

```
$ read3
Enter something: this is something else, really.
Word 1 is:  this
Word 2 is:  is
Word 3 is:  something else, really.
```

Table 11-4 lists some of the options supported by the read builtin.

Table 11-4 read options

Option	Function
–a *aname* (array)	Assigns each word of input to an element of array *aname*.
–d *delim* (delimiter)	Uses *delim* to terminate the input instead of NEWLINE.
–e (Readline)	If input is coming from a keyboard, use the Readline Library (page 305) to get input.

Table 11-4   read options (continued)

−n *num* (number of characters)	Reads *num* characters and returns. As soon as the user types *num* characters, read returns; there is no need to press RETURN.
−p *prompt* (prompt)	Displays *prompt* on standard error without a terminating NEWLINE before reading input. Displays *prompt* only when input comes from the keyboard.
−s (silent)	Does not echo characters.

−u*n* (file descriptor)	Uses the integer *n* as the file descriptor that read takes its input from.
	
	    `read −u4 arg1 arg2`
	
	is equivalent to
	
	    `read arg1 arg2 <&4`
	
	See "File Descriptors" (page 470) for a discussion of redirection and file descriptors.

The read builtin returns an exit status of 0 if it successfully reads any data. It has a nonzero exit status when it reaches the EOF (end of file). The following example runs a **while** loop from the command line. It takes its input from the **names** file and terminates after reading the last line from **names**.

```
$ cat names
Alice Jones
Robert Smith
Alice Paulson
John Q. Public

$ while read first rest
> do
> echo $rest, $first
> done < names
Jones, Alice
Smith, Robert
Paulson, Alice
Q. Public, John
$
```

The placement of the redirection symbol (<) for the **while** structure is critical. It is important that you place the redirection symbol at the **done** statement and not at the call to read.

optional   Each time you redirect input, the shell opens the input file and repositions the read pointer at the start of the file:

```
$ read line1 < names; echo $line1; read line2 < names; echo $line2
Alice Jones
Alice Jones
```

Here each read opens **names** and starts at the beginning of the **names** file. In the following example, **names** is opened once, as standard input of the subshell created by the parentheses. Each read then reads successive lines of standard input.

```
$ (read line1; echo $line1; read line2; echo $line2) < names
Alice Jones
Robert Smith
```

Another way to get the same effect is to open the input file with exec and hold it open (refer to "File Descriptors" on page 470):

```
$ exec 3< names
$ read -u3 line1; echo $line1; read -u3 line2; echo $line2
Alice Jones
Robert Smith
$ exec 3<&-
```

exec: EXECUTES A COMMAND

The exec builtin (not available in tcsh) has two primary purposes: to run a command without creating a new process and to redirect a file descriptor—including standard input, output, or error—of a shell script from within the script (page 470). When the shell executes a command that is not built into the shell, it typically creates a new process. The new process inherits environment (global or exported) variables from its parent but does not inherit variables that are not exported by the parent. (For more information refer to "Locality of Variables" on page 475.) In contrast, exec executes a command in place of (overlays) the current process.

exec versus . (dot) Insofar as exec runs a command in the environment of the original process, it is similar to the . (dot) command (page 259). However, unlike the . command, which can run only shell scripts, exec can run both scripts and compiled programs. Also, whereas the . command returns control to the original script when it finishes running, exec does not. Finally, the . command gives the new program access to local variables, whereas exec does not.

exec runs a The exec builtin used for running a command has the following syntax:
command

exec command arguments

exec does not Because the shell does not create a new process when you use exec, the command
return control runs more quickly. However, because exec does not return control to the original program, it can be used only as the last command that you want to run in a script. The following script shows that control is not returned to the script:

```
$ cat exec_demo
who
exec date
echo "This line is never displayed."
```

```
$ exec_demo
jenny    pts/7    May 30   7:05 (bravo.example.com)
hls      pts/1    May 30   6:59 (:0.0)
Mon May 30 11:42:56 PDT 2005
```

The next example, a modified version of the **out** script (page 442), uses **exec** to execute the final command the script runs. Because **out** runs either cat or less and then terminates, the new version, named **out2**, uses **exec** with both cat and less:

```
$ cat out2
if [ $# -eq 0 ]
    then
        echo "Usage: out2 [-v] filenames" 1>&2
        exit 1
fi
if [ "$1" = "-v" ]
    then
        shift
        exec less "$@"
    else
        exec cat -- "$@"

fi
```

exec redirects input and output   The second major use of **exec** is to redirect a file descriptor—including standard input, output, or error—from within a script. The next command causes all subsequent input to a script that would have come from standard input to come from the file named **infile**:

```
exec < infile
```

Similarly the following command redirects standard output and standard error to **outfile** and **errfile**, respectively:

```
exec > outfile 2> errfile
```

When you use **exec** in this manner, the current process is not replaced with a new process, and **exec** can be followed by other commands in the script.

/dev/tty   When you redirect the output from a script to a file, you must make sure that the user sees any prompts the script displays. The **/dev/tty** device is a pseudonym for the screen the user is working on; you can use this device to refer to the user's screen without knowing which device it is. (The tty utility displays the name of the device you are using.) By redirecting the output from a script to **/dev/tty**, you ensure that prompts and messages go to the user's terminal, regardless of which terminal the user is logged in on. Messages sent to **/dev/tty** are also not diverted if standard output and standard error from the script are redirected.

The **to_screen1** script sends output to three places: standard output, standard error, and the user's screen. When it is run with standard output and standard error redirected, **to_screen1** still displays the message sent to **/dev/tty** on the user's screen. The **out** and **err** files hold the output sent to standard output and standard error.

```
$ cat to_screen1
echo "message to standard output"
echo "message to standard error" 1>&2
echo "message to the user" > /dev/tty

$ to_screen1 > out 2> err
message to the user
$ cat out
message to standard output
$ cat err
message to standard error
```

The following command redirects the output from a script to the user's screen:

```
exec > /dev/tty
```

Putting this command at the beginning of the previous script changes where the output goes. In **to_screen2**, exec redirects standard output to the user's screen so the **> /dev/tty** is superfluous. Following the exec command, all output sent to standard output goes to **/dev/tty** (the screen). Output to standard error is not affected.

```
$ cat to_screen2
exec > /dev/tty
echo "message to standard output"
echo "message to standard error" 1>&2
echo "message to the user" > /dev/tty

$ to_screen2 > out 2> err
message to standard output
message to the user
```

One disadvantage of using exec to redirect the output to **/dev/tty** is that all subsequent output is redirected unless you use exec again in the script.

You can also redirect the input to read (standard input) so that it comes from **/dev/tty** (the keyboard):

```
read name < /dev/tty
```

or

```
exec < /dev/tty
```

trap: CATCHES A SIGNAL

A *signal* is a report to a process about a condition. Linux uses signals to report interrupts generated by the user (for example, pressing the interrupt key) as well as bad system calls, broken pipes, illegal instructions, and other conditions. The trap builtin (tcsh uses onintr) catches, or traps, one or more signals, allowing you to direct the actions a script takes when it receives a specified signal.

Table 11-5 Signals

Type	Name	Number	Generating condition
Not a real signal	EXIT	0	Exit because of exit command or reaching the end of the program (not an actual signal but useful in trap)
Hang up	SIGHUP or HUP	1	Disconnect the line
Terminal interrupt	SIGINT or INT	2	Press the interrupt key (usually CONTROL-C)
Quit	SIGQUIT or QUIT	3	Press the quit key (usually CONTROL-SHIFT-| or CONTROL-SHIFT-\\)
Kill	SIGKILL or KILL	9	The kill command with the **–9** option (cannot be trapped; use only as a last resort)
Software termination	SIGTERM or TERM	15	Default of the kill command
Stop	SIGTSTP or TSTP	20	Press the suspend key (usually CONTROL-Z)
Debug	DEBUG		Executes **commands** specified in the trap statement after each command (not an actual signal but useful in trap)
Error	ERR		Executes **commands** specified in the trap statement after each command that returns a nonzero exit status (not an actual signal but useful in trap)

This discussion covers six signals that are significant when you work with shell scripts. Table 11-5 lists these signals, the signal numbers that systems often ascribe to them, and the conditions that usually generate each signal. Give the command **kill –l, trap –l**, or **man 7 signal** for a list of signal names.

When it traps a signal, a script takes whatever action you specify: It can remove files or finish any other processing as needed, display a message, terminate execution immediately, or ignore the signal. If you do not use trap in a script, any of the six actual signals listed in Table 11-5 (not EXIT, DEBUG, or ERR) terminates the script. Because a process cannot trap a KILL signal, you can use **kill –KILL** (or **kill –9**) as a last resort to terminate a script or any other process. (See page 497 for more information on kill.)

The trap command has the following syntax:

> *trap ['**commands**'] [*signal*]*

The optional **commands** part specifies the commands that the shell executes when it catches one of the signals specified by *signal*. The *signal* can be a signal name or number—for example, INT or 2. If *commands* is not present, trap resets the trap to its initial condition, which is usually to exit from the script.

The trap builtin does not require single quotation marks around *commands* as shown in the preceding syntax, but it is a good practice to use them. The single quotation marks cause shell variables within the *commands* to be expanded when the signal occurs, not when the shell evaluates the arguments to trap. Even if you do not use any shell variables in the *commands,* you need to enclose any command that takes arguments within either single or double quotation marks. Quoting the *commands* causes the shell to pass to trap the entire command as a single argument.

After executing the *commands,* the shell resumes executing the script where it left off. If you want trap to prevent a script from exiting when it receives a signal but not to run any commands explicitly, you can specify a null (empty) *commands* string, as shown in the **locktty** script (page 458). The following command traps signal number 15 after which the script continues.

```
trap '' 15
```

The following script demonstrates how the trap builtin can catch the terminal interrupt signal (2). You can use SIGINT, INT, or 2 to specify this signal. The script returns an exit status of 1:

```
$ cat inter
#!/bin/bash
trap 'echo PROGRAM INTERRUPTED; exit 1' INT
while true
do
    echo "Program running."
    sleep 1
done
$ inter
Program running.
Program running.
Program running.
CONTROL-C
PROGRAM INTERRUPTED
$
```

: (null) builtin   The second line of **inter** sets up a trap for the terminal interrupt signal using INT. When trap catches the signal, the shell executes the two commands between the single quotation marks in the trap command. The echo builtin displays the message **PROGRAM INTERRUPTED**, exit terminates the shell running the script, and the parent shell displays a prompt. If exit were not there, the shell would return control to the **while** loop after displaying the message. The **while** loop repeats continuously until the script receives a signal because the true utility always returns a *true* exit status. In place of true you can use the : (null) builtin, which is written as a colon and always returns a 0 (*true*) status.

The trap builtin frequently removes temporary files when a script is terminated prematurely so that the files are not left to clutter the filesystem. The following shell script, named **addbanner,** uses two traps to remove a temporary file when the script terminates normally or owing to a hangup, software interrupt, quit, or software termination signal:

```
$ cat addbanner
#!/bin/bash
script=$(basename $0)

if [ ! -r "$HOME/banner" ]
    then
        echo "$script: need readable $HOME/banner file" 1>&2
        exit 1
fi

trap 'exit 1' 1 2 3 15
trap 'rm /tmp/$$.$script 2> /dev/null' 0

for file
do
    if [ -r "$file" -a -w "$file" ]
        then
            cat $HOME/banner $file > /tmp/$$.$script
            cp /tmp/$$.$script $file
            echo "$script: banner added to $file" 1>&2
        else
            echo "$script: need read and write permission for $file" 1>&2
        fi
done
```

When called with one or more filename arguments, **addbanner** loops through the files, adding a header to the top of each. This script is useful when you use a standard format at the top of your documents, such as a standard layout for memos, or when you want to add a standard header to shell scripts. The header is kept in a file named **~/banner**. Because **addbanner** uses the **HOME** variable, which contains the pathname of the user's home directory, the script can be used by several users without modification. If Alex had written the script with **/home/alex** in place of **$HOME** and then given the script to Jenny, either she would have had to change it or **addbanner** would have used Alex's **banner** file when Jenny ran it (assuming Jenny had read permission for the file).

The first trap in **addbanner** causes it to exit with a status of 1 when it receives a hangup, software interrupt (terminal interrupt or quit signal), or software termination signal. The second trap uses a 0 in place of **signal-number,** which causes trap to execute its command argument *whenever* the script exits because it receives an exit command or reaches its end. Together these traps remove a temporary file whether the script terminates normally or prematurely. Standard error of the second trap is sent to **/dev/null** for cases in which trap attempts to remove a nonexistent temporary file. In those cases rm sends an error message to standard error; because standard error is redirected, the user does not see this message.

See page 458 for another example that uses trap.

kill: ABORTS A PROCESS

The kill builtin sends a signal to a process or job. The kill command has the following syntax:

kill [–signal] PID

where *signal* is the signal name or number (for example, INT or 2) and *PID* is the process identification number of the process that is to receive the signal. You can specify a job number (page 125) as *%n* in place of *PID*. If you omit *signal*, kill sends a TERM (software termination, number 15) signal. For more information on signal names and numbers see Table 11-5 on page 494.

The following command sends the TERM signal to job number 1:

```
$ kill -TERM %1
```

Because TERM is the default signal for kill, you can also give this command as **kill %1**. Give the command **kill –l** (lowercase "l") to display a list of signal names.

A program that is interrupted often leaves matters in an unpredictable state: Temporary files may be left behind (when they are normally removed), and permissions may be changed. A well-written application traps, or detects, signals and cleans up before exiting. Most carefully written applications trap the INT, QUIT, and TERM signals.

To terminate a program, first try INT (press CONTROL-C, if the job is in the foreground). Because an application can be written to ignore these signals, you may need to use the KILL signal, which cannot be trapped or ignored; it is a "sure kill." Refer to page 693 for more information on kill. See also the related utility killall (page 695).

getopts: PARSES OPTIONS

The getopts builtin (not available in tcsh) parses command line arguments, thereby making it easier to write programs that follow the Linux argument conventions. The syntax for getopts is

getopts optstring varname [arg ...]

where *optstring* is a list of the valid option letters, *varname* is the variable that receives the options one at a time, and *arg* is the optional list of parameters to be processed. If *arg* is not present, getopts processes the command line arguments. If *optstring* starts with a colon (:), the script takes care of generating error messages; otherwise, getopts generates error messages.

The getopts builtin uses the **OPTIND** (option index) and **OPTARG** (option argument) variables to store option-related values. When a shell script starts, the value of **OPTIND** is 1. Each time getopts locates an argument, it increments **OPTIND** to the index of the next option to be processed. If the option takes an argument, bash assigns the value of the argument to **OPTARG**.

To indicate that an option takes an argument, follow the corresponding letter in *optstring* with a colon (:). The option string **dxo:lt:r** indicates that getopts should search for −d, −x, −o, −l, −t, and −r options and that the −o and −t options take arguments.

Using getopts as the *test-command* in a **while** control structure allows you to loop over the options one at a time. The getopts builtin checks the option list for options that are in *optstring*. Each time through the loop, getopts stores the option letter it finds in *varname*.

Suppose that you want to write a program that can take three options:

1. A −b option indicates that the program should ignore whitespace at the start of input lines.

2. A −t option followed by the name of a directory indicates that the program should use that directory for temporary files. Otherwise, it should use **/tmp**.

3. A −u option indicates that the program should translate all its output to uppercase.

In addition, the program should ignore all other options and end option processing when it encounters two hyphens (−−).

The problem is to write the portion of the program that determines which options the user has supplied. The following solution does not use getopts:

```
SKIPBLANKS=
TMPDIR=/tmp
CASE=lower
while [[ "$1" = -* ]] # [[ = ]] does pattern match
do
    case $1 in
        -b)     SKIPBLANKS=TRUE ;;
        -t)     if [ -d "$2" ]
                    then
                    TMPDIR=$2
                    shift
                else
                    echo "$0: -t takes a directory argument." >&2
                    exit 1
                fi ;;
        -u)     CASE=upper ;;
        --)     break    ;;        # Stop processing options
        *)      echo "$0: Invalid option $1 ignored." >&2 ;;
    esac
    shift
done
```

This program fragment uses a loop to check and shift arguments while the argument is not ––. As long as the argument is not two hyphens, the program continues to loop through a **case** statement that checks for possible options. The –– **case** label breaks out of the **while** loop. The ❖ **case** label recognizes any option; it appears as the last **case** label to catch any unknown options, displays an error message, and allows processing to continue. On each pass through the loop, the program does a shift to get to the next argument. If an option takes an argument, the program does an extra shift to get past that argument.

The following program fragment processes the same options, but uses getopts:

```
SKIPBLANKS=
TMPDIR=/tmp
CASE=lower

while getopts :bt:u arg
do
    case $arg in
        b)      SKIPBLANKS=TRUE ;;
        t)      if [ -d "$OPTARG" ]
                    then
                    TMPDIR=$OPTARG
                else
                    echo "$0: $OPTARG is not a directory." >&2
                    exit 1
                fi ;;
        u)      CASE=upper ;;
        :)      echo "$0: Must supply an argument to -$OPTARG." >&2
                exit 1 ;;
        \?)     echo "Invalid option -$OPTARG ignored." >&2 ;;
    esac
done
```

In this version of the code, the **while** structure evaluates the getopts builtin each time it comes to the top of the loop. The getopts builtin uses the **OPTIND** variable to keep track of the index of the argument it is to process the next time it is called. There is no need to call shift in this example.

In the getopts version of the script the **case** patterns do not start with a hyphen because the value of **arg** is just the option letter (getopts strips off the hyphen). Also, getopts recognizes –– as the end of the options, so you do not have to specify it explicitly as in the **case** statement in the first example.

Because you tell getopts which options are valid and which require arguments, it can detect errors in the command line and handle them in two ways. This example uses a leading colon in *optstring* to specify that you check for and handle errors in your code; when getopts finds an invalid option, it sets *varname* to ? and **OPTARG** to the option letter. When it finds an option that is missing an argument, getopts sets *varname* to : and **OPTARG** to the option lacking an argument.

The **\?** **case** pattern specifies the action to take when getopts detects an invalid option. The **:** **case** pattern specifies the action to take when getopts detects a missing option argument. In both cases getopts does not write any error message; it leaves that task to you.

If you omit the leading colon from *optstring*, both an invalid option and a missing option argument cause *varname* to be assigned the string **?**. **OPTARG** is not set and getopts writes its own diagnostic message to standard error. Generally this method is less desirable because you have less control over what the user sees when an error is made.

Using getopts will not necessarily make your programs shorter. Its principal advantages are that it provides a uniform programming interface and it enforces standard option handling.

A PARTIAL LIST OF BUILTINS

Table 11-6 lists some of the bash builtins. See "Listing bash builtins" on page 133 for instructions on how to display complete lists of builtins.

Table 11-6   bash builtins

Builtin	Function
:	Returns 0 or *true* (the null builtin; page 495)
. (dot)	Executes a shell script as part of the current process (page 259)
bg	Puts a suspended job in the background (page 273)
break	Exits from a looping control structure (page 459)
cd	Changes to another working directory (page 82)
continue	Starts with the next iteration of a looping control structure (page 459)
echo	Displays its arguments (page 53)
eval	Scans and evaluates the command line (page 318)
exec	Executes a shell script or program in place of the current process (page 491)
exit	Exits from the current shell (usually the same as CONTROL-D from an interactive shell; page 480)
export	Places the value of a variable in the calling environment (makes it global; page 475)
fg	Brings a job from the background into the foreground (page 272)
getopts	Parses arguments to a shell script (page 497)

Table 11-6   bash builtins (continued)

jobs	Displays list of background jobs (page 271)
kill	Sends a signal to a process or job (page 693)
pwd	Displays the name of the working directory (page 81)
read	Reads a line from standard input (page 487)
readonly	Declares a variable to be readonly (page 281)
set	Sets shell flags or command line argument variables; with no argument, lists all variables (pages 319, 356, and 484)
shift	Promotes each command line argument (page 483)
test	Compares arguments (pages 437 and 794)
times	Displays total times for the current shell and its children
trap	Traps a signal (page 493)
type	Displays how each argument would be interpreted as a command (page 487)
umask	Returns the value of the file-creation mask (page 810)
unset	Removes a variable or function (page 281)
wait	Waits for a background process to terminate (page 381)

EXPRESSIONS

An expression is composed of constants, variables, and operators that can be processed to return a value. This section covers arithmetic, logical, and conditional expressions as well as operators. Table 11-8 on page 505 lists the bash operators.

ARITHMETIC EVALUATION

The Bourne Again Shell can perform arithmetic assignments and evaluate many different types of arithmetic expressions, all using integers. The shell performs arithmetic assignments in a number of ways. One is with arguments to the let builtin:

```
$ let "VALUE=VALUE * 10 + NEW"
```

In the preceding example, the variables **VALUE** and **NEW** contain integer values. Within a let statement you do not need to use dollar signs ($) in front of variable names. Double quotation marks must enclose a single argument, or expression, that contains SPACES. Because most expressions contain SPACES and need to be quoted, bash accepts *((expression))* as a synonym for *let "expression"*, obviating the need for both quotation marks and dollar signs:

```
$ ((VALUE=VALUE * 10 + NEW))
```

You can use either form wherever a command is allowed and can remove the SPACES if you like. In the following example, the asterisk (*) does not need to be quoted because the shell does not perform pathname expansion on the right side of an assignment (page 280):

```
$ let VALUE=VALUE*10+NEW
```

Because each argument to let is evaluated as a separate expression, you can assign values to more than one variable on a single line:

```
$ let "COUNT = COUNT + 1" VALUE=VALUE*10+NEW
```

You need to use commas to separate multiple assignments within a set of double parentheses:

```
$ ((COUNT = COUNT + 1, VALUE=VALUE*10+NEW))
```

Arithmetic evaluation versus arithmetic expansion

tip   Arithmetic evaluation differs from arithmetic expansion. As explained on page 327, arithmetic expansion uses the syntax *$((expression))*, evaluates **expression**, and replaces *$((expression))* with the result. You can use arithmetic expansion to display the value of an expression or to assign that value to a variable.

Arithmetic evaluation uses the *let* **expression** or *((expression))* syntax, evaluates **expression**, and returns a status code. You can use arithmetic evaluation to perform a logical comparison or an assignment.

Logical expressions   You can use the *((expression))* syntax for logical expressions, although that task is frequently left to *[[expression]]*. The next example expands the **age_check** script (page 327) to include logical arithmetic evaluation in addition to arithmetic expansion:

```
$ cat age2
#!/bin/bash
echo -n "How old are you? "
read age
if ((30 < age && age < 60)); then
        echo "Wow, in $((60-age)) years, you'll be 60!"
    else
        echo "You are too young or too old to play."
fi

$ age2
How old are you? 25
You are too young or too old to play.
```

The *test-statement* for the **if** structure evaluates two logical comparisons joined by a Boolean AND and returns 0 (*true*) if they are both *true* or 1 (*false*) otherwise.

LOGICAL EVALUATION (CONDITIONAL EXPRESSIONS)

The syntax of a conditional expression is

[[expression]]

where *expression* is a Boolean (logical) expression. You must precede a variable name with a dollar sign ($) within *expression*. The result of executing this builtin, like the test builtin, is a return status. The *conditions* allowed within the brackets are almost a superset of those accepted by test (page 794). Where the test builtin uses –a as a Boolean AND operator, *[[expression]]* uses &&. Similarly, where test uses –o as a Boolean OR operator, *[[expression]]* uses ||.

You can replace the line that tests **age** in the **age2** script (preceding) with the following conditional expression. You must surround the [[and]] tokens with whitespace or a command terminator, and place dollar signs before the variables:

```
if [[ 30 < $age && $age < 60 ]]; then
```

You can also use test's relational operators –gt, –ge, –lt, –le, –eq, and –ne:

```
if [[ 30 -lt $age && $age -lt 60 ]]; then
```

String comparisons The test builtin tests whether strings are equal or unequal. The *[[expression]]* syntax adds comparison tests for string operators. The > and < operators compare strings for order (for example, "aa" < "bbb"). The = operator tests for pattern match, not just equality: *[[string = pattern]]* is *true* if *string* matches *pattern*. This operator is not symmetrical; the *pattern* must appear on the right side of the equal sign. For example, [[**artist = a***]] is *true* (= 0), whereas [[**a* = artist**]] is *false* (= 1):

```
$ [[ artist = a* ]]
$ echo $?
0
$ [[ a* = artist ]]
$ echo $?
1
```

The next example uses a command list that starts with a compound condition. The condition tests that the directory **bin** and the file **src/myscript.bash** exist. If this is *true,* cp copies **src/myscript.bash** to **bin/myscript**. If the copy succeeds, chmod makes **myscript** executable. If any of these steps fails, echo displays a message.

```
$ [[ -d bin && -f src/myscript.bash ]] && cp src/myscript.bash \
bin/myscript && chmod +x bin/myscript || echo "Cannot make \
executable version of myscript"
```

STRING PATTERN MATCHING

The Bourne Again Shell provides string pattern-matching operators that can manipulate pathnames and other strings. These operators can delete from strings prefixes or suffixes that match patterns. The four operators are listed in Table 11-7.

Table 11-7   String operators

Operator	Function
#	Removes minimal matching prefixes
##	Removes maximal matching prefixes
%	Removes minimal matching suffixes
%%	Removes maximal matching suffixes

The syntax for these operators is

   ${varname op pattern}

where *op* is one of the operators listed in Table 11-7 and *pattern* is a match pattern similar to that used for filename generation. These operators are commonly used to manipulate pathnames so as to extract or remove components or to change suffixes:

```
$ SOURCEFILE=/usr/local/src/prog.c
$ echo ${SOURCEFILE#*/}
local/src/prog.c
$ echo ${SOURCEFILE##*/}
prog.c
$ echo ${SOURCEFILE%/*}
/usr/local/src
$ echo ${SOURCEFILE%%/*}

$ echo ${SOURCEFILE%.c}
/usr/local/src/prog
$ CHOPFIRST=${SOURCEFILE#*/}
$ echo $CHOPFIRST
local/src/prog.c
$ NEXT=${CHOPFIRST%%/*}
$ echo $NEXT
local
```

Here the string-length operator, ${#*name*}, is replaced by the number of characters in the value of **name**:

```
$ echo $SOURCEFILE
/usr/local/src/prog.c
$ echo ${#SOURCEFILE}
21
```

OPERATORS

Arithmetic expansion and arithmetic evaluation use the same syntax, precedence, and associativity of expressions as the C language. Table 11-8 lists operators in order of decreasing precedence (priority of evaluation); each group of operators has equal precedence. Within an expression you can use parentheses to change the order of evaluation.

Table 11-8 Operators

Type of operator/operator	Function
Post	
var++	Postincrement
var−−	Postdecrement
Pre	
++*var*	Preincrement
−−*var*	Predecrement
Unary	
−	Unary minus
+	Unary plus
Negation	
!	Boolean NOT (logical negation)
~	Complement (bitwise negation)
Exponentiation	
**	Exponent
Multiplication, division, remainder	
*	Multiplication
/	Division
%	Remainder
Addition, subtraction	
−	Subtraction
+	Addition

Table 11-8 Operators (continued)

Bitwise shifts

<<	Left bitwise shift
>>	Right bitwise shift

Comparison

<=	Less than or equal
>=	Greater than or equal
<	Less than
>	Greater than

Equality, inequality

==	Equality
!=	Inequality

Bitwise

&	Bitwise AND
^	Bitwise XOR (exclusive OR)
|	Bitwise OR

Boolean (logical)

&&	Boolean AND
||	Boolean OR

Conditional evaluation

? :	Ternary operator

Assignment

=, *=, /=, %=, +=, -=, <<=, >>=, &=, ^=, |=	Assignment

Comma

,	Comma

Pipe   The pipe token has higher precedence than operators. You can use pipes anywhere in a command that you can use simple commands. For example, the command line

```
$ cmd1 | cmd2 || cmd3 | cmd4 && cmd5 | cmd6
```

is interpreted as if you had typed

```
$ ((cmd1 | cmd2) || (cmd3 | cmd4)) && (cmd5 | cmd6)
```

Do not rely on rules of precedence: use parentheses

tip   Do not rely on the precedence rules when you use compound commands. Instead, use parentheses to explicitly state the order in which you want the shell to interpret the commands.

Increment and decrement operators   The postincrement, postdecrement, preincrement, and predecrement operators work with variables. The pre- operators, which appear in front of the variable name as in **++COUNT** and **−−VALUE**, first change the value of the variable (**++** adds 1; **−−** subtracts 1) and then provide the result for use in the expression. The post- operators appear after the variable name as in **COUNT++** and **VALUE−−**; they first provide the unchanged value of the variable for use in the expression and then change the value of the variable.

```
$ N=10
$ echo $N
10
$ echo $((--N+3))
12
$ echo $N
9
$ echo $((N++ - 3))
6
$ echo $N
10
```

Remainder   The remainder operator (**%**) gives the remainder when its first operand is divided by its second. For example, the expression **$((15%7))** has the value 1.

Boolean   The result of a Boolean operation is either 0 (*false*) or 1 (*true*).

The **&&** (AND) and **||** (OR) Boolean operators are called *short-circuiting* operators. If the result of using one of these operators can be decided by looking only at the left operand, the right operand is not evaluated. The **&&** operator causes the shell to test the exit status of the command preceding it. If the command succeeded, bash executes the next command; otherwise, it skips the remaining commands on the command line. You can use this construct to execute commands conditionally:

```
$ mkdir bkup && cp -r src bkup
```

This compound command creates the directory **bkup**. If mkdir succeeds, the contents of directory **src** is copied recursively to **bkup**.

The **||** separator also causes bash to test the exit status of the first command but has the opposite effect: The remaining command(s) are executed only if the first one failed (that is, exited with nonzero status):

```
$ mkdir bkup || echo "mkdir of bkup failed" >> /tmp/log
```

The exit status of a command list is the exit status of the last command in the list. You can group lists with parentheses. For example, you could combine the previous two examples as

```
$ (mkdir bkup && cp -r src bkup) || echo "mkdir failed" >> /tmp/log
```

In the absence of parentheses, && and || have equal precedence and are grouped from left to right. The following examples use the true and false utilities. These utilities do nothing and return *true* (0) and *false* (1) exit statuses, respectively:

```
$ false; echo $?
1
```

The $? variable holds the exit status of the preceding command (page 479). The next two commands yield an exit status of 1 (*false*):

```
$ true || false && false
$ echo $?
1
$ (true || false) && false
$ echo $?
1
```

Similarly the next two commands yield an exit status of 0 (*true*):

```
$ false && false || true
$ echo $?
0
$ (false && false) || true
$ echo $?
0
```

Because || and && have equal precedence, the parentheses in the two preceding pairs of examples do nothing to change the order of operations.

Because the expression on the right side of a short-circuiting operator may never get executed, you must be careful with assignment statements in that location. The following example demonstrates what can happen:

```
$ ((N=10,Z=0))
$ echo $((N || ((Z+=1)) ))
1
$ echo $Z
0
```

Because the value of N is nonzero, the result of the || (OR) operation is 1 (*true*), no matter what the value of the right side is. As a consequence ((Z+=1)) is never evaluated and Z is not incremented.

Ternary   The ternary operator, ? :, decides which of two expressions should be evaluated, based on the value returned from a third expression:

expression1 ? expression2 : expression3

If *expression1* produces a *false* (0) value, *expression3* is evaluated; otherwise, *expression2* is evaluated. The value of the entire expression is the value of *expression2* or *expression3*, depending on which one is evaluated. If *expression1* is *true*, *expression3* is not evaluated. If *expression1* is *false expression2* is not evaluated:

```
$ ((N=10,Z=0,COUNT=1))
$ ((T=N>COUNT?++Z:--Z))
$ echo $T
1
$ echo $Z
1
```

Assignment The assignment operators, such as **+=**, are shorthand notations. For example, **N+=3** is the same as ((N=N+3)).

Other bases The following commands use the syntax *base#n* to assign base 2 (binary) values. First **v1** is assigned a value of 0101 (5 decimal) and **v2** is assigned a value of 0110 (6 decimal). The echo utility verifies the decimal values.

```
$ ((v1=2#0101))
$ ((v2=2#0110))
$ echo "$v1 and $v2"
5 and 6
```

Next the bitwise AND operator (**&**) selects the bits that are on in both 5 (0101 binary) and 6 (0110 binary). The result is binary 0100, which is 4 decimal.

```
$ echo $(( v1 & v2 ))
4
```

The Boolean AND operator (**&&**) produces a result of 1 if both of its operands are nonzero and a result of 0 otherwise. The bitwise inclusive OR operator (**|**) selects the bits that are on in either 0101 or 0110, resulting in 0111, which is 7 decimal. The Boolean OR operator (**||**) produces a result of 1 if either of its operands is non-zero and a result of 0 otherwise.

```
$ echo $(( v1 && v2 ))
1
$ echo $(( v1 | v2 ))
7
$ echo $(( v1 || v2 ))
1
```

Next the bitwise exclusive OR operator (**^**) selects the bits that are on in either, but not both, of the operands 0101 and 0110, yielding 0011, which is 3 decimal. The Boolean NOT operator (**!**) produces a result of 1 if its operand is 0 and a result of 0 otherwise. Because the exclamation point in **$((! v1))** is enclosed within double parentheses, it does not need to be escaped to prevent the shell from interpreting the exclamation point as a history event. The comparison operators produce a result of 1 if the comparison is *true* and a result of 0 otherwise.

```
$ echo $(( v1 ^ v2 ))
3
$ echo $(( ! v1 ))
0
$ echo $(( v1 < v2 ))
1
$ echo $(( v1 > v2 ))
0
```

Shell Programs

The Bourne Again Shell has many features that make it a good programming language. The structures that bash provides are not a random assortment. Rather, they have been chosen to provide most of the structural features that are in other procedural languages, such as C or Pascal. A procedural language provides the ability to

- Declare, assign, and manipulate variables and constant data. The Bourne Again Shell provides string variables, together with powerful string operators, and integer variables, along with a complete set of arithmetic operators.

- Break large problems into small ones by creating subprograms. The Bourne Again Shell allows you to create functions and call scripts from other scripts. Shell functions can be called recursively; that is, a Bourne Again Shell function can call itself. You may not need to use recursion often, but it may allow you to solve some apparently difficult problems with ease.

- Execute statements conditionally, using statements such as **if**.

- Execute statements iteratively, using statements such as **while** and **for**.

- Transfer data to and from the program, communicating with both data files and users.

Programming languages implement these capabilities in different ways but with the same ideas in mind. When you want to solve a problem by writing a program, you must first figure out a procedure that leads you to a solution—that is, an *algorithm*. Typically you can implement the same algorithm in roughly the same way in different programming languages, using the same kinds of constructs in each language.

Chapter 8 and this chapter have introduced numerous bash features, many of which are useful for interactive use as well as for shell programming. This section develops two complete shell programs, demonstrating how to combine some of these features effectively. The programs are presented as problems for you to solve along with sample solutions.

A Recursive Shell Script

A recursive construct is one that is defined in terms of itself. Alternatively, you might say that a recursive program is one that can call itself. This may seem circular, but it need not be. To avoid circularity a recursive definition must have a special case that is not self-referential. Recursive ideas occur in everyday life. For example, you can define an ancestor as your mother, your father, or one of their ancestors. This definition is not circular; it specifies unambiguously who your ancestors are: your mother or your father, or your mother's mother or father or your father's mother or father, and so on.

A number of Linux system utilities can operate recursively. See the **–R** option to the chmod (page 604), chown (page 608), and cp (page 616) utilities for examples.

Solve the following problem by using a recursive shell function:

Write a shell function named **makepath** that, given a pathname, creates all components in that pathname as directories. For example, the command **makepath a/b/c/d** should create directories **a**, **a/b**, **a/b/c**, and **a/b/c/d**. (The mkdir utility supports a **–p** option that does exactly this. Solve the problem without using **mkdir –p**.)

One algorithm for a recursive solution follows:

1. Examine the path argument. If it is a null string or if it names an existing directory, do nothing and return.

2. If it is a simple path component, create it (using mkdir) and return.

3. Otherwise, call **makepath** using the path prefix of the original argument. This step eventually creates all the directories up to the last component, which you can then create with mkdir.

In general, a recursive function must invoke itself with a simpler version of the problem than it was given until it is finally called with a simple case that does not need to call itself. Following is one possible solution based on this algorithm:

makepath
```
# this is a function
# enter it at the keyboard, do not run it as a shell script
#
function makepath()
{
    if [[ ${#1} -eq 0 || -d "$1" ]]
        then
            return 0          # Do nothing
    fi
    if [[ "${1%/*}" = "$1" ]]
        then
            mkdir $1
            return $?
    fi
    makepath ${1%/*} || return 1
    mkdir $1
    return $?
}
```

In the test for a simple component (the **if** statement in the middle of the function), the left expression is the argument after the shortest suffix that starts with a **/** character has been stripped away (page 504). If there is no such character (for example, if **$1** is **alex**), nothing is stripped off and the two sides are equal. If the argument is a simple filename preceded by a slash, such as **/usr**, the expression **${1%/*}** evaluates to a null string. To make the function work in this case, you must take two precautions: Put the left expression within quotation marks and ensure that the recursive function behaves sensibly when it is passed a null string as an argument. In general, good programs are robust: They should be prepared for borderline, invalid, or meaningless input and behave appropriately in such cases.

By giving the following command from the shell you are working in, you turn on debugging tracing so that you can watch the recursion work:

```
$ set -o xtrace
```

(Give the same command, but replace the hyphen with a plus sign (**+**) to turn debugging off.) With debugging turned on, the shell displays each line in its expanded form as it executes the line. A **+** precedes each line of debugging output. In the following example, the first line that starts with **+** shows the shell calling **makepath**. The **makepath** function is called from the command line with arguments of **a/b/c**. Subsequently it calls itself with arguments of **a/b** and finally **a**. All the work is done (using mkdir) as each call to **makepath** returns.

```
$ makepath a/b/c
+ makepath a/b/c
+ [[ 5 -eq 0 ]]
+ [[ -d a/b/c ]]
+ [[ a/b = \a\/\b\/\c ]]
+ makepath a/b
+ [[ 3 -eq 0 ]]
+ [[ -d a/b ]]
+ [[ a = \a\/\b ]]
+ makepath a
+ [[ 1 -eq 0 ]]
+ [[ -d a ]]
+ [[ a = \a ]]
+ mkdir a
+ return 0
+ mkdir a/b
+ return 0
+ mkdir a/b/c
+ return 0
```

The function works its way down the recursive path and back up again.

It is instructive to invoke **makepath** with an invalid path and see what happens. The following example, run with debugging turned on, tries to create the path **/a/b**, which requires that you create directory **a** in the root directory. Unless you have permission to write to the root directory, you are not permitted to create this directory.

```
$ makepath /a/b
+ makepath /a/b
+ [[ 4 -eq 0 ]]
+ [[ -d /a/b ]]
+ [[ /a = \/\a\/\b ]]
+ makepath /a
+ [[ 2 -eq 0 ]]
+ [[ -d /a ]]
+ [[ '' = \/\a ]]
+ makepath
+ [[ 0 -eq 0 ]]
+ return 0
+ mkdir /a
mkdir: cannot create directory '/a': Permission denied
+ return 1
+ return 1
```

The recursion stops when **makepath** is denied permission to create the **/a** directory. The error return is passed all the way back, so the original **makepath** exits with nonzero status.

Use local variables with recursive functions

tip The preceding example glossed over a potential problem that you may encounter when you use a recursive function. During the execution of a recursive function, many separate instances of that function may be active simultaneously. All but one of them are waiting for their child invocation to complete.

Because functions run in the same environment as the shell that calls them, variables are implicitly shared by a shell and a function it calls so that all instances of the function share a single copy of each variable. Sharing variables can give rise to side effects that are rarely what you want. As a rule, you should use **typeset** to make all variables of a recursive function be local variables. See page 477 for more information.

THE quiz SHELL SCRIPT

Solve the following problem using a bash script:

Write a generic multiple-choice quiz program. The program should get its questions from data files, present them to the user, and keep track of the number of correct and incorrect answers. The user must be able to exit from the program at any time with a summary of results to that point.

The detailed design of this program and even the detailed description of the problem depend on a number of choices: How will the program know which subjects are available for quizzes? How will the user choose a subject? How will the program know when the quiz is over? Should the program present the same questions (for a given subject) in the same order each time, or should it scramble them?

Of course, you can make many perfectly good choices that implement the specification of the problem. The following details narrow the problem specification:

- Each subject will correspond to a subdirectory of a master quiz directory. This directory will be named in the environment variable **QUIZDIR**, whose default will be **/usr/games/quiz**. For example, you could have the following directories correspond to the subjects engineering, art, and politics: **/usr/games/quiz/engineering**, **/usr/games/quiz/art**, and **/usr/games/quiz/politics**.

- Each subject can have several questions. Each question is represented by a file in its subject's directory.

- The first line of each file that represents a question is the text of the question. If it takes more than one line, you must escape the NEWLINE with a backslash. (This setup makes it easy to read a single question with the read builtin.) The second line of the file is an integer that specifies the number of choices. The next lines are the choices themselves. The last line is the correct answer. Following is a sample question file:

```
Who discovered the principle of the lever?
4
Euclid
Archimedes
Thomas Edison
The Lever Brothers
Archimedes
```

- The program presents all the questions in a subject directory. At any point the user can interrupt the quiz with CONTROL-C, whereupon the program will summarize the results so far and exit. If the user does not interrupt, the program summarizes the results and exits when it has asked all questions for the chosen subject.

- The program scrambles the questions in a subject before presenting them.

Following is a top-level design for this program:

1. Initialize. This involves a number of steps, such as setting the counts of the number of questions asked so far and the number of correct and wrong answers to zero. Sets up to trap CONTROL-C.

2. Present the user with a choice of subjects and get the user's response.

3. Change to the corresponding subject directory.

4. Determine the questions to be asked (that is, the filenames in that directory). Arrange them in random order.

5. Repeatedly present questions and ask for answers until the quiz is over or is interrupted by the user.

6. Present the results and exit.

Clearly some of these steps (such as step 3) are simple, whereas others (such as step 4) are complex and worthy of analysis on their own. Use shell functions for any complex step, and use the trap builtin to handle a user interrupt.

Here is a skeleton version of the program with empty shell functions:

```
function initialize
{
# Initializes variables.
}
function choose_subj
{
# Writes choice to standard output.
}

function scramble
{
# Stores names of question files, scrambled,
# in an array variable named questions.
}

function ask
{
# Reads a question file, asks the question, and checks the
# answer. Returns 1 if the answer was correct, 0 otherwise. If it
# encounters an invalid question file, exit with status 2.
}

function summarize
{
# Presents the user's score.
}

# Main program
initialize                              # Step 1 in top-level design

subject=$(choose_subj)                  # Step 2
[[ $? -eq 0 ]] || exit 2                # If no valid choice, exit

cd $subject || exit 2                   # Step 3
echo                                    # Skip a line
scramble                                # Step 4

for ques in ${questions[*]}; do         # Step 5
    ask $ques
    result=$?
    (( num_ques=num_ques+1 ))
    if [[ $result == 1 ]]; then
        (( num_correct += 1 ))
    fi
    echo                                # Skip a line between questions
    sleep ${QUIZDELAY:=1}
done

summarize                               # Step 6
exit 0
```

To make reading the results a bit easier for the user, a sleep call appears inside the question loop. It delays $QUIZDELAY seconds (default = 1) between questions.

Now the task is to fill in the missing pieces of the program. In a sense this program is being written backward. The details (the shell functions) come first in the file but come last in the development process. This common programming practice is called top-down design. In top-down design you fill in the broad outline of the program first and supply the details later. In this way you break the problem up into smaller problems, each of which you can work on independently. Shell functions are a great help in using the top-down approach.

One way to write the initialize function follows. The cd command causes **QUIZDIR** to be the working directory for the rest of the script and defaults to **/usr/games/quiz** if **QUIZDIR** is not set.

```
function initialize ()
{
trap 'summarize ; exit 0' INT      # Handle user interrupts
num_ques=0                         # Number of questions asked so far
num_correct=0                      # Number answered correctly so far
first_time=true                    # true until first question is asked
cd ${QUIZDIR:=/usr/games/quiz} || exit 2
}
```

Be prepared for the cd command to fail. The directory may be unsearchable or conceivably another user may have removed it. The preceding function exits with a status code of 2 if cd fails.

The next function, **choose_subj**, is a bit more complicated. It displays a menu using a **select** statement:

```
function choose_subj ()
{
subjects=($(ls))
PS3="Choose a subject for the quiz from the preceding list: "
select Subject in ${subjects[*]}; do
    if [[ -z "$Subject" ]]; then
        echo "No subject chosen.  Bye." >&2
        exit 1
    fi
    echo $Subject
    return 0
done
}
```

The function first uses an ls command and command substitution to put a list of subject directories in the **subjects** array. Next the **select** structure (page 466) presents the user with a list of subjects (the directories found by ls) and assigns the chosen directory name to the **Subject** variable. Finally the function writes the name of the subject directory to standard output. The main program uses command substitution to assign this value to the **subject** variable [**subject=$(choose_subj)**].

The **scramble** function presents a number of difficulties. In this solution it uses an array variable (**questions**) to hold the names of the questions. It scrambles the entries in an array using the **RANDOM** variable (each time you reference **RANDOM** it has the value of a [random] integer between 0 and 32767):

```
function scramble ()
{
typeset -i index quescount
questions=($(ls))
quescount=${#questions[*]}           # Number of elements
((index=quescount-1))
while [[ $index > 0 ]]; do
    ((target=RANDOM % index))
    exchange $target $index
    ((index -= 1))
done
}
```

This function initializes the array variable **questions** to the list of filenames (questions) in the working directory. The variable **quescount** is set to the number of such files. Then the following algorithm is used: Let the variable index count down from **quescount – 1** (the index of the last entry in the array variable). For each value of **index**, the function chooses a random value target between 0 and **index**, inclusive. The command

```
((target=RANDOM % index))
```

produces a random value between 0 and **index – 1** by taking the remainder (the **%** operator) when **$RANDOM** is divided by **index**. The function then exchanges the elements of **questions** at positions **target** and **index**. It is convenient to do this in another function named **exchange**:

```
function exchange ()
{
temp_value=${questions[$1]}
questions[$1]=${questions[$2]}
questions[$2]=$temp_value
}
```

The **ask** function also uses the **select** structure. It reads the question file named in its argument and uses the contents of that file to present the question, accept the answer, and determine whether the answer is correct. (See the code that follows.)

The **ask** function uses file descriptor 3 to read successive lines from the question file, whose name was passed as an argument and is represented by **$1** in the function. It reads the question into the **ques** variable and the number of questions into **num_opts**. The function constructs the variable **choices** by initializing it to a null string and successively appending the next choice. Then it sets **PS3** to the value of **ques** and uses a **select** structure to prompt the user with **ques**. The **select** structure places the user's answer in **answer,** and the function then checks it against the correct answer from the file.

The construction of the **choices** variable is done with an eye toward avoiding a potential problem. Suppose that one answer has some whitespace in it. Then it might appear as two or more arguments in **choices**. To avoid this problem, make sure that **choices** is an array variable. The **select** statement does the rest of the work:

quiz

```
$ cat quiz
#!/bin/bash

# remove the # on the following line to turn on debugging
# set -o xtrace

#===================
function initialize ()
{
trap 'summarize ; exit 0' INT      # Handle user interrupts
num_ques=0                         # Number of questions asked so far
num_correct=0                      # Number answered correctly so far
first_time=true                    # true until first question is asked
cd ${QUIZDIR:=/usr/games/quiz} || exit 2
}

#===================
function choose_subj ()
{
subjects=($(ls))
PS3="Choose a subject for the quiz from the preceding list: "
select Subject in ${subjects[*]}; do
    if [[ -z "$Subject" ]]; then
        echo "No subject chosen.  Bye." >&2
        exit 1
    fi
    echo $Subject
    return 0
done
}

#===================
function exchange ()
{
temp_value=${questions[$1]}
questions[$1]=${questions[$2]}
questions[$2]=$temp_value
}
```

```
#==================
function scramble ()
{
typeset -i index quescount
questions=($(ls))
quescount=${#questions[*]}              # Number of elements
((index=quescount-1))
while [[ $index > 0 ]]; do
    ((target=RANDOM % index))
    exchange $target $index
    ((index -= 1))
done
}


#==================
function ask ()
{
exec 3<$1
read -u3 ques || exit 2
read -u3 num_opts || exit 2

index=0
choices=()
while (( index < num_opts )) ; do
    read -u3 next_choice || exit 2
    choices=("${choices[@]}" "$next_choice")
    ((index += 1))
done
read -u3 correct_answer || exit 2
exec 3<&-

if [[ $first_time = true ]]; then
    first_time=false
    echo -e "You may press the interrupt key at any time to quit.\n"
fi

PS3=$ques" "                          # Make $ques the prompt for select
                                      # and add some spaces for legibility.
select answer in "${choices[@]}"; do
    if [[ -z "$answer" ]]; then
            echo  Not a valid choice. Please choose again.
        elif [[ "$answer" = "$correct_answer" ]]; then
            echo "Correct!"
            return 1
        else
            echo "No, the answer is $correct_answer."
            return 0
    fi
done
}
```

```
#===================
function summarize ()
{
echo                                  # Skip a line
if (( num_ques == 0 )); then
    echo "You did not answer any questions"
    exit 0
fi

(( percent=num_correct*100/num_ques ))
echo "You answered $num_correct questions correctly, out of \
$num_ques total questions."
echo "Your score is $percent percent."
}

#===================
# Main program
initialize                            # Step 1 in top-level design

subject=$(choose_subj)                # Step 2
[[ $? -eq 0 ]] || exit 2              # If no valid choice, exit

cd $subject || exit 2                 # Step 3
echo                                  # Skip a line
scramble                              # Step 4

for ques in ${questions[*]}; do       # Step 5
    ask $ques
    result=$?
    (( num_ques=num_ques+1 ))
    if [[ $result == 1 ]]; then
        (( num_correct += 1 ))
    fi
    echo                              # Skip a line between questions
    sleep ${QUIZDELAY:=1}
done

summarize                             # Step 6
exit 0
```

Chapter Summary

The shell is a programming language. Programs written in this language are called shell scripts, or simply scripts. Shell scripts provide the decision and looping control structures present in high-level programming languages while allowing easy access to system utilities and user programs. Shell scripts can use functions to modularize and simplify complex tasks.

Control structures   The control structures that use decisions to select alternatives are **if...then**, **if...then...else**, and **if...then...elif**. The **case** control structure provides a multiway branch and can be used when you want to express alternatives using a simple pattern-matching syntax.

The looping control structures are **for...in**, **for**, **until**, and **while**. These structures perform one or more tasks repetitively.

The **break** and **continue** control structures alter control within loops: **break** transfers control out of a loop, and **continue** transfers control immediately to the top of a loop.

The Here document allows input to a command in a shell script to come from within the script itself.

File descriptors The Bourne Again Shell provides the ability to manipulate file descriptors. Coupled with the read and echo builtins, file descriptors allow shell scripts to have as much control over input and output as programs written in lower-level languages.

Variables You assign attributes, such as readonly, to bash variables using the typeset builtin. The Bourne Again Shell provides operators to perform pattern matching on variables, provide default values for variables, and evaluate the length of variables. This shell also supports array variables and local variables for functions and provides built-in integer arithmetic capability, using the let builtin and an expression syntax similar to the C programming language.

Builtins Bourne Again Shell builtins include type, read, exec, trap, kill, and getopts. The type builtin displays information about a command, including its location; read allows a script to accept user input.

The **exec** builtin executes a command without creating a new process. The new command overlays the current process, assuming the same environment and PID number of that process. This builtin executes user programs and other Linux commands when it is *not* necessary to return control to the calling process.

The trap builtin catches a signal sent by Linux to the process running the script and allows you to specify actions to be taken upon receipt of one or more signals. You can use this builtin to cause a script to ignore the signal that is sent when the user presses the interrupt key.

The kill builtin allows you to terminate a running program. The getopts builtin parses command line arguments, making it easier to write programs that follow standard Linux conventions for command line arguments and options.

Utilities in scripts In addition to using control structures, builtins, and functions, shell scripts generally call Linux utilities. The find utility, for instance, is commonplace in shell scripts that search for files in the system hierarchy and can perform a vast range of tasks, from simple to complex.

A well-written shell script adheres to standard programming practices, such as specifying the shell to execute the script on the first line of the script, verifying the number and type of arguments that the script is called with, displaying a standard usage message to report command line errors, and redirecting all informational messages to standard error.

Expressions   There are two basic types of expressions: arithmetic and logical. Arithmetic expressions allow you to do arithmetic on constants and variables, yielding a numeric result. Logical (Boolean) expressions compare expressions or strings, or test conditions to yield a *true* or *false* result. As with all decisions within Linux shell scripts, a *true* status is represented by the value zero; *false*, by any nonzero value.

EXERCISES

1. Rewrite the **journal** script of Chapter 8 (question 5, page 335) by adding commands to verify that the user has write permission for a file named **journal-file** in the user's home directory, if such a file exists. The script should take appropriate actions if **journal-file** exists and the user does not have write permission to the file. Verify that the modified script works.

2. The special parameter "**$@**" is referenced twice in the **out** script (page 442). Explain what would be different if the parameter "**$＊**" were used in its place.

3. Write a filter that takes a list of files as input and outputs the basename (page 465) of each file in the list.

4. a. Write a function that takes a single filename as an argument and adds execute permission to the file for the user.

   b. When might such a function be useful?

   c. Revise the script so that it takes one or more filenames as arguments and adds execute permission for the user for each file argument.

   d. What can you do to make the function available every time you log in?

   e. Suppose that, in addition to having the function available on subsequent login sessions, you want to make the function available now in your current shell. How would you do so?

5. When might it be necessary or advisable to write a shell script instead of a shell function? Give as many reasons as you can think of.

6. Write a shell script that displays the names of all directory files, but no other types of files, in the working directory.

7. Write a script to display the time every 15 seconds. Read the date man page and display the time, using the %r field descriptor. Clear the window (using the clear command) each time before you display the time.

8. Enter the following script named **savefiles**, and give yourself execute permission to the file:

```
$ cat savefiles
#! /bin/bash
echo "Saving files in current directory in file savethem."
exec > savethem
for i in *
        do
        echo "=================================================="
        echo "File: $i"
        echo "=================================================="
        cat "$i"
        done
```

a. What error message do you get when you execute this script? Rewrite the script so that the error does not occur, making sure the output still goes to savethem.

b. What might be a problem with running this script twice in the same directory? Discuss a solution to this problem.

9. Read the bash man or info page, try some experiments, and answer the following questions:

a. How do you export a function?

b. What does the hash builtin do?

c. What happens if the argument to exec is not executable?

10. Using the find utility, perform the following tasks:

a. List all files in the working directory and all subdirectories that have been modified within the last day.

b. List all files that you have read access to on the system that are larger than 1 megabyte.

c. Remove all files named **core** from the directory structure rooted at your home directory.

d. List the inode numbers of all files in the working directory whose filenames end in .c.

e. List all files that you have read access to on the root filesystem that have been modified in the last 30 days.

11. Write a short script that tells you whether the permissions for two files, whose names are given as arguments to the script, are identical. If the permissions for the two files are identical, output the common permission field. Otherwise, output each filename followed by its permission field. (*Hint:* Try using the cut utility.)

12. Write a script that takes the name of a directory as an argument and searches the file hierarchy rooted at that directory for zero-length files. Write the names of all zero-length files to standard output. If there is no option on the command line, have the script delete the file after displaying its name, asking the user for confirmation, and receiving positive confirmation. A –f (force) option on the command line indicates that the script should display the filename but not ask for confirmation before deleting the file.

ADVANCED EXERCISES

13. Write a script that takes a colon-separated list of items and outputs the items, one per line, to standard output (without the colons).

14. Generalize the script written in exercise 13 so that the character separating the list items is given as an argument to the function. If this argument is absent, the separator should default to a colon.

15. Write a function named **funload** that takes as its single argument the name of a file containing other functions. The purpose of **funload** is to make all functions in the named file available in the current shell; that is, **funload** loads the functions from the named file. To locate the file, **funload** searches the colon-separated list of directories given by the environment variable **FUNPATH**. Assume that the format of **FUNPATH** is the same as **PATH** and that searching **FUNPATH** is similar to the shell's search of the **PATH** variable.

16. Rewrite **bundle** (page 469) so that the script it creates takes an optional list of filenames as arguments. If one or more filenames are given on the command line, only those files should be re-created; otherwise, all files in the shell archive should be re-created. For example, suppose that all files with the filename extension .c are bundled into an archive named **srcshell**, and you want to unbundle just the files **test1.c** and **test2.c**. The following command will unbundle just these two files:

```
$ bash srcshell test1.c test2.c
```

17. What kind of links will the **lnks** script (page 445) not find? Why?

18. In principle, recursion is never necessary. It can always be replaced by an iterative construct, such as **while** or **until**. Rewrite **makepath** (page 511) as a nonrecursive function. Which version do you prefer? Why?

19. Lists are commonly stored in environment variables by putting a colon (:) between each of the list elements. (Th e value of the **PATH** variable is a good example.) You can add an element to such a list by catenating the new element to the front of the list, as in

    ```
    PATH=/opt/bin:$PATH
    ```

    If the element you add is already in the list, you now have two copies of it in the list. Write a shell function named **addenv** that takes two arguments: (1) the name of a shell variable and (2) a string to prepend to the list that is the value of the shell variable only if that string is not already an element of the list. For example, the call

    ```
    addenv PATH /opt/bin
    ```

    would add **/opt/bin** to **PATH** only if that pathname is not already in **PATH**. Be sure that your solution works even if the shell variable starts out empty. Also make sure that you check the list elements carefully. If **/usr/opt/bin** is in **PATH** but **/opt/bin** is not, the example just given should still add **/opt/bin** to **PATH**. (*Hint:* You may find this exercise easier to complete if you first write a function **locate_field** that tells you whether a string is an element in the value of a variable.)

20. Write a function that takes a directory name as an argument and writes to standard output the maximum of the lengths of all filenames in that directory. If the function's argument is not a directory name, write an error message to standard output and exit with nonzero status.

21. Modify the function you wrote for exercise 20 to descend all subdirectories of the named directory recursively and to find the maximum length of any filename in that hierarchy.

22. Write a function that lists the number of regular files, directories, block special files, character special files, FIFOs, and symbolic links in the working directory. Do this in two different ways:

    a. Use the first letter of the output of **ls –l** to determine a file's type.

    b. Use the file type condition tests of the *[[expression]]* syntax to determine a file's type.

23. Modify the **quiz** program (page 518) so that the choices for a question are randomly arranged.

The gawk Pattern Processing Language

The gawk (GNU awk) utility is a pattern-scanning and processing language that searches one or more files to see whether they contain records (usually lines) that match specified patterns. It processes lines by performing actions, such as writing the record to standard output or incrementing a counter, each time it finds a match. As opposed to *procedural* languages, the gawk language is *data driven*: You describe the data you want to work with and tell gawk what to do with the data once it finds it.

You can use gawk to generate reports or filter text. It works equally well with numbers and text; when you mix the two, gawk usually comes up with the right answer. The authors of awk (Alfred V. Aho, Peter J. Weinberger, and Brian W. Kernighan), on which gawk is based, designed the original utility to be easy to use. To achieve this end they sacrificed execution speed.

The gawk utility takes many of its constructs from the C programming language. It includes the following features:

- Flexible format
- Conditional execution
- Looping statements
- Numeric variables
- String variables
- Regular expressions
- Relational expressions
- C's **printf**
- Coprocess execution
- Network data exchange

SYNTAX

A gawk command line has the following syntax:

gawk [options] [program] [file-list]
gawk [options] –f program-file [file-list]

The gawk utility takes its input from files you specify on the command line or from standard input. An advanced command, **getline**, gives you more choices about where input comes from and how you read it. Using a coprocess, gawk can interact with another program or exchange data over a network. Unless you redirect output from gawk, it goes to standard output.

ARGUMENTS

In the preceding syntax, *program* is a gawk program that you include on the command line. The *program-file* is the name of the file that holds a gawk program. Putting the program on the command line allows you to write short gawk programs without having to create a separate *program-file*. To prevent the shell from interpreting the gawk commands as shell commands, enclose the *program* within single quotation marks. Putting a long or complex program in a file can reduce errors and retyping.

The *file-list* contains pathnames of the ordinary files that gawk processes. These files are the input files. When you do not specify a *file-list*, gawk takes input from standard input or as specified by **getline** (page 554) or a coprocess (page 557).

OPTIONS

--field-separator *fs*
> **–F** *fs*
>> Uses *fs* as the value of the input field separator (**FS** variable).

--file *program-file*
> **–f** *program-file*
>> Reads the gawk program from the file named *program-file* instead of the command line. You can specify this option more than once on a command line.

--help **–W help**
> Summarizes how to use gawk.

--lint **–W lint**
> Warns about constructs that may not be correct or portable.

--posix **–W posix**
> Runs a POSIX-compliant version of gawk. This option introduces some restrictions; see the gawk man page for details.

--traditional **–W traditional**
> Ignores the new GNU features in a gawk program, making the program conform to UNIX awk.

--assign *var=value*
> **–v** *var=value*
>> Assigns *value* to the variable *var*. The assignment takes place prior to execution of the gawk program and is available within the **BEGIN** pattern (page 531). You can specify this option more than once on a command line.

NOTES

The gawk utility is the GNU version of UNIX awk. For convenience many Linux systems provide a link from **/bin/awk** to **/bin/gawk** so that you can run the program using either name.

See page 554 for advanced gawk commands and page 559 for examples of gawk error messages.

LANGUAGE BASICS

A gawk *program* (from the command line or from *program-file*) consists of one or more lines containing a *pattern* and/or *action* in the following format:

pattern { action }

The *pattern* selects lines from the input. The gawk utility performs the *action* on all lines that the *pattern* selects. The braces surrounding the *action* enable gawk to differentiate it from the *pattern*. If a *program* line does not contain a *pattern*, gawk selects all lines in the input. If a **program** line does not contain an *action*, gawk copies the selected lines to standard output.

To start, gawk compares the first line of input (from the *file-list* or standard input) with each *pattern* in the *program*. If a *pattern* selects the line (if there is a match), gawk takes the *action* associated with the *pattern*. If the line is not selected, gawk takes no *action*. When gawk has completed its comparisons for the first line of input, it repeats the process for the next line of input, continuing this process of comparing subsequent lines of input until it has read all of the input.

If several *patterns* select the same line, gawk takes the *actions* associated with each of the *patterns* in the order in which they appear in the *program*. It is possible for gawk to send a single line from the input to standard output more than once.

PATTERNS

You can use a regular expression (Appendix A), enclosed within slashes, as a *pattern*. The ~ operator tests whether a field or variable matches a regular expression. The !~ operator tests for no match. You can perform both numeric and string comparisons using the relational operators listed in Table 12-1. You can combine any of the *patterns* using the Boolean operators ‖ (OR) or && (AND).

Table 12-1   Relational operators

Relop	Meaning
<	Less than
<=	Less than or equal to
==	Equal to
!=	Not equal to
>=	Greater than or equal to
>	Greater than

BEGIN and **END** Two unique *patterns*, **BEGIN** and **END**, execute commands before gawk starts its processing and after it finishes. The gawk utility executes the *actions* associated with the **BEGIN** *pattern* before, and with the **END** *pattern* after, it processes all the input.

, (comma) The comma is the range operator. If you separate two *patterns* with a comma on a single gawk program line, gawk selects a range of lines, beginning with the first line that matches the first *pattern*. The last line gawk selects is the next subsequent line that matches the second *pattern*. If no line matches the second *pattern*, gawk selects every line through the end of the input. After gawk finds the second *pattern*, it begins the process again by looking for the first *pattern* again.

ACTIONS

The *action* portion of a gawk command causes gawk to take that *action* when it matches a *pattern*. When you do not specify an *action*, gawk performs the default *action*, which is the **print** command (explicitly represented as {**print**}). This *action* copies the record (normally a line—see "Variables") from the input to standard output.

When you follow a **print** command with arguments, gawk displays only the arguments you specify. These arguments can be variables or string constants. You can send the output from a **print** command to a file (**>**), append it to a file (**>>**), or send it through a pipe to the input of another program (**|**). A coprocess (**|&**) is a two-way pipe that exchanges data with a program running in the background (page 557).

Unless you separate items in a **print** command with commas, gawk catenates them. Commas cause gawk to separate the items with the output field separator (**OFS**, normally a SPACE—see "Variables").

You can include several *actions* on one line by separating them with semicolons.

COMMENTS

The gawk utility disregards anything on a program line following a pound sign (#). You can document a gawk program by preceding comments with this symbol.

VARIABLES

Although you do not need to declare gawk variables prior to their use, you can optionally assign initial values to them. Unassigned numeric variables are initialized to 0; string variables are initialized to the null string. In addition to user variables, gawk maintains program variables. You can use both user and program variables in the *pattern and* in the *action* portion of a gawk program. Table 12-2 lists a few program variables.

Table 12-2   Variables

Variable	Meaning
$0	The current record (as a single variable)
$1–$n	Fields in the current record
FILENAME	Name of the current input file (null for standard input)
FS	Input field separator (default: SPACE or TAB)
NF	Number of fields in the current record
NR	Record number of the current record
OFS	Output field separator (default: SPACE)
ORS	Output record separator (default: NEWLINE)
RS	Input record separator (default: NEWLINE)

In addition to initializing variables within a program, you can use the **––assign** (**–v**) option to initialize variables on the command line. This feature is useful when the value of a variable changes from one run of gawk to the next.

By default the input and output record separators are NEWLINE characters. Thus gawk takes each line of input to be a separate record and appends a NEWLINE to the end of each output record. By default the input field separators are SPACEs and TABs. The default output field separator is a SPACE. You can change the value of any of the separators at any time by assigning a new value to its associated variable either from within the program or from the command line by using the **––assign** (**–v**) option.

FUNCTIONS

Table 12-3 lists a few of the functions that gawk provides for manipulating numbers and strings.

Table 12-3   Functions

Function	Meaning
length(*str*)	Returns the number of characters in *str*; without an argument, returns the number of characters in the current record
int(*num*)	Returns the integer portion of *num*
index(*str1*, *str2*)	Returns the index of *str2* in *str1* or 0 if *str2* is not present
split(*str*, *arr*, *del*)	Places elements of *str*, delimited by *del*, in the array *arr*[1]...*arr*[*n*]; returns the number of elements in the array
sprintf(*fmt*, *args*)	Formats *args* according to *fmt* and returns the formatted string; mimics the C programming language function of the same name

Table 12-3   Functions

substr(*str,pos,len*)	Returns the substring of *str* that begins at *pos* and is *len* characters long
tolower(*str*)	Returns a copy of *str* in which all uppercase letters are replaced with their lowercase counterparts
toupper(*str*)	Returns a copy of *str* in which all lowercase letters are replaced with their uppercase counterparts

ARITHMETIC OPERATORS

The gawk arithmetic operators listed in Table 12-4 are from the C programming language.

Table 12-4   Arithmetic operators

Operator	Meaning
*	Multiplies the expression preceding the operator by the expression following it
/	Divides the expression preceding the operator by the expression following it
%	Takes the remainder after dividing the expression preceding the operator by the expression following it
+	Adds the expression preceding the operator to the expression following it
−	Subtracts the expression following the operator from the expression preceding it
=	Assigns the value of the expression following the operator to the variable preceding it
++	Increments the variable preceding the operator
−−	Decrements the variable preceding the operator
+=	Adds the expression following the operator to the variable preceding it and assigns the result to the variable preceding the operator
−=	Subtracts the expression following the operator from the variable preceding it and assigns the result to the variable preceding the operator
*=	Multiplies the variable preceding the operator by the expression following it and assigns the result to the variable preceding the operator
/=	Divides the variable preceding the operator by the expression following it and assigns the result to the variable preceding the operator
%=	Assigns the remainder, after dividing the variable preceding the operator by the expression following it, to the variable preceding the operator

ASSOCIATIVE ARRAYS

An associative array is one of gawk's most powerful features. These arrays use strings as indexes. Using an associative array, you can mimic a traditional array by using numeric strings as indexes.

You assign a value to an element of an associative array just as you would assign a value to any other gawk variable. The syntax is

array[string] = *value*

where *array* is the name of the array, *string* is the index of the element of the array you are assigning a value to, and *value* is the value you are assigning to that element.

You can use a special **for** structure with an associative array. The syntax is

for (elem in array) action

where *elem* is a variable that takes on the value of each element of the array as the **for** structure loops through them, *array* is the name of the array, and *action* is the action that gawk takes for each element in the array. You can use the *elem* variable in this *action*.

The "Examples" section found later in this chapter contains programs that use associative arrays.

printf

You can use the **printf** command in place of **print** to control the format of the output that gawk generates. The gawk version of **printf** is similar to that found in the C language. A **printf** command has the following syntax:

printf "control-string", arg1, arg2, ..., argn

The *control-string* determines how **printf** formats *arg1, arg2, ..., argn*. These arguments can be variables or other expressions. Within the *control-string* you can use **\n** to indicate a NEWLINE and **\t** to indicate a TAB. The *control-string* contains conversion specifications, one for each argument. A conversion specification has the following syntax:

%[−][x[.y]]conv

where − causes **printf** to left-justify the argument; *x* is the minimum field width, and *.y* is the number of places to the right of a decimal point in a number. The *conv* indicates the type of numeric conversion and can be selected from the letters in Table 12-5. Refer to "Examples" later in this chapter for examples of how to use **printf**.

Table 12-5   Numeric conversion

conv	Type of conversion
d	Decimal
e	Exponential notation

Table 12-5 Numeric conversion (continued)

f	Floating-point number
g	Use **f** or **e**, whichever is shorter
o	Unsigned octal
s	String of characters
x	Unsigned hexadecimal

CONTROL STRUCTURES

Control (flow) statements alter the order of execution of commands within a gawk program. This section details the **if...else, while,** and **for** control structures. In addition, the **break** and **continue** statements work in conjunction with the control structures to alter the order of execution of commands. See page 436 for more information on control structures. You do not need to use braces around *commands* when you specify a single, simple command.

if...else

The **if...else** control structure tests the status returned by the *condition* and transfers control based on this status. The syntax of an **if...else** structure is shown below. The **else** part is optional.

> *if (**condition**)*
>   *{**commands**}*
>   *[else*
>   *{**commands**}]*

The simple **if** statement shown here does not use braces:

```
if ($5 <= 5000) print $0
```

Next is a gawk program that uses a simple **if...else** structure. Again, there are no braces.

```
$ cat if1
BEGIN   {
        nam="sam"
        if (nam == "max")
                print "nam is max"
        else
                print "nam is not max, it is", nam
        }
$ gawk -f if1
nam is not max, it is sam
```

while

The **while** structure loops through and executes the *commands* as long as the *condition* is *true*. The syntax of a **while** structure is

> *while (condition)*
> > *{commands}*

The next gawk program uses a simple **while** structure to display powers of 2. This example uses braces because the **while** loop contains more than one statement.

```
$ cat while1
BEGIN{
    n = 1
    while (n <= 5)
        {
        print n "^2", 2**n
        n++
        }
    }

$ gawk -f while1
1^2 2
2^2 4
3^2 8
4^2 16
5^2 32
```

for

The syntax of a **for** control structure is

> *for (init; condition; increment)*
> > *{commands}*

A **for** structure starts by executing the *init* statement, which usually sets a counter to 0 or 1. It then loops through the *commands* as long as the *condition* is *true*. After each loop it executes the *increment* statement. The **for1** gawk program does the same thing as the preceding **while1** program except that it uses a **for** statement, which makes the program simpler:

```
$ cat for1
BEGIN   {
        for (n=1; n <= 5; n++)
        print n "^2", 2**n
        }
$ gawk -f for1
1^2 2
2^2 4
3^2 8
4^2 16
5^2 32
```

The gawk utility supports an alternative **for** syntax for working with associative arrays:

for (var in array)
  {commands}

This **for** structure loops through elements of the associative array named *array*, assigning the value of the index of each element of *array* to *var* each time through the loop.

```
END    {for (name in manuf) print name, manuf[name]}
```

break

The **break** statement transfers control out of a **for** or **while** loop, terminating execution of the innermost loop it appears in.

continue

The **continue** statement transfers control to the end of a **for** or **while** loop, causing execution of the innermost loop it appears in to continue with the next iteration.

EXAMPLES

cars data file   Many of the examples in this section work with the **cars** data file. From left to right the columns in the file contain each car's make, model, year of manufacture, mileage in thousands of miles, and price. All whitespace in this file is composed of single TABs (the file does not contain any SPACEs).

```
$ cat cars
plym    fury    1970    73    2500
chevy   malibu  1999    60    3000
ford    mustang 1965    45    10000
volvo   s80     1998    102   9850
ford    thundbd 2003    15    10500
chevy   malibu  2000    50    3500
bmw     325i    1985    115   450
honda   accord  2001    30    6000
ford    taurus  2004    10    17000
toyota  rav4    2002    180   750
chevy   impala  1985    85    1550
ford    explor  2003    25    9500
```

Missing pattern   A simple gawk program is

```
{ print }
```

This program consists of one program line that is an *action*. Because the *pattern* is missing, gawk selects all lines of input. When used without any arguments the **print** command displays each selected line in its entirety. This program copies the input to standard output.

```
$ gawk '{ print }' cars
plym    fury    1970    73      2500
chevy   malibu  1999    60      3000
ford    mustang 1965    45      10000
volvo   s80     1998    102     9850
...
```

Missing action   The next program has a *pattern* but no explicit *action*. The slashes indicate that **chevy** is a regular expression.

```
/chevy/
```

In this case gawk selects from the input all lines that contain the string **chevy**. When you do not specify an *action*, gawk assumes that the *action* is **print**. The following example copies to standard output all lines from the input that contain the string **chevy**:

```
$ gawk '/chevy/' cars
chevy   malibu  1999    60      3000
chevy   malibu  2000    50      3500
chevy   impala  1985    85      1550
```

Single quotation marks   Although neither gawk nor shell syntax requires single quotation marks on the command line, it is still a good idea to use them because they can prevent problems. If the gawk program you create on the command line includes SPACEs or special shell characters, you must quote them. Always enclosing the program in single quotation marks is the easiest way of making sure that you have quoted any characters that need to be quoted.

Fields   The next example selects all lines from the file (it has no *pattern*). The braces enclose the *action*; you must always use braces to delimit the *action* so that gawk can distinguish it from the *pattern*. This example displays the third field ($3), a SPACE (the output field separator, indicated by the comma), and the first field ($1) of each selected line:

```
$ gawk '{print $3, $1}' cars
1970 plym
1999 chevy
1965 ford
1998 volvo
...
```

The next example, which includes both a *pattern* and an *action*, selects all lines that contain the string **chevy** and displays the third and first fields from the lines it selects:

```
$ gawk '/chevy/ {print $3, $1}' cars
1999 chevy
2000 chevy
1985 chevy
```

Next gawk selects lines that contain a match for the regular expression **h**. Because there is no explicit *action*, gawk displays all the lines it selects:

```
$ gawk '/h/' cars
chevy    malibu  1999    60      3000
ford     thundbd 2003    15      10500
chevy    malibu  2000    50      3500
honda    accord  2001    30      6000
chevy    impala  1985    85      1550
```

~ (matches operator)   The next *pattern* uses the matches operator (~) to select all lines that contain the letter **h** in the first field:

```
$ gawk '$1 ~ /h/' cars
chevy    malibu  1999    60      3000
chevy    malibu  2000    50      3500
honda    accord  2001    30      6000
chevy    impala  1985    85      1550
```

The caret (**^**) in a regular expression forces a match at the beginning of the line (page 830) or, in this case, the beginning of the first field:

```
$ gawk '$1 ~ /^h/' cars
honda    accord  2001    30      6000
```

Brackets surround a character-class definition (page 829). In the next example, gawk selects lines that have a second field that begins with **t** or **m** and displays the third and second fields, a dollar sign, and the fifth field. Because there is no comma between the "**$**" and the **$5**, gawk does not put a SPACE between them in the output.

```
$ gawk '$2 ~ /^[tm]/ {print $3, $2, "$"  $5}' cars
1999 malibu $3000
1965 mustang $10000
2003 thundbd $10500
2000 malibu $3500
2004 taurus $17000
```

Dollar signs   The next example shows three roles a dollar sign can play in a gawk program. A dollar sign followed by a number names a field. Within a regular expression a dollar sign forces a match at the end of a line or field (**5$**). Within a string a dollar sign represents itself.

```
$ gawk '$3 ~ /5$/ {print $3, $1, "$"  $5}' cars
1965 ford $10000
1985 bmw $450
1985 chevy $1550
```

In the next example, the equal-to relational operator (**==**) causes gawk to perform a numeric comparison between the third field in each line and the number **1985**. The gawk command takes the default *action*, **print**, on each line where the comparison is *true*.

```
$ gawk '$3 == 1985' cars
bmw     325i    1985    115     450
chevy   impala  1985    85      1550
```

The next example finds all cars priced at or less than $3,000:

```
$ gawk '$5 <= 3000' cars
plym    fury    1970    73      2500
chevy   malibu  1999    60      3000
bmw     325i    1985    115     450
toyota  rav4    2002    180     750
chevy   impala  1985    85      1550
```

Textual comparisons
When you use double quotation marks, gawk performs textual comparisons by using the ASCII (or other local) collating sequence as the basis of the comparison. In the following example, gawk shows that the *strings* 450 and 750 fall in the range that lies between the *strings* 2000 and 9000, which is probably not the intended result:

```
$ gawk '"2000" <= $5 && $5 < "9000"' cars
plym    fury    1970    73      2500
chevy   malibu  1999    60      3000
chevy   malibu  2000    50      3500
bmw     325i    1985    115     450
honda   accord  2001    30      6000
toyota  rav4    2002    180     750
```

When you need to perform a numeric comparison, do not use quotation marks. The next example gives the intended result. It is the same as the previous example except that it omits the double quotation marks.

```
$ gawk '2000 <= $5 && $5 < 9000' cars
plym    fury    1970    73      2500
chevy   malibu  1999    60      3000
chevy   malibu  2000    50      3500
honda   accord  2001    30      6000
```

, (range operator)
The range operator (,) selects a group of lines. The first line it selects is the one specified by the *pattern* before the comma. The last line is the one selected by the *pattern* after the comma. If no line matches the *pattern* after the comma, gawk selects every line through the end of the input. The next example selects all lines, starting with the line that contains **volvo** and concluding with the line that contains **bmw**:

```
$ gawk '/volvo/ , /bmw/' cars
volvo   s80     1998    102     9850
ford    thundbd 2003    15      10500
chevy   malibu  2000    50      3500
bmw     325i    1985    115     450
```

After the range operator finds its first group of lines, it begins the process again, looking for a line that matches the *pattern* before the comma. In the following example, gawk finds three groups of lines that fall between **chevy** and **ford**.

Although the fifth line of input contains **ford**, gawk does not select it because at the time it is processing the fifth line, it is searching for **chevy**.

```
$ gawk '/chevy/ , /ford/' cars
chevy    malibu   1999   60     3000
ford     mustang  1965   45     10000
chevy    malibu   2000   50     3500
bmw      325i     1985   115    450
honda    accord   2001   30     6000
ford     taurus   2004   10     17000
chevy    impala   1985   85     1550
ford     explor   2003   25     9500
```

--file option When you are writing a longer gawk program, it is convenient to put the program in a file and reference the file on the command line. Use the **–f** or **--file** option followed by the name of the file containing the gawk program.

BEGIN The following gawk program, stored in a file named **pr_header,** has two *actions* and uses the **BEGIN** *pattern.* The gawk utility performs the *action* associated with **BEGIN** before processing any lines of the data file: It displays a header. The second *action,* {print}, has no *pattern* part and displays all the lines from the input.

```
$ cat pr_header
BEGIN   {print "Make      Model   Year    Miles   Price"}
        {print}


$ gawk -f pr_header cars
Make    Model   Year    Miles   Price
plym    fury    1970    73      2500
chevy   malibu  1999    60      3000
ford    mustang 1965    45      10000
volvo   s80     1998    102     9850
...
```

The next example expands the *action* associated with the BEGIN *pattern.* In the previous and following examples, the whitespace in the headers is composed of single TABs, so that the titles line up with the columns of data.

```
$ cat pr_header2
BEGIN   {
print "Make      Model   Year    Miles   Price"
print "----------------------------------------"
}
        {print}


$ gawk -f pr_header2 cars
Make    Model   Year    Miles   Price
----------------------------------------
plym    fury    1970    73      2500
chevy   malibu  1999    60      3000
ford    mustang 1965    45      10000
volvo   s80     1998    102     9850
...
```

length function   When you call the **length** function without an argument, it returns the number of characters in the current line, including field separators. The $0 variable always contains the value of the current line. In the next example, gawk prepends the line length to each line and then a pipe sends the output from gawk to sort (the **−n** option specifies a numeric sort; page 762) so that the lines of the **cars** file appear in order of length:

```
$ gawk '{print length, $0}' cars | sort -n
21 bmw   325i    1985    115     450
22 plym fury    1970    73      2500
23 volvo       s80     1998    102     9850
24 ford explor 2003    25      9500
24 toyota      rav4    2002    180     750
25 chevy       impala  1985    85      1550
25 chevy       malibu  1999    60      3000
25 chevy       malibu  2000    50      3500
25 ford taurus 2004    10      17000
25 honda       accord  2001    30      6000
26 ford mustang 1965   45      10000
26 ford thundbd 2003   15      10500
```

The formatting of this report depends on TABs for horizontal alignment. The three extra characters at the beginning of each line throw off the format of several lines. A remedy for this situation is covered shortly.

NR (record number)   The **NR** variable contains the record (line) number of the current line. The following *pattern* selects all lines that contain more than 24 characters. The *action* displays the line number of each of the selected lines.

```
$ gawk 'length > 24 {print NR}' cars
2
3
5
6
8
9
11
```

You can combine the range operator (**,**) and the **NR** variable to display a group of lines of a file based on their line numbers. The next example displays lines 2 through 4:

```
$ gawk 'NR == 2 , NR == 4' cars
chevy   malibu  1999    60      3000
ford    mustang 1965    45      10000
volvo   s80     1998    102     9850
```

END   The **END** *pattern* works in a manner similar to the **BEGIN** *pattern*, except that gawk takes the *actions* associated with it after processing the last line of input. The following report displays information only after it has processed all the input. The **NR** variable retains its value after gawk finishes processing the data file, so that an *action* associated with an **END** *pattern* can use it:

```
$ gawk 'END {print NR, "cars for sale." }' cars
12 cars for sale.
```

The next example uses **if** control structures to expand the abbreviations used in some of the first fields. As long as gawk does not change a record, it leaves the entire record—including separators—intact. Once it makes a change to a record, gawk changes all separators in that record to the value of the output field separator. The default output field separator is a SPACE.

```
$ cat separ_demo
      {
      if ($1 ~ /ply/)  $1 = "plymouth"
      if ($1 ~ /chev/) $1 = "chevrolet"
      print
      }

$ gawk -f separ_demo cars
plymouth fury 1970 73 2500
chevrolet malibu 1999 60 3000
ford     mustang 1965     45      10000
volvo    s80     1998     102     9850
ford     thundbd 2003     13      10500
chevrolet malibu 2000 50 3500
bmw      325i    1985     115     450
honda    accord  2001     30      6000
ford     taurus  2004     10      17000
toyota   rav4    2002     180     750
chevrolet impala 1985 85 1550
ford     explor  2003     25      9500
```

Stand-alone script Instead of calling gawk from the command line with the **–f** option and the name of the program you want to run, you can write a script that calls gawk with the commands you want to run. The next example is a stand-alone script that runs the same program as the previous example. The **#!/bin/gawk –f** command (page 265) runs the gawk utility directly. You need both read and execute permission to the file holding the script (page 263).

```
$ chmod u+rx separ_demo2
$ cat separ_demo2
#!/bin/gawk -f
      {
      if ($1 ~ /ply/)  $1 = "plymouth"
      if ($1 ~ /chev/) $1 = "chevrolet"
      print
      }

$ separ_demo2 cars
plymouth fury 1970 73 2500
chevrolet malibu 1999 60 3000
ford     mustang 1965     45      10000
...
```

OFS variable   You can change the value of the output field separator by assigning a value to the **OFS** variable. The following example assigns a TAB character to **OFS**, using the backslash escape sequence \t. This fix improves the appearance of the report but does not line up the columns properly.

```
$ cat ofs_demo
BEGIN   {OFS = "\t"}
        {
        if ($1 ~ /ply/)  $1 = "plymouth"
        if ($1 ~ /chev/) $1 = "chevrolet"
        print
        }
```

```
$ gawk -f ofs_demo cars
plymouth        fury    1970    73      2500
chevrolet       malibu  1999    60      3000
ford    mustang 1965    45      10000
volvo   s80     1998    102     9850
ford    thundbd 2003    15      10500
chevrolet       malibu  2000    50      3500
bmw     325i    1985    115     450
honda   accord  2001    30      6000
ford    taurus  2004    10      17000
toyota  rav4    2002    180     750
chevrolet       impala  1985    85      1550
ford    explor  2003    25      9500
```

printf   You can use **printf** (page 534) to refine the output format. The following example uses a backslash at the end of several program lines to quote the following NEWLINE. You can use this technique to continue a long line over one or more lines without affecting the outcome of the program.

```
$ cat printf_demo
BEGIN   {
    print "                                Miles"
    print "Make        Model       Year    (000)       Price"
    print \
    "-------------------------------------------------"
    }
    {
    if ($1 ~ /ply/)  $1 = "plymouth"
    if ($1 ~ /chev/) $1 = "chevrolet"
    printf "%-10s %-8s    %2d    %5d        $ %8.2f\n",\
        $1, $2, $3, $4, $5
    }
```

```
$ gawk -f printf_demo cars
                        Miles
Make        Model       Year    (000)       Price
-------------------------------------------------
plymouth    fury        1970    73      $  2500.00
chevrolet   malibu      1999    60      $  3000.00
ford        mustang     1965    45      $ 10000.00
volvo       s80         1998    102     $  9850.00
```

```
ford        thundbd    2003    15      $ 10500.00
chevrolet   malibu     2000    50      $  3500.00
bmw         325i       1985    115     $   450.00
honda       accord     2001    30      $  6000.00
ford        taurus     2004    10      $ 17000.00
toyota      rav4       2002    180     $   750.00
chevrolet   impala     1985    85      $  1550.00
ford        explor     2003    25      $  9500.00
```

Redirecting output   The next example creates two files: one with the lines that contain **chevy** and one with the lines that contain **ford**:

```
$ cat redirect_out
/chevy/     {print > "chevfile"}
/ford/      {print > "fordfile"}
END         {print "done."}

$ gawk -f redirect_out cars
done.

$ cat chevfile
chevy   malibu  1999    60      3000
chevy   malibu  2000    50      3500
chevy   impala  1985    85      1550
```

The **summary** program produces a summary report on all cars and newer cars. Although they are not required, the initializations at the beginning of the program represent good programming practice; gawk automatically declares and initializes variables as you use them. After reading all the input data, gawk computes and displays averages.

```
$ cat summary
BEGIN   {
        yearsum = 0 ; costsum = 0
        newcostsum = 0 ; newcount = 0
        }
        {
        yearsum += $3
        costsum += $5
        }
$3 > 2000 {newcostsum += $5 ; newcount ++}
END     {
        printf "Average age of cars is %4.1f years\n",\
            2006 - (yearsum/NR)
        printf "Average cost of cars is $%7.2f\n",\
            costsum/NR
            printf "Average cost of newer cars is $%7.2f\n",\
                newcostsum/newcount
        }

$ gawk -f summary cars
Average age of cars is 13.1 years
Average cost of cars is $6216.67
Average cost of newer cars is $8750.00
```

The following gawk command shows the format of a line from the **passwd** file that the next example uses:

```
$ awk '/mark/ {print}' /etc/passwd
mark:x:107:100:ext 112:/home/mark:/bin/tcsh
```

The next example demonstrates a technique for finding the largest number in a field. Because it works with the **passwd** file, which delimits fields with colons (**:**), the example changes the input field separator (**FS**) before reading any data. It reads the **passwd** file and determines the next available user ID number (field 3). The numbers do not have to be in order in the **passwd** file for this program to work.

The *pattern* (**$3 > saveit**) causes gawk to select records that contain a user ID number greater than any previous user ID number that it has processed. Each time it selects a record, gawk assigns the value of the new user ID number to the **saveit** variable. Then gawk uses the new value of **saveit** to test the user IDs of all subsequent records. Finally gawk adds 1 to the value of **saveit** and displays the result.

```
$ cat find_uid
BEGIN          {FS = ":"
                saveit = 0}
$3 > saveit    {saveit = $3}
END            {print "Next available UID is " saveit + 1}

$ gawk -f find_uid /etc/passwd
Next available UID is 192
```

The next example produces another report based on the **cars** file. This report uses nested **if...else** control structures to substitute values based on the contents of the price field. The program has no *pattern* part; it processes every record.

```
$ cat price_range
    {
    if            ($5 <= 5000)              $5 = "inexpensive"
        else if   (5000 < $5 && $5 < 10000) $5 = "please ask"
        else if   (10000 <= $5)            $5 = "expensive"
    #
    printf "%-10s %-8s   %2d   %5d   %-12s\n",\
    $1, $2, $3, $4, $5
    }

$ gawk -f price_range cars
plym     fury      1970      73    inexpensive
chevy    malibu    1999      60    inexpensive
ford     mustang   1965      45    expensive
volvo    s80       1998     102    please ask
ford     thundbd   2003      15    expensive
chevy    malibu    2000      50    inexpensive
bmw      325i      1985     115    inexpensive
```

honda	accord	2001	30	please ask
ford	taurus	2004	10	expensive
toyota	rav4	2002	180	inexpensive
chevy	impala	1985	85	inexpensive
ford	explor	2003	25	please ask

Associative arrays Next the **manuf** associative array uses the contents of the first field of each record in the **cars** file as an index. The array is composed of the elements **manuf[plym]**, **manuf[chevy]**, **manuf[ford]**, and so on. Each new element is initialized to 0 (zero) as it is created. The C language operator **++** increments the variable that it follows.

The *action* following the **END** *pattern* is the special **for** structure that loops through the elements of an associative array. A pipe sends the output through sort to produce an alphabetical list of cars and the quantities in stock. Because it is a shell script and not a gawk program file, you must have both read and execute permission to the **manuf** file to execute it as a command. Depending on how the **PATH** variable (page 284) is set, you may have to execute the script as **./manuf**.

```
$ cat manuf
gawk ' {manuf[$1]++}
END    {for (name in manuf) print name, manuf[name]}
' cars |
sort

$ manuf
bmw 1
chevy 3
ford 4
honda 1
plym 1
toyota 1
volvo 1
```

The next program, named **manuf.sh**, is a more general shell script that includes some error checking. This script lists and counts the contents of a column in a file, with both the column number and the name of the file being specified on the command line.

The first *action* (the one that starts with {**count**) uses the shell variable **$1** in the middle of the gawk program to specify an array index. Because of the way the single quotation marks are paired, the **$1** that appears to be within single quotation marks is actually not quoted: The two quoted strings in the gawk program surround, but do not include, the **$1**. Because the **$1** is not quoted, and because this is a shell script, the shell substitutes the value of the first command line argument in place of **$1** (page 481). As a result the **$1** is interpreted before the gawk command is invoked. The leading dollar sign (the one before the first single quotation mark on that line) causes gawk to interpret what the shell substitutes as a field number.

```
$ cat manuf.sh
if [ $# != 2 ]
    then
        echo "Usage: manuf.sh field file"
        exit 1
fi
gawk < $2 '
        {count[$'$1']++}
END     {for (item in count) printf "%-20s%-20s\n",\
            item, count[item]}' |
sort

$ manuf.sh
Usage: manuf.sh field file

$ manuf.sh 1 cars
bmw                 1
chevy               3
ford                4
honda               1
plym                1
toyota              1
volvo               1

$ manuf.sh 3 cars
1965                1
1970                1
1985                2
1998                1
1999                1
2000                1
2001                1
2002                1
2003                2
2004                1
```

A way around the tricky use of quotation marks that allow parameter expansion within the gawk program is to use the **-v** option on the command line to pass the field number to gawk as a variable. This change makes it easier for someone else to read and debug the script. You call the **manuf2.sh** script the same way you call **manuf.sh**:

```
$ cat manuf2.sh
if [ $# != 2 ]
        then
                echo "Usage: manuf.sh field file"
                exit 1
fi
gawk -v "field=$1" < $2 '
                {count[$field]++}
END             {for (item in count) printf "%-20s%-20s\n",\
                        item, count[item]}' |
sort
```

The **word_usage** script displays a word usage list for a file you specify on the command line. The tr utility (page 804) lists the words from standard input, one to a line. The sort utility orders the file, with the most frequently used words first. This script sorts groups of words that are used the same number of times in alphabetical order.

```
$ cat word_usage
tr -cs 'a-zA-Z' '[\n*]' < $1 |
gawk      '
          {count[$1]++}
END       {for (item in count) printf "%-15s%3s\n", item, count[item]}' |
sort +1nr +0f -1

$ word_usage textfile
the             42
file            29
fsck            27
system          22
you             22
to              21
it              17
SIZE            14
and             13
MODE            13
...
```

Following is a similar program in a different format. The style mimics that of a C program and may be easier to read and work with for more complex gawk programs:

```
$ cat word_count
tr -cs 'a-zA-Z' '[\n*]' < $1 |
gawk ' {
        count[$1]++
}
END     {
        for (item in count)
            {
            if (count[item] > 4)
                {
                printf "%-15s%3s\n", item, count[item]
                }
            }
} ' |
sort +1nr +0f -1
```

The tail utility displays the last ten lines of output, illustrating that words occurring fewer than five times are not listed:

```
$ word_count textfile | tail
directories     5
if              5
information     5
INODE           5
more            5
no              5
on              5
response        5
this            5
will            5
```

The next example shows one way to put a date on a report. The first line of input to the gawk program comes from date. The program reads this line as record number 1 (**NR == 1**), processes it accordingly, and processes all subsequent lines with the *action* associated with the next *pattern* (**NR > 1**).

```
$ cat report
if (test $# = 0) then
    echo "You must supply a filename."
    exit 1
fi
(date; cat $1) |
gawk '
NR == 1     {print "Report for", $1, $2, $3 ", " $6}
NR >  1     {print $5 "\t" $1}'

$ report cars
Report for Mon Jan 31, 2005
2500    plym
3000    chevy
10000   ford
9850    volvo
10500   ford
3500    chevy
450     bmw
6000    honda
17000   ford
750     toyota
1550    chevy
9500    ford
```

The next example sums each of the columns in a file you specify on the command line; it takes its input from the **numbers** file. The program performs error checking, reporting on and discarding rows that contain nonnumeric entries. It uses the **next** command (with the comment **skip bad records**) to skip the rest of the commands for the current record if the record contains a nonnumeric entry. At the end of the program, gawk displays a grand total for the file.

```
                    $ cat numbers
                    10      20      30.3    40.5
                    20      30      45.7    66.1
                    30      xyz     50      70
                    40      75      107.2   55.6
                    50      20      30.3    40.5
                    60      30      45.0    66.1
                    70      1134.7  50      70
                    80      75      107.2   55.6
                    90      176     30.3    40.5
                    100     1027.45 45.7    66.1
                    110     123     50      57a.5
                    120     75      107.2   55.6
```

```
$ cat tally
gawk ' BEGIN   {
               ORS = ""
               }

NR == 1 {                                   # first record only
    nfields = NF                            # set nfields to number of
    }                                       # fields in the record (NF)
    {
    if ($0 ~ /[^0-9. \t]/)                  # check each record to see if it contains
        {                                   # any characters that are not numbers,
        print "\nRecord " NR " skipped:\n\t"  # periods, spaces, or TABs
        print $0 "\n"
        next                                # skip bad records
        }
    else
        {
        for (count = 1; count <= nfields; count++)# for good records loop through fields
            {
            printf "%10.2f", $count > "tally.out"
            sum[count] += $count
            gtotal += $count
            }
        print "\n" > "tally.out"
        }
    }

END    {                                    # after processing last record
    for (count = 1; count <= nfields; count++)  # print summary
        {
        print "   -------" > "tally.out"
        }
    print "\n" > "tally.out"
    for (count = 1; count <= nfields; count++)
        {
        printf "%10.2f", sum[count] > "tally.out"
        }
    print "\n\n          Grand Total " gtotal "\n" > "tally.out"
} ' < numbers
```

```
$ tally
Record 3 skipped:
        30        xyz       50        70

Record 6 skipped:
        60        30        45.0      66.1

Record 11 skipped:
        110       123       50        57a.5

$ cat tally.out
        10.00     20.00     30.30     40.50
        20.00     30.00     45.70     66.10
        40.00     75.00    107.20     55.60
        50.00     20.00     30.30     40.50
        70.00   1134.70     50.00     70.00
        80.00     75.00    107.20     55.60
        90.00    176.00     30.30     40.50
       100.00   1027.45     45.70     66.10
       120.00     75.00    107.20     55.60
       -------   -------   -------   -------
       580.00   2633.15    553.90    490.50

        Grand Total 4257.55
```

The next example reads the **passwd** file, listing users who do not have passwords and users who have duplicate user ID numbers. (The pwck utility performs similar checks.)

```
$ cat /etc/passwd
bill::102:100:ext 123:/home/bill:/bin/bash
roy:x:104:100:ext 475:/home/roy:/bin/bash
tom:x:105:100:ext 476:/home/tom:/bin/bash
lynn:x:166:100:ext 500:/home/lynn:/bin/bash
mark:x:107:100:ext 112:/home/mark:/bin/bash
sales:x:108:100:ext 102:/m/market:/bin/bash
anne:x:109:100:ext 355:/home/anne:/bin/bash
toni::164:100:ext 357:/home/toni:/bin/bash
ginny:x:115:100:ext 109:/home/ginny:/bin/bash
chuck:x:116:100:ext 146:/home/chuck:/bin/bash
neil:x:164:100:ext 159:/home/neil:/bin/bash
rmi:x:118:100:ext 178:/home/rmi:/bin/bash
vern:x:119:100:ext 201:/home/vern:/bin/bash
bob:x:120:100:ext 227:/home/bob:/bin/bash
janet:x:122:100:ext 229:/home/janet:/bin/bash
maggie:x:124:100:ext 244:/home/maggie:/bin/bash
dan::126:100::/home/dan:/bin/bash
dave:x:108:100:ext 427:/home/dave:/bin/bash
mary:x:129:100:ext 303:/home/mary:/bin/bash
```

```
$ cat passwd_check
gawk < /etc/passwd '     BEGIN   {
    uid[void] = ""                        # tell gawk that uid is an array
    }
    {                                     # no pattern indicates process all records
    dup = 0                               # initialize duplicate flag
```

```
split($0, field, ":")                  # split into fields delimited by ":"
if (field[2] == "")                     # check for null password field
    {
    if (field[5] == "")                 # check for null info field
        {
        print field[1] " has no password."
        }
    else
        {
        print field[1] " ("field[5]") has no password."
        }
    }
for (name in uid)                       # loop through uid array
    {
    if (uid[name] == field[3])          # check for second use of UID
        {
        print field[1] " has the same UID as " name " : UID = " uid[name]
        dup = 1                         # set duplicate flag
        }
    }
if (!dup)                               # same as if (dup == 0)
                                        # assign UID and login name to uid array
    {
    uid[field[1]] = field[3]
    }
}'
```

```
$ passwd_check
bill (ext 123) has no password.
toni (ext 357) has no password.
neil has the same UID as toni : UID = 164
dan has no password.
dave has the same UID as sales : UID = 108
```

The next example shows a complete interactive shell script that uses gawk to generate a report on the cars file based on price ranges:

```
$ cat list_cars
trap 'rm -f $$.tem > /dev/null;echo $0 aborted.;exit 1' 1 2 15
echo -n "Price range (for example, 5000 7500):"
read lowrange hirange

echo '
                                   Miles
Make        Model      Year      (000)          Price
-------------------------------------------------------' > $$.tem
gawk < cars '
$5 >= '$lowrange' && $5 <= '$hirange' {
        if ($1 ~ /ply/)  $1 = "plymouth"
        if ($1 ~ /chev/) $1 = "chevrolet"
        printf "%-10s %-8s     %2d     %5d     $ %8.2f\n", $1, $2, $3, $4,
$5
        }' | sort -n +5 >> $$.tem
cat $$.tem
rm $$.tem
```

```
$ list_cars
Price range (for example, 5000 7500):3000 8000

                          Miles
Make        Model    Year (000)        Price
-------------------------------------------------
chevrolet   malibu   1999    60    $   3000.00
chevrolet   malibu   2000    50    $   3500.00
honda       accord   2001    30    $   6000.00

$ list_cars
Price range (for example, 5000 7500):0 2000

                          Miles
Make        Model    Year (000)        Price
-------------------------------------------------
bmw         325i     1985   115    $    450.00
toyota      rav4     2002   180    $    750.00
chevrolet   impala   1985    85    $   1550.00

$ list_cars
Price range (for example, 5000 7500):15000 100000

                          Miles
Make        Model    Year (000)        Price
-------------------------------------------------
ford        taurus   2004    10    $  17000.00
```

ADVANCED gawk PROGRAMMING

This section discusses some of the advanced features that the GNU developers added when they rewrote awk to create gawk. It covers how to control input using the **getline** statement, how to use a coprocess to exchange information between gawk and a program running in the background, and how to use a coprocess to exchange data over a network.

getline: CONTROLLING INPUT

The **getline** statement gives you more control over the data gawk reads than other methods of input do. When you give a variable name as an argument to **getline**, it reads data into that variable. The **BEGIN** block of the **g1** program uses **getline** to read one line into the variable **aa** from standard input:

```
$ cat g1
BEGIN   {
        getline aa
        print aa
        }
```

```
$ echo aaaa | gawk -f g1
aaaa
```

The **alpha** file is used in the next few examples:

```
$ cat alpha
aaaaaaaaa
bbbbbbbbb
ccccccccc
ddddddddd
```

Even when **g1** is given more than one line of input, it processes only the first line:

```
$ gawk -f g1 < alpha
aaaaaaaaa
```

When **getline** is not given an argument, it reads into $0 and modifies the field variables ($1, $2, . . .):

```
$ gawk 'BEGIN {getline;print $1}' < alpha
aaaaaaaaa
```

The **g2** program uses a **while** loop in the **BEGIN** block to loop over the lines in standard input. The **getline** statement reads each line into **holdme** and **print** outputs each value of **holdme**.

```
$ cat g2
BEGIN    {
         while (getline holdme)
             print holdme
         }
$ gawk -f g2 < alpha
aaaaaaaaa
bbbbbbbbb
ccccccccc
ddddddddd
```

The **g3** program demonstrates that gawk automatically reads each line of input into $0 when it has statements in its body (and not just a **BEGIN** block). This program outputs the record number (**NR**), the string $0:, and the value of $0 (the current record) for each line of input.

```
$ cat g3
        {print NR, "$0:", $0}

$ gawk -f g3 < alpha
1 $0: aaaaaaaaa
2 $0: bbbbbbbbb
3 $0: ccccccccc
4 $0: ddddddddd
```

Next **g4** demonstrates that **getline** works independently of gawk's automatic reads and $0. When **getline** reads into a variable, it does not modify $0 nor does it modify any of the fields in the current record ($1, $2, . . .). The first statement in **g4** is the same as the statement in **g3** and outputs the line that gawk has automatically read. The **getline** statement reads the next line of input into the variable named **aa**. The third statement outputs the record number, the string **aa:**, and the value of **aa**. The output from **g4** shows that **getline** processes records independently of gawk's automatic reads.

```
$ cat g4
        {
        print NR, "$0:", $0
        getline aa
        print NR, "aa:", aa
        }

$ gawk -f g4 < alpha
1 $0: aaaaaaaaa
2 aa: bbbbbbbbb
3 $0: ccccccccc
4 aa: ddddddddd
```

The **g5** program outputs each line of input except that it skips lines that begin with the letter **b**. The first **print** statement outputs each line that gawk reads automatically. Next the **/^b/** *pattern* selects all lines that begin with **b** for special processing. The *action* uses **getline** to read the next line of input into the variable **hold**, outputs the string **skip this line:** followed by the value of **hold**, and outputs the value of **$1**. The **$1** holds the value of the first field of the record that gawk read automatically, not the record read by **getline**. The final statement displays a string and the value of **NR**, the current record number. Even though **getline** does not change **$0** when it reads into a variable, gawk increments **NR**.

```
$ cat g5
        # print all lines except those read with getline
        {print "line #", NR, $0}

# if line begins with "b" process it specially
/^b/    {
        # use getline to read the next line into variable named hold
        getline hold

        # print value of hold
        print "skip this line:", hold

        # $0 is not affected when getline reads into a variable
        # $1 still holds previous value
        print "previous line began with:", $1
        }


        {
        print ">>>> finished processing line #", NR
        print ""
        }
```

```
$ gawk -f g5 < alpha
line # 1 aaaaaaaaa
>>>> finished processing line # 1

line # 2 bbbbbbbbb
skip this line: ccccccccc
previous line began with: bbbbbbbbb
>>>> finished processing line # 3

line # 4 ddddddddd
>>>> finished processing line # 4
```

COPROCESS: TWO-WAY I/O

A *coprocess* is a process that runs in parallel with another process. Starting with version 3.1, gawk can invoke a coprocess to exchange information directly with a background process. A coprocess can be useful when you are working in a client/server environment, setting up an *SQL* (page 902) front end/back end, or exchanging data with a remote system over a network. The gawk syntax identifies a coprocess by preceding the name of the program that starts the background process with a |& operator.

The coprocess command must be a filter (i.e., it reads from standard input and writes to standard output) and must flush its output whenever it has a complete line rather than accumulating lines for subsequent output. When a command is invoked as a coprocess, it is connected via a two-way pipe to a gawk program so that you can read from and write to the coprocess.

to_upper   When used alone the tr utility (page 804) does not flush its output after each line. The **to_upper** shell script is a wrapper for tr that does flush its output; this filter can be run as a coprocess. For each line read, **to_upper** writes the line, translated to uppercase, to standard output. Remove the # before **set –x** if you want **to_upper** to display debugging output.

```
$ cat to_upper
#!/bin/bash
#set -x
while read arg
do
    echo "$arg" | tr '[a-z]' '[A-Z]'
done

$ echo abcdef | to_upper
ABCDEF
```

The **g6** program invokes **to_upper** as a coprocess. This gawk program reads standard input or a file specified on the command line, translates the input to uppercase, and writes the translated data to standard output.

```
$ cat g6
    {
    print $0 |& "to_upper"
    "to_upper" |& getline hold
    print hold
    }

$ gawk -f g6 < alpha
AAAAAAAAA
BBBBBBBBB
CCCCCCCCC
DDDDDDDDD
```

The g6 program has one compound statement, enclosed within braces, comprising three statements. Because there is no *pattern,* gawk executes the compound statement once for each line of input.

In the first statement, **print $0** sends the current record to standard output. The **|&** operator redirects standard output to the program named **to_upper**, which is running as a coprocess. The quotation marks around the name of the program are required. The second statement redirects standard output from **to_upper** to a **getline** statement, which copies its standard input to the variable named **hold**. The third statement, **print hold**, sends the contents of the **hold** variable to standard output.

GETTING INPUT FROM A NETWORK

Building on the concept of a coprocess, gawk can exchange information with a process on another system via an IP network connection. When you specify one of the special filenames that begins with **/inet/**, gawk processes your request using a network connection. The format of these special filenames is

/inet/protocol/local-port/remote-host/remote-port

where *protocol* is usually **tcp** but can be **udp**, *local-port* is 0 (zero) if you want gawk to pick a port (otherwise it is the number of the port you want to use), *remote-host* is the *IP address* (page 882) or *fully qualified domain name* (page 876) of the remote host, and *remote-port* is the port number on the remote host. Instead of a port number in *local-port* and *remote-port*, you can specify a service name such as **http** or **ftp**.

The g7 program reads the **cars** file from the server at www.sobell.com; the author has set up this file for you to experiment with. On www.sobell.com the file is located at **/CMDREF1/code/chapter_12/cars**. The first statement in g7 assigns the special filename to the **server** variable. The filename specifies a TCP connection, allows the local system to select an appropriate port, and connects to www.sobell.com on port 80. You can use **http** in place of 80 to specify the standard HTTP port.

The second statement uses a coprocess to send a **GET** request to the remote server. This request includes the pathname of the file gawk is requesting. A **while** loop uses a coprocess to redirect lines from the server to **getline**. Because **getline** has no variable name as an argument, it saves its input in the current record buffer $0. The final **print** statement sends each record to standard output. Experiment with this script, replacing the final **print** statement with gawk statements that process the file.

```
$ cat g7
BEGIN   {
        # set variable named server
        # to special networking filename
        server = "/inet/tcp/0/www.sobell.com/80"

        # use coprocess to send GET request to remote server
        print "GET /CMDREF1/code/chapter_12/cars" |& server

        # while loop uses coprocess to redirect
        # output from server to getline
        while (server |& getline)
            print $0
        }

$ gawk -f g7
plym    fury    1970    73      2500
chevy   malibu  1999    60      3000
ford    mustang 1965    45      10000
volvo   s80     1998    102     9850
...
```

ERROR MESSAGES

The following examples show some of the more common causes of gawk error messages (and nonmessages). These examples are run under bash. When you use gawk with tcsh, the error messages from the shell will be different.

The first example leaves the single quotation marks off the command line, so the shell interprets $3 and $1 as shell variables. Also, because there are no single quotation marks, the shell passes gawk four arguments instead of two.

```
$ gawk {print $3, $1} cars
gawk: cmd. line:2: (END OF FILE)
gawk: cmd. line:2: syntax error
```

The next command line includes a typo (**prinnt**) that gawk does not catch. Instead of issuing an error message, gawk simply does not do anything useful.

```
$ gawk '$3 >= 83 {prinnt $1}' cars
```

The next example has no braces around the *action:*

```
$ gawk '/chevy/ print $3, $1' cars
gawk: cmd. line:1: /chevy/ print $3, $1
gawk: cmd. line:1:            ^ syntax error
```

There is no problem with the next example; gawk did just what you asked it to do (none of the lines in the file contains a z).

```
$ gawk '/z/' cars
```

The next example shows an improper *action* for which gawk does not issue an error message:

```
$ gawk '{$3  " made by "  $1}' cars
```

The following example does not display the heading because there is no backslash after the **print** command in the **BEGIN** block. The backslash is needed to quote the following NEWLINE so that the line can be continued. Without it, gawk sees two separate statements; the second does nothing.

```
$ cat print_cars
BEGIN   {print
"Model  Year    Price"}
/chevy/ {printf "%5s\t%4d\t%5d\n", $2, $3, $5}
$ gawk -f print_cars cars

malibu  1999    3000
malibu  2000    3500
impala  1985    1550
```

You must use double quotation marks, not single ones, to delimit strings.

```
$ cat print_cars2
BEGIN {OFS='\t'}
$3 ~ /5$/  {print $3, $1, "$" $5}

$ gawk -f print_cars2 cars
gawk: print_cars2:1: BEGIN {OFS='\t'}
gawk: print_cars2:1:                  ^ invalid char ''' in expression
```

CHAPTER SUMMARY

The gawk utility is a pattern-scanning and processing language that searches one or more files to see whether they contain records (usually lines) that match specified patterns. It processes lines by performing actions, such as writing the record to standard output or incrementing a counter, each time it finds a match.

A gawk *program* consists of one or more lines containing a *pattern* and/or *action* in the following format:

     pattern { action }

The *pattern* selects lines from the input. The gawk utility performs the *action* on all lines that the *pattern* selects. If a *program* line does not contain a *pattern,* gawk selects all lines in the input. If a program line does not contain an *action,* gawk copies the selected lines to standard output.

A gawk program can use variables, functions, arithmetic operators, associative arrays, control statements, and C's **printf** statement. Advanced gawk programming takes advantage of **getline** statements to fine-tune input, coprocesses to enable gawk to exchange data with other programs, and network connections to exchange data with programs running on remote systems on a network.

EXERCISES

1. Write a gawk program that numbers each line in a file and sends its output to standard output.

2. Write a gawk program that displays the number of characters in the first field followed by the first field and sends its output to standard output.

3. Write a gawk program that uses the **cars** file (page 537), displays all cars priced at more than $5000, and sends its output to standard output.

4. Use gawk to determine how many lines in **/etc/termcap** contain the string **vt100**. Verify your answer using grep.

ADVANCED EXERCISES

5. Experiment with pgawk. What does it do? How can it be useful?

6. Write a gawk program named **net_list** that reads from the **cars** file on www.sobell.com (see "Getting Input from a Network" on page 558) and displays a list of each of the cars' make, model, and price. Separate the output fields with TABs.

7. Expand the **net_list** program developed in exercise 6 to use **to_upper** (page 557) as a coprocess to display the list of cars with only the make of the cars in uppercase. The model and subsequent fields on each line should appear as they do in the **cars** file.

8. How can you get gawk to neatly format—that is "pretty print"—a gawk program file? (*Hint:* See the gawk man page.)

13

THE sed EDITOR

The sed (stream editor) utility is a batch (noninteractive) editor. It transforms an input stream that can come from a file or standard input. It is frequently used as a filter in a pipe. Because it makes only one pass through its input, sed is more efficient than an interactive editor such as ed. This chapter describes GNU sed.

SYNTAX

A sed command line has the following syntax:

sed [–n] **program** *[file-list]*
sed [–n] –f **program-file** *[file-list]*

The sed utility takes its input from files you specify on the command line or from standard input. Unless you direct output from sed elsewhere, it goes to standard output.

ARGUMENTS

The **program** is a sed program that is included on the command line. This format allows you to write simple, short sed programs without creating a separate **program-file**. The **program-file** is the pathname of a file containing a sed program (see "Editor Basics"). The **file-list** contains pathnames of the ordinary files that sed processes. These are the input files. When you do not specify a file, sed takes its input from standard input.

OPTIONS

––file *program-file*

–f **program-file**

Causes sed to read its program from the file named **program-file** instead of from the command line. You can use this option more than once on the command line.

––in-place[=*suffix*]

–i[*suffix*]

Edits files in place. Without this option sed sends its output to standard output. With this option sed replaces the file it is processing with its output. When you specify a **suffix**, sed makes a backup of the original file. This backup has the original filename with **suffix** appended. You must include a period in **suffix** if you want a period to appear between the original filename and **suffix**.

––help   Summarizes how to use sed.

––quiet *or* –n Causes sed not to copy lines to standard output except as specified by the Print
––silent   (**p**) instruction or flag.

EDITOR BASICS

A sed program consists of one or more lines with the following syntax:

[address[,address]] instruction [argument-list]

The *address*es are optional. If you omit the *address,* sed processes all lines from the input. The *instruction* is the editing instruction that modifies the text. The *address*es select the line(s) that the *instruction* part of the command operates on. The number and kinds of arguments in the *argument-list* depend on the *instruction.* If you want to put several sed commands on one line you can separate the commands with semicolons (;).

The sed utility processes input as follows:

1. Reads one line of input from *file-list* or standard input.

2. Reads the first instruction from the *program* or *program-file.* If the *address*(es) select the input line, acts on the input line as the *instruction* specifies.

3. Reads the next instruction from the *program* or *program-file.* If the *address*(es) select the input line, acts on the input line (possibly modified by the previous instruction) as the *instruction* specifies.

4. Repeats step 3 until it has executed all instructions in the *program* or *program-file.*

5. Starts over again with step 1 if there is another line of input; otherwise, it is finished.

ADDRESSES

A line number is an address that selects a line. As a special case, the line number $ represents the last line of input.

A regular expression (refer to Appendix A) is an address that selects those lines containing a string that the regular expression matches. Although slashes are often used to delimit these regular expressions, sed permits you to use any character other than a backslash or NEWLINE for this purpose.

Except as noted, zero, one, or two addresses (either line numbers or regular expressions) can precede an instruction. If you do not use an address, sed selects all lines, causing the instruction to act on every line of input. Providing one address causes the instruction to act on each input line that the address selects. Providing two addresses causes the instruction to act on groups of lines. The first address selects the first line in the first group. The second address selects the next subsequent line that it matches; this line is the last line in the first group. If no match for the second address is found, the second address points to the end of the file. After selecting the last line in a group, sed starts the selection process over again, looking for the next line that the first address matches. This line is the first line in the next group. The sed utility continues this process until it has finished going through the entire file.

INSTRUCTIONS

d (**delete**)   The Delete instruction causes sed not to write out the lines it selects and not to finish processing the lines. After sed executes a Delete instruction, it reads the next input line and begins over again with the first instruction from the *program* or *program-file*.

n (**next**)   The Next instruction writes out the currently selected line if appropriate, reads the next input line, and starts processing the new line with the next instruction from the *program* or *program-file*.

a (**append**)   The Append instruction appends one or more lines to the currently selected line. If you precede an Append instruction with two addresses, it appends to each line that is selected by the addresses; earlier versions of sed did not accept Append instructions with two addresses. If you do not precede an Append instruction with an address, it appends to each input line. An Append instruction has the following format:

> *[address[,address]] a*
> *text *
> *text *
> *...*
> *text*

You must end each line of appended text, except the last, with a backslash (the backslash quotes the following NEWLINE). The appended text concludes with a line that does not end with a backslash. The sed utility *always* writes out appended text, regardless of whether you use a **–n** flag on the command line. It even writes out the text if you delete the line to which you are appending the text.

i (**insert**)   The Insert instruction is identical to the Append instruction except that it places the new text *before* the selected line.

c (**change**)   The Change instruction is similar to Append and Insert except that it changes the selected lines so that they contain the new text. When you specify an address range, Change replaces the entire range of lines with a single occurrence of the new text.

s (**substitute**)   The Substitute instruction in sed is similar to that in vim (page 166). It has the following format:

[address[,address]] s/pattern/replacement-string/[g][p][w file]

The *pattern* is a regular expression (refer to Appendix A) that is delimited by any character other than a SPACE or NEWLINE, traditionally a slash (/). The *replacement-string* starts immediately following the second delimiter and must be terminated by the same delimiter. The final (third) delimiter is required. The *replacement-string* can contain an ampersand (&), which sed replaces with the matched *pattern*. Unless you use the **g** flag, the Substitute instruction replaces only the first occurrence of the *pattern* on each selected line.

The **g** (global) flag causes the Substitute instruction to replace all nonoverlapping occurrences of the *pattern* on the selected lines.

The **p** (print) flag causes sed to send all lines on which it makes substitutions to standard output. This flag overrides the –n option on the command line.

The **w** (write) flag is similar to the **p** flag but it sends its output to the file specified by *file*. A single SPACE and the name of the output file must follow a **w** flag.

p (**print**)   The Print instruction writes the selected lines to standard output, writing the lines immediately, and does not reflect the effects of subsequent instructions. This instruction overrides the –n option on the command line. (The –n option prevents sed from copying lines to standard output.)

w *file* (**write**)   This instruction is similar to the Print instruction except that it sends output to the file specified by *file*. A single SPACE and the name of the output file must follow a Write instruction.

r *file* (**read**)   The Read instruction reads the contents of the specified file and appends it to the selected line. A single SPACE and the name of the input file must follow a Read instruction.

q (**quit**)   The Quit instruction causes sed to terminate immediately.

CONTROL STRUCTURES

! (**NOT**)   Causes sed to apply the following instruction, located on the same line, to each of the lines *not* selected by the address portion of the instruction. For example, **3!d** deletes all lines except line 3 and **$!p** displays all lines except the last.

{ } (**group instructions**)   When you enclose a group of instructions within a pair of braces, a single address (or address pair) selects the lines on which the group of instructions operates. Use semicolons (;) to separate multiple commands appearing on a single line.

Branch instructions   The sed info page lists the branch instructions as "Commands for sed gurus" and suggests that if you need them you might be better off writing your program in awk or Perl.

: *label*   Identifies a location within a sed program. The *label* is useful as a target for the **b** and **t** branch instructions.

b [*label*]   Unconditionally transfers control (branches) to *label*. Without *label,* skips the rest of the instructions for the current line of input and reads the next line of input (page 565).

t [*label*]   Transfers control (branches) to *label* only if a Substitute instruction has been successful since the most recent line of input was read (conditional branch). Without *label*, skips the rest of the instructions for the current line of input and reads the next line of input (page 565).

THE PATTERN SPACE AND THE HOLD SPACE

The sed utility has two buffers. The commands reviewed up to this point work with the *Pattern space,* which initially holds the line of input that sed just read. The *Hold space* can hold data while you manipulate data in the Pattern space; it is a temporary buffer. Until you place data in the Hold space it is empty. This section discusses commands that move data between the Pattern space and the Hold space.

g   Copies the contents of the Hold space to the Pattern space. The original contents of the Pattern space is lost.

G   Appends a NEWLINE and the contents of the Hold space to the Pattern space.

h   Copies the contents of the Pattern space to the Hold space. The original contents of the Hold space is lost.

H   Appends a NEWLINE and the contents of the Pattern space to the Hold space.

x   Exchanges the contents of the Pattern space and the Hold space.

EXAMPLES

new data file   The following examples use the input file **new:**

```
$ cat new
Line one.
The second line.
The third.
This is line four.
Five.
This is the sixth sentence.
This is line seven.
Eighth and last.
```

Unless you instruct it not to, sed sends all lines—selected or not—to standard output. When you use the **–n** option on the command line, sed sends only certain lines, such as those selected by a Print (**p**) instruction, to standard output.

The following command line displays all the lines in the **new** file that contain the word **line** (all lowercase). In addition, because there is no **–n** option, sed displays all the lines of input. As a result the lines that contain the word **line** are displayed twice.

```
$ sed '/line/ p' new
Line one.
The second line.
The second line.
The third.
This is line four.
This is line four.
Five.
This is the sixth sentence.
This is line seven.
This is line seven.
Eighth and last.
```

The command uses the address **/line/**, a regular expression that is a simple string. The sed utility selects each of the lines that contains a match for that pattern. The Print (**p**) instruction displays each of the selected lines.

The following command uses the **–n** option so that sed displays only the selected lines:

```
$ sed -n '/line/ p' new
The second line.
This is line four.
This is line seven.
```

Next sed displays part of a file based on line numbers. The Print instruction selects and displays lines 3 through 6.

```
$ sed -n '3,6 p' new
The third.
This is line four.
Five.
This is the sixth sentence.
```

The next command line uses the Quit instruction to cause sed to display only the beginning of a file. In this case sed displays the first five lines of **new** just as a **head –5 new** command would.

```
$ sed '5 q' new
Line one.
The second line.
The third.
This is line four.
Five.
```

program-file When you need to give sed more complex or lengthy instructions, you can use a ***program-file***. The **print3_6** program performs the same function as the command line in a previous example. The **–f** option tells sed that it should read its program from the file named on the command line.

```
$ cat print3_6
3,6 p

$ sed -n -f print3_6 new
The third.
This is line four.
Five.
This is the sixth sentence.
```

Append   The next program selects line 2 and uses an Append instruction to append a NEWLINE and the text **AFTER.** to the selected line. Because the command line does not include the **–n** option, sed copies all the lines from the input file **new**.

```
$ cat append_demo
2 a\
AFTER.

$ sed -f append_demo new
Line one.
The second line.
AFTER.
The third.
This is line four.
Five.
This is the sixth sentence.
This is line seven.
Eighth and last.
```

Insert   The **insert_demo** program selects all the lines containing the string **This** and inserts a NEWLINE and the text **BEFORE.** before the selected lines.

```
$ cat insert_demo
/This/ i\
BEFORE.

$ sed -f insert_demo new
Line one.
The second line.
The third.
BEFORE.
This is line four.
Five.
BEFORE.
This is the sixth sentence.
BEFORE.
This is line seven.
Eighth and last.
```

Change   The next example demonstrates a Change instruction with an address range. When you specify a range of lines for a Change instruction, it does not change each line

within the range but rather changes the block of lines to a single occurrence of the
new text.

```
$ cat change_demo
2,4 c\
SED WILL INSERT THESE\
THREE LINES IN PLACE\
OF THE SELECTED LINES.

$ sed -f change_demo new
Line one.
SED WILL INSERT THESE
THREE LINES IN PLACE
OF THE SELECTED LINES.
Five.
This is the sixth sentence.
This is line seven.
Eighth and last.
```

Substitute The next example demonstrates a Substitute instruction. The sed utility selects all
lines because the instruction has no address. On each line **subs_demo** replaces the
first occurrence of **line** with **sentence**. The **p** flag displays each line where a substitution occurs. The command line calls sed with the **–n** option, so sed displays only the
lines that the program explicitly requests it to display.

```
$ cat subs_demo
s/line/sentence/p

$ sed -n -f subs_demo new
The second sentence.
This is sentence four.
This is sentence seven.
```

The next example is similar to the preceding one except that a **w** flag and filename
(**temp**) at the end of the Substitute instruction cause sed to create the file named
temp. The command line does not include the **–n** option, so it displays all lines in
addition to writing the changed lines to **temp**. The cat utility displays the contents of
the file **temp**. The word **Line** (starting with an uppercase L) is not changed.

```
$ cat write_demo1
s/line/sentence/w temp

$ sed -f write_demo1 new
Line one.
The second sentence.
The third.
This is sentence four.
Five.
This is the sixth sentence.
This is sentence seven.
Eighth and last.
```

```
$ cat temp
The second sentence.
This is sentence four.
This is sentence seven.
```

The following bash script changes all occurrences of **REPORT** to **report**, **FILE** to **file**, and **PROCESS** to **process** in a group of files. Because it is a shell script and not a sed program file, you must have read and execute permission to the **sub** file to execute it as a command (page 263). The **for** structure (page 451) loops through the list of files supplied on the command line. As it processes each file, the script displays each filename before processing the file with sed. This program uses multiline embedded sed commands. Because the NEWLINES between the commands are quoted (placed between single quotation marks), sed accepts multiple commands on a single, extended command line (within a shell script). Each Substitute instruction includes a **g** (global) flag to take care of the case where a string occurs more than one time on a line.

```
$ cat sub
for file
do
        echo $file
        mv $file $$.subhld
        sed 's/REPORT/report/g
            s/FILE/file/g
            s/PROCESS/process/g' $$.subhld > $file
done
rm $$.subhld

$ sub file1 file2 file3
file1
file2
file3
```

In the next example, a Write instruction copies part of a file to another file (**temp2**). The line numbers **2** and **4**, separated by a comma, select the range of lines sed is to copy. This program does not alter the lines.

```
$ cat write_demo2
2,4 w temp2

$ sed -n -f write_demo2 new

$ cat temp2
The second line.
The third.
This is line four.
```

The program **write_demo3** is very similar to **write_demo2** but precedes the Write instruction with the NOT operator (!), causing sed to write to the file those lines *not* selected by the address.

```
$ cat write_demo3
2,4 !w temp3

$ sed -n -f write_demo3 new

$ cat temp3
Line one.
Five.
This is the sixth sentence.
This is line seven.
Eighth and last.
```

The following example demonstrates the Next instruction. When it processes the selected line (line 3), sed immediately starts processing the next line without displaying line 3.

```
$ cat next_demo1
3 n
p

$ sed -n -f next_demo1 new
Line one.
The second line.
This is line four.
Five.
This is the sixth sentence.
This is line seven.
Eighth and last.
```

The next example uses a textual address. The sixth line contains the string **the**, so the Next instruction causes sed not to display it.

```
$ cat next_demo2
/the/ n
p

$ sed -n -f next_demo2 new
Line one.
The second line.
The third.
This is line four.
Five.
This is line seven.
Eighth and last.
```

The next set of examples uses the file **compound.in** to demonstrate how sed instructions work together.

```
$ cat compound.in
1. The words on this page...
2. The words on this page...
3. The words on this page...
4. The words on this page...
```

The following example substitutes the string **words** with **text** on lines 1, 2, and 3 and the string **text** with **TEXT** on lines 2, 3, and 4. The example also selects and deletes line 3. The result is **text** on line 1, **TEXT** on line 2, no line 3, and **words** on line 4. The sed utility made two substitutions on lines 2 and 3: **text** for **words** and **TEXT** for **text**. Then sed deleted line 3.

```
$ cat compound
1,3 s/words/text/
2,4 s/text/TEXT/
3 d

$ sed -f compound compound.in
1. The text on this page...
2. The TEXT on this page...
4. The words on this page...
```

The ordering of instructions within a sed program is critical. Both Substitute instructions are applied to the second line in the following example, as in the previous example, but the order in which the substitutions occur changes the result.

```
$ cat compound2
2,4 s/text/TEXT/
1,3 s/words/text/
3 d

$ sed -f compound2 compound.in
1. The text on this page...
2. The text on this page...
4. The words on this page...
```

Next **compound3** appends two lines to line 2. The sed utility displays all the lines from the file once because no **–n** option appears on the command line. The Print instruction at the end of the program file displays line 3 an additional time.

```
$ cat compound3
2 a\
This is line 2a.\
This is line 2b.
3 p

$ sed -f compound3 compound.in
1. The words on this page...
2. The words on this page...
This is line 2a.
This is line 2b.
3. The words on this page...
3. The words on this page...
4. The words on this page...
```

The next example shows that sed always displays appended text. Here line 2 is deleted but the Append instruction still displays the two lines that were appended to it. Appended lines are displayed even if you use the **–n** option on the command line.

```
$ cat compound4
2 a\
This is line 2a.\
This is line 2b.
2 d

$ sed -f compound4 compound.in
1. The words on this page...
This is line 2a.
This is line 2b.
3. The words on this page...
4. The words on this page...
```

The next example uses regular expressions in the addresses. The regular expression in the following instruction (^.) matches one character at the beginning of every line that is not empty. The replacement string (between the second and third slashes) contains a backslash escape sequence that represents a TAB character (\t) followed by an ampersand (&). The ampersand takes on the value of whatever the regular expression matched.

```
$ sed 's/^./\t&/' new
        Line one.
        The second line.
        The third.
...
```

This type of substitution is useful for indenting a file to create a left margin. See Appendix A for more information on regular expressions.

You can also use the simpler form **s/^/\t/** to add TABs to the beginnings of lines. However, in addition to placing TABs at the beginning of lines with text on them, this instruction places a TAB at the beginning of every empty line—something the preceding command does not do.

You may want to put the preceding sed instruction into a shell script so that you do not have to remember it (and retype it) each time you want to indent a file. The chmod utility gives you read and execute permission to the **ind** file.

```
$ cat ind
sed 's/^./\t&/' $*
$ chmod u+rx ind
$ ind new
        Line one.
        The second line.
        The third.
...
```

Stand-alone script   When you run the preceding shell script, it creates two processes: It calls a shell, which in turn calls sed. You can eliminate the overhead associated with the shell process by putting the line **#!/bin/sed –f** (page 265) at the start of the script, which runs the sed utility directly. You need read and execute permission to the file holding the script.

```
$ cat ind2
#!/bin/sed -f
s/^./\t&/
```

In the following sed program, the regular expression (two SPACEs followed by *$) matches one or more SPACEs at the end of a line. This program removes trailing SPACEs at the ends of lines, which is useful for cleaning up files that you created using vim.

```
$ cat cleanup
sed 's/ *$//' $*
```

The **cleanup2** script runs the same sed command as **cleanup** but stands alone: It calls sed directly with no intermediate shell.

```
$ cat cleanup2
#!/bin/sed -f
s/ *$//
```

Hold space   The next sed program makes use of the Hold space to exchange pairs of lines in a file.

```
$ cat s1
h # Copy Pattern space (line just read) to Hold space.
n # Read the next line of input into Pattern space.
p # Output Pattern space.
g # Copy Hold space to Pattern space.
p # Output Pattern space (which now holds the previous line).

$ sed -nf s1 new
The second line.
Line one.
This is line four.
The third.
This is the sixth sentence.
Five.
Eighth and last.
This is line seven.
```

The commands in the **s1** program process pairs of input lines. This program reads a line and stores it; reads another line and displays it; and then retrieves the stored line and displays it. After processing a pair of lines the program starts over with the next pair of lines.

The next sed program adds a blank line after each line in the input file (i.e., it double-spaces a file).

```
$ sed 'G' new
Line one.

The second line.

The third.

This is line four.

$
```

The **G** instruction appends a NEWLINE and the contents of the Hold space to the Pattern space. Unless you put something in the Hold space, it is empty. Thus the **G** instruction copies a NEWLINE to each line of input before **sed** displays the line(s) from the Pattern space.

The **s2** sed program reverses the order of the lines in a file just as the **tac** utility does.

```
$ cat s2
2,$G   # On all but the first line, append a NEWLINE and the
       # contents of the Hold space to the Pattern space.
h      # Copy the Pattern space to the Hold space.
$!d    # Delete all except the last line.

$ sed -f s2 new
Eighth and last.
This is line seven.
This is the sixth sentence.
Five.
This is line four.
The third.
The second line.
Line one.
```

This program includes three commands: **2,$G, h,** and **$!d.** To understand this script it is important to understand how the address of the last command works: The **$** is the address of the last line of input and the **!** negates the address. The result is an address that selects all except the last line of input. In the same fashion you could replace the first command with **1!G:** Select all except the first line for processing; the results would be the same.

Here is what happens as **s2** processes the **new** file:

1. The sed utility reads the first line of input (**Line one.**) into the Pattern space.

   a. The **2,$G** does not process the first line of input—because of its address the **G** instruction starts processing at the second line.

   b. The **h** copies **Line one.** from the Pattern space to the Hold space.

   c. The **$!d** deletes the contents of the Pattern space. Because there is nothing in the Pattern space, **sed** does not display anything.

2. The sed utility reads the second line of input (**The second line.**) into the Pattern space.

   a. The **2,$G** adds what is in the Hold space (**Line one.**) to the Pattern space. The Pattern space now has **The second line.**NEWLINE**Line one.**

   b. The **h** copies what is in the Pattern space to the Hold space.

   c. The **$!d** deletes the second line of input. Because it is deleted, sed does not display it.

3. The sed utility reads the third line of input (**The third.**) into the Pattern space.

   a. The **2,$G** adds what is in the Hold space (**The second line.**NEWLINE**Line one.**) to the Pattern space. The Pattern space now has **The third.**NEWLINE **The second line.**NEWLINE**Line one.**

   b. The **h** copies what is in the Pattern space to the Hold space.

   c. The **$!d** deletes the contents of the Pattern space. Because there is nothing in the Pattern space, sed does not display anything.

   . . .

8. The sed utility reads the eighth (last) line of input into the Pattern space.

   a. The **2,$G** adds what is in the Hold space to the Pattern space. The Pattern space now has all the lines from **new** in reverse order.

   b. The **h** copies what is in the Pattern space to the Hold space. This step is not necessary for the last line of input but does not alter the program's output.

   c. The **$!d** does not process the last line of input. Because of its address the **d** instruction does not delete the last line.

   d. The sed utility displays the contents of the Pattern space.

CHAPTER SUMMARY

The sed (stream editor) utility is a batch (noninteractive) editor. It takes its input from files you specify on the command line or from standard input. Unless you redirect the output from sed, it goes to standard output.

A sed program consists of one or more lines with the following syntax:

[address[,address]] instruction [argument-list]

The *address*es are optional. If you omit the *address,* sed processes all lines of input. The *instruction* is the editing instruction that modifies the text. The *address*es select the line(s) the *instruction* part of the command operates on. The number and kinds of arguments in the *argument-list* depend on the *instruction.*

In addition to basic instructions, sed includes some powerful advanced instructions. One set of these instructions allows sed programs to store data temporarily in a buffer called the Hold space. Other instructions provide unconditional and conditional branching in sed programs.

EXERCISES

1. Write a sed command that copies a file to standard output, removing all lines that begin with the word **Today**.

2. Write a sed command that copies only those lines of a file that begin with the word Today to standard output.

3. Write a sed command that copies a file to standard output, removing all blank lines (lines with no characters on them).

4. Write a sed program named **ins** that copies a file to standard output, changing all occurrences of **cat** to **dog** and preceding each modified line with a line that says **following line is modified**.

5. Write a sed program named **div** that copies a file to standard output, copies the first five lines to a file named **first**, and copies the rest of the file to a file named **last**.

6. Write a sed command that copies a file to standard output, replacing a single SPACE as the first character on a line with a 0 (zero) only if the SPACE is immediately followed by a number (0–9). For example:

```
abc  ⟶  abc
 abc  ⟶   abc
 85c  ⟶  085c
55b  ⟶  55b
 000  ⟶  0000
```

7. How can you use sed to triple-space (i.e., add two blank lines after each line in) a file?

PART V
COMMAND REFERENCE

COMMAND REFERENCE

The following tables list the utilities covered in this part of the book grouped by function and alphabetically within function. Although most of these are true utilities (programs that are separate from the shells), some are built into the shells (shell builtins). The sample utility on page 588 shows the format of the description of each utility in this part of the book.

Utilities That Display and Manipulate Files

aspell	Checks a file for spelling errors—page 589
bzip2	Compresses or decompresses files—page 596
cat	Joins and displays files—page 599
cmp	Compares two files—page 610
comm	Compares sorted files—page 612
cp	Copies files—page 616
cpio	Creates an archive or restores files from an archive—page 619
cut	Selects characters or fields from input lines—page 627
dd	Converts and copies a file—page 633
diff	Displays the differences between two files—page 638
find	Finds files based on criteria—page 655
fmt	Formats text very simply—page 664
gawk	Searches for and processes patterns in a file—page 527
grep	Searches for a pattern in files—page 683
gzip	Compresses or decompresses files—page 688
head	Displays the beginning of a file—page 691
less	Displays text files, one screen at a time—page 697
ln	Makes a link to a file—page 702
lpr	Sends files to printers—page 705

ls	Displays information about one or more files—page 708
man	Displays documentation for commands—page 721
mkdir	Creates a directory—page 724
mv	Renames or moves a file—page 732
od	Dumps the contents of a file—page 737
paste	Joins corresponding lines from files—page 742
pr	Paginates files for printing—page 744
rm	Removes a file (deletes a link)—page 753
rmdir	Removes a directory—page 755
sed	Edits a file (not interactively)—page 563
sort	Sorts and/or merges files—page 762
split	Divides a file into sections—page 771
strings	Displays strings of printable characters—page 777
tail	Displays the last part (tail) of a file—page 783
tar	Stores or retrieves files to/from an archive file—page 786
touch	Changes a file's access and/or modification time—page 801
uniq	Displays unique lines—page 812
wc	Displays the number of lines, words, and bytes—page 816

Network Utilities

ftp	Transfers files over a network—page 671
rcp	Copies one or more files to or from a remote system—page 750
rlogin	Logs in on a remote system—page 752
rsh	Executes commands on a remote system—page 756
scp	Securely copies one or more files to or from a remote system—page 758
ssh	Securely executes commands on a remote system—page 773
telnet	Connects to a remote system over a network—page 792

Utilities That Display and Alter Status

cd	Changes to another working directory—page 601
chgrp	Changes the group associated with a file—page 603
chmod	Changes the access mode (permissions) of a file—page 604
chown	Changes the owner of a file and/or the group the file is associated with—page 608
date	Displays or sets the system time and date—page 630
df	Displays disk space usage—page 636
du	Displays information on disk usage by file—page 644
file	Displays the classification of a file—page 653
finger	Displays information about users—page 661
kill	Terminates a process by PID—page 693
killall	Terminates a process by name—page 695
nice	Changes the priority of a command—page 734
nohup	Runs a command that keeps running after you log out—page 736
ps	Displays process status—page 746
sleep	Creates a process that sleeps for a specified interval—page 760
stty	Displays or sets terminal parameters—page 778
top	Dynamically displays process status—page 798
umask	Establishes the file-creation permissions mask—page 810
w	Displays information about system users—page 814
which	Shows where in PATH a command is located—page 817
who	Displays information about logged-in users—page 819

Utilities That Are Programming Tools

configure	Configures source code automatically—page 614
gcc	Compiles C and C++ programs—page 678
make	Keeps a set of programs current—page 715

Miscellaneous Utilities

at	Executes commands at a specified time—page 593
cal	Displays a calendar—page 598
crontab	Maintains crontab files—page 624
echo	Displays a message—page 647
expr	Evaluates an expression—page 649
fsck	Checks and repairs a filesystem—page 666
mkfs	Creates a filesystem on a device—page 725
Mtools	Uses DOS-style commands on files and directories—page 728
tee	Copies standard input to standard output and one or more files—page 791
test	Evaluates an expression—page 794
tr	Replaces specified characters—page 804
tty	Displays the terminal pathname—page 807
tune2fs	Changes parameters on an ext2 or ext3 filesystem—page 808
xargs	Converts standard input into command lines—page 821

Standard Multiplicative Suffixes

Several utilities allow you to use the suffixes listed in Table V-1 following byte counts. You can precede a multiplicative suffix with a number that is a multiplier. For example, 5K means 5×2^{10}. The absence of a multiplier indicates that the multiplicative suffix is to be multiplied by 1. The utilities that allow these suffixes are marked as such.

table V-1   Multiplicative suffixes

Suffix	Multiplicative value	Suffix	Multiplicative value
KB	1,000 (10^3)	PB	10^{15}
K	1,024 (2^{10})	P	2^{50}
MB	1,000,000 (10^6)	EB	10^{18}
M	1,048,576 (2^{20})	E	2^{60}

table V-1	Multiplicative suffixes (continued)		
GB	1,000,000,000 (10^9)	ZB	10^{21}
G	1,073,741,824 (2^{30})	Z	2^{70}
TB	10^{12}	YB	10^{24}
T	2^{40}	Y	2^{80}

Common Options

Several GNU utilities share the options listed in Table V-2. The utilities that use these options are marked as such.

table V-2	Common command line options
Option	**Effect**
–	A single hyphen appearing in place of a filename indicates that the utility will accept standard input in place of the file.
––	A double hyphen marks the end of the options on a command line. You can follow this option with an argument that begins with a hyphen. Without this option the utility assumes that an argument that begins with a hyphen is an option.
––help	Displays a help message for the utility. Some of these messages are quite long; you can pipe the output through less to display it one screen at a time. For example, you could give the command **ls ––help	less**. Alternatively you can pipe the output through grep if you are looking for specific information. For example, you could give the following command to get information on the **–d** option to ls: **ls ––help	grep –– –d**. See the preceding entry in this table for information on the double hyphen.
––version	Displays version information for the utility.

The sample Utility

The following description of the sample utility shows the format that is used to describe the utilities in this part of the book. These descriptions are similar to the man page descriptions (pages 30 and 721); however, most users find the descriptions in this book easier to read and understand. These descriptions emphasize the most useful features of the utilities and often leave out the more obscure features. For information about the less commonly used features, refer to the man and info pages or call the utility with the ––help option, which works with many utilities.

sample

Very brief description of what the utility does

sample [options] arguments

Following the syntax line is a description of the utility. The syntax line shows how to run the utility from the command line. Options and arguments enclosed in brackets (*[]*) are not required. Type words that appear in *this italic typeface* as is. Words that you must substitute when you type appear in *this bold italic typeface*. Words listed as arguments to a command identify single arguments (for example, *source-file*) or groups of similar arguments (for example, *directory-list*).

Arguments   This section describes the arguments that you can use when you run the utility. The argument itself, as shown in the preceding syntax line, is printed in *this bold italic typeface*.

Options   This section lists some of the options you can use with the command. Unless otherwise specified, you must precede options with one or two hyphens. Most commands accept a single hyphen before multiple options (page 109). Options in this section are ordered alphabetically by short (single-hyphen) options. If an option has only a long version (two hyphens), it is ordered by its long option. Following are some sample options:

––make-dirs –d   This option has a long and a short version. You can use either option; they are equivalent.

––delimiter=*dchar*

–d *dchar*   This option includes an argument. The argument is set in a *bold italic typeface* in both the heading and the description. You substitute another word (filename, string of characters, or other value) for any arguments you see in *this typeface*. Type characters that are in **bold type** (such as the **––delimiter** and **–d**) as is, letter for letter.

–t   (**table of contents**) This is an example of a simple option preceded by a single hyphen and not followed with any arguments. It has no long version. The **table of contents** appearing in parentheses at the beginning of the description is a cue, suggestive of what the option letter stands for.

Discussion   This optional section contains a discussion about how to use the utility and any quirks it may have.

Notes   This section contains miscellaneous notes—some important and others merely interesting.

Examples   This section contains examples of how to use the utility. This section is tutorial and is more casual than the preceding sections of the description.

aspell

Checks a file for spelling errors

aspell **check** *[options] filename*
aspell **list** *[options] < filename*
aspell **config**
aspell **help**

The aspell utility checks the spelling of words in a document against a standard dictionary. You can use aspell interactively: It displays each misspelled word in context, together with a menu that gives you the choice of accepting the word as is, choosing one of aspell's suggested replacements for the word, inserting the word into your personal dictionary, or replacing the word with one you enter. You can also use aspell in batch mode so that it reads from standard input and writes to standard output.

aspell **is not like other utilities regarding its input**

tip   Unlike many other utilities, aspell does not accept input from standard input when you do not specify a filename on the command line. Instead, the **action** specifies where aspell gets its input.

Action   You must choose one and only one *action* when you run aspell.

check   −c Runs aspell as an interactive spelling checker. Input comes from a single file named on the command line. Refer to "Discussion" on page 590.

config   Displays aspell's configuration, both default and current values. Send the output through a pipe to less for easier viewing, or use grep to find the option you are looking for (for example, **aspell config | grep backup**).

help   −? Displays an extensive page of help. Send the output through a pipe to less for easier viewing.

list   −l Runs aspell in batch mode (noninteractively) with input coming from standard input and output going to standard output.

Arguments   The *filename* is the name of the file you want to check. The aspell utility accepts this argument only when you use the **check** (−c) *action*. With the **list** (−l) *action*, input must come from standard input.

Options   The aspell utility has many options. A few of the more commonly used ones are listed in this section; see the manual for a complete list. Default values of many options are determined when aspell is compiled (see the **config** *action*).

You can specify options on the command line, in value of the **ASPELL_CONF** shell variable, or in your personal configuration file (**~/.aspell.conf**). Superuser can create a global configuration file (**/etc/aspell.conf**). Put one option per line in a configuration file; separate options with a semicolon (;) in **ASPELL_CONF**. Options on the command line override those in **ASPELL_CONF**, which override those in your personal configuration file, which override those in the global configuration file.

There are two types of options in the following list: Boolean and value. The Boolean options turn a feature on (enable the feature) or off (disable the feature). Precede a Boolean option with **dont–** to turn it off. For example, **––ignore-case** turns the **ignore-case** feature on and **––dont-ignore-case** turns it off.

Value options assign a value to a feature. Follow the option with an equal sign and a value—for example, **––ignore=4**.

For all options in a configuration file or in the **ASPELL_CONF** variable, drop the leading hyphens (**ignore-case** or **dont-ignore-case**).

aspell **options and leading hyphens**

caution   The way you specify options differs depending on whether you are specifying them on the command line, using the **ASPELL_CONF** shell variable, or in a configuration file.

On the command line prefix long options with two hyphens (for example, **––ignore-case** or **––dont-ignore-case**). In **ASPELL_CONF** and configuration files, drop the leading hyphens (for example, **ignore-case** or **dont-ignore-case**).

––dont-backup   Does not create a backup file named *filename*.**bak** (default is **––backup** when *action* is **check**).

––ignore=*n*   Ignores words with *n* or fewer characters (default is 1).

––ignore-case   Ignores the case of letters in words being checked (default is **––dont-ignore-case**).

––lang=*cc*   Specifies the two-letter language code (*cc*). The language code defaults to the value of **LC_MESSAGES** (page 291).

––mode=*mod*   Specifies a filter to use. Select *mod* from **url** (default), **none**, **sgml**, and others. The modes work as follows: **url**: skips URLs, hostnames, and email addresses; **none**: turns off all filters; **sgml**: skips SGML, HTML, XHTML, and XML commands.

––strip-accents   Removes accent marks from all the words in the dictionary before checking words (default is **––dont-strip-accents**).

Discussion   The aspell utility has two basic modes of operation: batch and interactive. You specify batch mode by using the **list** or **–l** *action*. In batch mode aspell takes the document you want to check for spelling errors as standard input and sends the list of potentially misspelled words to standard output.

You specify interactive mode by using the **check** or **–c** *action*. In interactive mode aspell displays a screen with the potentially misspelled word in context highlighted in the middle and a menu of choices at the bottom. See "Examples" for an illustation. The menu includes various commands (Table V-3) as well as some suggestions of similar, correctly spelled words. You either enter one of the numbers from the menu to select a suggested word to replace the word in question or enter a letter to give a command.

table V-3	Commands
Command	**Action**
SPACE	Takes no action and goes on to next the misspelled word.
n	Replaces the misspelled word with suggested word number *n*.
a	Adds the "misspelled" word to your personal dictionary.
b	Aborts aspell; does not save changes.
i *or* **I** (letter "i")	Ignores the misspelled word. **I** (uppercase "I") ignores all occurrences of this word; **i** ignores this occurrence only and is the same as SPACE.
l (lowercase "l")	Shifts the "misspelled" word to lowercase and adds it to your personal dictionary.
r *or* **R**	Replaces the misspelled word with the word that you enter at the bottom of the screen. **R** replaces all occurrences of this word; **r** replaces this occurrence only.
x	Saves the file as corrected so far and exits from aspell.

Notes

For more information refer to the **/usr/share/doc/aspell** directory with manuals in the **man-html** and **man-text** subdirectories and to the aspell home page located at aspell.sourceforge.net.

The aspell utility is not a foolproof way of finding spelling errors. It also does not check for misused, properly spelled words (such as *red* instead of *read*).

Spelling from emacs You can make it easy to use aspell from emacs by adding the following line to your **~/.emacs** file. This line causes emacs' ispell functions to call aspell:

```
(setq-default ispell-program-name "aspell")
```

Spelling from vim Similarly, you can make it easy to use aspell from vim by adding the following line to your **~/.vimrc** file:

```
map ^T :w!<CR>:!aspell check %<CR>:e! %<CR>
```

When you enter this line in **~/.vimrc** using vim, enter the **^T** as CONTROL-V CONTROL-T (page 159). With this line in **~/.vimrc**, CONTROL-T brings up aspell to spell check the file you are editing with vim.

Examples

The following examples use aspell to correct the spelling in the **memo.txt** file:

```
$ cat memo.txt
Here's a document for teh aspell utilitey
to check. It obviosly needs proofing
quiet badly.
```

The first example uses aspell with the **check** *action* and no options. The appearance of the screen for the first misspelled word, **teh,** is shown. At the bottom of the screen is the menu of commands and suggested words. The numbered words each differ slightly from the misspelled word:

```
$ aspell check memo.txt


Here's a document for teh aspell utilitey
to check. It obviosly needs proofing
quiet badly.


==========================================================
1) the                          6) th
2) Te                           7) tea
3) tech                         8) tee
4) Th                           9) Ted
5) eh                           0) tel
i) Ignore                       I) Ignore all
r) Replace                      R) Replace all
a) Add                          l) Add Lower
b) Abort                        x) Exit
==========================================================
?
```

Enter one of the menu choices in response to the preceding display; aspell will do your bidding and move the highlight to the next misspelled word (unless you choose to abort or exit).

The next example uses the **list** *action* to display a list of misspelled words. The word **quiet** is not in the list—it is not properly used but is properly spelled.

```
$ aspell list < memo.txt
teh
aspell
utilitey
obviosly
```

The last example also uses the uses the **list** *action*. It shows a quick way to check the spelling of a word or two with a single command. The user gives the **aspell list** command and then enters **seperate temperature** into aspell's standard input (the keyboard). After the user enters RETURN and CONTROL-D (to mark the end of file), aspell writes the misspelled word to standard output (the screen):

```
$ aspell list
seperate temperatureRETURN
CONTROL-D
seperate
```

at

Executes commands at a specified time

at [options] time [date | +increment]
atq
atrm job-list
batch [options] [time]

The at and batch utilities execute commands at a specified time. They accept commands from standard input or, with the –f option, from a file. Commands are executed in the same environment as the at or batch command. Unless redirected, standard output and standard error from commands are emailed to the user who ran at or batch. A *job* is the group of commands that is executed by one call to at. The batch utility differs from at in that it schedules jobs so that they run when the CPU load on the system is low.

The atq utility displays a list of at jobs you have queued; atrm cancels pending at jobs.

Arguments

The *time* is the time of day that at runs the job. You can specify the *time* as a one-, two-, or four-digit number. One- and two-digit numbers specify an hour, and four-digit numbers specify an hour and minute. You can also give the time in the form **hh:mm**. The at utility assumes a 24-hour clock unless you place **am** or **pm** immediately after the number, in which case it uses a 12-hour clock. You can also specify *time* as **now, midnight, noon,** or **teatime** (4:00 PM).

The *date* is the day of the week or day of the month on which you want at to execute the job. When you do not specify a day, at executes the job today if the hour you specify in *time* is greater than the current hour. If the hour is less than the current hour, at executes the job tomorrow.

You specify a day of the week by spelling it out or abbreviating it to three letters. You can also use the words **today** and **tomorrow**. Use the name of a month followed by the number of the day in the month to specify a date. You can follow the month and day number with a year.

The *increment* is a number followed by one of the following (plural or singular is allowed): **minutes, hours, days,** or **weeks**. The at utility adds the *increment* to *time*. You cannot specify an increment for a date.

When using atrm, *job-list* is a list of one or more at job numbers. You can list job numbers by running at with the –l option or by using atq.

Options

The –l and –d options are not for use when you initiate a job with at. You can use them only to determine the status of a job or to cancel a job.

–c *job-list*   (**cat**) Displays the environment and *commands* specified by *job-list*.

–d *job-list*   (**delete**) Cancels jobs that you previously submitted with at. The *job-list* argument is a list of one or more at job numbers to cancel. If you do not remember the job number, use the –l option or run atq to list your jobs and their numbers. Using this option with at is the same as running atrm.

–f *file*   (**file**) Specifies that *commands* come from *file* instead of standard input. This option is useful for long lists of *commands* or *commands* that are executed repeatedly.

–l   (**list**) Displays a list of your at jobs. Using this option with at is the same as running atq.

–m   (**mail**) Sends you email after a job is run, even when nothing is sent to standard output or standard error. When a job generates output, at always emails it to you, regardless of this option.

Notes

The shell saves the environment variables and the working directory at the time you submit an at job so that they are available when at executes *commands*.

*/etc/at.allow and */etc/at.deny*   The **root** user can always use at. The /etc/at.allow and /etc/at.deny files, which should be readable and writable by **root** only (mode 600), control which ordinary, local users can use at. When /etc/at.deny exists and is empty, all users can use at. When /etc/at.deny does not exist, only users listed in /etc/at.allow can use at. Users listed in /etc/at.deny cannot use at unless they are also listed in /etc/at.allow.

Jobs you submit using at are run by the at daemon (**atd**). This daemon stores jobs in /var/spool/at and output in /var/spool/at/spool, both of which should be set to mode 700 and owned by the user named **daemon**.

Examples

You can use any of the following techniques to paginate and print **long_file** tomorrow at 2:00 AM. The first example executes the command directly from the command line; the last two examples use the **pr_tonight** file, which contains the necessary command, and execute it using at.

```
$ at 2am
at> pr long_file | lpr
at>CONTROL-D<EOT>
job 8 at 2005-08-17 02:00

$ cat pr_tonight
#!/bin/bash
pr long_file | lpr

$ at -f pr_tonight 2am
job 9 at 2005-08-17 02:00

$ at 2am < pr_tonight
job 10 at 2005-08-17 02:00
```

If you execute commands directly from the command line, you must signal the end of the commands by pressing CONTROL-D at the beginning of a line. After you press CONTROL-D, at displays a line that begins with **job** followed by the job number and the time at will execute the job.

If you run atq after the preceding commands, it displays a list of jobs in its queue:

```
$ atq
8        2005-08-17 02:00 a
9        2005-08-17 02:00 a
10       2005-08-17 02:00 a
```

The following command removes job number 9 from the queue:

```
$ atrm 9
$ atq
8        2005-08-17 02:00 a
10       2005-08-17 02:00 a
```

The next example executes **cmdfile** at 3:30 PM (1530 hours) one week from today:

```
$ at -f cmdfile 1530 +1 week
job 12 at 2005-08-23 15:30
```

Next at executes a job at 7 PM on Thursday. This job uses find to create an intermediate file, redirects the output sent to standard error, and prints the file.

```
$ at 7pm Thursday
at> find / -name "core" -print >report.out 2>report.err
at> lpr report.out
at>CONTROL-D<EOT>
job 13 at 2005-08-18 19:00
```

The final example shows some of the output generated by the −c option when at is queried about the preceding job. Most of the lines show the environment; only the last few lines execute the *commands:*

```
$ at -c 13
#!/bin/sh
# atrun uid=500 gid=500
# mail     mark 0
umask 2
PATH=/usr/kerberos/bin:/usr/local/bin:/bin:/usr/bin:/usr/X11R6/bin:.;
export PATH
PWD=/home/mark/book.examples/99/cp; export PWD
EXINIT=set\ ai\ aw; export EXINIT
LANG=C; export LANG
PS1=\\\$\ ; export PS1
...
cd /home/mark/book\.examples/99/cp || {
        echo 'Execution directory inaccessible' >&2
        exit 1
}
find / -name "core" -print >report.out 2>report.err
lpr report.out
```

bzip2

Compresses or decompresses files

bzip2 [options] [file-list]
bunzip2 [options] [file-list]
bzcat [options] [file-list]
bzip2recover [file]

The bzip2 utility compresses files; bunzip2 restores files compressed with bzip2; bzcat displays files compressed with bzip2.

Arguments   The *file-list* is a list of one or more files (no directories) that are to be compressed or decompressed. If *file-list* is empty or if the special option – is present, bzip2 reads from standard input. The −−**stdout** option causes bzip2 to write to standard output.

Options   Accepts the common options described on page 587.

−−stdout   −c   Writes the results of compression or decompression to standard output.

−−decompress   −d   Decompresses a file compressed with bzip2. This option with bzip2 is equivalent to the bunzip2 command.

−−fast *or*   −*n*   Sets the block size when compressing a file. The *n* is a digit from 1 to 9, where
−−best   1 (−−**fast**) generates a block size of 100 kilobytes and 9 (−−**best**) generates a block size of 900 kilobytes. The default level is 9. The options −−**fast** and −−**best** are provided for compatibility with gzip and do not necessarily yield the fastest or best compression.

−−force   −f   Forces compression even if a file already exists, has multiple links, or comes directly from a terminal. The option has a similar effect with bunzip2.

−−keep   −k   Does not delete input files while compressing or decompressing them.

−−quiet   −q   Suppresses warning messages; does display critical messages.

−−test   −t   Verifies the integrity of a compressed file. Displays nothing if the file is OK.

−−verbose   −v   For each file being compressed displays the name of the file, the compression ratio, the percentage of space saved, and the sizes of the decompressed and compressed files.

Discussion   The bzip2 and bunzip2 utilities work similarly to gzip and gunzip; see the discussion of gzip (page 689) for more information. Normally bzip2 does not overwrite a file; you must use −−**force** to overwrite a file during compression or decompression.

Notes   The bzip2 home page is sources.redhat.com/bzip2.

The bzip2 utility does a better job of compressing files than gzip.

Use the **--bzip2** modifier with tar (page 788) to compress archive files with bzip2.

bzcat *file-list* Works like cat except that it uses bunzip2 to decompress *file-list* as it copies files to standard output.

bzip2recover Attempts to recover a damaged file that was compressed with bzip2.

Examples   In the following example, bzip2 compresses a file and gives the resulting file the same name with a **.bz2** filename extension. The **–v** option displays statistics about the compression.

```
$ ls -l
total 728
-rw-r--r--  1 sam sam 737414 Feb 20 19:05 bigfile
$ bzip2 -v bigfile
  bigfile: 3.926:1, 2.037 bits/byte, 74.53% saved, 737414 in, 187806 out
$ ls -l
total 188
-rw-r--r--  1 sam sam 187806 Feb 20 19:05 bigfile.bz2
```

Next touch creates a file with the same name as the original file; bunzip2 refuses to overwrite the file in the process of decompressing **bigfile.bz2**. The **--force** option enables bunzip2 to overwrite the file.

```
$ touch bigfile
$ bunzip2 bigfile.bz2
bunzip2: Output file bigfile already exists.
$ bunzip2 --force bigfile.bz2
$ ls -l
total 728
-rw-r--r--  1 sam sam 737414 Feb 20 19:05 bigfile
```

cal

Displays a calendar

cal [options] [[month] year]

The cal utility displays a calendar for a month or a year.

Arguments   The arguments specify the month and year for which cal displays a calendar. The *month* is a decimal integer from 1 to 12 and the *year* is a decimal integer. Without any arguments, cal displays a calendar for the current month. When you specify a single argument, it is taken to be the year.

Options

–j   (**Julian**) Displays a Julian calendar—a calendar that numbers the days consecutively from January 1 (1) through December 31 (365 or 366).

–m   (**Monday**) Makes Monday the first day of the week. Without this option, Sunday is the first day of the week.

–y   (**year**) Displays a calendar for the current year.

–3   (**three months**) Displays the previous, current, and next months.

Notes   Do not abbreviate the year. The year **05** is not the same as **2005**.

Examples   The following command displays a calendar for August 2007:

```
$ cal 8 2007
      August 2007
Su Mo Tu We Th Fr Sa
          1  2  3  4
 5  6  7  8  9 10 11
12 13 14 15 16 17 18
19 20 21 22 23 24 25
26 27 28 29 30 31
```

Next is a Julian calendar for 1949 with Monday as the first day of the week:

```
$ cal -jm 1949
                           1949
          January                        February
Mon Tue Wed Thu Fri Sat Sun    Mon Tue Wed Thu Fri Sat Sun
                      1   2     32  33  34  35  36  37
  3   4   5   6   7   8   9     38  39  40  41  42  43  44
 10  11  12  13  14  15  16     45  46  47  48  49  50  51
 17  18  19  20  21  22  23     52  53  54  55  56  57  58
 24  25  26  27  28  29  30     59
 31 ...
```

cat

Joins and displays files

cat [options] [file-list]

The cat utility copies files to standard output. You can use cat to display the contents of one or more text files on the screen.

Arguments   The *file-list* is a list of the pathnames of one or more files that cat processes. If you do not specify an argument or if you specify a hyphen (–) in place of a filename, cat reads from standard input.

Options   Accepts the common options described on page 587.

––show-all   –A   Same as –vET.

––number-nonblank
          –b   Numbers all lines that are not blank as they are written to standard output.

          –e   (**end**) Same as –vE.

––show-ends   –E   Marks the ends of lines with dollar signs.

––number   –n   (**number**) Numbers all lines as they are written to standard output.

––squeeze-blank   –s   Removes extra blank lines so there are never two or more blank lines in a row.

          –t   (**tab**) Same as –vT.

––show-tabs   –T   Marks each TAB with ^I.

––show-nonprinting
          –v   Displays CONTROL characters with the caret notation (^M) and displays characters that have the high bit set (META characters) with the **M-** notation. This option does not convert TABs and LINEFEEDs. Use **––show-tabs** if you want to display TABs as ^I. LINEFEEDs cannot be displayed as anything but themselves; otherwise, the line would be too long.

Notes   See page 115 for a discussion of cat, standard input, and standard output.

Use the od utility (page 737) to display the contents of a file that does not contain text (for example, an executable program file).

Use the tac utility to display lines of a text file in reverse order. See the tac info page for more information.

The name cat is derived from one of the functions of this utility, *catenate,* which means to join together sequentially, or end to end.

Set noclobber to avoid overwriting a file

caution   Despite cat's warning message, the shell destroys the input file (**letter**) before invoking cat in the following example:

```
$ cat memo letter > letter
cat: letter: input file is output file
```

You can prevent overwriting a file in this situation by setting the **noclobber** variable (pages 119 and 367).

Examples   The following command displays the contents of the **memo** text file on the terminal:

```
$ cat memo
...
```

The next example catenates three text files and redirects the output to the **all** file:

```
$ cat page1 letter memo > all
```

You can use cat to create short text files without using an editor. Enter the following command line, type (or paste) the text you want in the file, and press CONTROL-D on a line by itself:

```
$ cat > new_file
...
(text)
...
CONTROL-D
```

In this case cat takes input from standard input (the keyboard) and the shell redirects standard output (a copy of the input) to the file you specify. The CONTROL-D signals the EOF (end of file) and causes cat to return control to the shell (page 116).

In the next example, a pipe sends the output from who to standard input of cat. The shell redirects cat's output to the file named **output** that, after the commands have finished executing, contains the contents of the **header** file, the output of who, and **footer**. The hyphen on the command line causes cat to read standard input after reading **header** and before reading **footer**.

```
$ who | cat header - footer > output
```

cd

Changes to another working directory

cd [options] [directory]

The cd builtin makes *directory* the working directory.

Arguments   The *directory* is the pathname of the directory you want to be the new working directory. Without an argument, cd makes your home directory the working directory. Using a hyphen in place of *directory* changes to the previous working directory.

Notes   The cd command is a bash and tcsh builtin.

See page 82 for a discussion of cd.

Without an argument, cd makes your home directory the working directory; it uses the value of the **HOME** (bash; page 283) or **home** (tcsh, page 362) variable for this purpose.

With an argument of a hyphen, cd makes the previous working directory the working directory. It uses the value of the **OLDPWD** (bash) or **owd** (tcsh) variable for this purpose.

The **CDPATH** (bash; page 289) or **cdpath** (tcsh; page 362) variable contains a colon-separated list of directories that cd searches. Within the list a null directory name (::) or a period (:.:) represents the working directory. If CDPATH or cdpath is not set, cd searches only the working directory for *directory*. If this variable is set and *directory* is not an absolute pathname (does not begin with a slash), cd searches the directories in the list; if the search fails, cd searches the working directory. See page 289 for a discussion of **CDPATH**.

Examples   The following **cd** command makes Alex's home directory his working directory. The pwd builtin verifies the change:

```
$ pwd
/home/alex/literature
$ cd
$ pwd
/home/alex
```

The next command makes the **/home/alex/literature** directory the working directory:

```
$ cd /home/alex/literature
$ pwd
/home/alex/literature
```

Next the cd utility makes a subdirectory of the working directory the new working directory:

```
$ cd memos
$ pwd
/home/alex/literature/memos
```

Finally cd uses the .. reference to the parent of the working directory to make the parent the new working directory:

```
$ cd ..
$ pwd
/home/alex/literature
```

chgrp

Changes the group associated with a file

chgrp [options] group file-list
chgrp [options] --reference=rfile file-list

The chgrp utility changes the group associated with one or more files.

Arguments   The *group* is the name or numeric group ID of the new group. The *file-list* is a list of the pathnames of the files whose group association is to be changed. The *rfile* is the pathname of a file whose group is to become the new group associated with *file-list*.

Options

--changes	-c	Displays a message for each file whose group is changed.
--dereference		Changes the group IDs of the files symbolic links point to, not the symbolic links themselves. The default is **--no-dereference**.
--quiet *or* --silent	-f	Prevents the display of warning messages about files whose permissions prevent you from changing their group IDs.
--no-dereference	-h	Changes the group IDs of symbolic links, not the files that the links point to (default).
--recursive	-R	Recursively descends a directory specified in *file-list* and changes the group ID on all files in the directory hierarchy.
--reference=*rfile*		Changes the group of the files in *file-list* to that of *rfile*.
--verbose	-v	Displays for each file a message saying whether its group was retained or changed.

Notes   Only the owner of a file or **root** can change the group association of a file. Also, unless you are **root**, you must belong to the specified *group* to change the group ID of a file to that *group*.

See page 608 for information on how chown can change the group associated with, as well as the owner of, a file.

Examples   The following command changes the group that the **manuals** file is associated with; the new group is **pubs**.

```
$ chgrp pubs manuals
```

chmod

Changes the access mode (permissions) of a file

chmod [*options*] *who operator permission file-list (symbolic)*
chmod [*options*] *mode file-list (absolute)*
chmod [*options*] *--reference=rfile file-list (referential)*

The chmod utility changes the ways in which a file can be accessed by the owner of the file, the group to which the file belongs, and/or all other users. Only the owner of a file or Superuser can change the access mode, or permissions, of a file. You can specify the new access mode absolutely, symbolically, or referentially.

Arguments   Arguments specify which files are to have their modes changed in what ways.

Symbolic

You can specify multiple sets of symbolic modes (*who operator permission*) by separating each set from the next with a comma.

The chmod utility changes the access permission for the class of users specified by *who*. The class of users is designated by one or more of the letters specified in the *who* column of Table V-4.

table V-4	Symbolic mode user class specification	
who	**User class**	**Meaning**
u	User	Owner of the file
g	Group	Group to which the owner belongs
o	Other	All other users
a	All	Can be used in place of **ugo**

Table V-5 lists the symbolic mode *operators*.

table V-5	Symbolic mode operators
operator	**Meaning**
+	Adds permission for the specified user class
–	Removes permission for the specified user class
=	Sets permission for the specified user class—resets all other permissions for that user class

The access *permission* is specified by one or more of the letters listed in Table V-6.

table V-6	Symbolic mode permissions
permission	**Meaning**
r	Sets read permission
w	Sets write permission
x	Sets execute permission
s	Sets user ID or group ID (depending on the **who** argument) to that of the owner of the file while the file is being executed (For more information see page 94.)
t	Sets the sticky bit (Only Superuser can set the sticky bit, and it can be used only with **u**; see page 903.)
X	Makes the file executable only if it is a directory or if another user class has execute permission
u	Sets specified permissions to those of the owner
g	Sets specified permissions to those of the group
o	Sets specified permissions to those of others

Absolute

You can use an octal number to specify the access mode. Construct the number by ORing the appropriate values from Table V-7. To OR two octal numbers from this table, just add them. (Refer to Table V-8 for examples.)

table V-7	Absolute mode specifications
mode	**Meaning**
4000	Sets user ID when the program is executed (page 94)
2000	Sets group ID when the program is executed (page 94)
1000	Sticky bit (page 903)
0400	Owner can read the file
0200	Owner can write to the file
0100	Owner can execute the file
0040	Group can read the file
0020	Group can write to the file
0010	Group can execute the file
0004	Others can read the file
0002	Others can write to the file
0001	Others can execute the file

Table V-8 lists some typical modes.

table V-8	Examples of absolute mode specifications
Mode	**Meaning**
0777	Owner, group, and others can read, write, and execute file
0755	Owner can read, write, and execute file; group and others can read and execute file
0711	Owner can read, write, and execute file; group and others can execute file
0644	Owner can read and write file; group and others can read file
0640	Owner can read and write file, group can read file, and others cannot access file

Options

--changes	-c	Displays a message giving the new permissions for each file whose mode is changed.
--quiet *or* --silent	-f	Prevents the display of warning messages about files whose permissions prevent chmod from changing the permissions of the file.
--recursive	-R	Recursively descends a directory specified in *file-list* and changes the permissions on all files in the directory hierarchy.
--reference=*rfile*		Changes the permissions of the files in *file-list* to that of *rfile*.
--verbose	-v	Displays for each file a message saying that its permissions were changed (even if they were not changed) and specifying the permissions. Use --**changes** to display messages only when permissions are actually changed.

Notes

When you are using symbolic arguments, you can omit the *permission* from the command line only when the *operator* is =. This omission takes away all permissions. See the second example in the next section.

Examples

The following examples show how to use the chmod utility to change the permissions of the file named **temp**. The initial access mode of **temp** is shown by ls (see "Discussion" on page 710 for information about the ls display):

```
$ ls -l temp
-rw-rw-r-- 1 alex pubs 57 Jul 12 16:47 temp
```

When you do not follow an equal sign with a permission, chmod removes all permissions for the specified user class. The following command removes all access permissions for the group and all other users so that only the owner has access to the file:

```
$ chmod go= temp
$ ls -l temp
-rw------- 1 alex pubs 57 Jul 12 16:47 temp
```

The next command changes the access modes for all users (owner, group, and others) to read and write. Now anyone can read from or write to the file.

```
$ chmod a=rw temp
$ ls -l temp
-rw-rw-rw- 1 alex pubs 57 Jul 12 16:47 temp
```

Using an absolute argument, **a=rw** becomes **666**. The next command performs the same function as the previous one:

```
$ chmod 666 temp
```

The next command removes write access permission for other users. As a result members of the **pubs** group can still read from and write to the file, but other users can only read from the file:

```
$ chmod o-w temp
$ ls -l temp
-rw-rw-r-- 1 alex pubs 57 Jul 12 16:47 temp
```

The following command yields the same result, using an absolute argument:

```
$ chmod 664 temp
```

The next command adds execute access permission for all users:

```
$ chmod a+x temp
$ ls -l temp
-rwxrwxr-x 1 alex pubs 57 Jul 12 16:47 temp
```

If **temp** is a shell script or other executable file, all users can now execute it. (You need read and execute access to execute a shell script but only execute access to execute a binary file.) The absolute command that yields the same result is

```
$ chmod 775 temp
```

The final command uses symbolic arguments to achieve the same result as the preceding one. It sets permissions to read, write, and execute for the owner, and to read and write for the group and other users. A comma separates the sets of symbolic modes.

```
$ chmod u=rwx,go=rw temp
```

chown

Changes the owner of a file and/or the group the file is associated with

chown [options] owner file-list
chown [options] owner:group file-list
chown [options] owner: file-list
chown [options] :group file-list
chown [options] --reference=rfile file-list

The chown utility changes the owner of a file and/or the group the file is associated with. Only **root** can change the owner of a file. Only **root** or the owner of a file who belongs to the new group can change the group a file is associated with.

Arguments   The *owner* is the username or numeric user ID of the new owner. The *file-list* is a list of the pathnames of the files whose ownership and/or group association you want to change. The *group* is the group name or numeric group ID of the new group that the file is associated with. Table V-9 shows the ways you can specify the new *owner* and/or *group*.

table V-9   Specifying the new owner and/or group

Argument	Meaning
owner	The new owner of *file-list*; the group is not changed
owner:group	The new owner and new group association of *file-list*
owner:	The new owner of *file-list*; the group association is changed to that of the new owner's login group
:group	The new group associated with *file-list*; the owner is not changed

Options   Accepts the common options described on page 587.

--changes   **-c** Displays a message for each file whose ownership/group is changed.

--dereference   Changes the ownership/group of the files symbolic links point to, not the symbolic links themselves. The default is **--no-dereference**.

--quiet *or*   **-f** Prevents chown from displaying error messages when it is unable to change the
--silent   ownership/group of a file.

--no-dereference   **-h** Changes the ownership/group of symbolic links, not the files that the links point to (default).

--recursive   **-R** When you include directories in the *file-list*, this option descends the directory hierarchy, setting the specified ownership/group for all files encountered.

--reference=*rfile*	Changes the ownership and group association of the files in the *file-list* to that of *rfile*.
--verbose -v	Displays for each file a message saying whether its ownership/group was retained or changed.

Notes   The chown utility clears setuid and setgid bits when it changes the owner of a file.

Examples   The following command changes the owner of the **chapter1** file in the **manuals** directory. The new owner is Jenny:

```
# chown jenny manuals/chapter1
```

The following command makes Alex the owner of, and Alex's login group the group associated with, all files in the **/home/alex/literature** directory and in all its subdirectories:

```
# chown --recursive alex: /home/alex/literature
```

The next command changes the ownership of the files in **literature** to alex and the group associated with these files to **pubs**:

```
# chown alex:pubs /home/alex/literature/*
```

The final example changes the group association of the files in **manuals** to **pubs** without altering their ownership. The owner of the files, who is executing this command, must belong to the **pubs** group.

```
$ chown :pubs manuals/*
```

cmp

Compares two files

cmp [options] file1 [file2 [skip1 [skip2]]]

The cmp utility displays the differences between two files on a byte-by-byte basis. If the files are the same, cmp is silent. If the files differ, cmp displays the byte and line number of the first difference.

Arguments
The *file1* and *file2* are pathnames of the files that cmp compares. If *file2* is omitted, cmp uses standard input instead. Using a hyphen (–) in place of *file1* or *file2* causes cmp to read standard input instead of that file.

The *skip1* and *skip2* are decimal numbers indicating the number of bytes to skip in each file before beginning the comparison.

Options

––print–bytes   –b Displays more information, including filenames, byte and line number, as well as octal and ASCII values of the first differing byte.

––ignore–initial=*n*   –i *n*
Skips the first *n* bytes in both files before beginning the comparison.

––verbose   –l (lowercase "l") Instead of stopping at the first byte that differs, continues comparing the two files and displays both the location and the value of each byte that differs. Locations are displayed as decimal byte count offsets from the beginning of the files; byte values are displayed in octal. The comparison terminates when an EOF is encountered on either file.

––silent *or*   –s Suppresses output from cmp; only sets the exit status (see "Notes").
––quite

Notes
Byte and line numbering start at 1.

The cmp utility does not display a message if the files are identical; it only sets the exit status. This utility returns an exit status of 0 if the files are the same and 1 if they are different. An exit status greater than 1 means an error occurred.

When you use *skip1* (and *skip2*), the offset values cmp displays are based on the byte where the comparison began. You can use the standard multiplicative suffixes after *skip1* and *skip2;* see Table V-1 on page 586.

Unlike diff (page 638), cmp works with binary as well as ASCII files.

Examples   The examples use the files **a** and **b** shown below. These files have two differences. The first difference is that the word **lazy** in file **a** is replaced by **lasy** in file **b**. The second difference is more subtle: A TAB character appears just before the NEWLINE character in file **b**.

```
$ cat a
The quick brown fox jumped over the lazy dog.
$ cat b
The quick brown fox jumped over the lasy dog.TAB
```

The first example uses cmp without any options to compare the two files. The cmp utility reports that the files are different and identifies the offset from the start of the files where the first difference is found:

```
$ cmp a b
a b differ: char 39, line 1
```

You can display the values of the bytes at that location by adding the **--print-chars** option:

```
$ cmp --print-bytes a b
a b differ: char 39, line 1 is 172 z 163 s
```

The **–l** option displays all bytes that differ between the two files. Because this option creates a lot of output if the files have many differences, you may want to redirect the output to a file. The following example shows the two differences between files **a** and **b**. The **–b** option displays the values for the bytes as well. Where file **a** has a CONTROL-J (NEWLINE), file **b** has a CONTROL-I (TAB). The message saying that it has reached the end of file on file **a** indicates that file **b** is longer than file **a**.

```
$ cmp -lb a b
39 172 z     163 s
46  12 ^J     11 ^I
cmp: EOF on a
```

In the next example, the **--ignore-initial** option is used to skip over the first difference in the files. The cmp utility now reports on the second difference. The difference is put at character 7, which is the 46th character in the original file **b** (7 characters past the ignored 39 characters).

```
$ cmp --ignore-initial=39 a b
a b differ: char 7, line 1
```

You can use *skip1* and *skip2* in place of the **--ignore-initial** option used in the preceding example:

```
$ cmp a b 39 39
a b differ: char 7, line 1
```

comm

Compares sorted files

comm [options] file1 file2

The comm utility displays a line-by-line comparison of two sorted files. The first of the three columns it displays lists the lines found only in *file1*, the second column lists the lines found only in *file2*, and the third lists the lines common to both files.

Arguments   The *file1* and *file2* are pathnames of the files that comm compares. Using a hyphen (–) in place of *file1* or *file2* causes comm to read standard input instead of that file.

Options   You can combine the options.

–1   Does not display column 1 (does not display lines found only in **file1**).

–2   Does not display column 2 (does not display lines found only in **file2**).

–3   Does not display column 3 (does not display lines found in both files).

Notes   If the files have not been sorted, comm will not work properly.

Lines in the second column are preceded by one TAB, and those in the third column are preceded by two TABs.

The exit status indicates whether comm completed normally (0) or abnormally (not 0).

Examples   The following examples use two files, **c** and **d**, in the working directory. As with all input to comm, the files have already been sorted:

```
$ cat c
bbbbb
ccccc
ddddd
eeeee
fffff
$ cat d
aaaaa
ddddd
eeeee
ggggg
hhhhh
```

Refer to sort on page 762 for information on sorting files.

The following example calls comm without any options, so it displays three columns. The first column lists those lines found only in file **c**, the second column lists those found in **d**, and the third lists the lines found in both **c** and **d**:

```
$ comm c d
          aaaaa
bbbbb
ccccc
                    ddddd
                    eeeee
fffff
          ggggg
          hhhhh
```

The next example shows the use of options to prevent comm from displaying columns 1 and 2. The result is column 3, a list of the lines common to files **c** and **d**:

```
$ comm -12 c d
ddddd
eeeee
```

configure

Configures source code automatically

./configure options

The configure script is part of the GNU Configure and Build System. Software developers who supply source code for their products face the problem of making it easy for relatively naive users to build and install their software package on a wide variety of machine architectures, operating systems, and system software. Toward this end many software developers supply a shell script named configure with their source code.

When you run configure, it determines the capabilities of the local system. The data collected by configure is used to build the makefiles with which make (page 715) builds the executables and libraries. You can adjust the behavior of configure by specifying command line options and environment variables.

Options

––disable-*feature*   Works in the same manner as *––enable-feature* except that it disables support for *feature*.

––enable-*feature*   Replace *feature* with the name of a feature that can be supported by the software being configured. For example, configuring the Z Shell source code with the command **configure ––enable-zsh-mem** configures the source code to use the special memory allocation routines provided with zsh instead of using the system memory allocation routines. Check the **README** file supplied with the software distribution to see the choices available for *feature*.

––help   Displays a detailed list of all options available for use with configure. The contents of this list depends on the software distribution being configured.

––prefix=*directory*

By default configure builds makefiles that install software in the **/usr/local** directory (when you give the command **make install**). To install into a different directory, replace *directory* with the pathname of the directory you want to install the software in.

––with-*package*   Replace *package* with the name of an optional package that can be included with the software you are configuring. For example, if you configure the source code for the Windows emulator wine with the command **configure ––with-dll**, the source code is configured to build a shared library of Windows emulation support. Check the **README** file supplied with the software distribution to see the choices available for *package*. Also, **configure ––help** usually displays the choices available for *package*.

Discussion   The GNU Configure and Build System allows software developers to distribute software that can configure itself to be built on a variety of systems. This system builds a shell script named configure, which prepares the software distribution to be built and installed on a local system. The configure script searches the local system to find the various dependencies for the software distribution and constructs the appropriate makefiles. Once you have run configure, you can build the software with a **make** command and install the software with a **make install** command.

The configure script determines which C compiler to use (usually gcc) and specifies a set of flags to pass to that compiler. You can set the environment variables **CC** and **CFLAGS** to override these values with your own choices. (See the "Examples" section.)

Notes   Each package that uses the GNU autoconfiguration utility provides its own custom copy of configure, which the software developer created using the GNU autoconf utility. Read the **README** and **INSTALL** files that are provided with the package you are installing to obtain detailed information about the available options.

The configure scripts are self-contained and run correctly on a wide variety of systems. You do not need any special system resources to use configure.

Examples   The simplest way to call configure is to cd to the base directory for the software distribution you want to configure and then run the following command:

```
$ ./configure
```

The ./ is prepended to the command name to ensure that you are running the configure script that was supplied with the software distribution. To cause configure to build makefiles that pass the flags –**Wall** and –**O2** to gcc, use the following command from bash:

```
$ CFLAGS="-Wall -O2" ./configure
```

If you are using tcsh, use the following command:

```
tcsh $ env CFLAGS="-Wall -O2" ./configure
```

cp

Copies files

cp [options] source-file destination-file
cp [options] source-file-list destination-directory

The cp utility copies one or more files. It can either make a copy of a single file (first format) or it can copy one or more files to a directory (second format). With the **--recursive** option, cp can copy directories.

Arguments

The *source-file* is the pathname of the file that cp makes a copy of. The *destination-file* is the pathname that cp assigns to the resulting copy of the file.

The *source-file-list* is a list of one or more pathnames of files that cp makes copies of. The *destination-directory* is the pathname of the directory in which cp places the copied files. With this format, cp gives each of the copied files the same simple filename as its *source-file*.

The **--recursive** option enables cp to copy directories recursively from the *source-file-list* into the *destination-directory*.

Options

Accepts the common options described on page 587.

--archive   **-a**   Attempts to preserve as many attributes of *source-file* as possible. Same as **-dpPR**.

--backup   **-b**   If copying a file would remove or overwrite an existing file, this option makes a backup copy of the file that would be overwritten. The backup copy has the same name as the *destination-file* with a tilde (~) appended to it. When you use both **--backup** and **--force**, cp makes a backup copy when you try to copy a file over itself.

-d   Copies symbolic links, not the files that links point to. Also preserves hard links in *destination-files* that exist between corresponding *source-files*. This option is equivalent to **--no-dereference** and **--preserve=links**.

--force   **-f**   When the *destination-file* exists and cannot be opened for writing, this option causes cp to try to remove *destination-file* before copying *source-file*. This option is useful when the user copying a file does not have write permission to an existing *destination-file* but has write permission to the directory containing the *destination-file*. See also **--backup**.

--interactive   **-i**   Prompts you whenever cp would overwrite a file. If you respond with a string that starts with **y** or **Y**, cp continues. If you enter anything else, cp does not copy the file.

––dereference	**–L**	Copies the file that a symbolic link points to. See **––no-dereference**.
––preserve	**–p**	Creates a *destination-file* with the same owner, group, permissions, access date, and modification date as the *source-file*.
––no-dereference	**–P**	Copies symbolic links, not the files that the links point to. Without the **–R**, **–r**, or **––recursive** option, the default behavior is to dereference links (copy the files that links point to, not the links). With one of these options, cp does not dereference symbolic links (it copies the links, not the files that the links point to).
––parents		Copies a relative pathname to a directory, creating directories as needed. (See "Examples.")
––preserve=links		When recursively copying directories, attempts to preserve hard links in *destination-files* that exist between corresponding *source-files*.
––recursive	**–R** *or* **–r**	
		Recursively copies directory hierarchies including ordinary files. The **––no-dereference** option is implied.
––update	**–u**	Copies only when the *destination-file* does not exist or when it is older than the *source-file*.
––verbose	**–v**	Displays the name of each file as cp copies it.

Notes   If the *destination-file* exists before you execute cp, cp overwrites the file, destroying the contents but leaving the access privileges, owner, and group associated with the file as they were.

If the *destination-file* does not exist, cp uses the access privileges of the *source-file*. The user who copies the file becomes the owner of the *destination-file* and the user's group becomes the group associated with the *destination-file*.

With the **–p** option, cp attempts to set the owner, group, permissions, access date, and modification date to match those of the *source-file*.

Unlike ln (page 702), the *destination-file* that cp creates is independent of its *source-file*.

Examples   The first command makes a copy of the file **letter** in the working directory. The name of the copy is **letter.sav**.

```
$ cp letter letter.sav
```

The next command copies all files with filenames ending in **.c** into the **archives** directory, which is a subdirectory of the working directory. Each copied file retains its simple filename but has a new absolute pathname. Because of the **––preserve** option, the copied files in **archives** have the same owner, group, permissions, access date, and modification date as the source files.

```
$ cp --preserve *.c archives
```

The next example copies **memo** from **/home/jenny** to the working directory:

```
$ cp /home/jenny/memo .
```

The next example uses the **--parents** option to copy the file **memo/thursday/max** to the **dir** directory as **dir/memo/thursday/max**. The find utility shows the newly created directory hierarchy.

```
$ cp --parents memo/thursday/max dir
$ find dir
dir
dir/memo
dir/memo/thursday
dir/memo/thursday/max
```

The following command copies the files named **memo** and **letter** into another directory. The copies have the same simple filenames as the source files (**memo** and **letter**) but have different absolute pathnames. The absolute pathnames of the copied files are **/home/jenny/memo** and **/home/jenny/letter**.

```
$ cp memo letter /home/jenny
```

The final command demonstrates one use of the **--force** option. Alex owns the working directory and tries unsuccessfully to copy **one** onto a file (**me**) that he does not have write permission for. Because he has write permission to the directory that holds **me**, Alex can remove the file but not write to it. The **--force** option unlinks, or removes, **me** and then copies **one** to the new file named **me**.

```
$ ls -ld
drwxrwxr-x    2 alex alex 4096 Oct 21 22:55 .
$ ls -l
-rw-r--r--    1 root root 3555 Oct 21 22:54 me
-rw-rw-r--    1 alex alex 1222 Oct 21 22:55 one
$ cp one me
cp: cannot create regular file 'me': Permission denied
$ cp --force one me
$ ls -l
-rw-r--r--    1 alex alex 1222 Oct 21 22:58 me
-rw-rw-r--    1 alex alex 1222 Oct 21 22:55 one
```

If Alex had used the **--backup** option in addition to **--force**, cp would have created a backup of **me** named **me~**. Refer to "Directory Access Permissions" on page 94 for more information.

cpio

Creates an archive or restores files from an archive

cpio --create [options]
cpio --extract [options] [patterns]
cpio --pass-through [options] directory

The cpio utility has three modes of operation: Create mode places multiple files into a single archive file, extract mode restores files from an archive, and pass-through mode copies a directory hierarchy to another location. The archive file used by cpio may be saved on disk, tape, other removable media, or a remote system.

Create mode reads a list of ordinary or directory filenames from standard input and writes the resulting archive file to standard output. You can use this mode to create an archive. Extract mode reads the name of an archive from standard input and extracts files from that archive. You can decide to restore all the files from the archive or only those whose names match specific *patterns*. Pass-through mode reads ordinary or directory filenames from standard input and copies the files to another location on the disk.

Arguments   By default cpio in extract mode extracts all files found in the archive. You can choose to extract files selectively by supplying one or more *patterns*. If the name of a file in the archive matches one of the *patterns*, that file is extracted; otherwise, it is ignored. The cpio *patterns* are similar to shell wildcards (page 127) except that *patterns* match slashes (**/**) and a leading period (**.**) in a filename.

In pass-through mode you must give the name of the target *directory* as an argument to cpio.

Options

Major Options

Three options determine the mode in which cpio operates. You must include exactly one of these options whenever you use cpio.

--extract   **-i**   Reads the archive from standard input and extracts files. Without any *patterns* on the command line, cpio extracts all the files from the archive. With *patterns* specified, cpio extracts only files with names the *patterns* match. The following example extracts from the SCSI tape at **/dev/st0** only those files whose names end in **.c**:

```
$ cpio -i \*.c < /dev/st0
```

The backslash prevents the shell from expanding the * before it passes the argument to cpio.

--create   **-o**   Constructs an archive from the files named on standard input. These files may be ordinary or directory files, and each must appear on a separate line. The archive is written to standard output as it is built. The find utility frequently generates the filenames that cpio uses. The following command builds an archive of the entire local system and writes it to the SCSI tape at **/dev/st0**:

```
$ find / -depth -print | cpio -o >/dev/st0
```

The **--depth** option causes find to search for files in a depth-first search, reducing the likelihood of permissions problems when you restore the files from the archive. See the discussion of this option on page 622.

--pass-through   **-p**   Copies files from one place on the system to another. Instead of constructing an archive file containing the files named on standard input, cpio copies them into the *directory* (the last argument given to cpio). The effect is the same as if you had created an archive with copy-out mode and then extracted the files with copy-in mode, but using pass-through mode avoids creating an archive. The following example copies the files in the working directory and all subdirectories into **/home/alex/code**:

```
$ find . -depth -print | cpio -pdm ~alex/code
```

Other Options

The remaining options alter the behavior of cpio. These options work with one or more of the preceding major options.

--reset-access-time
   -a   Resets the access times of source files after copying them so that they have the same access time after copying as they did before.

   -B   (**block**) Sets the block size to 5,120 bytes instead of the default 512 bytes.

--block-size=n Sets the block size used for input and output to n 512-byte blocks.

   -c   (**compatible**) Writes header information in ASCII so that older (incompatible) cpio utilities on other systems can read the file. This option is rarely needed.

--make-directories
   -d   Creates directories as needed when copying files. For example, you need this option when you are extracting files from an archive with a file list generated by find with the **--depth** option. This option can be used only with the **--extract** and **--pass--through** options.

--pattern-file=*filename*
   -E *filename*
      Reads *patterns* from *filename*, one *pattern* per line. You can specify additional *patterns* on the command line.

—nonmatching	–f	Reverses the sense of the test done on *patterns* when extracting files from an archive. Files are extracted from the archive only if they do *not* match any of the *patterns*.
—file=*archive*	–F *archive*	
		Uses *archive* as the name of the archive file. In extract mode, reads from *archive* instead of standard input. In create mode, writes to *archive* instead of standard output. You can use this option to access a device on another system on a network; see the **——file** option to tar (page 787) for more information.
—help		Displays a list of options.
—link	–l	When possible, links files instead of copying them.
—dereference	–L	Copies the files that symbolic links point to, not the symbolic links themselves.
—preserve–modification–time		
	–m	Preserves the modification times of files that are extracted from an archive. Without this option the files show the time they were extracted. With this option the created files show the time they had when they were copied into the archive.
—no-absolute-filenames		
		In extract mode, creates all filenames relative to the working directory—even files that were archived with absolute pathnames.
—rename	–r	Allows you to rename files as cpio copies them. When cpio prompts you with the name of a file, you respond with the new name. The file is then copied with the new name. If you press RETURN instead, cpio does not copy the file.
—list	–t	(**table of contents**) Displays a table of contents of the archive. This option works only with the **——extract** option, although no files are actually extracted from the archive. With the **——verbose** option, it displays a detailed table of contents in a format similar to that used by ls –l.
—unconditional	–u	Overwrites existing files regardless of their modification times. Without this option cpio will not overwrite a more recently modified file with an older one; it simply displays a warning message.
—verbose	–v	Lists files as they are processed. With the **——list** option, it displays a detailed table of contents in a format similar to that used by ls –l.

Discussion   GNU cpio version 2.5 displays erroneous **truncating inode number** error messages; you can safely ignore these messages.

Without the **——unconditional** option, cpio will not overwrite a more recently modified file with an older file.

You can use both ordinary and directory filenames as input when you create an archive. If the name of an ordinary file appears in the input list before the name of its parent directory, the ordinary file appears before its parent directory in the archive as well. This order can lead to an avoidable error: When you extract files from the archive, the child has nowhere to go in the file structure if its parent has not yet been extracted.

Making sure that files appear after their parent directories in the archive is not always a solution. One problem occurs if the −−preserve−modification−time option is used when extracting files. Because the modification time of a parent directory is updated whenever a file is created within it, the original modification time of the parent directory is lost when the first file is written to it.

The solution to this potential problem is to ensure that all files appear *before* their parent directories when creating an archive *and* to create directories as needed when extracting files from an archive. When you use this technique, directories are extracted only after all files have been written to them and their modification times are preserved.

With the −depth option, the find utility generates a list of files with all children appearing in the list before their parent directories. If you use this list to create an archive, the files are in the proper order. (Refer to the first example in the next section.) When extracting files from an archive, the −−make−directories option causes cpio to create parent directories as needed and the −−preserve−modification−time option does just what its name says. Using this combination of utilities and options preserves directory modification times through a create/extract sequence.

This strategy also solves another potential problem. Sometimes a parent directory may not have permissions set so that you can extract files into it. When cpio automatically creates the directory with −−make−directories, you can be assured of write permission to the directory. When the directory is extracted from the archive (after all the files are written into the directory), it is extracted with its original permissions.

Examples   The first example creates an archive of the files in Jenny's home directory, writing the archive to a tape drive supported by the **ftape** driver:

```
$ find /home/jenny -depth -print | cpio -oB >/dev/ftape
```

The find utility produces the filenames that cpio uses to build the archive. The −depth option causes all entries in a directory to be listed before listing the directory name itself, making it possible for cpio to preserve the original modification times of directories (see the preceding "Discussion.") Use the −−make-directories and the −−preserve-modification-time when you extract files from this archive (see the following examples). The −B option blocks the tape at 5,120 bytes per block.

To check the contents of the archive file and display a detailed listing of the files it contains, use

```
$ cpio -itv < /dev/ftape
```

The following command restores the files that formerly were in the **memo** subdirectory of Jenny's home directory:

```
$ cpio -idm /home/jenny/memo/\* < /dev/ftape
```

The **–d** (**––make-directories**) option ensures that any subdirectories that were in the **memo** directory are re-created as needed. The **–m** (**––preserve-modification-time**) option preserves the modification times of files and directories. The asterisk in the regular expression is escaped to keep the shell from expanding it.

The next command is the same as the preceding command except that it uses the **––no-absolute-filenames** option to re-create the **memo** directory in the working directory, which is named **memocopy**. The pattern does not start with the slash that represents the root directory allowing cpio to create the files with relative pathnames.

```
$ pwd
/home/jenny/memocopy
$ cpio -idm --no-absolute-filenames home/jenny/memo/\* < /dev/ftape
```

The final example uses the **–f** option to restore all the files in the archive except those that were formerly in the **memo** subdirectory:

```
$ cpio -ivmdf /home/jenny/memo/\* < /dev/ftape
```

The **–v** option lists the extracted files as cpio processes the archive, verifying that the expected files are extracted.

crontab

Maintains crontab files

crontab [–u user-name] filename
crontab [–u user-name] option

A crontab file associates periodic times (such as 14:00 on Wednesdays) with commands. The cron utility executes each command at the specified time. When you are working as yourself, the crontab utility installs, removes, lists, and edits your crontab file. Superuser can work with any user's crontab file.

Arguments   The first format copies the contents of *filename* (which contains crontab commands) into the crontab file of the user who runs the command. When the user does not have a crontab file, this process creates a new one; when the user has a crontab file, this process overwrites the file. When you replace *filename* with a hyphen (–), crontab reads commands from standard input.

The second format lists, removes, or edits the crontab file, depending on which option you specify.

Options   Choose only one of the **–e**, **–l**, or **–r** options. Superuser can use **–u** with one of these options.

–e (**edit**) Runs the text editor specified by the **VISUAL** or **EDITOR** shell variable on the crontab file, enabling you to add, change, or delete entries. Installs the modified crontab file when you exit from the editor.

–l (**list**) Displays the contents of the crontab file.

–r (**remove**) Deletes the crontab file.

–u *username*
(**user**) Works on *username's* crontab file. Only Superuser can use this option and Superuser should always use this option.

Notes   This section covers the versions of cron, **crond**, crontab, and crontab files that were written by Paul Vixie—hence the term *Vixie cron*. These versions differ from an earlier version of Vixie cron as well as from the classic SVR3 syntax. This version is POSIX compliant.

User crontab files are kept in the **/var/spool/cron** directory, each named with the username of the user that it belongs to, owned by **root**, and associated with the user's primary group.

The system utility named cron reads the crontab files and runs the commands. If a command line in a crontab file does not redirect its output, output sent to standard output and standard error are mailed to the user unless you set the **MAILTO** variable within the crontab file to a different username.

To make the system administrator's job easier, the directories named **/etc/cron.hourly**, **/etc/cron.daily**, **/etc/cron.weekly**, and **/etc/cron.monthly** hold crontab files that are run by run-parts, which in turn are run by the **/etc/crontab** file. Each of these directories contains files that execute system tasks at the interval named by the directory. Superuser can add files to these directories instead of adding lines to **root**'s crontab file. A typical **/etc/crontab** file looks like this:

```
$ cat /etc/crontab
SHELL=/bin/bash
PATH=/sbin:/bin:/usr/sbin:/usr/bin
MAILTO=root
HOME=/

# run-parts
01 * * * * root run-parts /etc/cron.hourly
02 4 * * * root run-parts /etc/cron.daily
22 4 * * 0 root run-parts /etc/cron.weekly
42 4 1 * * root run-parts /etc/cron.monthly
```

Each entry in a crontab file begins with five fields that specify when the command is to run (minute, hour, day of the month, month, and day of the week). The cron utility interprets an asterisk appearing in place of a number as a wildcard representing all possible values. In the day-of-the-week field, you can use either 7 or 0 to represent Sunday.

It is a good practice to start cron jobs a variable number of minutes before or after the hour, half hour, or quarter hour. When you start them at these times, it becomes less likely that many processes will start at the same time, potentially overloading the system.

When cron starts (usually when the system is booted), it reads all of the crontab files into memory. The cron utility mostly sleeps but wakes up once a minute, reviews all crontab entries it has stored in memory, and runs whichever ones are due to be run at that time.

/etc/cron.allow
/etc/cron.deny
Superuser determines which users can run crontab by creating, editing, and removing the **/etc/cron.allow** and **/etc/cron.deny** files. When you create a **cron.deny** file with no entries and no **cron.allow** file exists, everyone can use crontab. When the **cron.allow** file exists, only users listed in that file can use crontab, regardless of the presence and contents of **cron.deny**. Otherwise, you can list in the **cron.allow** file those users who should be able to use crontab and in **cron.deny** those who should not be able to use it. (Listing a user in **cron.deny** is not necessary because, if a

cron.allow file exists and the user is not listed in it, the user will not be able to use crontab anyway.)

Examples   The following example uses **crontab –l** to list the contents of Jenny's crontab file (**/var/spool/cron/jenny**). All the scripts that Jenny runs are in her **~/bin** directory. The first line sets the **MAILTO** variable to **alex** so that Alex gets the output from commands run from Jenny's crontab file that is not redirected. The **sat.job** script runs every Saturday (day 6) at 2:05 AM, **twice.week** runs at 12:02 AM on Sunday and Thursday (days 0 and 4), and **twice.day** runs twice a day, every day, at 10 AM and 4 PM.

```
$ who am i
jenny

$ crontab -l
MAILTO=alex
05 02 * * 6          $HOME/bin/sat.job
00 02 * * 0,4        $HOME/bin/twice.week
05 10,16 * * *       $HOME/bin/twice.day
```

To add an entry to your crontab file, run the crontab utility with the –e (edit) option. Some Linux systems use a version of crontab that does not support the –e option. If the local system runs such a version, you need to make a copy of your existing **crontab** file, edit it, and then resubmit it, as in the example that follows. The **–l** (list) option displays a copy of your **crontab** file.

```
$ crontab -l > newcron
$ vim newcron
...
$ crontab newcron
```

cut

Selects characters or fields from input lines

cut [options] [file-list]

The cut utility selects characters or fields from lines of input and writes them to standard output. Character and field numbering start with 1.

Arguments   The *file-list* is a list of ordinary files. If you do not specify an argument or if you specify a hyphen (–) in place of a filename, cut reads from standard input.

Options   Accepts the common options described on page 587.

––characters=*clist*

–c *clist*

Selects the characters given by the column numbers in *clist*. The value of *clist* is one or more comma separated column numbers or column ranges. A range is specified by two column numbers separated by a hyphen. A range of *–n* means columns **1** through *n; n–* means columns *n* through the end of the line.

––delimiter=*dchar*

–d *dchar*

Specifies *dchar* as the input field delimiter. Also specifies *dchar* as the output field delimiter unless you use the **––output-delimiter** option. The default delimiter is a TAB character. Quote characters as necessary to protect them from shell expansion.

fields=*flist*   **–f** *flist*

Selects the fields specified in *flist*. The value of *flist* is one or more comma-separated field numbers or field ranges. A range is specified by two field numbers separated by a hyphen. A range of *–n* means fields **1** through *n; n–* means fields *n* through the last field. The field delimiter is a TAB character unless you use the **––delimiter** option to change it.

––output-delimiter=*ochar*

Specifies *ochar* as the output field delimiter. The default delimiter is the TAB character. You can specify a different delimiter by using the **––delimiter** option. Quote characters as necessary to protect them from shell expansion.

Notes   Although limited in functionality, cut is easy to learn and use and is a good choice when columns and fields can be selected without using pattern matching. Sometimes cut is used with paste (page 742).

Examples   For the next two examples, assume that an ls –l command produces the following output:

```
$ ls -l
total 2944
-rwxr-xr-x  1 zach pubs      259 Feb  1 00:12 countout
-rw-rw-r--  1 zach pubs     9453 Feb  4 23:17 headers
-rw-rw-r--  1 zach pubs  1474828 Jan 14 14:15 memo
-rw-rw-r--  1 zach pubs  1474828 Jan 14 14:33 memos_save
-rw-rw-r--  1 zach pubs     7134 Feb  4 23:18 tmp1
-rw-rw-r--  1 zach pubs     4770 Feb  4 23:26 tmp2
-rw-rw-r--  1 zach pubs    13580 Nov  7 08:01 typescript
```

The following command outputs the permissions of the files in the working directory. The cut utility with the –c option selects characters 2 through 10 from each input line. The characters in this range are written to standard output.

```
$ ls -l | cut -c2-10
otal 2944
rwxr-xr-x
rw-rw-r--
rw-rw-r--
rw-rw-r--
rw-rw-r--
rw-rw-r--
rw-rw-r--
```

The next command outputs the size and name of each file in the working directory. This time the –f option selects the fifth and ninth fields from the input lines. The –d option tells cut to use SPACEs, not TABs, as delimiters. The tr utility (page 804) with the –s option changes sequences of more than one SPACE character into a single SPACE; otherwise, cut counts the extra SPACE characters as separate fields.

```
$ ls -l | tr -s ' ' ' ' | cut -f5,9 -d' '

259 countout
9453 headers
1474828 memo
1474828 memos_save
7134 tmp1
4770 tmp2
13580 typescript
```

The last example displays a list of full names as stored in the fifth field of the /etc/passwd file. The –d option specifies that the colon character be used as the field delimiter.

```
$ cat /etc/passwd
root:x:0:0:Root:/:/bin/sh
jenny:x:401:50:Jenny Chen:/home/jenny:/bin/zsh
alex:x:402:50:Alex Watson:/home/alex:/bin/bash
scott:x:504:500:Scott Adams:/home/scott:/bin/tcsh
hls:x:505:500:Helen Simpson:/home/hls:/bin/bash
```

```
$ cut -d: -f5 /etc/passwd
Root
Jenny Chen
Alex Watson
Scott Adams
Helen Simpson
```

date

Displays or sets the system time and date

date [options] [+format]
date [options] [newdate]

The date utility displays the time and date known to the system. Superuser can use date to change the system clock.

Arguments The *+format* argument specifies the format for the output of date. The format string consisting of field descriptors and text follows a plus sign (+). The field descriptors are preceded by percent signs, and each one is replaced by its value in the output. Table V-10 lists some of the field descriptors.

table V-10	Selected field descriptors
Descriptor	**Meaning**
%a	Abbreviated weekday—Sun to Sat
%A	Unabbreviated weekday—Sunday to Saturday
%b	Abbreviated month—Jan to Dec
%B	Unabbreviated month—January to December
%c	Date and time in default format used by date
%d	Day of the month—01 to 31
%D	Date in mm/dd/yy format
%H	Hour—00 to 23
%I	Hour—00 to 12
%j	Julian date (day of the year—001 to 366)
%m	Month of the year—01 to 12
%M	Minutes—00 to 59
%n	NEWLINE character
%P	AM or PM
%r	Time in AM/PM notation
%s	Number of seconds since the beginning of January 1, 1970
%S	Seconds—00 to 60 (the 60 accommodates leap seconds)

table V-10	Selected field descriptors (continued)
%t	TAB character
%T	Time in HH:MM:SS format
%w	Day of the week—0 to 6 (0 = Sunday)
%y	Last two digits of the year—00 to 99
%Y	Year in four-digit format (for example, 2005)
%Z	Time zone (for example, PDT)

By default date zero fills numeric fields. Place an underscore (_) immediately following the percent sign (%) for a specific field to cause date to blank fill the field and with a hyphen (–) to cause date not to fill the field—that is, to left justify the field.

The date utility assumes that, in a format string, any character that is not a percent sign, an underscore or a hyphen following the percent sign, or a field descriptor is ordinary text and copies it to standard output. You can use ordinary text to add punctuation to the date and to add labels (for example, you can put the word **DATE:** in front of the date). Surround the format argument with single quotation marks if it contains SPACEs or other characters that have a special meaning to the shell.

Setting the date   When Superuser specifies *newdate,* the system changes the system clock to reflect the new date. The *newdate* argument has the format

   nnddhhmm[[cc]yy][.ss]

where *nn* is the number of the month (01–12), *dd* is the day of the month (01–31), *hh* is the hour based on a 24-hour clock (00–23), and *mm* is the minutes (00–59). When you change the date, you must specify at least these fields.

The optional *cc* specifies the first two digits of the year (the value of the century minus 1), and *yy* specifies the last two digits of the year. You can specify *yy* or *ccyy* following *mm*. When you do not specify a year, date assumes that the year has not changed.

You can specify the number of seconds past the start of the minute with *.ss*.

Options

Accepts the common options described on page 587.

--reference=*file*   –r *file*
        Displays the modification date and time of *file* in place of the current date and time.

--utc *or*   –u   Displays or sets the time and date using Universal Coordinated Time (UTC,
--universal   page 908; also called Greenwich Mean Time [GMT]).

Notes   If you set up a locale database, date uses that database to substitute terms appropriate to your *locale* (page 885).

Examples   The first example shows how to set the date for 2:07:30 PM on August 19 without changing the year:

```
# date 08191407.30
Sat Aug 19 14:07:30 PDT 2005
```

The next example shows the *format* argument, which causes date to display the date in a commonly used format:

```
$ date '+Today is %h %d, %Y'
Today is Aug 19, 2005
```

dd

Converts and copies a file

dd [arguments]

The dd (device-to-device copy) utility converts and copies a file. The primary use of dd is to copy files to and from such devices as tape and floppy drives. Often dd can handle the transfer of information to and from other operating systems when other methods fail. A rich set of arguments gives you precise control over the characteristics of the transfer.

Arguments

Accepts the common options described on page 587.

By default dd copies standard input to standard output.

bs=*n*	(**block size**) Reads and writes *n* bytes at a time. This argument overrides the **ibs** and **obs** arguments.
cbs=*n*	(**conversion block size**) When performing data conversion during the copy, converts *n* bytes at a time.
conv=*type[,type...]*	By applying conversion *types* in the order given on the command line, converts the data that is being copied. The *types* must be separated by commas with no SPACEs. The types of conversions are shown in Table V-11.
count=*numblocks*	Restricts to *numblocks* the number of blocks of input that dd copies. The size of each block is the number of bytes specified by the **ibs** argument.
ibs=*n*	(**input block size**) Reads *n* bytes at a time.
if=*filename*	(**input file**) Reads from *filename* instead of from standard input. You can use a device name for *filename* to read from that device.
obs=*n*	(**output block size**) Writes *n* bytes at a time.
of=*filename*	(**output file**) Writes to *filename* instead of to standard output. You can use a device name for *filename* to write to that device.
seek=*numblocks*	Skips *numblocks* blocks of output before writing any output. The size of each block is the number of bytes specified by the **obs** argument.
skip=*numblocks*	Skips *numblocks* blocks of input before starting to copy. The size of each block is the number of bytes specified by the **ibs** argument.

table V-11	Conversion types
type	**Meaning**
ascii	Converts EBCDIC-encoded characters to ASCII, allowing you to read tapes written on IBM mainframe and similar computers.
block	Each time a line of input is read (that is, a sequence of characters terminated with a NEWLINE character), outputs a block of text without the NEWLINE. Each output block has the size given by the **obs** or **bs** argument and is created by adding trailing SPACE characters to the text until it is the proper size.
ebcdic	Converts ASCII-encoded characters to EBCDIC, allowing you to write tapes for use on IBM mainframe and similar computers.
unblock	Performs the opposite of the block conversion.
lcase	Converts uppercase letters to lowercase while copying data.
noerror	If a read error occurs, dd normally terminates. This conversion allows dd to continue processing data. This conversion is useful when you are trying to recover data from bad media.
notrunc	Does not truncate the output file before writing to it.
ucase	Converts lowercase letters to uppercase while copying data.

Notes

You can use the standard multiplicative suffixes to make it easier to specify large block sizes. See Table V-1 on page 586.

Examples

You can use dd to create a file filled with pseudo-random bytes.

```
$ dd if=/dev/urandom of=randfile2 bs=1 count=100
```

The preceding command reads from the **/dev/urandom** file (an interface to the kernel's random number generator) and writes to the file named **randfile**. The block size is 1 and the count is 100 so **randfile** is 100 bytes long. For bytes that are more random, you can read from **/dev/random**. See the **urandom** and **random** man pages for more information.

Wiping a file   You can use a similar technique to wipe data from a file before deleting it, making it almost impossible to recover data from a deleted file. You might want to wipe a file for security reasons. Wipe a file several times for added security.

In the following example, ls shows the size of the file named **secret**; dd, with a block size of 1 and a count corresponding to the number of bytes in **secret**, then wipes the file. The **conv=notrunc** argument ensures that dd writes over the data in the file and not another place on the disk.

```
$ ls -l secret
-rw-rw-r--  1 max max 2494 Feb  6 00:56 secret
$ dd if=/dev/urandom of=secret bs=1 count=2494 conv=notrunc
2494+0 records in
2494+0 records out
$ rm secret
```

Copying a diskette You can use dd to make an exact copy of a floppy diskette. First copy the contents of the diskette to a file on the hard drive and then copy the file from the hard disk to a formatted diskette. This technique works regardless of what is on the floppy diskette. The next example copies a DOS-formatted diskette. The mount, ls, umount sequences at the beginning and end of the example verify that the original diskette and the copy hold the same files. You can use the **floppy.copy** file to make multiple copies of the diskette.

```
# mount -t msdos /dev/fd0H1440 /mnt
# ls /mnt
abprint.dat  bti.ini      setup.ins      supfiles.z    wbt.z
adbook.z     setup.exe    setup.pkg      telephon.z
# umount /mnt
# dd if=/dev/fd0 ibs=512 > floppy.copy
2880+0 records in
2880+0 records out
# ls -l floppy.copy
-rw-rw-r--    1 alex speedy 1474560 Oct 11 05:43 floppy.copy
# dd if=floppy.copy bs=512 of=/dev/fd0
2880+0 records in
2880+0 records out
# mount -t msdos /dev/fd0H1440 /mnt
# ls /mnt
abprint.dat  bti.ini      setup.ins      supfiles.z    wbt.z
adbook.z     setup.exe    setup.pkg      telephon.z
# umount /mnt
```

df

Displays disk space usage

df [options] [filesystem-list]

The df (disk free) utility reports on the total space and the free space on each mounted device.

Arguments   When you call df without an argument, it reports on the free space on each of the currently mounted devices.

The *filesystem-list* is an optional list of one or more pathnames that specify the file-systems you want the report to cover. You can refer to a mounted filesystem by its device pathname *or* by the pathname of the directory it is mounted on.

Options

—all   –a   Reports on filesystems with a size of 0 blocks, such as **/dev/proc**. Normally df does not report on these filesystems.

—block-size=*sz*   –B *sz*
   The *sz* specifies the units that the report uses (the default is 1-kilobyte blocks). For example, **—block-size=M** displays sizes in 1,048,576-byte units while **—block-size=MB** displays sizes in 1,000,000-byte units. See Table V-1 on page 586 for a complete list of multiplicative suffixes. See also the **—human-readable** option.

—human-readable
   –h   Displays sizes in K (kilobyte), M (megabyte), and G (gigabyte) blocks, as is appropriate. Uses powers of 1,024; use **—si** for powers of 1,000.

—inodes   –i   Reports the number of *inodes* (page 880) that are used and free instead of reporting on blocks.

–k   Same as **—block-size=K**.

—local   –l   Displays local filesystems only.

—type=*fstype*   –t *fstype*
   Reports information only about the filesystems of type *fstype*, such as DOS or NFS. Repeat this option to report on several types of filesystems.

—exclude-type=*fstype*
   –x *fstype*
   Reports information only about the filesystems *not* of type *fstype*.

Examples   In the following example, df displays information about all mounted filesystems on the local system:

```
$ df
Filesystem          1k-blocks      Used Available Use% Mounted on
/dev/hda12           1517920     53264   1387548   4% /
/dev/hda1              15522      4846      9875  33% /boot
/dev/hda8           1011928    110268    850256  11% /free1
/dev/hda9           1011928     30624    929900   3% /free2
/dev/hda10          1130540     78992    994120   7% /free3
/dev/hda5           4032092   1988080   1839188  52% /home
/dev/hda7           1011928        60    960464   0% /tmp
/dev/hda6           2522048    824084   1569848  34% /usr
zach:/c             2096160   1811392    284768  86% /zach_c
zach:/d             2096450   1935097    161353  92% /zach_d
```

Next df is called with the **–l** and **–h** options, generating a human-readable list of local filesystems. The sizes in this listing are given in terms of megabytes and gigabytes. The NFS mounted filesystems (from **zach**) are not visible.

```
$ df -lh
Filesystem         Size  Used Avail Use% Mounted on
/dev/hda12         1.4G   52M  1.3G   4% /
/dev/hda1           15M  4.7M  9.6M  33% /boot
/dev/hda8          988M  108M  830M  11% /free1
/dev/hda9          988M   30M  908M   3% /free2
/dev/hda10         1.1G   77M  971M   7% /free3
/dev/hda5          3.8G  1.9G  1.8G  52% /home
/dev/hda7          988M   60k  938M   0% /tmp
/dev/hda6          2.4G  805M  1.5G  34% /usr
```

The next example displays information about the **/free2** partition in megabyte units:

```
$ df -BM /free2
Filesystem          1M-blocks      Used Available Use% Mounted on
/dev/hda9                 988        30       908   3% /free2
```

The final example displays information about NFS filesystems in human-readable terms:

```
$ df -ht nfs
Filesystem         Size  Used Avail Use% Mounted on
zach:/c            2.0G  1.7G  278M  86% /zach_c
zach:/d            2.0G  1.8G  157M  92% /zach_d
```

diff

Displays the differences between two files

diff [options] file1 file2
diff [options] file1 directory
diff [options] directory file2
diff [options] directory1 directory2

The diff utility displays line-by-line differences between two files. By default diff displays the differences as instructions you can use to edit one of the files to make it the same as the other.

Arguments   The *file1* and *file2* are pathnames of ordinary files that diff works on. When the *directory* argument is used in place of *file2*, diff looks for a file in *directory* with the same name as *file1*. It works similarly when *directory* replaces *file1*. When you specify two directory arguments, diff compares the files in *directory1* with the files that have the same simple filenames in *directory2*.

Options   Accepts the common options described on page 587, with one exception: When one of the arguments is a directory and the other is an ordinary file, you cannot compare to standard input.

--ignore-space-change
    –b   Ignores whitespace (SPACEs and TABs) at the ends of lines and considers other strings of whitespace to be equal.

--ignore-blank-lines
    –B   Ignores differences that involve only blank lines.

--context[*=lines*]   **–C** [*lines*]
    Displays the sections of the two files that differ, including *lines* lines (the default is 3) around each line that differs to show the context. Each line in *file1* that is missing from *file2* is preceded by **–**; each extra line in *file2* is preceded by **+**; and lines that have different versions in the two files are marked with **!**. When lines that differ are within *lines* lines of each other, they are grouped together in the output.

--ed   **–e**   Creates and sends to standard output a script for the ed editor, which will edit *file1* to make it the same as *file2*. You must add **w** (write) and **q** (quit) instructions to the end of the script if you plan to redirect input to ed from the script. When you use **--ed**, diff displays the changes in reverse order: Changes to the end of the file are listed before changes to the top, preventing early changes from affecting later changes when the script is used as input to ed. For example, if a line near the top were deleted, subsequent line numbers in the script would be wrong.

--ignore-case   –i Ignores differences in case when comparing files.

--new-file –N When comparing directories, when a file is present in one of the directories only, considers it to be present and empty in the other directory.

--show-c-function
                –p Shows which C function each change affects.

--brief –q Does not display the differences between lines in the files. Instead, diff reports only that the files differ.

--recursive –r When using diff to compare the files in two directories, causes the comparisons to extend through subdirectories as well.

--unified[=*lines*] –U *lines*
                Uses the easier-to-read unified output format. See the discussion of diff on page 51 for more detail and an example. The *lines* is the number of lines of context; the default is three.

--ignore-all-space
                –w (**whitespace**) Ignores whitespace when comparing lines.

--width=*columns*
          –W *columns*
                Sets the width of the columns that diff uses to display the output to *columns*. This option is useful with the --side-by-side option. The sdiff utility uses a lowercase **w** to perform the same function: –w *columns*.

--side-by-side –y Displays output in a side-by-side format. This option generates the same output as sdiff. Use the --width=*columns* option with this option.

Notes

The sdiff utility is similar to diff but its output may be easier to read. The diff --side-by-side option produces the same output as sdiff. See the "Examples" section and refer to the diff and sdiff man and info pages for more information.

You can use the diff3 utility to compare three files.

Discussion

When you use diff without any options, it produces a series of lines containing Add (**a**), Delete (**d**), and Change (**c**) instructions. Each of these lines is followed by the lines from the file that you need to add, delete, or change to make the files the same. A *less than* symbol (<) precedes lines from **file1**. A *greater than* symbol (>) precedes lines from **file2**. The diff output appears in the format shown in Table V-12. A pair of line numbers separated by a comma represents a range of lines; a single line number represents a single line.

The diff utility assumes that you will convert *file1* to *file2*. The line numbers to the left of each of the **a**, **c**, or **d** instructions always pertain to *file1*; the line numbers to the right of the instructions apply to *file2*. To convert *file2* to *file1*, run diff again, reversing the order of the arguments.

table V-12   diff output

Instruction	Meaning (to change file1 to file2)
`line1 a line2,line3` `> lines from file2`	Append lines line2 through line3 from **file2** after line1 in **file1**.
`line1,line2 d line3` `< lines from file1`	Delete line1 through line2 from **file1**.

`line1,line2 c line3,line4`
`< lines from file1`
`---`
`> lines from file 2`
	Change line1 through line2 in **file1** to line3 through line 4 from **file2**.

Examples

The first example shows how diff displays the differences between two short, similar files:

```
$ cat m
aaaaa
bbbbb
ccccc

$ cat n
aaaaa
ccccc

$ diff m n
2d1
< bbbbb
```

The difference between files **m** and **n** is that the second line of file **m** (**bbbbb**) is missing from file **n**. The first line that diff displays (**2d1**) indicates that you need to delete the second line from *file1* (**m**) to make it the same as *file2* (**n**). The next line diff displays starts with a less than symbol (**<**), indicating that this line of text is from **file1**. In this example, you do not need this information—all you need to know is the line number so that you can delete the line.

The **--side-by-side** option and the sdiff utility, both with the output width set to 30 columns (characters), display the same output. In the output a less than symbol points to the extra line in file **m**, whereas diff/sdiff leaves a blank line in file **n** where the extra line would go to make the files the same.

```
$ diff --side-by-side --width=30 m n
aaaaa           aaaaa
bbbbb         <
ccccc           ccccc
```

```
$ sdiff -w 30 m n
aaaaa            aaaaa
bbbbb         <
ccccc            ccccc
```

The next example uses the same **m** file and a new file, **p**, to show diff issuing an **a** (append) instruction:

```
$ cat p
aaaaa
bbbbb
rrrrr
ccccc
$ diff m p
2a3
> rrrrr
```

In the preceding example, diff issues the instruction **2a3** to indicate that you must append a line to file **m**, after line 2, to make it the same as file **p**. The second line that diff displays indicates that the line is from file **p** (the line begins with **>**, indicating **file2**). In this example, you need the information on this line; the appended line must contain the text **rrrrr**.

The next example uses file **m** again, this time with file **r**, to show how diff indicates a line that needs to be changed:

```
$ cat r
aaaaa
-q
ccccc

$ diff m r
2c2
< bbbbb
---
> -q
```

The difference between the two files is in line 2: File **m** contains **bbbbb**, and file **r** contains **–q**. The diff utility displays **2c2** to indicate that you need to change line 2. After indicating that a change is needed, diff shows that you must change line 2 in file **m** (**bbbbb**) to line 2 in file **r** (**–q**) to make the files the same. The three hyphens indicate the end of the text in file **m** that needs to be changed and the start of the text in file **r** that is to replace it.

Comparing the same files using the side-by-side and width options (**–y** and **–W**) yields an easier-to-read result. The pipe symbol (l) indicates that the line on one side must replace the line on the other side to make the files the same:

```
$ diff -y -W 30 m r
aaaaa            aaaaa
bbbbb         |  -q
ccccc            ccccc
```

The next examples compare the two files **q** and **v**:

```
$ cat q            $ cat v
Monday             Monday
Tuesday            Wednesday
Wednesday          Thursday
Thursday           Thursday
Saturday           Friday
Sunday             Saturday
                   Sundae
```

Running in side-by-side mode diff shows that **Tuesday** is missing from file **v**, there is only one **Thursday** in file **q** (there are two in file **v**), and **Friday** is missing from file **q**. The last line is **Sunday** in file **q** and **Sundae** in file **v**: diff indicates that these lines are different. You can change file **q** to be the same as file **v** by removing **Tuesday**, adding one **Thursday** and **Friday**, and substituting **Sundae** from file **v** for Sunday from file **q**. Alternatively, you can change file **v** to be the same as file **q** by adding **Tuesday**, removing one **Thursday** and **Friday**, and substituting **Sunday** from file **q** for **Sundae** from file **v**.

```
$ diff -y -W 30 q v
Monday             Monday
Tuesday          <
Wednesday          Wednesday
Thursday           Thursday
                 > Thursday
                 > Friday
Saturday           Saturday
Sunday           | Sundae
```

Context diff   With the **--context** option (called a *context diff*), diff displays output that tells you how to turn the first file into the second. The top two lines identify the files and show that **q** is represented by asterisks, whereas **v** is represented by hyphens. Following a row of asterisks that indicates the start of a hunk of text is a row of asterisks with the numbers **1,6** in the middle. This line indicates that the instructions in the first section tell you what to remove from or change in file **q**—namely, lines 1 through 6 (that is, all the lines of file **q**; in a longer file it would mark the first hunk). The hyphen on the next line means that you need to remove the line with **Tuesday**. The line with an exclamation point indicates that you need to replace the line with **Sunday** with the corresponding line from file **v**. The row of hyphens with the numbers **1,7** in the middle indicates that the next section tells you which lines from file **v**—lines 1 through 7—you need to add or change in file **q**. You need to add a second line with **Thursday** and a line with **Friday**, and you need to change **Sunday** in file **q** to **Sundae** (from file **v**).

```
$ diff --context q v
*** q    Mon Aug 22 18:26:45 2005
--- v    Mon Aug 22 18:27:55 2005
***************
*** 1,6 ****
  Monday
- Tuesday
  Wednesday
  Thursday
  Saturday
! Sunday
--- 1,7 ----
  Monday
  Wednesday
  Thursday
+ Thursday
+ Friday
  Saturday
! Sundae
```

du

Displays information on disk usage by file

du [options] [path-list]

The du (disk usage) utility reports how much disk space is occupied by a directory (along with all its subdirectories and files) or a file. By default du displays the number of 1,024-byte blocks that are occupied by the directory or file.

Arguments

Without any arguments, du displays information about the working directory and its subdirectories. The *path-list* specifies the directories and files you want information on.

Options

Without any options, du displays the total storage used for each argument in *path-list*. For directories du displays this total after recursively listing the totals for each subdirectory.

--all	–a	Displays the space used by all ordinary files along with the total for each directory.
--block-size=*sz*	–B *sz*	The *sz* specifies the units the report uses. For example, **--block-size=M** displays sizes in 1,048,576-byte units while **--block-size=MB** displays sizes in 1,000,000-byte units. See Table V-1 on page 586 for a complete list of multiplicative suffixes. See also the **--human-readable** option.
--total	–c	Displays a grand total at the end of the output.
--human-readable	–h	Displays sizes in K (kilobyte), M (megabyte), and G (gigabyte) blocks, as appropriate. Uses powers of 1,024; use **--si** for powers of 1,000.
--kilobytes	–k	Displays sizes in 1-kilobyte blocks.
--dereference	–L	Includes the sizes of the files symbolic links point to, not the symbolic links themselves. The default is **--no-dereference**.
--megabytes	–m	Displays sizes in 1-megabyte blocks.
--no-dereference	–P	Includes the sizes of symbolic links, not the files that the links point to (default).
--summarize	–s	Displays only the total size for each directory or file you specify on the command line; subdirectory totals are not displayed.
--one-file-system	–x	Reports only on files and directories on the same filesystem as that of the argument being processed.

Examples   In the first example, du displays size information about subdirectories in the working directory. The last line contains the grand total for the working directory and its subdirectories.

```
$ du
26        ./Postscript
4         ./RCS
47        ./XIcon
4         ./Printer/RCS
12        ./Printer
105       .
```

The total (105) is the number of blocks occupied by all plain files and directories under the working directory. All files are counted, even though du displays only the sizes of directories.

Next using the **--summarize** option, du displays the total for each of the directories in **/home** but not for any subdirectories:

```
# du --summarize /home/*
68        /home/Desktop
1100      /home/doug
100108    /home/dump
62160     /home/ftp
6540      /home/httpd
16        /home/lost+found
1862104   /home/alex
176       /home/max
88        /home/jenny
4         /home/samba
4         /home/tom
```

Add to the previous example the **--total** option and you get the same listing with a grand total at the end:

```
# du --summarize --total /home/*
68        /home/Desktop
...
4         /home/tom
2032456 total
```

If you do not have read permission for a file or directory that du encounters, du sends a warning to standard error and skips that file or directory. The following example uses the **s** (summarize), **h** (human-readable), and **c** (total) options:

```
$ du -shc /usr/*
112M      /usr/X11R6
161M      /usr/bin
4.0K      /usr/dict
4.0K      /usr/doc
4.0K      /usr/etc
3.9M      /usr/games
...
```

```
du: cannot change to directory '/usr/lost+found': Permission denied
30M     /usr/sbin
du: cannot change to directory '/usr/share/ssl/CA': Permission denied
797M    /usr/share
188M    /usr/src
2.2G    total
```

The final example displays, in human-readable format, the total size of all the files the user can read in the **/usr** filesystem. Redirecting standard error to **/dev/null** discards all warnings about files and directories that are unreadable.

```
$ du --human-readable --summarize /usr 2>/dev/null
2.2G    /usr
```

echo

Displays a message

echo [options] message

The echo utility copies its arguments, followed by a NEWLINE, to standard output. The Bourne Again and TC Shells each has an echo builtin that works similarly to the echo utility.

Arguments   The *message* consists of one or more arguments, which can include quoted strings, ambiguous file references, and shell variables. A SPACE separates each argument from the next. The shell recognizes unquoted special characters in the arguments. For example, the shell expands an asterisk into a list of filenames in the working directory.

Options   You can configure the tcsh echo builtin to treat backslash escape sequences and the –n option in different ways. Refer to **echo_style** in the tcsh man page. The typical tcsh configuration recognizes the –n option, enables backslash escape sequences, and ignores the –e and –E options.

   –e   Enables the interpretation of backslash escape sequences such as \n.

   –E   Suppresses the interpretation of backslash escape sequences such as \n (bash and utility default).

   ––help   Gives a short summary of how to use echo. The summary includes a list of the backslash escape sequences interpreted by echo. This option works only with the echo utility (**/bin/echo**) and not with the echo builtins.

   –n   Suppresses the NEWLINE terminating the message.

Notes   You can use echo to send messages to the screen from a shell script. See page 129 for a discussion of how to use echo to display filenames using wildcard characters.

   The echo utility and builtins provide an escape notation to represent certain non-printing characters in *message* (Table V-13). You must use the –e option in order for these backslash escape sequences to work with the echo utility and the bash echo builtin. Typically you do not need the –e option with the tcsh echo builtin.

table V-13	Backslash escape sequences
Sequence	**Meaning**
\a	Bell
\c	Suppress trailing NEWLINE

table V-13	Backslash escape sequences (continued)
\n	NEWLINE
\t	HORIZONTAL TAB
\v	VERTICAL TAB
\\	BACKSLASH

Examples   Following are some echo commands. These commands will work with the echo utility (**/bin/echo**) and the bash and tcsh echo builtins, except for the last, which may not need the −e option under tcsh.

```
$ echo "This command displays a string."
This command displays a string.
$ echo -n "This displayed string is not followed by a NEWLINE."
This displayed string is not followed by a NEWLINE.$ echo hi
hi
$ echo -e "This message contains\v a vertical tab."
This message contains
                      a vertical tab.
$
```

The following examples contain messages with the backslash escape sequence \c. In the first example, the shell processes the arguments before calling echo. When the shell sees the \c, it replaces the \c with the character c. The next three examples show how to quote the \c so that the shell passes it to echo, which then does not append a NEWLINE to the end of the message. The first four examples are run under bash and require the −e option. The final example runs under tcsh, which typically does not use this option.

```
$ echo -e There is a newline after this.\c
There is a newline after this.c

$ echo -e 'There is no newline after this.\c'
There is no newline after this.$

$ echo -e "There is no newline after this.\c"
There is no newline after this.$

$ echo -e There is no newline after this.\\c
There is no newline after this.$

$ tcsh
tcsh $ echo 'There is no newline after this.\c'
There is no newline after this.$
```

You can use the **−n** option in place of **−e** and \c.

expr

Evaluates an expression

expr expression

The expr utility evaluates an expression and sends the result to standard output. It evaluates character strings that represent either numeric or nonnumeric values. Operators are used with the strings to form expressions.

Arguments The *expression* is composed of strings interspersed with operators. Each string and operator constitute a distinct argument that you must separate from other arguments with a SPACE. You must quote operators that have special meanings to the shell (for example, the multiplication operator, *).

The following list of expr operators is given in order of decreasing precedence. Each operator within a group of operators has the same precedence. You can change the order of evaluation by using parentheses.

:   (**comparison**) Compares two strings, starting with the first character in each string and ending with the last character in the second string. The second string is a regular expression with an implied caret (^) as its first character. If there is a match, expr displays the number of characters in the second string. If there is no match, expr displays a zero.

*   (**multiplication**)
/   (**division**)
%   (**remainder**)
Work only on strings that contain the numerals 0 through 9 and optionally a leading minus sign. Convert strings to integer numbers, perform the specified arithmetic operation on numbers, and convert the result back to a string before sending it to standard output.

+   (**addition**)
–   (**subtraction**)
Function in the same manner as the preceding group of operators.

<   (**less than**)
<=   (**less than or equal to**)
= *or* ==   (**equal to**)
!=   (**not equal to**)
>=   (**greater than or equal to**)
>   (**greater than**)
Relational operators work on both numeric and nonnumeric arguments. If one or both of the arguments are nonnumeric, the comparison is nonnumeric, using the machine collating sequence (typically ASCII). If both arguments are

numeric, the comparison is numeric. The expr utility displays a 1 (one) if the comparison is *true* and a 0 (zero) if it is *false*.

    &   **(AND)** Evaluates both of its arguments. If neither is 0 or a null string, expr displays the value of the first argument. Otherwise, it displays a 0. You must quote this operator.

    | **(OR)** Evaluates the first argument. If it is neither 0 nor a null string, expr displays the value of the first argument. Otherwise, it displays the value of the second argument. You must quote this operator.

Notes

The expr utility returns an exit status of 0 (zero) if the expression evaluates to other than a null string or the number 0, a status of 1 if the expression is null or 0, and a status of 2 if the expression is invalid.

Although expr and this discussion distinguish between numeric and nonnumeric arguments, all arguments to expr are nonnumeric (character strings). When applicable, expr attempts to convert an argument to a number (for example, when using the + operator). If a string contains characters other than 0 through 9 with an optional leading minus sign, expr cannot convert it. Specifically, if a string contains a plus sign or a decimal point, expr considers it to be nonnumeric. If both arguments are numeric, the comparison is numeric. If one is nonnumeric, the comparison is lexicographic.

Examples

The following examples show command lines that call expr to evaluate constants. You can also use expr to evaluate variables in a shell script. The fourth command displays an error message because of the illegal decimal point in **5.3**:

```
$ expr 17 + 40
57
$ expr 10 - 24
-14
$ expr -17 + 20
3
$ expr 5.3 + 4
expr: non-numeric argument
```

The multiplication (*), division (/), and remainder (%) operators provide additional arithmetic power. You must quote the multiplication operator (precede it with a backslash) so that the shell will not treat it as a special character (an ambiguous file reference). You cannot put quotation marks around the entire expression because each string and operator must be a separate argument.

```
$ expr 5 \* 4
20
$ expr 21 / 7
3
$ expr 23 % 7
2
```

The next two examples show how parentheses change the order of evaluation. You must quote each parenthesis and surround the backslash/parenthesis combination with SPACEs:

```
$ expr 2 \* 3 + 4
10
$ expr 2 \* \( 3 + 4 \)
14
```

You can use relational operators to determine the relationship between numeric or nonnumeric arguments. The following commands compare two strings to see if they are equal; expr displays a 0 when the relationship is *false* and a 1 when it is *true*.

```
$ expr fred == sam
0
$ expr sam == sam
1
```

In the following examples, the relational operators, which must be quoted, establish order between numeric or nonnumeric arguments. Again, if a relationship is *true*, expr displays a 1.

```
$ expr fred \> sam
0
$ expr fred \< sam
1
$ expr 5 \< 7
1
```

The next command compares 5 with **m**. When one of the arguments that expr is comparing with a relational operator is nonnumeric, expr considers the other to be nonnumeric. In this case because **m** is nonnumeric, expr treats 5 as a nonnumeric argument. The comparison is between the ASCII (on many systems) values of **m** and 5. The ASCII value of **m** is 109 and that of 5 is 53, so expr evaluates the relationship as *true*.

```
$ expr 5 \< m
1
```

The next example shows the matching operator determining that the four characters in the second string match the first four characters in the first string. The expr utility displays the number of matching characters (4).

```
$ expr abcdefghijkl : abcd
4
```

The & operator displays a 0 if one or both of its arguments are 0 or a null string; otherwise, it displays the first argument:

```
$ expr '' \& book
0
```

```
$ expr magazine \& book
magazine

$ expr 5 \& 0
0

$ expr 5 \& 6
5
```

The I operator displays the first argument if it is not 0 or a null string; otherwise, it displays the second argument:

```
$ expr '' \| book
book

$ expr magazine \| book
magazine

$ expr 5 \| 0
5

$ expr 0 \| 5
5

$ expr 5 \| 6
5
```

file

Displays the classification of a file

file [option] file-list

The file utility classifies files according to their contents.

Arguments   The *file-list* is a list of the pathnames of one or more files that file classifies. You can specify any kind of file, including ordinary, directory, and special files, in the *file-list*.

Options

--files-from=*file*   **–f** *file*
    Takes the names of files to be examined from *file* rather than from *file-list* on the command line. The names of the files must be listed one per line in *file*.

--mime   **–i** Displays *MIME* (page 887) type strings.

--help   Displays a help message.

--dereference   **–L** Reports on the files that symbolic links point to, not on the symbolic links themselves. The default is **--no-dereference**.

--uncompress   **–z** (**zip**) Attempts to classify files within a compressed file.

Notes   The file utility can classify more than 5, 000 file types. Some of the more common file types found on Linux systems, as displayed by file, are

```
archive
ascii text
c program text
commands text
core file
cpio archive
data
directory
ELF 32-bit LSB executable
empty
English text
executable
```

The file utility uses a maximum of three tests in its attempt to classify a file: filesystem, magic number, and language tests. When file identifies the type of a file, it ceases testing. The filesystem test examines the return from a **stat** system call to see whether the file is empty or a special file. The *magic number* (page 886) test looks for data in particular fixed formats near the beginning of the file. The language test, if needed, determines whether the file is a text file, what encoding it uses, and what language it is written in. Refer to the file man page for a more detailed description of how file works. The results of file are not always correct.

Examples

Some examples of file identification follow:

```
/etc/DIR_COLORS:    ASCII English text
/etc/X11:    directory
/etc/aliases.db:    regular file, no read permission
/etc/anacrontab:    ASCII text
/etc/asound.state:    ASCII text, with very long lines
/etc/at.deny:    empty
/etc/auto.net:    Bourne shell script text executable
/etc/grub.conf:    symbolic link to '../boot/grub/grub.conf'
/etc/localtime:    timezone data
/etc/named.conf:    C++ program text
/etc/rpc:    ASCII C program text
/etc/vimrc:    Composer 669 Module sound data
/usr/bin/GET:    perl script text executable
/usr/bin/HtFileType:    Bourne shell script text executable
/usr/bin/Maelstrom:    setgid ELF 32-bit LSB executable, Intel 80386, version 1 (SYSV), for
GNU/Linux 2.2.5, dynamically linked (uses shared libs), stripped
/usr/bin/X11:    symbolic link to '../X11R6/bin'
/usr/bin/[:    ELF 32-bit LSB executable, Intel 80386, version 1 (SYSV), for GNU/Linux
2.2.5, dynamically linked (uses shared libs), stripped
/usr/bin/at:    setuid ELF 32-bit LSB executable, Intel 80386, version 1 (SYSV), for
GNU/Linux 2.2.5, dynamically linked (uses shared libs), stripped
/usr/share/templates/linkHD.desktop:    UTF-8 Unicode text
/usr/share/templates/.source/Floppy.desktop:    UTF-8 Unicode text
/usr/share/templates/.source/TextFile.txt:    very short file (no magic)
/usr/share/autoconf/m4sugar/m4sugar.m4f:    ASCII M4 macro language pre-processor text
/usr/share/pygtk/2.0/defs/bonoboui.defs:    Lisp/Scheme program text
/usr/share/rhpl/extramodes:    C++ program text
/usr/share/apps/konquest/pics/planet1.xpm:    X pixmap image text
/usr/share/apps/konquest/pics/konquest-splash.png:    PNG image data, 600 x 550, 8-bit
colormap, non-interlaced
/usr/share/apps/konquest/konquestui.rc:    exported SGML document text
/usr/share/apps/templates/text/scripts/demo.php:    PHP script text
```

find

Finds files based on criteria

*find [**directory-list**] [**expression**]*

The find utility selects files that are located in specified directory hierarchies and that meet specified criteria.

Arguments

The *directory-list* specifies the directories that find is to search. When find searches a directory, it searches all subdirectories to all levels. When you do not specify a *directory-list*, find searches the working directory.

The *expression* contains criteria, as described in the "Criteria" section. The find utility tests each of the files in each of the directories in the *directory-list* to see whether it meets the criteria described by the *expression*. When you do not specify an *expression*, the *expression* defaults to **–print**.

A SPACE separating two criteria is a Boolean AND operator: The file must meet *both* criteria to be selected. A **–or** or **–o** separating the criteria is a Boolean OR operator: The file must meet one or the other (or both) of the criteria to be selected.

You can negate any criterion by preceding it with an exclamation point. The find utility evaluates criteria from left to right unless you group them using parentheses.

Within the *expression* you must quote special characters so that the shell will not interpret them but rather passes them to find. Special characters that you may frequently use with find are parentheses, brackets, question marks, and asterisks.

Each element within the *expression* is a separate argument. You must separate arguments from each other with SPACEs. There must be a SPACE on both sides of each parenthesis, exclamation point, criterion, or other element.

Criteria

You can use the following criteria within the *expression*. As used in this list, $\pm n$ is a decimal integer that can be expressed as **+n** (more than *n*), **–n** (fewer than *n*), or *n* (exactly *n*).

–anewer *filename*
 (**accessed newer**) The file being evaluated meets this criterion if it was accessed more recently than *filename*.

–atime $\pm n$
 (**access time**) The file being evaluated meets this criterion if it was last accessed $\pm n$ days ago. When you use this option, find changes the access times of directories it searches.

–depth

> The file being evaluated always meets this action criterion. It causes find to take action on entries in a directory before it acts on the directory itself. When you use find to send files to the cpio utility, the **–depth** criterion enables cpio to preserve the modification times of directories when you restore files (assuming that you use the **––preserve–modification–time** option to cpio). See the "Discussion" and "Examples" sections under cpio on pages 621 and 622.

–exec *command* \;

> The file being evaluated meets this action criterion if the *command* returns a 0 (zero [*true*]) exit status. You must terminate the *command* with a quoted semicolon. A pair of braces ({}) within the *command* represents the name of the file being evaluated. You can use the **–exec** action criterion at the end of a group of other criteria to execute the *command* if the preceding criteria are met. Refer to the following "Discussion" section for more information. See xargs on page 821 for a more efficient way of doing what this option does.

–follow

> (**dereference**) When this criterion is specified and find encounters a symbolic link, find follows the link.

–group *name*

> The file being evaluated meets this criterion if it is associated with the group named *name*. You can use a numeric group ID in place of *name*.

–inum *n*

> The file being evaluated meets this criterion if its inode number is *n*.

–links ±*n*

> The file being evaluated meets this criterion if it has ±*n* links.

–mount

> See –xdev.

–mtime ±*n*

> (**modify time**) The file being evaluated meets this criterion if it was last modified ±*n* days ago.

–name *filename*

> The file being evaluated meets this criterion the pattern *filename* matches its name. The *filename* can include wildcard characters (*, ?, and []) but these characters must be quoted.

–newer *filename*

> The file being evaluated meets this criterion if it was modified more recently than *filename*.

–nogroup

> The file being evaluated meets this criterion if it does not belong to a group that is listed in the **/etc/group** file.

–nouser

The file being evaluated meets this criterion if it does not belong to a user who is listed in the **/etc/passwd** file (that is, the user ID of the file does not correspond to a user on the local system).

–ok *command* \;

This action criterion is the same as **–exec** but displays each *command* to be executed enclosed in angle brackets and executes the *command* only if it receives a response that starts with a **y** or **Y** from standard input.

–perm [±]*mode*

The file being evaluated meets this criterion if it has the access permissions given by *mode*. If *mode* is preceded by a minus sign (–), the file access permissions must include all the bits in *mode*. If *mode* is preceded by a plus sign (+), the file access permissions must include at least one of the bits in *mode*. If no plus or minus sign precedes *mode,* the mode of the file must exactly match *mode*. You may use either a symbolic or octal representation for *mode* (see chmod on page 604).

–print

The file being evaluated always meets this action criterion. When evaluation of the *expression* reaches this criterion, find displays the pathname of the file it is evaluating. If **–print** is the only criterion in the *expression,* find displays the names of all files in the *directory-list*. If this criterion appears with other criteria, find displays the name only if the preceding criteria are met. If no action criteria appear in the *expression,* **–print** is assumed. (Refer to the following "Discussion" and "Notes" sections.)

–size ±*n*[clk]

The file being evaluated meets this criterion if it is the size specified by ±*n,* measured in 512-byte blocks. Follow *n* with the letter **c** to measure files in characters or **k** to measure files in kilobytes.

–type *filetype*

The file being evaluated meets this criterion if its file type is specified by *filetype*. Select a *filetype* from the following list:

b	Block special file
c	Character special file
d	Directory file
f	Ordinary file
l	Symbolic link
p	FIFO (named pipe)
s	Socket

–user *name*

The file being evaluated meets this criterion if it belongs to the user with the username *name*. You can use a numeric user ID in place of *name*.

–xdev

> The file being evaluated always meets this action criterion. It causes find not to search directories in filesystems other than the one specified by *directory-list*. Also **–mount**.

Discussion   Assume that **x** and **y** are criteria. The following command line never tests whether the file meets criterion **y** if it does not meet criterion **x**. Because the criteria are separated by a SPACE (the Boolean AND operator), once find determines that criterion **x** is not met, the file cannot meet the criteria so find does not continue testing. You can read the expression as "(test to see whether) the file meets criterion **x** *and* (SPACE means *and*) criterion **y**."

```
$ find dir x y
```

The next command line tests the file against criterion **y** if criterion **x** is not met. The file can still meet the criteria so find continues the evaluation. You can read the expression as "(test to see whether) the file meets criterion **x** *or* criterion **y**." If the file meets criterion **x**, find does not evaluate criterion **y** as there is no need to do so.

```
$ find dir x -or y
```

Action criteria   Certain "criteria" do not select files but rather cause find to take action. The action is triggered when find evaluates one of these *action criteria*. Therefore, the position of an action criterion on the command line—not the result of its evaluation—determines whether find takes the action.

The **–print** action criterion causes find to display the pathname of the file it is testing. The following command line displays the names of *all* files in the **dir** directory (and all its subdirectories), regardless of whether they meet the criterion **x**:

```
$ find dir -print x
```

The following command line displays only the names of the files in the **dir** directory that meet criterion **x**:

```
$ find dir x -print
```

This common use of **–print** after the testing criteria is the default action criterion. The following command line generates the same output as the previous one:

```
$ find dir x
```

Notes   You can use the **–a** operator between criteria for clarity. This operator is a Boolean AND operator, just as the SPACE is.

Examples   The simplest find command has no arguments and lists the files in the working directory and all subdirectories:

```
$ find
...
```

The following command finds the files in the working directory and subdirectories that have filenames beginning with **a**. The command uses a period to designate the working directory. To prevent the shell from interpreting the **a**✳ as an ambiguous file reference, it is enclosed within quotation marks.

```
$ find . -name 'a✳'
```

The **–print** criterion is implicit in the preceding command. If you omit the *directory-list* argument, find searches the working directory. The next command performs the same function as the preceding one without explicitly specifying the working directory:

```
$ find -name 'a✳'
```

The following command sends a list of selected filenames to the cpio utility, which writes them to tape. The first part of the command line ends with a pipe symbol, so the shell expects another command to follow and displays a secondary prompt (>) before accepting the rest of the command line. You can read this find command as "find, in the root directory and all subdirectories (/), ordinary files (**–type f**) that have been modified within the past day (**–mtime –1**), with the exception of files whose names are suffixed with .o (**! –name '✳.o'**)." (An object file carries a .o suffix and usually does not need to be preserved because it can be re-created from the corresponding source file.)

```
$ find / -type f -mtime -1 ! -name '✳.o' -print |
> cpio -oB > /dev/ftape
```

The following command finds, displays the filenames of, and deletes the files in the working directory and subdirectories named **core** or **junk**:

```
$ find . \( -name core -o -name junk \) -print -exec rm {} \;
...
```

The parentheses and the semicolon following **–exec** are quoted so that the shell does not treat them as special characters. SPACEs separate the quoted parentheses from other elements on the command line. Read this find command as "find, in the working directory and subdirectories (.), files named **core** (**–name core**) *or* (**–o**) **junk** (**–name junk**) [if a file meets these criteria, continue] *and* (SPACE) print the name of the file (**–print**) *and* (SPACE) delete the file (**–exec rm {}**)."

The next shell script uses find in conjunction with grep to identify files that contain a particular string. This script enables you to look for a file when you remember its contents but cannot remember its filename. The **finder** script locates files in the working directory and subdirectories that contain the string specified on the command line. The **–type f** criterion is necessary so that find will pass to grep only the names of ordinary files, not directory files.

```
$ cat finder
find . -type f -exec grep -l "$1" {} \;
$ finder "Executive Meeting"
./january/memo.0102
./april/memo.0415
```

When called with the string **Executive Meeting**, **finder** locates two files containing that string: **./january/memo.0102** and **./april/memo.0415**. The period (.) in the pathnames represents the working directory; **january** and **april** are subdirectories of the working directory. The **grep** utility with the **––recursive** option performs the same function as the **finder** script.

The next command looks in two user directories for files that are larger than 100 blocks (**–size +100**) and have been accessed only more than five days ago—that is, have not been accessed within the past five days (**–atime +5**). This find command then asks whether you want to delete the file (**–ok rm {}**). You must respond to each query with **y** (for *yes*) or **n** (for *no*). The rm command works only if you have write and execute access permission to the directory.

```
$ find /home/alex /home/barbara -size +100 -atime +5 -ok rm {} \;
< rm ... /home/alex/notes >? y
< rm ... /home/alex/letter >? n
...
```

In the next example, **/home/alex/memos** is a symbolic link to Jenny's directory named **/home/jenny/memos**. When you use the **–follow** option with find, the symbolic link is followed, and the contents of that directory are searched.

```
$ ls -l /home/alex
lrwxrwxrwx  1 alex    pubs      17 Aug 19 17:07 memos -> /home/jenny/memos
-rw-r--r--  1 alex    pubs    5119 Aug 19 17:08 report

$ find /home/alex -print
/home/alex
/home/alex/memos
/home/alex/report
/home/alex/.profile

$ find /home/alex -follow -print
/home/alex
/home/alex/memos
/home/alex/memos/memo.817
/home/alex/memos/memo.710
/home/alex/report
/home/alex/.profile
```

finger

Displays information about users

finger [options] [user-list]

The finger utility displays the usernames of users, together with their full names, terminal device numbers, times they logged in, and other information. The *options* control how much information finger displays, and the *user-list* specifies which users finger displays information about. The finger utility can retrieve information from both local and remote systems.

Arguments Without any arguments, finger provides a short (–s) report on users who are logged in on the local system. When you specify a *user-list*, finger provides a long (–l) report on each user in the *user-list*. Names in the *user-list* are not case sensitive.

If the name includes an at sign (@), the finger utility interprets the name following the @ as the name of a remote host to contact over the network. If there is also a name in front of the @ sign, finger provides information on that particular user on the remote system.

Options **–l** (**long**) Displays detailed information (the default display when *user-list* is specified).

–m (**match**) If a *user-list* is specified, displays entries only for those users whose username matches one of the names in *user-list*. Without this option the *user-list* names match usernames and full names.

–p (**no plan, project, or pgpkey**) Does not display the contents of .plan, .project, and .pgpkey files for users. Because these files may contain backslash escape sequences that can change the behavior of the screen, you may not wish to view them. Normally the long listing displays the contents of these files if they exist in the user's home directory.

–s (**short**) Provides a short report for each user (the default display when *user-list* is not present).

Discussion The long report provided by the finger utility includes the user's username, full name, home directory location, and login shell, plus information about when the user last logged in and how long it has been since the user last typed on the keyboard and read her email. After extracting this information from various system files, the finger utility displays the contents of the **~/.plan**, **~/.project**, and **~/.pgpkey** in the user's home directory. It is up to each user to create and maintain these files, which usually provide more information about the user (such as telephone number, postal mail address, schedule, interests, and pgp key).

The short report generated by finger is similar to that provided by the w utility; it includes the user's username, his full name, the device number of the user's terminal, the amount of time that has elapsed since the user last typed on the terminal keyboard, the time the user logged in, and the location of the user's terminal. If the user logged in over the network, the name of the remote system is displayed.

Notes   When you specify a network address, the finger utility queries a standard network service that runs on the remote system. Although this service is supplied with most Linux systems, some administrators choose not to run it (so as to minimize the load on their systems, to eliminate possible security risks, or simply to maintain privacy). If you try to use finger to get information on someone at such a site, the result may be an error message or nothing at all. The remote system determines how much information to share with the local system and in what format. As a result the report displayed for any given system may differ from the examples shown here. See also "finger: Lists Users on the System" on page 64.

A file named **~/.nofinger** causes finger to deny the existence of the person whose home directory it appears in. For this subterfuge to work, the finger query must originate from a system other than the local host and the **fingerd** daemon must be able to see the **.nofinger** file (generally the home directory must have its execute bit for other users set).

Examples   The first example displays information on the users logged in on the local system:

```
$ finger
Login    Name              Tty    Idle  Login Time   Office      Office
Phone
alex     Alex Watson       tty1   13:29 Jun 25 21:03
hls      Helen Simpson    *pts/1  13:29 Jun 25 21:02 (:0)
jenny    Jenny Chen        pts/2        Jun 26 07:47 (bravo.example.com)
```

The asterisk (*) in front of the name of Helen's terminal (TTY) line indicates that she has blocked others from sending messages directly to her terminal (see mesg on page 68). A long report displays the string **messages off** for users who have disabled messages.

The next two examples cause finger to contact the remote system named **kudos** over the network for information:

```
$ finger @kudos
[kudos]
Login    Name              Tty    Idle  Login Time   Office      Office
Phone
alex     Alex Watson       tty1   23:15 Jun 25 11:22
roy      Roy Wong          pts/2        Jun 25 11:22
```

```
$ finger watson@kudos
[kudos]
Login: alex                        Name: Alex Watson
Directory: /home/alex              Shell: /bin/zsh
On since Sat Jun 25 11:22 (PDT) on tty1,  idle 23:22
Last login Sun Jun 26 06:20 (PDT) on ttyp2 from speedy
Mail last read Thu Jun 23 08:10 2005 (PDT)
Plan:
For appointments contact Jenny Chen, x1963.
```

fmt

Formats text very simply

fmt [option] [file-list]

The fmt utility does simple text formatting by attempting to make all nonblank lines nearly the same length.

Arguments   The fmt utility reads the files in *file-list* and sends a formatted version of their contents to standard output. If you do not specify a filename or if you specify a filename of –, fmt reads from standard input.

Options

––split-only   **–s**   Splits long lines but does not fill short lines.

––tagged-paragraph
–t   Indents all but the first line of each paragraph.

––uniform-spacing
–u   Changes the formatted output so that one SPACE appears between words and two SPACES appear between sentences.

––width=*n*   **–w** *n*
Changes the output line width to *n* characters. Without this option, fmt keeps output lines close to 75 characters wide. You can also specify this option as *–n*.

Notes   The fmt utility works by moving NEWLINE characters. The indention of lines, as well as the spacing between words, is left intact.

This utility is often used to format text while you are using an editor, such as vim. For example, you can format a paragraph with the vim editor in command mode by positioning the cursor at the top of the paragraph and then entering **!}fmt –60**. This command replaces the paragraph with the output generated by feeding it through fmt, specifying a width of 60 characters. Type **u** immediately if you want to undo the formatting.

Examples   The following example shows how fmt attempts to make all the lines the same length. The **–w 50** option gives a target line length of 50 characters.

```
$ cat memo
One factor that is important to remember while administering the dietary
intake of Charcharodon carcharias is that there is, at least from
the point of view of the subject,
very little
differentiating the prepared morsels being proffered from your digits.

In other words, don't feed the sharks!

$ fmt -w 50 memo
One factor that is important to remember while
administering the dietary intake of Charcharodon
carcharias is that there is, at least from the
point of view of the subject, very little
differentiating the prepared morsels being
proffered from your digits.

In other words, don't feed the sharks!
```

The next example demonstrates the **--split-only** option. Long lines are broken so that none is longer than 50 characters; this option prevents fmt from filling short lines.

```
$ fmt -w 50 --split-only memo
One factor that is important to remember while
administering the dietary
intake of Charcharodon carcharias is that there
is, at least from
the point of view of the subject,
very little
differentiating the prepared morsels being
proffered from your digits.

In other words, don't feed the sharks!
```

fsck

Checks and repairs a filesystem

fsck [options] [filesystem-list]

The fsck utility verifies the integrity of a filesystem and reports on and optionally repairs problems it finds. It is a front end for filesystem checkers, each specific to a filesystem type.

Arguments

Without the **–A** option and with no *filesystem-list*, fsck checks the filesystems listed in the **/etc/fstab** file one at a time (serially). With the **–A** option and with no *filesystem-list*, fsck checks all the filesystems listed in the **/etc/fstab** file in parallel if possible. See the **–s** option for a discussion of checking filesystems in parallel.

The *filesystem-list* specifies the filesystems to be checked. It can either specify the name of the device that holds the filesystem (for example, **/dev/hda2**) or, if the filesystem appears in **/etc/fstab**, specify the mount point (for example, **/usr2**) for the filesystem. The *filesystem-list* can also specify the label for the filesystem from **/etc/fstab** (for example, **LABEL=home**).

Options

When you run fsck, you can specify both global options and options specific to the filesystem type that fsck is checking (for example, **ext2**, **ext3**, **msdos**, **reiserfs**). Global options must precede type-specific options.

Global Options

–A (**all**) Process all the filesystems listed in the **/etc/fstab** file, in parallel if possible. See the **–s** option for a discussion of checking filesystems in parallel. Do not specify a *filesystem-list* when you use this option; you can specify filesystem types to be checked with the **–t** option. Use this option with the **–a**, **–p**, or **–n** option so that fsck does not attempt to process filesystems in parallel *interactively* (in which case you would have no way of responding to its multiple prompts).

–N (**no**) Assumes a *no* response to any questions that arise while processing a filesystem. This option generates the messages you would normally see but causes fsck to take no action.

–R (**root-skip**) With the **–A** option does not check the root filesystem. Useful when the system boots, because the root filesystem may be mounted with read-write access.

–s (**serial**) Causes fsck to process filesystems one at a time. Without this option, fsck processes multiple filesystems that reside on separate physical disk drives in parallel. Parallel processing enables fsck to process multiple filesystems more quickly. This option is required if you want to process filesystems interactively. See the **–a**, **–p**, or **–n** option to turn off interactive processing.

–t *fstype*

(**filesystem type**) A comma-separated list that specifies the filesystem type(s) to process. With the **–A** option fsck processes all the filesystems in **/etc/fstab** that are of type *fstype*. Common filesystem types are **ext2**, **ext3**, **msdos**, and **reiserfs**. You do not typically check remote NFS filesystems.

–T (**title**) Causes fsck not to display its title.

–V (**verbose**) Displays more output, including filesystem type-specific commands.

Filesystem Type-Specific Options

The following command lists the filesystem checking utilities available on the local system. Files with the same inode numbers are linked (page 99).

```
$ ls -i /sbin/*fsck*
63801 /sbin/dosfsck   63856 /sbin/fsck.cramfs   63801 /sbin/fsck.msdos
63763 /sbin/e2fsck    63763 /sbin/fsck.ext2     63801 /sbin/fsck.vfat
63780 /sbin/fsck      63763 /sbin/fsck.ext3
```

Review the man page or give the pathname of the filesystem checking utility to determine which options the utility accepts:

```
$ /sbin/fsck.ext3
Usage: /sbin/fsck.ext3 [-panyrcdfvstDFSV] [-b superblock] [-B blocksize]
                [-I inode_buffer_blocks] [-P process_inode_size]
                [-l|-L bad_blocks_file] [-C fd] [-j ext-journal]
                [-E extended-options] device

Emergency help:
 -p                     Automatic repair (no questions)
 -n                     Make no changes to the filesystem
 -y                     Assume "yes" to all questions
  c                     Check for bad blocks and add them to the badblock list
 -f                     Force checking even if filesystem is marked clean
...
```

The following options apply to many filesystem types, including **ext2** and **ext3**:

–a (**automatic**) Same as the **–p** option; kept for backward compatibility.

–f (**force**) Forces fsck to check filesystems even if they are *clean*. A clean filesystem is one that was just successfully checked with fsck or was successfully unmounted and has not been mounted since. Clean filesystems are skipped by fsck, greatly speeding up system booting under normal conditions. For information on setting up periodic, automatic filesystem checking on **ext2** and **ext3** filesystems, see tune2fs on page 808.

–p (**preen**) Attempts to repair all minor inconsistencies it finds when processing a filesystem. If any problems are not repaired, fsck terminates with a nonzero exit status. This option runs fsck in batch mode so that it does not ask whether to correct each problem it finds. The **–p** option is commonly used with the **–A** option when checking filesystems while booting Linux.

–r   (**interactive**) Asks whether to correct or ignore each problem that is found. For many filesystem types, this behavior is the default.

–y   (**yes**) Assumes a *yes* response to any questions that fsck asks while processing a filesystem. Use this option with caution as it gives fsck free reign to do what it thinks is best to clean up a filesystem.

Notes

When a filesystem is consistent, fsck displays a report such as the following:

```
# /sbin/fsck -f /dev/hda1
fsck 1.35 (28-Feb-2004)
e2fsck 1.35 (28-Feb-2004)
Pass 1: Checking inodes, blocks, and sizes
Pass 2: Checking directory structure
Pass 3: Checking directory connectivity
Pass 4: Checking reference counts
Pass 5: Checking group summary information
/boot: 71/26104 files (15.5% non-contiguous), 37257/104391 blocks
```

Interactive mode   You can run fsck either interactively or in batch mode. For many filesystems, unless you use one of the **–a**, **–p**, **–y**, or **–n** options, fsck runs in interactive mode. In interactive mode, if fsck finds a problem with a filesystem, it reports the problem and allows you to choose whether to repair or ignore it. If you repair a problem you may lose some data; however, that is often the most reasonable alternative.

Although it is technically feasible to repair files that are damaged and that fsck says you should remove, this action is usually not practical. The best insurance against significant loss of data is frequent backups.

Order of checking   The fsck utility looks at the sixth column in the **/etc/fstab** file to determine if, and in what order, it should check filesystems. A 0 (zero) in this position indicates that the filesystem should not be checked. A **1** (one) indicates that it should be checked first and is usually reserved for the root filesystem. A **2** indicates that the filesystem should be checked after those marked with a **1**.

fsck is a front end   Similar to mkfs (page 725), fsck is a front end that calls other utilities to handle various types of filesystems. For example, fsck calls e2fsck to check the widely used **ext2** and **ext3** filesystems. (Refer to the e2fsck man page for more information.) Other utilities that fsck calls are typically named **fsck.***type,* where *type* is the filesystem type. By splitting fsck in this manner, filesystem developers can provide programs to check their filesystems without affecting the development of other filesystems or changing how system administrators use fsck.

Boot time   Run fsck on filesystems that are unmounted or mounted readonly. When Linux is booting, the root filesystem is first mounted readonly to allow it to be processed by fsck. If fsck finds no problems with the root filesystem, it is then remounted (using the **remount** option to the mount utility) read-write and fsck is typically run with the **–A**, **–R**, and **–p** options.

lost+found When it encounters a file that has lost its link to its filename, fsck asks whether to reconnect it. If you choose to reconnect it, the file is put in a directory named **lost+found** in the root directory of the filesystem that the file was found in. The reconnected file is given its inode number as a name. For fsck to restore files in this way, a **lost+found** directory must be in the root directory of each filesystem. For example, if a system uses the **/**, **/usr**, and **/tmp** filesystems, you should have these three **lost+found** directories: **/lost+found**, **/usr/lost+found**, and **/tmp/lost+found**. Each of the **lost+found** directories must have unused entries that fsck can use to store the inode numbers for files that have lost their links. When you create an **ext2** and **ext3** filesystem using mkfs (page 725), a **lost+found** directory with the required unused entries is created automatically. Alternatively, you can use the mklost+found utility to create this directory in **ext2** and **ext3** filesystems if needed. On other types of filesystems you can create the unused entries by adding many files to the directory and then removing them. Try using touch (page 801) to create 500 entries in the **lost+found** directory and then using rm to delete them.

Messages Table V-14 lists fsck's common messages. In general fsck suggests the most logical way of dealing with a problem in the file structure. Unless you have information that suggests another response, respond to the prompts with **yes**. Use the system backup tapes or disks to restore data that is lost as a result of this process.

table V-14   Common fsck messages

Phase (message)	What fsck checks
Phase 1 - Check inodes, blocks, and sizes	Checks inode information.
Phase 2 - Check directory structures	Looks for directories that point to bad inodes that fsck found in Phase 1.
Phase 3 - Check directory connectivity	Looks for unreferenced directories and a nonexistent or full **lost+found** directory.
Phase 4 - Check reference counts	Checks for unreferenced files, a nonexistent or full **lost+found** directory, bad link counts, bad blocks, duplicated blocks, and incorrect inode counts.
Phase 5 - Check group summary information	Checks whether the free list and other filesystem structures are OK. If any problems are found with the free list, Phase 6 is run.
Phase 6 - Salvage free list	If Phase 5 found any problems with the free list, Phase 6 fixes them.

Cleanup

Once it has repaired the filesystem, fsck informs you about the status of the filesystem. The fsck utility displays the following message after it repairs a filesystem:

```
*****File System Was Modified*****
```

On **ext2** and **ext3** filesystems, fsck displays the following message when it has finished checking a filesystem:

*filesys: **used/maximum** files (**percent** non-contiguous), **used/maximum** blocks*

This message tells you how many files and disk blocks are in use as well as how many files and disk blocks the filesystem can hold. The *percent* non-contiguous tells you how fragmented the disk is.

ftp

Transfers files over a network

ftp [options] [remote-system]

The ftp utility is a user interface to the standard File Transfer Protocol (FTP), which transfers files between systems that can communicate over a network. To establish an FTP connection, you must have an account (personal, guest, or anonymous) on the remote system.

Use FTP only to download public information

security   FTP is not a secure protocol. The ftp utility sends your password over the network as cleartext, which is not a secure practice. You can use scp (page 758) for many FTP functions other than allowing anonymous users to download information. Because scp uses an encrypted connection, user passwords and data cannot be sniffed.

Arguments   The *remote-system* is the name or network address of the server, running an ftpd daemon, that you want to exchange files with.

Options   –i (**interactive**) Turns off prompts during file transfers with **mget** and **mput**. See also **prompt**.

–n (**no automatic login**) Disables automatic logins.

–v (**verbose**) Tells you more about how ftp is working. Displays responses from the *remote-system* and reports transfer times and speeds.

Discussion   The ftp utility is interactive. After you start it, ftp prompts you to enter commands to set parameters and transfer files. You can use a number of commands in response to the **ftp>** prompt; following are some of the more common ones.

![command]   Escapes to (spawns) a shell on the local system (use CONTROL-D or **exit** to return to ftp when you are finished using the local shell). Follow the exclamation point with a command to execute that command only; ftp returns you to the **ftp>** prompt when the command completes executing. Because the shell that ftp spawns with this command is a child of the shell that is running ftp, no changes you make in this shell are preserved when you return to ftp. Specifically, when you want to copy files to a local directory other than the directory that you started ftp from, you need to use the ftp **lcd** command to change the local working directory: Issuing a **cd** command in the spawned shell will not make the change you desire. See "**lcd** (local cd)" on page 676 for an example.

ascii   Sets the file transfer type to ASCII. Allows you to transfer text files from systems that end lines with a RETURN/LINEFEED combination and automatically strip off the RETURN. This type of transfer is useful when the remote computer is a DOS or MS Windows machine. The **cr** command must be ON for **ascii** to work.

binary   Sets the file transfer type to binary. Allows you to transfer files that contain non-ASCII (unprintable) characters correctly. This option also works for ASCII files that do not require changes to the ends of lines.

bye   Closes the connection to a remote system and terminates ftp. Same as **quit**.

cd *remote-directory*

Changes to the working directory named *remote-directory* on the remote system.

close   Closes the connection with the remote system without exiting from ftp.

cr   Toggles RETURN stripping when you retrieve files in ASCII mode. See **ascii**.

dir *[directory [file]]*

Displays a listing of the directory named *directory* from the remote system. When you do not specify *directory,* the working directory is displayed. When you specify *file,* the listing is saved on the local system in a file named *file.*

get *remote-file [local-file]*

Copies *remote-file* to the local system under the name *local-file.* Without *local-file,* ftp uses *remote-file* as the filename on the local system. The *remote-file* and *local-file* names can be pathnames.

glob   Toggles filename expansion for **mget** and **mput** commands and displays the current state (**Globbing on** or **Globbing off**).

help   Displays a list of commands recognized by the ftp utility on the local system.

lcd *[local_directory]*

(**local change directory**) Changes the working directory on the local system to *local_directory.* Without an argument changes the working directory on the local system to your home directory (just as cd does without an argument).

ls *[directory [file]]*Similar to **dir** but produces a more concise listing on some remote computers. When you specify *file,* the listing is saved on the local system in a file named *file.*

mget *remote-file-list*

(**multiple get**) Unlike the **get** command, the **mget** command allows you to retrieve multiple files from the remote system. You can name the remote files literally or use wildcards (see **glob**). See also **prompt**.

mput *local-file-list*

(**multiple put**) The **mput** command allows you to copy multiple files from the local system to the remote system. You can name the local files literally or use wildcards (see **glob**). See also **prompt**.

open Interactively specifies the name of the remote system. This command is useful if you did not specify a remote system on the command line or if the attempt to connect to the system failed.

passive Toggles between active (PORT—the default) and passive (PASV) transfer modes and displays the transfer mode. See "Passive versus active connections" under "Notes."

prompt When using **mget** or **mput** to receive or send multiple files, ftp asks for verification (by default) before transferring each file. This command toggles that behavior and displays the current state (**Interactive mode off** or **Interactive mode on**).

put *local-file [remote-file]*
Copies *local-file* to the remote system under the name *remote-file*. Without *remote-file*, ftp uses *local-file* as the filename on the remote system. The *remote-file* and *local-file* names can be pathnames.

pwd Causes ftp to display the pathname of the remote working directory. Use **!pwd** to display the name of the local working directory.

quit Quits the ftp session. Same as **bye**.

user *[username]* If the ftp utility did not log you in automatically, you can specify your account name as *username*. Without *username*, ftp prompts you for your username.

Notes

A Linux system running ftp can exchange files with any of the many operating systems that support the FTP protocol. Many sites offer archives of free information on an FTP server, although many of these are merely alternatives to an easier-to-access Web site (for example, ftp://ftp.ibiblio.org/pub/Linux and http://www.ibiblio.org/pub/Linux). Most browsers can connect to and download files from FTP servers.

The ftp utility makes no assumptions about filesystem naming or structure because you can use ftp to exchange files with non-UNIX/Linux systems (whose filename conventions may be different).

Anonymous FTP — Many systems—most notably those from which you can download free software—allow you to log in as **anonymous**. Most systems that support anonymous logins accept the name **ftp** as an easier-to-spell and quicker-to-enter synonym for **anonymous**. An anonymous user is usually restricted to a portion of a filesystem set aside to hold files that are to be shared with remote users. When you log in as an anonymous user, the server prompts you to enter a password. Although any password may be accepted, by convention you are expected to supply your email address. Many systems that permit anonymous access store interesting files in the **pub** directory.

Passive versus active connections — A client can ask an FTP server to establish either a PASV (passive—the default) or a PORT (active) connection for data transfer. Some servers are limited to one type of connection. The difference between a passive and an active FTP connection lies in whether the client or server initiates the data connection. In passive mode, the client initiates the data connection to the server (on port 20 by default); in active mode, the server initiates the data connection (there is no default port). Neither type of connection is inherently more secure. Passive connections are more common because a client behind a *NAT* (page 889) firewall can connect to a passive server and because it is simpler to program a scalable passive server.

Automatic login You can store server-specific FTP username and password information so that you do not have to enter it each time you visit an FTP site. Each line of the **~/.netrc** file identifies a server. When you connect to an FTP server, ftp reads **~/.netrc** to determine whether you have an automatic login set up for that server. The format of a line in **~/.netrc** is

> **machine** *server* **login** *username* **password** *passwd*

where *server* is the name of the server, *username* is your username, and *passwd* is your password on *server*. Replace *machine* with **default** on the last line of the file to specify a username and password for systems not listed in **~/.netrc**. The **default** line is useful for logging in on anonymous servers. A sample **~/.netrc** file follows:

```
$ cat ~/.netrc
machine bravo login alex password mypassword
default login anonymous password alex@example.com
```

Protect the account information in **.netrc** by making it readable by only the user whose home directory it appears in. Refer to the **netrc** man page for more information.

Examples

Following are two ftp sessions wherein Alex transfers files from and to an FTP server named **bravo**. When Alex gives the command **ftp bravo**, the local ftp client connects to the server, which asks for a username and password. Because he is logged in on his local system as **alex**, ftp suggests that he log in on **bravo** as **alex**. To log in as **alex**, he could just press RETURN. His username on **bravo** is **watson**, however, so he types **watson** in response to the **Name (bravo:alex):** prompt. Alex responds to the **Password:** prompt with his normal system password, and the FTP server greets him and informs him that it is **Using binary mode to transfer files**. With ftp in binary mode, Alex can transfer ASCII and binary files.

Connect and log in
```
$ ftp bravo
Connected to bravo.
220 (vsFTPd 1.2.0)
530 Please login with USER and PASS.
530 Please login with USER and PASS.
KERBEROS_V4 rejected as an authentication type
Name (bravo:alex): watson
331 Please specify the password.
Password:
230 Login successful.
Remote system type is UNIX.
Using binary mode to transfer files.
ftp>
```

After logging in, Alex uses the ftp **ls** command to display the contents of his remote working directory, which is his home directory on **bravo**. Then he cds to the **memos** directory and displays the files there.

ls and **cd**

```
ftp> ls
227 Entering Passive Mode (192,168,0,6,79,105)
150 Here comes the directory listing.
drwxr-xr-x    2 500        500            4096 Oct 10 23:52 expenses
drwxr-xr-x    2 500        500            4096 Oct 10 23:59 memos
drwxrwxr-x   22 500        500            4096 Oct 10 23:32 tech
226 Directory send OK.

ftp> cd memos
250 Directory successfully changed.

ftp> ls
227 Entering Passive Mode (192,168,0,6,114,210)
150 Here comes the directory listing.
-rw-r--r--    1 500        500            4770 Oct 10 23:58 memo.0514
-rw-r--r--    1 500        500            7134 Oct 10 23:58 memo.0628
-rw-r--r--    1 500        500            9453 Oct 10 23:58 memo.0905
-rw-r--r--    1 500        500            3466 Oct 10 23:59 memo.0921
-rw-r--r--    1 500        500            1945 Oct 10 23:59 memo.1102
226 Directory send OK.
```

Next Alex uses the ftp **get** command to copy **memo.1102** from the server to the local system. Binary mode ensures that he will get a good copy of the file regardless of whether it is binary or ASCII. The server confirms that the file was copied successfully and notes the size of the file and the time it took to copy. Alex then copies the local file **memo.1114** to the remote system. The file is copied into his remote working directory, **memos**.

get and **put**

```
ftp> get memo.1102
local: memo.1102 remote: memo.1102
227 Entering Passive Mode (192,168,0,6,194,214)
150 Opening BINARY mode data connection for memo.1102 (1945 bytes).
226 File send OK.
1945 bytes received in 7.1e-05 secs (2.7e+04 Kbytes/sec)

ftp> put memo.1114
local: memo.1114 remote: memo.1114
227 Entering Passive Mode (192,168,0,6,174,97)
150 Ok to send data.
226 File receive OK.
1945 bytes sent in 2.8e-05 secs (6.8e+04 Kbytes/sec)
```

After a while Alex decides he wants to copy all the files in the **memo** directory on **bravo** to a new directory on his local system. He gives an **ls** command to make sure he is going to copy the right files, but ftp has timed out. Instead of exiting from ftp and giving another ftp command from the shell, Alex gives ftp an **open bravo** command to reconnect to the server. After logging in, he uses the ftp **cd** command to change directories to **memos** on the server.

Timeout and open

```
ftp> ls
421 Timeout.
Passive mode refused.
ftp> open bravo
Connected to bravo (192.168.0.6).
220 (vsFTPd 1.1.3)
...
ftp> cd memos
250 Directory successfully changed.
```

lcd (local cd) At this point, Alex realizes he has not created the new directory to hold the files he wants to download. Giving an ftp **mkdir** command would create a new directory on the server, but Alex wants a new directory on the local system. He uses an exclamation point (**!**) followed by a **mkdir memos.hold** command to invoke a shell and run mkdir on the local system, creating a directory named **memos.hold** in his working directory on the local system. (You can display the name of your working directory on the local system with **!pwd**.) Next, because he wants to copy files from the server to the **memos.hold** directory on his local system, he has to change his working directory on the local system. Giving the command **!cd memos.hold** will not accomplish what Alex wants to do because the exclamation point spawns a new shell on the local system and the **cd** command would be effective only in the new shell, which is not the shell that ftp is running under. For this situation, ftp provides the **lcd** (local **cd**) command, which changes the working directory for ftp and reports on the new local working directory.

```
ftp> !mkdir memos.hold

ftp> lcd memos.hold
Local directory now /home/alex/memos.hold
```

Alex uses the ftp **mget** (multiple get) command followed by the asterisk (*****) wildcard to copy all the files from the remote **memos** directory to the **memos.hold** directory on the local system. When ftp prompts him for the first file, he realizes that he forgot to turn off prompts, responds with **n**, and presses CONTROL-C to stop copying files in response to the second prompt. The server checks whether he wants to continue with his **mget** command.

Next Alex gives the ftp **prompt** command, which toggles the prompt action (turns it *off* if it is *on* and turns it *on* if it is *off*). Now when he gives an **mget *** command, ftp copies all the files without prompting him.

After getting the files he wants, Alex gives a **quit** command to close the connection with the server, exit from ftp, and return to the local shell prompt.

mget and **prompt**

```
ftp> mget *
mget memo.0514? n
mget memo.0628? CONTROL-C
Continue with mget? n
```

```
ftp> prompt
Interactive mode off.

ftp> mget *
local: memo.0514 remote: memo.0514
227 Entering Passive Mode (192,168,0,6,53,55)
150 Opening BINARY mode data connection for memo.0514 (4770 bytes).
226 File send OK.
4770 bytes received in 8.8e-05 secs (5.3e+04 Kbytes/sec)
local: memo.0628 remote: memo.0628
227 Entering Passive Mode (192,168,0,6,65,102)
150 Opening BINARY mode data connection for memo.0628 (7134 bytes).
226 File send OK.
...
150 Opening BINARY mode data connection for memo.1114 (1945 bytes).
226 File send OK.
1945 bytes received in 3.9e-05 secs (4.9e+04 Kbytes/sec)
ftp> quit
221 Goodbye.
```

gcc

Compiles C and C++ programs

gcc [options] file-list [–larg]
g++ [options] file-list [–larg]

The Linux operating system uses the GNU C compiler, gcc, to preprocess, compile, assemble, and link C language source files. The same compiler with a different front end, g++, processes C++ source code. The gcc and g++ compilers can also assemble and link assembly language source files, link object files only, or build object files for use in shared libraries.

These compilers take input from files you specify on the command line. Unless you use the –o option, they store the executable program in **a.out**.

The gcc and g++ compilers are part of GCC, the *GNU Compiler Collection*, which includes front ends for C, C++, Objective C, Fortran, Java, and Ada as well as libraries for these languages. Go to gcc.gnu.org for more information.

gcc and g++

tip   Although this section specifies the gcc compiler, most of it applies to g++ as well.

Arguments   The *file-list* is a list of the pathnames of the files that gcc is to process.

Options   Without any options gcc accepts C language source files, assembly language files, object files, and other files described in Table V-15 on page 681. The gcc utility pre-processes, compiles, assembles, and links these files as appropriate, producing an executable file named **a.out**. If gcc is used to create object files without linking them to produce an executable file, each object file is named by adding the extension **.o** to the basename of the corresponding source file. If gcc is used to create an executable file, it deletes the object files after linking.

Some of the most commonly used options are listed here. When certain filename extensions are associated with an option, you can assume that the extension is added to the basename of the source file.

–c   (**compile**) Suppresses the linking step of compilation. Compiles and/or assembles source code files and leaves the object code in files with the extension **.o**.

–D*name*[=*value*]

Usually **#define** preprocessor directives are given in header, or include, files. You can use this option to define symbolic names on the command line instead. For example, **–DLinux** is equivalent to having the line **#define Linux** in an include file, and **–DMACH=i586** is the same as **#define MACH i586**.

–E **(everything)** On source code files, suppresses all steps of compilation *except* preprocessing and writes the result to standard output. By convention the extension **.i** is used for preprocessed C source and **.ii** for preprocessed C++ source.

–fpic

Causes gcc to produce *position-independent* code, which is suitable for installing into a shared library.

–fwritable-strings

By default the GNU C compiler places string constants into *protected memory*, where they cannot be changed. Some (usually older) programs assume that you can modify string constants. This option changes the behavior of gcc so string constants can be modified.

–g **(gdb)** Embeds diagnostic information in the object files. This information is used by symbolic debuggers, such as gdb (page 412). Although it is necessary only if you later use a debugger, it is a good practice to include this option as a matter of course.

–I*directory*

Looks for include files in *directory* before looking in the standard locations. Give this option multiple times to look in more than one directory.

–l*arg*

(lowercase "l") Searches the directories **/lib** and **/usr/lib** for a library file named **lib***arg***.a**. If the file is found, gcc then searches this library for any required functions. Replace *arg* with the name of the library you want to search. For example, the **–lm** option normally links the standard math library **libm.a**. The position of this option is significant: It generally needs to go at the end of the command line but can be repeated multiple times to search different libraries. Libraries are searched in the order in which they appear on the command line. The linker uses the library only to resolve undefined symbols from modules that *precede* the library option on the command line. You can add other library paths to search for **lib***arg***.a** using the **–L** option.

–L*directory*

Adds *directory* to the list of directories to search for libraries given with the **–l** option. Directories that are added to the list with **–L** are searched before looking in the standard locations for libraries.

–o *file*

(output) Names the executable program that results from linking *file* instead of **a.out**.

–O*n*

(optimize) Attempts to improve (optimize) the object code produced by the compiler. The value of *n* may be **0**, **1**, **2**, or **3** (or **06** if you are compiling code for the Linux kernel). The default value of *n* is **1**. Larger values of *n* result in better optimization but may increase both the size of the object file and the time it takes gcc to run. Using –O0 turns off optimization. Many related options control precisely the types of optimizations attempted by gcc when you use –O. Refer to the gcc info page for details.

–pedantic

The C language accepted by the GNU C compiler includes features that are not part of the ANSI standard for the C language. Using this option forces gcc to reject these *language extensions* and accept only standard C programming language features.

–Q   Displays the names of functions as gcc compiles them. Also displays statistics about each pass.

–S   (**suppress**) Suppresses the assembling and linking steps of compilation on source code files. The resulting assembly language files have **.s** filename extensions.

–traditional

Causes gcc to accept only C programming language features that existed in the traditional Kernighan and Ritchie C programming language. This option allows you to compile correctly older programs written using the traditional C language that existed before the ANSI standard C language was defined.

–Wall

Causes gcc to warn you about questionable code in the source code files. Many related options control warning messages more precisely. See page 408.

Notes

The preceding list of options represents only a small fraction of the full set of options available with the GNU C compiler. See the gcc info page for a complete list.

See "Programming in C" on page 388 for more information about using the gcc compiler.

Although the –o option is generally used to specify a filename to store object code, this option also allows you to name files resulting from other compilation steps. In the following example, the –o option causes the assembly language produced by the gcc command to be stored in the file **acode** instead of **pgm.s,** the default:

```
$ gcc -S -o acode pgm.c
```

The lint utility found in many UNIX systems is not available on Linux. However, the **–Wall** option (page 408) performs many of the same checks and can be used in place of lint.

The conventions used by the C compiler for assigning filename extensions are summarized in Table V-15.

table V-15	Filename extensions
Extension	**Type of file**
.a	Library of object modules
.c	C language source file
.C, **.cc**, *or* **.cxx**	C++ language source file
.i	Preprocessed C language source file
.ii	Preprocessed C++ language source file
.o	Object file
.s	Assembly language source file
.S	Assembly language source file that needs preprocessing

Examples   The first example compiles, assembles, and links a single C program, **compute.c**. The executable output is put in **a.out**. The gcc utility deletes the object file.

```
$ gcc compute.c
```

The next example compiles the same program using the C optimizer (**–O** option). It assembles and links the optimized code. The **–o** option causes gcc to put the executable output in **compute**.

```
$ gcc -O -o compute compute.c
```

Next a C source file, an assembly language file, and an object file are compiled, assembled, and linked. The executable output goes in **progo**.

```
$ gcc -o progo procom.c profast.s proout.o
```

In the next example, gcc searches the standard math library stored in **/lib/libm.a** when it is linking the **himath** program and puts the executable output in **a.out**:

```
$ gcc himath.c -lm
```

In the following example, the C compiler compiles **topo.c** with options that check the code for questionable source code practices (**–Wall** option) and violations of the ANSI C standard (**–pedantic** option). The **–g** option embeds debugging support in the executable file, which is saved in **topo** with the **–o topo** option. Full optimization is enabled with the **–O3** option.

The warnings produced by the C compiler are sent to standard output. Here the first and last warnings result from the **–pedantic** option; the other warnings result from the **–Wall** option:

```
$ gcc -Wall -g -O3 -pedantic -o topo topo.c
In file included from topo.c:2:
/usr/include/ctype.h:65: warning: comma at end of enumerator list
topo.c:13: warning: return-type defaults to 'int'
topo.c: In function 'main':
topo.c:14: warning: unused variable 'c'
topo.c: In function 'getline':
topo.c:44: warning: 'c' might be used uninitialized in this function
```

When compiling programs that use the X11 include files and libraries, you may need to use the **–I** and **–L** options to tell gcc where to locate those include files and libraries. The next example uses those options and instructs gcc to link the program with the basic X11 library:

```
$ gcc -I/usr/X11R6/include plot.c -L/usr/X11R6/lib -lX11
```

grep

Searches for a pattern in files

grep [options] pattern [file-list]

The grep utility searches one or more files, line by line, for a *pattern*, which can be a simple string or another form of a regular expression. The grep utility takes various actions, specified by options, each time it finds a line that contains a match for the *pattern*. This utility takes its input from files you specify on the command line or from standard input.

Arguments The *pattern* is a regular expression, as defined in Appendix A. You must quote regular expressions that contain special characters, SPACEs, or TABs. An easy way to quote these characters is to enclose the entire expression within single quotation marks.

The *file-list* is a list of the pathnames of ordinary files that grep searches. With the –r option, *file-list* may contain directories whose contents are searched.

Options Without any options grep sends lines that contain a match for *pattern* to standard output. When you specify more than one file on the command line, grep precedes each line that it displays with the name of the file that it came from followed by a colon.

Major Options

You can use only one of the following three options at a time. Normally you do not need to use any, because grep defaults to –G, which is regular grep.

–E (**extended**) Interprets *pattern* as an extended regular expression (page 836). The command **grep –E** is the same as egrep. See "Notes" later in this section.

–F (**fixed**) Interprets *pattern* as a fixed string of characters. The command **grep –F** is the same as fgrep.

–G (**grep**) Interprets *pattern* as a basic regular expression. This is the default major option if none is specified.

Other Options

Accepts the common options described on page 587.

––count –c Displays only the number of lines that contain a match in each file.

––context=*n* –C *n*
 Displays *n* lines of context around each matching line.

––file=*file* –f *file*
 Reads *file*, which contains one pattern per line, and finds lines in the input that match each of the patterns.

--no-filename	–h	Does not display the filename at the beginning of each line when searching through multiple files.
--ignore-case	–i	Causes lowercase letters in the pattern to match uppercase letters in the file, and vice versa. Use this option when you are searching for a word that may be at the beginning of a sentence (that is, may or may not start with an uppercase letter).
--files-with-matches	–l	(lowercase "l") Displays only the name of each file that contains one or more matches. A filename is displayed only once, even if the file contains more than one match.
--max-count=*n*	–m *n*	Stops reading each file, or standard input, after displaying *n* lines containing matches.
--line-number	–n	Precedes each line by its line number in the file. The file does not need to contain line numbers.
--quiet *or* --silent	–q	Does not write anything to standard output; only sets the exit code.
--recursive	–r *or* –R	Recursively descends directories in *file-list* and processes files within these directories.
--no-messages	–s	(silent) Does not display an error message if a file in *file-list* does not exist or is not readable.
--invert-match	–v	Causes lines *not* containing a match to satisfy the search. When you use this option by itself, grep displays all lines that do not contain a match for the *pattern*.
--word-regexp	–w	With this option, the *pattern* must match a whole word. This option is helpful if you are searching for a specific word that may also appear as a substring of another word in the file.
--line-regexp	–x	The *pattern* matches whole lines only.

Notes   The grep utility returns an exit status of 0 if it finds a match, 1 if it does not find a match, and 2 if the file is not accessible or there is a syntax error.

egrep and fgrep   Two utilities perform functions similar to that of grep. The egrep utility (same as **grep –E**) allows you to use *extended regular expressions* (page 836), which include a different set of special characters than basic regular expressions (page 834). The fgrep utility (same as **grep –F**) is fast and compact but processes only simple strings, not regular expressions.

Examples The following examples assume that the working directory contains three files: **testa, testb,** and **testc:**

File testa	File testb	File testc
aaabb	aaaaa	AAAAA
bbbcc	bbbbb	BBBBB
ff-ff	ccccc	CCCCC
cccdd	ddddd	DDDDD
dddaa		

The grep utility can search for a pattern that is a simple string of characters. The following command line searches **testa** and displays each line containing the string **bb:**

```
$ grep bb testa
aaabb
bbbcc
```

The **−v** option reverses the sense of the test. The following example displays the lines in **testa** *without* **bb:**

```
$ grep -v bb testa
ff-ff
cccdd
dddaa
```

The **−n** option displays the line number of each displayed line:

```
$ grep -n bb testa
1:aaabb
2:bbbcc
```

The grep utility can search through more than one file. Here grep searches through each file in the working directory. The name of the file containing the string precedes each line of output.

```
$ grep bb *
testa:aaabb
testa:bbbcc
testb:bbbbb
```

When the search for the string **bb** is done with the **−w** option, grep produces no output because none of the files contains the string **bb** as a separate word:

```
$ grep -w bb *
$
```

The search that grep performs is case sensitive. Because the previous examples specified lowercase **bb,** grep did not find the uppercase string **BBBBB** in **testc.** The **−i** option causes both uppercase *and* lowercase letters to match either case of letter in the pattern:

```
$ grep -i bb *
testa:aaabb
testa:bbbcc
testb:bbbbb
testc:BBBBB
$ grep -i BB *
testa:aaabb
testa:bbbcc
testb:bbbbb
testc:BBBBB
```

The **–c** option displays the number of lines in each file that contain a match:

```
$ grep -c bb *
testa:2
testb:1
testc:0
```

The **–f** option finds matches for each pattern in a file of patterns. The next example shows **gfile**, which holds two patterns, one per line, and grep searching for matches to the patterns in **gfile**:

```
$ cat gfile
aaa
bbb
$ grep -f gfile test*
testa:aaabb
testa:bbbcc
testb:aaaaa
testb:bbbbb
```

The following command line displays from **text2** lines that contain a string of characters starting with **st**, followed by zero or more characters (**.** represents zero or more characters in a regular expression—see Appendix A), and ending in **ing**:

```
$ grep 'st.*ing' text2
...
```

The **^** regular expression, which matches the beginning of a line, can be used alone to match every line in a file. Together with the **–n** option, **^** can be used to display the lines in a file, preceded by their line numbers:

```
$ grep -n '^' testa
1:aaabb
2:bbbcc
3:ff-ff
4:cccdd
5:dddaa
```

The next command line counts the number of times **#include** statements appear in C source files in the working directory. The **–h** option causes grep to suppress the filenames from its output. The input to sort is all lines from *.c that match **#include**. The output from sort is an ordered list of lines that contains many duplicates. When uniq with the **–c** option processes this sorted list, it outputs repeated lines only once, along with a count of the number of repetitions in its input.

```
$ grep -h '#include' *.c | sort | uniq -c
9 #include "buff.h"
2 #include "poly.h"
1 #include "screen.h"
6 #include "window.h"
2 #include "x2.h"
2 #include "x3.h"
2 #include <math.h>
3 #include <stdio.h>
```

The final command calls the vim editor with a list of files in the working directory that contain the string **Sampson**. The $(...) command substitution construct (page 329) causes the shell to execute grep in place and supply vim with a list of filenames that you want to edit:

```
$ vim $(grep -l 'Sampson' *)
...
```

The single quotation marks are not necessary in this example, but they are required if the regular expression you are searching for contains special characters or SPACEs. It is generally a good habit to quote the pattern so that the shell does not interpret special characters it may contain.

gzip

Compresses or decompresses files

gzip [options] [file-list]
gunzip [options] [file-list]
zcat [file-list]

The gzip utility compresses files; gunzip restores files compressed with gzip; zcat displays files compressed with gzip.

Arguments

The *file-list* is a list of the names of one or more files that are to be compressed or decompressed. If a directory appears in *file-list* with no **--recursive** option, gzip/gunzip issues an error message and ignores the directory. With the **--recursive** option, gzip/gunzip recursively compresses/decompresses files within the directory hierarchy.

If *file-list* is empty or if the special option – is present, gzip reads from standard input. The **--stdout** option causes gzip and gunzip to write to standard output.

The information in this section also applies to gunzip, a link to gzip.

Options

Accepts the common options described on page 587.

--stdout   **–c** Writes the results of compression or decompression to standard output instead of overwriting the original file.

--decompress *or*   **–d** Decompresses a file compressed with gzip. This option with gzip is equivalent
--uncompress   to the gunzip command.

--fast *or*   **–n** Controls the tradeoff between the speed of compression and the amount of com-
--best   pression. The *n* is a digit from 1 to 9; level 1 is the fastest (least) compression and level 9 is the best (slowest and most) compression. The default level is 6. The options **--fast** and **--best** are synonyms for –1 and –9, respectively.

--force   **–f** Overwrites an existing output file on compression/decompression.

--list   **–l** For each compressed file in *file-list*, displays the file's compressed and decompressed sizes, the compression ratio, and the name of the file before compression. Use with **--verbose** for additional information.

--quiet   **–q** Suppresses warning messages.

--recursive   **–r** Recursively descends directories in *file-list* and compresses/decompresses files within these directories.

--test   **–t** Verifies the integrity of a compressed file. Displays nothing if the file is OK.

     --verbose   **-v**   Displays the name of the file, the name of the compressed file, and the amount of compression as each file is processed.

Discussion

Compressing files reduces disk space requirements and the time needed to transmit files between systems. When gzip compresses a file, it adds the extension **.gz** to the filename. For example, compressing the file **fname** creates the file **fname.gz** and deletes the original file. To restore **fname**, use the command **gunzip** with the argument **fname.gz**.

Almost all files become much smaller when compressed with gzip. On rare occasions a file will become larger, but only by a slight amount. The type of a file and its contents (as well as the *–n* option) determine how much smaller a file becomes; text files are often reduced by 60 to 70 percent.

The attributes of a file, such as its owner, permissions, and modification and access times, are left intact when gzip compresses and gunzip decompresses a file.

If the compressed version of a file already exists, gzip reports that fact and asks for your confirmation before overwriting the existing file. If a file has multiple links to it, gzip issues an error message and exits. The **--force** option overrides the default behavior in both of these situations.

Notes

For more information refer to "gzip: Compresses a File" on page 58.

In addition to the gzip format, gunzip recognizes several other compression formats, enabling gunzip to decompress files compressed with compress.

To see an example of a file that becomes larger when compressed with gzip, compare the size of a file that has been compressed once with the same file compressed with gzip again. Because gzip complains when you give it an argument with the extension **.gz**, you need to rename the file before compressing it a second time.

The tar utility with the *–z* modifier (page 789) calls gzip.

The following related utilities display and manipulate compressed files. None of these utilities changes the files that it works on.

zcat *file-list*   Works like cat except that it uses gunzip to decompress *file-list* as it copies files to standard output.

zdiff [*options*] *file1* [*file2*]

    Works like diff (page 638) except that *file1* and *file2* are decompressed with gunzip as needed. The zdiff utility accepts the same options as diff. If you omit *file2*, zdiff compares *file1* with the compressed version of *file1*.

zless *file-list*   Works like less except that it uses gunzip to decompress *file-list* as it displays files.

Examples   In the first example, gzip compresses two files. Then gunzip decompresses one of the
files. When a file is compressed and decompressed, its size changes but its modification time remains the same:

```
$ ls -l
total 175
-rw-rw-r-- 1 alex group 33557 Jul 20 17:32 patch-2.0.7
-rw-rw-r-- 1 alex group 143258 Jul 20 17:32 patch-2.0.8
$ gzip *
$ ls -l
total 51
-rw-rw-r-- 1 alex group 9693 Jul 20 17:32 patch-2.0.7.gz
-rw-rw-r-- 1 alex group 40426 Jul 20 17:32 patch-2.0.8.gz
$ gunzip patch-2.0.7.gz
$ ls -l
total 75
-rw-rw-r-- 1 alex group 33557 Jul 20 17:32 patch-2.0.7
-rw-rw-r-- 1 alex group 40426 Jul 20 17:32 patch-2.0.8.gz
```

In the next example, the files in Jenny's home directory are archived by using the cpio
utility (page 619). The archive is compressed with gzip before it is written to tape:

```
$ find /home/jenny -depth -print | cpio -oBm | gzip >/dev/ftape
```

head

Displays the beginning of a file

head [options] [file-list]

The head utility displays the beginning (head) of a file. The utility takes its input from one or more files you specify on the command line or from standard input.

Arguments   The *file-list* is a list of the pathnames of the files that head displays. When you specify more than one file, head displays the filename before displaying the first few lines of each file. When you do not specify a file, head takes its input from standard input.

Options   Accepts the common options described on page 587.

--bytes=*n[u]*   –c *n[u]*

Displays the first *n* bytes (characters) of a file. The *u* is an optional unit of measure that can be **b** (512-byte blocks), **k** (kilobyte or 1,024-byte blocks), or **m** (megabyte or 1,048,576-byte blocks). If you include the unit of measure, head counts by this unit instead of by bytes.

--lines=*n*   –n *n*

Displays the first *n* lines of a file. You can use *–n* to specify *n* lines without using the **lines** keyword or the –n option. If you specify a negative value for *n*, head displays all but the last *n* lines of the file.

--quiet   –q   Suppresses header information when you specify more than one filename on the command line.

Notes   The head utility displays the first ten lines of a file by default.

Examples   The examples in this section are based on the following file:

```
$ cat eleven
line one
line two
line three
line four
line five
line six
line seven
line eight
line nine
line ten
line eleven
```

Without any arguments head displays the first ten lines of a file:

```
$ head eleven
line one
line two
line three
line four
line five
line six
line seven
line eight
line nine
line ten
```

The next example displays the first three lines (--**lines 3**) of the file:

```
$ head --lines 3 eleven
line one
line two
line three
```

The following example is equivalent to the preceding one:

```
$ head -3 eleven
line one
line two
line three
```

The next example displays the first six characters (--**bytes 6**) in the file:

```
$ head --bytes 6 eleven
line o$
```

The final example displays all but the last seven lines of the file:

```
$ head --lines=-7 eleven
line one
line two
line three
line four
```

kill

Terminates a process by PID

kill [option] PID-list

The kill utility terminates one or more processes by sending them signals. By default kill sends a software termination signal (signal number 15). For kill to work, the process must belong to the user executing kill, with one exception: Superuser can terminate any process.

Arguments   The *PID-list* is a list of process identification (PID) numbers of processes that kill is to terminate.

Options   You can specify a signal number or name, preceded by a hyphen, as an option to cause kill to send the signal you specify to the *PID-list*.

–l   (list) Displays a list of signals. (Do not specify *PID-list*.)

Notes   See also killall on page 695.

See Table 11-5 on page 494 for a list of signals. The command **kill –l** displays a complete list of signal numbers and names.

In addition to the kill utility, kill is a builtin in the Bourne Again and TC Shells. The builtins work similarly to the utility described here. Give the command **/bin/kill** to use the kill utility and the command **kill** to use the builtin. It does not usually matter which you use.

The shell displays the PID number of a background process when you initiate the process. You can also use the ps utility to determine PID numbers.

If the software termination signal does not terminate a process, try using a KILL signal (signal number 9). A process can choose to ignore any signal except KILL.

The kill utility/builtin accepts job identifiers in place of the *PID-list*. Job identifiers consist of a percent sign (%) followed by either a job number or a string that uniquely identifies the job.

To terminate all processes that the current login process initiated and have the operating system log you out, give the command **kill –9 0**.

root: do not run kill with arguments of –9 0 or KILL 0

caution   If you run the command **kill –9 0** while you are logged in as Superuser, you will bring the system down.

Examples   The first example shows a command line executing the file **compute** as a background process and the kill utility terminating it:

```
$ compute &
[2] 259
$ kill 259
$ RETURN
[2]+  Terminated                compute
```

The next example shows the ps utility determining the PID number of the background process running a program named **xprog** and the kill utility terminating **xprog** with the TERM signal:

```
$ ps
PID TTY STAT   TIME COMMAND
116   1 S     0:00 -tcsh
128   1 S N   0:00 xinit /home/alex/.xinitrc --
137   1 S N   0:01 fvwm
138  p0 S N   0:00 -tcsh
161  p0 S N   0:10 xprog
262  p0 R N   0:00 ps
$ kill -TERM 161
$
```

killall

Terminates a process by name

killall [option] name-list

The killall utility sends signals to processes executing specified commands. For killall to work, the processes must belong to the user executing killall, with one exception: Superuser can terminate any process.

Arguments   The *name-list* is a SPACE-separated list of names of programs that are to receive signals.

Options   You can specify a signal number or name, preceded by a hyphen, as an option before the *name-list* to cause killall to send the signal you specify. By default killall sends software termination signals (signal number 15, SIGTERM).

––interactive   –i   Prompts for confirmation before killing a process.

––list   –l   Displays a list of signals (but **kill –l** displays a better list). With this option killall does not accept a *name-list*.

––quiet   –q   Does not display a message if killall fails to terminate a process.

Notes   See also kill on page 693.

See Table 11-5 on page 494 for a list of signals. The command **kill –l** displays a complete list of signal numbers and names.

If the software termination signal does not terminate the process, try using a KILL signal (signal number 9). A process can choose to ignore any signal except KILL.

You can use ps (page 746) to determine the name of the program you want to terminate.

Examples   You can give the following commands to experiment with killall:

```
$ sleep 60 &
[1] 23274
$ sleep 50 &
[2] 23275
$ sleep 40 &
[3] 23276
$ sleep 120 &
[4] 23277
$ killall sleep
$ RETURN
[1]   Terminated              sleep 60
[2]   Terminated              sleep 50
[3]-  Terminated              sleep 40
[4]+  Terminated              sleep 120
```

If you want to terminate all instances of the Firefox browser, give the following command to determine how Firefox was called:

```
$ ps -ef | grep -i firefox
max 17517 17512  0 Apr02 ?        00:00:54 /usr/local/firefox/firefox-bin
max 19340  2787  0 00:33 pts/6    00:00:00 grep firefox
```

The next command, run as **root**, terminates all instances of the Firefox browser:

```
# killall firefox-bin
```

less

Displays text files, one screen at a time

less [options] [file-list]

The less utility displays text files, one screen at a time.

Arguments   The *file-list* is the list of files you want to view. If there is no *file-list,* less reads from standard input.

Options   Accepts the common options described on page 587.

--clear-screen   –c   Repaints the screen from the top line down instead of scrolling.

--quit-at-eof   –e   (**exit**) Normally less requires you to enter **q** to terminate. This option exits automatically the *second* time less reads the end of file.

--QUIT-AT-EOF   –E   (**exit**) Similar to –e, except that less exits automatically the *first* time it reads the end of file.

--quit-if-one-screen
   –F   Displays the file and quits if the file can be displayed on a single screen.

--ignore-case   –i   Causes a search for a string of lowercase letters to match both uppercase and lowercase letters. This option is ignored if you give a pattern that includes uppercase letters.

--IGNORE-CASE
   –I   Causes a search for a string of letters of any case to match both uppercase and lowercase letters, regardless of the case of the search pattern.

--long-prompt   –m   Reports the percentage of the file that you have viewed with each prompt. This option causes less to display a prompt that is similar to the prompt used by more. It does not work when less reads from standard input because less has no way of determining how much input there is.

--LINE-NUMBERS
   –N   Displays a line number at the start of each line.

   –P*sprompt*
      Changes the short prompt string (the prompt that appears at the bottom of each screen of output) to *prompt*. Enclose *prompt* in quotation marks if it contains SPACEs. You can use special symbols in *prompt* that less will replace with other values when it displays the prompt. For example, less displays the current filename in place of **%f** in *prompt*. See the less man page for a list of these

special symbols and descriptions of other prompts. Custom prompts are useful if you are running less from within another program and want to give instructions or information to the person who is using the program. The default prompt is the name of the file displayed in reverse video.

--squeeze-blank-lines

−s   Displays multiple, adjacent blank lines as a single blank line. When you use less to display text that has been formatted for printing with blank space at the top and bottom of each page, this option shortens these headers and footers to a single line.

--tabs=*n*   −x*n*

Sets tab stops *n* characters apart. The default is eight characters.

--window=*n*   −[z]*n*

Sets the scrolling size to *n* lines. The default is the size of the display. Each time you move forward or backward a page, you move *n* lines.

+*command*

Any command you can give less while it is running can also be given as an option by preceding it with a plus sign (+) on the command line. See the "Commands" section. A command preceded by a plus sign on the command line is executed as soon as less starts and applies only to the first file.

++*command*

Similar to +*command* except that *command* is applied to every file in *file-list*, not just the first.

Notes   The phrase "less is more" explains the origin of this utility. The more utility is the original Berkeley UNIX pager (also available under Linux). The less utility is similar to more but includes many enhancements. After displaying a screen of text, less displays a prompt and waits for you to enter a command. You can skip forward and backward in the file, invoke an editor, search for a pattern, or perform a number of other tasks.

See the **v** command in the next section for information on how you can edit the file you are viewing with less.

You can set the options to less either from the command line when you call less or by setting the **LESS** environment variable. For example, you can use the following command from bash to use less with the −x4 and −s options.

```
$ export LESS="-x4 -s"
```

Normally you would set **LESS** in ~/.bash_profile if you are using bash or in ~/.login if you are using tcsh. Once you have set the **LESS** variable, less is invoked with the specified options each time you call it. Any options you give on the command line override the settings in the **LESS** variable. The **LESS** variable is used both when you call less from the command line and when less is invoked by another program, such as man. To specify less as the pager to use with man and other programs, set the environment variable **PAGER** to **less**. For example, with bash you can add the following line to ~/.bash_profile:

```
export PAGER=less
```

Commands Whenever less pauses, you can enter any of a large number of commands. This section describes some commonly used commands. Refer to the less man page for the full list of commands. The optional numeric argument n defaults to 1, with the exceptions noted. You do not need to follow these commands with a RETURN.

*n*b *or* *n*CONTROL-B **(backward)** Scrolls backward n lines. The default value of n is the size of the screen.

*n*d *or* *n*CONTROL-D **(down)** Scrolls forward n lines. The default value of n is one-half the screen size. When you specify n, it becomes the new default value for this command.

F **(forward)** Scrolls forward. If the end of the input is reached, this command waits for more input and then continues scrolling. This command allows you to use less in a manner similar to **tail –f** (page 783), except that less paginates the output as it appears.

*n*g **(go)** Goes to line number n. This command may not work if the file is read from standard input and you have moved too far into the file. The default value of n is 1.

h *or* H **(help)** Displays a summary of all available commands. The summary is displayed using less, as the list of commands is quite long.

*n*RETURN *or* *n*j **(jump)** Scrolls forward n lines. The default value of n is 1.

q *or* :q Terminates less.

*n*u *or* *n*CONTROL-U Scrolls backward n lines. The default value of n is one-half the screen size. When you specify n, it becomes the default value for this command.

v Brings the current file into an editor with the cursor on the current line. The less utility uses the editor specified in the **EDITOR** environment variable. If **EDITOR** is not set, less uses vi (which is typically linked to vim).

*n*w Scrolls backward like *n*b, except that the value of n becomes the new default value for this command.

*n*y *or* *n*k Scrolls backward n lines. The default value of n is 1.

*n*z Displays the next n lines like *n*SPACE except that the value of n, if present, becomes the new default value for the **z** and SPACE commands.

*n*SPACE   Displays the next *n* lines. Pressing SPACE by itself displays the next screen of text.

/*regular-expression*

Skips forward in the file, looking for lines that contain a match for *regular-expression*. If you begin *regular-expression* with an exclamation point (!), this command looks for lines that do *not* contain a match for *regular-expression*. If *regular-expression* begins with an asterisk (*), this command continues the search through *file-list*. (A normal search stops at the end of the current file.) If *regular-expression* begins with an at sign (@), this command begins the search at the start of *file-list* and continues to the end of *file-list*.

?*regular-expression*

This command is similar to the previous one but searches backward through the file (and *file-list*). An asterisk (*) as the first character in *regular-expression* causes the search to continue backward through *file-list* to the beginning of the first file. An at sign (@) causes the search to start with the last line of the last file in *file-list* and progress toward the first line of the first file.

{ *or* (*or* [If one of these characters appears in the top line of the display, this command scrolls forward to the matching right brace, parenthesis, or bracket. For example, typing { causes less to move the cursor forward to the matching }.

} *or*) *or*]   Similar to the preceding commands, these commands move the cursor backward to the matching left brace, parenthesis, or bracket.

CONTROL-L   Redraws the screen. This command is useful if the text on the screen has become garbled.

[n]:n   Skips to the next file in *file-list*. If *n* is given, skips to the *n*th next file in *file-list*.

!*[command line]*   Executes *command line* under the shell specified by the SHELL environment variable, or sh (usually linked to bash) by default. A percent sign (%) in *command line* is replaced by the name of the current file. If you omit *command line,* less starts an interactive shell.

Examples

The following example displays the file **memo.txt**. To see more of the file, the user presses the SPACE bar in response to the less prompt at the bottom left of the screen:

```
$ less memo.txt
...
memo.txt SPACE
...
```

In the next example, the user changes the prompt to a more meaningful message and uses the **–N** option to display line numbers. Finally the user instructs less to skip forward to the first line containing the string **procedure**.

```
$ less -Ps"Press SPACE to continue, q to quit" -N +/procedure ncut.icn
   28  procedure main(args)
   29      local filelist, arg, fields, delim
   30
   31      filelist:=[]
...
   45      # Check for real field list
   46      #
   47      if /fields then stop("-fFIELD_LIST is required.")
   48
   49      # Process the files and output the fields
Press SPACE to continue, q to quit
```

ln

Makes a link to a file

ln [options] existing-file [new-link]
ln [options] existing-file-list directory

The ln utility creates hard or symbolic links to one or more files. You can create a symbolic link, but not a hard link, to a directory.

Arguments   In the first format the *existing-file* is the pathname of the file you want to create a link to. The *new-link* is the pathname of the new link. When you are creating a symbolic link, the *existing-file* can be a directory. If you omit *new-link*, ln creates a link to *existing-file* in the working directory, and uses the same simple filename as *existing-file*.

In the second format the *existing-file-list* is a list of the pathnames of the ordinary files you want to create links to. The ln utility establishes the new links in the *directory*. The simple filenames of the entries in the *directory* are the same as the simple filenames of the files in the *existing-file-list*.

Options

--backup –b   If the ln utility will remove a file, this option makes a backup by appending ~ to the filename. This option works only with **--force**.

--force –f   Normally ln does not create the link if *new-link* already exists. This option removes *new-link* before creating the link. When you use **--force** and **--backup** together, ln makes a copy of *new-link* before removing it.

--interactive –i   If *new-link* already exists, this option prompts you before removing *new-link*. If you enter **y** or **yes**, ln removes *new-link* before creating the link. If you answer **n** or **no**, no new link is made.

--symbolic –s   Creates a symbolic link. When you use this option, the *existing-file* and *new-link* may be directories and may reside on different filesystems. Refer to "Symbolic Links" on page 99.

Notes

For more information refer to "Links" on page 96. The ls utility with the –l option displays the number of hard links to a file (Figure 4-12, page 92).

Hard links   By default ln creates *hard links*. A hard link to a file is indistinguishable from the original file. All hard links to a file must be in the same filesystem. For more information refer to "Hard Links" on page 97.

Symbolic links   You can also use ln to create *symbolic links*. Unlike a hard link, a symbolic link can exist in a different filesystem from the linked-to file. Also, a symbolic link can point to a directory. For more information refer to "Symbolic Links" on page 99.

If *new-link* is the name of an existing file, ln does not create the link unless you use the **−−force** option or answer **yes** when using the **−−interactive** option.

Examples

The following command creates a link between **memo2** in the **/home/zach/literature** directory and the working directory. The file appears as **memo2** (the simple filename of the existing file) in the working directory:

```
$ ln /home/zach/literature/memo2 .
```

You can omit the period that represents the working directory from the preceding command. When you give a single argument to ln, it creates a link in the working directory.

The next command creates a link to the same file. This time the file appears as **new_memo** in the working directory:

```
$ ln /home/zach/literature/memo2 new_memo
```

The following command creates a link that causes the file to appear in another user's directory:

```
$ ln /home/zach/literature/memo2 /home/jenny/new_memo
```

You must have write and execute access permission to the other user's directory for this command to work. If you own the file, you can use chmod to give the other user write access permission to the file.

The next command creates a symbolic link to a directory. The **ls −ld** command shows the link:

```
$ ln -s /usr/local/bin bin
$ ls -ld bin
lrwxrwxrwx  1 zach zach 14 Feb 10 13:26 bin -> /usr/local/bin
```

The final example attempts to create a symbolic link named **memo1** to the file **memo2**. Because the file **memo1** exists, ln refuses to make the link. When you use the **−−interactive** option, ln asks whether you want to replace the existing **memo1** file with the symbolic link. If you enter **y** or **yes**, ln creates the link and the old **memo1** disappears.

```
$ ls -l memo?
-rw-rw-r--   1 zach group 224 Jul 31 14:48 memo1
-rw-rw-r--   1 zach group 753 Jul 31 14:49 memo2
$ ln --symbolic memo2 memo1
ln: memo1: File exists
$ ln --symbolic --interactive memo2 memo1
ln: replace 'memo1'? y
$ ls -l memo?
lrwxrwxrwx   1 zach group 5 Jul 31 14:49 memo1 -> memo2
-rw-rw-r--   1 zach group 753 Jul 31 14:49 memo2
```

You can also use the **--force** option to cause ln to overwrite a file.

lpr

Sends files to printers

lpr [options] [file-list]
lpq [options] [job-identifiers]
lprm [options] [job-identifiers]

The lpr utility places one or more files into a print queue, providing orderly access to printers for several users or processes. The utility can work with printers attached to remote systems. You can use the lprm utility to remove files from the print queues and the lpq utility to check the status of files in the queues. Refer to "Notes" later in this section.

Arguments
The *file-list* is a list of one or more filenames for lpr to print. Often these files are text files, but many systems are configured so that lpr can accept and properly print a variety of file types. Without a *file-list,* lpr accepts input from standard input.

The *job-identifiers* is a list of job numbers or user names. If you do not know the job number of a print job, use lpq to display a list of print jobs.

Options
Some of the following options depend on the type of file being printed as well as on how the system is configured for printing.

−l (lowercase "l") Specifies that lpr should not preprocess (filter) the file being printed. Use this option when the file is already formatted for the printer.

−P *printer*
Routes the print jobs to the queue for the printer named *printer*. If you do not use this option, print jobs are routed to the default printer for the local system. The acceptable values for *printer* are found in the file **/etc/printcap** and vary from system to system.

−r (**remove**) Deletes the files in *file-list* after calling lpr.

−# *n*
Prints *n* copies of each file. Depending on which shell you are using, you may need to escape the # with a backslash to pass it to lpr.

Discussion
The lpr utility takes input from files you specify on the command line or from standard input and adds the files to the print queue as *print jobs*. The utility assigns a unique identification number to each print job. The lpq utility displays the job numbers of the print jobs that lpr has set up; you can use the lprm utility to remove a print job from the print queue.

lpq
The lpq utility displays information about jobs in a print queue. When called without any arguments, lpq lists all the print jobs queued for the default printer. Use lpr's

–P *printer* option with lpq to look at other print queues—even those for printers connected to other systems. With the –l option lpq displays more information about each job. If you give the username of a user as an argument, lpq displays only the printer jobs belonging to that user.

lprm   One item displayed by lpq is the job number for each print job in the queue. To remove a job from the print queue, use the job number as an argument to lprm. Unless you are Superuser, you can remove only your own jobs. Even as Superuser you may not be able to remove a job from a queue for a remote printer. If you do not give any arguments to lprm, it removes the currently active printer job (that is, the job that is now printing) from the queue, if you own that job.

Notes

If you normally use a printer other than the system default printer, you can set up lpr to use another printer as your personal default by assigning the name of this printer to the environment variable **PRINTER**. For example, if you use bash, you can add the following line to **~/.bash_profile** to set your default printer to the printer named **ps**:

```
export PRINTER=ps
```

LPD and LPR   Traditionally, UNIX had two printing systems: the BSD Line Printer Daemon (LPD) and the System V Line Printer system (LPR). Linux adopted those systems at first, and both UNIX and Linux have seen modifications to and replacements for these systems. Today CUPS is the default printing system under many Linux distributions.

CUPS   CUPS (Common UNIX Printing System) is a cross-platform print server built around IPP (Internet Printing Protocol), which is based on HTTP. CUPS provides a number of printer drivers and can print different types of files, including PostScript files. CUPS provides System V and BSD command line interfaces and, in addition to IPP, supports LPD/LPR, HTTP, SMB, and JetDirect (socket) protocols, among others.

This section describes the LPD command line interface that runs under CUPS and also in native mode on older systems.

Examples

The first command sends the file named **memo2** to the default printer:

```
$ lpr memo2
```

Next a pipe sends the output of ls to the printer named **deskjet**:

```
$ ls | lpr -Pdeskjet
```

The next example paginates and sends the file **memo** to the printer:

```
$ pr -h "Today's memo" memo | lpr
```

The next example shows a number of print jobs queued for the default printer. Alex owns all of these jobs, and the first one is currently being printed (active). Jobs 635 and 639 were created by sending input to lpr's standard input; job 638 was created by giving **ncut.icn** as an argument to the lpr command. The last column gives the size of each print job.

```
$ lpq
deskjet is ready and printing
Rank    Owner    Job  Files                          Total Size
active  alex     635  (stdin)                      38128 bytes
1st     alex     638  ncut.icn                      3587 bytes
2nd     alex     639  (stdin)                        3960 bytes
```

The next command removes job 638 from the default print queue:

```
$ lprm 638
```

ls

Displays information about one or more files

ls [options] [file-list]

The ls utility displays information about one or more files. It lists the information alphabetically by filename unless you use an option to change the order.

Arguments   When you do not provide an argument, ls displays the names of the visible files in the working directory (those files whose filenames do not begin with a period).

The *file-list* is a list of one or more pathnames of any ordinary, directory, or device files. It can include ambiguous file references.

When you specify a directory, ls displays the contents of the directory. It displays the name of the directory only when needed to avoid ambiguity, such as when the listing includes more than one directory. When you specify an ordinary file, ls displays information about that one file.

Options   The options determine the type of information ls displays, the manner in which it displays the information, and the order in which it is displayed. When you do not use an option, ls displays a short list that contains only the names of files.

--all   –a   Includes invisible files (those with filenames that begin with a period) in the listing. Without this option ls does not list information about invisible files unless you list the name of an invisible file in the *file-list*. When you use this option with a *file-list* that includes an appropriate ambiguous file reference, ls displays information about invisible files. The * ambiguous file reference does not match a leading period in a filename (see page 129).

--almost-all   –A   The same as --all but does not list the . and .. entries.

--escape   –b   Displays nonprinting characters in a filename, using backslash escape sequences similar to those used in C language strings. A partial list is given in Table V-16. Other nonprinting characters are displayed as a backslash followed by an octal number.

table V-16   Backslash escape sequences

Sequence	Meaning
\b	BACKSPACE
\n	NEWLINE

table V-16	Backslash escape sequences (continued)
\r	RETURN
\t	HORIZONTAL TAB
\v	VERTICAL TAB
\\	BACKSLASH

--color[=*when*] The ls utility can display various types of files in different colors but normally does not use colors (the same result as when you specify *when* as **none**). If you do not specify *when* or if you specify *when* as **always**, ls uses colors. When you specify *when* as **auto**, ls uses colors only when the output goes to a screen. See "Notes" for more information.

--directory **-d** Displays the names of directories without displaying their contents. Without an argument this option displays information about the working directory. It does not dereference symbolic links (it lists a link, not the directory it points to).

--format=*word* By default ls displays files sorted vertically. This option sorts files based on *word*: across (**-x**), separated by **commas** (**-m**), **horizontal** (**-x**), **long** (**-l**), or **single-column** (**-1**).

--classify **-F** Displays a slash (**/**) after each directory, an asterisk (*****) after each executable file, and an at sign (**@**) after a symbolic link.

--human-readable

-h Displays sizes in K (kilobyte), M (megabyte), and G (gigabyte) blocks, as appropriate. Works with the **-l** option only. This option uses powers of 1,024; use **--si** for powers of 1,000.

--inode **-i** Displays the inode number of each file. With the **-l** option this option displays the inode number in column 1 and shifts all other items one column to the right.

--format=long **-l** (lowercase "l") Lists more information about each file. Use this option with **-h** to make file sizes more readable. See "Discussion" for more information.

--dereference **-L** Lists information about the file referenced by a symbolic link rather than information about the link itself.

-m Displays a comma-separated list of files that fills the width of the screen.

--hide-control-chars

-q Displays nonprinting characters in a filename as question marks. When output is going to the screen, this is the default behavior.

--reverse	–r	Displays the list of filenames in reverse sorted order.
--recursive	–R	Recursively lists subdirectories.
--size	–s	Displays the number of 1,024-byte blocks allocated to the file. The size precedes the filename. With the –l option this option displays the size in column 1 and shifts all other items one column to the right. You can include the –h option to make the file sizes easier to read.
--sort=*word*		By default ls displays files in ASCII order. This option sorts the files based on *word*: filename **extension** (–X), **none** (–U), file **size** (–S), **access** time (–u), or modification **time** (–t). See --**time** for an exception.
--time=*word*		By default ls with the –l option displays the modification time of a file. Set *word* to **atime** to display the access time (or use the –t option) or to **ctime** to display the creation time. The list is sorted by *word* when you also give the --**sort=time** option.
	–x	Displays files sorted by lines (the default display is sorted by columns).
	–X	Displays files sorted by filename extension. Files with no filename extension are listed first.
	–1	(one) Displays files one per line.

Discussion   The ls long listing (--**format=long** or –l options) displays the seven columns shown in Figure 4-12 on page 92. The first column, which contains 11 characters, is divided as described in the following paragraphs. The first character describes the type of file, as shown in Table V-17.

table V-17   First character in a long ls display

Character	Meaning
–	Ordinary
b	Block device
c	Character device
d	Directory
p	FIFO (named pipe)
l	Symbolic link

The next nine characters of the first column represent the access permissions associated with the file. They are divided into three sets of three characters each.

The first three characters represent the owner's access permissions. If the owner has read access permission to the file, **r** appears in the first character position. If the owner is not permitted to read the file, a hyphen appears in this position. The next two positions represent the owner's write and execute access permissions. If **w** appears in the second position the owner is permitted to write to the file; if **x** appears in the third position the owner is permitted to execute the file. An **s** in the third position indicates that the file has setuid permission and execute permission. An **S** indicates setuid without execute permission. A hyphen indicates that the owner does not have the access permission associated with the character position.

In a similar manner the second and third sets of three characters represent the access permissions of the group the file is associated with and of other users. An **s** in the third position of the second set of characters indicates that the file has setgid permission with execute permission, and an **S** indicates setgid without execute permission.

The last character is **t** if the sticky bit (page 903) is set with execute permission and **T** if it is set without execute permission. Refer to chmod on page 604 for information on changing access permissions.

Figure 4-12 on page 92 illustrates the columns described in the following paragraphs.

The second column indicates the number of hard links to the file. Refer to page 96 for more information on links.

The third and fourth columns display the name of the owner of the file and the name of the group the file is associated with.

The fifth column indicates the size of the file in bytes or, if information about a device file is being displayed, the major and minor device numbers. In the case of a directory, this number is the size of the directory file, not the size of the files that are entries within the directory. (Use du to display the sum of the sizes of all files in a directory.) Use the **–h** option to display the size of files in kilobytes, megabytes, or gigabytes.

The last two columns display the date and time the file was last modified and the filename, respectively.

Notes

Refer to page 127 for examples of using ls with ambiguous file references.

With the **––color** option ls displays filenames of various types of files in different colors. By default executable files are green, directory files are blue, symbolic links are cyan, archives and compressed files are red, and ordinary text files are black. The manner in which ls colors the various file types is specified in the **/etc/DIR_COLORS** file. If this file does not exist on the local system, ls will not color filenames. You can modify **/etc/DIR_COLORS** to alter the default color/filetype mappings on a system-wide basis. For your personal use, you can copy **/etc/DIR_COLORS** to the **~/.dir_colors** file in your home directory and modify it. For your login, **~/.dir_colors** overrides the systemwide colors established in **/etc/DIR_COLORS**. Refer to the **dir_colors** and dircolors man pages for more information.

Examples

The first command line shows the ls utility with the **–x** option, which sorts the files horizontally. The ls utility displays an alphabetical list of the names of the files in the working directory:

```
$ ls -x
bin        c          calendar
execute    letters    shell
```

The **–F** option appends a slash (/) to files that are directories, an asterisk to files that are executable, and an at sign (@) after symbolic links:

```
$ ls -Fx
bin/     c/         calendar
execute* letters/   shell@
```

Next the **–l** (**long**) option displays a long list. The files are still in alphabetical order:

```
$ ls -l
total 8
drwxrwxr-x  2 jenny pubs    80  May 20 09:17 bin
drwxrwxr-x  2 jenny pubs   144  Mar 26 11:59 c
-rw-rw-r--  1 jenny pubs   104  May 28 11:44 calendar
-rwxrw-r--  1 jenny pubs    85  May  6 08:27 execute
drwxrwxr-x  2 jenny pubs    32  Oct  6 22:56 letters
drwxrwxr-x 16 jenny pubs  1296  Jun  6 17:33 shell
```

The **–a** (**all**) option lists all files, including invisible ones:

```
$ ls -a
.          .profile  c          execute    shell
..         bin       calendar   letters
```

Combining the **–a** and **–l** options displays a long listing of all files, including invisible files, in the working directory. This list is still in alphabetical order:

```
$ ls -al
total 12
drwxrwxr-x  6 jenny pubs  480 Jun  6 17:42 .
drwxrwx--- 26 root  root  816 Jun  6 14:45 ..
-rw-rw-r--  1 jenny pubs  161 Jun  6 17:15 .profile
drwxrwxr-x  2 jenny pubs   80 May 20 09:17 bin
```

```
drwxrwxr-x  2 jenny pubs   144 Mar 26 11:59 c
-rw-rw-r--  1 jenny pubs   104 May 28 11:44 calendar
-rwxrw-r--  1 jenny pubs    85 May  6 08:27 execute
drwxrwxr-x  2 jenny pubs    32 Oct  6 22:56 letters
drwxrwxr-x 16 jenny pubs  1296 Jun  6 17:33 shell
```

When you add the −r (reverse) option to the command line, ls produces a list in reverse alphabetical order:

```
$ ls -ral
total 12
drwxrwxr-x 16 jenny pubs  1296 Jun  6 17:33 shell
drwxrwxr-x  2 jenny pubs    32 Oct  6 22:56 letters
-rwxrw-r--  1 jenny pubs    85 May  6 08:27 execute
-rw-rw-r--  1 jenny pubs   104 May 28 11:44 calendar
drwxrwxr-x  2 jenny pubs   144 Mar 26 11:59 c
drwxrwxr-x  2 jenny pubs    80 May 20 09:17 bin
-rw-rw-r--  1 jenny pubs   161 Jun  6 17:15 .profile
drwxrwx--- 26  root  root   816 Jun  6 14:45 ..
drwxrwxr-x  6 jenny pubs   480 Jun  6 17:42 .
```

Use the −t and −l options to list files so that the most recently modified file appears at the top of the list:

```
$ ls -tl
total 8
drwxrwxr-x 16 jenny pubs  1296 Jun  6 17:33 shell
-rw-rw-r--  1 jenny pubs   104 May 28 11:44 calendar
drwxrwxr-x  2 jenny pubs    80 May 20 09:17 bin
-rwxrw-r--  1 jenny pubs    85 May  6 08:27 execute
drwxrwxr-x  2 jenny pubs   144 Mar 26 11:59 c
drwxrwxr-x  2 jenny pubs    32 Oct  6 22:56 letters
```

Together the −r and −t options cause the file you modified least recently to appear at the top of the list.

```
$ ls -trl
total 8
drwxrwxr-x  2 jenny pubs    32 Oct  6 22:56 letters
drwxrwxr-x  2 jenny pubs   144 Mar 26 11:59 c
-rwxrw-r--  1 jenny pubs    85 May  6 08:27 execute
drwxrwxr-x  2 jenny pubs    80 May 20 09:17 bin
-rw-rw-r--  1 jenny pubs   104 May 28 11:44 calendar
drwxrwxr-x 16 jenny pubs  1296 Jun  6 17:33 shell
```

The next example shows ls with a directory filename as an argument. The ls utility lists the contents of the directory in alphabetical order:

```
$ ls bin
c        e        lsdir
```

To display information about the directory file itself, use the **–d** (directory) option. This option lists information only about the directory:

```
$ ls -dl bin
drwxrwxr-x 2 jenny pubs 80 May 20 09:17 bin
```

You can use the following command to display a list of all invisible filenames (those starting with a period) in your home directory. This is a convenient way to list the initialization files in your home directory:

```
$ ls -d ~/.*
/home/sam/.                          /home/sam/.gtkrc-kde
/home/sam/..                         /home/sam/.history
...
```

make

Keeps a set of programs current

make [options] [target-files] [arguments]

The GNU make utility keeps a set of executable programs current, based on differences in the modification times of the programs and the source files that each program is dependent on.

Arguments   The *target-files* refer to targets on dependency lines in the makefile. When you do not specify a *target-file*, make updates the target on the first dependency line in the makefile. Command line *arguments* of the form *name=value* set the variable *name* to *value* inside the makefile. See "Discussion" for more information.

Options   If you do not use the **–f** option, make takes its input from a file named **GNUmakefile**, **makefile**, or **Makefile** (in that order) in the working directory. In this section, this input file is referred to as **makefile**. Many users prefer to use the name **Makefile** because it shows up earlier in directory listings.

–C *directory*
>   Changes directories to *directory* before starting.

–d   (**debug**) Displays information about how make decides what to do.

–f *file*
>   (**input file**) Uses *file* as input instead of **makefile**.

–j *n*
>   (**jobs**) Runs up to *n* commands at the same time instead of the default of one command. Running multiple commands simultaneously is especially effective if you are running Linux on a multiprocessor system. If you omit *n*, make does not limit the number of simultaneous jobs.

–k   Continues with the next file from the list of *target-files* instead of quitting when a construction command fails.

–n   (**no execution**) Displays, but does not execute, the commands that make would execute to bring the *target-files* up-to-date.

–s   (**silent**) Does not display the names of the commands being executed.

–t   (**touch**) Updates the modification times of target files but does not execute any construction commands (page 403). Refer to touch on page 801.

Discussion   The make utility bases its actions on the modification times of the programs and the source files that each program is dependent on. Each of the executable programs, or *target-files*, is dependent on one or more prerequisite files. The relationships between *target-files* and prerequisites are specified on *dependency lines* in a makefile. Construction commands follow the dependency line, specifying how make can update the *target-files*.

Documentation   Refer to page 399 for more information about make and makefiles. For additional information refer to www.gnu.org/software/make/manual/make.html and to the make info page.

Although the most common use of make is to build programs from source code, this general-purpose build utility is suitable for a wide range of applications. Anywhere you can define a set of dependencies to get from one state to another represents an ideal candidate for using make.

Much of make's power derives from the features you can set up in a makefile. For example, you can define variables using the same syntax found in the Bourne Again Shell. *Always* define the variable **SHELL** in a makefile; set it to the pathname of the shell you want to use when running construction commands. To define the variable and assign it a value, place the following line near the top of a makefile:

```
SHELL=/bin/sh
```

Assigning the value **/bin/sh** to **SHELL** allows you to use a makefile on other computer systems. On Linux systems **/bin/sh** is generally linked to **/bin/bash**. The make utility uses the value of the environment variable **SHELL** if you do not set **SHELL** in a makefile. If **SHELL** does not hold the path of the shell you intended to use and if you do not set **SHELL** in a makefile, the construction commands may fail.

Following is a list of additional features associated with make:

- You can run specific construction commands silently by preceding them with an @ sign. For example, the following lines will display a short help message when you run the command **make help**:

```
help:
        @echo "You can make the following:"
        @echo " "
        @echo "libbuf.a        -- the buffer library"
        @echo "Bufdisplay      -- display any-format buffer"
        @echo "Buf2ppm         -- convert buffer to pixmap"
```

Without the @ signs in the preceding example, make would display each of the echo commands before executing it. This way of displaying a message works because no file is named **help** in the working directory. As a result make runs the construction commands in an attempt to build this file. Because the construction commands display messages but do not build the file **help**, you can run **make help** repeatedly with the same result.

• You can cause make to ignore the exit status of a command by preceding the command with a hyphen (–). For example, the following line allows make to continue regardless of whether the call to **/bin/rm** is successful (the call to **/bin/rm** fails if **libbuf.a** does not exist):

```
-/bin/rm libbuf.a
```

• You can use special variables to refer to information that might change from one use of make to the next. Such information might include the files that need updating, the files that are newer than the target, or the files that match a pattern. For example, you can use the variable **$?** in a construction command to identify all prerequisite files that are newer than the target file. This variable allows you to print any files that have changed since the last time you printed files out:

```
list:       .list
.list:      Makefile buf.h xtbuff_ad.h buff.c buf_print.c xtbuff.c
pr $? | lpr
date >.list
```

The target list depends on the source files that might be printed. The construction command **pr $? | lpr** prints only those source files that are newer than the file **.list**. The line **date > .list** modifies the **.list** file so that it is newer than any of the source files. The next time you run the command **make list,** only the files that have been changed are printed.

• You can include other makefiles as if they were part of the current makefile. The following line causes make to read **Make.config** and treat the contents of that file as though it were part of the current makefile, allowing you to put information common to more than one makefile in a single place:

```
include Make.config
```

Notes   The section "make: Keeps a Set of Programs Current" on page 399 provides more information about make.

Examples   The first example causes make to bring the *target-file* named **analysis** up-to-date by issuing three **cc** commands. It uses a makefile named **GNUmakefile, makefile,** or **Makefile** in the working directory.

```
$ make analysis
cc -c analy.c
cc -c stats.c
cc -o analysis analy.o stats.o
```

The following example also updates **analysis** but uses a makefile named **analysis.mk** in the working directory:

```
$ make -f analysis.mk analysis
'analysis' is up to date.
```

The next example lists the commands make would execute to bring the *target-file* named **credit** up-to-date. Because of the **–n** (**no-execution**) option, make does not execute the commands.

```
$ make -n credit
cc -c -O credit.c
cc -c -O accounts.c
cc -c -O terms.c
cc -o credit credit.c accounts.c terms.c
```

The next example uses the **–t** option to update the modification time of the *target-file* named **credit**. After you use this option, make thinks that **credit** is up-to-date.

```
$ make -t credit
$ make credit
'credit' is up to date.
```

Next is a simple makefile for building a utility named ff. Because the cc command needed to build ff is complex, using a makefile allows you to rebuild ff easily, without having to remember and retype the cc command.

```
$ cat Makefile
# Build the ff command from the fastfind.c source
SHELL=/bin/sh

ff:
cc -traditional -O2 -g -DBIG=5120 -o ff fastfind.c myClib.a

$ make ff
cc -traditional -O2 -g -DBIG=5120 -o ff fastfind.c myClib.a
```

The following example shows a much more sophisticated makefile that uses features not discussed in this section. Refer to the sources cited under "Documentation" on page 716 for information about these and other advanced features.

```
$ cat Makefile
#########################################################
## build and maintain the buffer library
#########################################################
SHELL=/bin/sh

#########################################################
## Flags and libraries for compiling. The XLDLIBS are needed
#   whenever you build a program using the library. The CCFLAGS
```

```
#    give maximum optimization.
CC=gcc
CCFLAGS=-O2 $(CFLAGS)
XLDLIBS= -lXaw3d -lXt -lXmu -lXext -lX11 -lm
BUFLIB=libbuf.a


##########################################################
## Miscellaneous
INCLUDES=buf.h
XINCLUDES=xtbuff_ad.h
OBJS=buff.o buf_print.o xtbuff.o


##########################################################
## Just a 'make' generates a help message
help:   Help
        @echo "You can make the following:"
        @echo " "
        @echo " libbuf.a          -- the buffer library"
        @echo " bufdisplay        -- display any-format buffer"
        @echo " buf2ppm           -- convert buffer to pixmap"
##########################################################
## The main target is the library
libbuf.a:   $(OBJS)
    -/bin/rm libbuf.a

    ar rv libbuf.a $(OBJS)
    ranlib libbuf.a
##########################################################
## Secondary targets -- utilities built from the library
bufdisplay: bufdisplay.c libbuf.a
    $(CC) $(CCFLAGS) bufdisplay.c -o bufdisplay $(BUFLIB) $(XLDLIBS)

buf2ppm: buf2ppm.c libbuf.a
    $(CC) $(CCFLAGS) buf2ppm.c -o buf2ppm $(BUFLIB)


##########################################################
## Build the individual object units
buff.o: $(INCLUDES) buff.c
    $(CC) -c $(CCFLAGS) buff.c

buf_print.o:$(INCLUDES) buf_print.c
    $(CC) -c $(CCFLAGS) buf_print.c

xtbuff.o: $(INCLUDES) $(XINCLUDES) xtbuff.c
    $(CC) -c $(CCFLAGS) xtbuff.c
```

The make utility can be used for tasks other than compiling code. As a final example, assume that you have a database that lists IP addresses and the corresponding hostnames in two columns and that the database dumps these values to a file named

hosts.tab. You need to extract only the hostnames from this file and generate a Web page named **hosts.html** containing these names. The following makefile is a simple report writer:

```
$ cat makefile
#
SHELL=/bin/bash
#
hosts.html: hosts.tab
        @echo "<HTML><BODY>" > hosts.html
        @awk '{print $$2, "<br>"}' hosts.tab >> hosts.html
        @echo "</BODY></HTML>" >> hosts.html
```

man

Displays documentation for commands

man [options] [section] command
man –k keyword

The man utility provides online documentation for Linux commands. In addition to user commands, documentation is available for many other commands and details that relate to Linux. Because many Linux commands come from GNU, the GNU info utility (page 32) frequently provides more complete information.

A one-line header is associated with each manual page. This header consists of a command name, the section of the manual in which the command is found, and a brief description of what the command does. These headers are stored in a database so that you can perform quick searches on keywords associated with each man page.

Arguments The *section* argument tells man to limit its search to the specified section of the manual (see page 30 for a listing of manual sections). Without this argument man searches the sections in numerical order and displays the first man page it finds. In the second form of the man command, the –k option searches for the *keyword* in the database of man page headers; man displays a list of headers that contain the *keyword*. A **man –k** command performs the same function as apropos (page 62).

Options –a Displays man pages for all sections of the manual. Without this option man displays only the first page it finds. Use this option when you are not sure which section contains the information you are looking for.

–k *keyword*
Displays manual page headers that contain the string *keyword*. You can scan this list for commands of interest. This option is equivalent to the apropos command (page 62).

–K *keyword*
Searches for *keyword* in all man pages. This option can take a long time to run.

–M *path*
Searches the directories in *path* for man pages, where *path* is a colon-separated list of directories.

–t Formats the page for printing on a PostScript printer. The output goes to standard output.

Discussion The manual pages are organized in sections, each pertaining to a separate aspect of the Linux system. Section 1 contains user-callable commands and is the section most likely to be accessed by users who are not system administrators or programmers.

Other sections of the manual describe system calls, library functions, and commands used by system administrators. See page 30 for a listing of the manual sections.

Pager The man utility uses less to display manual pages that fill more than one screen. To change to another pager, set the environment variable **PAGER** to the pathname of the pager you want to use. For example, adding the following line to the **~/.bash_profile** file allows a bash user to use more instead of less:

```
export PAGER=/bin/more
```

MANPATH You can tell man where to look for man pages by setting the environment variable **MANPATH** to a colon-separated list of directories. For example, bash users can add the following line to **~/.bash_profile** to cause man to search the **/usr/man**, **/usr/local/man**, and **/usr/X11R6/man** directories:

```
export MANPATH=/usr/man:/usr/local/man:/usr/X11R6/man
```

You can edit **/etc/man.config** to further configure man. Refer to the man man page for more information.

Notes

The argument to man is not always a command name. For example, the command **man ascii** lists the ASCII characters and their various representations; the command **man –k postscript** lists man pages that pertain to PostScript.

The man pages are commonly stored in unformatted, compressed form. When you request a man page, it has to be decompressed and formatted before being displayed. To speed up subsequent requests for that man page, man attempts to save the formatted version of the page.

Some utilities described in the manual pages have the same name as shell builtin commands. The behavior of the shell builtin may differ slightly from the behavior of the utility as described in the manual page.

Examples

The following example uses man to display the documentation for the command write, which sends messages to another user's terminal:

```
$ man write

WRITE(1)              Linux Programmer's Manual            WRITE(1)

NAME
    write - send a message to another user
SYNOPSIS
    write user [ttyname]
DESCRIPTION
    Write allows you to communicate with other users, by copy-
    ing lines from your terminal to theirs.

    When you run the write command, the user you are writing
...
```

The next example displays the man page for another command—the man command itself, a good starting place for someone learning about the system:

```
$ man man
man(1)                                                              man(1)


NAME
        man - format and display the online manual pages
        manpath - determine users search path for man pages

SYNOPSIS
        man  [-acdfFhkKtwW]  [--path]  [-m system] [-p string] [-C
        config_file] [-M pathlist] [-P  pager] [-S  section_list]
        [section] name ...


DESCRIPTION
        man formats and displays the online manual pages.  If you
        specify section, man only looks in  that  section  of  the
...
```

The next example shows how you can use the man utility to find the man pages that pertain to a certain topic. In this case **man –k** displays man page headers containing the string **latex**. The apropos utility (a shell script stored in **/usr/bin/apropos**) functions similarly to **man –k**.

```
$ man -k latex
Pod::LaTeX            (3pm) - Convert Pod data to formatted Latex
einitex [elatex]     (1)  - extended TeX
elatex [latex]       (1)  - structured text formatting and typesetting
etex [elatex]        (1)  - extended TeX
evirtex [elatex]     (1)  - extended TeX
lambda [latex]       (1)  - structured text formatting and typesetting
latex                (1)  - structured text formatting and typesetting
...
```

The search for the keyword entered with the **–k** option is not case sensitive. Although the keyword entered on the command line is all lowercase, it matches the first header, which contains the string **LaTeX** (uppercase and lowercase). The **3pm** on the first line indicates that the man page is from Section 3 (Subroutines) of the Linux System Manual and comes from the *Perl Programmers Reference Guide* (it is a Perl subroutine; see www.perl.org for more information on the Perl programming language).

mkdir

Creates a directory

mkdir [option] directory-list

The mkdir utility creates one or more directories.

Arguments The *directory-list* is a list of one or more pathnames of directories that mkdir creates.

Options Accepts the common options described on page 587.

--mode=*mode* –m *mode*
>Sets the permission to **mode**. You can represent the **mode** absolutely by using an octal number (page 605) or symbolically (see Table V-4 on page 604).

--parents –p Creates any directories that do not exist in the path to the directory you wish to create.

--verbose –v Displays the name of each directory created. This option is helpful when used with the **--parents** option.

Notes You must have permission to write to and search (execute permission) the parent directory of the directory you are creating. The mkdir utility creates directories that contain the standard invisible entries (. and ..).

Examples The following command creates the **accounts** directory as a subdirectory of the working directory and the **prospective** directory as a subdirectory of **accounts**:

```
$ mkdir --parents accounts/prospective
```

Without changing working directories, the same user creates another subdirectory within the **accounts** directory:

```
$ mkdir accounts/existing
```

Next the user changes the working directory to the **accounts** directory and creates one more subdirectory:

```
$ cd accounts
$ mkdir closed
```

The last example shows the user creating another subdirectory. This time the **--mode** option removes all access permissions for group and others:

```
$ mkdir --mode go= accounts/past_due
```

mkfs

Creates a filesystem on a device

mkfs [options] device

The mkfs utility creates a filesystem on a device such as a floppy diskette or a partition of a hard disk. It acts as a front end for programs that create filesystems, each specific to a filesystem type.

mkfs **destroys all data on a device**

caution   Be careful when using mkfs, as it destroys all data on a device.

Arguments   The *device* is the name of the device that you want to create the filesystem on. If the device name is in **/etc/fstab**, you can use the mount point of the device instead of the device name.

Options   When you run mkfs, you can specify both global options and options specific to the filesystem type that mkfs is creating (for example, **ext2**, **ext3**, **msdos**, **reiserfs**). Global options must precede type-specific options.

Global Options

–t *fstype*

(**type**) The *fstype* is the type of filesystem you want to create—for example, **ext2**, **ext3**, **msdos**, or **reiserfs**. The default filesystem varies between Linux distributions.

–V   (**verbose**) Displays more output, including file-specific information.

Filesystem Type-Specific Options

The following options apply to many common filesystem types, including **ext2** and **ext3**. The following command lists the filesystem creation utilities available on the local system:

```
$ ls /sbin/mkfs.*
/sbin/mkfs.cramfs   /sbin/mkfs.ext3    /sbin/mkfs.vfat
/sbin/mkfs.ext2     /sbin/mkfs.msdos
```

There is frequently a link to **/sbin/mkfs.ext2** at **/sbin/mke2fs**. Review the man page or give the pathname of the filesystem creation utility to determine which options the utility accepts.

```
$ /sbin/mkfs.ext3
Usage: mkfs.ext3 [-c|-t|-l filename] [-b block-size] [-f fragment-size]
        [-i bytes-per-inode] [-j] [-J journal-options] [-N number-of-inodes]
        [-m reserved-blocks-percentage] [-o creator-os] [-g blocks-per-group]
        [-L volume-label] [-M last-mounted-directory] [-O feature[,...]]
        [-r fs-revision] [-R options] [-qvSV] device [blocks-count]
```

–b *size*

>(**block**) Specifies the size of blocks in bytes. On **ext2** and **ext3** filesystems valid block sizes are 1,024, 2,048, and 4,096 bytes.

–c (**check**) Checks for bad blocks on the device before creating a filesystem. Specify this option twice to perform a slow, destructive, read-write test.

Discussion

Before you can write to and read from a hard disk or floppy diskette in the usual fashion, there must be a filesystem on it. Typically a hard disk is divided into *partitions* (page 892), each with a separate filesystem. A floppy diskette normally holds a single filesystem. Refer to Chapter 4 for more information on filesystems.

Notes

You can use tune2fs (page 808) with the –j option to change an existing **ext2** filesystem into a *journaling filesystem* (page 883) of type **ext3**. (See "Examples.") You can also use tune2fs to change how often fsck (page 666) checks a filesystem.

mkfs is a front end   Much like fsck, mkfs is a front end that calls other utilities to handle various types of filesystems. For example, mkfs calls mke2fs (which is typically linked to mkfs.ext2 and mkfs.ext3) to create the widely used **ext2** and **ext3** filesystems. Refer to the mke2fs man page for more information. Other utilities that mkfs calls are typically named **mkfs.***type*, where *type* is the filesystem type. By splitting mkfs in this manner, filesystem developers can provide programs to create their filesystems without affecting the development of other filesystems or changing how system administrators use mkfs.

Examples

In the following example, mkfs creates a filesystem on the device at **/dev/hda8**. In this case the default filesystem type is **ext2**.

```
# /sbin/mkfs /dev/hda8
mke2fs 1.35 (28-Feb-2004)
max_blocks 1309867008, rsv_groups = 39974, rsv_gdb = 312
Filesystem label=
OS type: Linux
Block size=4096 (log=2)
Fragment size=4096 (log=2)
640000 inodes, 1279167 blocks
63958 blocks (5.00%) reserved for the super user
First data block=0
Maximum filesystem blocks=1312817152
40 block groups
32768 blocks per group, 32768 fragments per group
16000 inodes per group
Superblock backups stored on blocks:
32768, 98304, 163840, 229376, 294912, 819200, 884736

Writing inode tables:  0/40...39/40...done
inode.i_blocks = 19976, i_size = 4243456
```

```
Writing superblocks and filesystem accounting information: done

This filesystem will be automatically checked every 23 mounts or
180 days, whichever comes first.  Use tune2fs -c or -i to override.
```

Next the administrator uses tune2fs to convert the **ext2** filesystem to an **ext3** journaling filesystem:

```
# /sbin/tune2fs -j /dev/hda8
tune2fs 1.35 (28-Feb-2004)
Creating journal inode: done
This filesystem will be automatically checked every 23 mounts or
180 days, whichever comes first.  Use tune2fs -c or -i to override.
```

Mtools

Uses DOS-style commands on files and directories

*mcd [**directory**]*
*mcopy [**options**] **file-list target***
*mdel **file-list***
*mdir [–w] **directory***
*mformat [**options**] **device***
*mtype [**options**] **file-list***

These utilities mimic DOS commands and manipulate Linux files or DOS files. The mcopy utility provides an easy way to move files between a Linux filesystem and a DOS disk. The default drive for all commands is **/dev/fd0** or **A:**.

Utilities

Table V-18 lists some of the utilities in the Mtools collection.

table V-18	The Mtools collection
Utility	**Function**
mcd	Changes the working directory on the DOS disk
mcopy	Copies DOS files from one directory to another
mdel	Deletes DOS files
mdir	Lists contents of DOS directories
mformat	Adds DOS formatting information to a disk
mtype	Displays the contents of DOS files

Arguments

The *directory,* used with mcd and mdir, must be the name of a directory on a DOS disk. The *file-list,* used with mcopy and mtype, is a SPACE-separated list of filenames. The *target,* used with mcopy, is the name of a regular file or a directory. If you give mcopy a *file-list* with more than one filename, *target* must be the name of a directory. The *device,* used with mformat, is the DOS drive letter containing the disk to be formatted (for example, **A:**).

Options

mcopy

–n   Automatically replaces existing files without asking. Normally mcopy asks for verification before overwriting a file.

–p   (**preserve**) Preserves the attributes of files when they are copied.

–s (**recursive**) Copies directories and their contents recursively.

–t (**text**) Converts DOS text files for use on a Linux system, and vice versa. Lines in DOS text files are terminated with the character pair RETURN-NEWLINE; lines in Linux text files end in NEWLINE. This option removes the RETURN character while copying from a DOS file and adds it when copying from a Linux file.

mdir

–w (**wide**) Displays only filenames and fits as many as possible on each line. By default mdir lists information about each file on a separate line, showing filename, size, and creation time.

mformat

–f 1440

Specifies a 1,440K 3.5-inch HD floppy diskette.

–f 2880

Specifies a 2,880K 3.5-inch ED floppy diskette.

–v *vol*

(**label**) Puts *vol* as the volume label on the newly formatted DOS disk.

mtype

–t (**text**) Similar to the **–t** option for mcopy, this option replaces each RETURN-NEWLINE character pair in the DOS file with a single NEWLINE character before displaying the file.

Discussion   Although these utilities mimic their DOS counterparts, they do not attempt to match those tools exactly. In most cases restrictions imposed by DOS are removed. For example, the asterisk ambiguous file reference (✳) matches all filenames (as it does under Linux), including those filenames that DOS would require ✳.✳ to match.

Notes   In this discussion, the term **DOS disk** refers to either a DOS partition on a hard disk or a DOS floppy diskette.

You can download Mtools from the Mtools home page (mtools.linux.lu) or from rpmfind.net.

If the local kernel is configured to support DOS filesystems, you can mount DOS disks on a Linux filesystem and manipulate the files using Linux utilities. Although this feature is handy and reduces the need for Mtools, it may not be practical or efficient to mount and unmount DOS filesystems each time you need to access a DOS file. These tasks can be time-consuming, and some systems are set up so that regular users cannot mount and unmount filesystems.

Use caution when using Mtools. These utilities may not warn you if you are about to overwrite a file. Using explicit pathnames—not ambiguous file references—reduces the chance of overwriting a file.

The most common uses of the Mtools utilities are to examine files on DOS floppy diskettes (mdir) and to copy files between a DOS floppy diskette and the Linux filesystem (mcopy). You can identify DOS disks by using the usual DOS drive letters: **A:** for the first floppy drive, **C:** for the first hard disk, and so on. You can separate filenames in paths by using either the Linux forward slash (/) or the DOS backslash (\). You need to escape backslashes to prevent the shell from interpreting it before passing the pathname to the utility you are using.

Each of the Mtools utilities returns an exit code of 0 on success, 1 on complete failure, and 2 on partial failure.

Examples   In the first example, mdir displays the contents of a DOS floppy diskette in **/dev/fd0**:

```
$ mdir
 Volume in drive A is DOS UTY
 Directory for A:/

ACAD     LIF      419370    5-10-05   1:29p
CADVANCE LIF       40560    2-08-04  10:36a
CHIPTST  EXE        2209    4-26-05   4:22p
DISK     ID           31   12-27-05   4:49p
GENERIC  LIF       20983    2-08-04  10:37a
INSTALL  COM         896    7-05-05  10:23a
INSTALL  DAT       45277   12-27-05   4:49p
KDINSTAL EXE      110529    8-13-05  10:50a
LOTUS    LIF       44099    1-18-05   3:36p
PCAD     LIF       17846    5-01-05   3:46p
READID   EXE       17261    5-07-05   8:26a
README   TXT        9851    4-30-05  10:32a
UTILITY  LIF       51069    5-05-05   9:13a
WORD     LIF       16817    7-01-05   9:58a
WP       LIF       57992    8-29-05   4:22p
        15 File(s)     599040 bytes free
```

The next example uses mcopy to copy the *.**TXT** files from the DOS floppy diskette to the working directory on the Linux filesystem. Because only one file has the extension .**TXT**, only one file is copied. Because .**TXT** files are usually text files under DOS, the **–t** option strips off the unnecessary RETURN characters at the end of each line. The ambiguous file reference * is escaped on the command line to prevent the shell from attempting to expand it before passing the argument to mcopy. The mcopy utility locates the file **README.TXT** when given the pattern *.**txt** because DOS does not differentiate between uppercase and lowercase letters in filenames.

```
$ mcopy -t a:\*.txt .
Copying README.TXT
```

Finally, the DOS floppy diskette is reformatted using mformat, wiping all data from the diskette. If the diskette has not been low-level formatted, you need to use fdformat before giving the following commands:

```
$ mformat a:
```

A check with mdir shows the floppy diskette is empty after formatting:

```
$ mdir a:
 Volume in drive A has no label
 Directory for A:/

File "*" not found
```

mv

Renames or moves a file

mv [options] existing-file new-filename
mv [options] existing-file-list directory
mv [options] existing-directory new-directory

The mv utility, which renames or moves one or more files, has three formats. The first renames a single file with a new filename that you supply. The second renames one or more files so that they appear in a specified directory. The third renames a directory. The mv utility physically moves the file if it is not possible to rename it (that is, if you move the file from one filesystem to another).

Arguments   In the first form, the *existing-file* is a pathname that specifies the ordinary file that you want to rename. The *new-filename* is the new pathname of the file.

In the second form, the *existing-file-list* is a list of the pathnames of the files that you want to rename and the *directory* specifies the new parent directory for the files. The files you rename will have the same simple filenames as each of the files in the *existing-file-list* but new absolute pathnames.

The third form renames the *existing-directory* with the *new-directory* name. This form works only when the *new-directory* does not already exist.

Options   Accepts the common options described on page 587.

--backup   **–b**   Makes a backup copy (by appending ~ to the filename) of any file that would be overwritten.

--force   **–f**   Causes mv *not* to prompt you if a move would overwrite an existing file that you do not have write permission for. You must have write permission for the directory holding the target file.

--interactive   **–i**   Prompts you for confirmation if mv would overwrite a file. If your response begins with a **y** or **Y**, mv overwrites the file; otherwise, mv does not move the file.

--update   **–u**   If a move would overwrite an existing file, not a directory, this option causes mv to compare the modification times of the source and target files. If the target file has a more recent modification time (the target is newer than the source), mv does not replace it.

--verbose   **–v**   Lists files as they are moved.

Notes   GNU mv is implemented as cp (with the –a option) and rm. When you execute the mv utility, it first copies the *existing-file* to the *new-file*. It then deletes the *existing-file*. If the *new-file* already exists, mv may delete it before copying.

As with rm, you must have write and execute access permission to the parent directory of the *existing-file*, but you do not need read or write access permission to the file itself. If the move would overwrite a file that you do not have write permission for, mv displays the file's access permissions and waits for a response. If you enter **y** or **Y**, mv overwrites the file; otherwise, it does not move the file. If you use the –**f** option, mv does not prompt you for a response but simply overwrites the file.

Although earlier versions of mv could move only ordinary files between filesystems, mv can now move any type of file, including directories and device files.

Examples   The first command renames **letter**, a file in the working directory, as **letter.1201**:

```
$ mv letter letter.1201
```

The next command renames the file so that it appears, with the same simple filename, in the user's ~/**archives** directory:

```
$ mv letter.1201 ~/archives
```

The following command moves all files in the working directory whose names begin with **memo** so they appear in the /**p04/backup** directory:

```
$ mv memo* /p04/backup
```

Using the –**u** option prevents mv from replacing a newer file with an older one. After the **mv** –**u** command shown below, the newer file, **memo2**, has not been overwritten. The **mv** command without the –**u** option overwrites the newer file (**memo2**'s modification time and size have changed to those of **memo1**).

```
$ ls -l
-rw-rw-r--  1 sam sam 22 Mar 25 23:34 memo1
-rw-rw-r--  1 sam sam 19 Mar 25 23:40 memo2
$ mv -u memo1 memo2
$ ls -l
-rw-rw-r--  1 sam sam 22 Mar 25 23:34 memo1
-rw-rw-r--  1 sam sam 19 Mar 25 23:40 memo2
$ mv memo1 memo2
$ ls -l
-rw-rw-r--  1 sam sam 22 Mar 25 23:34 memo2
```

nice

Changes the priority of a command

nice [option] [command-line]

The nice utility reports the priority of the shell or alters the priority of a command. An ordinary user can decrease the priority of a command. Only Superuser can increase the priority of a command. The TC Shell has a nice builtin that has a different syntax. Refer to "Notes" for more information.

Arguments

The *command-line* is the command line you want to execute at a different priority. Without any options or arguments, nice displays the priority of the shell running nice.

Options

Without an option, nice defaults to an adjustment of 10, lowering the priority of the command by 10—typically from 0 to 10. As you raise the priority value, the command runs at a lower priority.

--adjustment=*value*
     –n *value*

Changes the priority by the increment (or decrement) specified by *value*. The range of priorities is from –20 (the highest priority) to 19 (the lowest priority). A positive *value* lowers the priority, whereas a negative *value* raises the priority. Only Superuser can specify a negative *value*. When you specify a value outside this range, the priority is set to the limit of the range.

Notes

You can use top's **r** command (page 799) to change the priority of a running process.

Higher (more positive) priority values mean that the kernel schedules a job less often. Lower (more negative) values cause the job to be scheduled more often.

When Superuser schedules a job to run at the highest priority, this change can affect the performance of the system for all other jobs, including the operating system itself. For this reason you should be careful when using nice with negative values.

The TC Shell has a nice builtin. Under tcsh, use the following syntax to change the priority at which *command-line* is run. The default priority is 4. You must include the plus sign for positive values.

nice [±value] command line

Examples

The following command executes find in the background at the lowest possible priority. The **ps –l** command displays the nice value of the command in the **NI** column:

```
# nice -n 19 find / -name core -print > corefiles.out &
[1] 2610
```

```
# ps -l
  F S   UID   PID  PPID  C PRI  NI ADDR     SZ WCHAN  TTY          TIME CMD
100 S     0  1099  1097  0  75   0    -    605 wait4  pts/0    00:00:00 bash
100 R     0  2610  1099  0  99  19    -    634 -      pts/0    00:00:03 find
100 R     0  2611  1099  0  76   0    -    747 -      pts/0    00:00:00 ps
```

The next command finds very large files and runs at a high priority (–15):

```
# nice -n -15 find / -size +50000k
```

nohup

Runs a command that keeps running after you log out

nohup command line

The nohup utility executes a command line such that the command keeps running after you log out. In other words, nohup causes a process to ignore a SIGHUP signal. Depending on how the shell is configured, it may kill your background processes when you log out. The TC Shell has a nohup builtin. Refer to "Notes" for more information.

Arguments The *command line* is the command line you want to execute.

Notes Accepts the common options described on page 587.

If you do not redirect the output from a command that you execute using nohup, both standard output *and* standard error are sent to the file named **nohup.out** in the working directory. If you do not have write permission for the working directory, nohup sends output to **~/nohup.out**.

Unlike the nohup utility, the TC Shell's nohup builtin does not send output to **nohup.out**. Background jobs started from tcsh continue to run after you log out.

Examples The following command executes find in the background, using nohup:

```
$ nohup find / -name core -print > corefiles.out &
[1] 14235
```

od

Dumps the contents of a file

od [options] [file-list]

The od (octal dump) utility dumps the contents of a file. The dump is useful for viewing executable (object) files and text files with embedded nonprinting characters. This utility takes its input from the file you specify on the command line or from standard input.

Arguments   The *file-list* specifies the pathnames of the files that od displays. When you do not specify a *file-list*, od reads from standard input.

Options   Accepts the common options described on page 587.

--address-radix=*base*

   -A *base*

Specifies the base used when displaying the offsets shown for positions in the file. By default offsets are given in octal. Possible values for *base* are **d** (decimal), **o** (octal), **x** (hexadecimal), and **n** (no offsets printed).

--skip-bytes=*n*   -j *n*

Skips *n* bytes before displaying data.

--read-bytes=*n*   -N *n*

Reads a maximum of *n* bytes and quits.

--strings=*n*   -s *n*

Outputs from the file only those bytes that contain runs of *n* or more printable ASCII characters that are terminated by a NULL byte. The default value for *n* is 3.

--format=*type[n]*

   -t *type[n]*

Specifies the output format to use when displaying data from a file. You can repeat this option with different format *types* to see the file in several different formats. Table V-19 lists the possible values for *type*.

By default od dumps a file as 2-byte octal numbers. You can specify the number of bytes od uses to compose each number by specifying a length indicator, *n*. You can specify a length indicator for all types except **a** and **c**. Table V-21 lists the possible values of *n*.

table V-19	Output formats
type	**Type of output**
a	Named character. Displays nonprinting control characters using their official ASCII names. For example, FORMFEED is displayed as **ff**.
c	ASCII character. Displays nonprinting control characters as backslash escape sequences (Table V-20) or three-digit octal numbers.
d	Signed decimal.
f	Floating point.
o	Octal (default).
u	Unsigned decimal.
x	Hexadecimal.

table V-20	Output format type **c** backslash escape sequences
Sequence	**Meaning**
\0	NULL
\a	BELL
\b	BACKSPACE
\f	FORMFEED
\n	NEWLINE
\r	RETURN
\t	HORIZONTAL TAB
\v	VERTICAL TAB

table V-21	Length indicators
n	Number of bytes to use
Integers (types d, o, u, and x)	
C (character)	Uses single characters for each decimal value
S (short integer)	Uses 2 bytes
I (integer)	Uses 4 bytes
L (long)	Uses 4 bytes on 32-bit machines and 8 bytes on 64-bit machines

table V-21	Length indicators (continued)
Floating point (type f)	
F (float)	Uses 4 bytes
D (double)	Uses 8 bytes
L (long double)	Typically uses 8 bytes

Notes

To retain backward compatibility with older, non-POSIX versions of od, the od utility includes the options listed in Table V-22 as shorthand versions of many of the preceding options.

table V-22	Shorthand format specifications
Shorthand	**Equivalent specification**
–a	–t a
–b	–t oC
–c	–t c
–d	–t u2
–f	–t fF
–h	–t x2
–i	–t d2
–l	–t d4
–o	–t o2
–x	–t x2

Examples

The file **ac**, used in the following examples, contains all the ASCII characters. In the first example, the bytes in this file are displayed as named characters. The first column shows the offset of each byte from the start of the file. The offsets are given as octal values.

```
$ od -t a ac
0000000 nul soh stx etx eot enq ack bel bs ht nl vt ff cr so si
0000020 dle dc1 dc2 dc3 dc4 nak syn etb can em sub esc fs gs rs us
0000040 sp ! " # $ % & ' ( ) * + , - . /
0000060 0 1 2 3 4 5 6 7 8 9 : ; < = > ?
0000100 @ A B C D E F G H I J K L M N O
0000120 P Q R S T U V W X Y Z [ \ ] ^ _
0000140 ` a b c d e f g h i j k l m n o
0000160 p q r s t u v w x y z { | } ~ del
```

```
0000200 nul soh stx etx eot enq ack bel bs ht nl vt ff cr so si
0000220 dle dc1 dc2 dc3 dc4 nak syn etb can em sub esc fs gs rs us
0000240 sp ! " # $ % & ' ( ) * + , - . /
0000260 0 1 2 3 4 5 6 7 8 9 : ; < = > ?
0000300 @ A B C D E F G H I J K L M N O
0000320 P Q R S T U V W X Y Z [ \ ] ^ _
0000340 ` a b c d e f g h i j k l m n o
0000360 p q r s t u v w x y z { | } ~ del
0000400 nl
0000401
```

In the next example, the bytes are displayed as octal numbers, ASCII characters, or printing characters preceded by a backslash (refer to Table V-20 on page 738):

```
$ od -t c ac
0000000 \0 001 002 003 004 005 006 \a \b \t \n \v \f \r 016 017
0000020 020 021 022 023 024 025 026 027 030 031 032 033 034 035 036 037
0000040 ! " # $ % & ' ( ) * + , - . /
0000060 0 1 2 3 4 5 6 7 8 9 : ; < = > ?
0000100 @ A B C D E F G H I J K L M N O
0000120 P Q R S T U V W X Y Z [ \ ] ^ _
0000140 ` a b c d e f g h i j k l m n o
0000160 p q r s t u v w x y z { | } ~ 177
0000200 200 201 202 203 204 205 206 207 210 211 212 213 214 215 216 217
0000220 220 221 222 223 224 225 226 227 230 231 232 233 234 235 236 237
0000240 240 241 242 243 244 245 246 247 250 251 252 253 254 255 256 257
0000260 260 261 262 263 264 265 266 267 270 271 272 273 274 275 276 277
0000300 300 301 302 303 304 305 306 307 310 311 312 313 314 315 316 317
0000320 320 321 322 323 324 325 326 327 330 331 332 333 334 335 336 337
0000340 340 341 342 343 344 345 346 347 350 351 352 353 354 355 356 357
0000360 360 361 362 363 364 365 366 367 370 371 372 373 374 375 376 377
0000400 \n
0000401
```

The final example finds in the file **/usr/bin/who** all strings that are at least three characters long (the default) and terminated by a null byte. See strings on page 777 for another way of displaying a similar list. The offset positions are given as decimal offsets instead of octal offsets.

```
$ $ od -A d --strings /usr/bin/who
...
0015170 Joseph Arceneaux
0015187 Michael Stone
0015201 David MacKenzie
0015217 5.2.1
0015223 who
0015227 too many arguments
0015568 %-8.8s%s %-12s %-12s%s%s %-8s%s
0016840 Warning: -i will be removed in a future release; use -u instead
0016906 write error
0016918 %s: %s
```

```
0016925 literal
0016933 shell
0016939 shell-always
0016952 escape
0016959 clocale
0017708 Copyright (C) 2004 Free Software Foundation, Inc.
0018352 memory exhausted
...
```

paste

Joins corresponding lines from files

paste [option] [file-list]

The paste utility reads lines from the *file-list* and joins corresponding lines in its output. By default output lines are separated by a TAB character.

Arguments The *file-list* is a list of ordinary files. When you omit the *file-list*, paste reads from standard input.

Options Accepts the common options described on page 587.

--delimiter=*dlist* -d *dlist*

The *dlist* is a list of characters to be used to separate output fields. If *dlist* contains a single character, paste uses that character instead of the default TAB character to separate fields. If *dlist* contains more than one character, the characters are used in turn to separate output lines and are then reused from the beginning of the list as necessary.

--serial -s Processes one file at a time; pastes horizontally. See "Examples."

Notes A common use of paste is to rearrange the columns of a table. A utility, such as cut, can place the desired columns in separate files, and then paste can join them in any order.

Examples The following example uses the files **fnames** and **acctinfo**. These files can easily be created by using cut (page 627) and the **/etc/passwd** file. The paste command puts the full-name field first, followed by the remaining user account information. A TAB character separates the two output fields.

```
$ cat fnames
Jenny Chen
Alex Watson
Scott Adams
Helen Simpson

$ cat acctinfo
jenny:x:401:50:/home/jenny:/bin/zsh
alex:x:402:50:/home/alex:/bin/bash
scott:x:504:500:/home/scott:/bin/tcsh
hls:x:505:500:/home/hls:/bin/bash
```

```
$ paste fnames acctinfo
Jenny Chen        jenny:x:401:50:/home/jenny:/bin/zsh
Alex Watson       alex:x:402:50:/home/alex:/bin/bash
Scott Adams       scott:x:504:500:/home/scott:/bin/tcsh
Helen Simpson     hls:x:505:500:/home/hls:/bin/bash
```

The next examples use the files **p1**, **p2**, **p3**, and **p4**. The last example in this group uses the **—delimiter** option to give paste a list of characters to use to separate output fields:

```
$ cat p1
1
one
ONE
$ cat p2
2
two
TWO
extra
$ cat p3
3
three
THREE
$ cat p4
4
four
FOUR

$ paste p4 p3 p2 p1
4       3       2       1
four    three   two     one
FOUR    THREE   TWO     ONE
                extra

$ paste --delimiter="+-" p3 p2 p1 p4
3+2-1=4
three+two-one=four
THREE+TWO-ONE=FOUR
+extra-=
```

The final example uses the **—serial** option to paste the files one at a time:

```
$ paste --serial p1 p2 p3 p4
1       one     ONE
2       two     TWO     extra
3       three   THREE
4       four    FOUR
```

pr

Paginates files for printing

pr [options] [file-list]

The pr utility breaks files into pages, usually in preparation for printing. Each page has a header with the name of the file, date, time, and page number.

The pr utility takes its input from files you specify on the command line or from standard input. The output from pr goes to standard output and is frequently redirected by a pipe to a printer.

Arguments

The *file-list* is a list of the pathnames of text files that you want pr to paginate. When you omit the *file-list*, pr reads from standard input.

Options

Accepts the common options described on page 587.

You can embed options within the *file-list*. An embedded option affects only those files following it on the command line.

--show-control-chars

−c   Displays control characters with a caret (^; for example, ^H). Displays other nonprinting characters as octal numbers preceded by a backslash.

--columns=*col*   **−*col***

Displays output in *col* columns with a default of one. This option may truncate lines and cannot be used with the **--merge** option.

--double-space   **−d**   Double-spaces the output.

--form-feed   **−f**   Uses a FORMFEED character to skip to the next page rather than filling the current page with NEWLINE characters.

--header=*head*   **−h *head***

Displays *head* at the top of each page instead of the filename. If *head* contains SPACEs, you must enclose it within quotation marks.

--length=*lines*   **−l *lines***

Sets the page length to *lines* lines. The default is 66 lines.

--merge   **−m**   Displays all specified files simultaneously in multiple columns. This option cannot be used with **−columns**.

--number-lines=*[c[num]]*

−n*[c[num]]*

Numbers the lines of output. The *c* is a character that pr appends to the number to separate it from the contents of the file (the default is a TAB). The *num* specifies the number of digits in each line number (the default is 5).

--indent=*spaces*   **−o** *spaces*

> Indents the output by *spaces* characters (specifies the left margin).

--separator=*c*   **−s**[*c*]

> Separates columns with the single character *c* (defaults to TAB when you omit *c*). By default pr uses TABs as separation characters to align columns unless you use the **−w** option, in which case nothing separates columns.

--omit-header   **−t** Causes pr not to display its five-line page header and trailer. The header that pr normally displays includes the name of the file, the date, time, and page number. The trailer is five blank lines.

--width=*num*   **−w** *num*

> Sets the page width to *num* columns. This option is effective only with multi-column output (the **−−merge** or **−−columns** option).

--*firstpage*[:*lastpage*]

    +*firstpage*[:*lastpage*]

> Output begins with the page numbered *firstpage* and ends with *lastpage*. Without *lastpage,* pr outputs through the last page of the document. The short version of this option begins with a plus sign, not a hyphen.

Notes

When you use the **−−columns** option to display the output in multiple columns, pr displays the same number of lines in each column (with the possible exception of the last).

Examples

The first command shows pr paginating a file named **memo** and sending its output through a pipe to lpr for printing:

```
$ pr memo | lpr
```

Now **memo** is sent to the printer again, this time with a special heading at the top of each page. The job is run in the background.

```
$ pr -h 'MEMO RE: BOOK' memo | lpr &
[1] 4904
```

Next pr displays the **memo** file on the screen, without any header, starting with page 3:

```
$ pr -t +3 memo
...
```

ps

Displays process status

ps [options] [process-list]

The ps utility displays status information about processes running on the local system.

Arguments   The *process-list* is a comma- or SPACE-separated list of PID numbers. When you specify a *process-list,* ps reports on just the processes in that list.

Options   The ps utility accepts three types of options, each preceded by a different prefix. You can intermix the options.

Two hyphens:	GNU (long) options
One hyphen:	UNIX98 (short) options
No hyphens:	BSD options

–A   (**all**) Reports on all processes. Also **–e**.

–e   (**everything**) Reports on all processes. Also **–A**.

–f   (**full**) Displays a listing with more columns of information.

––forest   Displays the process tree.

–l   (**long**) Produces a long listing showing more information about each process. See the "Discussion" section for a description of all the columns that this option displays.

––no-headers   Omits the header. This option is useful if you are sending the output to another program for further processing.

–u   (**user-oriented**) Adds to the display the username of the user running the process, the time the process was started, the percentage of CPU and memory the process is using, and other information.

––User=*username*   Reports on processes being run by *username,* which can be the name or UID of a user on the local system.

–w   (**wide**) Without this option ps truncates output lines at the right side of the screen. This option extends the display so it wraps around one more line, if needed.

Discussion   Without any options, ps displays the statuses of all active processes that your terminal/screen controls. Table V-23 lists the heading and content of each of the four columns that ps displays.

table V-23	Column headings I
Heading	**Meaning**
PID	The process identification number.
TTY (terminal)	The name of the terminal that controls the process.
TIME	The number of hours, minutes, and seconds the process has been running.
CMD	The command line the process was called with. The command is truncated to fit on one line. Use the **–w** option to see more of the command line.

The columns that ps displays depend on your choice of options. Table V-24 lists the headings and contents of the most common columns.

table V-24	Column headings II

The column titles differ, depending on the type of option you use. This table shows the headings for UNIX98 (one-hyphen) options.

Heading	**Meaning**
%CPU	The percentage of total CPU time that the process is using. Owing to the way that Linux handles process accounting, this figure is approximate, and the total of %CPU values for all processes may exceed 100%.
%MEM (memory)	The percentage of RAM that the process is using.
COMMAND *or* **CMD**	The command line the process was called with. The command is truncated to fit on one line. Use the **–w** option to see more of the command line. This column is always displayed last on a line.
F (flags)	The flags associated with the process.
PID	The process identification number.
PPID (parent PID)	The process identification number of the parent process.
PRI (priority)	The priority of the process.
RSS (resident set size)	The number of blocks of memory that the process is using.
SIZE *or* **SZ**	The size, in blocks, of the core image of the process.
STIME *or* **START**	The date the process started.

table V-24   Column headings II (continued)

STAT *or* **S** (status)	The status of the process as specified by one or more letters from the following list:

<	High priority
D	Sleeping and cannot be interrupted
L	Pages locked in memory (real-time and custom I/O)
N	Low priority
R	Available for execution (in the run queue)
S	Sleeping
T	Either stopped or being traced
W	Has no pages resident in RAM
X	Dead
Z	Zombie process that is waiting for its child processes to terminate before it terminates

TIME	The number of minutes and seconds that the process has been running.
TTY (terminal)	The name of the terminal controlling the process.
USER *or* **UID**	The username of the user who owns the process.
WCHAN (wait channel)	If the process is waiting for an event, the address of the kernel function that caused the process to wait. It is 0 for processes that are not waiting or sleeping.

Notes

Use top (page 798) to display process status information dynamically.

Examples

The first example shows ps, without any options, displaying the user's active processes. The first process is the shell (bash), and the second is the process executing the ps utility.

```
$ ps
  PID TTY          TIME CMD
 2697 pts/0    00:00:02 bash
 3299 pts/0    00:00:00 ps
```

With the –l (long) option, ps displays more information about the processes:

```
$ ps -l
  F S   UID   PID  PPID  C PRI  NI ADDR    SZ WCHAN  TTY          TIME CMD
000 S   500  2697  2696  0  75   0    -   639 wait4  pts/0    00:00:02 bash
000 R   500  3300  2697  0  76   0    -   744 -      pts/0    00:00:00 ps
```

The –u option shows various types of information about the processes, including how much of the local system CPU and memory each one is using:

```
$ ps -u
USER         PID %CPU %MEM  VSZ  RSS TTY     STAT START   TIME COMMAND
alex        2697  0.0  0.5 2556 1460 pts/0   S    Jul31  0:02 -bash
alex        3303  0.0  0.2 2476  616 pts/0   R    Jul31  0:00 ps -u
```

The **--forest** option causes ps to display what the man page describes as an "ASCII art process tree." Processes that are children of other processes appear indented under their parents, making the process hierarchy, or tree, easier to see.

```
$ ps -ef --forest
UID        PID  PPID  C STIME TTY          TIME CMD
root         1     0  0 Jul22 ?        00:00:03 init
root         2     1  0 Jul22 ?        00:00:00 [keventd]
...
root       785     1  0 Jul22 ?        00:00:00 /usr/sbin/apmd -p 10 -w 5 -W -P
root       839     1  0 Jul22 ?        00:00:01 /usr/sbin/sshd
root      3305   839  0 Aug01 ?        00:00:00  \_ /usr/sbin/sshd.
alex      3307  3305  0 Aug01 ?        00:00:00      \_ /usr/sbin/sshd
alex      3308  3307  0 Aug01 pts/1    00:00:00          \_ -bash
alex      3774  3308  0 Aug01 pts/1    00:00:00              \_ ps -ef --forest
...
root      1040     1  0 Jul22 ?        00:00:00 login -- root
root      3351  1040  0 Aug01 tty2     00:00:00  \_ -bash
root      3402  3351  0 Aug01 tty2     00:00:00      \_ make modules
root      3416  3402  0 Aug01 tty2     00:00:00          \_ make -C drivers CFLA
root      3764  3416  0 Aug01 tty2     00:00:00              \_ make -C scsi mod
root      3773  3764  0 Aug01 tty2     00:00:00                  \_ ld -m elf_i3
```

ps and kill The next sequence of commands shows how to use ps to determine the PID number of a process running in the background and how to terminate that process by using the kill command. In this case it is not necessary to use ps because the shell displays the PID number of the background processes. The ps utility verifies the PID number.

The first command executes find in the background. The shell displays the job and PID numbers of the process, followed by a prompt.

```
$ find ~ -name memo -print > memo.out &
[1] 3343
```

Next ps confirms the PID number of the background task. If you did not already know this number, using ps would be the only way to find it out.

```
$ ps
  PID TTY          TIME CMD
 3308 pts/1    00:00:00 bash
 3343 pts/1    00:00:00 find
 3344 pts/1    00:00:00 ps
```

Finally kill (page 693) terminates the process:

```
$ kill 3343
$ RETURN
[1]+ Terminated              find ~ -name memo -print >memo.out
$
```

rcp

Copies one or more files to or from a remote system

rcp [options] source-file destination-file
rcp [options] source-file-list destination-directory

The rcp utility copies one or more ordinary files between two systems that can communicate over a network.

---

rcp **is not secure**

security   The rcp utility uses host-based trust, which is not secure, to authorize files to be copied. Use scp (page 758) when it is available.

Arguments   The *source-file, source-file-list,* and *destination-file* are pathnames of the ordinary files, and the *destination-directory* is the pathname of a directory file. A pathname that does not contain a colon (**:**) is the name of a file on the local system. A pathname of the form *name@host:path* names a file on the remote system named *host*. The *path* is relative to the home directory of the user *name* (unless *path* is an absolute pathname). When you omit the *name@* portion of the destination, a relative pathname is relative to the home directory on the *host* of the user giving the rcp command.

Like cp, rcp has two modes of operation: The first copies one file to another, and the second copies one or more files to a directory. The *source-file[-list]* is a list of the name(s) of the file(s) that rcp will copy; *destination-file* is the name that rcp assigns to the resulting copy of the file, or *destination-directory* is the name of the directory that rcp puts the copied files in. When rcp copies files to a *destination-directory*, the files maintain their original simple filenames.

Options   –p   (**preserve**) Sets the modification times and file access permissions of each copy to match those of the *source-file*. When you do not use **–p**, rcp uses the file-creation mask (umask; see page 810) on the remote system to modify the access permissions.

   –r   (**recursive**) When a file in the *source-file-list* is a directory, copies the contents of that directory and any subdirectories into the *destination-directory*. You can use this option only when the destination is a directory.

Notes   You must have an account on the remote system to copy files to or from it using rcp. The rcp utility does not prompt for a password but uses several alternative methods to verify that you have the authority to read or write files on the remote system.

One method requires that the name of the local system be specified in the **/etc/hosts.equiv** file on the remote system. If the name is there, rcp allows you to copy files *if* your usernames are the same on both systems *and* your account on the remote system has the necessary permissions to access files there.

Authorization can also be specified on a per-user basis. Using this method the remote user's home directory must contain a file named **~/.rhosts** that lists trusted remote systems and users. With this method, your local and remote user names do not have to match but your local username must appear on the line in the remote **~/.rhosts** file that starts with the name of the local system. See "Examples" for rlogin (page 752) for a sample **.rhosts** file.

If you use a wildcard (such as *****) in a remote pathname, you must quote the wildcard character or pathname so that the wildcard is interpreted by the shell on the remote system and not by the local shell. As with cp, if the *destination-file* exists before you execute rcp, rcp overwrites the file.

Examples   The first example copies the files with filenames ending in **.c** into the **archives** directory on the remote system named **bravo**. Because a username is not specified, rcp uses the local user's username on the remote system. Because the full pathname of the **archives** directory is not specified, rcp assumes that it is a subdirectory of the user's home directory on **bravo**. Each of the copied files retains its simple filename.

```
$ rcp *.c bravo:archives
```

The next example copies **memo** from the **/home/jenny** directory on **bravo** to the working directory on the local system:

```
$ rcp bravo:/home/jenny/memo .
```

Next rcp copies the files named **memo.new** and **letter** to Jenny's home directory on the remote system **bravo**. The absolute pathnames of the copied files on **bravo** are **/home/jenny/memo.new** and **/home/jenny/letter**:

```
$ rcp memo.new letter bravo:/home/jenny
```

The final command copies all the files in Jenny's **reports** directory on **bravo** to the **oldreports** directory on the local system, preserving the original modification dates and file access permissions on the copies:

```
$ rcp -p 'bravo:reports/*' oldreports
```

rlogin

Logs in on a remote system

rlogin [option] remote-system

The rlogin utility establishes a login session on a remote system over a network.

rlogin **is not secure**

security   The rlogin utility uses host-based trust, which is not secure, to authorize your login. Alternatively, it sends your password over the network as cleartext, which is not a secure practice. Use ssh (page 773) when it is available.

Arguments

The *remote-system* is the name of a system that the local system can reach over a network.

Options

–l *username*   (**login**) Logs you in on the remote system as the user specified by *username*.

Notes

If the file named **/etc/hosts.equiv** located on the remote system specifies the name of the local system, the remote system will not prompt you to enter your password. Systems that are listed in the **/etc/hosts.equiv** file are considered as secure as the local system.

An alternative way to specify a trusted relationship is on a per-user basis. Each user's home directory can contain a file named **~/.rhosts** that holds a list of trusted remote systems and users. See "Examples" for a sample **.rhosts** file.

Examples

The following example illustrates the use of rlogin. On the local system, Alex's username is **alex**; on the remote system **bravo**, his username is **watson**. The remote system prompts Alex to enter a password because he is logging in using a username different from the one he uses on the local system.

```
$ who am i
alex         tty06          Oct 14 13:26
$ rlogin -l watson bravo
Password:
```

~/.rhosts file   If the local system is named **hurrah**, the following **.rhosts** file on **bravo** allows the user **alex** to log in as the user **watson** without entering a password:

```
$ cat /home/watson/.rhosts
hurrah alex
```

rm

Removes a file (deletes a link)

rm [options] file-list

The rm utility removes hard and/or symbolic links to one or more files. When you remove the last hard link to a file, the file is deleted.

Be careful when you use rm with wildcards

caution   Because you can remove a large number of files with a single command, use rm cautiously, especially when you are working with ambiguous file references. If you have doubts about the effect of an rm command with an ambiguous file reference, first use echo with the same file reference and evaluate the list of files the reference generates. Alternatively, you can use the **--interactive** option.

Arguments   The *file-list* is a list of the list of files that rm deletes.

Options   Accepts the common options described on page 587.

--force   **-f**   Without asking for your consent, removes files for which you do not have write access permission. This option also suppresses informative output if a file does not exist.

--interactive   **-i**   Asks before removing each file. If you use **--recursive** with this option, rm also asks you before examining each directory.

--recursive   **-r**   Deletes the contents of the specified directory, including all its subdirectories, and the directory itself. Use this option cautiously.

--verbose   **-v**   Displays the name of each file as it is removed.

Notes   To delete a file, you must have execute and write access permission to the parent directory of the file, but you do not need read or write access permission to the file itself. If you are running rm interactively (that is, if rm's standard input is coming from the keyboard) and you do not have write access permission to the file, rm displays your access permission and waits for you to respond. If your response starts with a **y** or **Y**, rm deletes the file; otherwise, it takes no action. If standard input is not coming from a keyboard, rm deletes the file without question.

Refer to page 97 for information on hard links and page 99 for information on symbolic links. Page 101 includes a discussion about removing links. Refer to the rmdir utility (page 755) if you need to remove an empty directory.

When you want to remove a file that begins with a hyphen, you must prevent rm from interpreting the filename as an option. One way to do so is to give the special option -- before the name of the file. This option tells rm that no more options follow: Any arguments that come after it are filenames, even if they look like options.

Use shred to remove a file securely

security   Using rm does not securely delete a file—it is possible to recover a file deleted with rm. Use the shred utility to delete files more securely. See the example "Wiping a file" on page 634 for another method of deleting files more securely.

Examples   The following commands delete files both in the working directory and in another directory:

```
$ rm memo
$ rm letter memo1 memo2
$ rm /home/jenny/temp
```

The next example asks the user before removing each file in the working directory and its subdirectories:

```
$ rm -ir .
```

This command is useful for removing filenames that contain special characters, especially SPACEs, TABs, and NEWLINEs. (You should not create filenames containing these characters on purpose, but it may happen accidentally.)

rmdir

Removes a directory

*rmdir **directory-list***

The rmdir utility deletes empty directories.

Arguments   The *directory-list* is a list of pathnames of empty directories that rmdir removes.

Options   Accepts the common options described on page 587.

––ignore-fail-on-non-empty

Suppresses the message rmdir normally displays when it fails because a directory is not empty. With the **––parents** option, rmdir does not quit when it finds a directory that is not empty.

––parents   **–p**   Removes a series of empty, nested directories, starting with the child.

––verbose   **–v**   Displays the names of directories as they are removed.

Notes   Use the rm utility with the **–r** option if you need to remove directories that are not empty, together with their contents.

Examples   The following command deletes the empty **literature** directory from the working directory:

```
$ rmdir literature
```

The next command removes the **letters** directory, using an absolute pathname:

```
$ rmdir /home/jenny/letters
```

The final command removes the **letters**, **march**, and **05** directories, assuming the directories are empty except for other directories named in the path:

```
$ rmdir --parents letters/march/05
```

rsh

Executes commands on a remote system

rsh [option] host [command-line]

The rsh utility runs *command-line* on *host* by starting a shell on the remote system. Without a *command-line* rsh calls rlogin, which logs you in on the remote system.

rsh **is not secure**

security   The rsh utility uses host-based trust, which is not secure, to authorize your login. Alternatively, it sends your password over the network as cleartext, which is not a secure practice. Use ssh (page 773) when it is available.

Arguments   The *host* is the name of the remote system. The rsh utility runs *command-line* on the remote system. You must quote special characters in *command-line* so that they are not expanded by the local shell prior to passing them to rsh.

Options

–l *username*   (**login**) Logs you in on the remote system as the user specified by *username*.

Notes   If the file named **/etc/hosts.equiv** located on the remote system specifies the name of the local system, the remote system will not prompt you to enter your password. Systems that are listed in the **/etc/hosts.equiv** file are considered as secure as the local system.

An alternative way to specify a trusted relationship is on a per-user basis. Each user's home directory can contain a file named **~/.rhosts** that holds a list of trusted remote systems and users. See "Examples" under rlogin (page 752) for a sample **.rhosts** file.

Examples   In the first example, Alex uses rsh to obtain a listing of the files in his home directory on **bravo**:

```
$ rsh bravo ls
cost_of_living
info
preferences
work
```

Next the output of the previous command is redirected into the file **bravo.ls**. Because the redirection character (>) is not escaped, it is interpreted by the local shell, and the file **bravo.ls** is created on the local system.

```
$ rsh bravo ls > bravo_ls
$ cat bravo_ls
cost_of_living
info
preferences
work
```

The next example quotes the redirection character (**>**) so that the file **bravo.ls** is created on the remote system (**bravo**), as shown by ls run on **bravo**:

```
$ rsh bravo ls ">" bravo.ls
$ rsh bravo ls
bravo.ls
cost_of_living
info
preferences
work
```

In the final example, rsh without *command-line* logs in on the remote system. Alex has used the **–l watson** option to log in on **bravo** as **watson**. The **/home/watson/.rhosts** file must be configured to allow Alex to log in on the account in this manner. See "Examples" under rlogin (page 752) for a sample **.rhosts** file.

```
$ rsh -l watson bravo
Last login: Sat Jul 30 16:13:53 from kudos
$ hostname
bravo
$ exit
rlogin: connection closed.
```

scp

Securely copies one or more files to or from a remote system

scp [[user@]from-host:]source-file [[user@]to-host:][destination-file]

The scp (secure copy) utility copies an ordinary or directory file from one system to another on a network. This utility uses ssh to transfer files and the same authentication mechanism as ssh; therefore it provides the same security as ssh. The scp utility asks you for a password when it is needed.

Arguments

The *from-host* is the name of the system you are copying files from and the *to-host* is the system you are copying to. When you do not specify a host, scp assumes the local system. The *user* on either system defaults to the user on the local system who is giving the command; you can specify a different user with *user@*. The scp utility permits you to copy between two remote systems.

The *source-file* is the file you are copying, and the *destination-file* is the resulting copy. You can specify plain or directory files as relative or absolute pathnames. A relative pathname is relative to the specified or implicit user's home directory. When the *source-file* is a directory, you must use the –r option to copy its contents. When the *destination-file* is a directory, each of the source files maintains its simple filename.

Options

–p (**preserve**) Preserves the modification and access times as well as the permissions of the original file.

–q (**quiet**) Does not display the progress meter.

–r (**recursive**) Recursively copies a directory hierarchy.

–v (**verbose**) Displays debugging messages about the connection and transfer. This option is useful if things are not going as expected.

Notes

The scp utility is one of the OpenSSH suite of secure network connectivity tools. See "Notes" on page 774 for a discussion of OpenSSH security. Refer to "Message on initial connection to a server" on page 774 for information about a message you may get when using scp to connect to a remote system for the first time.

You can copy from or to the local system or between two remote systems. Make sure that you have read permission for the file you are copying and write permission for the directory you are copying it into.

You must quote a wildcard character (such as *) in a remote pathname so that it is interpreted by the shell on the remote system and not by the local shell.

As with cp, if the *destination-file* exists before you run scp, scp overwrites the file.

Examples   The first example copies the files with filenames ending in **.c** from the working directory on the local system into the **~jenny/archives** directory on **bravo**. The wildcard character is not quoted so that the local shell will expand it. Because **archives** is a relative pathname, scp assumes that it is a subdirectory of Jenny's home directory on **bravo**. Each of the copied files retains its simple filename.

```
$ scp *.c jenny@bravo:archives
```

Next Alex copies the directory structure under **~alex/memos** on the system named **bravo** to **~jenny/alex.memos.bravo** on **kudos**. He must have the necessary permissions to write to Jenny's home directory on **kudos**.

```
$ scp -r bravo:memos jenny@kudos:alex.memos.bravo
```

Finally Alex copies the files with filenames ending in **.c** from Jenny's **archives** directory on **bravo** to the **jenny.c.bravo** directory in his working directory. The wildcard character is quoted to protect it from expansion by the local shell; it will be interpreted by the remote system, **bravo**.

```
$ scp -r 'jenny@bravo:archives/*.c' jenny.c.bravo
```

It is important to remember that whenever you copy multiple files or directories, the destination—either local or remote—must be an existing directory and not an ordinary or nonexistent file.

sleep

Creates a process that sleeps for a specified interval

sleep **time**
sleep **time-list**

The sleep utility causes the process executing it to go to sleep for the time specified.

Arguments

Traditionally the amount of time that a process sleeps is given as a single integer argument, *time*, which denotes a number of seconds. The *time* does not have to be an integer, however: You can specify a decimal fraction. You can also append a unit specification to *time*: **s** (seconds), **m** (minutes), **h** (hours), and **d** (days).

You can construct a *time-list* by including several times on the command line: The total time that the process sleeps is the sum of these times. For example, if you specify **1h 30m 100s**, the process will sleep for 91 minutes and 40 seconds.

Examples

You can use sleep from the command line to execute a command after a period of time. The following example executes in the background a process that reminds you to make a phone call in 20 minutes (1,200 seconds):

```
$ (sleep 1200; echo "Remember to make call.") &
[1] 4660
```

Alternatively, you could give the following command to get the same reminder:

```
$ (sleep 20m; echo "Remember to make call.") &
[2] 4667
```

You can also use sleep within a shell script to execute a command at regular intervals. The **per** shell script executes a program named **update** every 90 seconds:

```
$ cat per
#!/bin/bash
while true
do
    update
    sleep 90
done
```

If you execute a shell script such as **per** in the background, you can terminate it only by using kill.

The final shell script accepts the name of a file as an argument and waits for that file to appear on the disk. If the file does not exist, the script sleeps for 1 minute and 45 seconds before checking for the file again:

```
$ cat wait_for_file
#!/bin/bash

if [ $# != 1 ]; then
    echo "Usage: wait_for_file filename"
    exit 1
fi

while true
do
    if [ -f "$1" ]; then
        echo "$1 is here now"
        exit 0
    fi
    sleep 1m 45
done
```

sort

Sorts and/or merges files

sort [options] [file-list]

The sort utility sorts and/or merges one or more text files.

Arguments   The *file-list* is a list of pathnames of one or more ordinary files that contain the text to be sorted. If the *file-list* is omitted, sort takes its input from standard input. Without the **–o** option sort sends its output to standard output. This utility sorts and merges files unless you use the **–m** (merge only) or **–c** (check only) option.

Options   When you do not specify an option, sort orders the file in the machine collating sequence (usually ASCII). Without a **––key** option sort orders a file based on full lines. Use **––key** to specify sort fields within a line. You can follow a **––key** option with additional options without a leading hyphen; see "Discussion" for more information.

––ignore-leading-blanks

   –b   Blanks (TAB and SPACE characters) normally mark the beginning of fields in the input file. Without this option, sort considers leading blanks to be part of the field they precede. This option ignores leading blanks within a field, so sort does not consider these characters in sort comparisons.

––check   **–c**   Checks whether the file is properly sorted. The sort utility does not display anything if everything is in order. It displays a message if the file is not in sorted order and returns an exit status of 1.

––dictionary-order

   –d   Ignores all characters that are not alphanumeric characters or blanks. For example, sort does not consider punctuation with this option.

––ignore-case   **–f**   (**fold**) Considers all lowercase letters to be uppercase letters. Use this option when you are sorting a file that contains both uppercase and lowercase text.

––ignore-nonprinting

   –i   Ignores nonprinting characters. This option is overridden by the **––dictionary-order** option.

––key=*start[,stop]*

   –k *start[,stop]*

   Specifies a sort field within a line. Without this option sort orders a file based on full lines. The sort field starts at the position on the line specified by *start* and ends at *stop*, or the end of the line if *stop* is omitted. The *start* and *stop* positions are in the format *f[.c]*, where *f* is the field number and *c* is the optional character within the field. Numbering starts with 1. When *c* is omitted from *start,* it defaults to the first character in the field; when *c* is omitted from *stop,* it defaults to the last character in the field. See "Discussion" for further explanation of sort fields and "Examples" for illustrations of their use.

--merge –m Assumes that multiple input files are each in sorted order and merges them without verifying that they are sorted.

--numeric-sort –n Sorts in arithmetic sequence; does not order lines or sort fields in the machine collating sequence. With this option, minus signs and decimal points take on their arithmetic meaning.

--output=*filename*

   –o *filename*

   Sends output to *filename* instead of standard output; *filename* can be the same as one of the names in the *file-list.*

--reverse –r Reverses the sense of the sort (for example, **z** precedes **a**).

--field-separator=*x*

   –t *x*

   Specifies *x* as the field separator. See "Discussion" for more information.

--unique –u Outputs repeated lines only once. When you use this option with **--check,** sort displays a message if the same line appears more than once in the input file, even if the file is in sorted order.

Discussion

Without any *options* sort bases its ordering on full lines.

In the following description, a *field* is a sequence of characters in a line of input. Without the **--field-separator** option, fields are bounded by the empty string preceding a group of one or more blanks (TAB and SPACE characters). You cannot see the empty string that delimits the fields; it is an imaginary point between two fields. Fields are also bounded by the beginning and end of the line. The line shown in Figure V-1 holds the fields **Toni,** SPACE**Barnett,** and SPACESPACESPACESPACE55020. These fields are used to define sort fields. Sometime fields and sort fields are the same.

Sort field A *sort field* is a sequence of characters that sort uses to put lines in order. A sort field can contain all or part of one or more fields (Figure V-1).

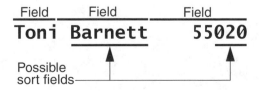

Figure V-1 Fields and sort fields

The **--key** option specifies pairs of pointers that define subsections of each line (sort fields) for comparison. See the **--key** option (page 762) for details.

Leading blanks   The **–b** option causes sort to ignore leading blanks in a sort field. If you do not use this option, sort considers each leading blank to be a character in the sort field and includes it in the sort comparison.

Options   You can specify options that pertain only to a given sort field by immediately following the *stop* pointer (or the *start* pointer if there is no *stop* pointer) with one of the options **b**, **d**, **f**, **i**, **n**, or **r**. In this case you must *not* precede the option with a hyphen.

Multiple sort fields   When you specify more than one sort field, sort examines them in the order you specify them on the command line. If the first sort field of two lines is the same, sort examines the second sort field. If these are again the same, sort looks at the third field. This process continues for all the sort fields you specify. If all the sort fields are the same, sort examines the entire line.

Examples

The examples in this section demonstrate some of the features and uses of the sort utility. The examples assume that the **list** file shown here is in the working directory:

```
$ cat list
Tom Winstrom         94201
Janet Dempsey        94111
Alice MacLeod        94114
David Mack           94114
Toni Barnett         95020
Jack Cooper          94072
Richard MacDonald    95510
```

This file contains a list of names and ZIP codes. Each line of the file contains three fields: the first name field, the last name field, and the ZIP code field. For the examples to work, make sure the blanks in the file are SPACEs, and not TABs.

The first example demonstrates sort without any options—the only argument is the name of the input file. In this case sort orders the file on a line-by-line basis. If the first characters on two lines are the same, sort looks at the second characters to determine the proper order. If the second characters are the same, sort looks at the third characters. This process continues until sort finds a character that differs between the lines. If the lines are identical, it does not matter which one sort puts first. In this example, sort needs to examine only the first three characters (at most) of each line. The sort utility displays a list that is in alphabetical order by first name.

```
$ sort list
Alice MacLeod        94114
David Mack           94114
Jack Cooper          94072
Janet Dempsey        94111
Richard MacDonald    95510
Tom Winstrom         94201
Toni Barnett         95020
```

You can instruct sort to skip any number of fields and characters on a line before beginning its comparison. Blanks normally mark the beginning of a field. The next example sorts the same list by last name, the second field. The --key=2 argument instructs sort to begin its comparison with the second field, the last name. Because there is no second pointer, the sort field extends to the end of the line. Now the list is almost in last-name order, but there is a problem with **Mac**.

```
$ sort --key=2 list
Toni Barnett          95020
Jack Cooper           94072
Janet Dempsey         94111
Richard MacDonald     95510
Alice MacLeod         94114
David Mack            94114
Tom Winstrom          94201
```

In the preceding example, **MacLeod** comes before **Mack**. After finding that the sort fields of these two lines were the same through the third letter (**Mac**), sort put **L** before **k** because it arranges lines based on ASCII character codes, in which uppercase letters come before lowercase ones.

The --ignore-case option makes sort treat uppercase and lowercase letters as equals and fixes the problem with **MacLeod** and **Mack**:

```
$ sort --ignore-case --key=2 list
Toni Barnett          95020
Jack Cooper           94072
Janet Dempsey         94111
Richard MacDonald     95510
David Mack            94114
Alice MacLeod         94114
Tom Winstrom          94201
```

The next example attempts to sort **list** on the third field, the ZIP code. In this case sort does not put the numbers in order but rather puts the shortest name first in the sorted list and the longest name last. The --key=3 argument instructs sort to begin its comparison with the third field, the ZIP code. A field starts with a blank and includes subsequent blanks. In the case of the **list** file, the blanks are SPACEs. The ASCII value of a SPACE character is less than that of any other printable character, so sort puts the ZIP code that is preceded by the most SPACEs first and the ZIP code that is preceded by the fewest SPACEs last.

```
$ sort --key=3 list
David Mack            94114
Jack Cooper           94072
Tom Winstrom          94201
Toni Barnett          95020
Janet Dempsey         94111
Alice MacLeod         94114
Richard MacDonald     95510
```

The –b (––ignore-leading-blanks) option causes sort to ignore leading SPACEs within a field. With this option, the ZIP codes come out in the proper order. When sort determines that **MacLeod** and **Mack** have the same ZIP codes, it compares the entire lines, putting **Alice MacLeod** before **David Mack** (because **A** comes before **D**).

```
$ sort -b --key=3 list
Jack Cooper          94072
Janet Dempsey        94111
Alice MacLeod        94114
David Mack           94114
Tom Winstrom         94201
Toni Barnett         95020
Richard MacDonald    95510
```

To sort alphabetically by last name when ZIP codes are the same, sort needs to make a second pass that sorts on the last name field. The next example shows how to make this second pass by specifying a second sort field and uses the –f (––ignore-case) option to keep the **Mack/MacLeod** problem from cropping up again:

```
$ sort -b -f --key=3 --key=2 list
Jack Cooper          94072
Janet Dempsey        94111
David Mack           94114
Alice MacLeod        94114
Tom Winstrom         94201
Toni Barnett         95020
Richard MacDonald    95510
```

The next example shows a **sort** command that skips not only fields but also characters. The **–k 3.4** option (equivalent to **––key=3.4**) causes sort to start its comparison with the fourth character of the third field. Because the command does not define an end to the sort field, it defaults to the end of the line. The sort field is the last two digits in the ZIP code.

```
$ sort -fb -k 3.4 list
Tom Winstrom         94201
Richard MacDonald    95510
Janet Dempsey        94111
Alice MacLeod        94114
David Mack           94114
Toni Barnett         95020
Jack Cooper          94072
```

The problem of how to sort by last name within the last two digits of the ZIP code is solved by a second pass covering the last-name field. The **f** option following the **–k 2** affects the second pass, which orders by last name only.

```
$ sort -b -k 3.4 -k 2f list
Tom Winstrom          94201
Richard MacDonald     95510
Janet Dempsey         94111
David Mack            94114
Alice MacLeod         94114
Toni Barnett          95020
Jack Cooper           94072
```

The next set of examples uses the **cars** data file. From left to right the columns in the file contain each car's make, model, year of manufacture, mileage, and price:

```
$ cat cars
plym    fury    1970    73      2500
chevy   malibu  1999    60      3000
ford    mustang 1965    45      10000
volvo   s80     1998    102     9850
ford    thundbd 2003    15      10500
chevy   malibu  2000    50      3500
bmw     325i    1985    115     450
honda   accord  2001    30      6000
ford    taurus  2004    10      17000
toyota  rav4    2002    180     750
chevy   impala  1985    85      1550
ford    explor  2003    25      9500
```

Without any options sort displays a sorted copy of the file:

```
$ sort cars
bmw     325i    1985    115     450
chevy   impala  1985    85      1550
chevy   malibu  1999    60      3000
chevy   malibu  2000    50      3500
ford    explor  2003    25      9500
ford    mustang 1965    45      10000
ford    taurus  2004    10      17000
ford    thundbd 2003    15      10500
honda   accord  2001    30      6000
plym    fury    1970    73      2500
toyota  rav4    2002    180     750
volvo   s80     1998    102     9850
```

The objective of the next example is to sort by manufacturer and by price within manufacturer. Unless you specify otherwise, a sort field extends to the end of the line. The **–k 1** sort field specifier sorts from the beginning of the line. The command line instructs sort to sort on the entire line and then make a second pass, sorting on the fifth field all lines whose first-pass sort fields were the same (**–k 5**):

```
$ sort -k 1 -k 5 cars
bmw      325i     1985    115     450
chevy    impala   1985    85      1550
chevy    malibu   1999    60      3000
chevy    malibu   2000    50      3500
ford     explor   2003    25      9500
ford     mustang  1965    45      10000
ford     taurus   2004    10      17000
ford     thundbd  2003    15      10500
honda    accord   2001    30      6000
plym     fury     1970    73      2500
toyota   rav4     2002    180     750
volvo    s80      1998    102     9850
```

Because no two lines are the same, sort makes only one pass, sorting on each entire line. (If two lines differed only in the fifth field, they would be sorted properly on the first pass anyway, so the second pass would be unnecessary.) Look at the lines containing **taurus** and **thundbd**. They are sorted by the second field rather than the fifth, demonstrating that sort never made a second pass and so never sorted on the fifth field.

The next example forces the first-pass sort to stop at the end of the first field. The –k 1,1 option specifies a *start* pointer of the first character of the first field and a *stop* pointer of the last character of the first field. When you do not specify a character within a *start* pointer, it defaults to the first character; when you do not specify a character within a *stop* pointer, it defaults to the last character. Now the **taurus** and **thundbd** are properly sorted by price. But look at the **explor**: It is less expensive than the other Fords, but sort has it positioned as the most expensive. The sort utility put the list in ASCII collating sequence order, not in numeric order: Thus **9500** comes after **10000** because **9** comes after **1**.

```
$ sort -k 1,1 -k 5 cars
bmw      325i     1985    115     450
chevy    impala   1985    85      1550
chevy    malibu   1999    60      3000
chevy    malibu   2000    50      3500
ford     mustang  1965    45      10000
ford     thundbd  2003    15      10500
ford     taurus   2004    10      17000
ford     explor   2003    25      9500
honda    accord   2001    30      6000
plym     fury     1970    73      2500
toyota   rav4     2002    180     750
volvo    s80      1998    102     9850
```

The –n (numeric) option on the second pass puts the list in the proper order:

```
$ sort -k 1,1 -k 5n cars
bmw      325i     1985    115     450
chevy    impala   1985    85      1550
chevy    malibu   1999    60      3000
chevy    malibu   2000    50      3500
ford     explor   2003    25      9500
ford     mustang  1965    45      10000
ford     thundbd  2003    15      10500
ford     taurus   2004    10      17000
honda    accord   2001    30      6000
plym     fury     1970    73      2500
toyota   rav4     2002    180     750
volvo    s80      1998    102     9850
```

The next example again demonstrates that, unless you instruct it otherwise, sort orders a file starting with the field you specify and continuing to the end of the line. It does not make a second pass unless two of the first sort fields are the same. Because there is no *stop* pointer on the first sort field specifier, the sort field for the first pass includes the third field through the end of the line. Although this example sorts the cars by years, it does not sort the cars by model within manufacturer within years (**ford thndbd** comes before **ford explor**, these lines should be reversed).

```
$ sort -k 3 -k 1 cars
ford     mustang  1965    45      10000
plym     fury     1970    73      2500
bmw      325i     1985    115     450
chevy    impala   1985    85      1550
volvo    s80      1998    102     9850
chevy    malibu   1999    60      3000
chevy    malibu   2000    50      3500
honda    accord   2001    30      6000
toyota   rav4     2002    180     750
ford     thundbd  2003    15      10500
ford     explor   2003    25      9500
ford     taurus   2004    10      17000
```

Specifying an end to the sort field for the first pass allows sort to perform its secondary sort properly:

```
$ sort -k 3,3 -k 1 cars
ford     mustang  1965    45      10000
plym     fury     1970    73      2500
bmw      325i     1985    115     450
chevy    impala   1985    85      1550
volvo    s80      1998    102     9850
chevy    malibu   1999    60      3000
chevy    malibu   2000    50      3500
honda    accord   2001    30      6000
toyota   rav4     2002    180     750
ford     explor   2003    25      9500
ford     thundbd  2003    15      10500
ford     taurus   2004    10      17000
```

The next examples demonstrate important sorting techniques: putting a list in alphabetical order, merging uppercase and lowercase entries, and eliminating duplicates. The unsorted list follows:

```
$ cat short
Pear
Pear
apple
pear
Apple
```

Following is a plain sort:

```
$ sort short
Apple
Pear
Pear
apple
pear
```

The following folded sort is a good start, but it does not eliminate duplicates:

```
$ sort -f short
Apple
apple
Pear
Pear
pear
```

The −u (unique) option eliminates duplicates but without the −f the uppercase entries come first:

```
$ sort -u short
Apple
Pear
apple
pear
```

When you attempt to use both −u and −f, some of the entries get lost:

```
$ sort -uf short
apple
Pear
```

Two passes is the answer. Both passes are unique sorts, and the first folds lowercase letters onto uppercase ones:

```
$ sort -u -k 1f -k 1 short
Apple
apple
Pear
pear
```

split

Divides a file into sections

split [options] [filename [prefix]]

The split utility breaks its input into 1000-line sections named **xaa, xab, xac,** and so on. The last section may be shorter. Options can change the sizes of the sections and lengths of the names.

Arguments   The *filename* is the pathname of the file that split processes. If you do not specify an argument or if you specify a hyphen (–) instead of the *filename*, split reads from standard input. The *prefix* is one or more characters that split uses to prefix the names of the files it creates. The default prefix is **x**.

Options   Accepts the common options described on page 587.

––suffix-length=*len*

–a *len*
Specifies that the filename suffix is *len* characters long (the default is 2).

––bytes=*n[u]*   **–b** *n[u]*
Breaks the input into files that are *n* bytes long. The *u* is an optional unit of measure that can be **b** (512-byte blocks), **k** (kilobyte or 1,024-byte blocks), or **m** (megabyte or 1,048,576-byte blocks). If you include the unit of measure, split counts by this unit in place of bytes.

––numeric-suffixes

–d   Specifies numeric suffixes instead of alphabetic suffixes.

––lines=*num*   **–l** *num*
Breaks the input into files that are *num* lines long (the default is 1,000).

Discussion   By default split names the first file it creates **xaa**. The **x** is the default prefix. You can change the prefix with the *prefix* argument on the command line. You can change the number of characters in each filename following the prefix with the **––suffix-length** option.

Examples   By default split breaks a file into 1,000-line sections with the names **xaa, xab, xac,** and so on. The wc utility with the **–l** option shows the number of lines in each file. The last file, **xar,** is smaller than the rest.

```
$ split /etc/termcap
$ wc -l *
  1000 xaa
  1000 xab
  1000 xac
...
  1000 xap
  1000 xaq
   103 xar
17103 total
```

The next example uses the *prefix* argument to specify a filename prefix of **SEC** and uses **--suffix-length** to change the number of letters in the filename suffix to 3:

```
$ split --suffix-length=3 /etc/termcap SEC
$ ls
SECaaa  SECaac  SECaae  SECaag  SECaai  SECaak  SECaam  SECaao  SECaaq
SECaab  SECaad  SECaaf  SECaah  SECaaj  SECaal  SECaan  SECaap  SECaar
```

ssh

Securely executes commands on a remote system

ssh [option] [user@]host [command-line]

The ssh utility runs ***command-line*** on ***host*** by starting a shell on the remote system or logs you in on ***host***. The ssh utility, which can replace rsh and rlogin, provides secure, encrypted communication between two systems on an insecure network.

Arguments   The ***host*** is the system that you want to log in or run a command on. Unless you have one of several kinds of authentication established, ssh prompts you for a username and password for the remote system. When ssh is able to log in automatically, it logs in as the user running the ssh command or as ***user*** if ***user@*** appears on the ssh command line.

The ***command-line*** runs on the remote system. Without ***command-line***, ssh logs you in on the remote system. You must quote special characters in ***command-line*** if you do not want them expanded by the local shell.

Options   **–f**   (**not foreground**) Sends ssh to the background after asking for a password and before executing ***command-line***. This option is useful when you want to run the ***command-line*** in the background but must supply a password. Its use implies **–n**.

–l *user*
    (**login**) Attempts to log in as *user*. This option is equivalent to using *user@* on the command line.

–n   (**null**) Redirects standard input to ssh to come from **/dev/null**. See **–f**.

–p *port*
    Connects to port ***port*** on the remote host.

–q   (**quiet**) Suppresses warning and diagnostic messages.

–t   (**tty**) Allocates a pseudo-tty to the ssh process on the remote system. Without this option, when you run a command on a remote system, ssh does not allocate a tty (terminal) to the process. Instead, ssh attaches standard input and standard output of the remote process to the ssh session—that is, normally, but not always, what you want. This option forces ssh to allocate a tty on the remote system so that programs that require a tty will work.

–v   (**verbose**) Displays debugging messages about the connection and transfer. This option is useful if things are not going as expected.

–x   (**X11**) Turns off X11 forwarding.

–X (X11) Turns on X11 forwarding. You may not need this option—X11 forwarding may be turned on in a configuration file.

Notes

OpenSSH Using public-key encryption, OpenSSH provides two levels of authentication: server and client/user. First, the client (ssh or scp) verifies that it is connected to the correct server and OpenSSH encrypts communication between the client and server. Second, once a secure, encrypted connection has been established, OpenSSH confirms that the user is authorized to log in on or copy files from/to the server. Once the system and user have been verified, OpenSSH allows different services to pass through the connection. These services include interactive shell sessions (ssh), remote command execution (ssh and scp), X11 client/server connections, and TCP/IP port tunneling.

Message on initial connection to a server When you connect to an OpenSSH server for the first time, the OpenSSH client prompts you to confirm that you are connected to the correct system. This checking can help prevent a person-in-the-middle attack.

```
The authenticity of host 'grape (192.168.0.3)' can't be established.
RSA key fingerprint is c9:03:c1:9d:c2:91:55:50:e8:19:2b:f4:36:ef:73:78.
Are you sure you want to continue connecting (yes/no)? yes
Warning: Permanently added 'grape,192.168.0.3' (RSA) to the list of
known hosts.
```

Before you respond to the preceding query, verify that you are logging in on the correct system and not an imposter. If you are not sure, a telephone call to someone who logs in on that system locally can verify that you are on the intended system. When you answer yes (you must spell it out), the client appends the server's public host key to the user's ~/.ssh/known_hosts file on the local system, creating the ~/.ssh directory if necessary. So that it can keep track of which line in known_hosts applies to which server, OpenSSH prepends the name of the server and the server's IP address to the line. Subsequently, when you use OpenSSH to connect to that server, the client verifies that it is connected to the correct server by comparing this key to the one supplied by the server.

Examples

In the first example, Alex uses ssh to display a list of the files in his home directory on kudos:

```
$ ssh kudos ls
alex@kudos's password:
Work
code
graphs
reports
```

Next the output of the previous command is redirected to the file **kudos_ls**. Because the redirection character (>) is not escaped, it is interpreted by the local shell, and the file **kudos_ls** is created on the local system.

```
$ ssh kudos ls > kudos_ls
alex@kudos's password:
$ cat kudos_ls
Work
code
graphs
reports
```

The next example quotes the entire command that will run on the remote system. As a result, the local shell does not interpret the redirection character (>) but rather passes it to the remote shell. The file **kudos.ls** is created on the remote system (**kudos**), as shown by ls run on **kudos**:

```
$ ssh kudos "ls > kudos.ls"
alex@kudos's password:
$ ssh kudos ls
alex@kudos's password:
Work
code
graphs
kudos.ls
reports
```

The next command does not quote the pipe symbol (|). As a result the pipe is interpreted by the local shell, which sends the output of the remote ls to standard input of less on the local system:

```
$ ssh kudos ls | less
```

Next ssh executes a series of commands, connected with pipes, on a remote system. The commands are enclosed within single quotation marks so that the local shell does not interpret the pipe symbols and all the commands are run on the remote system.

```
$ ssh kudos 'ps -ef | grep nmbd | grep -v grep | cut -c10-15 |xargs kill -1'
```

The output of ps is piped through grep, which passes all lines containing the string **nmbd** to another invocation of grep. The second grep passes all lines *not* containing the string **grep** to cut (page 627). The cut utility extracts the process ID numbers and passes them to xargs (page 821), which kills the listed processes with a HUP signal (**kill –1**).

In the following example, ssh without *command-line* logs in on the remote system. Here Alex has used **watson@kudos** to log in on **kudos** as **watson**:

```
$ ssh watson@kudos
watson@kudos's password:
Last login: Sat Sep 17 06:51:59 from bravo
$ hostname
kudos
$ exit
```

Alex now decides to change the password for his **watson** login on **kudos**.

```
$ ssh watson@kudos passwd
watson@kudos's password:
(current) UNIX password: por
```

Alex stops as soon as he sees passwd (running on **kudos**) displaying his password: He knows that something is wrong. For the passwd to work, it must run with a tty (terminal) so that it can turn off character echo (**stty –echo**) and thus not display passwords as the user enters them. The **–t** option solves the problem by associating a pseudo-tty with the process running passwd on the remote system:

```
$ ssh -t watson@kudos passwd
watson@kudos's password:
Changing password for watson
(current) UNIX password:
New UNIX password:
Retype new UNIX password:
passwd: all authentication tokens updated successfully
Connection to kudos closed.
$
```

The **–t** option is also useful when you are running a program that uses a character-based/pseudographical interface.

The following example uses tar (page 786) to create an archive file of the contents of the working directory hierarchy. The **f –** option causes tar to send its output to standard output. A pipe sends the output of tar running on the local system, via ssh, to dd (page 633) running on the remote system.

```
$ cat buwd
#! /bin/bash
# back up the working directory to the user's
# home directory on the remote system specified
# by $machine

# remote system:
machine=speedy

dir=$(basename $(pwd))
filename=$$.$dir.tar

echo Backing up $(pwd) to your home directory on $machine
tar -cf - . | ssh $machine "dd obs=256k of=$filename"
echo done. Name of file on $machine is $filename
```

strings

Displays strings of printable characters

strings [options] file-list

The strings utility displays strings of printable characters from object and other nontext files.

Arguments   The *file-list* is a list of files that strings processes.

Options

--all   **-a**   Processes whole files. Without this option strings processes only the initialized and loaded parts of an object file.

--bytes=*min*   -*min*
Displays strings of characters that are at least *min* characters long (the default is 4).

--print-file-name   **-f**   Precedes each string with the name of the file that the string comes from.

Discussion   The strings utility can help you determine the contents of nontext files. One application for strings is determining the owner of files in a **lost+found** directory.

Examples   The following example displays the strings of four or more printable characters in the executable file for the man utility. If you did not know what this file was, these strings could help you determine that it was the man executable.

```
$ strings /usr/bin/man
...
man: internal error - cannot find message %d
/unsafe/
my_xsprintf called with %s
Error parsing config file
No manual entry for %s
using %s as pager
%s, version %s
found man directory %s
found manpath map %s --> %s
corresponding catdir is %s
Line too long in config file
section: %s
...
```

stty

Displays or sets terminal parameters

stty [options] [arguments]

Without any arguments, stty displays certain parameters affecting the operation of the terminal/terminal emulator. For a list of some of these parameters and an explanation of each, see "Arguments." The arguments establish or change parameters.

Options

Accepts the common options described on page 587.

--all   –a   Reports on all parameters. This option does not accept arguments.

--file=/dev/*device*   –F /dev/*device*

Affects ***device***. Without this option stty affects the device attached to standard input. You can change the characteristics of a device only if you own its device file or if you are Superuser.

--save   –g   Generates a report of the current settings in a format you can use as arguments to another stty command. This option does not accept arguments.

Arguments

The arguments to stty specify which terminal parameters stty is to alter. Turn on each of the parameters that is preceded by an optional hyphen (indicated in the following list as [–]) by specifying the parameter without the hyphen. Turn it off by using the hyphen. Unless specified otherwise, this section describes the parameters in their *on* states.

Special Keys and Characteristics

columns *n*   Sets the line width to *n* columns.

ek   (**erase kill**) Sets the erase and line kill keys to their default values. Many systems use DELETE and CONTROL-U as the defaults.

erase *x*   Sets the erase key to *x*. To specify a control character, precede *x* with CONTROL-V (for example, use CONTROL-V CONTROL-H to indicate CONTROL-H) or use the notation **^h**, where **^** is a caret (SHIFT 6 on most keyboards).

intr *x*   Sets the interrupt key to *x*. See **erase *x*** for conventions.

kill *x*   Sets the line kill key to *x*. See **erase *x*** for conventions.

rows *n*   Sets the number of screen rows to *n*.

sane   Sets the terminal parameters to values that are usually acceptable. The **sane** argument is useful when several stty parameters have changed, making it difficult to use the terminal to run stty to set things right. If **sane** does not appear to work, try entering the following characters:

CONTROL-J **stty sane** CONTROL-J

susp *x* (**suspend**) Sets the suspend (terminal stop) key to *x*. See **erase** *x* for conventions.

werase *x* (**word erase**) Sets the word erase key to *x*. See **erase** *x* for conventions.

Modes of Data Transmission

[–]cooked See **raw**.

[–]cstopb (**stop bits**) Selects two stop bits (**–cstopb** specifies one stop bit).

[–]parenb (**parity enable**) Enables parity on input and output. When you specify **–parenb**, the system does not use or expect a parity bit when communicating with the terminal.

[–]parodd (**parity odd**) Selects odd parity (**–parodd** selects even parity).

[–]raw The normal state is **–raw**. When the system reads input in its raw form, it does not interpret the following special characters: erase (usually DELETE), line kill (usually CONTROL-U), interrupt execution (CONTROL-C), and EOF (CONTROL-D). In addition, the system does not use parity bits. Reflecting the humor that is typical of Linux's heritage, you can specify **–raw** as **cooked**.

Treatment of Characters

[–]echo Echoes characters as they are typed (full-duplex operation). If a terminal is half-duplex and displays two characters for each one it should display, turn the **echo** parameter off (**–echo**). Use **–echo** when the user is entering passwords.

[–]echoe (**echo erase**) The normal setting is **echoe**, which causes the kernel to echo the character sequence BACKSPACE SPACE BACKSPACE when you use the erase key to delete a character. The effect is to move the cursor backward across the line, removing characters as you delete them.

[–]echoke (**echo kill erase**) The normal setting is **echoke**. When you use the kill character to delete a line while this option is set, all characters back to the prompt are erased on the current line. When this option is negated, pressing the kill key moves the cursor to the beginning of the next line.

[–]echoprt (**echo print**) The normal setting is **–echoprt**, which causes characters to disappear as you erase them. When you set **echoprt**, characters that you erase are displayed between a backslash (\) and a slash (/). For example, if you type the word **sort** and then erase it by pressing BACKSPACE four times, Linux displays **sort\tros/** when **echoprt** is set. Also, if you use the kill character to delete the entire line, having **echoprt** set causes the entire line to be displayed as if you had BACKSPACEd to the beginning of the line.

[–]lcase   For uppercase-only terminals, translates all uppercase characters into lowercase as they are entered (also [–]**LCASE**).

[–]nl   Accepts only a NEWLINE character as a line terminator. With **–nl** in effect, the system accepts a RETURN character from the terminal as a NEWLINE but sends a RETURN followed by a NEWLINE to the terminal in place of a NEWLINE.

[–]tabs   Transmits each TAB character to the terminal as a TAB character. When **tabs** is turned off (**–tabs**), the kernel translates each TAB character into the appropriate number of SPACEs and transmits them to the terminal (also [–]**tab3**).

Job Control Parameters

[–]tostop   Stops background jobs if they attempt to send output to the terminal (**–tostop** allows background jobs to send output to the terminal).

Notes

The name stty is an abbreviation for *set teletypewriter,* or *set tty* (page 807), the first terminal that UNIX was run on. Today stty is commonly thought of as *set terminal.*

The shells retain some control over standard input when you use them interactively. As a consequence a number of the options available with stty appear to have no effect. For example, the command **stty –echo** appears to have no effect under tcsh:

```
tcsh $ stty -echo
tcsh $ date
Fri Feb 18 21:21:14 PST 2005
```

While **stty –echo** does work when you are using bash interactively, **stty –echoe** does not. However, you can still use these options to affect shell scripts and other utilities.

```
$ cat testit
#!/bin/bash
stty -echo
echo -n "Enter a value: "
read a
echo
echo "You entered: $a"
stty echo

$ testit
Enter a value:
You entered: 77
```

In the preceding example, the kernel does not display the user's response to the **Enter a value:** prompt. The value is retained by the **a** variable and is displayed by the **echo "You entered: $a"** statement.

Examples   The first example shows that stty without any arguments displays several terminal operation parameters. (Your system may display more or different parameters.) The character following the **erase =** is the erase key. A ^ preceding a character indicates a CONTROL key. In the example the erase key is set to CONTROL-H. If stty does not display the erase character, it is set to its default value of DELETE. If you do not see a kill character, it is set to its default of ^U.

```
$ stty
speed 38400 baud; line = 0;
erase = ^H;
```

Next the **ek** argument returns the erase and line kill keys to their default values:

```
$ stty ek
```

The next display verifies the change. The stty utility does not display either the erase character or the line kill character, indicating that both are set to their default values:

```
$ stty
speed 38400 baud; line = 0;
```

The next example sets the erase key to CONTROL-H. The CONTROL-V quotes the CONTROL-H so that the shell does not interpret it and it is passed to stty:

```
$ stty erase CONTROL-V CONTROL-H
$ stty
speed 38400 baud; line = 0;
erase = ^H;
```

Next stty sets the line kill key to CONTROL-X. This time the user entered a caret (^) followed by an **x** to represent CONTROL-X. You can use either a lowercase or uppercase letter.

```
$ stty kill ^X
$ stty
speed 38400 baud; line = 0;
erase = ^H; kill = ^X;
```

Now stty changes the interrupt key to CONTROL-C:

```
$ stty intr CONTROL-V CONTROL-C
```

In the following example, stty turns off TABs so that the appropriate number of SPACES is sent to the terminal in place of a TAB. Use this command if a terminal does not automatically expand TABs.

```
$ stty -tabs
```

If you log in and everything appears on the terminal in uppercase letters, give the following command and then check the CAPS LOCK key. If it is set, turn it off:

```
$ STTY -LCASE
```

Turn on **lcase** if you are using a very old terminal that cannot display lowercase characters.

Although no one usually changes the suspend key from its default of CONTROL-Z, you can. Give the following command to change the suspend key to CONTROL-T:

```
$ stty susp ^T
```

tail

Displays the last part (tail) of a file

tail [options] [file-list]

The tail utility displays the last part, or end, of a file.

Arguments The *file-list* is a list of pathnames of the files that tail displays. When you specify more than one file, tail displays the filename of each file before displaying the lines of the file. If you do not specify an argument or if you specify a hyphen (–) instead of a filename, tail reads from standard input.

Options Accepts the common options described on page 587.

––bytes=*[+]n[u]*   **–c** *[+]n[u]*

Counts by bytes (characters) instead of lines. The *n* is an integer that specifies the number of bytes. Thus the command **tail –c 5** displays the last five bytes of a file. The *u* is an optional unit of measure that can be **b** (512-byte blocks), **k** (kilobyte or 1,024-byte blocks), or **m** (megabyte or 1,048,576-byte blocks). If you include the unit of measure, tail counts by this unit instead of by bytes.

If you put a plus sign (**+**) in front of *n*, tail counts from the start of the file instead of the end. The tail utility still *displays to the end* of the file, even though it *starts counting* from the beginning. Thus **tail –c +5** causes tail to display from the fifth character through the end of the file.

––follow   **–f**   After copying the last line of the file, tail enters an endless loop, waiting and copying additional lines from the file if the file grows. If you specify multiple files in *file-list* with this option, tail includes a new header each time it displays output from a different file so that you know which file is being added to. This option is useful for tracking the progress of a process that is running in the background and sending its output to a file. The tail utility continues to wait indefinitely, so you must use the interrupt key to terminate it. See also the **–s** option.

––lines=*[+]n[u]*   **–n** *[+]n[u]*

Counts by lines (the default). The *n* is an integer that specifies the number of lines. The *u* is an optional unit of measure; see the **––bytes** option for an explanation of its use. Although it is not documented, you can use **±*n*** to specify a number of lines without using this option.

If you put a plus sign (**+**) in front of *n*, tail counts from the start of the file instead of the end. The tail utility still *displays to the end* of the file, even though it *starts counting* from the beginning. Thus **tail –n +5** causes tail to display from the fifth line through the last line of the file.

   --quiet **-q** Suppresses header information when you specify multiple files in *file-list*.

--sleep-interval=*n* **-s** *n*

      When used with **-f**, causes tail to sleep for *n* seconds between checks for additional output.

Notes

The tail utility displays the last ten lines of its input by default.

Examples

The examples are based on the **eleven** file:

```
$ cat eleven
line one
line two
line three
line four
line five
line six
line seven
line eight
line nine
line ten
line eleven
```

First tail displays the last ten lines of the **eleven** file (no options):

```
$ tail eleven
line two
line three
line four
line five
line six
line seven
line eight
line nine
line ten
line eleven
```

Next it displays the last three lines (**--lines 3**) of the file:

```
$ tail --lines 3 eleven
line nine
line ten
line eleven
```

The following example displays the file starting at line 8 (**+8**):

```
$ tail -n +8 eleven
line eight
line nine
line ten
line eleven
```

The next example displays the last six characters in the file (**--bytes 6**). Only five characters are evident (**leven**); the sixth is a NEWLINE.

```
$ tail --bytes 6 eleven
leven
```

The final example demonstrates the **–f** option. Here tail tracks the output of a make command, which is being sent to the file **accounts.out**:

```
$ make accounts > accounts.out &
$ tail -f accounts.out
        cc -c trans.c
        cc -c reports.c
...
CONTROL-C
$
```

In the preceding example, using tail with **–f** has the same effect as running make in the foreground and letting its output go to the terminal. However, using tail offers some advantages. First, the output of make is saved in a file. (The output would not be saved if you let it go to the terminal.) Second, if you decide to do something else while make is running, you can kill tail and the screen will be free for you to use while make continues in the background. When you are running a large job, such as compiling a large program, you can use tail with the **–f** option to check on its progress periodically.

tar

Stores or retrieves files to/from an archive file

tar option [modifiers] [file-list]

The tar (tape archive) utility creates, adds to, lists, and retrieves files from an archive file.

Arguments

The *file-list* is a list of pathnames of the files that tar archives or extracts.

Options

Use only one of the following options to indicate what type of action you want tar to take. You can alter the action of the option by following it with one or more modifiers.

––create   –c Creates an archive. This option stores the files named in *file-list* in a new archive. If the archive already exists, it is destroyed before the new archive is created. If a *file-list* argument is a directory, tar recursively copies the files within the directory into the archive. Without the **––file** option, the archive is sent to standard output.

––compare   –d (**diff**) Compares an archive with the corresponding disk files and reports on the differences.

––help Displays a list of options and modifiers, with short descriptions of each.

––append   –r Writes the files named in *file-list* to the end of the archive. This option leaves files that are already in the archive intact, so duplicate copies of files may appear in the archive after tar finishes. When tar extracts the files, the most recent copy of a file in the archive is the one that ends up on the disk.

––list   –t (**table of contents**) Without a *file-list*, this option produces a table of contents listing all files in an archive. With a *file-list*, it displays the name of each file in the *file-list* each time it occurs in the archive. You can use this option with the **––verbose** option to display detailed information about each file in an archive.

––update   –u Adds the files from *file-list* if they are not already in the archive or if they have been modified since they were last written to the archive. Because of the additional checking required, tar runs more slowly when you specify this option.

––extract   –x Extracts *file-list* from the archive and writes it to the disk. Overwrites existing files with the same names. Without a *file-list* this option extracts all files from the archive. If the *file-list* includes a directory, tar extracts that directory and all the files below it. The tar utility attempts to keep the owner, modification time, and access privileges the same as those of the original file. If tar reads the same file more than once, the last version read will appear on the disk when tar is finished.

Modifiers

You can specify one or more modifiers following an option. If you use the single-character form of the modifier, a leading hyphen is not required. In general, it is a good practice to use the hyphen unless you combine the modifier with other single-character modifiers.

If a modifier takes an argument, that modifier must be the last one in a group. For example, the arguments are arranged legally in the following tar command:

```
$ tar -cb 10 -f /dev/ftape memos
```

Conversely, the following tar command generates an error:

```
$ tar -cbf 10 /dev/ftape memos
tar: f: Invalid blocking factor
Try 'tar --help' for more information.
```

The error occurs because the –b modifier takes an argument but is not the last modifier in a group.

--blocking-factor=*n*
–b *n*

Uses *n* as the blocking factor for creating an archive. Use this option only when tar is creating an archive directly to a tape. (When tar reads a tape archive, it automatically determines the blocking factor.) The value of *n* is the number of 512-byte blocks to write as a single block on the tape.

--directory=*dir*   –C *dir*

Changes the working directory to *dir* before processing.

--checkpoint

Displays periodic messages. This option lets you know tar is running without displaying all the --verbose messages.

--file=*filename*   –f *filename*

Uses *filename* as the name of the file (device) to hold the archive. The *filename* can be the name of an ordinary file or a device (such as a tape drive). You can use a hyphen (–) instead of the *filename* to refer to standard input when creating an archive and to standard output when extracting files from an archive. The following two commands are equivalent ways of creating a compressed archive of the files under the /home directory on /dev/st0:

```
$ tar -zcf /dev/st0 /home
$ tar -cf - /home | gzip > /dev/st0
```

--dereference   –h   Archives the files that symbolic links point to, not the links themselves.

--exclude=*file*

Does not process the file named *file*. If *file* is a directory, no files or directories within that directory are processed. The *file* can be an ambiguous file reference; quote special characters as needed.

--ignore-failed-read

When creating an archive, tar normally quits with a nonzero exit status if any of the files in *file-list* is unreadable. This option causes tar to continue processing, skipping unreadable files.

--bzip   –j   Uses bzip2 (page 56) to compress/decompress files when creating an archive and extracting files from an archive.

--one-file-system   –l   (lowercase "l") When a directory name appears in *file-list* while creating an archive, tar recursively processes the files and directories below the named directory. With this option tar stays in the filesystem that contains the named directory and does not process directories in other filesystems.

**--tape–length=*n*   –L *n*   Asks for a new tape after writing *n* * 1,024 bytes to the current tape. This feature is useful when you are building archives that are too big to fit on a single tape.

--touch   –m   Sets the modification time of extracted files to the time of extraction. Without this option tar attempts to maintain the modification time of the original file.

--absolute-paths   –P   The default behavior of tar is to force all pathnames to be relative paths by stripping leading slashes. This option disables this feature, so absolute pathnames remain as absolute paths.

--sparse   –S   Linux allows you to have sparse files—that is, large, mostly empty files—on disk. The empty sections of sparse files do not take up any disk space. When tar copies a sparse file out of an archive, it normally expands the file to its full size. As a result, when you restore a sparse file from a tar backup, the file takes up its full space and may no longer fit in the same disk space as the original. This option causes tar to handle sparse files efficiently so that they do not take up unnecessary space either in the archive or when they are extracted.

--verbose   –v   Lists each file as tar reads or writes it. When combined with the –t option, –v causes tar to display a more detailed listing of the files in the archive, showing their ownership, permissions, size, and other information.

--interactive *or*   **–w**   Asks you for confirmation before reading or writing each file. Respond with y
--confirmation   if you want tar to take the action. Any other response causes tar not to take the action.

--exclude-from=*filename*
**   –X *filename***
Similar to the **--exclude** option except that *filename* specifies a file that contains a list of files to exclude from processing. Each file listed in *filename* must appear on a separate line.

	--gzip *or* **--gunzip**	**-z**	Causes tar to use gzip to compress an archive while it is being created and to decompress an archive when extracting files from it. This option also works to extract files from archives that have been compressed with the compress utility.
	--compress *or* **--uncompress**	**-Z**	Uses compress when creating an archive and uncompress when extracting files from an archive.

Notes

The **--help** option displays all the tar options and modifiers. The info page on tar provides extensive information, including a tutorial.

You can use ambiguous file references in *file-list* when you create an archive but not when you extract files from an archive.

The name of a directory file within the *file-list* references all files and subdirectories within that directory.

The file that tar sends its output to by default is compilation specific; typically it goes to standard output. Use the **-f** option to specify a different filename or device to hold the archive.

When you create an archive using a simple filename in *file-list,* the file appears in the working directory when you extract it. If you use a relative pathname when you create an archive, the file appears with that relative pathname, starting from the working directory when you extract it. If you use the **-P** option and an absolute pathname when you create an archive, tar extracts the file with the same pathname.

Examples

The following example makes a copy of the **/home/alex** directory hierarchy on a floppy tape device. The **v** modifier causes the command to list the files it writes to the tape. This command erases anything that was already on the tape. The message from tar explains that the default action is to store all pathnames as relative paths instead of absolute paths, thereby allowing you to extract the files into a different directory on the disk.

```
$ tar -cvf /dev/ftape /home/alex
tar: Removing leading '/' from member names.
home/alex/
home/alex/.bash_history
home/alex/.bash_profile
...
```

In the next example, the same directory is saved on the tape device **/dev/st0** with a blocking factor of 100. Without the **v** modifier, tar does not display the list of files it is writing to the tape. The command runs in the background and displays any messages after the shell issues a new prompt.

```
$ tar -cb 100 -f /dev/st0 /home/alex &
[1] 4298
$ tar: Removing leading '/' from member names.
```

The next command displays the table of contents of the archive on tape device /dev/ftape:

```
$ tar -tvf /dev/ftape
drwxrwxrwx alex/group          0 Jun 30 21:39 2004 home/alex/
-rw-r--r-- alex/group        678 Aug  6 14:12 2005 home/alex/.bash_history
-rw-r--r-- alex/group        571 Aug  6 14:06 2005 home/alex/.bash_profile
drwx------ alex/group          0 Nov  6 22:34 2005 home/alex/mail/
-rw------- alex/group       2799 Nov  6 22:34 2005 home/alex/mail/sent-mail
...
```

In the last example, Alex creates a gzipped tar archive in **/tmp/alex.tgz**. This approach is a popular way to bundle files that you want to transfer over a network or otherwise share with others. Ending a filename with **.tgz** is one convention for identifying gzipped tar archives. Another convention is to end the filename with **.tar.z**.

```
$ tar -czf /tmp/alex.tgz literature
```

The next command lists the files in the compressed archive **alex.tgz**:

```
$ tar -tzvf /tmp/alex.tgz
...
```

tee

Copies standard input to standard output and one or more files

tee [options] file-list

The tee utility copies standard input to standard output *and* to one or more files.

Arguments   The *file-list* is a list of the pathnames of files that receive output from tee.

Options   Without any options, tee overwrites the output files if they exist and responds to interrupts. If a file in *file-list* does not exist, tee creates it.

--append   –a   Appends output to existing files rather than overwriting them.

--ignore-interrupts

–i   Causes tee not to respond to interrupts.

Examples   In the following example, a pipe sends the output from make to tee, which copies it to standard output and the file **accounts.out**. The copy that goes to standard output appears on the screen. The cat utility displays the copy that was sent to the file:

```
$ make accounts | tee accounts.out
        cc -c trans.c
        cc -c reports.c
...
$ cat accounts.out
        cc -c trans.c
        cc -c reports.c
...
```

Refer to page 785 for a similar example that uses **tail –f** rather than tee.

telnet

Connects to a remote system over a network

telnet [options] [remote-system]

The telnet utility implements the TELNET protocol to connect to a remote system over a network.

telnet **is not secure**

security   The telnet utility is not secure. It sends your username and password over the network as cleartext, which is not a secure practice. Use ssh (page 773) when it is available.

Arguments   The *remote-system* is the name or IP address of the remote system that telnet connects to. When you do not specify a *remote-system,* telnet works interactively and prompts you to enter one of the commands described in this section.

Options   –e *c*

(**escape**) Changes the escape character from CONTROL-] to the character *c*.

–K   Prevents automatic login.

–l *username*

Attempts an automatic login on the remote system using *username*. If the remote system understands how to handle automatic login with telnet, you are prompted for a password.

Discussion   After telnet connects to a remote system, you can put telnet in command mode by typing the escape character (usually CONTROL-]). A remote system should report the escape character it recognizes. To leave command mode, type RETURN on a line by itself.

In command mode telnet displays the **telnet>** prompt. You can use the following commands in command mode:

? (**help**) Displays a list of commands recognized by the telnet utility on the local system.

close   Closes the connection to the remote system. If you specified the name of a system on the command line when you started telnet, **close** has the same effect as **quit**: The telnet program quits, and the shell displays a prompt. If you used the **open** command instead of specifying a remote system on the command line, **close** returns telnet to command mode.

logout   Logs you off of the remote system; similar to **close**.

open *remote-computer*

> If you did not specify a remote system on the command line or if the attempt to connect to the system failed, you can specify the name of a remote system interactively with the **open** command.

quit   Quits the telnet session.

z   Suspends the telnet session. When you suspend a session, you return to the login shell on the local system. To resume the suspended telnet session, type **fg** at a shell prompt.

Notes

Many computers, including non-Linux systems, support the TELNET protocol. The telnet utility is a user interface to this protocol for Linux systems that allows you to connect to many different types of systems. Although you typically use telnet to log in, the remote computer may offer other services through telnet, such as access to special databases.

Examples

In the following example, the user connects to the remote system named **bravo**. After running a few commands, the user escapes to command mode and uses the **z** command to suspend the telnet session so as to run a few commands on the local system. The user gives an **fg** command to the shell to resume using telnet. The **logout** command on the remote system ends the telnet session, and the local shell displays a prompt.

```
kudos% telnet bravo
Trying 192.168.0.55 ...
Connected to bravo.
Escape character is '^]'.

Fedora Core Release 2 (Tettnang)
Kernel 2.6.5-1.358 on an i686

login: watson
Password:
Last login: Wed Jul 31 10:37:16 from kudos
bravo $
...
bravo $CONTROL-]
telnet> z

[1]+ Stopped   telnet bravo
kudos $
...
kudos $fg
telnet bravo

bravo$ logout
Connection closed by foreign host.
kudos $
```

test

Evaluates an expression

*test **expression***
*[**expression**]*

The test utility evaluates an expression and returns a condition code indicating that the expression is either *true* (0) or *false* (not 0). You can place brackets ([]) around the expression instead of using the word **test** (second format).

Arguments   The *expression* contains one or more criteria (see the following list) that test evaluates. A **−a** separating two criteria is a Boolean AND operator: Both criteria must be *true* for test to return a condition code of *true*. A **−o** is a Boolean OR operator. When **−o** separates two criteria, one or the other (or both) of the criteria must be *true* for test to return a condition code of *true*.

You can negate any criterion by preceding it with an exclamation point (!). You can group criteria with parentheses. If there are no parentheses, **−a** takes precedence over **−o**, and test evaluates operators of equal precedence from left to right.

Within the ***expression*** you must quote special characters, such as parentheses, so that the shell does not interpret them but rather passes them to test.

Because each element, such as a criterion, string, or variable within the **expression**, is a separate argument, you must separate each element from other elements with a SPACE. Table V-25 lists the criteria you can use within the ***expression***. Table V-26 lists test's relational operators.

table V-25	Criteria
Criterion	**Meaning**
string	*True* if ***string*** is not a null string.
−n *string*	*True* if ***string*** has a length greater than zero.
−z *string*	*True* if ***string*** has a length of zero.
string1 = *string2*	*True* if ***string1*** is equal to ***string2***.
string1 != *string2*	*True* if ***string1*** is not equal to ***string2***.
int1 relop int2	*True* if integer ***int1*** has the specified algebraic relationship to integer ***int2***. The ***relop*** is a relational operator from Table V-26. As a special case, **−l** *string*, which gives the length of ***string***, may be used for ***int1*** or ***int2***.
file1 **−ef** *file2*	*True* if ***file1*** and ***file2*** have the same device and inode numbers.

table V-25	Criteria (continued)
file1 −nt *file2*	*True* if *file1* was modified after *file2* (the modification time of *file1* is newer than that of *file2*).
file1 −ot *file2*	*True* if *file1* was modified before *file2* (the modification time of *file1* is older than that of *file2*).
−b *filename*	*True* if the file named *filename* exists and is a block special file.
−c *filename*	*True* if the file named *filename* exists and is a character special file.
−d *filename*	*True* if the file named *filename* exists and is a directory.
−e *filename*	*True* if the file named *filename* exists.
−f *filename*	*True* if the file named *filename* exists and is an ordinary file.
−g *filename*	*True* if the file named *filename* exists and its setgid bit (page 94) is set.
−G *filename*	*True* if the file named *filename* exists and is associated with the group that is the primary group of the user running the command (same effective group ID).
−k *filename*	*True* if the file named *filename* exists and its sticky bit (page 903) is set.
−L *filename*	*True* if the file named *filename* exists and is a symbolic link.
−O *filename*	*True* if the file named *filename* exists and is owned by the user running the command (same effective user ID).
−p *filename*	*True* if the file named *filename* exists and is a named pipe.
−r *filename*	*True* if the file named *filename* exists and you have read permission for it.
−s *filename*	*True* if the file named *filename* exists and contains information (has a size greater than 0 bytes).
−t *file-descriptor*	*True* if *file-descriptor* is associated with the screen/keyboard. The *file-descriptor* for standard input is 0, for standard output is 1, and for standard error is 2.
−u *filename*	*True* if the file named *filename* exists and its setuid bit (page 94) is set.
−w *filename*	*True* if the file named *filename* exists and you have write permission for it.
−x *filename*	*True* if the file named *filename* exists and you have execute permission for it.

table V-26	Relational operators
Relop	**Meaning**
−eq	Equal to
−ge	Greater than or equal to
−gt	Greater than

table V-26	Relational operators (continued)
–le	Less than or equal to
–lt	Less than
–ne	Not equal to

Notes   The test command is built into the Bourne Again and TC Shells.

Examples   The following examples demonstrate the use of the test utility in Bourne Again Shell scripts. Although test works from a command line, it is more commonly employed in shell scripts to test input or verify access to a file.

The first example prompts the user, reads a line of input into a variable, and uses the synonym for test, [], to see whether the user entered yes:

```
$ cat user_in
echo -n "Input yes or no: "
read user_input
if [ "$user_input" = "yes" ]
    then
        echo You input yes.
fi
```

The next example prompts for a filename and then uses the synonym for test, [], to see whether the user has read access permission (–r) for the file *and* (–a) whether the file contains information (–s):

```
$ cat validate
echo -n "Enter filename: "
read filename
if [ -r "$filename" -a -s "$filename" ]
    then
        echo File $filename exists and contains information.
        echo You have read access permission to the file.
fi
```

The –t 1 criterion checks whether the process running test is sending standard output to the screen. If it is, the test utility returns a value of *true* (0). The shell stores the exit status of the last command it ran in the $? variable. The following script tests whether its output is going to a terminal:

```
$ cat term
test -t 1
echo "This program is (=0) or is not (=1)
sending its output to a terminal:" $?
```

First **term** is run with the output going to the terminal:

```
$ term
This program is (=0) or is not (=1)
sending its output to a terminal: 0
```

The next example runs **term** and redirects the output to a file. The contents of the file **temp** show that test returned 1, indicating that its output was not going to a terminal.

```
$ term > temp
$ cat temp
This program is (=0) or is not (=1)
sending its output to a terminal: 1
```

top

Dynamically displays process status

top [options]

The top utility displays information about the status of the local system including information about current processes.

Options

Although top does not require the use of hyphens with options, it is a good idea to include them for clarity and consistency with other utilities. You can cause top to run as though you had specified any of the options by giving commands to the utility while it is running. See "Discussion" for more information.

–d *ss.tt*

(**delay**) Specifies *ss.tt* as the number of seconds and tenths of seconds of delay from one display update to the next. The default is 3 seconds.

–i Ignores idle and zombie processes. (A zombie process is one without a parent.)

–n *n*

(**number**) Specifies the number of iterations: top updates the display *n* times and exits.

–p *n*

(PID) Monitors the process with a PID of *n*. You can use this option up to 20 times on a command line or specify *n* as a comma-separated list of up to 20 PID numbers.

–s (**secure**) Runs top in secure mode, restricting commands that you can use while top is running to those that pose less security risk.

–S (**sum**) Causes top to run in cumulative mode. In cumulative mode, the CPU times reported for processes include CPU times accumulated by child processes that are now dead.

Discussion

The first few lines that top displays summarize the status of the local system. You can turn each of these lines on or off with the toggle switches (interactive command keys) specified in the following descriptions. The first line is the same as the output of the uptime utility and shows the current time, the amount of time the local system has been running since it was last booted, the number of users logged in, and the load averages from the last 1, 5, and 15 minutes (toggle l [lowercase "l"]). The second line indicates the number of processes that are currently running (toggle t). The next three lines report on CPU (also toggle t), memory (toggle m), and swap space (also toggle m) use.

The rest of the display reports on individual processes, listed in descending order by current CPU usage (the most CPU-intensive process is listed first). By default top displays the number of processes that fit on the screen.

Table V-27 describes the meanings of the fields displayed for each process.

table V-27	Field names
Name	**Meaning**
PID	Process identification number
USER	Username of the owner of the process
PR	Priority of the process
NI	nice value (see page 734)
VIRT	Number of kilobytes of virtual memory used by the process
RES	Number of kilobytes of physical (nonswapped) memory used by the process
SHR	Number of kilobytes of shared memory used by the process
S	Status of the process (see **STAT** on page 748)
%CPU	Percentage of the total CPU time that the process is using
%MEM	Percentage of physical memory that the process is using
TIME[+]	Total CPU time used by the process
COMMAND	Command line that started the process or name of the program (toggle with **c**)

While top is running, you can use the following commands to modify its behavior. Some of these commands are disabled when you run top in secure mode (**–s** option).

h (**help**) Displays a summary of the commands you can use while top is running.

k (**kill**) Allows you to kill a process. Unless you are Superuser, you can kill only processes you own. When you use this command, top prompts you for the PID of the process and the signal to send to the process. You can enter either a signal number or name. (See Table 11-5 on page 494 for a list of signals.) This command is disabled in secure mode.

n (**number**) When you give this command, top asks you to enter the number of processes you want it to display. If you enter 0 (the default) top shows as many processes as fit on the screen.

q (**quit**) Terminates top.

r (**renice**) Changes the priority of a running process (refer to nice on page 734). Unless you are Superuser, you can change the priority of only your own processes and even then only to lower the priority by entering a positive value.

Superuser can enter a negative value, increasing the priority of the process. This command is disabled in secure mode.

s   (**seconds**) Prompts you for the number of seconds to delay between updates to the display (3 is the default). You may enter an integer, a fraction, or 0 (for continuous updates). This command is disabled in secure mode.

S   (**switch**) Switches top back and forth between cumulative mode and regular mode. See the –S option for details.

W   (**write**) Writes top's current configuration to your personal configuration file (**~/.toprc**).

SPACE
Refreshes the screen.

Notes

The top utility is similar to ps but periodically updates the display, enabling you to watch the behavior of the local system over time.

This utility shows only as much of the command line for each process as fits on a line. If a process is swapped out, top replaces the command line with the name of the command in parentheses.

The top utility uses the **proc** filesystem: When **proc** is not mounted, top does not work.

Requesting continuous updates is almost always a mistake. The display updates too quickly and the system load increases dramatically.

Examples

The following display is the result of a typical execution of top:

```
top - 23:30:31 up 18 days, 30 min,  6 users,  load average: 0.08, 0.07, 0.01
Tasks: 125 total,   1 running, 124 sleeping,   0 stopped,   0 zombie
Cpu(s):  0.9% us,  0.7% sy,  0.0% ni, 98.4% id,  0.0% wa,  0.0% hi,  0.0% si
Mem:   1037272k total,  1023048k used,    14224k free,   126684k buffers
Swap:  2048248k total,        0k used,  2048248k free,   382612k cached

  PID USER      PR  NI  VIRT  RES  SHR S %CPU %MEM    TIME+  COMMAND
 2029 root      15   0  227m  96m 132m S  0.4  9.5 192:12.51 X
 2214 sam       15   0 34728  20m  29m S  0.4  2.0 351:08.69 kdeinit
14314 sam       16   0 22736  12m  18m S  0.2  1.3   0:07.83 gaim
15476 sam       16   0  2760  932 1620 R  0.2  0.1   0:00.93 top
    1 root      16   0  1836  464 1316 S  0.0  0.0   0:06.74 init
    2 root      34  19     0    0    0 S  0.0  0.0   0:00.01 ksoftirqd/0
    3 root       5 -10     0    0    0 S  0.0  0.0   0:00.65 events/0
    4 root       5 -10     0    0    0 S  0.0  0.0   0:00.01 kblockd/0
    6 root       5 -10     0    0    0 S  0.0  0.0   0:00.06 khelper
    5 root      15   0     0    0    0 S  0.0  0.0   0:00.00 khubd
    7 root      15   0     0    0    0 S  0.0  0.0   0:03.36 pdflush
   10 root      11 -10     0    0    0 S  0.0  0.0   0:00.00 aio/0
    9 root      15   0     0    0    0 S  0.0  0.0   0:17.85 kswapd0
```

touch

Changes a file's access and/or modification time

touch [options] file-list

The touch utility changes the access and/or modification time of a file to the current time or a time you specify.

Arguments   The *file-list* is a list of the pathnames of the files that touch will update.

Options   Accepts the common options described on page 587. Without any options touch changes the access and modification times to the current time. When you do not specify the **--no-create** option, touch creates files that do not exist.

--time=atime *or* **-a**   Updates the access time only, leaving the modification time unchanged.
--time=access

--no-create **-c**   Does not create files that do not exist.

--date=*datestring* **-d** *datestring*
  Updates times with the date specified by *datestring*. Most familiar formats are permitted for *datestring*. Components of the date and time not included in *datestring* are assumed to be the current date and time. This option may not be used with **-t**.

--time=mtime *or* **-m**   Updates the modification time only, leaving the access time unchanged.
--time=modify

--reference=*file* **-r** *file*
  Updates times with the times of *file*.

-t [[*cc*]*yy*]*nnddhhmm*[.*ss*]
  Changes times to the date specified by the argument. The *nn* is the number of the month (01–12), *dd* is the day of the month (01–31), *hh* is the hour based on a 24-hour clock (00–23), and *mm* is the minutes (00–59). You must specify at least these fields. You can specify the number of seconds past the start of the minute with .*ss*.

  The optional *cc* specifies the first two digits of the year (the value of the century minus 1), and *yy* specifies the last two digits of the year. When you do not specify a year, touch assumes the current year. When you do not specify *cc*, touch assumes 20 for *yy* in the range 0–68 and 19 for *yy* in the range 69–99.

  This option may not be used with **-d**.

Examples   The first three commands show touch updating an existing file. The ls utility with the –l option displays the modification time of the file. The last three commands show touch creating a file.

```
$ ls -l program.c
-rw-r--r--   1 alex group 5860 Apr 21 09:54 program.c
$ touch program.c
$ ls -l program.c
-rw-r--r--   1 alex group 5860 Aug 13 19:01 program.c

$ ls -l read.c
ls: read.c: No such file or directory
$ touch read.c
$ ls -l read.c
-rw-rw-r--   1 alex group 0 Aug 13 19:01 read.c
```

The next example demonstrates the use of the –a option to change the access time only and the –d option to specify a date for touch to use instead of the current date and time. The first ls command displays the file *modification* times; the second ls (with the --time=atime option) displays file *access* times. In this case the touch command does not have the intended effect: The access times of the files **cases** and **excerpts** are changed to 7:00 on the current date and three unwanted files are created. Because the date was not quoted (by surrounding it with double quotation marks), touch assumed that 7:00 went with the –d option and created the **pm**, **Jul**, and **30** files.

```
$ ls -l
-rw-rw-r--   1 alex group 45 Nov 30  2005 cases
-rw-rw-rw-   1 alex group 14 Jan  8  2006 excerpts

$ ls -l --time=atime
-rw-rw-r--   1 alex group 45 Jul 17 19:47 cases
-rw-rw-rw-   1 alex group 14 Jul 17 19:47 excerpts

$ touch -a -d 7:00 pm Jul 30 cases excerpts

$ ls -l
-rw-rw-r--   1 alex group 0 Aug 11 12:23 30
-rw-rw-r--   1 alex group 0 Aug 11 12:23 Jul
-rw-rw-r--   1 alex group 45 Nov 30  2005 cases
-rw-rw-rw-   1 alex group 14 Jan  8  2006 excerpts
-rw-rw-r--   1 alex group 0 Aug 11 12:23 pm

$ ls -l --time=atime
-rw-rw-r--   1 alex group 0 Aug 11 07:00 30
-rw-rw-r--   1 alex group 0 Aug 11 07:00 Jul
-rw-rw-r--   1 alex group 45 Aug 11 07:00 cases
-rw-rw-rw-   1 alex group 14 Aug 11 07:00 excerpts
-rw-rw-r--   1 alex group 0 Aug 11 07:00 pm
```

The final example is the same as the preceding one but correctly encloses the date within double quotation marks. After the touch command is executed, ls shows that the access times of the files **cases** and **excerpts** have been updated as expected:

```
$ ls -l
-rw-rw-r--   1 alex group 45 Nov 30  2005 cases
-rw-rw-rw-   1 alex group 14 Jan  8  2006 excerpts
$ ls -l --time=atime
-rw-rw-r--   1 alex group 45 Jul 17 19:47 cases
-rw-rw-rw-   1 alex group 14 Jul 17 19:47 excerpts

$ touch -a -d "7:00 pm Jul 30" cases excerpts

$ ls -l
-rw-rw-r--   1 alex group 45 Nov 30  2005 cases
-rw-rw-rw-   1 alex group 14 Jan  8  2006 excerpts
$ ls -l --time=atime
-rw-rw-r--   1 alex group 45 Jul 30 19:00 cases
-rw-rw-rw-   1 alex group 14 Jul 30 19:00 excerpts
```

tr

Replaces specified characters

tr [options] string1 [string2]

The tr utility reads standard input and, for each input character, maps it to an alternate character, deletes the character, or leaves the character alone. This utility reads from standard input and writes to standard output.

Arguments   The tr utility is typically used with two arguments, *string1* and *string2*. The position of each character in the two strings is important: Each time tr finds a character from *string1* in its input, it replaces that character with the corresponding character from *string2*.

With one argument, *string1,* and the **--delete** option, tr deletes the characters specified in *string1*. The option **--squeeze-repeats** replaces multiple sequential occurrences of characters in *string1* with single occurrences (for example, **abbc** becomes **abc**).

Ranges

A range of characters is similar in function to a character class within a regular expression (page 829). GNU tr does not support ranges (character classes) enclosed within brackets. You can specify a range of characters by following the character that appears earlier in the collating sequence with a hyphen and then the character that comes later in the collating sequence. For example, **1–6** expands to **123456**. Although the range A–Z expands as you would expect in ASCII, this approach does not work when you use the EBCDIC collating sequence, as these characters are not sequential in EBCDIC. See "Character Classes" for a solution to this issue.

Character Classes

A tr character class is not the same as described elsewhere in this book. (GNU documentation uses the term *list operator* for what this book calls a *character class*.) You specify a character class as *'[:class:]'*, where *class* is a character class from Table V-28. You must specify a character class in *string1* unless you are performing case conversion (see "Examples" later in this section) or are using the **–d** and **–s** options together.

table V-28	Character classes
Class	**Meaning**
alnum	Letters and digits
alpha	Letters

table V-28	Character classes (continued)
blank	Whitespace
cntrl	CONTROL characters
digit	Digits
graph	Printable characters but not SPACES
lower	Lowercase letters
print	Printable characters including SPACES
punct	Punctuation characters
space	Horizontal or vertical whitespace
upper	Uppercase letters
xdigit	Hexadecimal digits

Options

--complement   **-c**   Complements *string1*, causing tr to match all characters *except* those in *string1*.

--delete   **-d**   Deletes characters that match those specified in *string1*. If you use this option with the **--squeeze-repeats** option, you must specify both *string1* and *string2* (see "Notes").

--help   Summarizes how to use tr, including the special symbols you can use in *string1* and *string2*.

--squeeze-repeats   **-s**   Replaces multiple sequential occurrences of a character in *string1* with a single occurrence of the character when you call tr with only one string argument. If you use both *string1* and *string2*, the tr utility first translates the characters in *string1* to those in *string2* and then reduces multiple sequential occurrences of characters in *string2*.

--truncate-set1   **-t**   Truncates *string1* so it is the same length as *string2* before processing input.

Notes

When *string1* is longer than *string2*, the initial portion of *string1* (equal in length to *string2*) is used in the translation. When *string1* is shorter than *string2*, tr uses the last character of *string1* to extend *string1* to the length of *string2*. In this case tr departs from the POSIX standard, which does not define a result.

If you use the **--delete** and **--squeeze-repeats** options at the same time, tr deletes the characters in *string1* and then reduces multiple sequential occurrences of characters in *string2*.

Examples   You can use a hyphen to represent a range of characters in *string1* or *string2*. The two command lines in the following example produce the same result:

```
$ echo abcdef | tr 'abcdef' 'xyzabc'
xyzabc
$ echo abcdef | tr 'a-f' 'x-za-c'
xyzabc
```

The next example demonstrates a popular method for disguising text, often called ROT13 (rotate 13) because it replaces the first letter of the alphabet with the thirteenth, the second with the fourteenth, and so forth.

```
$ echo The punchline of the joke is ... |
> tr 'A-M N-Z a-m n-z' 'N-Z A-M n-z a-m'
Gur chapuyvar bs gur wbxr vf ...
```

To make the text intelligible again, reverse the order of the arguments to tr:

```
$ echo Gur chapuyvar bs gur wbxr vf ... |
> tr 'N-Z A-M n-z a-m' 'A-M N-Z a-m n-z'
The punchline of the joke is ...
```

The --delete option causes tr to delete selected characters:

```
$ echo If you can read this, you can spot the missing vowels! |
> tr --delete 'aeiou'
If y cn rd ths, y cn spt th mssng vwls!
```

In the following example, tr replaces characters and reduces pairs of identical characters to single characters:

```
$ echo tennessee | tr -s 'tnse' 'srne'
serene
```

The next example replaces each sequence of nonalphabetic characters (the complement of all the alphabetic characters as specified by the character class **alpha**) in the file **draft1** with a single NEWLINE character. The output is a list of words, one per line.

```
$ tr --complement --squeeze-repeats '[:alpha:]' '\n' < draft1
```

The next example uses character classes to upshift the string **hi there**:

```
$ echo hi there | tr '[:lower:]' '[:upper:]'
HI THERE
```

tty

Displays the terminal pathname

tty [option]

The tty utility displays the pathname of standard input if it is a terminal and displays **not a tty** if it is not a terminal. The exit status is 0 if standard input is a terminal and 1 if it is not.

Arguments   There are no arguments.

Options   Accepts the common options described on page 587.

--**silent** *or*   --**s**   Causes tty not to print anything. The exit status of tty is set.
--**quiet**

Notes   The term *tty* is short for teletypewriter, the terminal device on which UNIX was first run. This command appears in UNIX, and Linux has kept it for the sake of consistency and tradition.

Examples   The following example illustrates the use of tty:

```
$ tty
/dev/pts/11
$ echo $?
0
$ tty < memo
not a tty
$ echo $?
1
```

tune2fs

Changes parameters on an ext2 or ext3 filesystem

tune2fs [options] device

The tune2fs utility displays and modifies filesystem parameters on **ext2** filesystems and on **ext3** filesystems, which are modified **ext2** filesystems. This utility can also set up journaling on an **ext2** filesystem, turning it into an **ext3** filesystem. With typical filesystem permissions, tune2fs must be run as **root**.

Arguments   The *device* is the name of the device, such as **/dev/hda8**, that holds the filesystem whose parameters you want to display or modify.

Options

–c *n*

(**count**) Sets the maximum number of times the filesystem can be mounted between filesystem checks to *n*. Set *n* to 0 (zero) to disregard this parameter.

–C *n*

(**count**) Sets the number of times the filesystem has been mounted without being checked to *n*. This option is useful for staggering filesystem checks (see "Discussion") and for forcing a check the next time the system boots.

–e *behavior*

(**error**) Specifies what the kernel will do when it detects an error. Set *behavior* to **continue** (continues execution), **remount-ro** (remounts the filesystem read-only), or **panic** (causes a kernel panic). Regardless of how you set this option, an error will cause fsck to check the filesystem next time the system boots.

–i *n[u]*

(**interval**) Sets the maximum time between filesystem checks to *n* time periods. Without *u* or with *u* set to **d**, the time period is days. Set *u* to **w** to set the time period to weeks; **m** for months. Set *n* to 0 (zero) to disregard this parameter. Because a filesystem check is forced only when the system is booted the time specified by this option may be exceeded.

–j   (**journal**) Adds an **ext3** journal to an **ext2** filesystem. For more information refer to "journaling filesystem" on page 883.

–l   (**list**) Lists information about the filesystem.

–T *date*

(**time**) Sets the time the filesystem was last checked to *date*. The *date* is the time and date in the format *yyymmdd[hh[mm]ss]]]*. Here *mm* is the number of the month (01–12) and *dd* is the day of the month (01–31). You must specify at least these fields. The *hh* is the hour based on a 24-hour clock (00–23), *mm* is the minutes (00–59), and *.ss* is the number of seconds past the start of the minute. You can also specify *date* as **now**.

Discussion Checking a large filesystem can take a long time. Use the –C and/or –T options to stagger filesystem checks so they do not all happen at the same time. When all the filesystem checks occur at the same time it can take a long time for the system to boot.

Examples Following is the output of tune2fs run with the –l option on a typical **ext3** filesystem:

```
# /sbin/tune2fs -l /dev/hda2
tune2fs 1.35 (28-Feb-2004)
Filesystem volume name:   /p04
Last mounted on:          <not available>
Filesystem UUID:          125be803-2f51-53ef-dfcf-292bf7e4ecc4
Filesystem magic number:  0xEF53
Filesystem revision #:    1 (dynamic)
Filesystem features:      has_journal filetype needs_recovery
sparse_super
Default mount options:    (none)
Filesystem state:         clean
Errors behavior:          Continue
Filesystem OS type:       Linux
Inode count:              2562240
Block count:              5120718
Reserved block count:     256035
Free blocks:              3194303
Free inodes:              2554160
First block:              0
Block size:               4096
Fragment size:            4096
Blocks per group:         32768
Fragments per group:      32768
Inodes per group:         16320
Inode blocks per group:   510
Filesystem created:       Sat May 17 15:22:29 2003
Last mount time:          Sun Jan 30 23:00:37 2005
Last write time:          Sun Jan 30 23:00:37 2005
Mount count:              5
Maximum mount count:      30
Last checked:             Thu Dec  2 01:02:46 2004
Check interval:           15552000 (6 months)
Next check after:         Tue May 31 02:02:46 2005
Reserved blocks uid:      0 (user root)
Reserved blocks gid:      0 (group root)
First inode:              11
Inode size:               128
Journal inode:            8
Default directory hash:   tea
Directory Hash Seed:      81345bv8-740d-4af5-c5bc-12033ed7c121
Journal backup:           inode blocks
```

umask

Establishes the file-creation permissions mask

umask [mask]

The umask builtin specifies a mask that the system uses to set access permissions when you create a file. This builtin works slightly differently in each of the shells.

Arguments   The *mask* can be a three-digit octal number (bash and tcsh) or a symbolic value (bash) such as you would use with chmod (page 604). The *mask* specifies the permissions that are *not* allowed.

When *mask* is an octal number, the digits correspond to the permissions for the owner of the file, members of the group the file is associated with, and everyone else. Because the *mask* specifies the permissions that are *not* allowed, the system subtracts each of these digits from 7 when you create a file. The resulting three octal numbers specify the access permissions for the file (the numbers you would use with chmod). A *mask* that you give as a symbolic value also specifies the permissions that are *not* allowed. See "Notes."

Without any arguments, umask displays the file-creation permissions *mask*.

Notes   Most utilities and applications do not attempt to create files with execute permissions, regardless of the value of *mask*; they assume that you do not want an executable file. As a result, when a utility or application such as touch creates a file, the system subtracts each of the digits in *mask* from 6. An exception occurs with mkdir, which does assume that you want the execute (access in the case of a directory) bit set. See "Examples."

The umask program is a builtin in bash and tcsh and generally goes in the initialization file for your shell (**~/.bash_profile** [bash] or **~/.login** [tcsh]).

Under bash the argument **g=r,o=r** turns *on* the write bit in the *mask* for groups and other users (the mask is 0033), causing those bits to be *off* in file permissions (744 or 644). Refer to chmod on page 604 for more information about symbolic permissions.

Examples   The following commands set the file-creation permissions mask and display the mask and its effect when you create a file and a directory. The mask of 022, when subtracted from 777, gives permissions of 644 (**rw–r––r––**) for a file and 755 (**rwxr–xr–x**) for a directory:

```
$ umask 022
$ umask
022
```

```
$ touch afile
$ mkdir adirectory
$ ls -ld afile adirectory
drwxr-xr-x  2 max max 4096 Jul 24 11:25 adirectory
-rw-r--r--  1 max max 0 Jul 24 11:25 afile
```

The next example sets the same mask value symbolically:

```
$ umask g=rx,o=rx
$ umask
022
```

uniq

Displays unique lines

uniq [options] [input-file] [output-file]

The uniq utility displays its input, removing all but one copy of successive repeated lines. If the file has been sorted (see sort on page 762), uniq ensures that no two lines that it displays are the same.

Arguments   When you do not specify the *input-file*, uniq reads from standard input. When you do not specify the *output-file*, uniq writes to standard output.

Options   Accepts the common options described on page 587. A *field* is a sequence of characters bounded by SPACEs, TABs, NEWLINEs, or a combination of these characters.

--count   –c   Precedes each line with the number of occurrences of the line in the input file.

--repeated   –d   Displays one copy of lines that are repeated; does not display lines that are not repeated.

--skip-fields=*nfield*

   –f *nfield*

   Ignores the first *nfield* blank-separated fields of each line. The uniq utility bases its comparison on the remainder of the line, including the leading blanks of the next field on the line (see the --skip-chars option).

--ignore-case   –i   Ignores case when comparing lines.

--skip-chars=*nchar*

   –s *nchar*

   Ignores the first *nchar* characters of each line. If you also use the --skip-fields option, uniq ignores the first *nfield* fields followed by *nchar* characters. You can use this option to skip over leading blanks of a field.

--unique   –u   Displays only lines that are *not* repeated.

--check-chars=*nchar*

   –w *nchar*

   Compares up to *nchars* characters on a line after honoring the --skip-fields and --skip-chars options. By default uniq compares the entire line.

Examples   These examples assume that the file named **test** in the working directory contains the following text:

```
$ cat test
boy took bat home
boy took bat home
girl took bat home
dog brought hat home
dog brought hat home
dog brought hat home
```

Without any options, uniq displays only one copy of successive repeated lines:

```
$ uniq test
boy took bat home
girl took bat home
dog brought hat home
```

The --count option displays the number of consecutive occurrences of each line in the file:

```
$ uniq --count test
     2 boy took bat home
     1 girl took bat home
     3 dog brought hat home
```

The --repeated option displays only lines that are consecutively repeated in the file.

```
$ uniq --repeated test
boy took bat home
dog brought hat home
```

The --unique option displays only lines that are *not* consecutively repeated in the file:

```
$ uniq --unique test
girl took bat home
```

Next the --skip-fields option skips the first field in each line, causing the lines that begin with **boy** and the one that begins with **girl** to appear to be consecutive repeated lines. The uniq utility displays only one occurrence of these lines:

```
$ uniq --skip-fields=1 test
boy took bat home
dog brought hat home
```

The next example uses both the –f (--skip-fields) and –s (--skip-chars) arguments first to skip two fields and then to skip two characters. The two characters this command skips include the SPACE that separates the second and third fields and the first character of the third field. Ignoring these characters, all the lines appear to be consecutive repeated lines containing the string **at home**. The uniq utility displays only the first of these lines:

```
$ uniq -f 2 -s 2 test
boy took bat home
```

w

Displays information about system users

w [options] [username]

The w utility displays the names of users who are currently logged in, together with their terminal device numbers, the times they logged in, the commands they are running, and other information.

Options

–f (**from**) Removes the **FROM** column. For users who are directly connected, this field contains a hyphen.

–h (**no header**) Suppresses the header line.

–s (**short**) Displays less information: username, terminal device, idle time, and command.

Arguments

The *username* restricts the display to information about that user.

Discussion

The first line that w displays is the same as that displayed by uptime. This line includes the time of day, how long the system has been running (in days, hours, and minutes), how many users are logged in, and how busy the system is (load average). From left to right, the load averages indicate the number of processes that have been waiting to run in the past 1 minute, 5 minutes, and 15 minutes.

The columns of information that w displays have the following headings:

```
USER TTY FROM LOGIN@ IDLE JCPU PCPU WHAT
```

The **USER** is the username of the user. The **TTY** is the device name for the line that the user is on. The **FROM** is the system name that a remote user is logged in from; it is a hyphen for a local user. The **LOGIN@** gives the date and time the user logged in. The **IDLE** indicates how many minutes have elapsed since the user last used the keyboard. The **JCPU** is the CPU time used by all processes attached to the user's tty, not including completed background jobs. The **PCPU** is the time used by the process named in the **WHAT** column. The **WHAT** is the command that user is running.

Examples

The first example shows the full list produced by the w utility:

```
$ w
 10:26am  up 1 day, 55 min,  6 users,  load average: 0.15, 0.03, 0.01
 USER      TTY      FROM            LOGIN@    IDLE   JCPU    PCPU   WHAT
 alex      tty1     -               Fri 9am   20:39m  0.22s  0.01s  vim td
 alex      tty2     -               Fri 5pm   17:16m  0.07s  0.07s  -bash
 root      pts/1    -               Fri 4pm   14:28m  0.20s  0.07s  -bash
 jenny     pts/2    -               Fri 5pm   3:23    0.08s  0.08s  /bin/bash
 hls       pts/3    potato          10:07am   0.00s   0.08s  0.02s  w
```

The next example shows the **–s** option producing an abbreviated listing:

```
$ w -s
 10:30am  up 1 day, 58 min,  6 users,  load average: 0.15, 0.03, 0.01
USER     TTY    FROM            IDLE  WHAT
alex     tty1   -              20:43m  vim td
alex     tty2   -              17:19m  -bash
root     pts/1  -              14:31m  -bash
jenny    pts/2  -               0.20s  vim memo.030125
hls      pts/3  potato          0.00s  w -s
```

The final example requests information only about Alex:

```
$ w alex
 10:35am  up 1 day,  1:04,  6 users,  load average: 0.06, 0.01, 0.00
USER     TTY    FROM           LOGIN@  IDLE   JCPU   PCPU  WHAT
alex     tty1   -              Fri 9am 20:48m 0.22s  0.01s vim td
alex     tty2   -              Fri 5pm 17:25m 0.07s  0.07s -bash
```

wc

Displays the number of lines, words, and bytes

wc [options] [file-list]

The wc utility displays the number of lines, words, and bytes in its input. When you specify more than one file on the command line, wc displays totals for each file as well as totals for the group of files.

Arguments   The *file-list* is a list of the pathnames of one or more files that wc analyzes. When you omit *file-list,* the wc utility takes its input from standard input.

Options   Accepts the common options described on page 587.

--bytes   –c   Displays only the number of bytes in the input.

--lines   –l   (lowercase "l") Displays only the number of lines (that is, NEWLINE characters) in the input.

--max-line-length   –L   Displays the length of the longest line in the input.

--chars   –m   Displays only the number of characters in the input.

--words   –w   Displays only the number of words in the input.

Notes   A *word* is a sequence of characters bounded by SPACEs, TABs, NEWLINEs, or a combination of these characters.

Examples   The following command analyzes the file named **memo**. The numbers in the output represent the number of lines, words, and bytes in the file:

```
$ wc memo
      5      31      146 memo
```

The next command displays the number of lines and words in three files. The line at the bottom, with the word **total** in the right column, contains the sum of each column.

```
$ wc -lw memo1 memo2 memo3
     10      62 memo1
     12      74 memo2
     12      68 memo3
     34     204 total
```

which

Shows where in **PATH** a command is located

which command-list

For each command in *command-list,* the which utility searches the directories in the **PATH** variable (page 284) and displays the absolute pathname of the first file it finds whose simple filename is the same as the command.

Arguments

The *command-list* is a list of one or more commands (utilities) that which searches for. For each command which searches the directories listed in the **PATH** environment variable, in order, and displays the full pathname of the first command (executable file) it finds. If which does not locate a command, it displays a message.

Options

––all	**–a**	Displays all matching executable files in **PATH**, not just the first.
––read-alias	**–i**	Reads aliases from standard input and reports on matching aliases in addition to executable files in **PATH** (turn off with **––skip-alias**).
––read-functions		Reads shell functions from standard input and reports on matching functions in addition to executable files in **PATH** (turn off with **––skip-functions**).
––show-dot		Displays **./** in place of the absolute pathname when a directory in **PATH** starts with a period and a matching executable file is in that directory (turn off with **––skip-dot**).
––show-tilde		Displays a tilde (**~**) in place of the absolute pathname of the user's home directory where appropriate. This option is ignored when Superuser runs which.
––tty-only		Do not process more options (to the right of this option) if the process running which is not attached to a terminal.

Notes

Many distributions define an alias for which such as the following:

```
$alias which
alias which='alias | /usr/bin/which --tty-only --read-alias --show-dot --show-tilde'
```

If which is not behaving as you would expect, verify that you are not running an alias. The preceding alias causes which to be effective only when it is run interactively (**––tty-only**) and to display aliases, display the working directory as a period when appropriate, and display the name of the user's home directory as a tilde.

The TC Shell includes a which builtin (see the tcsh man page) that works slightly differently from the which utility (**/usr/bin/which**). Without any options the which utility does not locate aliases, functions, and shell builtins because these do not appear in **PATH.** In contrast the tcsh which builtin locates aliases, functions, and shell builtins.

Examples   The first example quotes the first letter of the command (**\which**) to prevent the shell from invoking the alias (page 313) for which:

```
$ \which vim dir which
/usr/bin/vim
/usr/bin/dir
/usr/bin/which
```

The next example is the same as the first but uses the alias for which (which it displays):

```
$ which vim dir which
alias which='alias | /usr/bin/which --tty-only --read-alias --show-dot --show-tilde'
/usr/bin/which
/usr/bin/vim
/usr/bin/dir
```

The final example is the same as the previous one except that it is run from tcsh. The tcsh which builtin is used instead of the which utility:

```
tcsh $ which vim dir which
/usr/bin/vim
/usr/bin/dir
which: shell built-in command.
```

who

Displays information about logged-in users

who [options]
who am i

The who utility displays information about users who are logged in on the local system. This information includes each user's username, terminal device, login time, and, if applicable, the corresponding remote hostname or X display.

Arguments   When given two arguments (traditionally, **am i**), who displays information about the user giving the command. If applicable, the username is preceded by the hostname of the system running who (as in **kudos!alex**).

Options   Accepts the common options described on page 587.

--all	–a	Displays a lot of information.
--boot	–b	Displays the date and time the system was last booted.
--heading	–H	Displays a header.
--login	–l	(lowercase "l") Lists devices waiting for a user to log in.
--count	–q	(**quick**) Lists the usernames only, followed by the number of users logged in on the system.
--message *or* mesg	–T	Appends after each user's username a character that shows whether that user has messages enabled. A plus (+) means that messages are enabled, a hyphen (–) means that they are disabled, and a question mark (?) indicates that who cannot find the device. If messages are enabled, you can use write to communicate with the user. Refer to "mesg: Denies or Accepts Messages" on page 68.
--users	–u	Includes each user's idle time in the display. If the user has typed on her terminal in the past minute, a period (.) appears in this field. If no input has occurred for more than a day, the word **old** appears. In addition, this option includes the PID number and comment fields. See "Discussion."

Discussion   The line that who displays has the following syntax:

> *user [messages] line login-time [idle] [PID] comment*

The *user* is the username of the user. The *messages* indicates whether messages are enabled or disabled (see the **--message** option). The *line* is the device name associated with the line the user is logged in on. The *login-time* is the date and time that the user logged in. The *idle* is the length of time since the terminal was last used (the *idle time*; see the **--idle** option). The **PID** is the process identification number. The *comment* is the remote system or X display that the user is logged in from (blank for local users).

Notes   The finger utility (page 661) provides information similar to that given by who.

Examples   The following examples demonstrate the use of the who utility:

```
$ who
hls        tty1      Jul 30 06:01
jenny      tty2      Jul 30 06:02
alex       ttyp3     Jul 30 14:56 (bravo)

$ who am i
bravo!alex        ttyp3      Jul 30 14:56 (bravo)

$ who --heading --users -T
USER         LINE      TIME           IDLE       PID COMMENT
hls          - tty1    Jul 30 06:01 03:53       1821
jenny        + tty2    Jul 30 06:02 14:47       2235
alex         + ttyp3   Jul 30 14:56    .        14777  (bravo)
```

xargs

Converts standard input into command lines

xargs [options] [command]

The xargs utility is a convenient, efficient way to convert standard output of one command into arguments for another command. This utility reads from standard input, keeps track of the maximum allowable length of a command line, and avoids exceeding that limit by repeating *command* as needed. Finally xargs executes the constructed command line.

Arguments

The *command* is the command line you want xargs to use as a base for the command it constructs. If you omit *command,* it defaults to echo. The xargs utility appends to *command* the arguments it receives from standard input. If any arguments should precede the arguments from standard input, you must include them as part of *command*.

Options

––replace*[=marker]*
          –i*[marker]*

Allows you to place arguments from standard input anywhere within *command*. All occurrences of *marker* in *command* for xargs are replaced by the arguments generated from standard input of xargs. If you omit *marker,* it defaults to the string {}, which matches the syntax used in the find command –exec option. With this option *command* is executed for each input line; the ––**max-lines** option is ignored when you use ––**replace**.

––max–lines*[=num]*
          –l *[num]*

(lowercase "l") Executes *command* once for every *num* lines of input (*num* defaults to 1).

––max–args=*num* –n *num*

Executes *command* once for every *num* arguments in the input line.

  ––interactive –p Prompts the user prior to each execution of *command*.

––max–procs=*num*
          –P *num*

Allows xargs to run up to *maxprocs* instances of *command* simultaneously. (The default is 1, which runs *commands* sequentially.) This option may improve the throughput if you are running Linux on a multiprocessor system.

--no-run-if-empty

-r Causes xargs not to execute *command* if standard input is empty. Ordinarily xargs executes *command* at least once, even if standard input includes only blanks.

Discussion The xargs utility reads arguments to *command* from standard input, interpreting each whitespace-delimited string as a separate argument. It then constructs a command line from *command* and a series of arguments. When the maximum command line length would be exceeded by adding another argument, xargs runs the command line it has built. If there is more input, xargs repeats the process of building a command line and running it. This process continues until all input has been read.

Notes One common use of xargs is as an efficient alternative to the –exec option of find (page 656). If you call find with the –exec option to run a command, it runs the command once for each file it processes. Each execution of the command creates a new process, which can drain system resources when you are processing many files. By accumulating as many arguments as possible, xargs can greatly reduce the number of processes needed. The first example in the "Examples" section shows how to use xargs with find.

The --replace option changes how xargs handles whitespace in standard input. Without this option xargs treats sequences of blanks, TABS, and NEWLINES as equivalent. With this option xargs treats NEWLINE characters in a special way. If it encounters a NEWLINE in standard input when using the --replace option, xargs runs *command* using the argument list that has been built up to that point.

Examples To locate and remove all files whose names end in .o from the working directory and its subdirectories, you can use the find –exec option:

```
$ find . -name \*.o -exec rm --force {} \;
```

This approach calls the rm utility once for each .o file that find locates. Each invocation of rm requires a new process. If a lot of .o files exist, a significant amount of time is spent creating, starting, and then cleaning up these processes. You can reduce the number of processes by allowing xargs to accumulate as many filenames as possible before calling rm:

```
$ find . -name \*.o -print | xargs rm --force
```

In the next example, the contents of all *.txt files located by find are searched for lines containing the word **login**. All filenames that contain **login** are displayed by grep.

```
$ find . -name \*.txt -print | xargs grep -w -l login
```

The next example shows how you can use the **--replace** option to cause xargs to embed standard input within *command* instead of appending it to *command*. This option also causes *command* to be executed each time a NEWLINE character is encountered in standard input; **--max-lines** does not override this behavior.

```
$ cat names
Tom,
Dick,
and Harry
$ xargs echo "Hello, " < names
Hello, Tom, Dick, and Harry
$ xargs --replace echo "Hello {}.  Join me for lunch?" <names
Hello Tom,. Join me for lunch?
Hello Dick,. Join me for lunch?
Hello and Harry. Join me for lunch?
```

The final example uses the same input file as the previous example as well as the **--max-args** and **--max-lines** options:

```
$ xargs echo "Hi there" < names
Hi there Tom, Dick, and Harry
$ xargs   max-args-1 echo "Hi there" < names
Hi there Tom,
Hi there Dick,
Hi there and
Hi there Harry
$ xargs --max-lines=2 echo "Hi there" < names
Hi there Tom, Dick,
Hi there and Harry
```

See page 775 for another example of the use of xargs.

PART VI
Appendixes

REGULAR EXPRESSIONS

A regular expression defines a set of one or more strings of characters. A simple string of characters is a regular expression that defines one string of characters: itself. A more complex regular expression uses letters, numbers, and special characters to define many different strings of characters. A regular expression is said to *match* any string it defines.

This appendix describes the regular expressions used by ed, vim, emacs, grep, gawk, sed, and other utilities. The regular expressions used in shell ambiguous file references are different and are described in "Filename Generation/Pathname Expansion" on page 127.

CHARACTERS

As used in this appendix, a *character* is any character *except* a NEWLINE. Most characters represent themselves within a regular expression. A *special character* is one that does not represent itself. If you need to use a special character to represent itself, you must quote it as explained on page 831.

DELIMITERS

A character called a *delimiter* usually marks the beginning and end of a regular expression. The delimiter is always a special character for the regular expression it delimits (that is, it does not represent itself but marks the beginning and end of the expression). Although vim permits the use of other characters as a delimiter and grep does not use delimiters at all, the regular expressions in this appendix use a forward slash (/) as a delimiter. In some unambiguous cases, the second delimiter is not required. For example, you can sometimes omit the second delimiter when it would be followed immediately by RETURN.

SIMPLE STRINGS

The most basic regular expression is a simple string that contains no special characters except the delimiters. A simple string matches only itself (Table A-1). In the examples in this appendix, the strings that are matched are underlined and <u>look like this</u>.

Table A-1 Simple strings

Regular expression	Matches	Examples
/ring/	<u>ring</u>	<u>ring</u>, sp<u>ring</u>, <u>ring</u>ing, st<u>ring</u>ing
/Thursday/	<u>Thursday</u>	<u>Thursday</u>, <u>Thursday</u>'s
/or not/	<u>or not</u>	<u>or not</u>, po<u>or not</u>hing

SPECIAL CHARACTERS

You can use special characters within a regular expression to cause the regular expression to match more than one string. A regular expression that includes a special character always matches the longest possible string, starting as far toward the beginning (left) of the line as possible.

PERIODS

A period (.) matches any character (Table A-2).

Table A-2 Period

Regular expression	Matches	Examples
/.alk/	All strings consisting of a SPACE followed by any character followed by <u>alk</u>	will <u>talk</u>, may <u>balk</u>
/.ing/	All strings consisting of any character preceding <u>ing</u>	<u>sing</u> song, <u>ping</u>, before <u>ing</u>lenook

BRACKETS

Brackets ([]) define a *character class*[1] that matches any single character within the brackets (Table A-3). If the first character following the left bracket is a caret (^), the brackets define a character class that matches any single character not within the brackets. You can use a hyphen to indicate a range of characters. Within a character-class definition, backslashes and asterisks (described in the following sections) lose their special meanings. A right bracket (appearing as a member of the character class) can appear only as the first character following the left bracket. A caret is special only if it is the first character following the left bracket. A dollar sign is special only if it is followed immediately by the right bracket.

Table A-3 Brackets

Regular expression	Matches	Examples
/[bB]ill/	Member of the character class b and B followed by <u>ill</u>	<u>bill</u>, <u>Bill</u>, <u>bill</u>ed
/t[aeiou].k/	t followed by a lowercase vowel, any character, and a <u>k</u>	<u>talk</u>ative, <u>stink</u>, <u>teak</u>, <u>tank</u>er
/# [6–9]/	# followed by a SPACE and a member of the character class <u>6</u> through <u>9</u>	<u># 6</u>0, <u># 8</u>:, get <u># 9</u>
/[^a–zA–Z]/	Any character that is not a letter (ASCII character set only)	<u>1</u>, <u>7</u>, <u>@</u>, <u>.</u>, <u>}</u>, Stop<u>!</u>

---

1. GNU documentation calls these List Operators and defines Character Class operators as expressions that match a predefined group of characters, such as all numbers (see Table V-28 on page 804).

ASTERISKS

An asterisk can follow a regular expression that represents a single character (Table A-4). The asterisk represents *zero* or more occurrences of a match of the regular expression. An asterisk following a period matches any string of characters. (A period matches any character, and an asterisk matches zero or more occurrences of the preceding regular expression.) A character-class definition followed by an asterisk matches any string of characters that are members of the character class.

Table A-4   Asterisks

Regular expression	Matches	Examples
/ab*c/	<u>a</u> followed by zero or more <u>b</u>'s followed by a <u>c</u>	<u>ac</u>, <u>abc</u>, <u>abbc</u>, debbca<u>abbbc</u>
/ab.*c/	<u>ab</u> followed by zero or more characters followed by <u>c</u>	<u>abc</u>, <u>abxc</u>, <u>ab45c</u>, x<u>ab 756.345 x c</u>at
/t.*ing/	<u>t</u> followed by zero or more characters followed by <u>ing</u>	<u>thing</u>, <u>ting</u>, I <u>thought of going</u>
/[a–zA–Z]*/	A string composed only of letters and SPACES	1. <u>any string without numbers or punctuation</u>!
/(.*)/	As long a string as possible between (and)	Get <u>(this) and (that)</u>;
/([^)]*)/	The shortest string possible that starts with (and ends with)	<u>(this)</u>, Get <u>(this and that)</u>

CARETS AND DOLLAR SIGNS

A regular expression that begins with a caret (^) can match a string only at the beginning of a line. In a similar manner, a dollar sign ($) at the end of a regular expression matches the end of a line. The caret and dollar sign are called anchors because they force (anchor) a match to the beginning or end of a line (Table A-5).

Table A-5   Carets and dollar signs

Regular expression	Matches	Examples
/^T/	A <u>T</u> at the beginning of a line	<u>T</u>his line..., <u>T</u>hat Time..., In Time
/^+[0–9]/	A plus sign followed by a digit at the beginning of a line	<u>+5</u> +45.72, <u>+7</u>59 Keep this...
/:$/	A colon that ends a line	...below<u>:</u>

QUOTING SPECIAL CHARACTERS

You can quote any special character (but not a digit or a parenthesis) by preceding it with a backslash (Table A-6). Quoting a special character makes it represent itself.

Table A-6   Quoted special characters

Regular expression	Matches	Examples
/end\./	All strings that contain end followed by a period	The end., send., pretend.mail
/ \\/	A single backslash	\
/ */	An asterisk	*.c, an asterisk (*)
/ \[5\]/	[5]	it was five [5]
/and\/or/	and/or	and/or

RULES

The following rules govern the application of regular expressions.

LONGEST MATCH POSSIBLE

A regular expression always matches the longest possible string, starting as far toward the beginning of the line as possible. For example, given the string

```
This (rug) is not what it once was (a long time ago), is it?
```

the expression **/Th.*is/** matches

```
This (rug) is not what it once was (a long time ago), is
```

and **/(.*)/** matches

```
(rug) is not what it once was (a long time ago)
```

However, **/([^)]*)/** matches

```
(rug)
```

Given the string

    singing songs, singing more and more

the expression **/s.*ing/** matches

    singing songs, singing

and **/s.*ing song/** matches

    singing song

EMPTY REGULAR EXPRESSIONS

Within some utilities, such as vim and less (but not grep), an empty regular expression represents the last regular expression that you used. For example, suppose you give vim the following Substitute command:

    :s/mike/robert/

If you then want to make the same substitution again, you can use the following command:

    :s//robert/

Alternatively, you can use the following commands to search for the string **mike** and then make the substitution

    /mike/
    :s//robert/

The empty regular expression (**//**) represents the last regular expression you used (**/mike/**).

BRACKETING EXPRESSIONS

You can use quoted parentheses, \(and \), to *bracket* a regular expression. The string that the bracketed regular expression matches can be recalled, as explained in "Quoted Digit." A regular expression does not attempt to match quoted parentheses. Thus a regular expression enclosed within quoted parentheses matches what the same regular expression without the parentheses would match. The expression **/\(rexp\)/** matches what **/rexp/** would match; **/a\(b*\)c/** matches what **/ab*c/** would match.

You can nest quoted parentheses. The bracketed expressions are identified only by the opening \(, so no ambiguity arises in identifying them. The expression **/\([a–z]\([A–Z]*\)x\)/** consists of two bracketed expressions, one nested within the other. In the string **3 t dMNORx7 1 u**, the preceding regular expression matches **dMNORx**, with the first bracketed expression matching **dMNORx** and the second matching **MNOR**.

THE REPLACEMENT STRING

The vim and sed editors use regular expressions as search strings within Substitute commands. You can use the ampersand (**&**) and quoted digits (**\n**) special characters to represent the matched strings within the corresponding replacement string.

AMPERSAND

Within a replacement string, an ampersand (**&**) takes on the value of the string that the search string (regular expression) matched. For example, the following vim Substitute command surrounds a string of one or more digits with **NN**. The ampersand in the replacement string matches whatever string of digits the regular expression (search string) matched.

```
:s/[0-9][0-9]*/NN&NN/
```

Two character-class definitions are required because the regular expression [0–9]* matches *zero* or more occurrences of a digit, and *any* character string constitutes zero or more occurrences of a digit.

QUOTED DIGIT

Within the search string, a bracketed regular expression, **\(xxx\)**, matches what the regular expression would have matched without the quoted parentheses, **xxx**. Within the replacement string, a quoted digit, **\n**, represents the string that the bracketed regular expression (portion of the search string) beginning with the *n*th **\(** matched. For example, you can take a list of people in the form

```
last-name, first-name initial
```

and put it in the form

```
first-name initial last-name
```

with the following vim command:

```
:1,$s/\([^,]*\), \(.*\)/\2 \1/
```

This command addresses all the lines in the file (**1,$**). The Substitute command (**s**) uses a search string and a replacement string delimited by forward slashes. The first bracketed regular expression within the search string, **\([^,]*\)**, matches what the same unbracketed regular expression, [^,]*, would match: zero or more characters not containing a comma (the **last-name**). Following the first bracketed regular expression are a comma and a SPACE that match themselves. The second bracketed expression, \(.*\), matches any string of characters (the **first-name** and **initial**).

The replacement string consists of what the second bracketed regular expression matched (\2), followed by a SPACE and what the first bracketed regular expression matched (\1).

EXTENDED REGULAR EXPRESSIONS

The three utilities egrep, grep when run with the –E option (similar to egrep), and gawk provide all the special characters that are included in ordinary regular expressions, except for \(and \), as well as several others. The vim editor includes the additional characters as well as \(and \). Patterns using the extended set of special characters are called *full regular expressions* or *extended regular expressions*.

Two of the additional special characters are the plus sign (+) and the question mark (?). They are similar to *, which matches *zero* or more occurrences of the previous character. The plus sign matches *one* or more occurrences of the previous character, whereas the question mark matches *zero* or *one* occurrence. You can use any one of the special characters *, +, and ? following parentheses, causing the special character to apply to the string surrounded by the parentheses. Unlike the parentheses in bracketed regular expressions, these parentheses are not quoted (Table A-7).

Table A-7   Extended regular expressions

Regular expression	Matches	Examples
/ab+c/	a followed by one or more b's followed by a c	yabcw, abbc57
/ab?c/	a followed by zero or one b followed by c	back, abcdef
/(ab)+c/	One or more occurrences of the string ab followed by c	zabcd, ababc!
/(ab)?c/	Zero or one occurrence of the string ab followed by c	xc, abcc

In full regular expressions, the vertical bar (|) special character is a Boolean OR operator. Within vim, you must quote the vertical bar by preceding it with a backslash to make it special (\|). A vertical bar between two regular expressions causes a match with strings that match the first expression, the second expression, or both. You can use the vertical bar with parentheses to separate from the rest of the regular expression the two expressions that are being ORed (Table A-8).

Table A-8   Full regular expressions

Regular expression	Meaning	Examples
/ab|ac/	Either <u>ab</u> or <u>ac</u>	<u>ab</u>, <u>ac</u>, <u>abac</u> (**abac** is two matches of the regular expression)
/^Exit|^Quit/	Lines that begin with <u>Exit</u> or <u>Quit</u>	<u>Exit</u>, <u>Quit</u>, No Exit
/(D|N)\. Jones/	<u>D. Jones</u> or <u>N. Jones</u>	P.<u>D. Jones</u>, <u>N. Jones</u>

APPENDIX SUMMARY

A regular expression defines a set of one or more strings of characters. A regular expression is said to match any string it defines.

In a regular expression, a special character is one that does not represent itself. Table A-9 lists special characters.

Table A-9   Special characters

Character	Meaning
.	Matches any single character
*	Matches zero or more occurrences of a match of the preceding character
^	Forces a match to the beginning of a line
$	A match to the end of a line
\	Used to quote special characters
\<	Forces a match to the beginning of a word
\>	Forces a match to the end of a word

Table A-10 lists ways of representing character classes and bracketed regular expressions.

Table A-10   Character classes and bracketed regular expressions

Class	Defines
[*xyz*]	Defines a character class that matches *x*, *y*, or *z*
[^*xyz*]	Defines a character class that matches any character except *x*, *y*, or *z*
[*x–z*]	Defines a character class that matches any character *x* through *z* inclusive
\(*xyz*\)	Matches what *xyz* matches (a bracketed regular expression)

In addition to the preceding special characters and strings (excluding quoted parentheses, except in vim), the characters given in Table A-11 are special within full, or extended, regular expressions.

Table A-11   Extended regular expressions

Expression	Matches
+	Matches one or more occurrences of the preceding character
?	Matches zero or one occurrence of the preceding character
(*xyz*)+	One or more occurrences of what *xyz* matches
(*xyz*)?	Zero or one occurrence of what *xyz* matches
(*xyz*)*	Zero or more occurrences of what *xyz* matches
xyz|*abc*	Either what *xyz* or what *abc* matches (use \\| in vim)
(*xy*|*ab*)*c*	Either what *xyc* or what *abc* matches (use \\| in vim)

Table A-12 lists characters that are special within a replacement string in sed and vim.

Table A-12   Replacement strings

String	Represents
&	Represents what the regular expression (search string) matched
n	A quoted number, *n*, represents what the *n*th bracketed regular expression in the search string matched

B

Help

You need not act as a user or system administrator in isolation. A large community of Linux experts is willing to assist you in learning about, helping you solve your problems with, and getting the most out of your Linux system. Before you ask for help, however, make sure you have done everything you can to solve the problem by yourself. No doubt, someone has experienced the same problem before you and the answer to your question can be found somewhere on the Internet. Your job is to find it. This appendix lists resources and describes methods that can help you in that task.

SOLVING A PROBLEM

Following is a list of steps that can help you solve a problem without asking someone else for help. Depending on your understanding of and experience with the hardware and software involved, these steps may lead to a solution.

1. Most Linux distributions come with extensive documentation. Read the documentation on the specific hardware or software you are having a problem with. If it is a GNU product, use info; otherwise, use man to find local information. For more information refer to "Getting the Facts: Where to Find Documentation" on page 29.

2. When the problem involves some type of error or other message, use a search engine, such as Google (www.google.com) or Google Groups (groups.google.com), to look up the message on the Internet. If the message is long, pick a unique part of the message to search for; 10 to 20 characters should be enough. Enclose the search string within double quotation marks.

3. Check whether the Linux Documentation Project (www.tldp.org) has a HOWTO or mini-HOWTO on the subject in question. Search on keywords that relate directly to the product and your problem. Read the FAQs.

4. See Table B-1 for other sources of documentation.

5. Use Google or Google Groups to search on keywords that relate directly to the product and your problem.

6. When all else fails (or perhaps before you try anything else) examine the system logs in **/var/log**. Running as Superuser, first look at the end of the **messages** file using the following command:

```
# tail -20 /var/log/messages
```

If **messages** contains nothing useful, run the following command. It displays the names of the log files in chronological order, with the most recently modified files appearing at the bottom of the list:

```
$ ls -ltr /var/log
```

If your problem involves a network connection, review the **secure** log file (some systems may use a different name) on the local and remote systems. Also look at **messages** on the remote system.

7. The **/var/spool** directory contains subdirectories with useful information: **cups** holds the print queues, **mail** holds the user's mail files, and so on.

If you are unable to solve a problem yourself, a thoughtful question to an appropriate newsgroup (page 841) or mailing list (page 841) can elicit useful information. When you send or post a question, make sure you describe the problem and identify the local system carefully. Include the version numbers of the operating system and any software packages that relate to the problem. Describe your hardware, if appropriate.

The author's home page (www.sobell.com) contains corrections to this book, answers to selected chapter exercises, and pointers to other Linux sites.

FINDING LINUX-RELATED INFORMATION

Distributions of Linux come with reference pages stored online. You can read these documents by using the info (page 32) or man (page 30) utilities. You can read man and info pages to get more information about specific topics while reading this book or to determine which features are available with Linux. You can search for topics by using apropos (see page 62 or give the command **man apropos**).

DOCUMENTATION

Good books are available on various aspects of using and administrating UNIX systems in general and Linux systems in particular. In addition, you may find the sites listed in Table B-1 useful.[1]

Table B-1 Documentation

Site	About the site	URL
freedesktop.org	Creates standards for interoperability between open source desktop environments.	freedesktop.org
GNOME	GNOME home page.	www.gnome.org
GNU Manuals	GNU manuals. GNU manual on info.	www.gnu.org/manual www.gnu.org/software/texinfo/manual/info
Internet FAQ Archives	Searchable FAQ archives.	www.faqs.org
Info	Instructions for using the info utility.	www.gnu.org/software/texinfo/manual/info

---

1. The right-hand columns of most of the tables in this appendix show Internet addresses (URLs). All sites have an implicit http:// prefix unless ftp:// or https:// is shown. Refer to "URLs (Web addresses)" on page 23.

Table B-1 Documentation *(continued)*

KDE Documentation	KDE documentation.	kde.org/documentation
KDE News	KDE news.	dot.kde.org
RFCs	Request for Comments; see *RFC* (page 898).	www.rfc-editor.org
System Administrators Guild (SAGE)	SAGE is a group for system administrators.	www.sage.org
The Linux Documentation Project	All things related to Linux documentation (in many languages): HOWTOs, guides, FAQs, man pages, and magazines. This is the best overall source for Linux documentation. Make sure to visit its Links page.	www.tldp.org

USEFUL LINUX SITES

Sometimes the sites listed in Table B-2 are so busy that you cannot log in. When this happens, you are usually given a list of alternative, or *mirror*, sites to try.

Table B-2 Useful Linux sites

Site	About the site	URL
GNU	GNU Project Web server.	www.gnu.org
ibiblio	A large library and digital archive. Formerly Metalab; formerly Sunsite.	www.ibiblio.org www.ibiblio.org/pub/linux www.ibiblio.org/pub/historic-linux
Linux Knowledge Portal	A configurable site that gathers information from other sites and sources and presents it in a well-organized format. Sources include KDE News, GNOME News, Slashdot, and many more. In English and German.	www.linux-knowledge-portal.org
Linux Standard Base (LSB)	A group dedicated to standardizing Linux.	www.linuxbase.org
Sobell	The author's home page contains useful links, errata for this book, code for many of the examples in this book, and answers to selected exercises.	www.sobell.com

Table B-2   Useful Linux sites *(continued)*

USENIX	A large, well-established UNIX group. This site has many links, including a list of conferences.	www.usenix.org
X.Org	The X Window System home.	www.x.org

LINUX NEWSGROUPS

One of the best ways of getting specific information is through a newsgroup. Frequently you can find the answer to your question by reading postings to the newsgroup. Try using Google Groups (groups.google.com) to search through newsgroups to see whether your question has already been asked and answered. Or open a newsreader program and subscribe to appropriate newsgroups. If necessary, you can post your question for someone to answer. Before you do so, make sure you are posting to the correct group and that your question has not been answered. There is an etiquette to posting questions—see www.catb.org/~esr/faqs/smart-questions.html for a good paper by Eric S. Raymond and Rick Moen titled "How To Ask Questions the Smart Way."

The newsgroup **comp.os.linux.answers** provides postings of solutions to common problems and periodic postings of the most up-to-date versions of the FAQ and HOWTO documents. The **comp.os.linux.misc** newsgroup has answers to miscellaneous Linux-related questions.

MAILING LISTS

Subscribing to a mailing list allows you to participate in an electronic discussion. With most lists, you can send and receive email dedicated to a specific topic to and from a group of users. Moderated lists do not tend to stray as much as unmoderated lists, assuming the list has a good moderator. The disadvantage of a moderated list is that some discussions may be cut off when they get interesting if the moderator deems that the discussion has gone on for too long. Mailing lists described as bulletins are strictly unidirectional: You cannot post information to these lists but can only receive periodic bulletins. If you have the subscription address for a mailing list but are not sure how to subscribe, put the word **help** in the body and/or header of email that you send to the address. You will usually receive instructions via return email. You can also use a search engine to search for **mailing list linux**.

WORDS

Many dictionaries, thesauruses, and glossaries are available online. Table B-3 lists a few of them.

Table B-3   Looking up words

Site	About the site	URL
Apt	Apt installs, removes, and updates system software packages	apt.freshrpms.net
ARTFL Project: ROGET'S Thesaurus	Thesaurus	humanities.uchicago.edu/forms_unrest/ROGET.html
BitTorrent	BitTorrent efficiently distributes large amounts of static data	www.bittorrent.com
DICT.org	Multiple database search for words	www.dict.org
Dictionary.com	Everything related to words	www.dictionary.com
DNS Glossary	DNS Glossary	www.menandmice.com/online_docs_and_faq/glossary/glossarytoc.htm
FOLDOC (The Free On-Line Dictionary of Computing)	Computer terms	www.foldoc.org
Merriam-Webster	English language	www.m-w.com
OneLook	Multiple-site word search with a single query	www.onelook.com
The Jargon File	An online version of *The New Hacker's Dictionary*	www.catb.org/~esr/jargon
Webopedia	Commercial technical dictionary	www.webopedia.com
Wikipedia	An open-source (user-contributed) encyclopedia project	wikipedia.org
Wordsmyth	Dictionary and thesaurus	www.wordsmyth.net
Yahoo Reference	Search multiple sources at the same time	education.yahoo.com/reference
yum	The yum utility installs, removes, and updates system software packages	linux.duke.edu/projects/yum apt.freshrpms.net

SOFTWARE

There are many ways to learn about interesting software packages and where they are available on the Internet. Table B-4 lists sites that you can download software from. Another way to learn about software packages is through a newsgroup (page 841).

Table B-4 Software

Site	About the site	URL
CVS	CVS (Concurrent Versions System) is a version control system	www.cvshome.org
ddd	The ddd utility is a graphical front end for command line debuggers such as gdb	www.gnu.org/software/ddd
Free Software Directory	Categorized, searchable lists of free software	www.gnu.org/directory savannah.gnu.org
Freshmeat	A large index of UNIX and cross-platform software, themes, and Palm OS software	freshmeat.net
gdb	The gdb utility is a command line debugger	www.gnu.org/software/gdb
GNOME Project	Links to all GNOME projects	www.gnome.org/projects
IceWALKERS	Categorized, searchable lists of free software	www.iccwalkorc.com
kdbg	The kdbg utility is a graphical user interface to gdb	freshmeat.net/projects/kdbg
Linux Software Map	A database of packages written for, ported to, or compiled for Linux	www.boutell.com/lsm
linuxapps	Categorized, searchable list of free software	www.linuxapps.com
Mtools	A collection of utilities to access DOS floppy diskettes from Linux without mounting the diskettes	mtools.linux.lu
Network Calculators	Subnet mask calculator	www.subnetmask.info
rpmfind.net	Searchable list of rpm files for various Linux distributions and versions	rpmfind.net/linux/RPM
SourceForge	A development Web site with a large repository of open-source code and applications	sourceforge.net
strace	The strace utility is a system call trace debugging tool	www.liacs.nl/~wichert/strace sourceforge.net/projects/strace

Table B-4 Software (continued)

Tucows-Linux	Commercial, categorized, searchable list of software	linux.tucows.com
ups	The ups utility is a graphical source-level debugger	ups.sourceforge.net

OFFICE SUITES AND WORD PROCESSORS

Several office suites and many word processors are available for Linux. Table B-5 lists a few of them. If you are exchanging documents with people using Windows, make sure the import from/export to MS Word functionality covers your needs.

Table B-5 Office suites and word processors

Product name	What it does	URL
AbiWord	Word processor (free)	www.abisource.com
KOffice	Integrated suite of office applications including the Kword word processing program (free, KDE-based)	www.koffice.org
OpenOffice	An open-source version of StarOffice	www.openoffice.org www.gnome.org/projects/ooo
Xcoral	A programmer's multiwindow mouse-based editor that runs under X (free)	xcoral.free.fr

SPECIFYING A TERMINAL

Because vim, emacs, konsole, and other programs take advantage of features that are specific to various kinds of terminals and terminal emulators, you must tell these programs the name of the terminal you are using or the terminal that your terminal emulator is emulating. On many systems your terminal name is set for you. If your terminal name is not specified or is not specified correctly, your screen will look garbled or, when you start a program, the program will ask what type of terminal you are using.

Terminal names describe the functional characteristics of your terminal or terminal emulator to programs that require this information. Although terminal names are referred to as either Terminfo or Termcap names, the difference relates to the method that each system uses to store the terminal characteristics internally, not in the manner that you specify the name of a terminal. Terminal names that are often used with Linux terminal emulators and with graphical monitors while they are run in text mode are **ansi**, **linux**, **vt100**, **vt102**, **vt220**, and **xterm**.

When you are running a terminal emulator, you can specify the type of terminal you want to emulate. Set the emulator to either **vt100** or **vt220**, and set **TERM** to the same value.

When you log in, you may be prompted to identify the type of terminal you are using:

```
TERM = (vt100)
```

There are two ways to respond to this prompt. You can press RETURN to set your terminal type to the name in parentheses. When that name does not describe the terminal you are using, you can enter the correct name and then press RETURN.

```
TERM = (vt100) ansi
```

You may also receive the following prompt:

```
TERM = (unknown)
```

This prompt indicates that the system does not know what type of terminal you are using. If you plan to run programs that require this information, enter the name of the terminal or terminal emulator you are using before you press RETURN.

TERM If you do not receive a prompt, you can give the following command to display the value of the **TERM** variable and check whether your terminal type has been set:

```
$ echo $TERM
```

If the system responds with the wrong name, a blank line, or an error message, set or change the terminal name. From the Bourne Again Shell (bash), enter a command similar to the following to set the **TERM** variable so that the system knows the type of terminal you are using:

export TERM=name

Replace *name* with the terminal name for the terminal you are using, making sure that you do not put a SPACE before or after the equal sign. If you always use the same type of terminal, you can place this command in your **~/.bashrc** file (page 257), causing the shell to set the terminal type each time you log in. For example, give the following command to set your terminal name to **vt100**:

```
$ export TERM=vt100
```

Use the following format under the TC Shell (tcsh).

setenv TERM name

Again replace *name* with the terminal name for the terminal you are using. Under tcsh you can place this command in your **~/.login** file (page 342). For example, under tcsh you can give this command to set your terminal name to **vt100**:

```
$ setenv TERM vt100
```

LANG   For some programs to display information correctly you may need to set the **LANG** variable (page 290). Frequently you can set this variable to **C**. Under bash use the command

```
$ export LANG=C
```

and under tcsh use

```
$ setenv LANG C
```

C

KEEPING THE SYSTEM UP-TO-DATE

Apt and yum both fill the same role: They install and update software packages. Both utilities compare the files in a repository (generally on the Internet) with those on the local system and update the files on the local system according to your instructions. Both utilities automatically install and update any additional files that a package is dependent on. Apt is slightly faster, especially over slow connections, and it supports a few more features, such as undoing upgrades. The yum utility is easier to configure and use than Apt. If you are familiar with Debian systems or find that yum lacks some features you need, try using Apt; otherwise use yum. The examples in this section are from a Fedora Core system; although the files, input, and output on your system may look different, how you use the tools and the results will be the same.

Contrasted with Apt and yum, BitTorrent efficiently distributes large amounts of static data, such as installation ISO images. It does not check files on the local system and does no dependency checking.

yum: UPDATES AND INSTALLS PACKAGES

Early releases of Linux did not include a tool for managing updates. The RPM tool could install or upgrade individual software packages, but it was up to the user to locate the packages and the packages they were dependent on. When Terra Soft produced its Linux distribution for the PowerPC, the company created the Yellow Dog Updater to fill this gap. This program has since been ported to other architectures and distributions. The result, named Yellow Dog Updater, Modified (yum), is included with many Linux distributions. The yum home page is linux.duke.edu/projects/yum and more information is available at apt.freshrpms.net.

CONFIGURING yum

The yum utility is designed to be easy to use. The configuration file, **/etc/yum.conf**, has two parts: The [**main**] section contains general settings and the rest of the file holds a list of servers.

The [**main**] section must be present for yum to function. The **cachedir** specifies the directory yum uses to store downloaded packages and **logfile** specifies where yum keeps its log. The amount of information logged is specified by **debuglevel**, with a value of 10 producing the most information.

```
$ cat /etc/yum.conf
[main]
cachedir=/var/cache/yum
debuglevel=2
logfile=/var/log/yum.log
pkgpolicy=newest
distroverpkg=fedora-release
tolerant=1
exactarch=1
...
```

The **pkgpolicy** defines which version of a software package yum installs; always set it to **newest** to install the newest version of a package. You can also configure yum to try to install from a specific server, falling back to other servers on failure and ignoring package versions. The **distroverpkg** specifies which distribution the system is running.

With **tolerant** set to **1**, yum automatically corrects simple command line errors, such as attempting to install a package already on the system. Setting **tolerant** to **0** turns this feature off. Setting **exactarch** to **1** causes yum to update packages only with packages of the same architecture—preventing an i686 package from replacing an i386 one, for example.

The last sections contain lists of servers holding updates. They are marked with [core], [updates], or other similar labels. Frequently the last section contains updates that are not ready for release and is commented out; do not uncomment it unless you are testing unstable packages. Never uncomment this section on production systems. Each server section contains a **name, baseurl,** and **gpgcheck** flag:

```
$ cat /etc/yum.conf
...
[core]
name=Fedora Linux $releasever - $basearch - core
baseurl=http://ayo.freshrpms.net/fedora/linux/$releasever/$basearch/core
gpgcheck=1
...
```

The **name** provides a friendly name for the server. The **baseurl** indicates the location of the server. Set **gpgcheck** to **1** if you want yum to check the gpg signatures of the packages it downloads. Set it to **0** otherwise. These definitions use two variables: yum sets **$basearch** to the architecture of the system and **$releasever** to the version of the release. Refer to the **yum.conf** man page for more options.

USING yum

Working as **root,** you can run yum from a command line. Its behavior depends on the options you specify. The **update** option updates all installed packages: It downloads package headers for installed packages, prompts you to proceed, and downloads and installs the updated packages.

```
# yum update
Gathering header information file(s) from server(s)
Server: Fedora Core 3 - i386 - Base
Server: Fedora Core 3 - i386 - Released Updates
Finding updated packages
Downloading needed headers
getting /var/cache/yum/updates-released/headers/pango-0-1.6.07.i386.hdr
pango-0-1.6.0-7.i386.hdr  100% |=========================| 6.5 kB 00:00
...
[update: rhn-applet 2.1.4-3.i386]
Is this ok [y/N]: y
Getting pango-1.6.0-7.i386.rpm
pango-1.6.0-7.i386.rpm    100% |=========================| 341 kB 00:06
...
```

You can update individual packages by specifying the names of the packages on the command line following the word **update.**

To install a new package together with the packages it is dependent on, give the command **yum install** followed by the name of the package as shown on the next page.

```
# yum install tcsh
Gathering header information file(s) from server(s)
Server: Fedora Core 3 - i386 - Base
Server: Fedora Core 3 - i386 - Released Updates
Finding updated packages
Downloading needed headers
getting /var/cache/yum/base/headers/tcsh-0-6.13-9.i386.hdr
tcsh-0-6.13-9.i386.hdr     100% |=========================| 3.8 kB    00:00
Resolving dependencies
Dependencies resolved
I will do the following:
[install: tcsh 6.13-9.i386]
Is this ok [y/N]: y
Getting tcsh-6.13-9.i386.rpm
tcsh-6.13-9.i386.rpm       100% |=========================| 443 kB    00:10
Running test transaction:
Test transaction complete, Success!
tcsh 100 % done 1/1
Installed:  tcsh 6.13-9.i386
Transaction(s) Complete
```

You can also use yum to remove packages, using a similar syntax:

```
# yum remove tcsh
Gathering header information file(s) from server(s)
Server: Fedora Core 3 - i386 - Base
Server: Fedora Core 3 - i386 - Released Updates
Finding updated packages
Downloading needed headers
Resolving dependencies
Dependencies resolved
I will do the following:
[erase: tcsh 6.13-9.i386]
Is this ok [y/N]: y
Running test transaction:
Test transaction complete, Success!
Erasing: tcsh 1/1
Erased:  tcsh 6.13-9.i386
Transaction(s) Complete
```

APT: AN ALTERNATIVE TO yum

The Apt (Advanced Package Tool) utility can help with the issue of dependencies: Apt tries to resolve package dependencies automatically by looking for the packages that the package you are installing is dependent on. Since starting life as part of the Debian Linux distribution using Debian's **.deb** package format, Apt has been ported to rpm-based distributions. For more information go to apt.freshrpms.net.

The Apt utility uses repositories of rpm files as the basis for its actions. To make things quicker, Apt keeps locally a list of packages that are held in each of the repositories it uses. Any software you want to install or update must reside in a repository.

When you give Apt a command to install a package, Apt looks for the package in its local package list. If the package appears in the list, Apt fetches both that package and any packages that the package you are installing is dependent on and calls rpm to install the packages. Because Apt uses rpm, it maintains the rpm database.

USING APT

This section describes how to configure Apt.

INSTALLING AND SETTING UP APT

Once you have downloaded the **apt＊.rpm** file, you must install it (your Apt version number will be different):

```
# rpm -Uvh apt-0.5.15cnc6-1.1.fc3.fr.i386.rpm
Preparing...                ###########################################[100%]
   1:apt                    ###########################################[100%]
```

Update the local package list The primary Apt command is apt-get; its arguments determine what the command does. After you install Apt, give the command **apt-get update** to update the local package list:

```
# apt-get update
Get:1 http://ayo.freshrpms.net fedora/linux/3/i386 release [1991B]
Fetched 1991B in 0s (4922B/s)
Get:1 http://ayo.freshrpms.net fedora/linux/3/i386/core pkglist [1445kB]
Get:2 http://ayo.freshrpms.net fedora/linux/3/i386/core release [151B]
Get:3 http://ayo.freshrpms.net fedora/linux/3/i386/updates pkglist [251kB]
Get:4 http://ayo.freshrpms.net fedora/linux/3/i386/updates release [157B]
Get:5 http://ayo.freshrpms.net fedora/linux/3/i386/freshrpms pkglist [98kB]
Get:6 http://ayo.freshrpms.net fedora/linux/3/i386/freshrpms release [161B]
Fetched 1847kB in 28s (64.7kB/s)
Reading Package Lists... Done
Building Dependency Tree... Done
```

Because the available packages change frequently, it is a good idea to create a cron job to update the local package list automatically. Create the following file to perform this task daily:

```
$ cat /etc/cron.daily/apt-update
apt-get update
```

Check the dependency tree The Apt utility does not tolerate a broken rpm dependency tree. To check the status of the local dependency tree, run **apt-get check**:

```
# apt-get check
Reading Package Lists... Done
Building Dependency Tree... Done
```

The easiest way to fix errors that apt-get reveals is to erase the offending packages and then reinstall them using Apt.

At the time this book was written, Apt was incompatible with the Ximian Desktop.

Update the system Two arguments to apt-get cause it upgrade all packages on the system: **upgrade** upgrades all packages on the system that do not require new packages to be installed and **dist-upgrade** upgrades all packages on the system, installing new packages as needed.

The following command updates all rpm-based packages on the system that depend only on packages that are already installed:

```
# apt-get upgrade
Reading Package Lists... Done
Building Dependency Tree... Done
The following packages will be upgraded
  bash binutils dia ethereal foomatic gaim gdm ghostscript gimp-print
...
   rhn-applet rsync sed slocate strace vnc-server yum
The following packages have been kept back
  gstreamer-plugins gthumb rhythmbox
57 upgraded, 0 newly installed, 0 removed and 3 not upgraded.
Need to get 59.7MB/87.9MB of archives.
After unpacking 11.8MB of additional disk space will be used.
Do you want to continue? [Y/n]
```

Enter **Y** to upgrade the listed packages; otherwise, enter **N**. Packages that are not upgraded because they depend on packages that are not already installed are listed as **kept back**.

Use **dist-upgrade** to upgrade all packages, including packages that are dependent on packages that are not installed. This command also installs dependencies.

```
# apt-get dist-upgrade
Reading Package Lists... Done
Building Dependency Tree... Done
Calculating Upgrade... Done
The following packages will be upgraded
  gstreamer-plugins gthumb rhythmbox
The following NEW packages will be installed:
  Hermes flac libexif libid3tag
3 upgraded, 4 newly installed, 0 removed and 0 not upgraded.
Need to get 4510kB of archives.
After unpacking 6527kB of additional disk space will be used.
Do you want to continue? [Y/n]
```

ADDING AND REMOVING INDIVIDUAL PACKAGES

The format of a command to install a specific software package and the packages it is dependent on is *apt-get install **package***

where ***package*** is the name of the package, such as **zsh**, and not the name of the rpm, which usually includes version and architecture information (for example, **zsh-1.2.i386.rpm**).

```
# apt-get install zsh
Reading Package Lists... Done
Building Dependency Tree... Done
The following NEW packages will be installed:
  zsh
0 upgraded, 1 newly installed, 0 removed and 0 not upgraded.
Need to get 1435kB of archives.
After unpacking 2831kB of additional disk space will be used.
Get:1 http://ayo.freshrpms.net fedora/linux/3/i386/core zsh 4.2.0-3 [1435kB]
Fetched 1435kB in 21s (66.0kB/s)
Committing changes...
Preparing...                ########################################### [100%]
   1:zsh                    ########################################### [100%]
Done.
```

Remove a package the same way you install a package, substituting **remove** for **install**:

```
# apt-get remove zsh
Reading Package Lists... Done
Building Dependency Tree... Done
The following packages will be REMOVED:
  zsh
0 upgraded, 0 newly installed, 1 removed and 0 not upgraded.
Need to get 0B of archives.
After unpacking 2831kB disk space will be freed.
Do you want to continue? [Y/n] y
Committing changes...
Preparing...                ########################################### [100%]
Done.
```

To ensure that you can later reinstall a package with the same configuration, the **apt-get remove** command does not remove configuration files from the **/etc** directory hierarchy. Although it is not recommended, you can use the **--purge** option to remove all of these files, including configuration files. Alternatively, you can move these files to an archive so you can restore them later if necessary.

apt.conf: Configuring Apt

The **/etc/apt/apt.conf** file contains Apt configuration information and is split into three sections: **APT**, which contains global settings for the Apt tools; **Acquire**, which describes settings related to the package-fetching mechanism; and **RPM**, which contains rpm-specific settings. In this file semicolons (**;**) separate statements and double forward slashes (**//**) introduce comments.

APT section   The **APT** section is shown following:

```
$ cat /etc/apt/apt.conf
APT {
    Clean-Installed "false";
    Get {
        Assume-Yes "false";
        Download-Only "false";
        Show-Upgraded "true";
        Fix-Broken "false";
        Ignore-Missing "false";
        Compile "false";
    };
};
...
```

When you set **Clean-Installed** to TRUE, Apt removes packages that are no longer in the repository.

The options in the **Get** subsection listed here apply to the apt-get utility (the apt-get utility has command line arguments with the same names as these options):

Assume-Yes   TRUE runs apt-get in batch mode, automatically answering YES whenever it would otherwise prompt you for input.

Download-Only   TRUE retrieves packages from the repository but does not install them. FALSE retrieves and installs the packages.

Show-Upgraded   TRUE displays a list of upgraded packages.

Fix-Broken   TRUE attempts to fix dependency tree problems with varying degrees of success. FALSE quits if it finds a dependency tree problem.

Ignore-Missing   TRUE holds back missing or corrupt packages and continues to install other packages. FALSE aborts the entire install or upgrade upon finding a missing or corrupt package.

Compile   TRUE compiles and installs source rpm (SRPM) packages that you ask apt-get to retrieve. FALSE downloads these files without compiling or installing them.

Acquire section   The **Acquire** section controls options related to fetching packages.

```
$ cat /etc/apt/apt.conf
...
Acquire {
Retries "0";
Http {
Proxy ""; // http://user:pass@host:port/
}
};
...
```

The **Retries** option specifies the number of times Apt attempts to fetch a package when an attempt fails. The **Http Proxy** setting specifies the proxy to use when fetching packages using HTTP. The argument to this option is blank by default, indicating that Apt should not use a proxy. An example proxy is shown as a comment.

RPM section   Following is the **RPM** section of **apt.conf**:

```
$ cat /etc/apt/apt.conf
...
RPM {
    Ignore { };
    Hold { };
    Allow-Duplicated { "^kernel$"; "^kernel-"; "^kmodule-"; "^gpg-pukey$"
};
    Options { };
    Install-Options "";
    Erase-Options "";
    Source {
        Build-Command "rpmbuild --rebuild";
    };
};
```

The **Ignore** and **Hold** options perform similar functions and contain lists of packages that Apt ignores or holds (does not upgrade). They are usually blank.

The **Allow-Duplicated** section lists packages that can have more than one version on the system at one time. In general you do not want to have multiple versions of the same package on a system. The kernel is an exception: It is good practice to leave the old kernel installed when you install a new kernel in case you are unable to boot the new one.

The **Options** section contains options that are passed to rpm. The **Install-Options** and **Erase-Options** sections contain options that are passed to rpm whenever it is used to install or erase a package.

The **Source Build-Command** option specifies the command that Apt uses to build a source rpm file.

BITTORRENT

The BitTorrent protocol implements a hybrid client/server and *P2P* (page 891) file transfer mechanism. BitTorrent efficiently distributes large amounts of static data, such as installation ISO images. It can replace protocols such as anonymous FTP, where client authentication is not required. Each BitTorrent client that downloads a file provides additional bandwidth for uploading the file, reducing the load on the initial source. In general BitTorrent downloads proceed more rapidly than FTP downloads.

Unlike protocols such as FTP, BitTorrent groups multiple files into a single package called a *torrent*. For example, you can typically download several installation ISO images as a single torrent.

Like other P2P systems, BitTorrent does not use a dedicated server. Instead, the functions of a server are performed by the tracker, peers, and seeds. The *tracker* allows clients to communicate with each other. A client—called a *peer* when it has downloaded part of the torrent and a *seed* once it has downloaded the entire torrent—acts as an additional source for the torrent. As with a P2P network, each peer and seed that downloads a torrent uploads to other clients the sections of the torrent it already has. There is nothing special about a seed: It can be removed at any time once the torrent is available for download from other seeds.

The BitTorrent program is available from www.bittorrent.com. After you download and install BitTorrent, the first step in downloading a torrent using BitTorrent is to locate or acquire a **.torrent** file. A **.torrent** file contains the information about the torrent, such as its size and the location of the tracker. You can use a **.torrent** file using its *URI* (page 908) or you can acquire it via the Web, an email attachment, or other means. The next step is for the BitTorrent client to connect to the tracker to learn the locations of other clients that it can download the torrent from.

Once you have downloaded a torrent, it is good manners to allow BitTorrent to continue to run so other clients can upload *at least* as much information as you have downloaded.

PREREQUISITES

If no BitTorrent rpm file exists for your version of Linux, use an rpm file for a similar version. Because BitTorrent is written in Python and runs on any platform with a Python interpreter, it is not dependent on system architecture. The **noarch** in the name of the rpm file stands for no architecture.

To run, BitTorrent requires Python, which is installed as **/usr/bin/python** on many systems. Python is available in the **python** rpm package.

HOW BITTORRENT WORKS

The official BitTorrent distribution includes three client applications. You can use any of these applications to download BitTorrent files:

- **btdownloadheadless.py**   A text-based client that writes the status to standard output. Good for unattended downloads where the output is redirected to a file.

- **btdownloadcurses.py**   A text-based client that provides a pseudographical interface. Good for attended downloads to machines not running a GUI.

- **btdownloadgui.py**   A graphical client.

In addition to the official clients, several other clients provide extra features. Some of these clients are available on sourceforge.net.

Using BitTorrent

To use BitTorrent, first locate the **.torrent** file for the torrent you want to download. You can copy the **.torrent** file to the working directory (the first format shown below) or specify it with a **--url** option (second format). The simplest BitTorrent command lines have the following formats:

$ *btdownloadheadless.py --responsefile* **tfile.torrent** *[--saveas* **savefile**]

or

$ *btdownloadheadless.py --url* **http://domain/tfile.torrent** *[--saveas* **savefile**]

where **tfile.torrent** is the name of, or **http://domain/tfile.torrent** is the URI for, the .torrent file, and *savefile* is the location to save the torrent in. In the case of torrents containing a single file, the file is saved as *savefile*. For torrents containing multiple files, the files are saved in a directory named *savefile*. If you omit the **--saveas** argument, the files are saved in the name specified in the **.torrent** file. Because each of the **btdownload*.py** applications takes the same arguments, the preceding formats work for all three applications.

The next example shows how to download Fedora Core 3 ISO images. These large files take considerable time to download. To start the download, give the following command. Because the command line is long, it is broken by a backslash (\). Make sure no character follows the backslash, or else the backslash will not quote the following RETURN and the command will fail. (The shell supplies the > on the second line.)

```
$ btdownloadheadless.py --max_upload_rate 8 \
> --url http://torrent.dulug.duke.edu/heidelberg-binary-i386.torrent
```

The preceding command uses a URI to specify a **.torrent** file and saves the downloaded files in a directory named **heidelberg** (the name of the Fedora release) as specified by the **.torrent** file.

The **--max_upload_rate** 8 option prevents BitTorrent from using more than 8 kilobytes per second of upstream bandwidth. BitTorrent usually gives higher download rates to clients that upload more, so feel free to increase this value if you have spare bandwidth. You need to leave enough free upstream bandwidth for the acknowledgment packets from your download to get through or your download will be very slow. By default the client uploads to a maximum of seven other clients at once. You can change this value by specifying the **--max_uploads** argument, followed by the maximum number of concurrent uploads you wish to permit. The default value of 7 is usually appropriate for typical broadband connections.

After you give the preceding command, the screen quickly fills with output that looks similar to the following:

```
saving:              heidelberg-binary-i386
percent done:        0.0
time left:           finishing in 27:09:04
download to:         /home/max/heidelberg-binary-i386
download rate:       32.9 KB/s
upload rate:         0.0 KB/s
share rating:        0.000  (0.0 MB up / 1.2 MB down)
seed status:         30 seen now, plus 1 distributed copies (2:81.5%, 3:23.0%, 4:2.1%)
peer status:         5 seen now
```

The file size is that of all the files you are downloading: four ISO images and several smaller files. To abort the download, press CONTROL-C. The download will automatically resume from where it left off when you download the same torrent to the same location again.

Use the following command to perform the same download as in the previous example, this time throttling the rate and number of uploads to values sensible for modem users. (The shell supplies the > on the second line, you do not enter it.)

```
$ btdownloadcurses.py --max_upload_rate 3 --max_uploads 2 \
> --url http://torrent.dulug.duke.edu/heidelberg-binary-i386.torrent
```

The preceding command displays output similar to the following:

```
---------------------------------------------------------------------
| file:     heidelberg-binary-i386                                    |
| size:     2,467,681,047 (2 GiB)                                     |
| dest:     /home/max/heidelberg-binary-i386                          |
| progress: _____ |
| status:   finishing in 6:40:42 (1.0%)                               |
| dl speed: 285.6 KB/s                                                 |
| ul speed: 2.6 KB/s                                                   |
| sharing:  0.009  (0.1 MB up / 15.1 MB down)                         |
| seeds:    29 seen now, plus 0 distributed copies (1:0.8%, 2:0.0%, 3:0.0%)  |
| peers:    1 seen now                                                |
|                                                                     |
---------------------------------------------------------------------
```

GLOSSARY

All entries marked with FOLDOC are based on definitions in the Free Online Dictionary of Computing (www.foldoc.org), Denis Howe, editor. Used with permission.

10.0.0.0	See *private address space* on page 894.
172.16.0.0	See *private address space* on page 894.
192.168.0.0	See *private address space* on page 894.
802.11	A family of specifications developed by IEEE for wireless LAN technology, including 802.11 (1–2 megabits per second), 802.11a (54 megabits per second), 802.11b (11 megabits per second), and 802.11g (20+ megabits per second).
absolute pathname	A pathname that starts with the root directory (/). An absolute pathname locates a file without regard to the working directory.
access	In computer jargon, a verb meaning to use, read from, or write to. To access a file means to read from or write to the file.
Access Control List	See *ACL*.
access permission	Permission to read from, write to, or execute a file. If you have write access permission to a file, you can write to the file. Also *access privilege*.
ACL	Access Control List. A system that performs a function similar to file permissions but with much finer-grain control.
active window	On a desktop, the window that receives the characters you type on the keyboard. Same as *focus, desktop* (page 875).
address mask	See *subnet mask* on page 903.
alias	A mechanism of a shell that enables you to define new commands.
alphanumeric character	One of the characters, either uppercase or lowercase, from A to Z and 0 to 9, inclusive.
ambiguous file reference	A reference to a file that does not necessarily specify any one file but can be used to specify a group of files. The shell expands an ambiguous file reference into a list of filenames. Special characters represent single characters (?), strings of zero or more characters (*), and character classes ([]) within ambiguous file references. An ambiguous file reference is a type of *regular expression* (page 897).
angle bracket	A left angle bracket (<) and a right angle bracket (>). The shell uses < to redirect a command's standard input to come from a file and > to redirect the standard output. The shell uses the characters << to signify the start of a Here document and >> to append output to a file.
animate	When referring to a window action, means that the action is slowed down so the user can view it. For example, when you minimize a window, it can disappear all at once (not animated) or it can slowly telescope into the panel so you can get a visual feel for what is happening (animated).

anti-aliasing	Adding gray pixels at the edge of a diagonal line to get rid of the jagged appearance and thereby make the line look smoother. Anti-aliasing sometimes makes type on a screen look better and sometimes worse; it works best on small and large fonts and is less effective on fonts from 8 to 15 points. See also *subpixel hinting* (page 904).
API	Application Program Interface. The interface (calling conventions) by which an application program accesses an operating system and other services. An API is defined at the source code level and provides a level of abstraction between the application and the kernel (or other privileged utilities) to ensure the portability of the code.ꜰᴏʟᴅᴏᴄ
append	To add something to the end of something else. To append text to a file means to add the text to the end of the file. The shell uses >> to append a command's output to a file.
applet	A small program that runs within a larger program. Examples are Java applets that run in a browser and panel applets that run from a desktop panel.
argument	A number, letter, filename, or another string that gives some information to a command and is passed to the command when it is called. A command line argument is anything on a command line following the command name that is passed to the command. An option is a kind of argument.
arithmetic expression	A group of numbers, operators, and parentheses that can be evaluated. When you evaluate an arithmetic expression, you end up with a number. The Bourne Again Shell uses the expr command to evaluate arithmetic expressions; the TC Shell uses @; and the Z Shell uses let.
array	An arrangement of elements (numbers or strings of characters) in one or more dimensions. The TC and Z Shells and gawk can store and process arrays.
ASCII	American Standard Code for Information Interchange. A code that uses seven bits to represent both graphic (letters, numbers, and punctuation) and control characters. You can represent textual information, including program source code and English text, in ASCII code. Because ASCII is a standard, it is frequently used when exchanging information between computers. See the file **/usr/pub/ascii** or give the command **man ascii** to see a list of ASCII codes.
	Extensions of the ASCII character set use eight bits. The seven-bit set is common; the eight-bit extensions are still coming into popular use. The eighth bit is sometimes referred to as the metabit.
ASCII terminal	A text-based terminal. Contrast with *graphical display* (page 877).
ASP	Application Service Provider. A company that provides applications over the Internet.

asynchronous event An event that does not occur regularly or synchronously with another event. Linux system signals are asynchronous; they can occur at any time because they can be initiated by any number of nonregular events.

attachment A file that is attached to, but is not part of, a piece of email. Attachments are frequently opened by programs (including your Internet browser) that are called by your mail program so you may not be aware that they are not an integral part of an email message.

authentication The verification of the identity of a person or process. In a communication system, authentication verifies that a message comes from its stated source. Methods of authentication on a Linux system include the **/etc/passwd** and **/etc/shadow** files, LDAP, Kerberos 5, and SMB authentication.FOLDOC

automatic mounting A way of demand mounting directories from remote hosts without having them hard configured into **/etc/fstab**. Also called *automounting*.

avoided An object, such as a panel, that should not normally be covered by another object, such as a window.

back door A security hole deliberately left in place by the designers or maintainers of a system. The motivation for creating such holes is not always sinister; some operating systems, for example, come out of the box with privileged accounts intended for use by field service technicians or the vendor's maintenance programmers.

Ken Thompson's 1983 Turing Award lecture to the ACM revealed the existence, in early UNIX versions, of a back door that may be the most fiendishly clever security hack of all time. The C compiler contained code that would recognize when the **login** command was being recompiled and would insert some code recognizing a password chosen by Thompson, giving him entry to the system whether or not an account had been created for him.

Normally such a back door could be removed by removing it from the source code for the compiler and recompiling the compiler. But to recompile the compiler, you have to *use* the compiler, so Thompson arranged that the compiler would *recognize when it was compiling a version of itself*. It would insert into the recompiled compiler the code to insert into the recompiled **login** the code to allow Thompson entry, and, of course, the code to recognize itself and do the whole thing again the next time around. Having done this once, he was then able to recompile the compiler from the original sources; the hack perpetuated itself invisibly, leaving the back door in place and active but with no trace in the sources.

Sometimes called a wormhole. Also *trap door*.FOLDOC

background process	A process that is not run in the foreground. Also called a *detached process*, a background process is initiated by a command line that ends with an ampersand (&). You do not have to wait for a background process to run to completion before giving the shell additional commands. If you have job control, you can move background processes to the foreground, and vice versa.
basename	The name of a file that, in contrast with a pathname, does not mention any of the directories containing the file (and therefore does not contain any slashes [/]). For example, **hosts** is the basename of **/etc/hosts**.<small>FOLDOC</small>
baud	The maximum information-carrying capacity of a communication channel in symbols (state transitions or level transitions) per second. It coincides with bits per second only for two-level modulation with no framing or stop bits. A symbol is a unique state of the communication channel, distinguishable by the receiver from all other possible states. For example, it may be one of two voltage levels on a wire for a direct digital connection, or it might be the phase or frequency of a carrier.<small>FOLDOC</small>
	Baud is often mistakenly used as a synonym for bits per second.
baud rate	Transmission speed. Usually used to measure terminal or modem speed. Common baud rates range from 110 to 38,400 baud. See *baud*.
Berkeley UNIX	One of the two major versions of the UNIX operating system. Berkeley UNIX was developed at the University of California at Berkeley by the Computer Systems Research Group and is often referred to as *BSD* (Berkeley Software Distribution).
BIND	Berkeley Internet Name Domain. An implementation of a *DNS* (page 872) server developed and distributed by the University of California at Berkeley
BIOS	Basic Input/Output System. On PCs, *EEPROM*-based (page 873) system software that provides the lowest-level interface to peripheral devices and controls the first stage of the *bootstrap* (page 864) process, which loads the operating system. The BIOS can be stored in different types of memory. The memory must be nonvolatile so that it remembers the system's settings even when the system is turned off. Also BIOS ROM.
bit	The smallest piece of information a computer can handle. A *bit* is a binary digit: either 1 or 0 (*on* or *off*).
bit depth	Same as *color depth* (page 868).
bit-mapped display	A graphical display device in which each pixel on the screen is controlled by an underlying representation of zeros and ones.

blank character   Either a SPACE or a TAB character, also called *whitespace* (page 909). In some contexts, NEWLINEs are considered blank characters.

block   A section of a disk or tape (usually 1,024 bytes long but shorter or longer on some systems) that is written at one time.

block device   A disk or tape drive. A block device stores information in blocks of characters. A block device is represented by a block device (block special) file. Contrast with *character device* (page 866).

block number   Disk and tape *blocks* are numbered so that Linux can keep track of the data on the device.

blocking factor   The number of logical blocks that make up a physical block on a tape or disk. When you write 1K logical blocks to a tape with a physical block size of 30K, the blocking factor is 30.

boot   See *bootstrap*.

boot loader   A very small program that takes its place in the *bootstrap* process that brings a computer from off or reset to a fully functional state.

bootstrap   Derived from "Pull oneself up by one's own bootstraps," the incremental process of loading an operating system kernel into memory and starting it running without any outside assistance. Frequently shortened to *boot*.

Bourne Again Shell   bash. GNU's command interpreter for UNIX, bash is a POSIX-compliant shell with full Bourne Shell syntax and some C Shell commands built in. The Bourne Again Shell supports emacs-style command line editing, job control, functions, and online help.FOLDOC

Bourne Shell   sh. This UNIX command processor was developed by Steve Bourne at AT&T Bell Laboratories.

brace   A left brace ({) and a right brace (}). Braces have special meanings to the shell.

bracket   A *square bracket* (page 902) or an *angle bracket* (page 860).

branch   In a tree structure, a branch connects nodes, leaves, and the root. The Linux filesystem hierarchy is often conceptualized as an upside-down tree. The branches connect files and directories. In a source code control system, such as SCCS or RCS, a branch occurs when a revision is made to a file and is not included in subsequent revisions to the file.

bridge   Typically a two-port device originally used for extending networks at layer 2 (data link) of the Internet Protocol model.

broadcast	A transmission to multiple, unspecified recipients. On Ethernet a broadcast packet is a special type of multicast packet that has a special address indicating that all devices that receive it should process it. Broadcast traffic exists at several layers of the network stack, including Ethernet and IP. Broadcast traffic has one source but indeterminate destinations (all hosts on the local network).
broadcast address	The last address on a subnet (usually 255), reserved as shorthand to mean all hosts.
broadcast network	A type of network, such as Ethernet, in which any system can transmit information at any time, and all systems receive every message.
BSD	See *Berkeley UNIX* on page 863.
buffer	An area of memory that stores data until it can be used. When you write information to a file on a disk, Linux stores the information in a disk buffer until there is enough to write to the disk or until the disk is ready to receive the information.
bug	An unwanted and unintended program property, especially one that causes the program to malfunction.^{FOLDOC}
builtin (command)	A command that is built into a shell. Each of the three major shells—the Bourne Again, TC, and Z Shells—has its own set of builtins. Refer to "Builtins" on page 132.
byte	A component in the machine data hierarchy, usually larger than a bit and smaller than a word; now most often eight bits and the smallest addressable unit of storage. A byte typically holds one character.^{FOLDOC}
C programming language	A modern systems language that has high-level features for efficient, modular programming as well as lower-level features that make it suitable for use as a systems programming language. It is machine independent so that carefully written C programs can be easily transported to run on different machines. Most of the Linux operating system is written in C, and Linux provides an ideal environment for programming in C.
C Shell	csh. The C Shell command processor was developed by Bill Joy for BSD UNIX. It was named for the C programming language because its programming constructs are similar to those of C. See *shell* on page 900.
cable modem	A type of modem that allows you to access the Internet by using your cable television connection.

cache Holding recently accessed data, a small, fast memory designed to speed up subsequent access to the same data. Most often applied to processor-memory access but also used for a local copy of data accessible over a network, from a hard disk, and so on.^{FOLDOC}

calling environment A list of variables and their values that is made available to a called program. Refer to "Executing a Command" on page 294.

cascading stylesheet See *CSS* on page 870.

cascading windows An arrangement of windows such that they overlap, generally with at least part of the title bar visible. Opposite of *tiled windows* (page 906).

case sensitive Able to distinguish between uppercase and lowercase characters. Unless you set the **ignorecase** parameter, vim performs case-sensitive searches. The grep utility performs case-sensitive searches unless you use the –i option.

catenate To join sequentially, or end to end. The Linux cat utility catenates files: It displays them one after the other. Also *concatenate*.

chain loading The technique used by a boot loader to load unsupported operating systems. Used for loading such operating systems as DOS or Windows, it works by loading another boot loader.

character-based A program, utility, or interface that works only with *ASCII* (page 861) characters. This set of characters includes some simple graphics, such as lines and corners, and can display colored characters. It cannot display true graphics. Contrast with *GUI* (page 877).

character-based terminal A terminal that displays only characters and very limited graphics. See *character-based*.

character class In a regular expression, a group of characters that defines which characters can occupy a single character position. A character-class definition is usually surrounded by square brackets. The character class defined by [abcr] represents a character position that can be occupied by **a**, **b**, **c**, or **r**. Also *list operator*.

character device A terminal, printer, or modem. A character device stores or displays characters one at a time. A character device is represented by a character device (character special) file. Contrast with *block device* (page 864).

checksum   A computed value that depends on the contents of a block of data and is transmitted or stored along with the data to detect corruption of the data. The receiving system recomputes the checksum based on the received data and compares this value with the one sent with the data. If the two values are the same, the receiver has some confidence that the data was received correctly.

The checksum may be 8, 16, or 32 bits, or some other size. It is computed by summing the bytes or words of the data block, ignoring overflow. The checksum may be negated so that the total of the data words plus the checksum is zero.

Internet packets use a 32-bit checksum._{FOLDOC}

child process   A process that is created by another process, the parent process. Every process is a child process except for the first process, which is started when Linux begins execution. When you run a command from the shell, the shell spawns a child process to run the command. See *process* on page 894.

CIDR   Classless Inter-Domain Routing. A scheme that allocates blocks of Internet addresses in a way that allows summarization into a smaller number of routing table entries. A CIDR block is a block of Internet addresses assigned to an ISP by the Internic._{FOLDOC}

CIFS   Common Internet File System. An Internet filesystem protocol based on *SMB* (page 901). CIFS runs on top of TCP/IP, uses DNS, and is optimized to support slower dial-up Internet connections. SMB and CIFS are used interchangeably._{FOLDOC}

CIPE   Crypto IP *Encapsulation* (page 874). This *protocol* (page 895) *tunnels* (page 907) IP packets within encrypted *UDP* (page 907) packets, is lightweight and simple, and works over dynamic addresses, *NAT* (page 889), and *SOCKS* (page 901) *proxies* (page 895).

cipher (cypher)   A cryptographic system that uses a key to transpose/substitute characters within a message, the key itself, or the message.

ciphertext   Text that is encrypted. Contrast with *plaintext* (page 893).

Classless Inter-Domain Routing   See *CIDR*.

cleartext   Text that is not encrypted; also *plaintext*. Contrast with *ciphertext*.

CLI   Command line interface. See also *character-based* (page 866).

client   A computer or program that requests one or more services from a server.

CODEC   Coder/decoder or compressor/decompressor. A hardware and/or software technology that codes and decodes data. MPEG is a popular CODEC for computer video.

color depth   The number of bits used to generate a pixel—usually 8, 16, 24, or 32. The color depth is directly related to the number of colors that can be generated. The number of colors that can be generated is 2 raised to the color-depth power. Thus that a 24-bit video adapter can generate about 16.7 million colors.

color quality   See *color depth*.

combo box   A combination of a list and text entry box. A user can either select an option from a provided list or enter his own option.

command   What you give the shell in response to a prompt. When you give the shell a command, it executes a utility, another program, a builtin command, or a shell script. Utilities are often referred to as commands. When you are using an interactive utility, such as vim or mail, you use commands that are appropriate to that utility.

command line   A line containing instructions and arguments that executes a command. This term usually refers to a line that you enter in response to a shell prompt on a character-based terminal or terminal emulator.

command substitution   Replacing a command with its output. The shells perform command substitution when you enclose a command between $(and) or between a pair of back ticks (` `), also called grave accent marks.

component architecture   A notion in object-oriented programming where "components" of a program are completely generic. Instead of having a specialized set of methods and fields, they have generic methods through which the component can advertise the functionality it supports to the system into which it is loaded. This strategy enables completely dynamic loading of objects. JavaBeans is an example of a component architecture.ᶠᴼᴸᴰᴼᶜ

concatenate   See *catenate* on page 866.

condition code   See *exit status* on page 874.

connection-oriented protocol   A type of transport layer data communication service that allows a host to send data in a continuous stream to another host. The transport service guarantees that all data will be delivered to the other end in the same order as sent and without duplication. Communication proceeds through three well-defined phases: connection establishment, data transfer, and connection release. The most common example is *TCP* (page 905).

Also called connection-based protocol and stream-oriented protocol. Contrast with *connectionless protocol* and *datagram* (page 870).ᶠᴼᴸᴰᴼᶜ

connectionless protocol   The data communication method in which communication occurs between hosts with no previous setup. Packets sent between two hosts may take different routes. There is no guarantee that packets will arrive as transmitted or even that they will arrive at the destination at all. *UDP* (page 907) is a connectionless protocol. Also called packet switching. Contrast with circuit switching and *connection-oriented protocol.*^{FOLDOC}

console   See *system console* on page 904.

console terminal   See *system console* on page 904.

control character   A character that is not a graphic character, such as a letter, number, or punctuation mark. Such characters are called control characters because they frequently act to control a peripheral device. RETURN and FORMFEED are control characters that control a terminal or printer.

The word CONTROL is shown in this book in THIS FONT because it is a key that appears on most terminal keyboards. Control characters are represented by ASCII codes less than 32 (decimal). See also *nonprinting character* on page 890.

control structure   A statement used to change the order of execution of commands in a shell script or other program. Each shell provides control structures (for example, **If** and **While**) as well as other commands that alter the order of execution (for example, **exec**). Also *control flow commands.*

cookie   Data stored on a client system by a server. The client system browser sends the cookie back to the server each time it accesses that server. For example, a catalog shopping service may store a cookie on your system when you place your first order. When you return to the site, it knows who you are and can supply your name and address for subsequent orders. You may consider cookies to be an invasion of privacy.

CPU   Central processing unit. The part of a computer that controls all the other parts. The CPU includes the control unit and the arithmetic and logic unit (ALU). The control unit fetches instructions from memory and decodes them to produce signals that control the other parts of the computer. These signals can cause data to be transferred between memory and ALU or peripherals to perform input or output. A CPU that is housed on a single chip is called a microprocessor. Also *processor* and *central processor.*

cracker   An individual who attempts to gain unauthorized access to a computer system. These individuals are often malicious and have many means at their disposal for breaking into a system. Contrast with *hacker* (page 877).^{FOLDOC}

crash   The system suddenly and unexpectedly stops or fails. Derived from the action of the hard disk heads on the surface of the disk when the air gap between the two collapses.

cryptography   The practice and study of encryption and decryption—encoding data so that only a specific individual or machine can decode it. A system for encrypting and decrypting data is a cryptosystem. Such systems usually rely on an algorithm for combining the original data (plaintext) with one or more keys—numbers or strings of characters known only to the sender and/or recipient. The resulting output is called *ciphertext* (page 867).

The security of a cryptosystem usually depends on the secrecy of keys rather than on the supposed secrecy of an algorithm. Because a strong cryptosystem has a large range of keys, it is not possible to try all of them. Ciphertext appears random to standard statistical tests and resists known methods for breaking codes.FOLDOC

.cshrc file   In your home directory, a file that the TC Shell executes each time you invoke a new TC Shell. You can use this file to establish variables and aliases.

CSS   Cascading stylesheet. Describes how documents are presented on screen and in print. Attaching a stylesheet to a structured document can affect the way it looks without adding new HTML (or other) tags and without giving up device independence. Also *stylesheet*.

current (process, line, character, directory, event, and so on)   The item that is immediately available, working, or being used. The current process controls the program you are running, the current line or character is the one the cursor is on, and the current directory is the working directory.

cursor   A small lighted rectangle, underscore, or vertical bar that appears on the terminal screen and indicates where the next character will appear. Differs from the *mouse pointer* (page 888).

daemon   A program that is not invoked explicitly but lies dormant, waiting for some condition(s) to occur. The perpetrator of the condition need not be aware that a daemon is lurking (although often a program will commit an action only because it knows that it will implicitly invoke a daemon). From the mythological meaning, later rationalized as the acronym Disk And Execution MONitor.FOLDOC

data structure   A particular format for storing, organizing, working with, and retrieving data. Frequently, data structures are designed to work with specific algorithms that facilitate these tasks. Common data structures include trees, files, records, tables, arrays, and so on.

datagram   A self-contained, independent entity of data carrying sufficient information to be routed from the source to the destination computer without reliance on earlier exchanges between this source and destination computer and the transporting network. *UDP* (page 907) uses datagrams; *IP* (page 882) uses *packets* (page 892). Packets are indivisible at the network layer; datagrams are not.FOLDOC See also *frame* (page 876).

dataless A computer, usually a workstation, that uses a local disk to boot a copy of the operating system and access system files but does not use a local disk to store user files.

dbm A standard, simple database manager. Implemented as **gdbm** (GNU database manager), it uses hashes to speed searching. The most common versions of the **dbm** database are **dbm**, **ndbm**, and **gdbm**.

DDoS attack Distributed denial of service attack. A *DoS attack* (page 873) from many systems that do not belong to the perpetrator of the attack.

debug To correct a program by removing its bugs (that is, errors).

default Something that is selected without being explicitly specified. For example, when used without an argument, ls displays a list of the files in the working directory by default.

delta A set of changes made to a file that has been encoded by the Source Code Control System (SCCS).

denial of service See *DoS attack* on page 873.

dereference When speaking of symbolic links, follow the link rather than working with the reference to the link. For example, the –L or ––dereference option causes ls to list the entry that a symbolic link points to rather than the symbolic link (the reference) itself.

desktop A collection of windows, toolbars, icons, and buttons, some or all of which appear on your display. A desktop comprises one or more *workspaces* (page 910).

desktop manager An icon- and menu-based user interface to system services that allows you to run applications and use the filesystem without using the system's command line interface.

detached process See *background process* on page 863.

device A disk drive, printer, terminal, plotter, or other input/output unit that can be attached to the computer.

device driver Part of the Linux kernel that controls a device, such as a terminal, disk drive, or printer.

device file A file that represents a device. Also *special file*.

device filename The pathname of a device file. All Linux systems have two kinds of device files: block and character device files. Linux also has FIFOs (named pipes) and sockets. Device files are traditionally located in the **/dev** directory.

device number   See *major device number* (page 886) and *minor device number* (page 887).

DHCP   Dynamic Host Configuration Protocol. A protocol that dynamically allocates IP addresses to computers on a LAN._{FOLDOC}

directory   Short for *directory file*. A file that contains a list of other files.

directory hierarchy   A directory, called the root of the directory hierarchy, and all the directory and ordinary files below it (its children).

directory service   A structured repository of information on people and resources within an organization, facilitating management and communication._{FOLDOC}

disk partition   See *partition* on page 892.

diskless   A computer, usually a workstation, that has no disk and must contact another computer (a server) to boot a copy of the operating system and access the necessary system files.

distributed computing   A style of computing in which tasks or services are performed by a network of cooperating systems, some of which may be specialized.

DMZ   Demilitarized zone. A host or small network that is a neutral zone between a LAN and the Internet. It can serve Web pages and other data to the Internet and allow local systems access to the Internet while preventing LAN access to unauthorized Internet users. Even if a DMZ is compromised, it holds no data that is private and none that cannot be easily reproduced.

DNS   Domain Name Service. A distributed service that manages the correspondence of full hostnames (those that include a domain name) to IP addresses and other system characteristics.

DNS domain name   See *domain name*.

document object model   See *DOM*.

DOM   Document Object Model. A platform-/language-independent interface that enables a program to update the content, structure, and style of a document dynamically. The changes can then be made part of the displayed document. Go to www.w3.org/DOM for more information.

domain name A name associated with an organization, or part of an organization, to help identify systems uniquely. Technically, the part of the *FQDN* (page 876) to the right of the leftmost period. Domain names are assigned hierarchically. The domain berkeley.edu refers to the University of California at Berkeley, for example; it is part of the top-level edu (education) domain. Also DNS domain name. Different than *NIS domain name* (page 890).

Domain Name Service See *DNS*.

door An evolving filesystem-based *RPC* (page 899) mechanism.

DoS attack Denial of service attack. An attack that attempts to make the target host or network unusable by flooding it with spurious traffic.

DPMS Display Power Management Signaling. A standard that can extend the life of CRT monitors and conserve energy. DPMS supports four modes for a monitor: Normal, Standby (power supply on, monitor ready to come to display images almost instantly), Suspend (power supply off, monitor takes up to ten seconds to display an image), and Off.

drag To move an icon from one position or application to another, usually in the context of a window manager. The motion part of drag-and-drop.

druid In role-playing games, a character that represents a magical user. Red Hat uses the term *druid* at the ends of names of programs that guide you through a task-driven chain of steps. Other operating systems call these types of programs *wizards*.

DSA Digital Signature Algorithm. A public key cipher used to generate digital signatures.

DSL Digital Subscriber Line/Loop. Provides high-speed digital communication over a specialized, conditioned telephone line. See also *xDSL* (page 911).

Dynamic Host Configuration Protocol See *DHCP* on page 872.

editor A utility, such as vim or emacs, that creates and modifies text files.

EEPROM Electrically erasable, programmable, readonly memory. A *PROM* (page 895) that can be written to.

effective user ID The user ID that a process appears to have; usually the same as the user ID. For example, while you are running a setuid program, the effective user ID of the process running the program is that of the owner of the program.

element	One thing; usually a basic part of a group of things. An element of a numeric array is one of the numbers stored in the array.
emoticon	See *smiley* on page 901.
encapsulation	See *tunneling* on page 907.
environment	See *calling environment* on page 866.
EOF	End of file.
EPROM	Erasable, programmable, readonly memory. A *PROM* (page 895) that can be written to by applying a higher than normal voltage.
escape	See *quote* on page 896.
Ethernet	A type of *LAN* (page 884) capable of transfer rates as high as 1,000 megabits per second.
event	An occurrence, or happening, of significance to a task or program—for example, the completion of an asynchronous input/output operation, such as a keypress or mouse click.<small>FOLDOC</small>
exabyte	2^{60} bytes or about 10^{18} bytes. See also *large number* (page 884).
exit status	The status returned by a process; either successful (usually 0) or unsuccessful (usually 1).
exploit	A security hole or an instance of taking advantage of a security hole.<small>FOLDOC</small>
expression	See *logical expression* (page 885) and *arithmetic expression* (page 861).
extranet	A network extension for a subset of users (such as students at a particular school or engineers working for the same company). An extranet limits access to private information even though it travels on the public Internet.
failsafe session	A session that allows you to log in on a minimal desktop in case your standard login does not work well enough to allow you to log in to fix a login problem.
FDDI	Fiber Distributed Data Interface. A type of *LAN* (page 884) designed to transport data at the rate of 100 million bits per second over fiberoptic cable.
file	A collection of related information referred to with a *filename* and frequently stored on a disk. Text files typically contain memos, reports, messages, program source code, lists, or manuscripts. Binary or executable files contain utilities or programs that you can run. Refer to "Directory and Ordinary Files" on page 77.

filename	The name of a *file*. A filename refers to a file.
filename completion	Automatic completion of a filename after you specify a unique prefix.
filename extension	The part of a filename following a period.
filename generation	What occurs when the shell expands ambiguous file references. See *ambiguous file reference* on page 860.
filesystem	A *data structure* (page 870) that usually resides on part of a disk. All Linux systems have a root filesystem, and most have at least a few other filesystems. Each filesystem is composed of some number of blocks, depending on the size of the disk partition that has been assigned to the filesystem. Each filesystem has a control block, named the superblock, that contains information about the filesystem. The other blocks in a filesystem are inodes, which contain control information about individual files, and data blocks, which contain the information in the files.
filling	A variant of maximizing in which window edges are pushed out as far as they can go without overlapping another window.
filter	A command that can take its input from standard input and send its output to standard output. A filter transforms the input stream of data and sends it to standard output. A pipe usually connects a filter's input to standard output of one command, and a second pipe connects the filter's output to standard input of another command. The grep and sort utilities are commonly used as filters.
firewall	A device for policy-based traffic management used to keep a network secure. A firewall can be implemented in a single router that filters out unwanted packets, or it can rely on a combination of routers, proxy servers, and other devices. Firewalls are widely used to give users access to the Internet in a secure fashion and to separate a company's public WWW server from its internal network. They are also employed to keep internal network segments more secure.

Recently the term has come to be defined more loosely to include a simple packet filter running on an endpoint machine.

See also *proxy server* on page 895. |
| **focus, desktop** | On a desktop the window that is active. The window with the desktop focus receives the characters you type on the keyboard. Same as *active window* (page 860). |
| **footer** | The part of a format that goes at the bottom (or foot) of a page. Contrast with *header* (page 878). |

foreground process When you run a command in the foreground, the shell waits for the command to finish before giving you another prompt. You must wait for a foreground process to run to completion before you can give the shell another command. If you have job control, you can move background processes to the foreground, and vice versa. See *job control* on page 883. Contrast with *background process* (page 863).

fork To create a process. When one process creates another process, it forks a process. Also *spawn*.

FQDN Fully qualified domain name. The full name of a system, consisting of its hostname and its domain name, including the top-level domain. Technically the name that **gethostbyname**(2) returns for the host named by **gethostname**(2). For example, **speedy** is a hostname and **speedy.example.com** is an FQDN. An FQDN is sufficient to determine a unique Internet address for a machine on the Internet.^{FOLDOC}

frame A data link layer packet that contains, in addition to data, the header and trailer information required by the physical medium. Network layer packets are encapsulated to become frames.^{FOLDOC} See also *datagram* (page 870) and *packet* (page 892).

free list In a filesystem, the list of blocks that are available for use. Information about the free list is kept in the superblock of the filesystem.

free space The portion of a hard disk that is not within a partition. A new hard disk has no partitions and contains all free space.

full duplex The ability to receive and transmit data simultaneously. A *network switch* (page 890) is typically a full-duplex device. Contrast with *half-duplex* (page 877).

fully qualified domain name See *FQDN*.

function See *shell function* on page 900.

gateway A generic term for a computer or a special device connected to more than one dissimilar type of network to pass data between them. Unlike a router, a gateway often must convert the information into a different format before passing it on. The historical usage of gateway to designate a router is deprecated.

GCOS See *GECOS*.

GECOS General Electric Comprehensive Operating System. For historical reasons, the user information field in the **/etc/passwd** file is called the GECOS field. Also *GCOS*.

giga- In the binary system, the prefix *giga-* multiplies by 2^{30} (i.e., 1,073,741,824). Gigabit and gigabyte are common uses of this prefix. Abbreviated as *G*. See also *large number* on page 884.

glyph A symbol that communicates a specific piece of information nonverbally. A *smiley* (page 901) is a glyph.

GMT Greenwich Mean Time. See *UTC* on page 908.

graphical display A bitmapped monitor that can display graphical images. Contrast with *ASCII terminal* (page 861).

graphical user interface See *GUI*.

group (of users) A collection of users. Groups are used as a basis for determining file access permissions. If you are not the owner of a file and you belong to the group the file is assigned to, you are subject to the group access permissions for the file. A user can simultaneously belong to several groups.

group (of windows) A way to identify similar windows so they can be displayed and acted on similarly. Typically windows started by a given application belong to the same group.

group ID A unique number that identifies a set of users. It is stored in the password and group databases (**/etc/passwd** and **/etc/group** files or their NIS equivalents). The group database associates group IDs with group names.

GUI Graphical user interface. A GUI provides a way to interact with a computer system by choosing items from menus or manipulating pictures drawn on a display screen instead of by typing command lines. Under Linux, the X Window System provides a graphical display and mouse/keyboard input. GNOME and KDE are two popular desktop managers that run under X. Contrast with *character-based* (page 866).

hacker A person who enjoys exploring the details of programmable systems and learning how to stretch their capabilities, as opposed to users, who prefer to learn only the minimum necessary. One who programs enthusiastically (even obsessively) or who enjoys programming rather than just theorizing about programming.^{FOLDOC} Contrast with *cracker* (page 869).

half-duplex A half-duplex device can only receive or transmit at a given moment; it cannot do both. A *hub* (page 880) is typically a half-duplex device. Contrast with *full duplex* (page 876).

hard link A directory entry that contains the filename and inode number for a file. The inode number identifies the location of control information for the file on the disk, which in turn identifies the location of the file's contents on the disk. Every file has at least one hard link, which locates the file in a directory. When you remove the last hard link to a file, you can no longer access the file. See *link* (page 884) and *symbolic link* (page 904).

hash A string that is generated from another string. See *one-way hash function* on page 891. When used for security, a hash can prove, almost to a certainty, that a message has not been tampered with during transmission: The sender generates a hash of a message, encrypts the message and hash, and sends the encrypted message and hash to the recipient. The recipient decrypts the message and hash, generates a second hash from the message, and compares the hash that the sender generated to the new hash. When they are the same, the message has probably not been tampered with. A hash can also be used to create an index called a *hash table*. Also *hash value*.

hash table An index created from hashes of the items to be indexed. The hash function makes it highly unlikely that two items will create the same hash. To look up an item in the index, create a hash of the item and search for the hash. Because the hash is typically shorter than the item, the search is more efficient.

header When you are formatting a document, the header goes at the top, or head, of a page. In electronic mail the header identifies who sent the message, when it was sent, what the subject of the message is, and so forth.

Here document A shell script that takes its input from the file that contains the script.

hesiod The name server of project Athena. Hesiod is a name service library that is derived from *BIND* (page 863) and leverages a DNS infrastructure.

heterogeneous Consisting of different parts. A heterogeneous network includes systems produced by different manufacturers and/or running different operating systems.

hexadecimal number A base 16 number. Hexadecimal (or *hex*) numbers are composed of the hexadecimal digits 0–9 and A–F. See Table G-1.

hidden file See *invisible file* on page 882.

hierarchy An organization with a few things, or thing—one at the top—and with several things below each other thing. An inverted tree structure. Examples in computing include a file tree where each directory may contain files or other directories, a hierarchical network, and a class hierarchy in object-oriented programming.FOLDOC Refer to "The Hierarchical Filesystem" on page 76.

Table G-1 Decimal, octal, and hexadecimal numbers

Decimal	Octal	Hex	Decimal	Octal	Hex
1	1	1	17	21	11
2	2	2	18	22	12
3	3	3	19	23	13
4	4	4	20	24	14
5	5	5	21	25	15
6	6	6	31	37	1F
7	7	7	32	40	20
8	10	8	33	41	21
9	11	9	64	100	40
10	12	A	96	140	60
11	13	B	100	144	64
12	14	C	128	200	80
13	15	D	254	376	FE
14	16	E	255	377	FF
15	17	F	256	400	100
16	20	10	257	401	101

history A shell mechanism that enables you to modify and reexecute recent commands.

home directory The directory that is your working directory when you first log in. The pathname of this directory is stored in the **HOME** shell variable.

hover To leave the mouse pointer stationary for a moment over an object. In many cases hovering displays a *tooltip* (page 906).

HTML Hypertext Markup Language. A *hypertext* (page 880) document format used on the World Wide Web. Tags, which are embedded in the text, consist of a less than sign (<), a directive, zero or more parameters, and a greater than sign (>). Matched pairs of directives, such as <TITLE> and </TITLE>, delimit text that is to appear in a special place or style.ᶠᴼᴸᴰᴼᶜ For more information on HTML, go to www.htmlhelp.com/faq/html/all.html.

HTTP Hypertext Transfer Protocol. The client/server TCP/IP protocol used on the World Wide Web for the exchange of *HTML* documents.

hub A multiport repeater. A hub rebroadcasts all packets it receives on all ports. This term is frequently used to refer to small hubs and switches, regardless of the device's intelligence. It is a generic term for a layer 2 shared-media networking device. Today the term *hub* is sometimes used to refer to small intelligent devices, although that was not its original meaning. Contrast with *network switch* (page 890).

hypertext A collection of documents/nodes containing (usually highlighted or underlined) cross-references or links, which, with the aid of an interactive browser program, allow the reader to move easily from one document to another.FOLDOC

Hypertext Markup Language See *HTML* on page 879.

Hypertext Transfer Protocol See *HTTP* on page 879.

i/o device Input/output device. See *device* on page 871.

IANA Internet Assigned Numbers Authority. A group that maintains a database of all permanent, registered system services (www.iana.org).

ICMP Internet Control Message Protocol. A type of network packet that carries only messages, no data.

icon In a GUI, a small picture representing a file, directory, action, program, and so on. When you click an icon, an action, such as opening a window and starting a program or displaying a directory or Web site, takes place. From miniature religious statues.FOLDOC

iconify The process of changing a window into an *icon*. Contrast with *restore* (page 897).

ignored window A state in which a window has no decoration and therefore no buttons or titlebar to control it with.

indentation See *indention*.

indention The blank space between the margin and the beginning of a line that is set in from the margin.

inode A *data structure* (page 870) that contains information about a file. An inode for a file contains the file's length, the times the file was last accessed and modified, the time the inode was last modified, owner and group IDs, access privileges, number of links, and pointers to the data blocks that contain the file itself. Each directory entry associates a filename with an inode. Although a single file may have several filenames (one for each link), it has only one inode.

input   Information that is fed to a program from a terminal or other file. See *standard input* on page 902.

installation   A computer at a specific location. Some aspects of the Linux system are installation dependent. Also *site*.

interactive   A program that allows ongoing dialog with the user. When you give commands in response to shell prompts, you are using the shell interactively. Also, when you give commands to utilities, such as vim and mail, you are using the utilities interactively.

interface   The meeting point of two subsystems. When two programs work together, their interface includes every aspect of either program that the other deals with. The *user interface* (page 908) of a program includes every program aspect the user comes into contact with: the syntax and semantics involved in invoking the program, the input and output of the program, and its error and informational messages. The shell and each of the utilities and built-in commands have a user interface.

International Organization for Standardization   See *ISO* on page 882.

internet   A large network that encompasses other, smaller networks.

Internet   The largest internet in the world. The Internet (uppercase "I") is a multilevel hierarchy composed of backbone networks (ARPANET, NSFnet, MILNET, and others), midlevel networks, and stub networks. These include commercial (**.com** or **.co**), university (**.ac** or **.edu**), research (**.org** or **.net**), and military (**.mil**) networks and span many different physical networks around the world with various protocols, including the Internet Protocol (IP). Outside the United States, country code domains are popular (**.us**, **.es**, **.mx**, **.de**, and so forth), although you will see them used within the United States as well.

Internet Protocol   See *IP*.

Internet Service Provider   See *ISP* on page 883.

intranet   An inhouse network designed to serve a group of people such as a corporation or school. The general public on the Internet does not have access to the intranet.

invisible file   A file whose filename starts with a period. These files are called invisible because the ls utility does not normally list them. Use the –a option of ls to list all files, including invisible ones. The shell does not expand a leading asterisk (*) in an ambiguous file reference to match the filename of an invisible file. Also *hidden file.*

IP   Internet Protocol. The network layer for TCP/IP. IP is a best-effort, packet-switching, *connectionless protocol* (page 869) that provides packet routing, fragmentation, and reassembly through the data link layer. *IPv4* is slowly giving way to *IPv6.*FOLDOC

IP address   Internet Protocol address. A four-part address associated with a particular network connection for a system using the Internet Protocol (IP). A system that is attached to multiple networks that use the IP will have a different IP address for each network interface.

IP multicast   See *multicast* on page 888.

IP spoofing   A technique used to gain unauthorized access to a computer. The would-be intruder sends messages to the target machine. These messages contain an IP address indicating that the messages are coming from a trusted host. The target machine responds to the messages, giving the intruder (privileged) access to the target.

IPC   Interprocess communication. A method to communicate specific information between programs.

IPv4   *IP* version 4. See *IP* and *IPv6.*

IPv6   *IP* version 6. The next generation of Internet Protocol, which provides a much larger address space (2^{128} bits versus 2^{32} bits for IPv4) that is designed to accommodate the rapidly growing number of Internet addressable devices. IPv6 also has built-in autoconfiguration, enhanced security, better multicast support, and many other features.

ISDN   Integrated Services Digital Network. A set of communications standards that allows a single pair of digital or standard telephone wires to carry voice, data, and video at a rate of 64 kilobits per second.

ISO   International Organization for Standardization. A voluntary, nontreaty organization founded in 1946. It is responsible for creating international standards in many areas, including computers and communications. Its members are the national standards organizations of 89 countries, including the American National Standards Institute.FOLDOC

ISO9660   The *ISO* standard defining a filesystem for CD-ROMs.

ISP   Internet service provider. Provides Internet access to its customers.

job control   A facility that enables you to move commands from the foreground to the background and vice versa. Job control enables you to stop commands temporarily.

journaling filesystem   A filesystem that maintains a noncached log file, or journal, which records all transactions involving the filesystem. When a transaction is complete, it is marked as complete in the log file.

The log file results in greatly reduced time spent recovering a filesystem after a crash, making it particularly valuable in systems where high availability is an issue.

JPEG   Joint Photographic Experts Group. This committee designed the standard image-compression algorithm. JPEG is intended for compressing either full-color or gray-scale digital images of natural, real-world scenes and does not work as well on nonrealistic images, such as cartoons or line drawings. Filename extensions: **.jpg**, **.jpeg**.^{FOLDOC}

justify   To expand a line of type in the process of formatting text. A justified line has even margins. A line is justified by increasing the space between words and sometimes between letters on the line.

Kerberos   An MIT-developed security system that authenticates users and machines. It does not provide authorization to services or databases; it establishes identity at logon, which is used throughout the session. Once you are authenticated, you can open as many terminals, windows, services, or other network accesses as you like until your session expires.

kernel   The part of the operating system that allocates machine resources, including memory, disk space, and *CPU* (page 869) cycles, to all other programs that run on a computer. The kernel includes the low-level hardware interfaces (drivers) and manages *processes* (page 894), the means by which Linux executes programs. The kernel is the part of the Linux system that Linus Torvalds originally wrote (see the beginning of Chapter 1).

kernelspace   The part of memory (RAM) where the kernel resides. Code running in kernelspace has full access to hardware and all other processes in memory. See the *KernelAnalysis-HOWTO*.

key binding   A *keyboard* key is said to be bound to the action that results from pressing it. Typically keys are bound to the letters that appear on the keycaps: When you press **A**, an **A** appears on the screen. Key binding usually refers to what happens when you press a combination of keys, one of which is CONTROL, ALT, META, or SHIFT, or when you press a series of keys, the first of which is typically ESCAPE.

keyboard	A hardware input device consisting of a number of mechanical buttons (keys) that the user presses to input characters to a computer. By default a keyboard is connected to standard input of a shell.^{FOLDOC}

keyboard

A hardware input device consisting of a number of mechanical buttons (keys) that the user presses to input characters to a computer. By default a keyboard is connected to standard input of a shell.<small>FOLDOC</small>

kilo-

In the binary system, the prefix *kilo-* multiplies by 2^{10} (i.e., 1,024). Kilobit and kilobyte are common uses of this prefix. Abbreviated as *k*.

Korn Shell

ksh. A command processor, developed by David Korn at AT&T Bell Laboratories, that is compatible with the Bourne Shell but includes many extensions. See also *shell* on page 900.

LAN

Local area network. A network that connects computers within a localized area (such as a single site, building, or department).

large number

Go to mathworld.wolfram.com/LargeNumber.html for a comprehensive list.

LDAP

Lightweight Directory Access Protocol. A simple protocol for accessing online directory services. Traditionally LDAP has been used to access information such as email directories; in some cases, it can be used as an alternative for services such as NIS. Given a name, many mail clients can use LDAP to discover the corresponding email address. See *directory service* on page 872.

leaf

In a tree structure, the end of a branch that cannot support other branches. When the Linux filesystem hierarchy is conceptualized as a tree, files that are not directories are leaves. See *node* on page 890.

least privilege, concept of

Mistakes that Superuser makes can be much more devastating than those made by an ordinary user. When you are working on the computer, especially when you are working as the system administrator, always perform any task using the least privilege possible. If you can perform a task logged in as an ordinary user, do so. If you must be logged in as Superuser, do as much as you can as an ordinary user, log in as su so that you are Superuser, do as much of the task that has to be done as Superuser, and revert to being an ordinary user as soon as you can.

Because you are more likely to make a mistake when you are rushing, this concept becomes more important when you have less time to apply it. Also **root** user or just **root**.

Lightweight Directory Access Protocol

See *LDAP*.

link

A pointer to a file. Two kinds of links exist: hard links and symbolic (soft) links. A hard link associates a filename with a place on the disk where the contents of the file is located. A symbolic link associates a filename with the pathname of a hard link to a file. See *hard link* (page 878) and *symbolic link* (page 904).

Linux-PAM	See *PAM* on page 892.
Linux-Pluggable Authentication Modules	See *PAM* on page 892.
loadable kernel module	See *loadable module*.
loadable module	A portion of the operating system that controls a special device and that can be loaded automatically into a running kernel as needed to access that device.
local area network	See *LAN* on page 884.
locale	The language; date, time, and currency formats; character sets; and so forth that pertain to a geopolitical place or area. For example, en_US specifies English as spoken in the United States and dollars; en_UK specifies English as spoken in the United Kingdom and pounds. See the **locale** (5) man page for more information. Also the locale utility.
log in	To gain access to a computer system by responding correctly to the **login:** and **Password:** prompts. Also *log on, login*.
log out	To end your session by exiting from your login shell. Also *log off*.
logical expression	A collection of strings separated by logical operators (>, >=, =, !=, <=, and <) that can be evaluated as *true* or *false*. Also *Boolean expression*.
.login file	A file in a user's home directory that the TC Shell executes when you log in. You can use this file to set environment variables and to run commands that you want executed at the beginning of each session.
login name	The name you enter in response to the **login:** prompt. Other users use your login name when they send you mail or write to you. Each login name has a corresponding user ID, which is the numeric identifier for the user. Both the login name and the user ID are stored in the **passwd** database (**/etc/passwd** or the NIS equivalent).
login shell	The shell that you are using when you log in. The login shell can fork other processes that can run other shells, utilities, and programs.
.logout file	A file in a user's home directory that the TC Shell executes when you log out, assuming that the TC Shell is your login shell. You can put in the **.logout** file commands that you want run each time you log out.

MAC address   Media Access Control address. The unique hardware address of a device connected to a shared network medium. Each Ethernet adapter has a globally unique MAC address in ROM. MAC addresses are 6 bytes long, enabling 256^6 (about 300 trillion) possible addresses or 65,536 addresses for each possible IPv4 address.

A MAC address performs the same role for Ethernet that an IP address performs for TCP/IP: It provides a unique way to identify a host.

machine collating sequence   The sequence in which the computer orders characters. The machine collating sequence affects the outcome of sorts and other procedures that put lists in alphabetical order. Many computers use ASCII codes so their machine collating sequences correspond to the ordering of the ASCII codes for characters.

macro   A single instruction that a program replaces by several (usually more complex) instructions. The C compiler recognizes macros, which are defined using a **#define** instruction to the preprocessor.

magic number   A magic number, which occurs in the first 512 bytes of a binary file, is a 1-, 2-, or 4-byte numeric value or character string that uniquely identifies the type of file (much like a DOS 3-character filename extension). See **/usr/share/magic** and the **magic** man page (5) for more information.

main memory   Random access memory (RAM), an integral part of the computer. Although disk storage is sometimes referred to as memory, it is never referred to as main memory.

major device number   A number assigned to a class of devices, such as terminals, printers, or disk drives. Using the **ls** utility with the **–l** option to list the contents of the **/dev** directory displays the major and minor device numbers of many devices (as major, minor).

MAN   Metropolitan area network. A network that connects computers and *LANs* (page 884) at multiple sites in a small regional area, such as a city.

masquerade   To appear to come from one domain or IP address when actually coming from another. Said of a packet (**iptables**) or message (**sendmail**).

MD5   Message Digest 5. A *one-way hash function* (page 891).

MDA   Mail delivery agent. One of the three components of a mail system; the other two are the MTA and MUA. An MDA accepts inbound mail from an MTA and delivers it to a local user.

mega-   In the binary system, the prefix *mega-* multiplies by 2^{20} (i.e., 1,048,576). Megabit and megabyte are common uses of this prefix. Abbreviated as *M*.

menu A list from which the user may select an operation to be performed. This selection is often made with a mouse or other pointing device under a GUI but may also be controlled from the keyboard. Very convenient for beginners, menus show which commands are available and facilitate experimenting with a new program, often reducing the need for user documentation. Experienced users usually prefer keyboard commands, especially for frequently used operations, because they are faster to use.[FOLDOC]

merge To combine two ordered lists so that the resulting list is still in order. The sort utility can merge files.

META key On the keyboard, a key that is labeled META or ALT. Use this key as you would the SHIFT key. While holding it down, press another key. The emacs editor makes extensive use of the META key.

metacharacter A character that has a special meaning to the shell or another program in a particular context. Metacharacters are used in the ambiguous file references recognized by the shell and in the regular expressions recognized by several utilities. You must quote a metacharacter if you want to use it without invoking its special meaning. See *regular character* (page 897) and *special character* (page 902).

metadata Data about data. In data processing, metadata is definitional data that provides information about, or documentation of, other data managed within an application or environment.

For example, metadata can document data about data elements or attributes (name, size, data type, and so on), records or *data structures* (page 870) (length, fields, columns, and so on), and data itself (where it is located, how it is associated, who owns it, and so on). Metadata can include descriptive information about the context, quality and condition, or characteristics of the data.[FOLDOC]

metropolitan area network See *MAN* on page 886.

MIME Multipurpose Internet Mail Extension. Originally used to describe how specific types of files that were attached to email were to be handled. Today MIME types describe how a file is to be opened or worked with, based on its filename extension.

minimize See *iconify* on page 880.

minor device number A number assigned to a specific device within a class of devices. See *major device number* on page 886.

modem	Modulator/demodulator. A peripheral device that modulates digital data into analog data for transmission over a voice-grade telephone line. Another modem demodulates the data at the other end.
module	See *loadable module* on page 885.
mount	To make a filesystem accessible to system users. When a filesystem is not mounted, you cannot read from or write to files it contains.
mount point	A directory that you mount a local or remote filesystem on.
mouse	A device you use to point to a particular location on a display screen, typically so you can choose a menu item, draw a line, or highlight some text. You control a pointer on the screen by sliding a mouse around on a flat surface; the position of the pointer moves relative to the movement of the mouse. You select items by pressing one or more buttons on the mouse.
mouse pointer	In a GUI, a marker that moves in correspondence with the mouse. It is usually a small black **X** with a white border or an arrow. Differs from the *cursor* (page 870).
mouseover	The action of passing the mouse pointer over an icon or other object on the screen.
MTA	Mail transfer agent. One of the three components of a mail system; the other two are the MDA and MUA. An MTA accepts mail from users and MTAs.
MUA	Mail user agent. One of the three components of a mail system; the other two are the MDA and MTA. An MUA is an end-user mail program such as Kmail, mutt, or Outlook.
multiboot specification	Specifies an interface between a boot loader and an operating system. With compliant boot loaders and operating systems, any boot loader should be able to load any operating system. The object of this specification is to ensure that different operating systems will work on a single machine. For more information, go to odin-os.sourceforge.net/guides/multiboot.html.
multicast	A multicast packet has one source and multiple destinations. In multicast, source hosts register at a special address to transmit data. Destination hosts register at the same address to receive data. In contrast to *broadcast* (page 865), which is LAN-based, multicast traffic is designed to work across routed networks on a subscription basis. Multicast reduces network traffic by transmitting a packet one time, with the router at the end of the path breaking it apart as needed for multiple recipients.

multitasking	A computer system that allows a user to run more than one job at a time. A multitasking system, such as Linux, allows you to run a job in the background while running a job in the foreground.
multiuser system	A computer system that can be used by more than one person at a time. Linux is a multiuser operating system. Contrast with *single-user system* (page 900).
NAT	Network Address Translation. A scheme that enables a LAN to use one set of IP addresses internally and a different set externally. The internal set is for LAN (private) use. The external set is typically used on the Internet and is Internet unique. NAT provides some privacy by hiding internal IP addresses and allows multiple internal addresses to connect to the Internet through a single external IP address.
NBT	NetBIOS over TCP/IP. A protocol that supports NetBIOS services in a TCP/IP environment. Also *NetBT*.
NetBIOS	Network Basic Input/Output System. An *API* (page 861) for writing network-aware applications.
netboot	To boot a computer over the network (as opposed to booting from a local disk).
netiquette	The conventions of etiquette—that is, polite behavior—recognized on Usenet and in mailing lists, such as not (cross-)posting to inappropriate groups and refraining from commercial advertising outside the business groups.
	The most important rule of netiquette is "Think before you post." If what you intend to post will not make a positive contribution to the newsgroup and be of interest to several readers, do not post it. Personal messages to one or two individuals should not be posted to newsgroups; use private email instead.FOLDOC
netmask	A 32-bit mask (for IPv4), that shows how an Internet address is to be divided into network, subnet, and host parts. The netmask has ones in the bit positions in the 32-bit address that are to be used for the network and subnet parts and zeros for the host part. The mask should contain at least the standard network portion (as determined by the address class). The subnet field should be contiguous with the network portion.FOLDOC
network address	The network portion (**netid**) of an IP address. For a class A network, it is the first byte, or segment, of the IP address; for a class B network, it is the first two bytes; and for a class C network, it is the first three bytes. In each case the balance of the IP address is the host address (**hostid**). Assigned network addresses are globally unique within the Internet. Also *network number*.
Network Filesystem	See *NFS* on page 890.

Network Information Service	See *NIS*.
network number	See *network address*.
network segment	A part of an Ethernet or other network on which all message traffic is common to all nodes; that is, it is broadcast from one node on the segment and received by all others. This commonality normally occurs because the segment is a single continuous conductor. Communication between nodes on different segments is via one or more routers.[FOLDOC]
network switch	A connecting device in networks. Switches are increasingly replacing shared media hubs in an effort to increase bandwidth. For example, a 16-port 10BaseT hub shares the total 10 megabits per second bandwidth with all 16 attached nodes. By replacing the hub with a switch, both sender and receiver can take advantage of the full 10 megabits per second capacity. Each port on the switch can give full bandwidth to a single server or client station or to a hub with several stations. *Network switch* refers to a device with intelligence. Contrast with *hub* (page 880).
Network Time Protocol	See *NTP* on page 891.
NFS	Network Filesystem. A remote filesystem designed by Sun Microsystems, available on computers from most UNIX system vendors.
NIC	Network interface card (or controller). An adapter circuit board installed in a computer to provide a physical connection to a network.[FOLDOC]
NIS	Network Information Service. A distributed service built on a shared database to manage system-independent information (such as login names and passwords).
NIS domain name	A name that describes a group of systems that share a set of NIS files. Different from *domain name* (page 873).
NNTP	Network News Transfer Protocol.
node	In a tree structure, the end of a branch that can support other branches. When the Linux filesystem hierarchy is conceptualized as a tree, directories are nodes. See *leaf* on page 884.
nonprinting character	See *control character* on page 869. Also *nonprintable character*.

nonvolatile storage   A storage device whose contents are preserved when its power is off. Also NVS and persistent storage. Some examples are CD-ROM, paper punch tape, hard disk, *ROM* (page 898), *PROM* (page 895), *EPROM* (page 874), and *EEPROM* (page 873). Contrast with *RAM* (page 896).

NTP   Network Time Protocol. Built on top of TCP/IP, NTP maintains accurate local time by referring to known accurate clocks on the Internet.

null string   A string that could contain characters but does not. A string of zero length.

octal number   A base 8 number. Octal numbers are composed of the digits 0–7, inclusive. Refer to Table G-1 on page 879.

one-way hash function   A one-way function that takes a variable-length message and produces a fixed-length hash. Given the hash, it is computationally infeasible to find a message with that hash; in fact, you cannot determine any usable information about a message with that hash. Also *message digest function*. See also *hash* (page 878).

OpenSSH   A free version of the SSH (secure shell) protocol suite that replaces TELNET, rlogin, and more with secure programs that encrypt all communication—even passwords—over a network.

operating system   A control program for a computer that allocates computer resources, schedules tasks, and provides the user with a way to access resources.

option   A command line argument that modifies the effects of a command. Options are usually preceded by hyphens on the command line and traditionally have single-character names (such as **–h** or **–n**). Some commands allow you to group options following a single hyphen (for example, **–hn**). GNU utilities frequently have two arguments that do the same thing: a single-character argument and a longer, more descriptive argument that is preceded by two hyphens (such as **––show-all** and **––invert-match**).

ordinary file   A file that is used to store a program, text, or other user data. See *directory* (page 872) and *device file* (page 871).

output   Information that a program sends to the terminal or another file. See *standard output* on page 902.

P2P   Peer-to-Peer. A network that does not divide nodes into clients and servers. Each computer on a P2P network can fulfill the roles of client and server. In the context of a file-sharing network, this ability means that once a node has downloaded (part of) a file, it can act as a server. BitTorrent implements a P2P network.

packet	A unit of data sent across a network. *Packet* is a generic term used to describe a unit of data at any layer of the OSI protocol stack, but it is most correctly used to describe network or application layer data units ("application protocol data unit," APDU).ᶠᵒᴸᴰᴼᶜ See also *frame* (page 876) and *datagram* (page 870).
packet filtering	A technique used to block network traffic based on specified criteria, such as the origin, destination, or type of each packet. See also *firewall* (page 875).
packet sniffer	A program or device that monitors packets on a network. See *sniff* on page 901.
pager	A utility that allows you to view a file one screen at a time (for example, less and more).
paging	The process by which virtual memory is maintained by the operating system. The contents of process memory is moved (paged out) to the *swap space* (page 904) as needed to make room for other processes.
PAM	Linux-PAM or Linux-Pluggable Authentication Modules. These modules allow a system administrator to determine how various applications authenticate users.
parent process	A process that forks other processes. See *process* (page 894) and *child process* (page 867).
partition	A section of a (hard) disk that has a name so you can address it separately from other sections. A disk partition can hold a filesystem or another structure, such as the swap area. Under DOS and Windows, partitions (and sometimes whole disks) are labeled C:, D:, and so on. Also *disk partition* and *slice*.
passive FTP	Allows FTP to work through a firewall by allowing the flow of data to be initiated and controlled by the client FTP program instead of the server. Also called *PASV FTP* because it uses the FTP PASV command.
passphrase	A string of words and characters that you type in to authenticate yourself. A passphrase differs from a *password* only in length. A password is usually short—6 to 10 characters. A passphrase is usually much longer—up to 100 characters or more. The greater length makes a passphrase harder to guess or reproduce than a password and therefore more secure.ᶠᵒᴸᴰᴼᶜ
password	To prevent unauthorized access to a user's account, an arbitrary string of characters chosen by the user or system administrator and used to authenticate the user when attempting to log in.ᶠᵒᴸᴰᴼᶜ See also *passphrase*.
PASV FTP	See *passive FTP*.

pathname	A list of directories separated by slashes (/) and ending with the name of a file, which can be a directory. A pathname is used to trace a path through the file structure to locate or identify a file.
pathname, last element of a	The part of a pathname following the final /, or the whole filename if there is no /. A simple filename. Also *basename*.
pathname element	One of the filenames that forms a pathname.
peripheral device	See *device* on page 871.
persistent	Data that is stored on nonvolatile media, such as a hard disk.
physical device	A tangible device, such as a disk drive, that is physically separate from other, similar devices.
PID	Process identification, usually followed by the word *number*. Linux assigns a unique PID number as each process is initiated.
pipe	A connection between programs such that standard output of one program is connected to standard input of the next. Also *pipeline*.
pixel	The smallest element of a picture, typically a single dot on a display screen.
plaintext	Text that is not encrypted. Also *cleartext*. Contrast with *ciphertext* (page 867).
Pluggable Authentication Modules	See *PAM* on page 892.
point-to-point link	A connection limited to two endpoints, such as the connection between a pair of modems.
port	A logical channel or channel endpoint in a communications system. The *TCP* (page 905) and *UDP* (page 907) transport layer protocols used on Ethernet use port numbers to distinguish between different logical channels on the same network interface on the same computer.
	The **/etc/services** file (see the beginning of this file for more information) or the *NIS* (page 890) **services** database specifies a unique port number for each application program. The number links incoming data to the correct service (program). Standard, well-known ports are used by everyone: Port 80 is used for HTTP (Web) traffic. Some protocols, such as TELNET and HTTP (which is a special form of TELNET), have default ports specified as mentioned earlier but can use other ports as well.^{FOLDOC}

port forwarding	The process by which a network *port* on one computer is transparently connected to a port on another computer. If port X is forwarded from system A to system B, any data sent to port X on system A is sent to system B automatically. The connection can be between different ports on the two systems.
portmapper	A server that converts TCP/IP port numbers into *RPC* (page 899) program numbers.
printable character	One of the graphic characters: a letter, number, or punctuation mark. Contrast with a nonprintable, or control, character. Also *printing character*.
private address space	*IANA* (page 880) has reserved three blocks of IP addresses for private internets or LANs:

```
10.0.0.0 - 10.255.255.255
172.16.0.0 - 172.31.255.255
192.168.0.0 - 192.168.255.255
```

You can use these addresses without coordinating with anyone outside of your LAN (you do not have to register the system name or address). Systems using these IP addresses cannot communicate directly with hosts using the global address space but must go through a gateway. Because private addresses have no global meaning, routing information is not stored by DNSs and most ISPs reject privately addressed packets. Make sure that your router is set up not to forward these packets onto the Internet.

privileged port	A *port* (page 893) with a number less than 1,024. On Linux and other UNIX-like systems, only **root** can bind to a privileged port. Any user on Windows 98 and earlier Windows systems can bind to any port.
procedure	A sequence of instructions for performing a particular task. Most programming languages, including machine languages, enable a programmer to define procedures that allow the procedure code to be called from multiple places. Also *subroutine*.FOLDOC
process	The execution of a command by Linux. See "Processes" on page 292.
.profile file	A startup file in a user's home directory that the Bourne Again Shell executes when you log in. The TC Shell executes **.login** instead. You can use the **.profile** file to run commands, set variables, and define functions.
program	A sequence of executable computer instructions contained in a file. Linux utilities, applications, and shell scripts are all programs. Whenever you run a command that is not built into a shell, you are executing a program.

PROM   Programmable readonly memory. A kind of nonvolatile storage. *ROM* (page 898) that can be written to using a PROM programmer.

prompt   A cue from a program, usually displayed on the screen, indicating that it is waiting for input. The shell displays a prompt, as do some of the interactive utilities, such as mail. By default the Bourne Again and Z Shells use a dollar sign ($) as a prompt, and the TC Shell uses a percent sign (%).

protocol   A set of formal rules describing how to transmit data, especially across a network. Low-level protocols define the electrical and physical standards, bit and byte ordering, and transmission, error detection, and correction of the bit stream. High-level protocols deal with data formatting, including message syntax, terminal-to-computer dialog, character sets, and sequencing of messages.[FOLDOC]

proxy   A service that is authorized to act for a system while not being part of that system. See also *proxy gateway* and *proxy server*.

proxy gateway   A computer that separates clients (such as browsers) from the Internet, working as a trusted agent that accesses the Internet on their behalf. A proxy gateway passes a request for data from an Internet service, such as HTTP from a browser/client, to a remote server. The data that the server returns goes back through the proxy gateway to the requesting service. A proxy gateway should be transparent to the user.

A proxy gateway often runs on a *firewall* (page 875) system and acts as a barrier to malicious users. It hides the IP addresses of the local computers inside the firewall from Internet users outside the firewall.

You can configure browsers, such as Mozilla and Netscape, to use a different proxy gateway or to use no proxy for each URL access method including FTP, nctnews, SNMP, HTTPS, and HTTP. See also *proxy*.

proxy server   A *proxy gateway* that usually includes a *cache* (page 866) that holds frequently used Web pages so that the next request for that page is available locally (and therefore more quickly). The terms *proxy server* and *proxy gateway* are frequently interchanged so that the use of cache does not rest exclusively with the proxy server. See also *proxy*.

Python   A simple, high-level, interpreted, object-oriented, interactive language that bridges the gap between C and shell programming. Suitable for rapid prototyping or as an extension language for C applications, Python supports packages, modules, classes, user-defined exceptions, a good C interface, and dynamic loading of C modules. It has no arbitrary restrictions. For more information, see www.python.org[FOLDOC]

quote When you quote a character, you take away any special meaning that it has in the current context. You can quote a character by preceding it with a backslash. When you are interacting with the shell, you can also quote a character by surrounding it with single quotation marks. For example, the command **echo *** or **echo '*'** displays *. The command **echo *** displays a list of the files in the working directory. See *ambiguous file reference* (page 860), *metacharacter* (page 887), *regular character* (page 897), *regular expression* (page 897), and *special character* (page 902). Also *escape*.

radio button One of a group of buttons similar to those used to select the station on a radio. Only one button can be selected at a time.

RAID Redundant array of inexpensive/independent disks. Two or more (hard) disk drives used in combination to improve fault tolerance and performance. RAID can be implemented in hardware or software.

RAM Random access memory. A kind of volatile storage. A data storage device for which the order of access to different locations does not affect the speed of access. Contrast with a hard disk or tape drive, which provides quicker access to sequential data because accessing a nonsequential location requires physical movement of the storage medium and/or read/write head rather than just electronic switching. Contrast with *nonvolatile storage* (page 891).ᶠᵒˡᴰᴼᶜ

RAM disk *RAM* that is made to look like a floppy diskette or hard disk. A RAM disk is frequently used as part of the *boot* (page 864) process.

RAS Remote access server. In a network, a computer that provides access to remote users via analog modem or ISDN connections. RAS includes the dial-up protocols and access control (authentication). It may be a regular file server with remote access software or a proprietary system, such as Shiva's LANRover. The modems may be internal or external to the device.

RDF Resource Description Framework. Being developed by W3C (the main standards body for the World Wide Web), a standard that specifies a mechanism for encoding and transferring *metadata* (page 887). RDF does not specify what the metadata should or can be. It can integrate many kinds of applications and data, using XML as an interchange syntax. Examples of the data that can be integrated include library catalogs and worldwide directories; syndication and aggregation of news, software, and content; and collections of music and photographs. Go to www.w3.org/RDF for more information.

redirection The process of directing standard input for a program to come from a file rather than from the keyboard. Also, directing standard output or standard error to go to a file rather than to the screen.

reentrant	Code that can have multiple simultaneous, interleaved, or nested invocations that do not interfere with one another. Noninterference is important for parallel processing, recursive programming, and interrupt handling.

It is usually easy to arrange for multiple invocations (that is, calls to a subroutine) to share one copy of the code and any readonly data. For the code to be reentrant, however, each invocation must use its own copy of any modifiable data (or synchronized access to shared data). This goal is most often achieved by using a stack and allocating local variables in a new stack frame for each invocation. Alternatively, the caller may pass in a pointer to a block of memory that that invocation can use (usually for output), or the code may allocate some memory on a heap, especially if the data must survive after the routine returns.

Reentrant code is often found in system software, such as operating systems and teleprocessing monitors. It is also a crucial component of multithreaded programs, where the term *thread-safe* is often used instead of reentrant.ᶠᴼᴸᴰᴼᶜ |
regular character	A character that always represents itself in an ambiguous file reference or another type of regular expression. Contrast with *special character*.
regular expression	A string—composed of letters, numbers, and special symbols—that defines one or more strings. See Appendix A.
relative pathname	A pathname that starts from the working directory. Contrast with *absolute pathname* (page 860).
remote access server	See *RAS* on page 896.
remote filesystem	A filesystem on a remote computer that has been set up so that you can access (usually over a network) its files as though they were stored on your local computer's disks. An example of a remote filesystem is NFS.
remote procedure call	See *RPC* on page 899.
resolver	The TCP/IP library software that formats requests to be sent to the *DNS* (page 872) for hostname-to-Internet address conversion.ᶠᴼᴸᴰᴼᶜ
Resource Description Framework	See *RDF* on page 896.
restore	The process of turning an icon into a window. Contrast with *iconify* (page 880)
return code	See *exit status* on page 874.

RFC   Request for comments. Begun in 1969, one of a series of numbered Internet informational documents and standards widely followed by commercial software and freeware in the Internet and UNIX/Linux communities. Few RFCs are standards but all Internet standards are recorded in RFCs. Perhaps the single most influential RFC has been RFC 822, the Internet electronic mail format standard.

The RFCs are unusual in that they are floated by technical experts acting on their own initiative and reviewed by the Internet at large rather than being formally promulgated through an institution such as ANSI. For this reason they remain known as RFCs, even after they are adopted as standards. The RFC tradition of pragmatic, experience-driven, after-the-fact standard writing done by individuals or small working groups has important advantages over the more formal, committee-driven process typical of ANSI or ISO. For a complete list of RFCs, go to www.rfc-editor.org.FOLDOC

roam   To move a computer between *wireless access points* (page 910) on a wireless network without the user or applications being aware of the transition. Moving between access points typically results in some packet loss, although this loss is transparent to programs that use TCP.

ROM   Readonly memory. A kind of nonvolatile storage. A data storage device that is manufactured with fixed contents. In general, ROM describes any storage system whose contents cannot be altered, such as a phonograph record or printed book. When used in reference to electronics and computers, ROM describes semiconductor integrated circuit memories, of which several types exist, and CD-ROM.

ROM is nonvolatile storage—it retains its contents even after power has been removed. ROM is often used to hold programs for embedded systems, as these usually have a fixed purpose. ROM is also used for storage of the *BIOS* (page 863) in a computer. Contrast with *RAM* (page 896).FOLDOC

root directory   The ancestor of all directories and the start of all absolute pathnames. The name of the root directory is /.

root filesystem   The filesystem that is available when the system is brought up in single-user mode. The name of this filesystem is always /. You cannot unmount or mount the root filesystem. You can remount root to change its mount options.

root login   Usually the login name of *Superuser* (page 904).

root (user)   Another name for *Superuser* (page 904).

rotate   When a file, such as a log file, gets indefinitely larger, you must keep it from taking up too much space on the disk. Because you may need to refer to the information in the log files in the near future, it is generally not a good idea to delete the contents of the file until it has aged. Instead you can periodically save the current log file under a new name and create a new, empty file as the current log file. You can keep a series of these files, renaming each as a new one is saved. You will then *rotate* the files. For example, you might remove **xyzlog.4**, **xyzlog.3** → **xyzlog.4**, **xyzlog.2** → **xyzlog.3**, **xyzlog.1** → **xyzlog.2**, **xyzlog** → **xyzlog.1**, and create a new **xyzlog** file. By the time you remove **xyzlog.4**, it will not contain any information more recent than you want to remove.

router   A device (often a computer) that is connected to more than one similar type of network to pass data between them. See *gateway* on page 876.

RPC   Remote procedure call. A call to a *procedure* (page 894) that acts transparently across a network. The procedure itself is responsible for accessing and using the network. The RPC libraries make sure that network access is transparent to the application. RPC runs on top of TCP/IP or UDP/IP.

RSA   A public key encryption technology that is based on the lack of an efficient way to factor very large numbers. Because of this lack, it takes an extraordinary amount of computer processing time and power to deduce an RSA key. The RSA algorithm is the de facto standard for data sent over the Internet.

run   To execute a program.

Samba   A free suite of programs that implement the Server Message Block (SMB) protocol. See *SMB* (page 901).

schema   Within a GUI, a pattern that helps you see and interpret the information that is presented in a window, making it easier to understand new information that is presented using the same schema.

scroll   To move lines on a terminal or window up and down or left and right.

scrollbar   A widget found in graphical user interfaces that controls (scrolls) which part of a document is visible in the window. A window can have a horizontal scroll bar, a vertical scroll bar (more common), or both.FOLDOC

server   A powerful centralized computer (or program) designed to provide information to clients (smaller computers or programs) on request.

session   The lifetime of a process. For a desktop, it is the desktop session manager. For a character-based terminal, it is the user's login shell process. In KDE, it is launched by kdeinit. A session may also be the sequence of events between when you start using a program, such as an editor, and when you finish.

setgid   When you execute a file that has setgid (set group ID) permission, the process executing the file takes on the privileges of the group the file belongs to. The ls utility shows setgid permission as an **s** in the group's executable position. See also *setuid*.

setuid   When you execute a file that has setuid (set user ID) permission, the process executing the file takes on the privileges of the owner of the file. As an example, if you run a setuid program that removes all the files in a directory, you can remove files in any of the file owner's directories, even if you do not normally have permission to do so. When the program is owned by **root**, you can remove files in any directory that **root** can remove files from. The ls utility shows setuid permission as an **s** in the owner's executable position. See also *setgid*.

sexillion   In the British system, 10^{36}. In the American system, this number is named *undecillion*. See also *large number* (page 884).

share   A directory and the filesystem hierarchy below it that are shared with another system using *SMB* (page 901). Also *Windows share* (page 910).

shared network topology   A network, such as Ethernet, in which each packet may be seen by systems other than its destination system. *Shared* means that the network bandwidth is shared by all users.

shell   A Linux system command processor. The three major shells are the *Bourne Again Shell* (page 864), the *TC Shell* (page 905), and the *Z Shell* (page 911).

shell function   A series of commands that the shell stores for execution at a later time. Shell functions are like shell scripts but run more quickly because they are stored in the computer's main memory rather than in files. Also, a shell function is run in the environment of the shell that calls it (unlike a shell script, which is typically run in a subshell).

shell script   An ASCII file containing shell commands. Also *shell program*.

signal   A very brief message that the UNIX system can send to a process, apart from the process's standard input. Refer to "trap: Catches a Signal" on page 493.

simple filename   A single filename containing no slashes (*/*). A simple filename is the simplest form of pathname. Also the last element of a pathname. Also *basename* (page 863).

single-user system   A computer system that only one person can use at a time. Contrast with *multiuser system* (page 889).

SMB Server Message Block. Developed in the early 1980s by Intel, Microsoft, and IBM, SMB is a client/server protocol that is the native method of file and printer sharing for Windows. In addition, SMB can share serial ports and communications abstractions, such as named pipes and mail slots. SMB is similar to a remote procedure call (*RPC;* page 899) that has been customized for filesystem access. Also *Microsoft Networking.*^{FOLDOC}

smiley A character-based *glyph* (page 877), typically used in email, that conveys an emotion. The characters :-) in a message portray a smiley face (look at it sideways). Because it can be difficult to tell when the writer of an electronic message is saying something in jest or in seriousness, email users often use :-) to indicate humor. The two original smileys, designed by Scott Fahlman, were :-) and :-(. Also *emoticon, smileys,* and *smilies.* For more information search on **smiley** on the Internet.

smilies See *smiley.*

SMTP Simple Mail Transfer Protocol. A protocol used to transfer electronic mail between computers. It is a server-to-server protocol, so other protocols are used to access the messages. The SMTP dialog usually happens in the background under the control of a message transport system such as sendmail.^{FOLDOC}

snap (windows) As you drag a window toward another window or edge of the workspace, it can move suddenly so that it is adjacent to the other window/edge. Thus the window *snaps* into position.

sneakernet Using hand-carried magnetic media to transfer files between machines.

sniff To monitor packets on a network. A system administrator can legitimately sniff packets and a malicious user can sniff packets to obtain information such as usernames and passwords. See also *packet sniffer* (page 892).

SOCKS A networking proxy protocol embodied in a SOCKS server, which performs the same functions as a *proxy gateway* (page 895) or *proxy server* (page 895). SOCKS works at the application level, requiring that an application be modified to work with the SOCKS protocol, whereas a *proxy* (page 895) makes no demands on the application.

SOCKSv4 does not support authentication or UDP proxy. SOCKSv5 supports a variety of authentication methods and UDP proxy.

sort To put in a specified order, usually alphabetic or numeric.

SPACE character A character that appears as the absence of a visible character. Even though you cannot see it, a SPACE is a printable character. It is represented by the ASCII code 32 (decimal). A SPACE character is considered a *blank* or *whitespace* (page 909).

spam   Posting irrelevant or inappropriate messages to one or more Usenet newsgroups or mailing lists in deliberate or accidental violation of *netiquette* (page 889). Also, sending large amounts of unsolicited email indiscriminately. This email usually promotes a product or service. Spam is the electronic equivalent of junk mail. From the Monty Python "Spam" song.ᶠᴼᴸᴰᴼᶜ

sparse file   A file that is large but takes up little disk space. The data in a sparse file is not dense (thus its name). Examples of sparse files are core files, dbm files, and **/etc/utmp** ($\rightarrow$ **/var/adm/utmp**).

spawn   See *fork* on page 876.

special character   A character that has a special meaning when it occurs in an ambiguous file reference or another type of regular expression, unless it is quoted. The special characters most commonly used with the shell are * and ?. Also *metacharacter* (page 887) and *wildcard*.

special file   See *device file* on page 871.

spinner   In a GUI, a type of *text box* (page 905) that holds a number you can change by typing over it or using the up and down arrows at the end of the box.

spoofing   See *IP spoofing* on page 882.

spool   To place items in a queue, each waiting its turn for some action. Often used when speaking about printers. Also used to describe the queue.

SQL   Structured Query Language. A language that provides a user interface to relational database management systems (RDBMS). SQL, the de facto standard, is also an ISO and ANSI standard and is often embedded in other programming languages.ᶠᴼᴸᴰᴼᶜ

square bracket   A left square bracket ([) or a right square bracket (]). These special characters define character classes in ambiguous file references and other regular expressions.

SSH Communications Security   The company that created the original SSH (secure shell) protocol suite (www.ssh.com). Linux uses OpenSSH. See *OpenSSH* on page 891.

standard error   A file to which a program can send output. Usually only error messages are sent to this file. Unless you instruct the shell otherwise, it directs this output to the screen (that is, to the device file that represents the screen).

standard input   A file from which a program can receive input. Unless you instruct the shell otherwise, it directs this input so that it comes from the keyboard (that is, from the device file that represents the keyboard).

standard output   A file to which a program can send output. Unless you instruct the shell otherwise, it directs this output to the screen (that is, to the device file that represents the screen).

startup file A file that the login shell runs when you log in. The Bourne Again and Z Shells run **.profile**, and the TC Shell runs **.login**. The TC Shell also runs **.cshrc** whenever a new TC Shell or a subshell is invoked. The Z Shell runs an analogous file whose name is identified by the **ENV** variable.

status line The bottom (usually the twenty-fourth) line of the terminal. The vim editor uses the status line to display information about what is happening during an editing session.

sticky bit An access permission bit that causes an executable program to remain on the swap area of the disk. It takes less time to load a program that has its sticky bit set than one that does not. Only Superuser can set the sticky bit. If the sticky bit is set on a directory that is publicly writable, only the owner of a file in that directory can remove the file.

streaming tape A tape that moves at a constant speed past the read/write heads rather than speeding up and slowing down, which can slow the process of writing to or reading from the tape. A proper blocking factor helps ensure that the tape device will be kept streaming.

streams See *connection-oriented protocol* on page 868.

string A sequence of characters.

stylesheet See *CSS* on page 870.

subdirectory A directory that is located within another directory. Every directory except the root directory is a subdirectory.

subnet Subnetwork. A portion of a network, which may be a physically independent network segment, that shares a network address with other portions of the network and is distinguished by a subnet number. A subnet is to a network as a network is to an internet.^FOLDOC

subnet address The subnet portion of an IP address. In a subnetted network, the host portion of an IP address is split into a subnet portion and a host portion using a subnet mask (also address mask). See also *subnet number*.

subnet mask A bit mask used to identify which bits in an IP address correspond to the network address and subnet portions of the address. Called a subnet mask because the network portion of the address is determined by the number of bits that are set in the mask. The subnet mask has ones in positions corresponding to the network and subnet numbers and zeros in the host number positions. Also *address mask*.

subnet number The subnet portion of an IP address. In a subnetted network, the host portion of an IP address is split into a subnet portion and a host portion using a *subnet mask* (also address mask). See also *subnet address*.

subpixel hinting Similar to *anti-aliasing* (page 861) but takes advantage of colors to do the anti-aliasing. Particularly useful on LCD screens.

subroutine See *procedure* on page 894.

subshell A shell that is forked as a duplicate of its parent shell. When you run an executable file that contains a shell script by using its filename on the command line, the shell forks a subshell to run the script. Also, commands surrounded with parentheses are run in a subshell.

superblock A block that contains control information for a filesystem. The superblock contains housekeeping information, such as the number of inodes in the filesystem and free list information.

superserver The extended Internet services daemon.

Superuser A privileged user having access to anything any other system user has access to and more. The system administrator must be able to become Superuser to establish new accounts, change passwords, and perform other administrative tasks. The login name of Superuser is usually **root**. Also *root* or *root user*.

swap The operating system moving a process from main memory to a disk, or vice versa. Swapping a process to the disk allows another process to begin or continue execution.

swap space An area of a disk (that is, a swap file) used to store the portion of a process's memory that has been paged out. Under a virtual memory system, the amount of swap space—rather than the amount of physical memory—determines the maximum size of a single process and the maximum total size of all active processes. Also *swap area* or *swapping area*.FOLDOC

switch See *network switch* on page 890.

symbolic link A directory entry that points to the pathname of another file. In most cases a symbolic link to a file can be used in the same ways a hard link can be used. Unlike a hard link, a symbolic link can span filesystems and can connect to a directory.

system administrator The person responsible for the upkeep of the system. The system administrator has the ability to log in as Superuser. See *Superuser*.

system console The main system terminal, usually directly connected to the computer and the one that receives system error messages. Also *console* and *console terminal*.

system mode	The designation for the state of the system while it is doing system work. Some examples are making system calls, running NFS and **autofs**, processing network traffic, and performing kernel operations on behalf of the system. Contrast with *user mode* (page 908).
System V	One of the two major versions of the UNIX system.
TC Shell	tcsh. An enhanced but completely compatible version of the BSD UNIX C shell, csh.
TCP	Transmission Control Protocol. The most common transport layer protocol used on the Internet. This connection-oriented protocol is built on top of *IP* (page 882) and is nearly always seen in the combination TCP/IP (TCP over *IP*). TCP adds reliable communication, sequencing, and flow control and provides full-duplex, process-to-process connections. *UDP* (page 907), although connectionless, is the other protocol that runs on top of *IP*.FOLDOC
tera-	In the binary system, the prefix *tera-* multiplies by 2^{40} (1,099,511,627,776). Terabyte is a common use of this prefix. Abbreviated as *T*. See also *large number* on page 884.
termcap	Terminal capability. The **/etc/termcap** file contains a list of various types of terminals and their characteristics. *System V* replaced the function of this file with the *terminfo* system.
terminal	Differentiated from a *workstation* (page 910) by its lack of intelligence, a terminal connects to a computer that runs Linux. A workstation runs Linux on itself.
terminfo	Terminal information. The **/usr/lib/terminfo** directory contains many subdirectories, each containing several files. Each of those files is named for and holds a summary of the functional characteristics of a particular terminal. Visually oriented text-based programs, such as vim, use these files. An alternative to the **termcap** file.
text box	In a GUI, a box you can type in.
theme	Defined as an implicit or recurrent idea, *theme* is used in a GUI to describe a look that is consistent for all elements of a desktop. Go to themes.freshmeat.net for examples.
thicknet	A type of coaxial cable (thick) used for an Ethernet network. Devices are attached to thicknet by tapping the cable at fixed points.

thinnet	A type of coaxial cable (thin) used for an Ethernet network. Thinnet cable is smaller in diameter and more flexible than *thicknet* cable. Each device is typically attached to two separate cable segments by using a T-shaped connector; one segment leads to the device ahead of it on the network and one to the device that follows it.
thread-safe	See *reentrant* on page 897.
thumb	The movable button in the scrollbar that positions the image in the window. The size of the thumb reflects the amount of information in the buffer. Also *bubble*.
TIFF	Tagged Image File Format. A file format used for still-image bitmaps, stored in tagged fields. Application programs can use the tags to accept or ignore fields, depending on their capabilities.FOLDOC
tiled windows	An arrangement of windows such that no window overlaps another. The opposite of *cascading windows* (page 866).
time to live	See *TTL* on page 907.
toggle	To switch between one of two positions. For example, the ftp **glob** command toggles the **glob** feature: Give the command once, and it turns the feature on or off; give the command again, and it sets the feature back to its original state.
token	A basic, grammatically indivisible unit of a language, such as a keyword, operator, or identifier.FOLDOC
token ring	A type of *LAN* (page 884) in which computers are attached to a ring of cable. A token packet circulates continuously around the ring. A computer can transmit information only when it holds the token.
tooltip	A minicontext help system that you activate by allowing your mouse pointer to *hover* (page 879) over a button, icon, or applet (such as those on a panel).
transient window	A dialog or other window that is displayed for only a short time.
Transmission Control Protocol	See *TCP* on page 905.
Trojan horse	A program that does something destructive or disruptive to your system. Its action is not documented, and the system administrator would not approve of it if she were aware of it.
	The term *Trojan horse* was coined by MIT-hacker-turned-NSA-spook Dan Edwards. It refers to a malicious security-breaking program that is disguised as something benign, such as a directory lister, archive utility, game, or (in one notorious 1990 case on the Mac) a program to find and destroy viruses. Similar to *back door* (page 862).FOLDOC

TTL	Time to live.

1. All DNS records specify how long they are good for—usually up to a week at most. This time is called the record's *time to live*. When a DNS server or an application stores this record in *cache* (page 866), it decrements the TTL value and removes the record from cache when the value reaches zero. A DNS server passes a cached record to another server with the current (decremented) TTL guaranteeing the proper TTL, no matter how many servers the record passes through.

2. In the IP header, a field that indicates how many more hops the packet should be allowed to make before being discarded or returned.

TTY	Teletypewriter. The terminal device that UNIX was first run from. Today TTY refers to the screen (or window, in the case of a terminal emulator), keyboard, and mouse that are connected to a computer. This term appears in UNIX, and Linux has kept the term for the sake of consistency and tradition.
tunneling	Encapsulation of protocol A within packets carried by protocol B, such that A treats B as though it were a data link layer. Tunneling is used to transfer data between administrative domains that use a protocol not supported by the internet connecting those domains. It can also be used to encrypt data sent over a public internet, as when you use ssh to tunnel a protocol over the Internet.FOLDOC See also *VPN* (page 909).
UDP	User Datagram Protocol. The Internet standard transport layer protocol that provides simple but unreliable datagram services. UDP is a *connectionless protocol* (page 869) that, like *TCP* (page 905), is layered on top of *IP* (page 882).
	Unlike *TCP*, UDP neither guarantees delivery nor requires a connection. As a result it is lightweight and efficient, but the application program must handle all error processing and retransmission. UDP is often used for sending time-sensitive data that is not particularly sensitive to minor loss, such as audio and video data.FOLDOC
UID	User ID. A number that the **passwd** database associates with a login name.
undecillion	In the American system, 10^{36}. In the British system, this number is named *sexillion*. See also *large number* (page 884).
unicast	A packet sent from one host to another host. Unicast means one source and one destination.
unmanaged window	See *ignored window* on page 880.

URI	Uniform Resource Identifier. The generic set of all names and addresses that are short strings referring to objects (typically on the Internet). The most common kinds of URIs are *URLs*.FOLDOC
URL	Uniform (was Universal) Resource Locator. A standard way of specifying the location of an object, typically a Web page, on the Internet. URLs are a subset of *URIs*.
usage message	A message displayed by a command when you call the command using incorrect command line arguments.
User Datagram Protocol	See *UDP*.
User ID	See *UID*.
user interface	See *interface* on page 881.
user mode	The designation for the state of the system while it is doing user work, such as running a user program (but not the system calls made by the program). Contrast with *system mode* (page 905).
userspace	The part of memory (RAM) where applications reside. Code running in userspace cannot access hardware directly and cannot access memory allocated to other applications. Also *userland*. See the *KernelAnalysis-HOWTO*.
UTC	Coordinated Universal Time. UTC is the equivalent to the mean solar time at the prime meridian (0 degrees longitude). Also called Zulu time (Z stands for longitude zero) and GMT (Greenwich Mean Time).
utility	A program included as a standard part of Linux. You typically invoke a utility either by giving a command in response to a shell prompt or by calling it from within a shell script. Utilities are often referred to as commands. Contrast with *builtin (command)* (page 865).
variable	A name and an associated value. The shell allows you to create variables and use them in shell scripts. Also, the shell inherits several variables when it is invoked, and it maintains those and other variables while it is running. Some shell variables establish characteristics of the shell environment; others have values that reflect different aspects of your ongoing interaction with the shell.
viewport	Same as *workspace* (page 910).
virtual console	Additional consoles, or displays, that you can view on the system, or physical, console.

virus	A *cracker* (page 869) program that searches out other programs and "infects" them by embedding a copy of itself in them, so that they become *Trojan horses* (page 906). When these programs are executed, the embedded virus is executed as well, propagating the "infection," usually without the user's knowledge. By analogy with biological viruses.^{FOLDOC}
VLAN	Virtual LAN. A logical grouping of two or more nodes that are not necessarily on the same physical network segment but that share the same network number. A VLAN is often associated with switched Ethernet.^{FOLDOC}
VPN	Virtual Private Network. A private network that exists on a public network, such as the Internet. A VPN is a less expensive substitute for company-owned/leased lines and uses encryption to ensure privacy. A nice side effect is that you can send non-Internet protocols, such as Appletalk, IPX, or NetBIOS, over the VPN connection by *tunneling* (page 907) them through the VPN IP stream.
W2K	Windows 2000 Professional or Server.
W3C	World Wide Web Consortium (www.w3.org).
WAN	Wide area network. A network that interconnects *LANs* (page 884) and *MANs* (page 886), spanning a large geographic area (typically states or countries).
WAP	See *wireless access point* on page 910.
Web ring	A collection of Web sites that provide information on a single topic or group of related topics. Each home page that is part of the Web ring has a series of links that let you go from site to site.
whitespace	A collective name for SPACEs and/or TABs and occasionally NEWLINEs. Also *white space*.
wide area network	See *WAN*.
widget	The basic objects of a graphical user interface. Buttons, text fields, and scrollbars are examples of widgets.
wild card	See *metacharacter* on page 887.
Wi-Fi	Wireless Fidelity. A generic term that refers to any type of *802.11* (page 860) wireless network.
window	On a display screen, a region that runs or is controlled by a particular program.

window manager   A program that controls how windows appear on a display screen and how you manipulate them.

Windows share   See *share* on page 900.

WINS   Windows Internet Naming Service. The service responsible for mapping NetBIOS names to IP addresses. WINS has the same relationship to NetBIOS names that DNS has to Internet domain names.

WINS server   The program responsible for handling WINS requests. This program caches name information about hosts on a local network and resolves them to IP addresses.

wireless access point   A bridge or router between wired and wireless networks. Wireless access points typically support some form of access control to prevent unauthorized clients from connecting to the network. Also *WAP*.

word   A sequence of one or more nonblank characters separated from other words by TABs, SPACEs, or NEWLINEs. Used to refer to individual command line arguments. In vim, a word is similar to a word in the English language—a string of one or more characters bounded by a punctuation mark, a numeral, a TAB, a SPACE, or a NEWLINE.

Work buffer   A location where vim stores text while it is being edited. The information in the Work buffer is not written to the file on the disk until you give the editor a command to write it.

working directory   The directory that you are associated with at any given time. The relative pathnames you use are *relative to* the working directory. Also *current directory*.

workspace   A subdivision of a *desktop* (page 871) that occupies the entire display.

workstation   A small computer, typically designed to fit in an office and be used by one person and usually equipped with a bit-mapped graphical display, keyboard, and mouse. Differentiated from a *terminal* (page 905) by its intelligence. A workstation runs Linux on itself while a terminal connects to a computer that runs Linux.

worm   A program that propagates itself over a network, reproducing itself as it goes. Today the term has negative connotations, as it is assumed that only *crackers* (page 869) write worms. Compare to *virus* (page 909) and *Trojan horse* (page 906). From **Tapeworm** in John Brunner's novel, *The Shockwave Rider*, Ballantine Books, 1990 (via XEROX PARC).FOLDOC

WYSIWYG   What You See Is What You Get. A graphical application, such as a word processor, whose display is similar to its printed output.

X terminal	A graphics terminal designed to run the X Window System.
X Window System	A design and set of tools for writing flexible, portable windowing applications, created jointly by researchers at MIT and several leading computer manufacturers.
XDMCP	X Display Manager Control Protocol. XDMCP allows the login server to accept requests from network displays. XDMCP is built into many X terminals.
xDSL	Different types of *DSL* (page 873) are identified by a prefix—for example, ADSL, HDSL, SDSL, and VDSL.
Xinerama	An extension to XFree86 release 6 version 4.0 (X4.0). Xinerama allows window managers and applications to use two or more physical displays as one large virtual display. Refer to *Xinerama-HOWTO*.
XML	Extensible Markup Language. A universal format for structured documents and data on the Web. Developed by *W3C* (page 909), XML is a pared-down version of SGML.
	See www.w3.org/XML and www.w3.org/XML/1999/XML-in-10-points.
XSM	X Session Manager. This program allows you to create a session that includes certain applications. While the session is running, you can perform a *checkpoint* (saves the application state) or a *shutdown* (saves the state and exits from the session). When you log back in, you can load your session so that everything in your session is running just as it was when you logged off.
Z Shell	zsh. A *shell* (page 900) that incorporates many of the features of the *Bourne Again Shell* (page 864), *Korn Shell* (page 884), and *TC Shell* (page 905), as well as many original features.
Zulu time	See *UTC* on page 908.

INDEX

Note: Only variables that must always appear with a leading dollar sign are indexed with a leading dollar sign. Other variables are indexed without a leading dollar sign.

SYMBOLS

Also Available from Mark G. Sobell

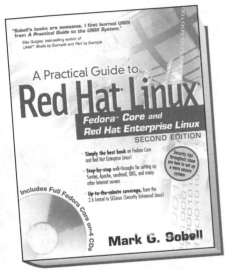

0-13-147024-8

A Practical Guide to Red Hat® Linux®: Fedora™ Core and Red Hat Enterprise Linux, Second Edition, explains Linux clearly and effectively—with a focus on the features you care about, including system security, Internet server setup, and sharing files and printers with Windows systems. This indispensable guide walks you through *everything* that matters, from installing Fedora Core—using the CDs included with the book—to GNOME, KDE, Samba-3, sendmail, Apache, DNS, NIS, and iptables. Along the way, you learn the "hows" and the "whys." Whether you are a user, an administrator, or a programmer, *this book gives you all you need and more.*

A Practical Guide to Solaris enables both novice and experienced users to quickly learn Sun Microsystems' popular Solaris operating system. Designed to maximize accessibility, the book is divided into three parts. Part I is a tutorial that brings novice users—those with no UNIX/Solaris background, or no programming experience at all—quickly up to speed. Part II is geared toward intermediate and advanced users. Part III is a comprehensive reference guide covering more than ninety Solaris utilities with clear explanations and a wide range of examples not available from any other source.

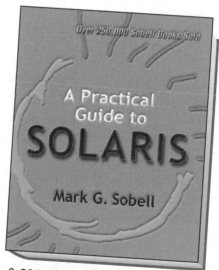

0-201-89548-X

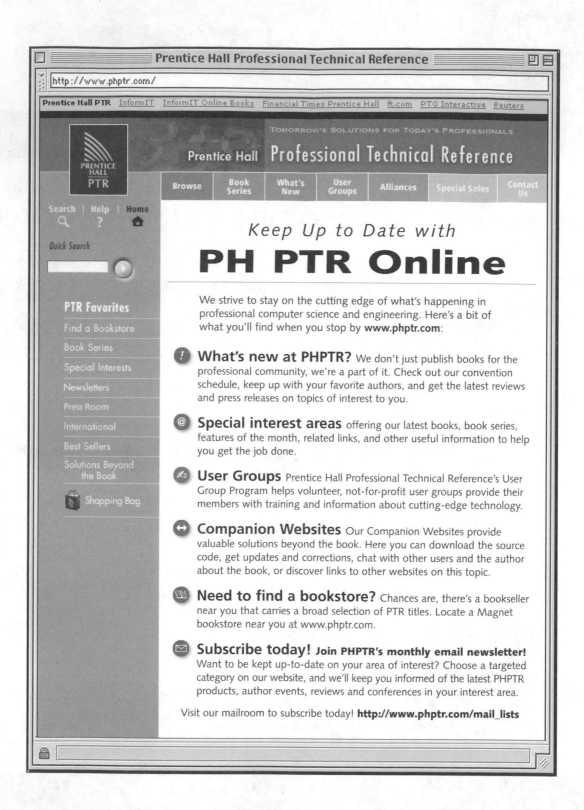